# FIRE IN THE BELLY

*Our Town:*
*A Heartland Lynching, a Haunted Town,*
*and the Hidden History of White America*

*On Edge:*
*Performance at the End of the*
*Twentieth Century* (as C. Carr)

# FIRE IN THE BELLY

## THE LIFE AND TIMES OF
## DAVID WOJNAROWICZ

### CYNTHIA CARR

BLOOMSBURY

NEW YORK • LONDON • NEW DELHI • SYDNEY

Published by Bloomsbury USA, New York

Certain passages first appeared in the *Village Voice* in slightly different form. Used by permission.

Photograph on title page by Marion Scemama.

Every reasonable effort has been made to trace copyright holders and to secure permission for material reproduced in this book.

All papers used by Bloomsbury USA are natural, recyclable products made from wood grown in well-managed forests. The manufacturing processes conform to the environmental regulations of the country of origin.

LIBRARY OF CONGRESS CATALOGING-IN-PUBLICATION DATA

Carr, C.
Fire in the belly : the life and times of David Wojnarowicz / Cynthia Carr.—1st U.S. ed.
p.   cm.
Includes bibliographical references (p.) and index.
ISBN: 978-1-59691-533-6
1. Wojnarowicz, David.   2. Artists—United States—Biography.   I. Title.
N6537.W63C37 2012
700.92—dc23
[B]
2012000684

First U.S. edition 2012

1  3  5  7  9  10  8  6  4  2

Designed by Sara Stemen

Typeset by Westchester Book Group
Printed in the U.S.A. by Quad/Graphics, Fairfield, Pennsylvania

## For Tom Rauffenbart

### And in memory of those who could not be interviewed

Arthur Bressan Jr. 1943–1987

Steve Brown 1954–1995

Iolo Carew 1955–1987

Emilio Cubiero 1947–2001

Keith Davis 1954–1987

Tim Dlugos 1950–1990

Ethyl Eichelberger 1945–1990

Luis Frangella 1944–1990

Steve Gliboff 1949–1991

Timothy Greathouse 1950–1998

Keith Haring 1958–1990

Montana Hewson c. 1952–1990

Peter Hujar 1934–1987

Greer Lankton 1958–1996

Haoui Montaug 1952–1991

Michael Morais 1945–1991

Nicolas Moufarrege 1947–1985

Cookie Mueller 1949–1989

Paul Proveaux 1948–1988

Bill Rice 1931–2006

Tom Rubnitz 1956–1992

Dean Savard 1958–1990

Huck Snyder 1953–1993

Paul Thek 1933–1988

Phil Zwickler 1954–1991

# CONTENTS

# THE TRUTH: AN INTRODUCTION

**It was November 30, 2010**—the eve of World AIDS Day. Smithsonian Secretary G. Wayne Clough ordered the National Portrait Gallery to remove David Wojnarowicz's film *A Fire in My Belly* from a landmark exhibition about gay identity in art, "Hide/Seek: Difference and Desire in American Portraiture." The eleven-second sequence deemed offensive showed ants crawling over a crucifix.

According to Bill Donohue, president of the far-right Catholic League, this was "hate speech," and he urged Congress to cut the museum's funding. The top two House Republicans, Speaker John Boehner and Majority Leader Eric Cantor, chimed in immediately, calling for "Hide/Seek" to be closed. The museum would face "tough scrutiny" now, Boehner promised, while Cantor called *A Fire in My Belly*, which had been on view since October 30, "an obvious attempt to offend Christians during the Christmas season."

Once again, David Wojnarowicz (pronounced *Voyna-ROW-vich*) was a targeted artist. Late in 1989, his catalog essay for another landmark show—this one about AIDS—became the catalyst for a row between the National Endowment for the Arts and a major nonprofit institution, Artists Space. That was just the opening salvo in David's battle with the right-wing culture warriors. By autumn 1990, however, increasingly weak and sick with AIDS, he prepared work for what would be his last show and told a friend in a letter that he was done butting heads with the bigots, adding "I'm tired of being perceived as a radical when I know I ain't particularly radical."

Even when he aggravated the powerful, David never saw his work as provocation. He saw it as a way to speak his truth, a way to challenge or at least to illuminate what many accept as given. That's what the ants actually represented to him—humanity rushing along heedless of what lies under

Untitled from the Ant Series (Spirituality), *1988. Gelatin-silver print, 29½ × 39 inches. (Courtesy of the Estate of David Wojnarowicz and P·P·O·W Gallery, New York)*

its tiny feet, indifferent to the structures that surround it. When he went to Teotihuacán late in 1986, knowing that he would find nests of fire ants among the Aztec ruins, he brought other props with him besides a crucifix (to represent spirituality). He also filmed and photographed ants crawling over watchfaces (time), coins (money), a toy soldier (control), and other charged symbols. This ant action accounts for very little screen time.

More than eighteen years after his death, David's blunt, disquieting imagery had apparently lost none of its power. But his intentions were completely misinterpreted. His detractors called it blasphemous and sacrilegious; his defenders said it was all about AIDS. But it was neither. He disparaged the policies of the Catholic Church on other occasions (while lamenting the death of American spirituality, the title of one of his paintings). And he had plenty to say about AIDS. But not in this film.

In a 1988 letter to Barry Blinderman, who curated David's retrospective "Tongues of Flame" he explained what *A Fire in My Belly* meant to him: "The film deals with ancient myth and its modern counterpart. It explores structures of power and control—using at times the fire ants north of Mexico City as a metaphor for social structure."

As David saw it, people were brutalized into fitting those structures. That was a core issue for him. So, while not specifically about AIDS, *A Fire in My Belly* is certainly a piece about suffering.

Both his art and his politics were rooted in life experience, beginning with his almost Dickensian childhood. David was an abused kid, a teen runaway, and a former Times Square hustler who used art to re-create himself. This was someone who never went to art school, who barely finished high school, who never owned a suit, a couch, or (until the last two years of his life) a credit card, but who came to believe in the truth of his own experience and desire.

David was a major figure in what is now a lost world, in part because he happened to come along when New York City was as raw as he was. Manhattan still had uncolonized space: from the rotting piers along the Hudson River where gay men went for sex to cheap empty storefronts in the drug-infested East Village. There, in what David called "the picturesque ruins," so much seemed possible and permissible. Then, in the late seventies and early eighties, the art world went through one of its seismic shifts—goodbye minimalism, hello expressionism—and fissures opened up that allowed a few outsiders in. By 1983, the art world was agog over what was happening in the above-mentioned funky storefronts: East Village art. The whole neighborhood seemed to be experimenting, expressing, and neo-expressing. When I wrote about the scene, because I too was part of what we used to term "downtown," I categorized it as schizo-culture, built from the alternating currents of postmodern theory and nightclub energy. My favorite quote came from Edit deAk, art critic and denizen of the nightclub generation: "We are prospectors of slum vintage. Who renamed the city after our own names. . . . We have taken your garbage all our lives and are selling it back at an inconceivable mark-up."

None of us would have thought so at the time, but those were innocent days—before gentrification flattened our options, and AIDS changed the world for the worse, and congressional leaders started weighing in on artists who filmed ants. We had no way to know how much was ending.

David has been called everything from "the last outsider" to "the last romantic." The era I've covered in this book surely was the end of some-thing. The East Villagers were the last subterraneans who actually had a terrain, because during the 1980s the whole concept of marginality changed. Once the demimonde had served as a community of like minds for people alienated from middle-class values (artistic, sexual, political). Then, in the eighties, it became the "hot bottom" of the torrid art market, a place for col-lectors to seek out the Next Big Thing. The discovery, exploitation, and de-mise of New York's last bohemia coincided with—among other things—the new visibility of queer culture, due in part to the advancing horror of AIDS. In brief, the media spotlight suddenly illuminated what had once been the cultural margin, exposing artists (especially gay artists) to an audience guar-anteed to find them intolerable.

About a year before his death from AIDS, David was one of the writers included in *High Risk: An Anthology of Forbidden Writings*. While topics like homosexuality, drug addiction, and sadomasochism no longer seem so forbidden, the fact remains that David was part of a community of people who felt compelled to be themselves even if that meant risking everything. Many of them died. Some of those names appear on the dedication page in this book—not all of them AIDS deaths but all of them among the novas who lit that era and disappeared from our firmament.

In his painting, writing, film, photography, sculpture, and performance, David was committed to facing uncomfortable truths. Even as a kid of six or seven, he told me, he was the one who ran down the block one day, giddy with what he'd just learned. "We all die! One day we're all going to be dead!" As he told his little friends, they burst into tears, parents rushed out of their houses, and David was seen as a very sick little kid for exposing the Real Deal. Recalling that memory, David smiled: "That's a metaphor for the rest of my life."

But David was also an elusive character—a truth teller who kept se-crets, a loner who loved to collaborate, an artist who craved recognition but did not want to be seen.

I met him in 1982 and interviewed him in 1990 for a *Village Voice* cover story. At the time, David was still working on the book he would eventually call *Close to the Knives: A Memoir of Disintegration.* He told me that he was going to let the publisher classify it as nonfiction, even though he thought of it as "a fusion of fiction and nonfiction." He had decided to let everything in his emotional history become part of his palette, whether or not he remembered it accurately.

I knew David best during the last eight months of his life. We also had some mutual friends, and a couple of them warned me that if I chose to write about David, I would have to deal with what they called "the mythology." Not that anyone knew of any specific myth. Or lie. But those stories! In 1989, when David prepared a Biographical Dateline for the catalog accompanying "Tongues of Flame," one of the first readers remarked (though not to David), "It's like effing Candide!" The Dateline ends in 1982, as David began his art career. Certainly, some of the facts he laid out on his early life are skewed or exaggerated or just wrong. His account emphasizes the hardships and omits a lot. But the Dateline does not vary from the accounts of his life he'd been giving since he first became a public figure.

So his childhood wasn't as bad as he said? I think it was worse. For one thing, the real David was never as hard-bitten as the persona toughing it out through those stories. Nor did he include much of what his siblings and half-siblings endured, which really provides context.

I don't think David understood the pathos in his own story. He emphasized the hardship he went through, and the hardship was there. But the central struggle in his life was about how much of himself to reveal. Who was safe? What could he tell? He felt he was an alien, that something at his core was suspect and would make people hate him. This feeling persisted until the last few years of his life.

David once told me that he used to long for acceptance from other people. Then he began to value the way he didn't fit in. He realized that his uneasiness with the world was where his work came from.

David learned to be daring when he lived on the street, when he came out as a gay man and refused to hide it, and then when he met his great mentor, Peter Hujar—part of an older generation of high-riskers and, for David, a guiding light. Hujar could not tell David how to have a career, since he was no good at that, but he could show him how to be an artist. David did not know much art history but realized he didn't need that in order to develop an iconography. In a yellow steno pad found among his papers, he wrote, "I had always believed that the content of paintings were always some denial of history—images preserved by and for a particular class of people. So it was in them that I reached for images of chaos—images that weren't used in paintings—maybe obscure books detailing the human efforts of power structures—also in growing up in a world without role models where all institutions relegated homosexual matters to snide johns or things to be exterminated. . . . I had always believed that change came down to personal action—not just language but the idea of self truth. / Peter's search for self-truth / All this in my work."

# 1 WHERE SOMETHING BROKE

**One day in** September 1954, Ed Wojnarowicz lost his salary gambling. All of it. This led to a quarrel with his wife, Dolores, and he went out to get plastered. When he came home drunk, he seized Dolores by the throat, choking her, muttering that he'd kill her. He grabbed a gun, threatening to shoot her, the children, and then himself. Dolores locked herself in the bedroom with the kids and heard Ed fire three shots. Silence. She crept downstairs to find him slumped over the kitchen table. Dead? When she approached, he jumped up laughing, waving the gun in her face. The divorce petition describing this incident does not specify whether it occurred just before or just after the birth of the couple's third child, David, on September 14.

Ed Wojnarowicz was a seaman on passenger ships, working the boiler room. He stood a wiry five foot ten, hawklike around the eyes and nose, with a tattoo on his left upper arm. He had met Dolores McGuinness in Sydney, Australia—at a soda shop. At least that was the story. She'd been raised in a convent. Or in an orphanage. Or in a fractured family where she'd been abused. So their three children variously told me. None of them knew much about her. Nor the year their parents had married. Nor whether they had family in Australia. Dolores was a brunette with delicate features, a beauty. The divorce papers state that she'd married Ed in Sydney in 1948, on September 14—the same day as David's eventual birth. She was sixteen to Ed's twenty-six.

Dolores had just turned eighteen when their daughter, Pat, was born in January 1950. In the short marriage of Ed and Dolores, major events clocked in at two-year intervals. After Pat came Steven in 1952, then David in '54, and the parents' separation in '56.

David, Steven, and Pat experienced childhood without stability or

*Ed Wojnarowicz at his mother's house in Michigan with (from left) Steven, Pat, and David. (Courtesy of Steven Wojnarowicz)*

security, spiked for some years with violence, then chaos, then neglect. Ed committed suicide for real in 1976. Dolores did not respond to repeated phone calls and a letter to her home in Manhattan requesting an interview. She was not in touch with David at the end of his life. Nor had she been in touch with her two surviving children since the early 1980s. Pat attempted to reconnect in 2002, but it didn't work out. (Dolores called her daughter late in 2011, but the upshot was unclear.) Nor did Pat and Steven have any contact with each other. This family was beyond dysfunctional; it had shattered.

Childhood was painful to resurrect for David's brothers and sisters, including his half-siblings from Ed's second marriage, Peter and Linda. All but Pat cried at some point while talking to me, and Pat had big holes in her memory. She has lived in Paris since the late 1970s and goes for weeks at a time without speaking the language in which these things happened. As she put it: "I have a lot of stuff that's been blocked out."

Pat insisted, however, that her very early years were happy—the years spent in or near Red Bank, New Jersey, where David was born. Asked for an example, she recalled sitting under a big tree with Steven and David when she was probably six, and suddenly feeling an overwhelming love for them. What Steven remembered of the years when his parents were mar-

*Steven (left), David, and Pat on their way to visit relatives in Massachusetts. David is about five. (Courtesy of Steven Wojnarowicz)*

ried was that Dolores would occasionally lock all three of them in the attic and leave for the day while their father was at sea. Steven remembered the attic's intense heat, and having to pee out the window. Pat said that usually they were locked in there as punishment, sometimes for a long time—"we'd amuse ourselves by going to the toilet in boxes." David remembered nothing from this period of his life. If he had, he might have mentioned the corrective braces he had to wear on his legs at night because he was pigeon-toed.

When Dolores filed for divorce in October 1956, she alleged that Ed's cruelty had started in May 1948, five months *before* the wedding. The date is mentioned three times, including once in Ed's rebuttal, so it can't be a typo. But the cruelty didn't turn physical until the month of David's birth. Before that, Ed was often drunk, verbally abusive, and absent from home without explanation. But he was just beginning his alcoholic spiral in the 1950s, and the violence was intermittent. In 1955, he threw a mirror at Dolores, cutting her on her face and head. In 1956, he came home drunk, chased Dolores upstairs, then closed all the windows and turned on the gas. She heard a crash and came downstairs to find Ed on the floor, laughing. A few months later, Ed again threatened to kill her.

In his counterclaim, Ed denied everything, adding that in August 1954 he had won six hundred dollars gambling and had given it all to Dolores. He pointed out that they had reaffirmed their wedding vows in July 1951, at a

Catholic church in Highlands, New Jersey. (They had married in Australia under the auspices of the Church of England, and Ed was a serious Roman Catholic.) Ed also claimed that Dolores had deserted him in the summer of 1956. That was when the couple separated. Dolores moved, with the children, to the Molly Pitcher Village Apartments in Red Bank. When the divorce papers were filed that fall, Ed gave his address as Pier 86 in Manhattan, his ship's berth—later the site of the Intrepid Sea, Air and Space Museum. He was paying seventy-five dollars a week in support and getting two or three hours with the children every sixteen days.

David was too young to have any memories of the year or so spent at the Molly Pitcher Village Apartments, but it was probably here that he was hit by a car and broke his leg. His lifelong fascination with creeping crawling things was already apparent. Pat recalled that he once brought dozens of caterpillars into the apartment in a paper bag. They were in the curtains. On the chairs. "You could just scoop them up," said Pat. He would also pick up big black ants and eat them.

Ed did not contest the divorce, which was granted in June 1957, but he'd been petitioning the court since the beginning of that year to get more time with his children. With the court's permission, he took them to his relatives in Michigan for the month of August 1957. A couple of months later, he sued for custody, even though he was seldom home. He told the court that he would place the children either with his mother in Detroit or in an institution in New Jersey. Meanwhile, Dolores had converted to Methodism and was unhappy with the court's order that she raise the children as Catholics. In January 1958, the court ruled that it could not decide a religious difference of opinion between parents and a month later confirmed that Dolores had custody, again ordering Ed to pay seventy-five dollars a week in alimony and child support.

For reasons none of the children understood, Dolores placed them in what David, then three years old, later called "either an orphanage or boarding home." It was the latter, but clearly felt like the former, and Dolores may have taken them there within weeks of getting custody. At least, that would be Ed's claim, and she never rebutted it. All three children hated this home, their memories differing only on which religion they were force-fed. The woman who ran the place with her teenage son was strict and abusive. Pat said that when kids misbehaved, "she would take a thorn branch, smack their butts," and that they had to sit by the piano every Sunday and sing hymns because the woman was Baptist. Steven hated the food, was thrown into cold showers for bed-wetting, and remembered spending every Saturday night reading Scripture because the woman was Jewish. David recalled a lack of food, cold showers, beatings, and standing at attention for hours while the woman played piano. Dolores came to visit on weekends, according to Pat. David remembered just one visit—when he followed Dolores outside to a waiting taxi to tell her how awful the place was, and Dolores replied that there was nothing she could do. Steven thought their father visited more than their mother did. Ed would usually take them to stay with him at a hotel for the weekend.

In September 1958, just before David's fourth birthday, Dolores applied to the court for permission to move the children to New York City. She'd been commuting back and forth, she said, looking for work as a model. And she asked that Ed be held in contempt of court because he hadn't paid any support since March. Ed's reply was that Dolores had "abandoned" the children in March and that she'd been "gainfully employed" since April—so he'd decided to send her just sixty dollars a week, the kids' share. According to Ed, she was already living in New York City, which would explain why the children weren't just in daycare but boarded full-time.

The court never had a chance to adjudicate on any of these claims. On November 9, Ed kidnapped his children. He showed up at the boarding home during one of his visitation weekends, told them to pack their bags because he was taking them to stay at the shore, and soon they were all on a plane to Detroit. Before they boarded, however, Ed called Dolores from the airport to tell her that the children wanted to live with him on a farm. Directed, no doubt, by her father, Pat then got on the phone to reiterate, "I want to live with Daddy on a farm." Years later, Pat still felt guilty about possibly saying such a thing. (Pat didn't recall doing this, but Dolores told her later that she had, and that it broke her heart.) In December, the court issued a warrant for Ed's arrest.

An important unstated point about the kidnapping is that Dolores would have known exactly where her children were going. Ed's sister Jean lived on a Michigan farm. That's where Ed had taken the children for the previous summer's court-approved vacation. That's where the family had always vacationed.

Ed's roots were in Michigan. He'd grown up in Hamtramck, a city that was completely surrounded by Detroit and, during his youth, mostly Polish. Ed's parents were immigrants. His father committed suicide during the Depression—by drinking ammonia, or so Ed eventually told Steven. Ed began working on a banana truck shortly after that. Working and drinking. He'd been eight years old. Ed brought Dolores to Michigan after they married, and Pat was born there. By the 1950s, most of the Wojnarowiczes had moved to Dearborn. But Michigan was not a convenient location for a merchant seaman. Ed moved his family to New Jersey after Pat was born in 1950. By the time he kidnapped the children and fled back to Michigan, he was working as an assistant engineer on the S.S. *United States*.

None of the children remembered when the kidnapping occurred. (The November '58 date comes from court records.) When David created the "Biographical Dateline" for his retrospective, "Tongues of Flame," he placed it a year earlier, in 1957: "Ended up with distant relatives on a chicken farm." His aunt and uncle. Distant? But then, David never felt much connection with his extended family or took any interest in his ancestry. He also had an imperfect sense of time, often situating events in the wrong year in his own account of his life.

Pat and Steven both said they'd lived mostly in Dearborn after the kidnapping—with their grandmother and Ed's two unmarried siblings, Helen and John. A few undated snapshots exist, with the children posed outside a small brick house. Here we get the first faint intimations of the menace Ed later became to his kids. Steven remembered Uncle Johnny intervening: "Eddie, that's enough. I'm not going to let you beat 'em." Or, "Eddie, that's enough. Leave 'em alone." And Pat still thought of Uncle Johnny as her hero. "He would stick up for me," she said, though she couldn't remember how.

Nor could either of them remember how long they were in Michigan or when they returned to New Jersey. Pat knows for sure that she attended school in Michigan—because it was a Catholic boarding school she hated. Then one day, Ed returned from one of his sailing trips with a woman he introduced as their new mother. This was Moira Banks—known as

Marion—a native of Scotland who'd been working as a nanny on Long Island. She'd met Ed on the ship while returning to New York from a visit with her family. She was two years younger than Dolores and, like her, had no family support or resources in this country.

The children spent, at most, a year in Michigan. In 1959, David appeared in a class picture at the Dryden Street School in Westbury, Long Island, with a Thanksgiving mural on the wall behind him. And his half-brother, Pete, was born there in December. After David published his Dateline, he was surprised to learn from his sister that they'd once lived on Long Island. He thought they'd been in New Jersey the whole time. But then, the geography of childhood had been something of a blur for them all. None of them could remember the names of all the schools they'd attended.

They didn't live on the Island for long. Ed didn't like it there. So in 1960, he moved the family back to New Jersey, renting in Parlin at 3108 Bordentown Avenue. Their one-story house was part of a long row all built from the same blueprint, like unlinked boxcars on a track. The area was just developing then, still farm country. And here David begins to come into focus as an individual. He made trips alone into the woods to look for critters. He found a kid who'd give him three dollars for a frog. He developed a risky game with a friend: lying down on busy Bordentown Avenue, just beyond the crest of a hill, so semitrailer trucks nosing over the top would suddenly have to hit the brakes while David and his friend got up and ran away.

David's half-sister, Linda—Ed's fifth child—was born in August '61 while they were living in Parlin. Soon after, Ed bought his first house, a split-level with a one-car garage at 9 Huntington Road in nearby East Brunswick. Here David lived until he left New Jersey for good.

In 1990, before he published *Close to the Knives*, his "memoir of disintegration," David called his sister and said he needed her to sign a permission form, agreeing to let him report "the private facts concerning her abuse," as the Random House legal department put it. David had included a story about their father picking her up and slamming her to the ground, then kicking her, while "brown stuff" came out of her ears and mouth. Pat had no memory of this—which David found shocking—but she signed the paper, thinking it could easily have been an incident she forgot. Or blocked out. "Because there was so much violence going on," she explained.

Still, Pat tried to emphasize the positive when possible. She had some memories from Huntington Road when her father "could be OK. And we weren't scared." That's when Ed was sober. But it seemed that he was rarely sober. Ed was an alcoholic who would never hit bottom, who would just keep falling. And when he was home, the family lived in a state of terror.

Steven remembered a kind of physical intensity their father had: how his lips would curl and spit would come out of his mouth, how the look in his eye said he wanted to kill, how—quite apart from the physical pain—he inflicted psychological pain that Steven thought more severe. He'd wave a beer can, demanding, "Know what I'm gonna do with this?" till Steven assumed that he was going to get it jammed down his throat, and then Ed would say, "I'm gonna drink it." He'd go into a tirade, telling them how worthless they were, how stupid, how like a seagull. ("All you do is eat, shit, and squawk.") He loved to lecture. He'd ramble through "the same old hunting story of how he caught a deer," as Pat put it. "You had to sit there for hours. You'd just die." He'd lash out if a kid's attention wavered. During one of these interminable sessions, Steven dared to scratch his legs, only to have his father pick up a jar of pickles and heave it at him.

Then there were the beatings. David usually didn't go into specifics apart from "got beat," but Pat and Steven both recalled their father using his fists, or his belt, or a stick, or a dog leash, or a two-by-four. He never broke their bones, said Pat, but they would be black and blue, and afraid for their lives. Steven felt he was treated differently by their father—treated worse—because he was the big boy, chubby and growing fast. (Eventually David would be taller than any of them, at six feet four, but he was both short and scrawny during the Jersey years.) Steven remembered bleeding from his eyes, ears, and nose, then being sent to the market with lips swollen "out to here" and people staring but not inquiring. Years later, David would say that he felt compelled to tell the Real Deal in his work because he never forgot the way the neighbors averted their eyes and shut their mouths.

In David's telling, the Catholic school he attended for at least first grade offered little sanctuary. He was frequently punished for not writing down assignments. (He needed glasses and couldn't see the blackboard.) The nuns beat him, he said, and made him kneel on bags of marbles. His siblings attended the same school. Yes, Pat said, they had to kneel in the corner as punishment, but she didn't recall any marbles. Steven did not recall any kneeling, just nuns hitting his hand with a ruler. According to David, they were all kicked out of Catholic school when they didn't bring in five bucks for the Mother Superior's birthday. Steven recalled being thrown out for fighting and remembered how glad he was when they all transferred to a public school, Irwin Elementary, in East Brunswick.

For David, the woods became safe haven. He especially adored the unlovable reptile and insect realms. He always said that if he brought home some injured creature, his father would "take it in the yard" and make David "watch him shoot it." How many wounded animals could he have found? His brother said, "I believe David saw things very magnified as a child." So, while David spoke of his father firing guns in the house, both Pat and Steven said that didn't happen. Not while they were living in East Brunswick. That came later. But they all remembered the rabbit story. In David's words, Ed "killed our pet rabbit and fed it to us claiming it was 'New York steak.'" David remembered their father revealing that it was their pet after forcing them to eat every bite. But Pat and Steven both said that he told them it was lamb, and that they only found out later that they'd eaten their own rabbit. They all thought it was disgusting, said Pat, "but David took it really, really bad."

One year, just before Christmas—probably in 1962—Ed gave each of the children five or six dollars to buy gifts and drove them to a five-and-dime store at a shopping center. When they finished and called home for a ride, their stepmother, Marion, told them, "I can't get your father up." He'd passed out drunk and Marion didn't yet drive. They would have to walk home—roughly three and a half miles—in a snowstorm that was fast becoming a blizzard. Half their route lay along Highway 18, a major thoroughfare that was unsafe for pedestrians. David had purchased a couple of turtles, which he carried in a Chinese food container. They trudged out through the wind and drifting snow for a mile and a half till they reached the Colonial Diner, and David insisted they stop. He was worried about his turtles. As Pat remembered it, a waitress approached because David was crying;

the turtles had frozen to death. The waitress called the police when she learned they were walking and had some two miles to go. Suddenly they had a police escort. Pat and Steven both spoke of how terrified they felt as the officers drove them home. When they arrived, the officers made Marion wake their father up so they could talk to him. But apparently no punishment was leveled. Steven speculated that "he was probably too scared to kick the shit out of us five minutes after the police left."

Once, when Ed confronted David over some transgression, David simply lied. Said he hadn't done it, and his father believed him. David knew that lying was a sin, but he felt that God would surely understand if someone could just tell Him what Ed was like. So David folded his hands and prayed: "Meet me outside in five minutes. I'll explain everything."

David had his first sexual encounters when he was too young to understand what they were. The first occurred with a boy who was fourteen when David was probably seven. He remembered asking the older boy, "Are we allowed to do this?"—and the older kid telling him, "Yeah."

An incident soon after this led to a nasty encounter with his father. Playing in one of the unfinished houses in the subdivision one day, David encountered a boy of about eighteen. The teenager took David to the attic and had David tie his hands to an overhead beam and take his pants down, then directed David to pull on his penis. David didn't want to keep touching it, so he picked up some insulation, wrapped it around the older kid's dick, and pulled. The kid screamed and David ran. His father got a phone call from the kid's father, stripped and beat David, then pulled out his own penis and said to David, "Wanna play with it? Go ahead." David refused and his father hit him again.

David loved drawing from a very young age. Marion recalled that she could keep him occupied when the older two kids were in school by giving him a paper and pencil. Once he was in school though, he started tracing—and telling people he'd drawn the pictures freehand. Teachers never called his bluff. But at some point, his schoolmates confronted him. They made him draw a sheep. David surprised himself by actually doing it. "Looked pretty good," he told me. "That's when I started drawing my own things." His young writing career developed through the same self-trickery. He'd lift stories from books and claim they were his own. That would explain the (regrettably lost) piece he wrote during this period about chasing wild anacondas through Africa, using deer as bait to lure them into cages. Then David began to invent his own stories.

This was life without Ed, the life less visible in David's Dateline and recollections.

Work took Ed blessedly away from home for weeks, and occasionally months, at a time. Then life was regular, with restrictions. Marion wasn't abusive, but she had her rules. They could not watch TV, listen to the radio, or play music. No snacks, no soda, no butter, no milk after breakfast. Marion was always conserving. Pat, David, and Steven changed their clothing and underwear once a week, and all had to bathe in the same bathwater.

Of course, as Steven admitted, they "were a handful." Steven and David fought so much they finally had to have separate bedrooms. In Parlin, when David would have been five or six, their father broke up a fight one night that Steven saw, in retrospect, as "typical kid stuff." But he was relegated to the furnace room—after Ed beat him—and his bed remained there until they moved. On Huntington Road, he and David shared a room again, if briefly. This time, it was Marion who moved Steven downstairs to the rec room. "They never had a hate for each other," said Pat, who remembered the brothers conspiring in their kid way to gang up on her.

Mostly, during the years in New Jersey, they were a team. David remembered the three of them sitting together behind Lee's gas station, Pat reading a story to calm them after one of their dad's beatings. Steven thought that might have been in Parlin, where there was a gas station two houses away. He used to go there to take naps in the bathroom.

Once they got to Huntington Road, they would team up on occasional weekends to break into the nearby Dag Hammarskjöld Middle School. Pat would unlatch a window in the home economics room on Fridays, and the three of them would crawl through it the next day. There they could engage in at least one activity forbidden at home: Pat would bake cookies.

Marion did not let them open the refrigerator without permission, much less allow Pat to bake. Sometimes they also broke into the school's cafeteria. (Steven would brace a door open with a rock on Fridays.) They could open the freezer just enough to grab some ice cream bars or Popsicles. Sometimes they'd steal frozen burgers and hot dogs, take them to a nearby park, start a fire, and cook them.

David also claimed, in his Dateline, that he'd stolen science equipment from Dag Hammarskjöld Middle School for Steven to sell. No, said Steven, laughing: "Who would I have sold it to?" But David did help him steal some money. Steven had gotten himself into a jam. Their father was a comic book reader. He never shared them, but he'd leave them in the bathroom, and one day Steven found an ad in the back pages promising that you could make a fortune selling flower seeds. He sent away for the seeds, then intercepted them at the mailbox. Neither his dad nor his stepmother knew a thing about it. He went door to door and sold the whole shipment, then spent the money on ice cream, cake, and soda. Now he was in trouble. He had no money to pay for the seeds; his dad would find out; he'd get a beating. David, apparently a regular at the school library, let Steven know that there was a fine box on the librarian's desk. On Friday, David unlatched the library window. On Saturday, the brothers went over to Hammarskjöld and David boosted Steven through the window. He found almost twenty-five dollars in the fine box, big money for a kid back in the sixties, enough that he could pay for the seeds and treat himself and David to snacks at Mom's Market.

"We just broke in to try to save my life," as Steven put it. Still, when David went back to the library the next Monday, he worried. He told Steven that night that he thought the librarian suspected him. He didn't relish breaking the rules. Not at this point in his life.

The children never knew when Ed was due back from one of his voyages. He would go directly from the boat to a local bar and call home from there. Then Marion would pick him up and tell him on the way home what the kids had been doing wrong. That's always when Ed would deliver his worst beatings. "You were never warned," said Pat. "That was the worst thing. Mentally, you were not prepared." Walking home from school, if they saw that the station wagon was gone, they panicked. Marion never left without forewarning them, unless it was to pick up their father. They'd become completely unnerved. They'd be anguished. That was Pat's word: *anguished*. Because none of them had keys, they had to wait out in the yard. "We'd be waiting for half an hour," Pat said. "And half an hour would turn into forty-five minutes, and we'd start going, 'Oh my god, oh my god, please don't let it be him, please, please, please.'" Ed would arrive home drunk and raging as he got out of the car—"YOOOOOU! GET IN HERE!"

One day, said Pat, she cracked: "I couldn't take it anymore." He'd returned from his weeks at sea and ordered them to sit in the yard and "don't move" while he took them one at a time to the basement for a beating. "He took Steven first, and I could hear the screams of Steven—with David and I just sitting there. Then David went down—or maybe they went down vice versa. I can't remember. I heard the screams. I just said, I have to get out of here. I have to run. I have to get us away from this." She got up and sprinted toward Dag Hammarskjöld Middle School—more terrified than ever, since she'd now violated the order not to move—and screamed at the crossing guard: "Call the police! I want to go to the police! I want to go to the police!"

The crossing guard took the hysterical Pat inside to the principal's office, but she wouldn't tell anybody what was wrong. "It's like I didn't want them to know what was going on in our home. Just—I want the police." Suddenly she heard her father's voice out in the hallway. "And when I heard his voice," she said. "I freaked out again. I just climbed the walls. I said, 'Get him away from me. I don't want to see him. I don't want to see him. I want the police!'"

Steven remembered this incident vividly. When their father saw that Pat was not in the yard, he put David and Steven in the car. "I remember the two of us just crying and yelling, 'Patty, Patty, Patty.' We were so worried about her," he said. Ed prowled the neighborhood, demanding, "You gotta tell. Where would she go?" One of the boys suggested the school; it had always been their refuge and resource.

Officials at the school did not hand Pat back to her father. They called the cops. But when the police finally came, they didn't know what to do. Pat kept telling them, "I am not going back to that house. He beats us." She was twelve or thirteen at the time. So they took her to the police station, "trying to find a solution" that would work for her. They promised Pat that if she went home, they'd make sure her father didn't hurt her. "I said, 'No way.' I was not going. Because sense came back to my head. I said, 'He's gonna kill me.'" Finally, one of the officers said she could stay with his family for a few days.

Ed did change his behavior after Pat returned to Huntington Road. "He never touched us again," Pat declared. But Steven was startled to hear that. He said his father never stopped beating him or David.

Suddenly, some five years after the kidnapping, Dolores reappeared. No one remembers how or why, but she showed up at a meeting after Pat had "cracked," a meeting at a local Catholic church that Steven didn't know about, that Marion didn't recall, and whose purpose can only be surmised. But Pat was there, and she remembered having "such a strange feeling" when she saw her mother again "after all the years of not seeing her." Dolores told Pat then that she could take her to live in Manhattan, but couldn't afford to take all three of them, so she thought it best to take no one.

In January 1964, Ed lost his job on the United States Lines, which had employed him since 1945. According to Marion, he got into an argument and quit. According to Steven, he was fired. David seemed to confirm that version when he wrote in one of his journals that Ed had started a fight on board and broke a whiskey bottle over someone's head.

For a while, Ed found work on ships that had just come into port, repairing or maintaining the engines while the crew was ashore. One day he arrived home with a Manhattan phone book, and Steven looked through it for his mother's name: Voyna. He couldn't remember how he knew that she'd taken the name Voyna. But there it was. And he whispered to Pat and David, "I found Mommy's number."

Ed lay passed out in a drunken stupor, and Steven went through his pockets for change. Then, all three of them rode their bikes together to the nearest phone booth and crowded inside. Steven dialed and said, "Are you my mother?" They told Dolores they wanted to see her.

So began a series of surreptitious visits. They'd tell Marion they were going to the park for the day, she'd give them a sandwich, and they'd ride their bikes to the bus stop. Dolores met them there, took them into the city to her apartment or to a museum, then brought them back. As long as they were home by five, there was never a problem. Pat thought they made five or six of these trips. David seemed to remember only the one that included a visit to the Museum of Modern Art. No doubt this was the first time he ever set foot in an art museum; he was impressed by a painting of a tree with babies in its branches (probably Pavel Tchelitchew's surrealist *Leaf Children*). He said later that this was what inspired him to become an artist, though when he went home and tried to re-create the piece, he utterly failed.

"There was a catalyst that got my mother to call," said Steven, but he couldn't remember what that was. Just that Dolores finally did call the house on Huntington Road. She got Marion and said she wanted to see her kids.

"I was in shock," Marion said.

It wasn't just that Marion hadn't known about the children's secret visits. She'd been told, by Ed, that he legally had custody and that Dolores had left them "to shack up with some millionaire." Marion believed this.

So she told Dolores that she'd have to talk to Ed about it, and he wasn't home. But when he did get home—"Oh, he had a fit," said Marion. "After all them years. All of a sudden, she wants to be involved." But they made arrangements. Dolores would come to the house to get her children on certain Saturdays and keep them till Sunday. She would take a taxi from the bus station, or drive. "I guess she borrowed a car from somebody," Marion said. "I know she had a boyfriend. I think he worked for Mattel Toys. Because the kids used to come home with all these toys from the weekends. I wasn't able to control 'em after she had 'em. Then she would get on the phone and start telling me how rotten Ed was. I told her, 'I don't want to hear this. Don't call me again.'" When Ed found out about that, he got them an unlisted phone number. Then, when Dolores wanted to see the kids, she had to send a telegram.

This went on for a while. Then one weekend, a taxi showed up without Dolores and the driver announced that he was there to take the children to the bus. Marion thought he looked scruffy and suspicious. Ed sent him away and took the kids to church. Dolores soon showed up and said something nasty to Marion—who slapped her.

Neither Pat nor Steven remembered Dolores coming to the house, or sending taxis, or tangling with Marion.

Pat thought it was all her fault that they were suddenly, unceremoniously, and permanently banished from their father's house. She had started writing Dolores letters. On one of them, fifteen pages long, she did not use enough postage. When it came back, Marion and Ed both read it. "The worst thing that ever happened," Pat said. "My father called me to come talk to him, and he had the letter in his hand. Scared the hell out of me. Because I had written 'my stepmother buys me ugly shoes' and, you know, stuff kids will say to their mom. And my father said, 'Pack your shit. You guys are going back to your mother. You don't appreciate anything.' My mother wasn't even aware we were coming until we arrived. He threw us at her doorstep."

But Marion didn't recall anything about a letter. She thought the breaking point for Ed came when Dolores appeared at the house. "He says, 'You want the kids? You take the kids. I can't go through this and neither can Marion. After all these years you want 'em, take 'em. But there's no money.'" Marion said she packed the children's things and then Ed drove them to Dolores's apartment.

David remembered the handoff happening at a restaurant near Port Authority and that they sat there while Ed told Dolores what little shits these kids were, what a waste of money. It was Horn and Hardart's, Steven clarified, inside Port Authority. He remembered sitting at a table for more than an hour while their parents talked and he ate a piece of spice cake. Pat had no memory of being in or near Port Authority at all. She was certain their father dropped them directly at Dolores's door. She could picture it.

No one could tell me when this happened. Not the year, much less the month. Not whether it was hot out or cold. Not even Marion. Here the timeline just disintegrates. Steven felt sure he was in the eighth grade, so— 1965 or '66. Pat couldn't remember what grade or even what school she was in. David situated the whole mess in 1963, which is certainly too early. According to his and Steven's school records, they entered the New York City system on January 10, 1966. They still could have arrived late in 1965. When their father shoved them into Dolores's care, he probably didn't bring their school records.

David would have been eleven. But, wherever and whenever this transfer—this trauma—occurred, one thing that stayed with all the children was the coldness of their father's fury. He just abruptly left. "Dumped us. No goodbye. No nothing," said Steven. Nor in the years that followed would any of them get so much as a phone call or a birthday card from Ed.

"So we finally find our mother. This is going to be our salvation," Steven said to me, his voice shaking, thinking no doubt of what had happened instead.

# 2 DISSOLUTION

**Dolores lived in** a one-bedroom apartment just west of Eighth Avenue, a short walk from Times Square. She and Pat shared the bedroom, while David and Steven slept in the living room on a mat and a fold-up cot. Certainly Dolores had not expected her children to ever move in. But once they were there, she told them that she'd been hunting and tracking them for years, and that every time she found them, Ed would move again, rooting them out of school and away from friends. As Pat remembered it, "She said, 'Guys, I never disappeared from your life. I just thought that I had to give you some stability.'" To do that, Dolores explained, she had to stop chasing them.

But if she'd been looking—and finding—why had she never taken legal action? Especially after the children found *her*. Pat speculated that her mother never had the money to hire a lawyer. Steven wondered whether his mother had ever even looked. But David believed she had. As did Pat, who cited a day back in Michigan at the Catholic boarding school she hated, when she thought she heard her mother's voice in the hallway. "Apparently she found me and tried to get in touch, but the school said she did not have permission. They did not have permission from my father." Pat thought her mother had worked in Detroit as a model at auto shows. Among Ed's papers, I found evidence that Dolores had indeed been in Michigan at that time. Ed filled out a document related to his service in the Naval Reserve, listing his ex-wife's address as "Detroit." It's dated August 1959. A month later, Ed married Marion and moved east, probably to be closer to his ship rather than to evade Dolores.

Marion knew nothing about Dolores ever hunting them, or finding them, or propelling Ed to move—until after Dolores had the children living with her. According to Marion, Dolores then bought clothes for them at Macy's and charged it to Ed's credit card. He refused to pay, ignored the subsequent letter from a lawyer, and then decided to leave East Brunswick so Dolores wouldn't know where he was. He moved his remaining family to nearby Spotswood in May 1966.


When I interviewed David in 1990, he told me that Dolores had decided within two or three days that taking her kids back had been a mistake.

None of them knew when she'd arrived in New York City, or what she'd been doing since the day they were kidnapped. Modeling, Pat thought. Showrooms and runways. Dolores does not show up in a Manhattan phone directory until 1962–63, living on East Seventy-first Street. She's not in the directory for 1963–64, then reappears in 1964–65 on the relatively angelic eastern edge of Hell's Kitchen. She was working as a secretary/receptionist by then, but living in a doorman building. David described her as "sophisticated, arty."

She encouraged the children to express themselves, where their father had beaten them for showing emotion of any kind. So, after years of pent-up rage, they erupted. "Once she gave us the green light, we were having these ransacking fights," David recalled. "Beds would get thrown. Shelves would come tumbling down. Basically we were trying to kill each other." It wasn't that the battles were new. It's that now they didn't stop. Back in Jersey, Pat said, they "could never play a game together because it would always end up in a fight. Someone would cheat or something." And of course, David and Steven had a history of squabbling. But in Jersey, they'd also shared moments of camaraderie, building forts together or breaking into the school. Suburban life came with built-in chances to get away from each other—to the woods, friends' houses, or their own backyard. Now they were inhabiting cramped quarters in a tough neighborhood. And whatever bond they'd had as a threesome began to come apart.

Her life suddenly akimbo, Dolores tried taking her angry kids to family counseling at an East Side church. Steven remembered going for individual sessions, getting help with his nightmares. As Pat remembered it, though, they often spent group sessions complaining to the therapist—about Dolores. That didn't last long. Dolores got fed up. Soon she also had to apply for welfare and food stamps, since her job didn't pay enough to support three children. Pat remembered waiting hours with "a hundred people sitting in chairs" to see what she called "the welfare dentist." Ed never gave them a dime.

Dolores had put a life together that didn't exactly jibe with full-time motherhood. Steven recalled that one hot summer day they went to use the swimming pool at a hotel on Forty-second Street. Dolores had a boyfriend who could get them access. When Steven called to her from the pool, "Mom, Mom, look," she marched to the water's edge and glared at him, declaring, "Don't call me 'Mom.'" Steven figured she was worried about impressing "some dude," but he found it quite painful. Eventually—no one remembered who started it or when—they all just called her "Dolores." Meanwhile, the children all began using the last name "Voyna."

After Pat turned sixteen in January 1966, Dolores took her to the nearest Woolworth's to apply for a job. Pat began working there every weekday after school and all day Saturday, turning at least half her salary over to Dolores. Pat attended Charles Evans Hughes High School, then an institution in serious decline. (Disciplinary problems were so bad by 1981 that teachers picketed, and the school closed shortly thereafter.)

David had entered Public School 111 on West Fifty-third Street in the second semester of sixth grade, no doubt reeling with culture shock. New York in the late sixties was a city in crisis—filthy, polluted, chaotic, violent, and roiling with racial tensions. The parks were dangerous and scarred by vandals. The subways were veritable trains through hell, un-air-conditioned, stinking, and often breaking down. Litter and dog shit fouled every piece of pavement. And Hell's Kitchen was still dominated by gangs like the notorious Westies. David addressed none of it in his Dateline for that first year in Manhattan. "Made cash drawing classmates sexual fantasies for lunch money," he wrote. An evaluation at the end of the school year said he was reading at the tenth grade level and seemed to like science. He had missed just one half day of school. But he got an "unsatisfactory" in half the social behavior categories (such as "gets along well with other children"). He didn't always pay attention. Nor did he participate in class discussions. He kept to himself.

During their first summer in New York, 1966, Dolores got both David and Steven into a Boys' Club summer camp. Pat, who stayed in the city to work, recalled that David sent Dolores a postcard describing the dangers he

*David in Hell's Kitchen with his friend Stephie in spring 1967. He was twelve. (Courtesy of Steven Wojnarowicz)*

had been facing at camp—how he'd gone to swim alone at a lake where no one was supposed to swim, how he'd encountered a huge snake. "My mother was shaking," Pat said. "She goes, 'He's going to drive me nuts.'"

The stories David told later about this part of his life emphasized his sexual encounters, first with predators and then with tricks. "I got molested almost immediately," he told me. "The second month." A man asked David to take him to what was then the RCA building in Rockefeller Center, and David agreed, proud that he knew where it was. As they got to the entrance, however, the man latched onto David's arm and dragged him through the whole RCA tour and then downstairs into the basement catacombs. David thought he was about to be murdered. Instead the man pulled David into a bathroom and tried to show him his dick. David somehow got out of this by asking if they could go back to the TV studio part of the tour, then pushing the man as they went through a revolving door. The man fell and David ran. "At home, no one wanted to deal with it," David complained. "I got yelled at." This had been a narrow escape, not a sexual escapade, and it would have been his mother who did the yelling. Neither Pat nor Steven recalled hearing a thing about it.

Nor could they imagine David, fresh from Jersey, as a hustler—though he would imply later that he began turning tricks almost as soon as he got to Manhattan. Pat was especially adamant about this. She recalled that David made friends with a girl in the building named Stephie. "I know what David was like then," Pat declared. "He was more interested in Stephie and his hamsters."

He began hanging out at a gaming arcade a block from home. Later he would tell Pat that this was where he had his first encounter with a potential trick. He told me the same thing—that he was in the game room, where there was a joke and novelty counter. One day as David stood admiring the fake noses and exploding cigars, a man came up and fondled him, asking him if he'd like to make ten bucks: "Come to my house and rub my shoulder." David snatched the ten and scooted off on his skateboard. He was beginning to figure out that the predators might be good for some money.

This story rings true for a boy of eleven, twelve, thirteen—as does his account of his first actual trick. He met the man in Central Park. He'd been told: Never get into a stranger's vehicle. So David took a bus to the guy's apartment, while the man followed in his car. David still remembered the weight of the man's body on top of him, the Polaroid shot, the man's cum. David asked for two dollars so he could get an ice cream sundae.

In September 1967, when he turned thirteen, David was in ninth grade at P.S. 17, a junior high. He earned the highest grades he would get in his secondary schooling, with a 79 average and no failures. He had skipped eighth grade, probably because of high achievement test scores.

As for the other things David said he was doing at this time, like stealing lizards and turtles from pet shops and letting them go in Central Park— "I could see him doing that," said Pat, though she never heard him speak of it. Steven remembered going to Central Park with David to fish with hooks made from bobby pins. The two brothers would go to a grocery store on Fifty-seventh Street and offer to carry people's bags to earn tips. They played pranks on their mother with items purchased from the above-mentioned joke and novelty counter—placing fake dog shit in the apartment of one of her boyfriends and pasting a fake crack on the television, then calling her at work to tell her Pat had broken it.

Underneath the kid stuff, however, lay an undercurrent of tension and strife. And David's life would change after 1968, when both Pat and Steven were booted out of the house.

Steven was the first to go. He had had the hardest time adjusting to life with his mother. Pat and David became allies, and would remain so. Steven was designated as the troublemaker.

In ninth grade, Steven found work at a nearby grocery store, pricing and shelving and sorting after school, sometimes till eleven P.M. He was paid in cash and handed most of it over to Dolores. "I was looking for approval," he explained. "Never did get it. I got a little pissed when she came home in a rabbit fur coat. She never spent the money on us."

Steven looked for ways to avoid being home, like going to the lobby to talk to the doorman. Soon he was hanging out with the doorman's brother, Johnny, who ran a newsstand on the corner of Fifty-first Street and Eighth Avenue. "I was adopted by all the street people, from derelicts to prostitutes," Steven said. "They called me 'the kid.' And I would work the stands until three or four or five o'clock in the morning." Johnny, a black man who was legally blind, became Steven's best friend. He was the first adult Steven ever met who encouraged him, saw potential in him, and told him things like "someday you're going to be the president of a company." Talks with Johnny lifted his spirits. Often on Saturday nights Steven would help him put the Sunday paper together, and in the morning Johnny would take him to Harlem for breakfast.

Steven was also cutting school a lot, and some nights he slept in the doorman's room. The doorman left at eleven P.M. and Steven had figured out how to pull the slats out so he could get his hand under the door and open it. He would put the doorman's heavy maroon coat down and sleep on the floor.

Pat thought her mother worried about Steven hanging out with his street friends all the time. Dolores couldn't control him, but didn't seem to try. Or didn't know how to try. "When she told him to do something, he just slammed out of the house," Pat said.

He felt abandoned—not just by his mother but also by David and Pat.

After he graduated from junior high in June 1967, Steven decided to run away, maybe become a hobo. So one day he headed down the West Side railroad tracks. But when he heard an unfamiliar noise, he realized this was just going to be too scary. Instead he took a bus back to East Brunswick. There he moved in with an old school friend for a few days, then went to his father's house in Spotswood. Ed was out of town. (He'd found work with the merchant marine on ships delivering supplies to Vietnam.) Marion let Steven move in for a week or two.

But she knew it couldn't be permanent. She called Aunt Helen in Michigan. "I said, 'Steve showed up here. I don't know what I'm going to do, Helen.' I said, 'There's no home.' And she says, 'Well, how about Steve comes and lives with me?' That's what we were going to arrange. For him to go live with Aunt Helen. But he took off on one of the kid's bikes and went way up to East Brunswick." He'd gone back to his friend's house. Marion couldn't remember how she found out where he was, but she drove over and put the bike—probably his half-brother Pete's—back in the car. Marion said she told him, "'Don't bother coming back here. I can't do this.' [We had an] argument over it, and after that I never saw him."

That July, Steven turned fifteen.

When her husband got home, Marion told him what had happened. "[Ed] said, 'If he ever comes to the door, don't you let him in this house.' So he did come to the door one night and I said, 'Steve, I'm sorry but you can't come in. Your father told me that I wasn't to let you in the house.' And he went away."

Steven moved in with some people Pat knew in East Brunswick, and someone—not Steven—let Dolores know where he was. In late August, Dolores drove out with her boyfriend, and Pat and David, to pick Steven up. Years later, he could still remember hearing the song "Red Rubber Ball" on the car radio as they drove back to Manhattan: "I should have known you'd bid me farewell . . . ."

The next night, at dinner, Dolores told Steven that he would have to move out, that Pat and David agreed with her on this.

As Pat remembered it, Dolores had come to her and David and said, "'Who agrees that Steven should live someplace else?' She's the one who set it up, so what were we going to do? We're not going to say no."

"I was told a vote was taken," said Steven, who was devastated, who could still barely speak about it more than forty years later. This was the most painful moment of his life. "I remember locking myself in the bathroom and crying. I had never felt such abandonment and grief." He stayed in the bathroom at least an hour. When he came back out, he "begged and begged and pleaded—to stay." Dolores gave in. He could stay.

One day soon after that, Steven took the elevator to the lobby and found Ed sitting there. It was the first time he'd seen his father since Ed "dumped" them. There were no "how are you's." Ed got to his feet and declared, "I'm gonna kill you, you fuckin' son of a bitch." He was furious that Steven had come to the house in Spotswood. He was drunk, and he had that terrible look with the curled lips that Steven remembered so well. Steven bolted for the door and ran toward Ninth Avenue and on for another eight or nine blocks. Ed could not catch him.

That Thanksgiving, Steven woke up in the doorman's room, where he'd spent the night, and walked to the newsstand. There sat one of the so-called derelicts he'd gotten to know, a man named Raymond who made a few dollars a day at the newsstand helping out. He asked Steven why he wasn't home for the holiday. Steven said something about his circumstances at home, his feeling that he wasn't welcome there. Raymond got another local vagrant to take over and said to Steven, "Follow me, kid."

Raymond took Steven to the Salvation Army on Tenth Avenue and handed over his last three dollars. "We'll take a Thanksgiving meal for two, please." They went down the cafeteria line and got their turkey and trimmings. Once they sat down, Raymond talked to Steven, telling him that many of the people seated around them had once been professionals, had once had families, and now they had nothing. He thought there were things Steven could do to avoid this destitution. What the specific advice was, Steven couldn't remember. But he never forgot this act of great kindness extended to him by someone who'd been labeled "a bum."

Steven and David had returned to their familiar pattern of fighting. One day early in 1968, in the midst of some ruckus, Dolores announced that she was going to call a girl Steven liked and, in his words, "tell her what a

*David at thirteen or fourteen in an early photo booth picture. Few, if any, photos exist from the rest of his teen years. (Courtesy of Steven Wojnarowicz)*

rotten shit I was." So Steven grabbed the address book out of Dolores's purse and ran to the newsstand. He did not come home that night.

The next day, David appeared at the newsstand, demanding that Steven return the address book. He refused, and David stabbed him in the arm with a pocketknife. Steven walked to the nearest hospital, where he got four or five stitches. Police were called. They took him to the precinct station, where the cops were waiting with David and Dolores. Steven didn't want to press charges. As he saw it, Dolores could manipulate David, who was "trying to protect Mommy." Apparently this incident hardened her resolve—either Steven or David would have to go.

Dolores was dating a policeman at the time. A couple of weeks after the stabbing, the police picked Steven up at the newsstand. They sat in the police car and told him he now had a choice. He could go immediately to Rikers Island. Or he could go to Brooklyn, to an orphanage. Steven had no idea that the cops couldn't just pick up a minor, someone charged with no crime, and deposit him at Rikers. He had no advocate.

So this was how, sometime in March or April 1968, Steven entered St. Vincent's Home of the City of Brooklyn for the Care and Instruction of Poor and Friendless Boys.

Years later, Steven would say that entering St. Vincent's had been "a gift," the best thing that ever happened to him. But he floundered at first, as he adjusted to living with 150 other "friendless boys." St. Vincent's was just a residence. He remained a student at Charles Evans Hughes High School in Manhattan, though he could have opted for a school in Bay Ridge and later thought he should have. He was a minority at Hughes as a white kid, and the late sixties were the days of rage. He got smacked around and threatened, and he started cutting school. But he stayed at Hughes because he wanted no more changes in his life—and because Hughes put him just two subway stops from the newsstand, still the epicenter of his emotional life. He returned there just two days after the police delivered him to St. Vincent's—and he ran into Dolores on the street. "I knew she was livid," said Steven. "She thought she had me locked up."

Or she was concerned that he was still hanging out with "street people." But if so, she'd never said it. Never said "I'm worried about you." The machinations that she used to get Steven into "the Home," as he called St. Vincent's—that's what he couldn't recover from. Voted out of the family! And to feel that both Pat and David had a hand in it. The bitterness he felt was slow to dissolve. It rankled. It hurt.

The major irony here is that Steven would prove to be the one who most valued family life, while David became the one with a life on the street.


Pat, meanwhile, had been transferred to the Woolworth's at Fifty-ninth and Broadway. There she met Bob Fitzgerald, who'd just been hired as assistant manager and, in his own judgment, was doing a horrible job. "If it wasn't for her, I probably would have gotten fired. She'd tell me what to do," Fitzgerald said. He and Pat started dating in March and would eventually marry.

Fitzgerald observed that Dolores thought she deserved a medal for taking in her three screwed-up kids. She felt abused by them. She told Fitzgerald she'd had to put Steven in a home because he tried to burn down the apartment. (Both Pat and Steven say this is not true.) "No sooner had she gotten rid of Steven than she started on Pat," said Fitzgerald. "Pat was getting the blunt end of everything at that point."

On the Fourth of July that summer of '68, Pat told her mother that Fitzgerald had invited her to go to Coney Island to watch fireworks. She promised to be home by eleven. Dolores said no. She wanted Pat to stay home, telling her, "We never spend enough time together." They argued and finally Dolores said, "If you go out the door, you're not coming back." Pat didn't take the threat seriously—though Dolores took Pat's keys.

That night, when Pat returned at eleven as promised, she found her suitcase downstairs in the lobby. Pat tried ringing the apartment. And ringing and ringing. Dolores didn't respond. Pat spent the next three days in a hotel. (Fitzgerald paid for it.) Then she went home to talk it over, and Dolores suggested that maybe Pat could move to the YWCA.

Pat was eighteen, about to enter her senior year of high school. She found herself a place at a women-only residence on the Upper West Side. The room was tiny, with a bathroom and a kitchen down the hall. Pat paid for everything out of her part-time Woolworth's salary. Soon she was struggling and had to apply for welfare.

David was still acting as his mother's protector. Dolores sent him up to Woolworth's in November to invite Pat home for Thanksgiving. "I was at the cash register taking care of people," Pat said, "and he kept insisting, and I said, 'Look—tell her I said no. What do I have to be thankful for?' And that upset him. He was really pissed off, and he just—he left. It's something that's always stayed in my mind, because I knew I had hurt him. I would have been glad to be with him. But I was not having anything to do with my mother."

One weekend, Dolores and David went to visit Steven at St. Vincent's. David told his brother that Pat had moved out, that she had no money but needed a winter coat. Steven, who'd been working as a messenger, decided that he could give her a hundred dollars. He was able to track her down at her Woolworth's job and gave her the money. For a winter coat, he told her. "And then I never really saw her after that." Pat could not recall getting this gift from Steven.


That fall, David had turned fourteen and entered the High School of Music and Art with a portfolio he'd thrown together overnight and a shoebox full of painted rocks. Applying there was probably his mother's idea. Pat remembered that Dolores wanted him to get into a good school.

"There was one teacher I met when I first got into school, who I really loved," David told me. "One art teacher. All I remember is this image of her standing on the desk, excitedly yelling about purple in the tree across the street. 'Look at that purple.' And I loved her." She was Betty Ann Hogan, the only teacher he connected with in high school, and the only one I could find who even remembered young David Voyna. She taught Introduction to Studio Practice, where David learned how to mix colors, stretch a canvas, paint a still life.

Hogan had no idea that David Voyna had become David Wojnarowicz until I contacted her, yet he'd stayed in her mind. "I was always sort of attracted to the ones who were afraid to be noticed," she said. As a fourteen-year-old sophomore, David wasn't just younger than his classmates; he was shorter than most of them. "Puny-looking," as Hogan put it. She allowed talking in Studio Practice, but David did not participate. He always sat by himself. He did not seem neglected. He was clean and still wore his hair short. He liked to do figurative line drawings of mythological or fantasy creatures. "There really was a hidden person that he wasn't sharing with anybody," Hogan said.

That year, David became friends at school with another skinny nerdy kid, John Hall. They were both misfits, both loners, and by no means constant companions, but sometimes they skipped school together to go on adventures. (David missed twenty-three days of school sophomore year.) John Hall remembered David taking him, for example, to Inwood Hill Park at the northern tip of Manhattan, the last patch of natural forest on the island and territory David had clearly explored before. He showed Hall a cave big enough to sleep in. Once or twice, David took Hall home, where he joked about Dolores's multitudinous cosmetics. "The preservatives," he called them. If Hall wasn't the only friend David made in high school, he was one of the very few.

David hated the High School of Music and Art. He said Hogan was the only teacher he respected. She taught there just a couple of years, but observed that there was a style the students had to emulate to get a good mark, a "bastardized Cezanne-ish, Matisse-y kind of look"—while she encouraged the kids to explore their own way of seeing things. Indeed, he got his best grades that year in Hogan's class—an 85 both semesters. He failed French once and math twice, and in four other classes he was right on the "passing" line with a 65.

After that year, David called Hogan a few times to complain about other teachers. He had given her a stone frog as a gift, assuring her that it was quite old. He said he bought it on a trip. A souvenir. When I called her, she still had it.

He began an affair with a mentally handicapped twenty-year-old named Anthony. Their two mothers were friends, and they had sex on the roof the night they met. David remembered the young man's penis against his face, remembered that for the first time he connected to someone emotionally through sex. This scared him so badly he thought he might have to kill the guy, so no one would know he was a homo.

"I tried to get information in the local library about what a 'fag' was," David wrote later in his Dateline. "The limited information I found depressed me." The "date" part of the Dateline has broken down here, but the affair had probably begun by the time he entered Music and Art.

At some point, they went to Florida together. Dolores had been invited by her friend, Anthony's mother. And Dolores in turn invited Pat, who paid her own way with help from Bob Fitzgerald. She wondered whether her mother had gone there to look for a rich man, but if so, they were in the wrong part of Florida. "The boondocks," said Pat. Far from the beach and the glitz. Staying in a trailer. Two dramas unfolded there.

First, Pat remembered that David and the young man who was "slow" stayed together in a dilapidated shack out back because there wasn't room in the trailer. They were in there during the day, with the door locked. "I don't know if they were caught in the act or not," Pat said, "but I remember there was a hoopla about it and my mother was really upset, and I think that's where her friendship with this woman ended." According to David, he and his friend "fucked the vacation away," and the family found out when they made a brief visit to the coast, where David considered suicide, standing in the motel bathroom with a razor pressed to his wrist. Pat recalled nothing about a visit to the coast or David with a razor.

What she remembered was the conflict she had with her mother when Dolores decided that they were all going to return to New York. Pat had connected with some young people her age, a brother and sister—in fact, with their whole family. They invited Pat to stay on and she wanted to do it. Dolores announced that she had hidden Pat's return ticket and wouldn't give it to her unless she came along to the airport. Anticipating trouble, Pat had already found the ticket. "She went bananas and came at me," Pat said. Now there was no way she was getting on a plane with her mother. In the end, Dolores steamed off to the airport with David. Pat did not see her mother again until she married Bob Fitzgerald in 1972.

David still found it bewildering years later: "My brother running away, then getting put in a boys' home. My sister's clothes all dumped in the hallway because she went on a date." He never knew how to read the mixed messages he got from his mother.

"I still have to struggle," he told me more than twenty years later. "I've never been able to fully [overlook her] responsibility for what she did or didn't do, and I feel anger about it. Yet at the same time, I just think she had a miserable life. She seems to have come through it somehow, but she did not do well. This was very weird to me my whole life. She seemed like such an intelligent woman. And I remember she could sing. She had this voice that would go up and down scales with like bird sounds . . . so full of life. And beautiful. The sounds and the way she thought, what she talked about.

"Then all of sudden—boom—it just vanished. And suddenly she couldn't do very simple things. She made this decision or emotionally came to this point where she felt she was losing her beauty after years of making a living off her looks, and her reaction to it was horrifying. She became full of fear. She had this obsession about meeting someone who was rich. And all the tension that went with that. Dating these absolute assholes. These guys—I hated them. Revolting oily characters. She denied that we were her kids. She introduced us as her little friends if we ran into her on the street. Horrible stuff. The messages were all over the place. I threw myself heavily into sex—for money or no money. Whenever I could get the money, I'd ask for it. But then, I also was very attracted to certain guys. It escalated faster

and faster till there were periods when I'd run away for like a week, sometimes for the summer, or just take off. And she was falling apart physically
and mentally and playing out all kinds of psychological stuff with me that
was very frightening, very upsetting, and I was becoming very violent in
reaction to things outside in the streets. At some point, I even stabbed my
brother."

# 3 THE STREET

**In late 1978** or early '79, a decade after these events, David began writing what he called his "street novel," based closely on his own experience. He abandoned the project after composing nearly sixty single-spaced pages, but it seems to have established a template for how he would speak of his life later. The book's narrator, a kid of unspecified age, begins in New Jersey with a drunken brute of a father and a beautiful mother he doesn't remember because she left so long ago. The kid runs away from home, thus eliminating family from the story and getting right to the crux of it: life in Times Square.

David's descriptions of the teeming square are surely drawn from his own observations. Already our child narrator knows that the "hustling strip" extends from Forty-third Street down Eighth Avenue to Thirty-eighth. He studies the crowd of sailors, runaways, winos, pushers, and prostitutes in two-foot-tall wigs. "Pimps lean in shadowy doorways with carved ebony sword canes and deadly looking fat peepshow operators chew cigars under the flashing entrances." He is enthralled. "The sense of it, be it anarchy or just exploding mad energy, grabs hold of you and shakes you through to the bone. My movements became animated and there was something stirring within, some valve opening and I was ready to go in all directions at once."

He finds a hotel where, for six dollars, he can spend the night in a squalid room smelling of decay and old food, where he has a bed with a bulge in the mattress and two water bugs to kill. A day later and nearly broke, our narrator describes the moment when—seated in the Automat with a plate of rice and beans—he decides to become a hustler. "I didn't have a fear of the sexual contact at all. Actually that seemed interesting." But he feels uncertain about "whether [he]'d be able to discern the fine line between a fella out for a good time or a knife wielding lunatic."

He then turns his first trick with a man he meets in front of a sporting goods store on Forty-second Street. They go to a hotel much like the one where the boy spent his first night. The narrator earns fifteen dollars and gets to keep the room after the guy leaves to catch a bus to New Jersey. "In the bathroom I slumped into the corner by the sink and stared at my face in the mirror illuminated by the fluorescent overhead light. I could hardly recognize myself."

David's school record indicates that by the time he was fifteen and in eleventh grade, something had gone very wrong. He missed seventy-two days of school that year, arrived late on fifty-three of the days he did attend, failed four classes, and just barely passed three others. His overall grade point average was 62—passing was 65. Eight out of twelve teachers gave him a personality rating of "N," for "needs improvement." (He'd earned just one "N" the year before.) He also fell out with John Hall—needling him over something. Hall couldn't remember the details, but he was certain that David had dropped out. He stopped seeing him at school.

This is most likely the point when David began his double life. In Times Square, he easily tapped into the man/boy underground and sold himself once a week or so. In the "street novel," he had assessed his narrator's desirability in a way that does not seem fictionalized. Customers had a type in mind when they searched among the boys on the street, wrote David, who was skinny and had glasses. "So I wasn't numbered among the most desired, though that gave me little trouble in scoring. Most of the Johns had it going for blonde kids, kids who were young and 'pretty' and had an eternal air of innocence about them. Some of this was just fantasy material from the porno shops, but I found a good deal of the characters who seemed to get a kick out of 'corrupting' a young boy. Johns would pull out a sheaf of porno magazines and ask you to page through it as they sucked you off. Others would just sit there with a gleam in their eyes jerking themselves off as you paged through a magazine filled with lurid photos."

David was still living at home, still more or less in school, and still more interested in lonely-kid things: wandering through the Museum of Natural History, walking over the George Washington Bridge to play on the cliffs, riding the motorized scaffolds at construction sites. Dolores always tried to send him to summer camp. At one, he met a kid who became one of his hustling buddies.

This was Keenan, a wild character a year younger than David. Keenan was already so jaded that, as David put it, "the only thing that kept him running now was a plunge in the Times Square and city scenes for a pure sensation of the unknown and unexpected. He was on a death trip continually." David ran into Keenan again in a gay bar in 1978 and wrote up his memories of one of their teenage encounters in his journal. He then fleshed it out in his "street novel" with dialogue and descriptions of decor that differ from those in the journal, but the basics are the same.

As a rule, the two boys would sit on the subway post railing at Seventh Avenue and Forty-second Street to wait for customers. Keenan was prettier and got more attention, but no matter who went first, they'd make a plan for where to meet later. One day, however, a man approached Keenan to say "my friend wants you," and Keenan declared that he wouldn't go without David. They walked to a parking lot on Forty-first Street where a limo sat, bearing "a fat guy with a face like a gizzard." In the "novel," this man promises both of them fifty dollars—more than David usually got. The limo then ferried them all to a doorman building in the East Seventies. Once inside, the fat guy told them he was "connected"—with the Mafia. He pulled out an authentic police badge to show them, and a German luger.

"He wanted to get it on with the two of us at once but we said: no," David wrote in his journal. "We were still new to hustling together and to have sex in front of each other would confirm what we were doing in each other's minds—it would make concrete the act of selling one's body."

So Keenan stayed in the bedroom with the guy while David waited his turn in the living room.

> A few minutes later [Keenan] came out holding his ass—he mumbled "He wants to try and fuck you—he tried me and said he'll give both of us $25 more if we allow him. . . . So don't say no." I didn't wanna do it but the guy grabbed me as I took off my clothes and wrestled me onto the bed—he had a huge bloated belly hospital white body like a huge codfish—he turned me over and got on top of me—it hurt and I struggled

I thought I was suffocating and finally with one thrust managed to throw the both of us over the side of the bed. . . . [Keenan's] story was bullshit—the guy had never promised 25.00 extra and I realized that the guy had forcibly fucked him and he was into one of his rationalizations, that I should have the same happen to me so he wouldn't lose face. We got our promised money and split the place, heading back to the Square for a balcony movie on some horror theme—bloody monsters and eyeballs plucked out in between soda and ice cream.

Usually, of course, David was hustling by himself. One night a man picked him up and took him not to a hotel but to a parking lot for city buses around Tenth or Eleventh Avenue. There he announced that he was a vice cop and that David was under arrest. When David began to cry, the "cop" said, OK, just give me all your money. David told him he had seventy cents. The man tried to fuck him, then pulled a knife, and David finally put it together: This was no cop. The man was marching him toward Twelfth Avenue when suddenly a city bus pulled up—empty, at the end of its route. David shoved the phony cop and ran screaming toward the bus driver, who sat there openmouthed. The phony cop turned away. David felt he'd come very close to being murdered by a madman.

Another Music and Art graduate, artist David Saunders, remembered meeting David Voyna, probably during the 1969–70 school year, eleventh grade for both of them. Saunders had run away from home the year before and realized that Voyna was a kid he already knew from the streets, specifically from Bethesda Fountain in Central Park, then a hippie hangout. "Sundown would come and rain would come, and you'd see that only a small group of people actually had nowhere to go. So we would band together and someone would say, 'I know a place to crash.'"

In those days, Saunders assured me, it was easy to survive as a street kid in New York. "We'd just eat out of the garbage," he said. "There was practically a half-eaten hot dog on every corner." And there were plenty of places to stay. New York was a broken city then, dotted with a large assortment of abandoned buildings. Anyone could just pry the barricade off a window, crawl in, and light a candle. When it was cold, Saunders said, he would just troll through the trash cans for something to insulate him at night. "You could stuff your clothing with newspaper, but that was a last resort."

David had changed physically by this time. He'd finally begun to shoot up toward his eventual six feet four, and he'd grown his hair out. Saunders described him as angular, goofy-looking, sloppily dressed. The two Davids were never close, just part of the same circle: "heads" at school, "dirty filthy freaks" on the street. According to Saunders, "heads" got together for inspiring discussions about philosophy, mind-blowing books—and drugs. David Voyna smoked pot and hash if someone passed it around. "While he was in my world, we were all pretending to be the same basic kind of character—a disgruntled leftist misanthrope or something. So we were hating the establishment, trying to find a new world, questioning everything, and just trying to be virtuous hippies."

As Saunders remembers it, he and David Voyna spent nights in the same place maybe four times. Along Columbus Avenue, from Seventy-second Street to Harlem, stood hundreds of empty tenements. In one around Ninety-second Street, Saunders himself crashed probably fifteen to twenty times. Five people were squatting there, with "cans of old baked beans sitting around, candles on the floor." David Voyna stayed there with him just once. On another night they both ended up in a building on the Bowery near Fourth Street. Then on a couple of warm nights, they slept in Central Park. That was always a group experience, everyone sleeping in a circle like a wagon train so if one was attacked, they would all wake up.

David was by no means living on the street full-time. He would still return to his mother's place, and occasionally he'd spend the night in a hotel room some trick had rented. He didn't bathe when he was gone from home for extended periods. Instead he began the practice of taking a bus out into Jersey, begging his way off when he spotted a good lake or pond, and wading out into it fully dressed. He'd lost touch with his siblings. He never visited Steven. He rarely saw Pat. She had moved to Jamaica, Queens, with Bob Fitzgerald and never called home, since she didn't want to speak to Dolores.

In his art classes, David began making very violent images—three-dimensional riot scenes with pig policemen and Black Panthers firing scope rifles from windows. He'd been going to antiwar and Black Panther demonstrations, and these were among the few things that made sense to him. He wore a black leather glove on his right fist. He told me that teachers destroyed his work or begged him not to pull it out when the principal came around, though I could not find anyone to corroborate this. He tried to set the school on fire with some *Anarchist Cookbook* device, but failed. (Both ex-teachers and ex-students remembered such a fire, in a stairwell, but no one knew who'd set it.) He disappeared from school for weeks at a time, but one of his hustling lines became "I need money for art supplies."

The two Davids never once spoke about their home lives. And Saunders never knew that the other David was hustling. By the time Saunders got off the streets in 1971, David Voyna had disappeared from school and Central Park both. At least, Saunders didn't see him anymore and assumed he'd dropped out.

He hadn't. At sixteen, he entered twelfth grade and his life somehow stabilized. This was apparently when he met a man named Syd in Times Square. Syd was thirty-five. He became one of David's "regulars" and then became something more. As David explained it, "He gave me some emotional warmth that I just was totally lacking and maintained contact with me up till I got off the streets." David used a street name with tricks, but he soon dropped it with Syd and told him who he really was. He loved Syd and felt he could have lived with him forever, if Syd hadn't been married with kids of his own. Sometimes when his family was away, Syd would bring David home. Syd stayed in touch after they stopped having sex, always encouraging David to write and draw. And David would call him when he was desperate for money.

David claimed that he met Syd when he was "around fourteen." Syd himself insisted that David was sixteen—when he came to David's memorial in 1992 and spoke to David's boyfriend, Tom Rauffenbart. While men who have sex with boys aren't above boosting the age of the boys in question, sixteen seems the likelier age in this case.

That last year at Music and Art, David missed twenty-one days of school and was tardy fifty-seven times, but his grade point average was in the 70s. He didn't fail any class, though he was right on the cusp in three of them. He just didn't have enough credits to graduate in June 1971.

Apparently David then tried summer school but—something happened. The record says, "Grades earned in summer 1971 are not included in high school average."

In August 1971, David traveled to Hurricane Island Outward Bound Camp off the coast of Maine. He would have qualified as an "at-risk youth." Given that he kept a journal here for the first time, he may have expected a life-changing experience. But the premise of Outward Bound seemed lost on him—the notion that an adventure in the wild would build character and self-esteem. David had had his share of physical challenges in the city. So the weeks spent rock climbing, sailing, and rappelling down cliffs simply taught him that he'd rather be in New York. There, he wrote, at least if you were starving, you could steal something.

Friends who knew David later in his life spoke of how grouchy and even mean he would get when he was hungry. He began his stay at Hurricane Island by giving up his last cigarette. Already he hated the other boys in his "watch" (a group of twelve) who wouldn't let him smoke it. But the main issue was food. He commented, usually negatively, on each meal. ("I am about to have hot cocoa in a pan. What a way to live.") About twelve days into his stay, he had to spend three days alone on an island, living off the land. This taught him how much he'd taken for granted. His first day there, he ate clams and limpets—and longed for Blimpie's. The next day, he gathered cattails and glasswort to eat. He got dizzy. He threw up. He developed cramps. He couldn't sleep. He thought of the sandwiches available at his local undistinguished deli. He vomited again. He felt like crying. If it was this bad after a couple of days, he wrote, what must the starving children in India be going through? He dreamed of eating licorice. He gathered and ate wild raspberries. He felt nauseated. At the airport, there would be doughnuts and coffee. And a candy stand. He'd buy a Milky Way.

He had some good moments on the island—when he found snakes. So beautiful. He captured one he wanted to take home, but it escaped, and some kid in another watch caught it. He hoped the snake would get back to him "alive without any broken ribs." But he didn't mention it again. "Thank Swami" he wrote at moments of blessed relief.

In this unadulterated glimpse into the mind of teenage David, he does not seem alienated from his family. He can't wait to see them, though he notes, "Things don't seem to be going right at home between Mom and Steve." (Steven explained that one summer he didn't want to go to St. Vincent's summer camp. "I wound up at Dolores's place," he said. "I don't recall what went on, but I didn't like it. I might have been there for several weeks.") David was sure his mother would let him come home early, when the camp called to ask her permission. He had thought of the excuse he needed to get out. He had to have time before school started "to adjust to the city." Clearly, he intended to take another swing at those missing credits. He mentions school more than once in this journal.

He got back to the city in September, just a few days short of his seventeenth birthday. But he didn't go back to school. It would be another two years before he got his diploma.


David said he did not recall his last day at home with his mother, or why he left. "Something happened. It may have been her who just said, 'Don't ever come back.' I can't remember."

That seems so unlikely. But I can only speculate that David recalled his ejection from the apartment as vividly as Steven and Pat remembered theirs. David never told anyone—at least anyone still living—how he ended up on the street soon after turning seventeen. Until the end of his life, a part of David wanted to protect his mother. He saw his father as a monster, so it was hard to even consider forgiving Ed. But David's feelings about Dolores were more complicated. He'd cast her as a tragic figure and didn't want to cause her pain. Despite the rage he would finally allow himself to feel. Despite everything.

David placed his move to the streets in 1970, a year before it actually happened. Usually he was off by two or three years. All the siblings tended to move events back in time. For example, Steven wrote a piece for his local paper about Thanksgiving with Raymond at the Salvation Army, stating that it happened when he was twelve. In fact, he'd been fifteen. Pat was certain that she'd been thrown out of the apartment when she was seventeen, if not sixteen and a half, when in fact she'd been eighteen. Neither one of them was trying to dissemble. Both made a real effort to help me pin down actual dates. Unlike Steven and Pat, David consciously created a persona or mask, but I think all the siblings shared some internal sense that they were too young to be experiencing these things. Misremembering is one way to protect oneself from a violating reality.

If David didn't remember how he ended up on the street, he did remember sexy encounters with sailors and sleeping in doorways and jumping naked from an ex-con's apartment during a raid. He remembered being drugged, raped, and beaten. But there's no chronology to these events. David was probably homeless from sometime in autumn 1971, after Outward Bound, until sometime in 1973. He did two stints in a halfway house, possibly living there for as long as a year.

For a while, he stayed at the Gay Activists Alliance (GAA) Firehouse on Wooster Street in SoHo, then a gloomy neighborhood, deserted after dark. A night watchman took pity on him and let him crash at the Firehouse for months. In exchange, David had to sell Lambda pins at meetings. He'd pocket half the money. Though he was hustling, he still did not identify as gay and wasn't politically involved. He just listened to the factions arguing. He particularly remembered the night German filmmaker Rosa von Praunheim screened *It's Not the Homosexual Who Is Perverse but the Situation in Which He Lives*. The film's critique of superficial gay sexual behavior and bourgeois striving outraged most of the GAA audience. David had been asleep upstairs and woke to find this foreigner facing an audience out for his blood. Years later, David would make a film with von Praunheim himself (*Silence=Death*, 1990), but as a teenager, he found the director intimidating. And sexy. After the screening, David followed him through the streets but never worked up the nerve to speak to him. The screening occurred sometime in 1972. An arson fire destroyed the Firehouse in 1974.

In Times Square, David met a man who was working as a counselor at a halfway house and passing bad checks to supplement his income. David couldn't remember the man's name. "He always liked to have sex with me and give me a little money." The guy had an apartment near Forty-fifth and Eighth Avenue and he invited David to move in. David was going through another phase of shoplifting lizards, snakes, and toads from pet stores and Woolworth's. Once he moved in with the man, he started building terrariums for the animals out of old chests of drawers and other detritus found on the street. The man put up with it for a few months, and then managed to make a case with his colleagues at the halfway house for admitting David as a potential jail risk. So David entered a halfway house on the West Side of Manhattan that had been set up for kids coming out of jail. "They gave me a room. It was great. I fattened up."

During the "street" years, the one family member David stayed in touch with was Pat, though their contact was limited. Occasionally he called her, and they'd meet in Chinatown for a meal or Pat would treat him to a movie. At first, she assumed he was living with Dolores. He never told her otherwise. "Never. He knows I would have freaked out," she said. But at some point, Pat did become aware that David was living in a halfway house.

He was probably there when Pat married Bob Fitzgerald in September 1972, at a Catholic church on Manhattan's Fourteenth Street. David served as an usher. As a wedding gift, he created nine colored-pencil drawings in the style of Edward Gorey, labeled "The Undiscovered Works of an Antiquated Photographer by David Voyna 1972." Pat had invited her mother—the first contact they'd had since the trip to Florida. Not only that, but Pat chose to get ready at the Hell's Kitchen apartment. There she argued with Dolores, who insisted on wearing a white dress. (Traditionally, of course, only the bride wears white.) Meanwhile, back at the church, the time for the wedding came and went, with no sign of Pat, and the organist was threatening to leave; she'd been hired just for an hour and had other appointments. Finally Pat arrived, with Dolores, an hour late. Both were in white. So as the mother of the bride marched down the aisle on David's arm, the organist saw a white dress and launched into "Here Comes the Bride" while everyone in the church stood up. Dolores had stolen Pat's moment.

The people running the halfway house wanted David to find work. They gave him some decent clothes to wear, and he went out with good intentions, soft-spoken. He remembered getting rejected from loading dock jobs, janitorial jobs. He'd walk in for an interview and see shock on the foreman's face. He realized that he carried some peculiar energy from the street. He embodied rejection now. "People who spend a certain amount of time on the streets—something happens. There's no way they can just drop what that feels like." David never did find a job during that first stint at the half-way house, but he did meet Willy.

David's descriptions of Willy present him as unpredictable, danger-ous, a risk taker, a criminal. Willy had done time for trying to kill his foster parents. They'd go on vacation and lock him in the attic with a box of ce-real and jugs of water. So he dumped roach poison in their soup. At least, that was Willy's story. David never mentioned Willy's last name, but talked and wrote about him for years afterward. In one story dating from the mid-seventies, he described meeting him in the dining hall at the residence. Willy walked in with a boom box he'd rigged up with Christmas lights that would brighten or dim according to the music's volume. David sat there drawing obese birdlike creatures. David and Willy became inseparable, and they moved out of the halfway house together. David wrote that he was kicked out "for refusing to get a job," but he said in the same piece that a counselor told him he could return if he came back without Willy, who was thought to be a bad influence. In one story, David said he'd been at the halfway house for a few months; in another, he said he'd been there for a year.

Pat and Bob Fitzgerald were living by then in Forest Hills, Queens. They had an extra room, and Pat offered it to David. He chose not to take it, but Pat always regarded it as "David's room" and sometimes he'd spend the night. For one thing, Pat was the only person he trusted to cut his hair, so he came whenever he needed a trim. She remembered him talking about a friend he'd made, and how he'd come to hate the halfway house. So she actually found an apartment for him to rent with this friend, probably Willy. Pat could not remember the friend's name or the apartment's location, ex-cept that it was in western Queens close to Manhattan. Pat paid the secu-rity deposit and the first month's rent and told David that he and his friend would have to pay from then on. They'd have to get jobs. She was certain that they moved in for a while but concluded, "I should have known he was too immature."

One day David's friend called Pat to say that David was in the hospital. This must have occurred during his brief interlude in Queens, because he'd entered a hospital in that borough. Pat couldn't remember details but thought the problem had something to do with his teeth. Steven remembered a hospitalization David had—though he thought it came a few years later—when "his teeth were so rotten he OD'd on aspirin. He would dissolve these aspirin on his teeth because he was in so much pain." Pat rushed to the hospital and then tried to contact Dolores. "Mother was nowhere to be found," Pat recalled, "and David said to me, 'No, there's no point.' I found out later she was on a trip to the Bahamas."

David told me he once went to his mother when his head was exploding in pain and his mouth was bleeding. He wanted her Medicaid card so he could go to the hospital. This is probably when that occurred and the trip out of town would explain why she told him to just slip the card under the door when he was done.

But the order of events during his time on the street with Willy is really unknowable. Obviously, David did not hang on to the Queens apartment. For a while, he and Willy stayed with an ex-con who had an apartment across from the Bowery Mission on Third Street. At some point, they went to Wooster Street because there was an abandoned bus there where they could sleep. Some nights they made their way to rooftops or boiler rooms. David also told a story about finding an abandoned bus on Houston Street, already occupied by an old bum who tried to choke him as he squeezed through a window. In that story, he and Willy ended up at a dive waterfront coffee shop where they slept in a booth till the counterman held a bottle of ammonia under their noses. David also told me that Willy tried to kill him a couple of times, once slamming him in the face with a marble slab. "He'd go on these jags where he'd suddenly get so ragey he'd try to stab me or something." Yet he stayed with him. Some nights they'd walk hundreds of blocks, practically the whole island of Manhattan, on opposite sides of the streets picking up every wino bottle they found and throwing it ten feet in the air so it crashed a few inches from the other one's feet. "On nights that called for it, every pane of glass in every phone booth from Midtown to South Street Seaport would dissolve in a shower of light. We slept good after a night of this in some abandoned car, boiler room, rooftop, or lonely drag queen's palace."

He could not remember who offered them the place near the Brooklyn Academy of Music, then a high-crime area. Some lesbians who owned a building there had awakened one night in the middle of a robbery and decided to clear out. David and Willy were told they could stay in the building if they guarded it. David said, "We tried. We were getting robbed in our sleep. We were nailing down windows and people were scaling the walls and coming in." David wrote two accounts of this sojourn—one in a letter to a friend. He and Willy found the place loaded with books and a guitar. They set up rooms for themselves, stole groceries, and cooked steaks over a fire in the hard dirt backyard, living unmolested for a week. When the robberies started, they couldn't figure out how people were getting in. Thieves got the guitar and all the food. One night, the women who owned the place suddenly showed up, screaming, since no one had informed them that they had house sitters. One of them was very pregnant and gave birth a day later in what passed for the living room, surrounded by candles. (There was no electricity.) A guy who was in the building courtesy of David and Willy proceeded to steal this woman's money (seven dollars) while she was in labor. Naturally, her friends then threw them all out.

David headed back into Manhattan with Willy, who knew some transsexuals they could crash with for a few days. But David's street life was winding down at this point. He'd become skeletal. During the last days in the Brooklyn house, he felt dizzy and had what he called "a massive toothache." He could no longer sell himself except to the worst creeps, including guys who would beat him up. He stopped trying to hustle. He and Willy were now hoping they could get on welfare. "We waited days in these offices," he told me. "I remember going to the Salvation Army, and this son of a bitch—I'll never forget it—he just took one look and said, 'We don't help people like you.'" Somewhere they secured two night's stay in a welfare hotel. "They sawed the bottom and top off the doors so it was like a barroom door," said David, "and these creeps would crawl in. You're trying to sleep and some salivating creep would drag himself into your room. We didn't even last one night there."

"Willy and me got so weak after awhile our judgment was bad," he wrote in one of his unpublished accounts of this period. Meaning—they went to Macy's kitchen department and stole meat cleavers they could use to mug people. For several nights, they prowled Park Avenue, looking for someone rich and alone to rob. A gay man picked them up, but when they got to his front door, a cleaver dropped out of Willy's pants and the intended victim began to scream. The next night, they spotted a man in a business suit and ran for him, but he turned in terror at the sound of their running feet, and they saw that he was just an old bum, filthy and wearing a found suit jacket with rips in the shoulders. "I almost burst into tears," David wrote.

Back when they first met, David and Willy had fantasized together about going upstate to search for Willy's real father, who supposedly owned a large farm. They would ask him for just a few acres. Whatever they intended to do with those acres, David never said, but they argued over it in the end. David was beginning to understand that he had to separate from Willy.

In another one of the stories he later wrote, he gave Willy the name "Lipsy" but the incidents, again, seem drawn from their real life together. They hang out in the Village after meeting in a halfway house. Lipsy had been in jail for trying to poison his parents. The narrator had left home after years of a double life split between home and Times Square. He and Lipsy steal meat cleavers at Macy's but can't pull off the robbery they plan. Briefly they move in with a transsexual. And so on. At the end, the narrator and Lipsy walk out onto a pier at Twenty-ninth Street where they share a stick of weed and talk about the end of their friendship. "I was getting too crazy and needed a break," says the narrator, "after a year of sleeping in boiler rooms, abandoned autos, gas station trailers and rooftops." They head over to a deserted diner near the river to spend the night. Inside it looks like a neutron bomb had gone off—no humans, but dried food still sitting on plates along the counter. "We cleared out the back room where a mattress lay sideways along the wall. . . . After setting the mattress on the floor we lay down ignoring the roaches flitting across our bodies and fell into deep sleep. . . . The next morning when I woke up, Lipsy was gone leaving behind his coat and a dollar in coins and two joints."

David begged the people at the halfway house to take him back. They said yes—if he promised to return to school. He agreed and became what he called "a model A citizen," earning his high school diploma around the time he turned nineteen in September 1973. He graduated 403rd in a class of 440.

Bob Fitzgerald remembered vividly the day he and Pat went to visit David at the halfway house. They decided on the spot that they were taking David with them, back to Forest Hills. To Fitzgerald, the place looked like a flophouse. Drunks everywhere. Cockroaches everywhere. And when he walked into David's tiny room, he saw a rat on the windowsill, just outside.

David had been feeding it.

# 4 THE SECRET LIFE

**He found a** job at the original Pottery Barn on Tenth Avenue in Chelsea—then really a barn, actually selling pottery. When co-worker Wendy Wolosoff-Hayes met him, he was still David Voyna. She invited him over for dinner, and in the sketchbook where she was collecting recipes, he drew a bare-breasted woman—one hand holding a breast while her other hand touches a long-eared rabbit. He labeled it "David's first porno drawing 1973."

David worked in the basement with the discounted items, but his main job was packing bags and loading them onto a dumbwaiter. Working with him was a young writer named John Ensslin, who eventually became David's best friend and co-editor of the literary magazine they started: *RedM*. By the time they met, David had taken back the surname "Wojnaro-wicz." (The change to "Voyna" was never official.) Ensslin described his new friend as a voracious self-directed reader. The two of them spent hours in the Pottery Barn basement discussing poetry.

In this era, poetry was braided into the counterculture. Every coffee-house and bar boasted a reading series, or so it seemed, while small presses and little magazines proliferated. When David came off the streets and re-turned to school, he'd discovered Rimbaud, Kerouac, and Genet. While he still drew constantly, he hadn't gone past quirky line drawings, occasionally funny, sometimes tentative, often derivative. He hadn't yet found a way to connect his art to what moved him. But with poetry, he'd discovered a path quivering with hallucination, euphoria, dissociation, and rage—the hot spots on his own internal map. And the legends must have resonated too: Rimbaud leaving Charleville, wandering beneath the stars in torn clothes, sleeping in a Paris doorway, getting arrested and sent home as a vagrant. Kerouac hitting the road with Neal, rhapsodizing over diner food, conversing with bums.

David romanticized that life. Certainly he saw it as a model for how to think about his own experience.

By late '73 or early '74, David had left town to live on a farm outside Churubusco, New York, near Plattsburgh and just a few miles south of the Canadian border. Exactly how David came to be living with a couple named Paul and Jane Braun remains a mystery, but apparently he knew both Paul's father and brother from Pottery Barn.

Among his contact sheets are three—in an envelope he labeled "FIRST PHOTOS (AWFUL)"—that come from this location: a hippie couple, a dwelling that looks like two connected yurts, a haymow, a potbelly stove, snow-covered farmland, and young, long-haired David. What appears to be his first letter to Ensslin from Churubusco is postmarked February 23, 1974. He reports that he's practicing the harmonica and will soon help someone build a fieldstone fireplace. In subsequent letters, David mentions planting a half-acre garden, building compost bins, and tearing down an old house "for lumber to build the barn."

He and Ensslin were also exchanging poems in the mail. Responding to one critique Ensslin does not recall making, David wrote, "I understand what you are saying about my poetry as far as its bordering on self pity." In another letter, he says he is "trying to refrain from being hung up on depressing things as all I've been writing is about some sad gray dismal thing in life. . . . people wandering in the great grey void of the world, endless littered streets, sagging docks and railroad cars rusting in the oily rain. . . . I can't change what I write about or rather feel so it's a never ending cycle which really throws me around." He hopes to do primal scream therapy "so as to work out the tension." And he wants to take writing classes, "as I need them terribly."

Ensslin lived in North Bergen, New Jersey, and organized poetry readings in nearby Weehawken for an antiwar, pro-farmworker co-op called the Community Store. He also edited its mimeographed magazine, *Novae Res* (*New Things*), filled with poets who'd read at the store. Though David had never read there—or anywhere—Ensslin invited him to contribute. The

*John Ensslin, co-editor of* RedM, *hosting a poetry reading at Morning Star Arts Center, where he got David his first reading. (Courtesy of John Ensslin)*

one and only issue appeared in April 1974, with David's first published work: several illustrations, including the cover, and four untitled poems. "Running through the dense underbrush / twigs snapping angrily scattering rabbits / quail and others I fought my enemies / treading softly among the moss and ferns / stumbling over logs I waylaid my father . . . ."

The other three poems include imagery of farm life, a dream that he and a girl are "enveloped in each other's feelings," and a childhood memory of ice-skating on a pond. For the cover, David created a careful pen-and-ink drawing of the Sea-Port Diner in Lower Manhattan. Inside he illustrated some of the other poems—here a caterpillar on a branch, there a hand lifting a child's drawing from a garbage can. He hadn't found his style.

In a letter postmarked April 23, 1974, he asked Ensslin to send copies of *Novae Res* to his sister's house in Queens because he was leaving Churubusco for a while. Obsessed with going to California, David had come up with a mad plan. Later, his claim that he tried to ride a bicycle to California and made it as far as Ohio would seem especially unbelievable. But he really did this. (He just, typically, had the date wrong.) That spring, he returned to his sister's place in Forest Hills to prepare. Somehow David had acquired a nineteenth-century edition of the complete works of Shakespeare, which he sold for two hundred dollars—to Fitzgerald, who wasn't sure they were worth that much. But this allowed David to buy a bicycle.

Fitzgerald recalled the day David left for the West Coast. "Pat and I went out to bid him farewell, out in front of the house in Forest Hills. He got on his bicycle with a knapsack on his back and started wobbling up the block, and I said to Pat, 'He's not going to make it to the Brooklyn Bridge. He's just ridiculous.' And she goes, 'You're always putting him down,' and I said, 'Pat I'm not putting him down. I'm realistic.'"

They did not hear from David for two weeks. Finally he called collect—from Ohio. He'd been sleeping on the ground and someone had stolen his wallet, leaving him flat broke. He was also very sick. Pat and Bob wired him money, telling him to ship the bicycle and take a bus back to New York. Fitzgerald recalled David going into the hospital with pneumonia upon his return. Then he went back to Churubusco. In an undated letter to Ensslin he reported, "I am doing a lot better after abandoning my insane cross-country trek to primal therapy."

The sojourn upstate is most notable for David's changing perspective on it over the years. In a letter to a friend written in 1976, he described his time there this way: "I did an acre of organic vegetables and an acre of grass in the backwoods in a clearing. . . . The people who owned the property were almost never there it seemed & I had no vehicle other than my own legs so I spent weeks wandering through the woods & streams & sitting in a rocker in one of two domes we built burning cherry wood and letting the mind wander out into the dusty fields." But when he constructed his Date-line in 1989, he wrote: "Worked as a farmer on Canadian border. Was supposed to share profit from ten acre vegetable garden. When time to pick crop, the vet tried to run me down in a pick-up truck. Left for n.y.c." Both accounts could be true: An idyll that ended badly. But it's like hearing from two different Davids and it's right there in the syntax—from breezy long lines to telegraph staccato.


David returned to the city by late August 1974. In September, Pat left for Europe—a move she never expected to become permanent. She had signed with the Stewart Modeling Agency sometime in '73, and the agents there decided she should go to Europe "to build her book." Within a year, she was on the cover of L'Officiel. She appeared in a Vitalis commercial that ran during the Super Bowl. Her modeling career would continue until 1986.

Steven had left New York City in '71, after taking an extra six months to graduate from high school. (He too had had excessive absence.) "I had turned my life around in the Home," he said. "I started to understand conceptually how you can get ahead if you just cooperate. And so I was given an honor from St. Vincent's for being an excellent child and student, and consequently they agreed to pay all of my college tuition." St. Vincent's also gave him money for rent and, when he was ill, paid his medical bills. Steven began his studies at Middlesex County College in Edison, New Jersey, about fifteen miles from his father's place in Spotswood. He began trying to reconnect. He'd go see his father at five in the morning. "It was the only time he was sober. He would take me to the bar at seven, and he and Tuna Fish Charlie would have five or six shots of Seagram's. Then I'd take off and leave him be."

David and Pat visited their father once after Pat's marriage. She wanted him to meet Bob Fitzgerald. Pat and David hadn't seen the house in Spotswood before. What stayed with Pat is that her father wanted to show her the upstairs. "As I started to walk up the steps, he smacked my behind. I had a short skirt on. So I turned around and he said, 'Oh come on. I changed your diaper when you were a baby.' And I said, fuck this, and never went back. *Couldn't* go back."

As Fitzgerald remembered it, Ed had been friendly, nice, doting, giving them food. When Pat announced as soon as they left that she would never go back, he didn't know why. As for David's experience of the visit, Fitzgerald said, "I can picture him right now. He sits in this chair with this long hair. He had very long hair. Way down past his shoulders. With glasses. And he sat there and said nothing. Sat there and listened all day."

Sometime in 1974, David visited Steven in New Jersey and drew some pictures for him. They would not really spend time together again for ten years.


After his sister left for Europe, David moved in again with Bob Fitzgerald in Forest Hills and got a job in Manhattan at Barnes and Noble, where he met poet Laura Glenn. There was a flirtation, "a little bit of a romantic entanglement that we had just briefly," as Glenn put it. But David scared her with his stories about living on the street. "There was a seamy side to his life." She also thought he was gay. David told her he was not. Ultimately, they were "just friends," but there'd been a spark. When Glenn left for a job at Marloff Books on Sheridan Square, David would visit her there.

He soon left Barnes and Noble himself for a job at Bookmasters, a chain with several stores in Manhattan. There he hit if off immediately with a co-worker, Peeka Trenkle, who was living with her boyfriend in a large apartment at 104th and West End. David had moved in with them by January 1975.

David lived at the West End apartment for at least a year and a half. Peeka's boyfriend, Lenny, was a part-time musician and full-time purveyor of Thai stick. He had a music room lined with cork, a living room covered with red felt, a cat named Spider, and three extra bedrooms to rent out. David had a mattress on the floor, a pile of books, a Patti Smith poster, and a manual typewriter, at which he worked diligently on poems and stories. He sported a droopy mustache and hair down to his collar. The roommates took to calling him "Woj-narrow-witz" and recalled that, despite his shyness, he could be cuttingly funny, and though he wanted to be a writer, he also did a lot of drawing. "That was almost compulsive," Peeka said.

On January 31, David gave his first public reading at Morning Star Arts Center in Union City, New Jersey, thanks to Ensslin, who organized it and acted as MC. The next day, David wrote a rapturous three-page letter to Ensslin, though by then Ensslin was ensconced nearby, in a Columbia University dorm. "Oh joy," David began. He'd been so nervous, so keyed up, he wrote. "But when you gave that introduction, it bang-knocked away all fears inside." A world had opened and David was feeling expansive. So, if the Community Store in Weehawken needed anything—a political cartoon for the newsletter, a painting to sell (the co-op could keep all the money), any resources he had—he would give it. He wrote that he was again anxious to travel but said, "I get this vision that I'll lose all I'm hoping to do if I leave now. Just starting to get slowly in touch with work (writing) and I have so far to go before I can successfully release my unspeakable images, visions, whatever. I'm glad having friends like you. . . . Maybe it's all inside me and it takes certain people to strike a thing inside that releases it all or in parts."

Ensslin was dating a woman named Lee Adler, who lived on Court

Street in Brooklyn with two young gay poets, Dennis DeForge and Michael Morais. Ensslin had invited DeForge and Morais to read in Union City along with David. Though David doesn't mention them in his letter to Ensslin, this had been a significant encounter. The poets at West End began to socialize with the poets on Court Street. Morais was editing Brooklyn College's undergraduate literary magazine, *riverrun*, and David drew the cover and an illustration for it that year.

He also had an affair with Morais, much to the surprise of everyone who heard about it later, including DeForge, who did not think David was gay. David was not even sure he was gay at this point. He kept the relationship secret, but Morais told DeForge about it. People who knew Morais seemed to be in awe, describing him as not just a dynamic performer of his own poetry but also "a muse" and "creativity personified." He'd been part of the Negro Ensemble Company. He was also bisexual. Within a year or two, Morais had married and moved to Montreal, where David kept in touch with him by letter.

The West End apartment was convivial most of the time, with occasional agitation—and there David stepped in. Lenny, thirty-eight years old to Peeka's nineteen, was constantly criticizing and browbeating her. David would sneak up behind Lenny, mimicking all the huffing and puffing, making faces. One night, a roommate named Leo—a black belt in kung fu—tried to break down the bathroom door so he could beat his wife, who'd taken cover there, and David stopped him.

On Easter they were all sitting around, too broke to do anything festive, when David caught one of the cockroaches that infested the place, cut out bunny ears, gave it a cotton tail, and set it down on the kitchen table, where it lurched along in its costume to the delight of the roommates. Years later, David would name these critters "cock-a-bunnies."

He spent hours in the kitchen talking to Peeka. She was the one he spoke to about his father's violence, perhaps because she too had had a rough childhood. Her memories of these conversations were vague, but she recalled their "heart connection," that David was troubled, that they talked at length about painful things, and that he would cry. She felt there was a

*Peeka Trenkle became a confidant of David's while they were roommates at the West End apartment. (Courtesy of Peeka Trenkle)*

softheartedness in him that he was not interested in cultivating. After he moved out, in 1976, they lost touch. "He was very enamored of William Burroughs and Jack Kerouac and this sort of self-destructive brilliance—he loved that and we used to have talks about it," Peeka said. "My big question was, do we have to destroy ourselves in order to be creative. I felt like he was kind of hell-bent on it. He wanted that. He wanted the dark part."

By early '75, David was working at the Bookmasters in Times Square. Sometime during that year, he ran into his old high school pal John Hall—either at Bookmasters or on the street. They hadn't seen each other since David was fifteen and they'd squabbled over something. John Hall couldn't get over how much better David looked. Aviator glasses instead of "goofy" glasses. A decent haircut. "I remember thinking pleasantly . . . he looks more normal now, whatever that means."

Late in the summer of '75, David went on vacation and finally made it to California, the first of many cross-country trips. This time, he took the bus. First stop: San Francisco, where he made the neo-Beat's pilgrimage to City Lights Bookstore. "A three floor rush," he reported via postcard to Richard Benz, another poet and a colleague at Bookmasters. He dipped into Mexico, which he found difficult—"as I know little Espagnol (?)"—and spent his twenty-first birthday at a religious youth hostel in New Mexico.

He wrote prose poems about both the Nashville and Denver bus stations, along with a short story set in the El Paso terminal. All those bus stations. If he wasn't yet ready to write about his own experience, the transients

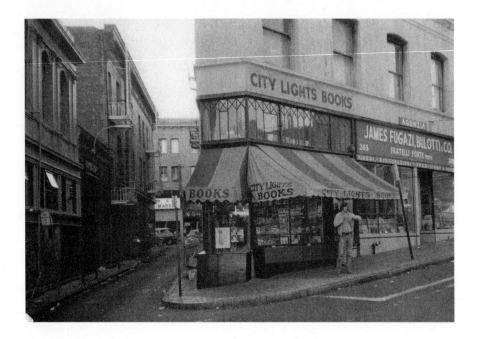

*In 1975, David took the bus to San Francisco and made his first pilgrimage to City Lights Bookstore where he asked someone to photograph him. (David Wojnarowicz Papers, Fales Library, NYU)*

and lowlifes often found in such spaces, especially in the seventies, would do nicely. David identified with street people and outcasts right to the end. "Every stinking bum should wear a crown," reads one of the epigraphs to his book *Close to the Knives*.

By the time David returned, Ensslin had taken a room at the West End apartment. Earlier that year, Peeka's sister Sauna had moved in. She was just seventeen or eighteen but soon found herself going to readings with David and Ensslin, immersed in their ongoing raptures and debates over poetry.

Bob Fitzgerald also accompanied David to readings occasionally. Fitzgerald described David's poems as "letters" because they didn't rhyme. "He was very introverted," Fitzgerald said. "Until he got up on those little stages and he started reading his letters, wailing about something that was bothering him in society. He'd go to these sleazy little coffee shops and there'd be about eight readers. He could stand up in front of a crowd, which always amazed me, because he was so shy."

That fall, David signed up for Bill Zavatsky's free workshop at St. Mark's Poetry Project. The class met one night a week from September to May and constituted the whole of David's higher education. Zavatsky remembered him—a beanpole, very gentle, very soft-spoken. "You kind of had to pry stuff out of him." David's work from this period could be dense if not overwritten and purplish. Zavatasky would tell him, "Cut back, cut back, find a spine here somewhere." But he encouraged David because he worked so hard, while some in the class produced very little. Zavatsky advised his students to do readings, do magazines, proliferate. At some point during this workshop year, David decided he'd start a journal—with Ensslin, who was not part of the class.

Eileen Myles was. She, of course, developed into a well-regarded poet, novelist, and critic. But she and David didn't get acquainted until the East Village years, the 1980s. In Zavatsky's class, she said, "We were not interested in each other." She thought him passive, laid-back, and she didn't remember his poems. In retrospect, she felt he'd used poetry as a launching pad. "Part of the reason poetry gets sneered at as a form so often is because it's where so many people began," she says. "Poetry is very often a plan. Like a list. At the beginning of a career, it can be a list of the directions you'd like to go."

David brought Richard Benz, his buddy from Bookmasters, into Zavatsky's class, and Benz recruited four poet friends from Staten Island. David then invited the Staten Island poets to contribute to his magazine, but not Eileen Myles. One of those Staten Islanders, Richard Bandanza, recalled that David also got him some poetry gigs. Ensslin set up readings at West End Café, and David often suggested people to him.

Around the time he started at the Poetry Project in the autumn of 1975, David began a love affair with Jezebel Cook, who was sixteen and Sauna Trenkle's best friend. Jezebel had dropped out of school and left home, and she liked to go to Sauna's and hang out with the bohos. "He actually pursued me and had this crush on me," Jezebel said, "and I remember him bringing me a ring back from Mexico." She'd just left another boyfriend, a "crazy, sick, nutty relationship." She moved in with David. "I'm not really sure why it didn't work out. I was very kind of hurt by not understanding. Seemed like I was madly in love with him, although I remember in the beginning it was

*David with his girlfriend
Jezebel, probably late in 1975.
(Courtesy of Peeka Trenkle)*

the other way around." The affair lasted for a few months. Jezebel is certain that it was over before she turned seventeen, in February 1976.

A decade or so later, David was long out of touch with his friends from West End and the Poetry Project, but as he became a public figure and spoke about his background, the old friends were stunned to hear the stories. Each brought up doubts when I spoke to them, even Peeka, one of the few to hear the stories from David directly. Throughout his life, David selected certain people to hear certain things and kept people he knew apart from each other, which Peeka understood. "It's what the psyche needs to do when there's been a lot of trauma. There's no way to have a continuous linear reality. You have to compartmentalize. Otherwise it can flood your consciousness." He had told Ensslin and Peeka about his hustling years. He'd talked to Peeka about his abusive father. But she found it hard to put his stories together with the David she knew. Even as she heard the anecdotes, she sometimes wondered "where it was reality and where it was elaborated on and where it was fictional."

When Richard Benz heard about David's past, he discussed it with others who'd known him. "Hearing some of the backstory about him being on the street, the piers—we were just saying to each other, when did this happen? Because he wasn't doing that when we knew him, and he didn't seem to be that kind of person. That sounds terrible, but it didn't seem like he had come out of that life." This was actually a general consensus. As Richard Bandanza put it, "Drama was absent from my recollection of this guy. A lot of people felt—wow, this is very counter the kind of guy he seemed to be. In the poetry scene, there was speculation that he sort of made it up—some of it."

None of them had known he was gay. Eileen Myles, who wasn't yet out herself in 1975, said that the David who came to Poetry Project "looked like a straight guy with a lot of hair."

His ex-girlfriend Jezebel said, "That he was gay was weird to us because we had no idea. When we knew him, that wasn't part of his story." And she wondered why he hadn't talked to her about it. She was not judgmental. "I have become a social worker because I'm the kind of person people tell all that shit to. I just find it odd that I wouldn't know anything about that." But it was how David handled his conflicted feelings. He just didn't bring those feelings to the surface. Jezebel didn't know what to think about the idea that he'd had a terrible childhood. "My impression is that some of that is how he invented himself."

Certainly, his letters from this period indicate that he'd honed a cheery affect.

David was hiding, maybe even from himself during the poetry years. But part of him would always wear camouflage. No one who ever knew him—not even those closest to him—saw all of David.

Sauna Trenkle was most surprised to learn that he'd become an activist. She'd always had the impression that "he felt he had to keep a low profile." She also used to notice him crying over "things you wouldn't assume some-one would cry about." Like some poignant moment on a television show or "a beautiful meal with people all being nice to each other." He and Sauna talked about "how overwhelming the good things could be," she said. "Because nei-ther of us had had a lot of good stuff happening in our lives." Even with these sisters, he compartmentalized. Sauna knew nothing of his emotional talks with Peeka. And Ensslin knew nothing of the crying, but said, "There were times he would just retreat to his room and you knew to leave him alone."

On November 29, 1975, David wrote to his sister Pat. "I really want to show you what I've been heading towards in my life," he explained. So he composed a manifesto, a first articulation of his resistance to what he would later call "the pre-invented world."

He wanted to explain his "feelings on the voice within the body, the voice of the subconscious." While he had to follow this voice, or be unhappy, he knew that it would take "a separation from the normal levels of existence," a rejection of "the foundation that really covers over the real world underneath. . . . The reasons for my wanting to reach this level . . . is to find the entirety of my own soul . . . to find that area in the vast cosmos both internally and externally where the true voice is to be found. Rimbaud came close to it, he came so close but turned his back to it on its very steps, either out of fright from what he saw or because he was unprepared to meet it. . . . I am a poet, one who hasn't found the true voice yet. . . . I won't worry about total acceptance once I break through the immediate binds around me which hold me back. What is really more important is that I at least give my life up to it."

He did not mail this letter.

In December 1975, Lee Adler was murdered in the Manhattan neighborhood of Washington Heights. Though she and Ensslin had split up by spring of that year, he was still quite traumatized and remembered what a good friend David was to him then, talking to him about it, not letting him isolate. Police never figured out who killed Adler. She was one of 1,631 homicide victims in New York City that year.

David had begun to work, with Ensslin, on the journal they would eventually title *RedM*—and dedicate to the memory of Lee Adler. The title stood for "red mirage," or as David used to say, "Red M I Rage." Ensslin explained: "It had to do with this thing David talked about. There's what you see in front of you and then there's this movie that plays in your head, this internal vision that you have of what's going on around you. He used to call it 'the film behind the eyeball.' That was his expression. So the magazine, if it had any kind of collective reason for being—it was a celebration of people's individual visions."

By 1976, David was making some headway with his poetry connections. Peter Cherches had taken over as editor at *riverrun*, and he accepted a poem along with two of David's photographs: a winter woodland scene and an old man alone in a coffee shop. Zavatsky's class did a xeroxed zine,

*Life Without Parole*, which included two poems by David, one on the Nashville bus station. But the big coup was getting a poem accepted by *Coldspring Journal*. Not only did the other contributors include Aram Saroyan and Gerald Stern, but one of the editors was Charles Plymell, a poet who'd lived with Neal Cassady for a while and counted all the Beats as friends. *Coldspring* no. 10 included David's prose poem on the Denver bus station ("7 blocks from station / the sidewalk in fronta liquor store filled w/great assortment of bums old/young all w/the same looka shock in their eyes / standing/leaning w/taut bristled faces").

On February 22, David went with John Hall to hear Plymell read at the Fugue Saloon. Plymell called in sick, but the other reader that afternoon inspired David to write a fan letter. That poet was Janine Pommy Vega, younger than the other Beats but also part of their scene. She didn't reply to that letter, but David wrote to her again in May, asking her to contribute to his then-unnamed magazine. He had decided to just write blind to poets he admired. He even tracked down Carl Solomon, the man who'd inspired Allen Ginsberg to write "Howl." David found Solomon working in the appliance department at Korvette's. In the end, *RedM* included Lawrence Ferlinghetti, Bernadette Mayer, Ron Padgettt, Charles Bernstein, Plymell, Solomon, and Pommy Vega along with friends like Benz and Bandanza, De-Forge and Morais. While they had no trouble drawing contributors, David and Ensslin hadn't realized how much labor would be involved. Producing *RedM* would take more than a year. They published only one issue.

Among David's papers, I found answers to a questionnaire about his poetry life. "I have plenty of interests besides writing but I devote no time at all towards them," he reported. "I gave up the application of paint to paper some time ago because I found writing a much more effective release for me." Prompted to say where he'd published, he omitted *Novae Res* but listed the other publications above, along with *Zone* (where his work appeared in 1977). That was the extent of his poetry career.

And once he began to tell his own story, David erased it all. Even the people closest to him at the end of his life knew nothing about *RedM* or Forest Hills or Pottery Barn. Fales Library at New York University ended up with 175 boxes of material. Along with his diaries, correspondence, and photos, the collection includes torn to-do lists, envelopes with footprints on them, wads of ATM receipts—but not a single one of the literary magazines that published David's poetry except for one copy of his beloved *RedM*.

The poetry in particular seems an odd thing to hide. Maybe David regarded his poetic output as juvenilia he couldn't be proud of. Maybe it was just too much the conventional path into the artist's, or certainly the writer's, life and didn't suit the persona he'd crafted. Certain friends of David's from the mid-seventies came to feel that this was about more than creating a persona, however—that David had willed himself into becoming someone else.

David yearned to hit the road, and later in his life he would speak of his many hitchhiking and freight-hopping trips across America. He certainly hitched to Montreal and back at least once to visit Michael Morais. But he made just one round-trip to the West Coast and back that way, with very little freight-hopping, in summer 1976.

He intended to head, once again, for the holy grail of City Lights Bookstore, this time with his tall, skinny buddy, John Hall. They studied *The Hitchhiker's Field Manual*, with its state-by-state suggestions about where it was safe to thumb a ride, and they found Michael Mathers' photo book *Riding the Rails* a great inspiration. Hall said they knew they wouldn't be able to hop a train until they were away from the eastern seaboard. Not that it couldn't be done. But it was "like secret hobo knowledge and more advanced than we were capable of."

David had hoped to finish production work on *RedM* before he left town. But a friend who was going to surreptitiously typeset the poems at his shop had been too busy to do more than one a week. Ensslin had left Columbia, broke, and gone up to the Berkshires to work for the summer. Early in June, David wrote him to say they'd have to do most of it on an IBM Selectric at the Print Center in Brooklyn. David used vacation days from the bookstore to type. In another letter to Ensslin he said he'd found an image for the cover in the twenty-five-cent bin at Argosy Books—a geological survey plate showing a cave town cut into a cliff, and a man in a cowboy hat seated on the cliff edge. This "gaucho," as David described him in a letter to Janine Pommy Vega, was staring in a trancelike way, "like someone who has seen behind the eyes for the first time." At that point, *RedM* went into limbo. The nonprofit Print Center had shut down till October for lack of funds.

On July 15, 1976, David left town with John Hall and Peeka Trenkle, who drove them to Massachusetts in a borrowed VW bus. They wanted to visit Ensslin before the hitching began. For the first time since his Outward Bound trip, David would keep a journal, and he waxed Kerouacian as he recorded day one: "into dense sound of all of America rushing forward—destinations—shaved forests—lonely tollbooth guards with empty holsters—all the country moving . . . crossing state lines into areas unknown myself now homeless (no base place) makes me feel that disconnectedness."

Ensslin had rented a room in West Stockbridge from Rosemarie Beenk, a former Isadora Duncan dancer then in her midsixties. David was entranced by Rosemarie, someone who had lived for her art. At her little house on the Williams River, he and John Hall spent a five-day idyll, swimming in a nearby marble quarry and hiking. They also created the first of their "Trail-o-Grams," news on their travels that they would send to friends back home. David drew R. Crumb–style illustrations and they both wrote, though David wrote most.

While at Rosemarie's, David also worked on a "story about brief time doing the streets," the account in which he refers to Willy as Lipsy. "I no longer have any scars on myself in any sense of the word," he wrote in an introductory paragraph. "Confronted by the past I take it as the present. . . . Regret hasn't any meaning."

On July 20, two hopeful hitchhikers bound for California left Rosemarie's place near the western edge of Massachusetts carrying a sign that said "Syracuse." After some initial good luck—a ride to Albany—their first twenty-four hours developed into an almost comical ordeal: the hours of waiting on an entrance ramp in the rain, the three other hitchers jumping ahead of them into the one car that stopped, the decision to then camp in a marsh infested with mosquitoes and potato bugs, the scramble back to the highway, the can of fruit cocktail split for dinner, and finally the ride near midnight to a rest stop east of Utica, where they slept behind a state police station in the rain and nearly got arrested in the morning.

They finally got to Syracuse on their second day, after someone dropped them a mile away and they walked. David went to the university library and read half of Kerouac's *Tristessa*—a novel almost impossible to find in 1976—in the Rare Books Department.

Already David was collecting stories from people he encountered, some of them destined for his book *Sounds in the Distance* (reissued after his death as *The Waterfront Journals*). He never taped, just listened intently, and the storytellers I've been able to find vouch for his accuracy. At this point, however, he didn't have publication in mind. The first "monologue" he'd recorded was Rosemarie Beenk's warped account of the American Revolution—how it started when the king ordered people to drink tea instead of coffee. Then, as he moved across the country, David also wanted to hear, for example, from a guy he met who took his nephew rail-riding and who never looked for work until his money got below fifty dollars. David wanted stories from those who'd opted out of society, or had never gotten in—the footloose, the pariahs, those who did what they wanted, paid the price, and didn't care. David treated these (usually) marginal people as if their positions on the margin gave them access to secret truths.

In Northfield, Minnesota, they stayed a couple of days with a friend of David's, a poet he'd known in New York as a "burning Cassady character." But now that energy was gone. The friend was a forklift operator. "He'd given up in a way I never thought he would," David wrote to Ensslin, disquieted. While they were in Northfield, David and John Hall assembled their second and final Trail-o-Gram.

From here, the trip became arduous as they began trying to freight-hop. In St. Paul, they prowled the train yards, consulted hoboes for advice, snuck into open cars that would back up instead of move forward, and kept running into security guards. Then someone shot at them from a car full of kids, and David felt the bullet go through his hair. But later he wrote in his journal about what he considered the truly disturbing moment of that day—he'd gotten a haircut, thinking it would make travel easier. He assured himself, that, while his new image felt unnatural, he still saw through the same eyes. And if the people driving the cars or sitting at counters could see behind his eyes, he'd be in trouble.

After another bungling day or two at the rail yard, he and John Hall went back to hitching. In North Dakota, they waited twenty-four hours for a train they then rode for four hours. (They had to ditch when workers began

*David and John Hall on their cross-country trip. David joined the two separate photos, taping them onto a three-ring binder labeled "Journal New York–California 1976." (David Wojnarowicz Papers, Fales Library, NYU)*

searching the cars.) They were halfway through Montana before they had consistent success with rail-riding. Finally they put their hammocks up inside a freight car and rolled toward the coast. Nearly broke by the time they hit Portland, Oregon, they spent a day there in fruitless job hunting. David decided then that they better head for San Francisco, where he would "either find work or slowly fall into becoming a bum."

They were able to freight-hop for one more night, until the train stopped just south of Mount Shasta and two officers of the law chased them away, brandishing clubs. That ended David's rail-riding career. They hitched the rest of the way, arriving in San Francisco on August 12, only twenty-three miserable and exhilarating days since western Massachusetts.

\* \* \*

John Hall took a bus back to New York after about a week. They'd moved into the San Francisco YMCA, where David remained as he started looking for a job. "Oh silent San Francisco with your long streets of movement yr New Yorkian times square with pomegranate nosed winos leafing through the trash where is your secret," he wrote in his journal. "Do I stand a chance in your woeful streets?"

By his second week, he was heading out at six A.M. for the Casual Labor Office. There he found work sorting eggs for the V-C Egg Company. The Viet Cong Company, he liked to joke. His job was to sort by size, removing any that were cracked or misshapen, for $2.50 an hour. But his major work in San Francisco became the collection of stories and voices. At the Labor Office. At the Y. And every day during lunch at a Chinatown greasy spoon where he listened to the regulars—junkies and "dull gangsters"—and made notes on napkins. Later he included many of these stories in *Sounds in the Distance*.

David and Ensslin were corresponding about *RedM*, still adding and subtracting poems. "At this point have lost touch with old self" he informed Ensslin on September 7, but it was too much for longhand. He needed a typewriter "to explode on." He hoped John Hall would send his soon. By September 9 he had a machine, and his explosion produced a seventeen-page, single-spaced epistle to Ensslin—"a letter I could only write to you and maybe John Hall," he said. He was trying to explain his "attraction to extreme social outcasts." He'd been talking night after night "till 1 2 3 4 am" to his next-door neighbor at the Y, a "strange Genet-ian character." This man had checked in with the clothes on his back, one extra cotton shirt, *The Tibetan Book of the Dead*, and a pack of Pall Malls. He told David a long, complex tale about his "self-imposed hermitude in a boarded-up house in New Orleans"—which is part of the title David gave it in *Sounds in the Distance*. David thought he needed to associate with certain characters, like this man.

"One of my fantasies for a long time," he wrote Ensslin, "had been to withdraw again into the streets away from the social mainstream of society and hang out again with every kind of social 'monster' and keep secret notebooks hidden beneath my coat . . . writing the grim sagas of that experience. But I don't need that fantasy any longer. I no longer entertain it 'cause it's inevitable—I'll end up there. Whether in a few years, or more likely when I am an old man, toothless and benumbed. . . . Ah hell. The way in which I'm living reflects the end."

He'd had a cushy situation in New York—an easy job, an apartment with good, energetic roommates, comfort, money, books—and he'd tossed it all. Now he had a tiny room, few friends, and twenty bucks to his name. But he was happier this way! "Why? Because I'm experiencing the more important things in my thought of life. I'm associating with people who interest me and it's that strange unknown beauty that I touch when riding into a town for the first time, not knowing a single person. It's an unexplainable excitement I feel when approaching unknown things."

He related more of his neighbor's saga, even some of the guy's dreams. He quoted Genet, from *A Thief's Journal*, the part where Genet takes money that belongs to a friend—money the friend desperately needs—and tears it up, then thinks better of it, pastes it back together, and buys himself a big meal. To "purify" himself, says Genet. To break his emotional bonds. David couldn't remember all the conversations with the fellow next door, but he remembered the feelings: that the guy was purging himself of everything programmed into him by society. The Genet-ian character wondered why David wrote, assuring him that it was useless.

The night before David wrote this letter, he began to feel he was disintegrating inside. As he explained it to Ensslin, "I went too far into an area I was incapable of handling at this point." The area where you let go of the constraining walls that fence in your thoughts. Where you lose your opinions and "thought molds." Where you see each and every thing as nothing. Where time isn't understandable and politics are useless. "It's an almost total abandonment of social ties," a place in society he'd discovered two years ago when he first read Rimbaud. That night in San Francisco he had "this weird sense of [his] death drawing near." He felt there was someone in the room with him. He heard a voice like his sister's whispering his name, then felt what seemed like a jolt of electricity into his head. At three in the morning, the next door neighbor banged and kicked his door till David opened up. The neighbor came in and asked angrily, you have to work and I woke you, so why are you so calm? David didn't know. The man walked out. Then David too left his room. It was "as if it contained all the things that I dislike," he wrote, "all emotional and disruptive energies that I've come in contact with inside of myself in the last so many years—that I had rid myself of during the last two years at west end avenue." The Genet-ian character checked out the next day.

On October 23, after learning that Bookmasters would take him back, David set out to hitchhike back to New York. Again, he started with great luck, as someone gave him a ride to Reno in a single-engine Cherokee aircraft.

Out on the interstate, he was fixing his sign ("East I-80 New York") when another hitchhiker showed up. They stood there for four hours—the other hitcher walking back some yards to snag the first ride. No fair, David thought. But he didn't say anything. Finally a battered pickup pulled over and, sure enough, the other hitcher got into the cab with two guys. As the truck cruised by slowly, looking for a place to nose back into the interstate flow, the hitcher yelled at David: "We're going to Denver." David yelled, "Can I come?" The truck stopped and he climbed into the back.

He was headed into the most dangerous ride of his hitchhiking life. The teens who'd picked him up had stolen the truck, and they began stopping to rob what David described as "supermarkets." The other hitchhiker joined right in as their accomplice. According to David's account in the Dateline, the self-described outlaws showed him their shotguns and said they were going to kill him, and if the police tried to stop them at any point, they intended to shoot it out. The account David gave Janine Pommy Vega in a letter was less dramatic; he'd pared it down to a couple of sentences: The outlaws did two burglaries and a robbery and "one hung out all night in the back of the truck with me talking about going to Mars."

Later, when David typed out the entire journal he kept on the trip west, he wrote what he labeled "an intro of sorts" for John Hall. Here he tried to explain why he had not tried to escape from these kids, because he *had* had a chance, and whatever the exact details, he did feel his life was in danger. "After I had accepted all foggy notions of death," he told Hall, "and slipped into that quiet reflective stage where I would think of anything and it was savored slowly . . . all I can remember is wanting to get out of it alive enough so I could tell you the story." The outlaws had entered one market with the other hitchhiker, leaving David alone in the truck with their two shotguns. He could have run. Yet he just sat there. "I *had* to live it through," wrote David, "regardless of what it led to—oh gee! Adventure! That's all it really is sometimes and that's all that matters to me in a series of systems that attempt to quash that kind of rush. Sure I get afraid, but somewhere in the midst of the action of following through an experience, there comes a sense that's incomparable to any other. Ah, that's what I strive for."

He wrote this up for Hall by way of thanking him. He might never have jumped into that first railroad car without his presence. "I believe that it takes a number of things (objects or people) to stimulate certain currents inherent in one's own system."

He spent at least twenty-four hours with the outlaws. In the Dateline, he wrote that, when they finally dropped him off on a dirt road, he assumed they were going to shoot him and he ran into the woods. Later, a woman and her daughter picked him up in another stolen vehicle. As he told Pommy Vega, the women ducked every time a cop came into view, "which made the car swerve."

Into the back of his journal, David pasted a warning issued to him by the Indiana State Police on October 27, 1976, for hitchhiking.


Soon after returning to New York, David moved to Court Street in Brooklyn with the other poets—the other gay poets. David had a long talk with Ensslin at the end of a pier on the Hudson and told his friend that he thought he was gay. He also came out to Laura Glenn, but added that he'd give up men for her if she'd have him. She declined.

Poet Steve Lackow drove David and his belongings from the Upper West Side to Court Street in Lackow Sr.'s old Chrysler New Yorker. It was snowing, the car had bad brakes, and they cruised into Brooklyn on a controlled skid. Lackow moved into Court Street shortly afterward. He remembered a David who drew compulsively on anything available and who survived almost exclusively on cheese sandwiches. David, Lackow, and Dennis DeForge shared the typewriter always in place on the dining room table.

That autumn, David read at the Prospect Park band shell in a series sponsored by *Mouth of the Dragon*, the first gay male poetry magazine. Among the spectators was Brian Butterick. "As soon as I saw him read," Brian said, "I was like, 'Wow, I want to meet him.'" David soon realized that he'd read one of Brian's poems in the window at Brentano's bookstore in 1973—and loved it. That year, Brian had won second prize in the New York City high school poetry contest, earning the display of his poem. David was either living on the street or at the halfway house.

Shortly after he met David, Brian moved to Provincetown, Massachusetts. But he would return almost a year later and become one of the few people from this era to stay at least semi-connected to David for the rest of his life.


Steve Lackow met David in 1975 and felt certain that David hadn't seen his mother in years.

Actually, David had had some contact with her. In a letter to his sister, Pat, dated February 21, 1976, he wrote, "Dolores has been pretty quiet, getting in touch now and then out of a sense of motherly duty, I guess. . . . She's sort of coming into her own and leading a life in her interests. I feel happy about that and don't mind at all not hearing from her 'cause that means she's happy." About a week later he wrote again and mentioned that Dolores was on vacation—though he'd only heard that from Bob Fitzgerald and didn't know where she'd gone. Clearly, he and Dolores weren't close, but she did make the list of people who got Trail-o-Grams that summer.

After David moved to Court Street, she apparently made more of an effort to connect. "She caught up with him on the phone and then she came on over one day," Lackow remembered. The moment stayed with him because, as he put it, he "couldn't help hating her guts." Lackow had had such an emotional response to David's stories about living on the street. None of the other friends remembered this reunion, but in the end, everyone from the Court Street era met Dolores—and liked her. No one from West End had ever met her and didn't remember David ever talking about her.

"Dolores is probably the most guilt-ridden individual I ever met in my life," said Lackow. "Totally filled with regret about her life, about what happened with her and David. She did everything she could to remake that re-lationship. At first I don't think David was all that interested, but ultimately he really was won over to it, and responded in kind." Dolores was charming, vivacious, almost "puppy-doggish" as she sought her son's approval. "She won us over. Basically we were following David's lead," he said. "He bent over backwards. I don't know where he found it within himself."

Since age eleven, David had seen his father for just a few hours, the day he visited with Pat and Bob Fitzgerald. Now David was twenty-two, and even as he reconnected with his mother, Ed Wojnarowicz was in a state of seri-ous self-inflicted decline.

Ed's alcoholism had worsened after he sent his three oldest children away. He had also left the merchant marine, after working on ships that took cargo to Vietnam, so his family no longer had the respite of his weeks at sea. He found boiler room jobs at local factories and schools, but he was always fired for drinking. He lost his driver's license three times for DUI, first for six months, then for two years, then for ten years. He bought himself a moped. But usually Marion had to drive him to work. When he had work.

Marion now took the brunt of his beatings, though his two youngest children also lived in a state of terror. What came through in Pete's and Lin-da's stories was their father's constant childlike need for attention: Waking Pete one morning to tell him some interminable story and giving him a fat lip when he didn't appear to be listening closely. Coming home one night when Marion, Pete, and Linda were in the middle of dinner and heaving a plate of spaghetti against the wall when they didn't stop eating to listen to him. Picking up the family dog by the neck and threatening to kill it if he didn't get a reaction.

Marion took to shutting herself in the bathroom when Ed's rampages began. It was the only room with a good lock. She'd bring a book and sit in there until he gave up or passed out. "He had a hatchet, and you'd see the marks [on the lock]," Linda said. Pete began trying to intervene in the attacks on his mother when he was thirteen or fourteen. Linda, Pete, and Marion all testified against him in court at some point. The police were now regu-lars at the house.

When he was unemployed, he'd head for the bar as the kids headed to school. Coming home from school was always fraught for them. Sometimes he'd be sitting in the front yard with a baseball bat. They could always dodge him when he took a swing, or outrun him—he was so drunk. But usually, they'd keep going, past the house to hang out with friends in the neighborhood. "We would stay for hours and hope for him to pass out on the couch," Linda said.

"We were petrified whenever he'd start fooling around with a gun," Pete said. Ed kept his rifles in a locked cabinet: a .30-06 rifle, a shotgun, an M1 carbine (now banned as an assault weapon), a .22, a .32 Marlin, and a BB gun. He hunted, but also liked firing the guns at home "outside the door for no apparent reason," said Pete. "Just to be angry."

He fired a gun in the house only once that anyone knows of: three shots through the downstairs bathroom ceiling with his .32 Marlin. Marion swears she was sitting on the couch when this happened, though both Pete and Steven believed her to be *in* that bathroom. Linda was the only other person home at the time, but she was upstairs, thinking her dad had just shot her mother dead. The bullets tore through the upstairs bathroom and out the roof. That night, the police arrested Ed and confiscated his rifles.

Marion began to stand up to him after she joined Al-Anon. Ed hated this, of course. He'd take her keys away and lock her out of the house when she went to a meeting. But she persisted and had the kids join Alateen. "I wanted them to understand they weren't the only kids going through what they were going through," she said, fighting back tears. For years, Ed had had the habit of stopping the car at some bar and telling the family to wait for him while he went in and drank. Sometimes they'd sit out there for an hour. Then, one day Marion decided to just leave him there. She drove away.

For eight or ten years, Marion worked a minimum-wage job at a blouse factory, sorting the pieces cut from patterns. She had to, since Ed was drinking up his pension check. Marion knew he hid his Seagram's in a tire in the garage, and she tried pouring it out, especially when there wasn't enough money to replace it. But the bar always gave him credit.

One night he came at Marion with the baseball bat and chased her out of the house. She called the police, who hauled him off to jail again. Several times, the court ordered him into psychiatric institutions for rehab. He'd detox. He'd work the program. He'd be pleasant when the family came to visit. But once he returned home, Ed was never sober for more than a day.

In December 1976, there'd been much talk in the family about Pete getting his license and helping to chauffeur the still-unlicensed Ed. Steven came to the house to confront his father. He was worried about Pete, knowing from his own experience that Ed saw his growing sons as a challenge to his authority. Steven pushed his father up against a wall and said, "Do you realize what it is to be so fucking afraid of you? Do you know what you've done to your children? I'm not afraid of you anymore. But I love you." Ed broke down crying. Steven urged him to get away from the family and straighten out his life.

Pete turned seventeen on December 21, and Steven drove him to the Department of Motor Vehicles to take his driving test. The next day, Pete was the first one home from school. Walking in from the breezeway, he could see straight down into the basement. And there he saw his father's feet. Off the floor.

"I got a knife and I cut him down," Pete said. "And when I cut him down, an exhale of air came out of his lungs. I tried to give him mouth-to-mouth. And realized he was gone. I'm looking at him thinking, 'This can't be. This is friggin' surreal.' And I sat down on the steps. I cried maybe ten seconds, and then I stopped. And as I sat there—this was the oddest thing that ever happened to me—but the weight of years and years of abuse, it lifted off my shoulders. An unbelievable feeling. You never know the burden that you're carrying until it's lifted, but someone just pulled it right off me. And I felt free. There'd be no more abuse. It was over."

Pat happened to be back from Paris for the holidays. Bob Fitzgerald drove her and David to New Jersey for the funeral. Three or four times, David begged Fitzgerald to pull over and stop so he could throw up. Since these pit stops followed an already late start, they actually missed the church service and joined the rest of the family graveside. Ed had drinking buddies but few friends. The funeral home had had to hire pallbearers.

That year, David spent Christmas Eve with his sister, his brother-in-law, and his mother at the Hell's Kitchen apartment. David had been very quiet, when he suddenly stood up and said, "I have an announcement to make." They sat there waiting until he blurted, "I'm gay!" and ran out of the room crying.

"Dolores really got pissed off," Fitzgerald remembered. Not about David being gay. She just thought he'd ruined Christmas.

# 5 AT THE SHATTERED EDGE OF THE MAP

"HE SAID THAT TO TRULY DREAM ONE MUST NOT DO ANYTHING THAT RE-
STRICTS EVEN AS IN LIVING BY THAT CODE SO HE DID LITTLE AND LIVED
FULLY IN HIS OWN QUIET WAY HE ACHIEVED A STRANGE STATE OF GRACE."

Those are the words of Emanuel Pancake, an alter ego David experimented with. Briefly. The "PANCAKE" piece consists of unpunctuated
uppercase type whose lower lines dip and bend at the bottom into a photo of
two unsmiling men who could be French race car drivers from the 1920s, or
a couple of scrappy surrealists. David went through a little surrealist phase
at Court Street. Entrusted with a stuffed dog's head that belonged to Brian
Butterick, David and Steve Lackow began taking it out on a leash, dragging
it behind them down Montague Street or the Promenade. They'd heard
about Gérard de Nerval taking a lobster for walks along the Seine. "We
were into outraging people," Lackow said.

They'd become students of the outré and obscure. They got a gig at a
club near Brooklyn College—as an opening act for a folk duo (friends of
Lackow's). So they decided to do something neo-Dada. After David had introduced him for forty-five minutes, Lackow walked out wearing only an
American flag and read a haiku. They'd modeled this presentation on Robert Filliou's "Yes—an Action Poem" performed at Café au Go-Go in 1965
and discovered in an anthology they turned up in a remainder bin.

The first issue of *Zone*—Lackow and DeForge were among the
editors—appeared in spring 1977, with three of David's short prose pieces,
written in three different styles. He did incantatory ("I bring it to you silently
with your head beneath the pillows. I bring it to you sleeping like unseen
gifts"). He did ellipses (". . . men wearing military masks walk the streets . . .
defunct railroads . . . an Indian walks by pounding his forehead . . . what

race are you. . . ."). He did surreal ("The caped man takes a wild shot and three dogs fall from the sky"). But he never attached his poetic language to an inner life, so he never managed to create a character. The stories slide through the reader's brain without making much impact. Here, for the first time, he was asked for a brief bio to run at the end of the magazine. So he said he came to the city at age eight, moved into a trailer with a street buddy at fourteen, and lived on the streets for a year "around a load of transvestite gangsters." He also mentioned that he'd "painted Nathan's downstairs night club ala Pollock" from twenty bottles of ketchup. He was playing.

*RedM* finally went to press in May 1977; it was 5½ by 8½ with the gaucho-on-a-cliff cover engraving in red. "Gaucho on cliff is staring at mirage of self in surroundings and within," reads the least cryptic line on the contents page explaining it all. But then, this was David's cryptic period. One of the two prose poems he contributed to his own magazine, "2Dream Ash2, for John Hall," is almost unintelligible in its dream imagery, but the bones of Times Square and hustling are there deep down. He just can't bring it to the surface. Like many young writers, he was struggling to disgorge his real subject matter and let it blurt.

That same month, at an Atlantic Avenue Laundromat, David struck up a conversation with another guy doing his wash. He turned out to be Louis Cartwright, who was living nearby with the notorious and legendary Herbert Huncke. Lackow was there doing laundry too, and he couldn't believe David would want to be associated with these lowlifes. But David was enthralled.

Huncke, after all, was the original Beat—a petty criminal, drug addict, jailbird, former Times Square hustler, and sometimes writer who'd given his autobiographical writing the apt title *Guilty of Everything*. He'd introduced William Burroughs to narcotics. He'd inadvertently landed Ginsberg in the mental hospital where he met Carl Solomon.* And he'd given Kerouac (or was it Ginsberg? or John Clellon Holmes?) the word "beat" to describe his

---

* When Huncke had nowhere to go after a jail stint in 1949, the kindhearted Ginsberg took him in, and soon Huncke and two burglar friends were storing stolen goods in the poet's apartment. After the burglars crashed a stolen car filled with more stolen goods, and some of Ginsberg's papers, the police arrested Ginsberg. Powerful friends among the Columbia University faculty managed to get him time in a mental hospital instead of a prison.

downtrodden hipster lifestyle. He'd appeared as a character in Burroughs's *Junkie*, in Kerouac's *On the Road*, and in Ginsberg's "Howl" ("who walked all night with their shoes full of blood on the snowbank docks waiting for a door in the East River to open to a room full of steamheat and opium").

One study of the Beat Generation, John Tytell's *Naked Angels*, analyzed Huncke's appeal: "Ginsberg was intrigued by an ominous aura of danger that enveloped Huncke. Here was a man who seemed self-damned, who believed death was imminent and regarded that eventuality with morbid complacence, a man who suffered greatly, and who possessed almost supersensory perceptions. Huncke was egoless completely rootless, with no sense of permanence, possession or property." Yet somehow, he would outlive both Cartwright and David.

When David met them, Huncke was sixty-two years old and Cartwright about thirty. According to filmmaker Laki Vazakas, whose *Huncke and Louis* documented the last years of both their lives, the two had met in Ginsberg's kitchen, probably late in the sixties. Huncke and Cartwright were not lovers. In fact, when David knew them, Cartwright's girlfriend Ondine Andriazzi was also part of the household, and for part of that time, Huncke was living with R'lene Dahlberg. Vazakas described Cartwright as a photographer. Indeed, his portrait of Huncke adorns the cover of *The Evening Sun Turned Crimson* (second edition), and more of his photos appear in *The Huncke Reader*. But there's no evidence he ever exhibited or worked anywhere as a photographer. What he and Huncke clearly shared was an abiding dedication to drugs.

As Janine Pommy Vega saw the relationship, however, "that was deep love there." She regarded Huncke as her oldest friend. (And the only Beat who was not sexist. She'd known them all.) Pommy Vega had left home at seventeen just to be near them and had ended up living with Huncke, who was fresh from another prison stint for burglary. That was 1959, when Huncke had an apartment at 170 East Second Street in the East Village, upstairs from Ginsberg and Peter Orlovsky. The building served for a while as a veritable nest of Beats. Poet Bob Kaufman also lived there, as did Jack Micheline, John Wieners, and Elise Cowen, who was hopelessly in love with Ginsberg and typed his manuscripts.

In late May 1977, David recounted an evening with Huncke and

Cartwright in a letter to Pommy Vega: "I spent the other night hanging out till twelve hearing a couple of great storytellers talk on about Afghanistan of '70 or '71 in a way where the voice gets all dreamy and soft from both subject recall and late hours and by the time I left, I was ready to pull on these beat-up boots of mine and haul off across a couple of large bodies of water in search of a sun-scorched hotel roof and some number one hashish as they call it and watch all these characters brought up like one-legged smugglers and desert bandits."

While David identified with the Beat tradition, he'd never expressed interest in punk—except for Patti Smith. But then, she was a poet who revered other poets. Ensslin reported that they had played her album *Horses* incessantly at the West End apartment. And David did love to pogo. His friend Susan Gauthier went with him to CBGB's for that. "A great show every night for two dollars," she said.

No wave would get his attention later. Certainly it was the caterwauling soundtrack best suited to the ravaged New York he took for granted. There's a photo from the late seventies, taken by David Godlis outside CBGB's, that captures a certain essence of the city at that time. It shows a group including Diego Cortez, Anya Phillips, Lydia Lunch, and James Chance lounging against a car—or on top of it, in Lydia's case. These are some of the major stars of no wave. But the photo shows no clamor, no glamour. Just another gritty night. Behind them we can see a closed hardware store, one passing cab on the Bowery, and two sets of headlights on Bleecker. We're a block and a half from the worst men's shelter in the system. But it all fits. Punk embraced ugliness and turned your "wretched refuse" into a style.

Later David would come to know and respect Lydia. "New York City during the 1970s," she writes in her foreword to the book *No Wave*, "was a beautiful ravaged slag—impoverished and neglected after suffering from decades of abuse and battery. She stunk of sewage, sex, rotting fish, and day-old diapers. She leaked from every pore."


The apartment at 115 Court Street was in downtown Brooklyn, just above a Yemenite social club where the sounds of men playing Ping-Pong could be heard at all hours. David's friends at this point included not just Ensslin and his new roommates, Lackow and DeForge, but also a young artist from Oklahoma named Jim McLauchlin. McLauchlin had lived briefly at Court Street early in '76, during David's fling with Michael Morais, but he had fallen ill with hepatitis and gone home to Oklahoma to recuperate.

When McLauchlin returned to New York in September '76, he brought a friend, Dirk Rowntree, who was then a musician. The two had performed together in Oklahoma—McLauchlin's poetry backed by Rowntree's experimental rock—and they wanted to try their luck in the big city. Among all the people David got to know during the Court Street days, the one person he stayed in touch with till the end of his life was Rowntree (who happened to be the only heterosexual in the group). Soon after arriving in New York, Rowntree and McLauchlin performed at a new gay arts space called the Glines. When McLauchlin did a second theater piece there in '77, he gave David a silent role in it. McLauchlin thought David had a "sinister grin"—as if he was on to some inside joke and wouldn't share it. He wanted that wry presence in his piece, so he instructed David to sit on a couch and look bored.

According to Lackow, David learned something from both McLauchlin and Morais about how to put some emotion into his readings. His affect during their neo-Dada performance had been "deadpan," as Lackow put it, while Morais' readings were "ablaze." McLauchlin could also light up a room when he appeared as his alter ego, Jimmy James Strange, "the rearranged Son of Cain who was feeling to blame for inflicting the pain but was not ashamed because he was just part of the scenery." Strange delivered his "rock and roll poetry" at venues like CBGB's, sometimes with musical accompaniment.

Since there was no longer room for him at Court Street, McLauchlin moved into a basement under a SoHo storefront. He created, in the space above him, the sort of magical installations that would call for, say, covering the floor with rose petals six inches deep. Sometime after the citywide blackout in the summer of '77, McLauchlin and his boyfriend, Luis Seralta Rivera, moved to a loft at West Fourth and Barrow. Here they began to hold salon evenings every Saturday where gay men in the arts would discuss their current projects. Regulars included writer Perry Brass, performer Emilio Cubiero, and the legendary drag queen skater Rollerina—though she never appeared there in her trademark '50s hat, rhinestone glasses, and dress. (No one at the salon ever learned her real name or occupation.) Nor could anyone remember David reading at the salon. Instead, he brought small sketchbooks filled with quirky comic line drawings to share with the group.

McLauchlin described the David he first met, in '76, as a hippie, a dweeb in straggly hair and overalls. Perry Brass remembered him from the salon, in '77, as "un-pretty," with bad skin and bad teeth, rail thin, not very well groomed. Though David wasn't in overalls anymore, he hadn't become a "clone" either, and this was the clone era, when gay men walked Christopher Street in army/navy surplus, short hair, and often a mustache.

Brass was seven years older than David and a self-described member of the "liberation generation" when he began to attend David's readings. To him, David was shy and vulnerable "with a standoffish affect, but," Brass recalled, "attractive in that it was unique and very, very self-contained. Some of us were still kind of put off by him because he was so far-out. We weren't quite sure what to make of him, and his poetry—it was sort of deforming itself. It was hard to get a bead on it, to figure out, was this even poetry?"

Back at Court Street, David collaborated with Lackow on a screenplay about a CIA assassination plot against Idi Amin. He was drawing "in small formats," Lackow remembered—thumbnail sketches about his cross-country trip and the people he'd encountered. David and Ensslin were also meeting to prepare a second *RedM*. They'd added a third editor, a friend of David's from Bookmasters named Alex Rodriguez.

This activity too he erased from his life story—*Zone*, the salon, and the performances with Lackow and McLauchlin.

When David went back to journal writing in July 1977—the first time since his cross-country trip—he'd just been to court with Huncke. This time the old Beat had been arrested for buying four Valiums from a pill pusher on Fourteenth Street. David waited with him from nine thirty in the morning till four, when his legal aid lawyer showed up and Huncke presented the judge with two letters, one from his methadone clinic and one from an unidentified professor of English. The judge allowed Huncke to plead guilty to disorderly conduct and let him off. David had paid for lunch—two oranges, a Coke, and a shared candy bar. Neither had enough money at the end of the day for subway fare—fifty cents—so they walked home across the Brooklyn Bridge. Back at his building, Huncke borrowed five singles from a neighbor and handed one of them to David, saying, "Here's a fin for ya."

David had begun taping Louis Cartwright's stories. Here was another lost voice from the margin—an important one, in David's opinion. A "monologue" wouldn't be enough. Cartwright deserved a full book. After all, he'd ridden a bike over the twisting mountain roads of Nepal, visiting monasteries "where they worshiped love and light on one side, death and darkness on the other." He'd passed a winter in Kabul, sleeping on a rope bed for five cents a night. He'd learned how to press powder into hash from "rogue Afghanies." He'd taken drugs so pure people died from them. David transcribed one of the tapes and labeled it "an excerpt from *Morpheus*, a book forthcoming from Redd Herring Press." David never actually set up Redd Herring, nor did he finish this project. But the taping went on for several months.

He was working by then at Bookmasters' Pennsylvania Station store. Huncke came in one day in July to ask for a loan, and David gave him five dollars. Suddenly he saw that Huncke looked exactly like his father, heavier but with "the same scowl grin." A couple of days later, after Huncke had paid David twelve of the twenty-two dollars he currently owed him, David wrote in his journal that Huncke was "a kind of model in roles that I form my life after."

"Met a fella." That's the phrase David often used in his journal when he wrote about his sexual encounters. He'd stop at Julius's or another West Village bar before taking the subway to Brooklyn. Or he'd walk the Brooklyn Promenade before heading to Court Street. And he'd meet a fella.

Much of what he wrote in his journal during this period was about sex. He had two or three lovers at any given time, a fact that he never remarked on, for indeed it was not remarkable in the seventies. During that wild era, a gay male friend of mine told me that if he went out to post a letter, he could find someone to have sex with between his front door and the mail-box. Another told me that, if he wanted, he could find a sex partner every day after work on the subway between the Village and the Upper West Side. (I *had* these friends. Both are dead.) In comparison, David wasn't particu-larly promiscuous. He enjoyed one-night stands ("sensuality among strang-ers is unmatched for some reason"). But more often, he found something praiseworthy and intriguing about each guy and wanted to know him better. It just usually didn't work out.

The first five weeks of journal entries, beginning in late July, are fairly representative. David said goodbye to Don Muir, who was leaving New York ("one of the few people I've really communicated with"). He broke up with Charlie, who hadn't treated him well ("even a friendship would be diffi-cult"). He spent the night with Paul, who worked at Pace University ("I feel a lot of warmth in him"). He agonized over his feelings for Susan Gauthier, a cashier at Bookmasters who'd been a good friend since 1975 ("I love her, entertain ideas of a relationship, but realize that my desire for men af-fects this. I can't do both"). He kept in touch, through the mail, with his old boyfriend Michael Morais and his future boyfriend Brian Butterick. He spent the night with a "big brute" he met on the Promenade ("said he wrote a little poetry so I went with him"). He began an affair—contact of some kind almost daily for two weeks—with Ken Sterling (handsome, self-taught in five languages, "sensitive as hell"). He began an affair with a lawyer named Randy that would continue intermittently into the eighties. He worried about coming out to John Hall (who might feel "uneasy"). He considered going to Identity House for counseling on it all. And on Sep-tember 1, he went to the Promenade and "wondered if I could feel sexual. Um yeah . . . met a fella."

Still, he wasn't quite sure he was gay. "I don't profess to be of any kind of sexuality," he wrote on September 4, ten days before his twenty-third birthday. "I have a terrible sexual desire for men—emotional at times in a certain way. . . . I don't know what my capabilities are in reference to women. . . . Don't know and may never as I rarely give myself a chance."

So, although he'd been sexually active since he was a teenager, he was still coming out, a process with many layers. With Ken Sterling, for example, he felt relaxed enough for the first time in his life to accept the touch of another man in public: once at a restaurant, when Ken touched his hand below the table; another time at a movie theater, when Ken put an arm around David's shoulders. Affection in public scared him, but he thought the fear was good to go through. That was mid-August. By the end of September, he was embarrassed to realize during a phone call at work that he couldn't remember Ken's name.

At the end of September—a point when he was involved with three men—David called Syd, the lawyer who'd been a regular during his hustling days. They had not spoken in two years. "I was afraid to call at first as I didn't know what was going on in his life, like maybe everything had changed and he was no longer interested in going out anymore." David never states the obvious—that the date they set up was a sexual assignation, and it would be for money—but Syd picked him up near Port Authority and they went to a motel in New Jersey. David always said he could spend the rest of his life with Syd. He wrote that in 1977. He said it to me in 1990 when he told me his life story. But he said it knowing that it could never happen. Syd was married, with kids and a complex career.

That fall, when Brian Butterick returned from Provincetown, he and David became lovers. Brian joined the salon at the McLauchlin-Rivera loft, and David got him a job at Bookmasters. They set up readings to do together. David mentioned none of this in the journal—not because Brian meant so little to him but because he meant so much. This was a pattern that would continue for the rest of David's life. The men he loved the most got the least ink, at least in the journals (with the exception of a man he would meet in Paris). In fact, David stopped keeping his journal in early November of '77, and did not take it up again until April of '78. By that time, he had stopped talking about his attraction to women.

Susan Gauthier was surprised when David finally came out to her; she'd long figured he was gay and never knew he had a crush on her. "When he first came out to a lot of people, it was as if it was the worst thing that could happen," she said. "He literally took everyone I knew [aside] and told them separately, like it was a big pronouncement. I never understood why he felt he had to do this. It was quite distressing for him."

*David with Brian Butterick, probably early in 1978. (Photograph by Dirk Rowntree)*

Alex Rodriguez also had a vivid memory of David coming out to him, because David had been so hesitant and tense.

He was drifting, accomplishing little, and very much aware of it. He thought he might join the merchant marine. Not to emulate his father, but to follow the example of ex-seamen Kerouac, Ginsberg, and Huncke. On September 19, 1977, David wrote in the journal, "I feel a need to make a vast decision soon! Regarding my going out to sea on the merchant marine or maintaining my position as a clerk among books writing so little and feeling things come through the fingertips disappearing into the tabletop. . . . I have to leave this city this country soon and make my way into the depths of foreign soil where all will turn about."

In the journal about a week later, he articulated his plan, for the first time, to "put together a collection of voices—overheard monologues or character monologues that'll consist of junkies in a Chinese/American restaurant in Frisco, junkie on 8th avenue and 43rd, Arthur Treacher's Fish & Chips, Mike the bookstore guard, and the kid in Reno pickup truck, Huncke and others. Illustrations will be photos of odd moments / people retreating into darkness / around corners / sliding off tables in old restaurants / back views / views from the shoulders down."

He'd recently collected a monologue from Huncke about "finding" four thousand dollars in Canadian money. Of course, Huncke had stolen the money from the front seat of what was probably a company car, as it was plastered with Canadian Club signs. He boosted two bottles of whiskey while he was at it. When David finally published these monologues in 1982 as *Sounds in the Distance*, he did not identify Huncke (or any other participant) and simply titled this piece "Man Lying Back on a Couch in 90-Degree Weather."

The directness and emotional power of the monologues stand in contrast to what he was writing creatively at this time.


What could he reveal of himself? What could he write, for example, about what had happened in his family? In September 1977, David pasted one of his poems into his journal: "My Father as the Red Lark Moving in a Photograph of Gypsies by the Sea." Ed Wojnarowicz? A lark? David was still using imagery to conceal more than reveal. The last lines read: "You are passing through, unable to make music among those / shadows. A sad but musing smile playing across your lips / Everyone else in the room must breathe."

What did he dare say about his sexuality? The second issue of *Zone* appeared that fall with David's story about the El Paso bus station, "Cutting Through the South." He writes about sitting on the toilet in the bus station restroom only to have a guy crawl under the partition and grab his ankle, wanting sex. Later the same creep hits on a cowboy, who calls the police. Our narrator knows where this predator has gone but does not tell. Here, for the first time, he dealt in print with homosexuality—though in this case not his own and not in a situation most would find sexy or even palatable.

One day in October 1977, he went to the McLauchlin-Rivera loft for a photo session with Dirk Rowntree. David was impressed by a woman named Linda who showed up to do the styling, looking "like she stepped out of a dark Parisian s/m night club." Linda added French hair tonic to David's shaggy mop top and combed it straight back, off his face. "I was racing beneath my skin. I was wild," he wrote in his journal, because he wasn't sure he liked what he saw in the mirror. He needed that hair to hide. When Dirk took the picture, "it was an image I thought I would <u>never</u> let anybody see 'cause it made me uncomfortable—I was too stark—felt naked naked like the word ain't been used—hairless and all."

Two days later, Janine Pommy Vega moved into the Court Street apartment, taking the spare room—actually a walk-in closet they'd turned into their "library." Pommy Vega lived in Woodstock but spent four days a week in the city as part of the Poets in the Schools program. Adding her to the household had been David's idea. He'd cleaned the small room, put up some art (Magritte, Ira Cohen, a Japanese print), and set out books (Rimbaud, Elizabeth Bishop). They threw a mattress on the floor. "There's things I wanna do for people," he wrote in his journal. "There are emotions, thoughts, ideas, concerns, loves that I wanna grab some people—like Janine—and tell 'em but then there's a false sense—a fear of not being what I really am—a sense of straying from the inner core; the hot rhythms of all that we are."

"A fear of not being what I really am." Yet David, in his cryptic phase, continued to experiment with ways to camouflage himself. McLauchlin remembered that for a while David took to spelling his surname "Wjnaro-wicz," to make it even more mysterious and unpronounceable.

David had started to see less of Huncke. The old Beat had called him, very upset, early in August 1977. Cartwright thought that Huncke was telling stories about him to David. And for Huncke, Cartwright came first. So Huncke and David agreed not to hang out with each other. David was still working on *Morpheus*, the book of Cartwright's monologues, though Cartwright was worried about that too. He thought the taping sessions with David were going too much into drugs.

David still wanted Brian to meet Huncke, who had by then vagabonded further east—maybe Red Hook, Brian speculated—to a terrible apartment furnished with discards from the street. Brian thought that

Huncke and Cartwright had a "weird enabling codependent relationship" and that "there was something dangerous about the two of them." He and David talked about not getting too tangled up with these friends. "The drugs were heavier than we'd ever seen before. At that time," Brian said. "Even though we didn't do drugs with them, you could tell." So Brian just withdrew, though, he pointed out, "Had I run into them a few years later, I would have welcomed them with open arms." Brian did heroin for most of the eighties.

David wrote his last journal entry about Huncke on the day Pommy Vega moved in, in October 1977. David took her over to Cartwright's place and Huncke happened to be there.

A few days later, David was at the Small Press Book Fair, where *RedM* had rented a table. David sat there all day and sold one copy of the magazine.

His sister, Pat, remembered that when David was a boy, he always had vivid dreams, and he would wake up screaming from his nightmares. The journals he kept in the late 1970s are filled with descriptions of dreams. Often he remembered three a night. And he began to find imagery there that he would use as a visual artist.

This dream from October 1977 could describe one of his later paintings, with its multiple layers, its poetry, and its intimation of ruin: He is in a desolate town where there's an "acute sense of disrepair in the space, a sense that something has taken place, occupied and executed a change, something irreversible." He's clerking in a store when his father walks in and says, "Go up there. They're short and need somebody." When he puts on his work boots, David realizes that they've turned black. He is walking with his father, who is not drunk and not angry, but instead a comforting presence. "With him there, it's a representation of a whole lot of security somehow—structure in my life somewhere behind me." David sees a toad and picks it up so it won't get run over. He realizes then that it's a special toad with suction cups on its body so it can stick to things. He shows it to his dad, then tosses the toad up the lawn—but it turns back to the site of original danger. Suddenly David notices that the black shoe polish is "crumbling" off his boots. He pulls his dad's arm, saying, look—someone messed up my shoes with this polish. His dad has a "funny sad look" on his face and splits into the house. David stays outside, trying to scrape the polish off his boots with sand. "The black scrapes away and I see a blue sky—there are clouds in it as if drifting away thru it all—as I keep scraping, the sky crumbles away and there's a panorama of the Grand Canyon with a real little family parked at the edge of the canyon watching a sunrise or sunset. . . . I suddenly flashed on the thought that Dad might have polished my shoes as a help to me and didn't realize that they wouldn't stay polished."

During the year and a half that followed his father's suicide, David was more connected to his family than usual, though the contact was still minimal and he didn't see Steven at all. In July 1977, however, he went crabbing once in New Jersey with his half-brother, Pete. In October of that year, he went to Spotswood to mow the lawn and trim hedges for his step-mother and to help Pete cut down a tree. Pete visited David in New York City a couple of times, most memorably when they went to CBGB's to see the Steel Tips. Pete loved the whole atmosphere of the place, including the other spectators, like a girl dressed completely in vinyl, and then the band came on and the lead singer lit some firecrackers he'd taped to his chest and broke a bottle over his own head, and Pete was saying, "Man, what a place this is."

Dolores began attending David's occasional readings. She was not homophobic. She met and liked his friends and seemed intrigued to have a poet son. Dolores had begun studying at Fordham, and in the fall of '77 she joined the school newspaper staff, contributing a story on David and his circle. Instead of interviewing them, she asked him and some of his poet friends (Ensslin, Lackow, Morais, and DeForge) to fill out a questionnaire she'd prepared. "When did you realize you were going to become a poet?" And so on. David wrote five single-spaced pages for her, with an apology for his "short" replies. In light of his later work, his most interesting answer is to the question "Do you have a message to convey through your poetry?" No, he said. He had no message. "I don't sit down with an idea formed in my head and then try to put it onto paper. I usually sit down with a mental film running—one composed of visual and emotional images and I will start out with a few unimportant lines and then things connect and I write quickly onto the paper whatever comes through my fingers. . . . That's the excitement for me, the discoveries and connections of thought that suddenly appear. . . . If there's no discovery involved, writing . . . isn't fulfilling for me."

Dolores eventually created a scrapbook for each respondent, filled with their answers plus photos of the poets. David kept a few of his answer pages among his papers. But he didn't keep the rest. Years later, Ensslin was the only one who still had the whole scrapbook. He remembered David being mortified by it.

David saw Syd again in late April 1978, filled this time with ambivalence. "I feel stilted in seeing him. Seeing him means money for sex." But they met at a burger joint and just talked. David even collected a monologue ("Man in Brew & Burger . . ." about Syd's need for sex with teenagers). As they parted out on the street, Syd wanted to know if David needed money. He did. He really did. Syd handed him a hundred dollars. David began to tremble, and he told Syd, "Man . . . I don't know what to say, all these years I've wanted to tell you things but didn't know how. I mean, at this point, I'm happy with what I'm doing in my life, but when I was hustling, when I was in the Square at a certain point in my life, I really needed to connect with someone and you were really important then. You helped me through so many things, in ways you might not even be aware of." Syd said he was happy to hear it. They shook hands and walked off in different directions. David started to cry. It was the last time he ever saw Syd.

Two weeks later he dreamt that he was coasting the New Jersey highways in a car, musing on the diners, auto parts shops, lawn figurines, and oil refineries, the strangers in their ugly houses, "instant death in the heart over the whole sad business of everywhere USA," when he suddenly turned and saw that Syd was driving. He felt terrible about taking the hundred dollars and woke up so depressed that he called into work sick.

He wanted the reassuring arms of some man around him. Someone he could love for the rest of his life. He felt scared, and he didn't know why. Just an ominous feeling, "like a passage coming to an end somewhere soon."

\* \* \*

On April 5, David and Brian presented a performance at the Glines called "Leaning with That Grey Beast of Desire." Brian described it later as "David's poetry and my songs."

David did not yet think of himself as a visual artist, but he met a couple of men that spring who may have influenced his later work. Ron the translator did not last long as a boyfriend, because David thought Ron wanted him only for sex. David wrote, "I should strengthen my character by not submitting to just loose fucking. . . . I want or desire more than just that from a person." But Ron did show him some artwork by Catalina Parra, daughter of Chilean poet Nicanor Parra. David sketched her piece *Diariamente* and described it in detail in his journal. It's a newspaper page—the bottom half is made up of obituaries torn out and then sewn together with rough stitching; the top half is an ad for bread, five slices folding forward wrapped in newsprint and stitched. The ad has been torn open, revealing another newspaper page: a photo. Someone is being seized. Parra's piece was a response to Pinochet's 1973 coup and the subsequent disappearance of so many Chileans. Ron told David that the stitching represented an old custom people had of sewing up the mouths, nose, ears, and eyes of an infant thought to possess evil spirits. In about 1988, he would create a photo of his own sewn mouth—though it looks very different from Parra's piece—and, in 1987, an image of two hands stitching together a loaf of bread.

Within days of meeting Ron, David also began seeing Arthur Tress, one of the few photographers in the art world at that time dealing with upfront gay imagery. Though their affair lasted only about a month, Tress encouraged David's artistry. He learned of an artists' postcard contest and urged David to enter. David planned to make a collage that would show Arthur Rimbaud spraying words from a ray gun, but the Rimbaud photo he'd found in a thrift shop was too big. Instead he came up with an image of a man "concealing messages behind a false eyeball" which he's plucked out. Lines of poetry curve over a map behind him. The design is fine, the meaning opaque. It didn't win.

Tress lived at Seventy-second and Riverside, near an abandoned Pennsylvania Railroad yard and a series of abandoned piers where gay men went for nude sunbathing. At the time of his affair with David, Tress had taken over the crumbling railroad workers' YMCA on the property and was using it as a studio, filling it with props gathered from the street and recruiting models from among the sunbathers to act out what he called "dark erotic fantasies."

With David, though, he was almost romantic—sex on a deserted pier after dark in a soft rain, sex followed by a comparison of poetic fantasies. In one interaction David recorded, Tress said he imagined himself on the edge of the Grand Canyon, and David said, "I was on the highway in a truck with the Vermeer gleam of fields hot insect whine screaming through the sunburnt brush." David read Tress some passages from his journal and was moved by the older man's reaction. (Tress was thirty-eight.) David wondered if he could live with him—an option he sometimes considered when the man in question was not really available. Tress was about to move to California.

David invited Tress to a big party he and his roommates were throwing at Court Street on May 6. The night of May 5, David went to the Promenade, "hoping to find someone to lay down with for awhile, to make love to and communicate with; a stranger—someone totally devoid of any mental connection with my past, present, or future." He met Ken the construction worker. He needed this, he decided, because of the way he'd been rejected by Ron and another fella who no longer called, Bob Culver. He wrote two pages of neo-Beat prosody on his night with Ken—the sensuousness of it all.

He was still figuring out what he wanted from a relationship. Not the amyl nitrate–fueled "cold loveless sex" notorious during the disco era. Not an exclusive partnership either. He tried to imagine sitting in an apartment with the same guy every night—"the dreariness of it, the inability to be moving." At times, though, he wondered if his hustling days had stunted his ability to actually have a relationship. That was the word he used. *Stunted*. More often, he saw no reason to question his nightly walks through New York searching for sexual contact and conversations with various street characters. Why question this need "when the fulfillment is not only a sense fulfillment but an education"?

"What I want is to know someone that I am sexually attracted to so well that we are kin, we are more than two lovers; we share something in common like a recorded sense of each other's characteristics . . . where the communication is complete to the point of not having to speak to convey everything one feels."

The Court Street poets threw their big party on May 6, 1978, to celebrate *RedM*, *Zone*, and Dennis DeForge's thirtieth birthday. David had also invited Louis Cartwright, John Hall, Susan Gauthier, and her boyfriend, Steve Gliboff. David took "Susie the blonde cashier" to his room to show her a mobile he'd made: a globe with animals hanging from it on strings, or as he described it in his journal, "falling from earth when gravity has failed." He'd gotten the idea from a third grade science book. This was the first piece of sculpture he ever made, at least the first he made note of, and the first of his pieces to deal with gravity, one of the forces he would ponder in his work for the rest of his life. He would re-create it early in his art career.

Another guest at the Court Street party was Dolores. She'd taken up photography, with David's encouragement, and had a photo published in *Zone 2* under her maiden name, Dolores McGuinness. It's a black-and-white image of a house with something rushing by, blurry but evocative. Pat's boyfriend, Jean-Pierre Pillu, showed up with Dolores. (He was a model, like Pat, and in town to work.)* Pillu encouraged David to think about coming to Paris. David did not need much encouragement. Before Pillu left town, he offered more good news: He and Pat would try to find David a job there.

David's teeth still bothered him, and he was facing serious dental work. But he decided that once he finished with all the dentistry, he would go to Paris. Pat wrote to say that she would pay his airfare, and she wondered, if she sent David another three hundred dollars, would that be enough "if paying your bills off is delaying you"?

By May 1978, David had nearly finished his monologue project—the first work he completed that would matter later on. The monologues were central to a life's mission he hadn't even articulated yet. David saw the world as

---

* Pat's divorce from Bob Fitzgerald was amicable. They were clearly just headed in different directions.

devolving, and here were those residing at the shattered edge of the map. An ex-con, a pedophile, a witness to murder, sex workers and johns, druggies, con men, and tramps—some were victims, but some were perps. These are lives characterized by risk and uncertainty. Here the social order does not protect, and does not apply. It's broken.

And hadn't he learned that as a boy?

After a childhood that had bred a kind of hopelessness, he and his brother—so different in every other way—had both thought about becoming hoboes. Steven considered it the day he ran from Hell's Kitchen back to their brutal father, while David thought for the rest of his life that he might end up back on the street. In the seventeen-page epistle to Ensslin written in '76 at the San Francisco Y, he'd fantasized about withdrawing from society to hang out with social monsters, and he concluded, "It's inevitable—I'll end up there."

So he put himself into the book of monologues too. "Young Guy Hanging Out on Market Street—San Francisco" is the story of David and Keenan getting picked up by the Mafia guy on Seventh Avenue, followed by a somewhat fictionalized account of the night he and Willy spotted a man in a business suit and ran up to mug him, armed with stolen meat cleavers, and saw that he was a terrified old bum. In the real-life account, David almost bursts into tears. In the monologue, the street kid bursts out laughing. But the monologues are about creating characters who inhabit the edge. They are devoid of self-pity—and devoid of pity. He may have moved the action to San Francisco just so all the hustling stories didn't come from New York. In "Young Boy in Times Square 4 A.M.," for example, we get the story he told many times of a john hiring him to take his clothes off and watch a man and a female prostitute through a peephole as they have a quickie; and David sees that the woman's torso is covered with scars. "Fresh scars with stitches in them."*

In April 1978, David had hitchhiked to Montreal to visit his old boyfriend Michael Morais, and one trucker who gave him a ride ended up

---

* He's also the central character in four others: "Boy in Coffee Shop on Third Avenue," "Young Man in Silver Dollar Restaurant," "Young Boy in Seafood Restaurant—NYC," and "Boy in Horn & Hardart's on Forty-second Street."

among the monologues. The trucker told David that there weren't hoboes like there used to be; he'd picked up lots of them—guys who were former dentists, scientists, teachers who "got started on the bottle . . . see these guys—something happens to 'em in their lives and they end up not wanting to do anything but move on. . . . They consider life one big zero and they themselves show what they think by becoming the same thing—no aim or point."

Maybe now they're called "homeless" and they don't move around as much, but David wanted to understand how people got to that shattered place. During his San Francisco sojourn in '76, David wrote an early version of the monologue "Man in Casual Labor Office 6:30 A.M." David himself was a regular at that office until he got his egg-sorting job, and he titled this first draft "Journal of Daily Labor." In the final draft, a tramp he meets there takes over the monologue, the tramp who announces, "I'm tired of being a tramp." In that second version, David deleted his own reflections, though they go to the heart of his project: "What is the beginning of tramping? Digging thru garbage? Smelly rooms with liquor store signs haunting the windows all night? What lines enclose or remove tramphood? Is it a figure of speech alien to one's own condition, used to describe other than yourself? Is it a state of mind or body? Is it a style of walking? Does the idea of it hit you suddenly at a particular age: hold me close. . . . I just had a vision of myself after the tenth grade."

David would identify with the tramps and outcasts of the world his entire life. It's what he saw in Louis Cartwright, this destitute and minimally educated "lowlife" who'd traveled to exotic locales and acquired special knowledge, though admittedly most of that was drug-related. By the spring of '78, David was feeling bad that he'd failed to get Cartwright's book launched, and he still intended to do it. In May, Cartwright brought him photos he'd taken of William Burroughs preparing dinner, which David very much wanted to publish in the second issue of *RedM*. He brought Cartwright along to a *RedM* meeting to show the pictures off to Ensslin and Rodriquez. "He is growing immensely in his thought, spirit/psychically," David wrote of Cartwright. David kept, with his own papers, two autobiographical pieces Cartwright wrote out in his big grade-school handwriting. One was about his bicycle trip through Nepal. In the other, "Confidence," dated

1974, Cartwright described his orphanhood and how he'd come to see eventually that he wasn't "born bad" but was "a good open free man who stopped being second class." David probably hoped to incorporate these pieces into the proposed book. But he was still making a hundred dollars a week in salary and would never have the money to publish even a small book in modest quantity. Not in the seventies. Nor would there be another issue of *RedM*.

By the early 1990s, Huncke and Cartwright were living in the East Village between Avenues C and D, a short walk from David's loft, but he had long ago left their orbits. (Nor was he willing to cope anymore with drug addicts.) Filmmaker Laki Vazakas began documenting Huncke and Cartwright in 1993. They were "using," of course—but organized. And coping. Then Huncke got hurt and went into the hospital, moving afterward to the Chelsea Hotel to convalesce. Without Huncke, Cartwright fell apart. His habit got worse, the apartment grew squalid, and he couldn't pay the rent since he spent what he had on drugs. He ended up in a flophouse on the Bowery.

On June 6, 1994, nearly two years after David's death, Louis Cartwright was murdered in broad daylight on Second Avenue near Seventh Street, a crime that remains unsolved. Police were astonished when several Lower East Side poets came to the precinct to make inquiries into the death of this . . . bum.


In summer 1978, David moved in with Brian Butterick, who had a loft in Manhattan on Orchard Street above a button seller. David stayed there rent-free, saving money for the trip to Paris. He would leave September 6.

On August 25, he began a passionate affair with a guy he met at Julius's, Phillip Seymour. At least, it was passionate on David's part. Phillip didn't want a relationship; he'd just broken up with someone and was depressed to be back in New York after a cross-country trip. David accepted this. But, the day after their second meeting, he felt compelled to explain the connection he sensed with Phillip in a three-page single-spaced letter. Through Phillip—who loved camping and had branches, rocks, and a wasp nest on display at home—David suddenly saw how he'd abandoned his own interest in nature. Through Phillip—who did ceramics David thought exquisite—he came to question why he'd stopped drawing. Phillip lived on Christopher Street, and when he said he was troubled by the gay male life-style surrounding him there, the constant cruising and constant tempta-tion, David said he felt the same way. He just didn't know an alternative to it. "His feelings were so completely like my own," David wrote in the jour-nal. "This unspoken connection of two figures moving about this dark planet at two separate times and finally connecting." He decided he had to give Phillip a piece of driftwood he'd found years earlier on his Outward Bound trip and then presented to his mother. Dolores was upset when it disappeared from her apartment, but David reasoned that he had to give it to Phillip "to show him my feelings."

However, as soon as he delivered the letter and driftwood to Phillip, David began to worry. And this was already a familiar worry: Had he re-vealed too much of himself? Maybe he'd been too open. What if the letter frightened Phillip, or produced some other effect that he "wouldn't wish for"? Even after they met for lunch the next day and Phillip called the letter "beautiful," David couldn't stop obsessing. Back at Bookmasters, where his co-workers were throwing him a bon voyage party, David was tense and unhappy. He'd been so anxious with Phillip that he hadn't enjoyed seeing him. He worried that he'd "done silliness again in [his] life—the big risk of the heart communication." That night, David went back to Julius's—and there he found Phillip again. This time David put it to him directly; he was "feeling funny about the letter, how it might have been taken." Phillip told him again; the letter was beautiful.

Years later, what Phillip most remembered about David was how little he'd known about him. He could never quite figure out where David lived, for example. Then, after digging through an old box, Phillip managed to find what I figured must be one bombshell of a letter. But no. It's cautious and rambling. David tells him, "Watching the excited and animated way in which you described thoughts and theories of your art and life somehow opened up an area which helped me connect with those important senses that I had somehow lost hold of."

Brian drove him to the airport. Brian had been there, through all the other fellas for the past ten months, but David had mentioned him in the journal only in passing. On the day he left town, however, David wrote: "Brian is gonna be missed in a way I can't explain—writing of him and what he means to me is too heartfelt and unintendedly personal that I haven't written the senses down. I wish he were going with me—if I do get money I will send for him."

Once David got to Paris, he and Phillip Seymour exchanged a few letters, but when they passed each other on Christopher Street sometime in the 1980s, Phillip didn't speak. He realized that David hadn't recognized him.

# 6 THE FLANEUR

**David thought he** might live in Paris for the rest of his life. So, during a last itchy week in New York, he attended to things he'd been putting off. He took his driver's test—and passed. He finally came out to his old buddy John Hall—who did not reject him, as David had feared. And he called Dolores, who said she'd contacted a medium on his behalf. David would find success, get his hot temper under control, and be healthy all of his later life.

David was so filled with tension, that something seemed to have cracked open in him. When he said his last goodbye to Phillip Seymour, he hallucinated—he saw a wolf's head and felt his own jaws elongating. A few days before that, he'd written in the journal, "feeling animalistic. Feeling hyena. Feeling wolf. Feeling dog. I am tongue and heart. Stillness in the morning. I reject all other thoughts of love and friendship." And in that same piece came the line, "My heritage is a calculated fuck"—the first sentence of a book he would write more than ten years later, *Close to the Knives*.

His life was about to change, and everywhere he looked were signs and portents. Everything was magnified now. Everything signified.

Two days before leaving town, David witnessed the legendary Marsha P. Johnson "flipping out" on Christopher Street. The Stonewall veteran and cofounder of the Street Transvestite Action Revolutionaries was walking toward the river, rifling through garbage cans, stuffing bits of trash into a white gift box, "saying in mock suburban housewife: my my what a pretty gift," David wrote in his journal. One minute, she was jumping—shoeless but in white athletic socks—and the next, lying in the street, where people who knew her tried to help her up, "the green glitter making her eyes more manic." She wanted money: "I ain't eaten in three fuckin' days." And David handed her some. He couldn't articulate just why this scene so disturbed him, beyond feeling "a sense of imprisonment." But this was his old street life, his hopelessness, turned into spectacle.

On September 5, 1978—the night before he left for Paris—he had dinner with John Hall and then stopped by Dirk Rowntree's apartment in the West Village to give him a poster. He suggested that Dirk might document this momentous occasion, do a portrait of the artist walking toward Europe. Out on the corner of Seventh Avenue and Tenth Street, Dirk photographed David's legs stepping from the curb, then David's head almost haloed in a blur of passing headlights, mouth open, eyes full of eagerness—and trepidation.

David took to Europe everything he owned. Two big bags. Heavier perhaps were the plans and goals with which he'd weighted himself: He would write a novel. He would find a publisher for the monologues. He would create illuminations for Rimbaud's *Illuminations*. He would illustrate Dennis DeForge's new poetry manuscript—and the children's book Phillip Seymour planned to write. He would make money from his drawings and writings, then send for Brian. He would work daily on the journal and correspond with friends. He would take Brian's old guitar, learn to play it, then write songs. And, of course, he would master the language. Finally. He had failed second-year French for three consecutive school terms.

In fact, his nine months in Paris would change him profoundly, though he accomplished few of the goals he'd set for himself. Instead, he fell in love for the first time, found his voice as a writer, and discovered that he was rather hopelessly American.

The plan was to meet Pat on September 8 in Normandy, where her boyfriend, Jean-Pierre Pillu, had a house. David flew to London. There he caught the train to Southampton and began recording the foreign. The grass out there! English grass! While waiting for the Channel ferry the next day, he pictured French docks right out of Genet: "a hooded area of fog and broken sliding piers populated with cutthroat sailors." I don't think this was willful naiveté so much as—hope.

After six days in Normandy, he and Pat and Pillu arrived in Paris on David's twenty-fourth birthday, September 14. His first impressions shocked him. So bourgeois. Where was the city of Rimbaud? Or, as he put it to Pillu, "Where's the underworld?" Pillu promised that some night soon he'd drive David through the Bois de Boulogne to show him "the travesties"— transvestites. Which was not, of course, what David had in mind.

Then, just blocks from their apartment in the Ninth Arrondissement, he discovered the Pigalle: "very much like Times Square with leather suited pale ghostwhite anemic boys—some muscled brutes with lowset eyes," transvestites, and "sailor types straight from the pages of Genet . . . prostitutes. . . . bag ladies . . . young Cocteauian boys struggling through the gas and heat of passing cars." Now he felt more at home. Even better was his discovery the next night of the Left Bank. Here Brassaï and all the writers he loved had sipped coffees in cafes, and he was walking where they had walked. He slept on cushions on his sister's floor. Out the window, he noted the "starlit world over Cezanne rooftops." Pat and Pillu bought him an Underwood typewriter at a flea market for his birthday. Now he could write poems and start the novel and do some letter writing, though he wondered how he was going to afford the postage.

During his first full day in Paris, he visited the Louvre, and the first painting to really catch his eye was *Le sommeil d'Endymion* by Anne-Louis Girodet-Trioson: a naked young man swoons in a forest glade, while a grinning cherub hovers in the air. David glued a postcard of it into his journal. For him, the painting was all about sex. "Sexual tension is in my loins at this point," he wrote. "The departure from the sexual life of NYC now up in my smooth throat—like a gasp—the body of the fallen male—intoxication. . . . I could put my mouth to his and taste wine." The next day, back at the Louvre, he found *Un coin de table*, Henri Fantin-Latour's group portrait of Rimbaud, Verlaine, and their circle. After leaving the museum to walk along the Seine, he unexpectedly had a sexual encounter—outdoors—with a man who parted from him by drawing, as David put it, "an 'X' in invisible red lines over my heart. . . . I tasted blood on my lips and walked delirious through the side streets of the Louvre." It would take him another ten days to figure out that the big gay cruising ground in Paris after dark—and maybe even during the day—was the Tuileries, the large formal garden just west of the museum.

Within his first week at his sister's apartment, he'd outlined a "a semi-surreal erotic novel," *Auto Noir.* He intended to base this on his own journey from New York to Paris. Sort of. Apparently it would be about sense impressions, and probably more "surreal" than "semi." In a letter to Michael Morais written on October 1, 1978, he explained the term "auto noir" as "automatic entry into the subconscious in foreign spaces . . . the black auto that waits around every corner; black auto of fear or groundlessness . . . black auto containing within its trunk all the unspoken desires and actions; black auto of chance." There would also be photos in this book: a snake, a whirl of "light lengths," desolate passageways beneath bridges, moon- or lamp-illuminated statues in public gardens, and "daytime photos of symbols that reflect areas of thinking."

David kept trying to access his subconscious through lofty imagery and a kind of automatic writing, hoping no doubt that something "real" would shake out. He was terribly afraid of his actual subject matter, and finally admitted as much in a letter to his old girlfriend Jezebel Cook. He told her he'd started to overcome this fear—because he was outlining the "street novel" based on his life. He'd started it three times in New York and given up each time.

By the beginning of October, he was a regular at the Tuileries. On October 9, for example, he squatted outside the Louvre in the afternoon listening to a street musician, went home for a nap, and returned after dark, noting the bums and bag ladies at the Metro station "laid out like mortuary bundles on the slatted benches." He squeezed between the locked gates at the Tuileries and immediately encountered a blond guy in a black leather jumpsuit, who approached David and grabbed his crotch. "I felt as if I could only surrender to it. . . . I have never felt any need or desire for exhibitionism . . . but there was a great sense of pleasure in doing this all within eyeball of any number of buildings and national monuments." They were close enough to the fountain to hear fish splashing.

He'd noticed the characters hanging out at Place Saint-Michel by the fountain. "Just low down beaten people with a wild look of criminality in their eyes." He wished he could speak to them. His French-deprived muteness was already starting to get him down. "I'm doing so much writing so's to keep a hold of my sanity and language," he wrote several days later in letters to Brian Butterick and John Hall, ". . . never thought so deeply as this."

He began a new project called "Study of the Internal Anatomy of the Face," a visual record of places where something had occurred to effect his life, his consciousness—events now over but "forever fixed in the non-seeing eye." With his sister's camera, he roamed the city photographing, for example, candles at Notre Dame—because he'd lit a candle there for his father weeks earlier. If and when he returned to New York, he would, of course, add Times Square.

He went to a Wim Wenders film, in German with French subtitles, so he could measure "the effect of seeing a film that [he] could only respond to either on a visual level or else on the level of voice intonations." He concluded that the sensations he had were the same ones he'd experienced "in cross country buses, in the silent dozing seats of a stranger's automobile . . . following the spinal cord of highway in a way that transcends the timeclock of the heart . . . so that one is a viable coasting vehicle of thought and response not held in by boundaries created in the fusion of society and physical law."

He wrote a set of letters to his mother, advising her to keep a journal, commiserating over the death of her cat: "For the cat its all completed and for you its an experience to assimilate and then continue with your life, with the realization of the great things that came from that contact. . . . Since we can't totally conceive of death as far as all the elements involved, then we owe it to ourselves and the creatures involved (whether it be people animals or senses) to learn as much as we can from it." In another missive, he commented on her observation that there was "a veil" between them. It was because he couldn't tell her everything, he said. He was interested in characters and lifestyles that "seem to go against the established order," and it might cause her pain.

David enjoyed just hanging out in a sexual milieu like the Tuileries—so forbidden and potentially dangerous. This was the heart of the tourist district, after all, and on many nights, the police raided, sending men scurrying over the fences. One night when David arrived, a man he identified as "an arab" managed to convey the question, "Any cops?" No. The man put his hand on David's crotch, then dropped his pants and bent over with his arms around a tree so David could fuck him. Afterward David went to the fountain and washed, watching other men in the shadows as he pulled some

*One panel from a two-page cartoon strip David drew in the style of Bill "Zippy the Pinhead" Griffith for his friend Susan Gauthier. (David Wojnarowicz Papers, Fales Library, NYU)*

bread and ham from a sack and made sandwiches for himself. Leaning his head against the stone side of the fountain, he stared "up at the spiralling sky" and thought about the distances he'd come in his life.

He wrote daily now unless he was traveling, and sometimes even then. During his first six weeks in France, he spent almost half his time in Normandy, where he stayed in an old house across from Pillu's place. He wrote, drew pictures of the chickens in the yard, created a cartoon for his friend Susan Gauthier, and raced over the country roads on Pillu's motorbike. On about half those Normandy days, Pat and Pillu were with him. He was completely dependent on them now, and their apartment at 6 rue Laferrière was just a studio. He let them know that he had friends in Paris he could stay with, so he didn't always have to intrude. But who would that have been? In fact, he had no one even to talk to except Pat and Pillu. In the journal, he wrote, "[I would] sleep out under the seine bridges and in the gardens and elsewhere . . . staying up all night if I have to among the street characters along St. Michel in my grubby coat with my notebooks and scribbling. . . . The experiences are needed . . . necessary."

He dreamt that his face was no longer his own. "Realizing that my life has been composed of series of strange and seemingly wounding incidents; time, places and situations that one would suppose would leave deep scars of the invisible forehead. . . . What I am realizing is that all those periods of my life, all the experiences no matter how some of them smell of shit and others are wrapt in stinking rags. What surfaces in the image mind is that of a brilliant white heart metamorphoses."

Before leaving New York, he'd sent the monologues to City Lights, where he wanted so badly to be published that he even dreamt about it. They wrote him in Paris to say that they weren't looking at new manuscripts now. He decided to try for a European publisher. After a month in France, nothing was coming together for him. He was in free fall, "a viable coasting vehicle," and he couldn't really see what he was doing.

Just observing. Just writing. Just thinking. France would prove to be his education, and this was the homework.

But he had made no effort to learn French, or to get a job. By the end of October, he was talking in the journal about a return to the United States and his plans for "extended hoboing." He wrote, "I need constant intense experience so that I feel I'm living and alive . . . as opposed to dreary existence of stabilization. But for whom? . . . . Who am I illuminating with my writings—myself and a handful of known people or what?"

That night he dreamt that the sun and moon had merged. Then two suns appeared, spinning like pinwheels, much like Van Gogh's *Starry Night*. He knew he was dreaming and would want to write it down later. So he observed carefully, trying to memorize the shapes. There were two skies now, and strange objects zooming through them. "They represented some important knowledge or symbol I couldn't understand."

"Met a fella towards dark dark evening." It was November 1, 1978. David had spent the day reading a book on surrealism that he'd found in a West Village garbage can and brought with him. He made a sandwich to eat on a bench on rue Guillaume-Apollinaire. He took a Nico poster from a Saint-Michel wall, thinking he'd write a letter on it to Brian. He thought about *Auto Noir*, imagining himself at an artsy dinner party where someone would ask, "and what do you write?" and he'd reply, "It's the same as asking me what I see; both before my eyes and behind them." He headed for the Tuileries.

There he met Jean Pierre Delage, "a stranger leanin against the midnight doors of the Louvre," as David, ever the romantic, wrote a couple of days later on the Nico poster. Actually, JP told me, they'd met "in a bush." David went home with him. He wrote: "It's hard to relate the changes I went through as a result of meeting a fella so fucking genuine and sincere and full of warmth—to lie down in a bed; on a mattress nude with another man whom you feel is both sexy and sensitive is a relief that wipes the brow clean of all insecurities and frustrations." They put the mattress on the floor so it wouldn't squeak as much and stayed in bed for about four hours. "First time in two months aside from Brian's great letters that I've laughed and felt good in such a way," David wrote later. "It was marvelous. Felt the old energy stirring within my veins finally."

JP had a rough Gallic handsomeness. He was eight years older than David and worked as a hairdresser. He showed David a book he was reading about Sufism. He didn't practice, he explained—just had an interest in Eastern philosophy. When they discussed some French traveler who'd gone to South America, David recommended he get Burroughs's *Yage Letters*. Jean Pierre apologized for speaking poor English; he was self-taught. David wrote: "I took his beautiful face in my hands and said, look man; I should be the one apologizing. . . . Communication was in the eyes and fingertips; the senses we traded back and forth in small gestures would make statues blush. I felt so good and comfortable in his arms, in contact with his body and mind, that I coulda wept at the release it provided; it was a sudden and great unleashing of sexual tensions and held-in desires."

JP took David's face in his hands and said that it would be difficult to say goodnight to him. David felt the same, but declined JP's invitation to spend the night. He'd promised Pat that he'd come home. "Plus" he wrote, "there's a sense I get when I'm having such an intense and good time—I need to get away so I can assimilate the feelings/emotions that run so wildly in those periods of release; release of tensions sexual and otherwise." He was writing all this back at Pat's apartment, at three A.M. "I can't find the words for what took place tonight and what is still taking place down in that bird within the chest." JP had driven him home.

David underlined the following in red: "I slumped into the corner of the elevator and stared at my face in the big mirror on the opposite wall illuminated by fluorescent light. God I could hardly recognize myself. . . . I could hardly see with all that racing movement behind the eyes."

*Jean Pierre Delage. (Courtesy
of Jean Pierre Delage)*

He continued, "At one point late in the evening as we sat cross-legged smoking, talking, and stroking each other, he picked up the dictionary and looked up a word; looked at me and said: ah yeah . . . 'caress' . . . and smiled happily."

That was written on a Thursday, in the wee hours. He didn't see JP again till Saturday after work.

In between, he came up with three arty (and never realized) film ideas, advised himself on the direction of *Auto Noir* (never completed), dreamt that he was traveling the world to photograph "optic designs" and drew those he could remember, dreamt that he restored two dried-up snakes to life by putting them in water, watched *The Hound of the Baskervilles* dubbed into French, trolled the Latin Quarter (but noted, "I don't find myself searching . . . now that I met this fella"), copied quotes from Paul Éluard, Benjamin Péret, René Crevel, Jack Kerouac, and Giorgio de Chirico into his journal, drew someone leaning on a table, face not visible, with a bottle and some spillage, above the caption: "lost words of the loveless surviving the night." And wrote a sort of prose poem, which became increasingly incoherent but began: "For Jean Pierre Delage: I'm resting on the surface of the Seine; a giant whose legs fit end external beneath the curved stanchions of the bridges; an anchoring down of this sometimes terrifying weight; my hands and arms made of sky."

He couldn't calm down.

He wrote to Janine Pommy Vega and Alex Rodriquez to say that he'd started talking to himself so he didn't lose his English and that he could hear the music in the trees and the earth now: "little creatures wonkin among the grassblades, but contact and sensation has always been the jumpin point of departure for me; that swift journeylike sensation of being a viable living vehicle among the elements of the earth's turning." And now he had this new love. He'd have to clear old baggage, which was hard work—"like deciding to move the tree ten or fifteen years after we planted it."

On Saturday night, he waited nervously for JP at Saint-Georges Metro station, thinking maybe he'd screwed up the time, maybe this wasn't going to work. But JP was just late. David's account of their dinner, their talk, their lovemaking is one long breathless sentence. JP showed David that he'd bought a French translation of *The Yage Letters*, and he'd nearly finished it. This time David spent the night, but neither of them slept well on the tiny bed. In the morning, Jean Pierre heated coffee on a camp stove and took a tiny package of butter and half a loaf of bread from the window ledge overlooking the courtyard six flights down. David wrote, "It tasted like food from the banquets of Monarchs but EVEN BETTER!"

They drove to Normandy. David was to spend the next two weeks there, but JP had to leave after two days. They had wine and wonderful meals (cooked by JP) and walks on the beach and "delicious sexual contact." David even thought his French was improving; he could speak a full sentence now, with maybe an English word here or there. David began trying to recapture it all in words as soon as JP was gone. He remembered feeling near the end of the three-hour drive from Paris as if JP's mind and body had suddenly merged with his own. "I'm breathing a sense of him in such a way that we are just about indistinguishable," he wrote. "This is all in silence in the car with landscape drifting and what I suddenly feel is that he is mine and in some sense possessed within my coursing blood in my pores, not a selfish owning sense but just a total merge within and at that exact moment in comes arrowlike a realization that he is an entirely separate person and living independent of me and my blood and that it's a subtle unknown thing that has drawn us together that is by no means certain or everlasting and from that I feel a striking and sudden faintness, a fever in my throat and forehead and my hands tremble invisibly and I'm about to black out in this fever and wanna grab onto something for all the frightening bareness I feel."

He would revisit these feelings in a piece he made for his last show, in 1990 in a world devastated by AIDS. David took a photo of skeletons exposed in a Native American burial ground, then silk-screened over it words inspired by his yearning for connection and his fear of impending and constant loss: "When I put my hands on your body on your flesh I feel the history of that body. Not just the beginning of its forming in that distant lake but all the way beyond its ending. . . . If I could attach our blood vessels in order to anchor you to the earth to this present time to me I would. If I could open your body and slip up inside your skin and look out your eyes and forever have my lips fuse with yours I would."

During one of their talks that weekend in Normandy, David felt he had explained himself "fully and justly" to Jean Pierre. His life. His work. So now, David concluded, "wherever this goes, it will at least go open-hearted." As JP left and said he felt funny about going, David decided to stop pretending that it wasn't affecting him. "You know . . . I feel," he began, but realized he couldn't articulate it. So he stopped and JP said, "Yes? What do you feel?"

David said, "Ah, never mind. It's nothing."

That night when he got into bed alone, he began talking to calm himself down: "My hands my arms my thoughts and all I can do is write yes that's all I could do."


David typed a letter to Brian on the Nico poster, covering both sides. It was all about meeting JP, his feelings for JP, including much of what he'd written in his journal. "I've changed since New York," he announced. He was now "less afraid of emotional commitment." And he had no intention of returning to America. "All it contains when I visualize the place is you . . . nothing else but fading photographs." He hoped Brian would make it to Paris and maybe the two of them could go on to India together. "I still think much of you and still love ya." He also wrote that he'd typed till three A.M. and thought he might tear the poster up now, "because of its personal sense."

Again, he was afraid that he had said too much. But he didn't tear it up. He just never mailed it.

Jean Pierre returned to Normandy the next weekend. The weekend after that, David took the train back to Paris. JP was feeling ill with a bad cold and got into bed, while David sat cross-legged on the edge talking about how angry and hurt he felt that he had to stay out in the country for such long periods of time. He also felt unable "to fully protest the situation as I am 'guest' and 'being supported.'"

Three days later he had a huge screaming argument with his sister. She thought he should go back to New York after Christmas. David was furious. She'd encouraged him to come, with the idea that he could stay for a long time. So he'd broken up his life in New York, sold his books, torn away from his friends—and developed a relationship with Jean Pierre. "She and her boyfriend encouraged me to explore life here, open up to it here—so I've done so and am faced with all this shit in the end." David didn't record her side of it, except to say that she called him selfish and told him to grow up. He told her he *had* grown up—to the point where he didn't fear emotional commitment to JP.

"She doesn't understand the depth of my emotions at this point—she said ask Jean Pierre to move to America—I could've slapped her at that point—she threatened to slap me." She told him that now he'd seen what existed in Europe; he could save up and return. He told her he'd live on the fucking street before he'd return to New York.

Finally he walked out, toward the Seine. "I wanted to kill myself so fucking bad—nothing mattered anymore—but the idea that she would suffer for it made me not do it; the idea that I would never put these lips to JP's again made me cease the action—I don't want to die and yet I can't face New York after all this. I CAN'T!!!"

He went back to Pat's apartment and took a bath. She came in, but left again before he was out of the bathroom. He wrote her an eight-page letter to convey his confusion. By five P.M. he was walking the streets, waiting to call JP at six. He'd have to move in with him. That was his only hope. "The descending night," he wrote in the journal he always had with him. "Auto noir—it is for sure delineated; the sense of the man spiraling on the tracks of oblivion."

Just as he wrote those lines, standing by the Saint-George Metro, Pat stopped in front of him talking to some male model she knew. Pat and David then walked home together, talking more quietly. Later he would admit in a letter to a friend that both Pat and Pillu were having trouble finding work; "the responsibility of my being here is a little more than they expected," he wrote. He loved Pat. He felt awful that they'd fought.

The next day, November 22, he went to the Alliance Française to inquire about enrollment in a French class and the requirements to get working papers. On November 23, he walked around Paris, realizing he didn't have the faintest idea how to find work. He thought about his many plans: the illustrations for Rimbaud's *Illuminations*, the "sensory journal surreal illustrations of day and night," the *Auto Noir* project, the photos he still wanted to take in Paris, the novel, a book of surreal dream sketches, the song lyrics he'd begun to write. And he thought about Jean Pierre, the completeness he felt when lying against him. "I get hit with sudden fearful concern for all I know and all those I love . . . the vulnerability of things . . . the death that hatches . . . unravels like a seed in all of us."

"Who the fuck am I and what am I racing towards?"

Within a week, David had moved in with Jean Pierre at 78 avenue de la Bourdonnais, near the Eiffel Tower. This was probably the wealthiest district in Paris, but JP had a maid's room on the top floor, with a toilet down the hall and a shower in the basement—even a separate elevator. Someone had given him the place for free; he was saving to buy an apartment. He worked nearby at a salon called New Wave, and that's the style he specialized in. "Hair in flame and in fire with red, pink, any kind of color and very strange shapes," he said. "My job was like a show." Passing window shoppers would stand outside and watch him work. "David saw that. He was laughing."

At the Alliance Française, David took an admissions test, then watched as the instructor slashed it with red marks and threw it in a wastebasket. He and JP picked up a larger mattress from an empty apartment filled with

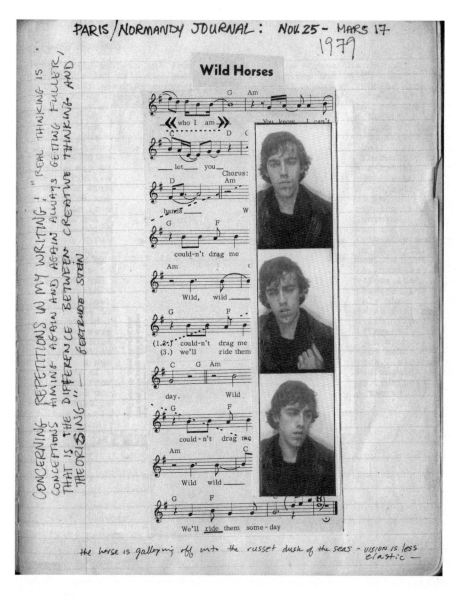

*During his nine months in France, David worked on his journal nearly every day. (David Wojnarowicz Papers, Fales Library, NYU)*

"tiny tiny rooms like for midgets." He was reading Lautréamont's *Maldoror*, in English of course.

He wrote to two French publishers, Nidra Poller at Soleil Noir and Christian Bourgois at Editions Christian Bourgois, asking for work and making queries about their possible interest in the monologues. It took just two days for a rejection letter to arrive from Bourgois. But Poller invited him to make an appointment, "to talk about your writing and your situation in Paris," she said.

He also had a letter from Sylvia Pogorzalek in Bonn, whom he'd queried earlier. She'd published German editions of works by Patti Smith and Tom Verlaine. She would find it difficult to publish an unknown, Pogorzalek wrote, but would be interested in seeing the manuscript. Maybe a piece of it would work for her magazine, *Gasolin*. David spent two days preparing a cover letter, then almost immediately regretted spending the seven francs postage. That could have bought two chocolate bars.

On December 4, he met with Nidra Poller, "a great woman." They talked for two hours. It was probably the first literary-philosophical conversation he'd had since coming to Paris. "I did it all shakily, not having had that kinda contact in a long time," he wrote, "also not having <u>spoken</u> on the book before." She pronounced herself interested in looking at the manuscript, but knew of no work prospects.

Where and how could he even look for a job without knowing French? The American embassy? He actually tried there. JP had made no demands of him; David just didn't like being dependent. As he explained in a letter to Dennis DeForge, "Being dependent on people always hooks into the Times Square senses, even though it's not the same. That's a sense I may never rid myself of."

He began a series of drawings in hopes of getting a gallery interested, getting "some food money rolling in." One drawing showed a huge dog walking behind mountains "filled with planets, stars, peep holes, rays, lines, lightning bolts, rain and the most obsessively pure eyes I've ever drawn. The mountains have huge reptile/hieroglyph carvings in them." He called the piece *Night Arrives on the Mayan Coastline,* and felt he'd had a kind of breakthrough. "I finally figured out how to draw black and white mountains; mountains that wouldn't be flat and signboard hollywoodian looking." He hated the thought of selling this. He liked it. Indeed, with its Western landscape, animal presence, and cosmic symbols, it's the first drawing he ever did that seems connected to the mythic style he later developed.

In his journal, late in December, he drew what looked like a Dürer wing, probably because he'd dreamt of a birdman—human legs and wings for arms, "sad man's eye's, gnashing beak as if he's trying to get out of bird appearance." He wanted to describe it to Brian, who'd been with him in the dream. But the wing was a prescient image to inscribe, as it would figure later in his life.

By the end of 1978, he'd stopped looking for a job. He would drop his French class after a month or two (by JP's estimate). And he never did tour the Paris galleries to try to interest them in his work.

On New Year's Eve, he dreamt that he'd joined the army or navy—he didn't know which—and they ordered him into a helicopter, flew him over the Arctic, and threw him out. He crashed through the ice, only to be rescued via rope and taken back to America.

Nidra Poller sent David a letter early in January 1979 to say that she saw the monologues as a writing exercise, "an apprencticeship to the craft." She wrote, "I feel like there's no poetry to be distilled from these experiences, that they are lived with a language so minimal that to enrich it would be a betrayal of the reality. And I think that is a serious dilemma for the writer. Barren soil. I wonder what you think?" While David had plenty of thoughts, he did not answer immediately.

In Normandy for the last time at the end of February, he was still pondering what he called her question on why he loved "sleeping thugs and wandering men and women who made nothing of their lives." His handwritten draft was tucked into a journal with an empty envelope from Bonn, probably another rejection, and he wrote in such a rush of emotion that it's hard to decipher, apart from lines like "the sleeping thug represents a sense of life more important to me than whatever I have learned of my own so far."

He would give up, for the time being, on trying to place the monologues.

He'd begun "a personal notebook of drawings," each maybe four inches by three of "pure bloody madness," with many of the images drawn from dreams. This would be the visual equivalent of automatic writing—permission to draw anything, to let go. He felt he had an internal censor "constantly at work prodding vision/image with a subtle 'no.'" Certainly the whole journey to Paris had been about giving himself a jolt, a way to remove himself from internal restraints.

He also began the practice, continued for the rest of his life, of writing instructions to himself. In regard to the street novel, for example: "Walk the streets and accept the return of those senses and return home and push them through the typewriter."

He felt that his writing had changed. "The continual silence here, the lack of creative American-style energy and dreams has slowed me down and calmed my writings," he said in a letter to Ensslin. Still, he was far from done with surrealism, an art form made for the removal of internal restraint.

He wondered if he should rewrite the street novel in symbolist language.

He wrote song lyrics like "Louis Bunuel / . . . can ya enter this cell / take a cinematic photograph of my soundless scream / cut the eye, make it die, before it starts to dream."

He outlined ideas for a piece on "a hallucinated America," another "supportive glimpse into the netherworld," but this time using dreams.

He began a project called "the Bolt book,"* dreams again, plus emotionally charged moments from his journals, and surreal stories combined with images.

He completed none of these projects.

But he was beginning to find bits of his visual vocabulary. In 1991, David would create what he very consciously decided would be his last piece, a photograph of his own face partly buried in loose dirt. In the Bolt book, in 1979, he wrote what seems to be a description of it: "I am the face beneath the sand still breathing while day pulls down from the sky, and I leaned back thinking he should have guaranteed entrance into heaven."

He knew he would have to leave Paris. His love for JP was the only thing holding him there.

He was having many dreams about the American West and wanted to make another cross-country trip. He missed the wildness of New York. In

---

* He'd started drawing what he called his "Arthur Rimbaud lightning bolt" in the journal as soon as he got to France, perhaps to mark possible material for this, or just to mark auspicious entries. The bolt was his symbol for what he called "the vision behind the eyes."

Paris, he'd observed, "the only anarchy I see is in the public parks after dusk; the ballet of pick-ups and pickpockets, Arabs runnin' from the police . . . hoods and local toughs playing soccer with beer cans . . . dreaming ladies walking their poodles in the midst of all this." He noted in a letter to Ensslin that France had now discovered the Beats and "wished it was fifties all over again." He described boys hanging out around Saint-Michel in slicked-back James Dean haircuts and leather jackets with Elvis Presley buttons. He was very aware of missing the cultural moment in New York—the club energy, "schizo-culture," and what was left of punk. He wanted to be part of that vibrant, growing scene. Also, he wasn't sure the change in his writing was for the better.

Left unsaid was the fact that David just missed his friends. On February 21, he woke up with a shout, sweating and frightened. Michael Morais! David had dreamt that he'd walked into an upstairs room where Michael was sleeping. Suddenly a spirit entered, mostly invisible though he saw "bare folds of clothing." David felt an overwhelming chill and terror. He suppressed a scream, then saw Michael sit up zombie-like with a luminous yellow blaze behind his eyes, then a flicker as if something was falling inside his head past his eyes—like a window shutting. David then saw that Brian was asleep in another bed, and while the "thing" went straight into Michael, its close proximity to Brian made him groan as if in pain. David got up wondering if Michael had died and immediately wrote him a letter. Brian too. He apologized for feeling susceptible to dream imagery and symbols; he'd been reading Jung. But the dream had truly frightened him and left him in a fog for a week. Michael wrote back to say that on February 22 his wife had given birth to a stillborn baby.

David walked to the Seine just about every day to observe: an interesting rock, a bandaged hobo, another who'd made a pillow of two Tintin books. That spring the river overflowed, throwing up pieces of crockery that stayed on the banks when the water receded. David found a bottle with a water-proof cap. He wrote his name and Brian's on a piece of paper with the words "the sea revolving in the eye of the horse, the distances of the forest in the eye of the fish," then sealed it in the bottle and tossed it into the current.

\* \* \*

*David working at his sister's apartment on rue Laferrière, Paris. (Courtesy of Jean Pierre Delage)*

That March both Pat and Pillu got work that took them out of the country, so David moved back into their place. Nothing had changed between him and JP, but Pat's studio was roomier, with better light, and she had a dog for him to walk.

Just before moving in, he completed the first collage that would remain part of his oeuvre, *Bill Burroughs' Recurring Dream*—using a photo of Burroughs bought in a Left Bank shop and an image of a centipede bought from a Seine stall.

In March, he made a drawing of a man in a suit falling onto some tracks, based on a warning sign posted everywhere in the Paris Metro. This later became one of David's stencils and an image sprayed onto many walls in Lower Manhattan.

On March 30, he drew *Rimbaud J.O. Study #1* in pencil, with the poet clothed, and at the end of April he made a colored-pencil version, *Rimbaud Masturbation Study #2*, with the poet naked.

Bill Burroughs' Recurring Dream, *1979. Collage, 6½ × 7 inches. (David Wojnarowicz Papers, Fales Library, NYU)*

Surely David had seen the cheap newsprint Rimbaud posters plastered everywhere in Paris in 1978–79. French artist Ernest Pignon-Ernest had attached the famous 1871 photo of the poet's head (then on the cover of *Illuminations*) to a photo of a leather-jacketed young man with a coat or perhaps a bundle thrown over his shoulder. The posters were life-size and plastered on walls, phone booths, and billboards. David would begin photographing his *Rimbaud in New York* series during the summer of '79.

By the beginning of April he'd made no solid plan to leave Paris, only knew that he had to. Sometime during the first week of that month, he met an Englishman his own age in the Tuileries and took him back to Pat's place for sex. It was the first time since meeting Jean Pierre that he'd had sex with someone else, and he did it very consciously. "It was sort of a removal point." To help him leave JP.

Still, he made excuses to himself about what a "breakthrough" it was to go to bed with someone his own age. Usually his lovers were older, and he liked that maturity, the extra years of reflection those guys had behind them. Plus, the age difference created an inherent separation. Making love with someone like this Englishman, Alan—that was frightening, but now he'd overcome it.

He made plans to meet Alan again, on April 10. But he decided he'd better tell JP. He fretted over this for a couple of days. Maybe he was wrong. But "then came senses of myself as a human being who needed freedom to do exactly what he desired in way of contact, sexual or otherwise." So he told Jean Pierre, I'm having dinner with this guy, and I'm sleeping with him. He was still committed to JP, but he said, "I . . . just need to explore things as they move my way." JP told him he had to feel free to do as he wished. Though David worried whether JP truly understood.

The night with Alan was almost comical, and completely foolish. First, David got lost trying to find the right street. Alan had a student room on the seventh floor at the top of a creaking staircase, and down dank hallways with dripping pipes. When David arrived, Alan was in red rubber gloves, chopping celery and apples for their meal. He struggled out of one to shake David's hand. David took a wobbly chair, noted the crumb-littered rug, the tiny cot, and the skylight with one broken pane. They listened to the BBC news while Alan finished chopping fruit and vegetables and poured nuts over them: their dinner. David knew immediately that he and Alan weren't clicking. "At one point I wanted to leave quite badly." But he wouldn't. He'd told JP he was going to spend the night; therefore he would. Alan's bed was so small that David felt he couldn't move an inch without falling out. He lay there—rain tapping his head through the broken skylight, a cat yowling in the alley, his thoughts on JP. Alan, meanwhile, wondered if David would be interested in a threesome next time.

Not really.

At six, David got up and scurried back to Jean Pierre, picking up a croissant for him on the way. They exchanged *ça va*'s and sat down to coffee. JP told him he was making plans to go to the shore for a week by himself. He needed some time alone.

They didn't discuss the affair for another three days. JP then admitted that it had hurt his feelings. David admitted that he hadn't enjoyed it, but he would not apologize. Though he concluded that "all this shoulda been spared from the typewriter," David not only typed it—he also pasted it into his journal. And when JP went off for his week of vacation, he took David with him.

David's relationship with Jean Pierre would prove to be one of the two major love affairs of his life, yet for all his talk of "emotional commitment," it seems likely that he allowed himself to fall in love with JP (and actually write about him in his journal) because he knew from the start that it would have to end. He'd never taken any step needed to stay in Paris.

For all his talk of needing to "explore things" moving his way, David sometimes wondered whether to trust his instincts. While he did not want to continue a sexual relationship with Alan, he thought they could socialize. Alan gave him a book, *Christopher and His Kind*, in which David immediately found two quotes to support him in what he'd done.

Author Christopher Isherwood had seized upon the same quotes: "There is only one sin: disobedience to the inner law of our own nature." (This from anthropologist John Layard, who seems to have picked it up from psychologist Homer Lane.) Isherwood was talking about his decision to go to Berlin in 1929. To go there to meet boys. When he meets one who becomes a magical figure for him and he can't explain why, Isherwood tells himself what he thinks Layard would have said—and this was a major one for David: "*Anything* one invents about oneself is part of one's personal myth and therefore true."

For one thing, this eased David's mind about the "fiction" he'd included in letters to friends, "the distortion or make up of events—for entertaining reasons or for reasons illustrating senses."

Like writing in a letter that he'd met JP "leanin against the midnight doors of the Louvre" instead of "in a bush"? After reading many letters, both those pasted into the journal and those gathered from friends, that seems a typical distortion.

The bigger truth-telling issue he had at this point was with Brian. He had written to him about JP on the Nico poster, but never mailed that—or any other letter explaining that he had a new boyfriend. Brian thought David was still at his sister's place, where he continued to get his mail. In fact, David was coy with many friends about Jean Pierre. "Mon ami," he would call him. My friend.

On April 25, David talked to Brian on the phone for ten minutes, and they made a plan. Brian would arrive in Paris for a visit on May 7. They would return to New York together on June 1.

David admitted to the journal that he was feeling nervous, feeling strange—maybe because Brian was coming. And he was depressed about leaving JP. Into that emotional mélange dropped a mind-blowing letter from John Hall, who confessed that he was having fantasies about making love with David. He currently had a girlfriend but was interested in exploring his "homosexual aspect." He'd never said this to another man, he wrote, adding, "I hope this isn't anything heavy for you."

David was startled but took it in stride. Sex was easy for David, something he could always handle without self-consciousness or awkwardness. It's the emotions that were hard, though distance from the person in question made them easier. His reply to John Hall was gracious and thoughtful. "Its a damn nice compliment in the form of trust that you've given me," David wrote. "It really brought about some intense feelings on this end, a sense of gladness that you felt comfortable enough to share those feelings with me." David told Hall of the fear he'd had about coming out to him, how he'd never allowed himself "to consider you in a sexual way," so now he would have to push back that sense—but sure, David would like to make love to him. "I just see so many things arising from it and want you to understand some of them before we attempt it." There was a possibility that Hall wouldn't like it, and if it was his first time, it had to be approached "openly and with talk and also with the idea that if you feel uncomfortable at any point then we don't go on. . . . The most pressing thought I have is that I don't want anything to get in the way of our friendship." Plus Hall needed to think about his relationships with women. David had always thought it difficult to do both at once.

Meanwhile, post-Alan, he'd gone back to cruising. Just a bit. And it was just sex, without emotion or expectation. Most interesting is the way he writes about it. As if observing from a little outside himself, where he connects this moment to a wider world. This is his voice—or it's getting to be: the directness of the monologues infused with reflection, the result no doubt of his many months of forced introspection and day after day of tapping that keyboard:

Standing in the semi darkness of a strangers room, shadow light on blue walls blue lamp blue blankets and sliding blue sheets, pulling on my dusty pro keds dirty rubber sides, dirty laces, socks all smudgy dirty, pants ill fitting, shirt green and too big neck space slipping over shoulder blade, underwear fulla holes and the elastic broken smell of perspiration I look at my hands, my chest, my young arms and lazy stomach muscles and think of age and rest and movement and drawings, think of my rimbaud masturbation drawings while some guy in another room is talking about how he's heading for rio then on to the islands and later spain itlay Greece oh Greece is so fabulous this time of year and then mexico in the fall and he's waiting for me to get dressed, we've just made love and when I've gone to fuck him he says: oh I'm not sure I'm perfect down there—me wonderin if that means the clap or what and in a few minutes we're to get into his Mercedes down in sub basement level two of this monolithic highrise . . . what things can I write about anymore what with all my senses having swung towards the exploration of sensuality and sexuality and the images the symbols the refracting light off object and flesh movement beneath clothes light covers and trees, in dark rainy doorways, from the corner windows of autos, in silhouette passing gardens in the misty night, along rivers where once I made love to a hobo down there young guy with his tiny fire beneath tunnel and rough face weathered and old clothes with musty smell and thinking about the changes of time and circumstance; reflecting on lovemaking with that almost penniless character and now this guy with his south-

american suntan afric chairs greek statues and gold Egyptian ashtrays
with ceramic beetles climbing the sides and what of it all matters really
in this strange sense of just the world of solitary character being made
up of transient moments in all levels and walks and how little important
most of it seems in hindsight.

All through the journals—and this piece is no exception—he has written with no cross-outs, no words added in margins, no second thoughts.

David met Brian at Gare du Nord on May 7. JP cooked dinner for them at
rue Laferrière. (Pat and Pillu were still out of town.) Then Brian turned in,
suffering from jet lag.

The next day, David took Brian to Versailles. Out where Marie Antoi-
nette used to play at milking the cows, he informed Brian that he was really
in love with Jean Pierre. And—so sorry I asked you to come. This shameful
incident David "spared from the typewriter." He never mentioned it, and
Brian never forgot it.

"I won't say I was misled, because I went into every direction in my life,
including him, with my eyes open," Brian said. "But—he wrote such loving
letters—'You have to come, you have to stay with me, I miss you so much.'
He was often confused about things. If he'd said, 'I'm involved with someone in Paris but I love you too, so come over,' I wouldn't have had a problem
with it." Brian took a train out of town for probably a day, in romantic despair, then returned.

"I was not a very jealous person," he said. "How could you be in the
seventies? Everyone was fucking everyone." Also, he thought JP was nice
and "very entertaining."

David moved Jean Pierre into Pat's apartment with him. Brian would
stay alone over at JP's place. By May 10, David was showing Brian his favorite spots—like Pont des Arts, a footbridge leading from the Louvre to Saint-
Germain-des-Prés, and of course, the Tuileries. There they even got to
experience a police raid and clamber over a fence.

That weekend, JP drove them to Vaux le Vicomte, a castle thirty-five
miles from Paris. "A royal bore," David thought, but not a total loss. He was

*David visited Père Lachaise cemetery with Brian Butterick, where they took turns posing at the graves of cultural heroes. (David Wojnarowicz Papers, Fales Library, NYU)*

able to photograph a dead and bloated rat. He was doing the tourist things he hadn't done in nine months of living in France. Like the visit to Père Lachaise, the final resting place of many artistic heroes: Gertrude and Alice, Oscar Wilde, Sarah Bernhardt, Molière, Chopin, La Fontaine. Brian took a picture (much reprinted since) of David next to Apollinaire's grave, holding his head to mimic the head wound that led to the poet's premature death.

One night as he, JP, and Brian hung out, the tension got to David, who said, "so long," and rushed to the nearest Metro, willing to go anywhere. There, on a train, he witnessed a robbery, and it left him feeling nauseated. The psychic tension that entered the car with the thieves, the practiced motions, the weary tourists they'd robbed—farmer types in their Sunday best. It only added to the emotional overload.

He couldn't quite parse everything he was feeling in those last days in Paris but told himself he felt rearranged. On May 31, he sat down, crying, to write Jean Pierre a goodbye letter, then rushed outside to walk, feeling displaced, "seeing so suddenly my faults laid bare, how I coulda done it all differently." JP had gone back to his place on Bourdonnais, so David took the letter there, with a painted rock JP had particularly liked. He sat tensely as

JP read the letter for what seemed to him a long time. Was the English too difficult? Finally, Jean Pierre told him it was beautiful. "We embraced and held each other as strongly as possible. [JP] said, 'I never told you how much I love you because I was afraid to make it too heavy. I thought you might one day leave and I didn't want it to be difficult.' I held him and felt such a harsh love for him, a thick fist rising in my throat. He said, 'You know I'm sad you go back to America, but I'm happy I had the chance to love you for this time." They both cried.

The reentry into Brooklyn was such a shock. He and Brian took a cab to Court Street through the clattering din, the grainy night light, the filthy chaotic streets. New York—he felt a sense of "almost horror" at being part of the place again.

# 7 GO RIMBAUD

**"Coming back here** after that time in Paris so many scenes I once embraced as a living movement now seem weary and burlesque, a step outta rhythm," he wrote two weeks into his return, still adjusting to the new pace and timbre of his life. It wasn't just what he'd added while in Paris, but what he'd subtracted: "the removal from media, hard street energies, manic violence . . . and tension." He didn't specify what he now found "vapid, harsh and useless," only observed that there was "an energy here that destroys the most subtle responses in human nature." That same day he made notes for a new piece called "Wounded Wild Boy."

He pulled back into his shell. At least in what he recorded about his life. (The passage above is unusually ruminative.) The effusiveness and reflection he'd accessed so instantly in France—gone. Maybe he just didn't have the time.

Once again he had nowhere to live. And no job. He wrote a letter or postcard to Jean Pierre roughly every other day, mostly to say that he loved him. Brian had remained a faithful friend despite everything and was basically supporting him at this point. They'd moved into Court Street temporarily with friends of Brian's, downstairs from David's old place.

The first thing David covered in his journal after his return, on June 6, 1979, was a trip with Brian to the West Village—"its immediate visual effect," which he doesn't describe except to agree with his ex-roommate Dennis De-Forge's assessment: It's an outdoor whorehouse. "Don't think I'll ever forget that initial sense of shock." He didn't elaborate, but clearly he wasn't talking about cruising on Christopher Street. He meant the piers, which would become the center of his life for the next year and a half.

These rotting treacherous structures along the Hudson River provided cover for acres of public sex. The waterfront from Christopher to Fourteenth

Streets was the unofficial gay men's playground. Separating the piers from the edge of the Village was the elevated West Side Highway, which had been closed to traffic since '73 but still provided shelter to transvestite hookers among its stanchions. On the city side of the highway were gay bars like the Ramrod, Peter Rabbit, and Alex in Wonderland. This big libidinous play district included the trucks parked along the highway every night and somehow never locked. Certain men preferred the truck ambience to the piers for casual sex. David would surely have been familiar with this area. He'd been frequenting the nearest dive coffee shop, the Silver Dollar, since his street days with Willy, but he usually picked up men on the streets or in bars. The piers could be dangerous, not just because they were falling apart and pockmarked with holes open to the river. Men had been murdered there. For many, the lawlessness and risk only added to the excitement. This was an autonomous zone.

Sex among the ruins—David found it fascinating. He wanted to cruise the piers, but he also wanted to paint them, photograph them, and record what happened in them. Soon he was back with Brian and a can of spray paint. He drew a crude Rimbaud face on a windowpane. On a wall, he sprayed a male torso shooting up with a big hypodermic needle. Elsewhere he painted a target. Then he sprayed a kind of a haiku onto a wall: "Did you watch the dogfight yesterday (under Mexican sky)." He graffitied a line often quoted by William Burroughs: "'There is no truth / Everything is possible' Hassan I Sabbah" and added his own ten-line poem underneath, beginning, "Some men gun fast trucks down red roads / Down into distant valleys where mountains / Are slowly eaten by deserts."

Other artists had already seen the possibilities in these abandoned structures. Gordon Matta-Clark, for example, had cut a large half-moon shape from the end of Pier 52, off Gansevoort Street, to create *Day's End* in 1975, but David may not have known about this. While in Paris, he'd discovered Joseph Beuys—in a book. He'd been especially excited to learn of *I Like America and America Likes Me*, a piece in which Beuys lived in a gallery with a coyote for three days. A Beuys retrospective was scheduled for the Guggenheim that fall. In homage, he sprayed a Beuys statement on another wall: "THE SILENCE OF MARCEL DUCHAMP IS OVERRATED."

David had one short-lived minimum-wage job that summer. In mid-

June, an ad agency trained him to print photographs and to run a photostat machine. They fired him when he almost immediately started using his sick days. But while there, he was able to photostat the cover of *Illuminations* to create a life-size mask of Arthur Rimbaud.

Rimbaud was a kind of lodestar for David at this point in his life. He identified with the poet. They'd been born a hundred years apart—Rimbaud in October 1854 and David in September 1954. Both were deserted by their fathers and unhappy with their mothers. Both ran away as teenagers. Both were impoverished and unwilling to live by the rules. Both were queer. Both tried to wring visionary work out of suffering. David just didn't yet know the rest—that he would soon meet an older man and mentor who would change his life (as Paul Verlaine had changed Rimbaud's), and that he too would die at the age of thirty-seven.

He began photographing *Rimbaud in New York* that summer with a borrowed camera, using Brian as his model. In 1990, the first time these photos were exhibited as a series, David told an interviewer from the *New York Native*, "I felt, at that time, that I wanted it to be the last thing I did before I ended up back on the streets or died or disappeared. Over the years, I've periodically found myself in situations that felt desperate and, in those moments, I'd feel that I needed to make certain things. . . . I had Rimbaud come through a vague biographical outline of what my past had been—the places I had hung out in as a kid, the places I starved in or haunted on some level."

Brian posed in the Rimbaud mask on Forty-second Street between Seventh and Eighth Avenues, a block then lined with porn theaters. He stood in front of dangling cow carcasses in the meatpacking district. He rode a graffiti-scarred subway. He spent quite a bit of time at the Hudson River sex piers and wandered among various other crumbling eyesores. He posed at the dancing-chicken booth in Chinatown. He stood outside the Terminal Bar. He shot heroin.

David wrote two "35mm photo scripts," with dozens of ideas for the poet's adventures. He had a narrative in mind. Rimbaud would arrive by ship, alighting at the Brooklyn Navy Yard in one script and at Coney Island in the other. Eventually he would die of a heroin overdose. Most of these scenarios were never photographed—like Rimbaud eating in the Salvation

Arthur Rimbaud in New York (Pier, Junkie), *1979. From a series of twenty-four gelatin-silver prints, 10 × 8 inches each. (Courtesy of the Estate of David Wojnarowicz and P·P·O·W Gallery, New York)*

Army cafeteria, Rimbaud inside Port Authority, Rimbaud making rude gestures at St. Patrick's during mass—probably because David lacked money for film and processing. Usually he economized on what he did shoot. Rimbaud on the subway: two exposures, one printed. For the heroin shot, he removed the needle and replaced it with a pin, its point inside the hypo, which he'd glued to Brian's arm. "The head of the pin was pressed into the flesh," Brian said. "It looked like it was *in* the flesh."

John Hall also took part in the Rimbaud project, though he doesn't remember when. He posed at the piers and in the meat-packing district as Brian had. (David used the images of Brian from those locations.) He was also Rimbaud wounded (bandaged hand) and Rimbaud with a Dubuffet sculpture. Most famously, though, John Hall was Rimbaud masturbating. He remembers nothing about where this photo was taken or how it came about, only that David put him at ease when he thought he was too skinny

Arthur Rimbaud in New York (Coney Island), *1979. From a series of twenty-four gelatin-silver prints, 10 × 8 inches each. (Courtesy of the Estate of David Wojnarowicz and P·P·O·W Gallery, New York)*

and didn't have a good body. Brian thought the photo might have happened when David went to photograph Hall's apartment, whose disarray he found fascinating. Indeed, David even described the place in his journal: "The hurricane dive that seems to be John's symbol, obsessively in turmoil—wild in a sense—I photographed parts of it for the images—the clash of headlines and food containers and loops of stereo wires and bass guitar—piles of papers sliding down hills of music magazines and newspapers. Posters of the Slits and James White on the walls—ashtrays of cigarette butts from guests who came and departed weeks ago." The Ludlow Street building was so old and decrepit that, according to Hall, tenants had been known "to fall through their living room floors into the apartment below."

When Jean Pierre came to visit, David quickly incorporated him into the project as well. JP became Rimbaud at Coney Island. JP remembered going two or three times. They'd leave at five A.M. to get there when it was deserted. He remembered the black jacket and white T-shirt he wore. Alone on the beach. Alone at the closed kebab stand. Alone in front of the parachute drop. JP could not remember where they stayed. Not Brooklyn, he thought. David still hadn't found a place to live.

All that summer and fall, David and Brian bounced around. After Court Street, they lived with Dolores for a couple of months, taking the bedroom while she slept on the couch. They crashed in a photographer's studio. They stayed briefly with Susan Gauthier and Steve Gliboff in the East Village. Sometimes David talked about looking for work, but he didn't look. He was drifting again.

During this first year after Paris, he devoted a great deal of time to the piers. He'd spent his first night there with John Hall early in July. Just as John's presence had once helped him to cross the country freight-hopping, now it seemed to reassure him about beginning to cruise the piers. He did his graffiti there during the day, but at night, you couldn't even see the floor until your eyes adjusted. David and Hall just dipped into the warehouse between Perry and Charles Streets and watched men drifting through it, then headed back to the Silver Dollar for English muffins. They dropped in at Dirk Rowntree's place, where Dirk photographed them. David and Hall walked out talking about no-wave bands, how good it was that they always broke up so fast and "nothing gets stale." They moved on to Tiffany's, a Sheridan Square coffee shop with terrible food and a colorful Christopher Street clientele. Then on to the Bank Street pier, which was open, and there they discussed the propriety of watching public sex—while they watched it "from a discreet distance . . . as it is an intense visual to be confronted with," David reported. That's when Hall proposed, for the first time since suggesting it by letter, that he and David should have sex, and David decided that if they were ever going to do it, this was the right place. They entered the warehouse again, but just as they started to make love, they heard shrieks and terrified, moved out along the river, where they found themselves trapped. Then the source of the racket, a gaggle of drag queens, burst out through the doors a few yards away. Outside, along a "U-shaped arena of warehouse walls and windows," they found "miraculously" a cheap

Arthur Rimbaud in New York (on the subway), *1979. From a series of twenty-four gelatin-silver prints, 10 × 8 inches each. (Courtesy of the Estate of David Wojnarowicz and P·P·O·W Gallery, New York)*

rug to lie down on, where they watched the disappearing night, the waves slapping up from tugboats and barges, and they finally made love. All night, David had been carrying Burroughs's *Algebra of Need.* He lit a cigarette and looked up at the World Trade Center, "the very top of it emerging into a dim sunlight of rising dawn. It was framed by crossbars of metal on top of the far warehouse roof and it was like some kinda vision in all this."

While the Rimbaud project was under way, he wrote nothing about it in his journals. He said nothing to the posing Rimbauds about what it meant to him. And he wrote nothing about Jean Pierre, who visited for most of August.

That summer he pasted into the journal his first drawing of a burning house. Somewhere he had seen the work of Saul Ostrow. "Desire one of his fire images," he wrote. "Stuff haunts the head." David was then having an affair with a guy acquainted with Ostrow. By September, he'd begun corresponding with Ostrow himself. David told me, "Ostrow was doing paintings of burning houses, and we had a correspondence of at least six or seven letters between us where we sent each other burning houses in the mail. Like, I'd find a logbook for a fire department from 1950 and do dotted lines in bold that he could cut, and make a burning house out of this paper. Things like that." It would take another two years for the burning house to become one of David's stencils, and one of the first images associated with him. In the journal, on lined paper, the burning house just sits behind a man in the foreground with a dog-head puppet on one hand saying, "If he's following my scent . . . this'll throw him off."

He'd started making "to do" lists. One from September includes this instruction to self: "Do a Saint Genet collage—go to Strand for a copy of his photo on Funeral Rites."

He also made a first rough sketch for this. *Untitled (Genet)* became controversial in 1990 because it includes an image of Christ shooting up. When he began it, he was working with images of the sacred and profane and seems simply to be questioning, what is evil? And by extension, what is good? He was just beginning to find his subject matter.

The original sketch is overly busy. He wants to set this scene at the waterfront, with Genet in the center, a Madonna and child looking down from a fortress at the right, and a large ship "possibly with flame inside" at the left. Salamanders without legs rain down on the ship. There's an eclipse. Onshore, left, two men are fucking. He's thinking the Madonna should have a weapon, maybe a cigarette. His second sketch is much simpler—just Genet on the left and the Madonna and child in a window to the right. He still thinks it should be set at the waterfront, and this time the baby Jesus holds a pistol.

But no. The waterfront suggests his own life—the piers, and his father the sailor. Madonna and child—that would be the Catholicism he knew as a young boy. It would take him till the end of the year to work this out, to see that the piece had a meaning beyond his own life, and that it is about sorrow. In the final version, he replaces the waterfront with a war-ravaged church. David had been very aware in France of all the people around him

*Untitled (Genet, after Brassaï), 1979. Photocopied collage, 8½ × 11 inches. (Private collection)*

who'd come through the war, often at great cost. Genet's lover had died "on the barricades" in 1944. *Funeral Rites* is the story of his grief. David has angels flying in from the left side of the picture and at bottom, one comic-book machine-gunner firing bullets toward heaven. Genet wears a nimbus.* David may well have skipped Sartre's critical study, drawing inspiration simply from the title *Saint Genet*. But he'd read all the novels. He particularly loved *The Thief's Journal*, telling JP in a letter that the book had made him feel good about his own early life. *The Thief's Journal* presents a world of inverted values, where criminality is a way to oppose the social order and evil can be the path to sainthood. David may also have noted lines such as, "Going into mourning means first submitting to a sorrow from which I shall escape, for I transform it into the strength necessary for departing from conventional morality."

As for the junkie Christ destined to so upset the American Family

---

* He did make a separate small collage (two by three inches) called *Madonna and Child with Gun*. In comparison, it seems a joke.

Association, it creates balance with the criminal Genet who's been exalted into sainthood. But where Genet wants to transcend his sorrow, Christ wants to embrace it, because he has chosen to identify with "the least of these." Jesus describes this to his followers who will get into heaven by saying, *I was hungry, I was sick*—and you fed *me*, you visited *me*. "Inasmuch as ye have done it unto one of the least of these my brethren, ye have done it unto me." In David's mind, he could have added, *I was a junkie, I was a bum, I was a lonely drag queen trolling the piers*.

One night David and Brian went to the Christopher Street pier and sat on the loading dock of the abandoned warehouse under a streetlamp, reading Genet's *Funeral Rites* out loud. David had begun the practice of going to the piers to write. He'd pick up a cup of coffee at the Silver Dollar and sit with his journal in the yellow streetlamp glow that came through the side of the warehouse. He was there to record the whole scene, including its architecture and ambience—headlights moving across a wall, the sound of tin doors banging, water slashing at pier posts. Later, he would tell me that he saw these dying structures as symbols of what was essentially a dying country. In the first journal entry he made after visiting the pier with John Hall, he wrote, "It's so simple, the man without the eye against a receding wall, the dog's head impaled against the surface: the subtleties of weather, of shading."

It was the first draft of a piece he would include in *Close to the Knives* in 1991: "Surrounded by shadows, the mudcaked floors and harsh scent of urine in damp corners, men moving with unbuttoned shirts, teeshirts tied around thick waists, dreams falling in dense heaps along the stairways, last flies of summer circling the busted windows, his hands red and moving thickly where his lips traced lines down on the belly."

By mid-September 1979, David had noticed that his "Marcel Duchamp" line was flaking off the wall, and someone had thrown rocks through the Rimbaud face he'd painted on a window.

But he would have heard nothing of the following news, also from September '79: Two young gay male New Yorkers went to their doctors complaining of odd purplish lesions on their bodies. Kaposi's sarcoma, declared the doctors—baffled, since KS was a rare cancer that usually appeared among elderly men of Mediterranean or Middle Eastern descent.

The disease these young men would soon die from would not get the acronym "AIDS" until 1982.

One day, David went to the piers to draw, but the wind made it hard to manage his paper. He ended up helping the warehouse's self-appointed artist in residence, Tava, carry paint cans inside. Tava was working on a huge mural of two men masturbating that would cover the back wall. David had encountered Tava before, in a former washroom among the broken shards of porcelain, and had watched him paint a giant hand on a giant cock. David thought of Tava's work as "thug frescoes." Outside, facing every passing boat, Tava had painted two men with huge erections, like two caryatids, as tall as the central doorway.

David loved just hanging out in this ambience. The piers were a glimpse of life outside the approved social structure. And the pier denizens were more than sexual objects. They represented what the hoboes in Paris had represented. "They can be seen as a physical rejection of society's priorities; which elevates many of these characters in my eyes," he'd written to a friend regarding the hoboes. Sex just added to the fascination—and the layers of meaning.

In October, David had a sexual encounter at the piers that he mused over for days:

> I'm losing myself in the language of his movements—he drifted, turned on his heel in grey light and passed into a quiet room with torn walls and glass "paymaster" windows boarded over on the other side. A hermaphrodite was scrawled on the wall near the broken window, lines of rain slowing to a halt. . . . I moved towards the stranger in the leather jacket, the brief motion of his body eyes and hands a brief shuffle in the vacant room, the swirling of fine shadows in the corners, the grace of his movements, all contributed to erasing the formality of being strangers, we eased towards one another and my jacket swung loose and to the side; blue colors of light, blue moving effortlessly over his face, the red glow of the skin making the hands luminous as they passed over my legs to my crotch. I slipped my hand between his shirt and smooth chest,

fingers touching lightly to his nipples as he rubbed slow and hard with his hand. I felt his neck and grew hard and he unzipped my trousers, drew them down slightly, a strong palm beneath my balls, face lowering slowly as he squatted and took me into his mouth. I bent my torso forward and rolled my hands down the linings of his collar, smoothed out the shadows and the heat of his skin, felt my blood had been removed, boiled slowly and then replaced, warm currents in the forehead and stomach, sleep rolling outside in the hallways in coils like rope. He stood up briefly as I tongued his chest, running my lips over his belly and chest, sucking at his nipples, caressing his smooth sides, his arms encased in leather, the leather becoming an extension of his flesh only in the way that belongs to men who have graceful animal movements and sexual energies running through their corded arms and legs. I felt a sweat run down my body in the cold air as is the case, rare that it is, when I'm in the company of a man like this; a culminating sense of time and age and direction coasting on a single track towards walls of life lived, felt naked as I came and grabbed his shoulders and shook him violently ramming my cock into his mouth with each movement, grabbed his hair between my fingers and stroked his face and neck and skull and embraced his back and shoulders and blew out shadows and bleak visions of sky and rain and water and blew out delirium from the base of my skull, felt heavy and lightweight simultaneously, felt a pitch of heat in my chest and belly, and he rose to his feet, said: whoah . . . really good, and I blushed slightly, all these unspoken sentences at the tip of my tongue.

Before they parted, David learned that the man was originally from Texas—and though the guy didn't live there anymore, David added that image to his musings. The cowboy. The pickup truck. The drive toward endless vistas with a bullet in the dashboard—the romance of that. This was about freedom. The fact that he connected anonymous sex with possibility. He decided that he'd never yet lived the life he wanted. "Really it's this lawlessness and anonymity simultaneously that I desire, living among thugs, but men who live under no degree of law or demand, just continual motion and robbery and light roguishness and motion, reading Genet out loud to the falling sun overlooking the vast lines of the desert . . . aimlessness in terms of the senseless striving to be something, the huge realization of the senselessness of that conscious attempt in the way this living is really constructed."

David decided that if he was living his life for anything, it was for this man from Texas—not that individual so much as what the encounter represented, "the combination of time, elements, visuals, visions, light, movements, all associations . . . as if that past moment holds everything that will make my life valid, that will save my life." That was the sense he had until he wrote it down, and then he was faced with emptiness, "having tasted a real freedom, a freeing of myself from this life from this city rotating with the world on its axis."

Writing about sex at the piers always sent him into these reveries, even when he was not personally involved. One day he watched as men drifted toward a corner of a warehouse to watch a blow job—like metal filings drawn to a magnet—and the scene spiraled out in his mind to the vistas he wished to travel and then back again, to his own mortality, to his wish to extend time, to turn sunsets "into lifelong moments, unbreathing, no need for food, no need to scratch or shift, the lengths of measure contained in the dragging feet of the large man who follows me from room to room, emptiness shadowed by rusting floor safes and broken glass that holds pieces of sky along the dark floorboards."

One of the men he met "along the river" took to him to see his first opera, *Le Prophète*. Tedious, David thought, except for the parts where he had to pinch his leg to keep from laughing. Afterward, David showed this man his artwork and could see that he didn't like it. How was it, he wondered, that his imagery was so threatening to those who enjoyed the established order? How could he explain that his images reflected energy he'd picked up "in society, in movement through these times? It's just a translation of what takes place in the world." But sometimes he questioned himself about why he was so drawn to imagery that unsettled and disturbed. Once he'd kept his life hidden. He wondered, did he now keep beauty hidden?

In November, David and Brian finally moved into their own apartment, in a desolate Brooklyn neighborhood called Vinegar Hill just north of DUMBO (down under the Manhattan Bridge overpass). DUMBO felt deserted and dangerous in the Seventies. A few artists had moved into old industrial buildings, but there were no grocery stores, newsstands, or Laundromats. Just one seedy bar stood between the York Street subway stop and the Brooklyn Bridge. Vinegar Hill was even harsher and more isolated. The blocks between the subway and their apartment at 59 Hudson Avenue were industrial, mostly cobblestone, and inhabited at night only by packs of stray dogs. It was a fifteen-minute walk that felt like an hour. But the apartment had five rooms. Out the back window they could see the Brooklyn Navy Yard. Out the front they could see the Manhattan Bridge, and beyond it the Brooklyn Bridge. They kept a three-ring binder to which, every day, they would each add an artwork: a drawing, a found object, a poem, a collage. They had no telephone.

Brian paid the rent. He worked the graveyard shift at the Empire Diner in Chelsea, as a short-order cook. David had a few short-lived jobs, often acquired through men he met cruising. Mostly he painted the occasional apartment, though one guy got him a job with decent pay in a piano factory. David quit after a week. The labor was exhausting, the commute too long. Early in November, David went to a clinic on Forty-second Street and sold some blood. Then for a couple of months that winter, he worked at a bookstore again, but it folded.

For David, these were "grey and confusing times." This was the year he began admitting to his sense of mortality, at least in the journals. He was now twenty-five.

He dreamt he'd been buried in coarse brown earth, all the way up to his teeth. That image again—of his own partly buried face. But it doesn't seem to be a death dream. One molar's been exposed to air, it's throbbing, and after running "with cutthroats," he returns to his own burial spot to lift out the aching tooth. He sees that it's rotten, filled with maggots. He feels he mustn't scream since it's his own tooth. He's given a shot of morphine and feels secure. "The matter of having no home becomes something relegated to the self of the past."

By the end of 1979, he'd rewritten the piece about the piers, which he now called "Losing the Form in Darkness." The four paragraphs in his journal appear almost verbatim in the final version:

It's so simple: the man without the eye against a receding wall, the subtle deteriorations of weather, of shading, of images in the flaking walls. Seeing the quiet outline of a dog in the plaster, simple as the splashing of a fish in dreaming, and then the hole in the wall further along, framing a jagged sky swarming with glints of silver and light. So simple, the sudden appearance of night in a room filled with strangers, the maze of hallways wandered as in films, the fracturing of bodies from darkness into light, sounds of plane engines easing into the distance.

He did the first of many drawings of a factory with one large smokestack, like the one on the Jersey side of the Hudson that he could see from the West Side piers. He drew this factory, with reindeer, on his Christmas card for JP.

He still wrote to Jean Pierre once or twice a week. For all his fantasies about "freedom" and living with thugs, he also fantasized about going back to JP. This would be a lifelong internal struggle: the urge to roam versus the longing for stability. He responded to warmth in others with such hunger, wanting to connect. But when he did, it scared him. On December 30, he wrote to JP: "For the first time in my life, I don't have any idea what will happen to me—I think sometimes that I would like to return to Paris."

On that same day, December 30, a tremor hit the downtown art world, but the shift in tectonic plates was so small that few noticed it at the time. This was the day that some thirty-five artists—their bolt cutters in a guitar case—broke into an abandoned city-owned building on Delancey Street and set up "The Real Estate Show." The artwork, in every medium, addressed how "artists, working people, the poor are systematically screwed out of decent places to exist in," according to the *East Village Eye*. Few people ever saw this exhibit, which opened on January 1, 1980, and included works by Rebecca Howland, Jane Dickson, Bobby G, Christy Rupp, Mike Glier, Edit DeAk, and others. Police closed it on January 2. But no matter. In retrospect, "The Real Estate Show" was a conceptual project, and the idea that it had happened was much more consequential than anything exhibited. The city responded to the break-in and attendant agitprop by giving the artists another building on nearby Rivington Street. It became ABC No Rio,

its name lifted from a sign fragment across the street. No Rio not only preceded the East Village galleries but also outlasted them.

Ironically enough, the artists had never intended to start an "alternative space" in the neighborhood. They were members of Colab (a.k.a. Collaborative Projects), a nonprofit set up to do thematic shows and access
funding. They were the harbingers of new energy in a stultified art world.
Members included Jenny Holzer, John Ahearn, Kiki Smith, and others
who felt they had no access to that closed world. They were also "political"
and acutely conscious of what it meant to bring their work into a neighborhood off the art world's beaten path. In 1978, Colab member Stefan Eins
had opened a storefront art space called Fashion Moda in the famously
blighted South Bronx. Fashion Moda connected graffiti and hip-hop artists
with the downtown scene. Graffiti writers were beautifully "bombing" the
trains. At least, most artists thought so. Wait on any platform and a masterpiece might roll in.

Charlie Ahearn, also a Colab member, would begin working on *Wild
Style* in 1981. The film starred real graffiti writers and rappers like Lee Quinones, Fab 5 Freddy, and Lady Pink, with a small featured role for Patti
Astor as the intrepid journalist who goes to the Bronx to do a story on them.
Astor was an actress in no-wave films and a self-styled blonde bombshell
who would open the first East Village gallery in the summer of '81. "There
seems to be little doubt these days that the story of the '80s is going to center on the merger of the South Bronx and the East Village," wrote Steven
Hager in a cover story on Astor for the *East Village Eye*. Who knows? Maybe
that could have happened if artists were really in charge. *Wild Style* ends by
making an uptown-downtown connection when rappers and break-dancers
perform at the East River Park amphitheater just off the Lower East Side—a
vandalized eyesore until Quinones paints it into glory.

In 1980, gentrification seemed eons away in the South Bronx, while
Delancey Street—and Rivington, and Grand—were literally within walking distance of Soho, then the epicenter of the art world. The artists could
foresee the changes in which they would soon play a part. One of the ide-
alists involved in "The Real Estate Show" promised in a letter to the architecture magazine *Skyline*, "In the past, artists have been forced to move on
once they had adequately defined new real estate values. This time, on the

Lower East Side, they intend to stay put and help determine the area's evolution."

Shortly after the New Year, David had a big argument with his mother and told her he'd never see her again. That night, he dreamt that he'd run into Jean Pierre on the subway. They talked like old friends. JP had just found an apartment in Chicago, or was it Washington, D.C.? After they parted, David realized that he didn't know and had no address for him. "Jean Pierre is lost to me," he thought inside the dream. "He feels for me but feels its best not to continue. World seems to be crashing apart for me. I feel upset as hell." Then, still in the dream, he rationalizes it. Birth always meant there'd be loneliness. He goes home with a guy he meets on the street, a "jerk." Looking out the window in the jerk's apartment, he sees Dolores scaling the side of the building. They're on at least the tenth floor. She's huffing and puffing and losing hold. He opens the window and grabs her hand, pulling her inside. She gives him a look. "Sadness in there." He turns and now his mother is on the couch with some wealthy middle-age man. The guy is pulling out gifts. David is disgusted, thinking his mother must be going for money. "I sit there wondering if I'm made of the same desperate actions."

Though he did not yet identify himself as a visual artist, he entered three pieces in a juried show at Washington Square East Gallery. The art had to be a foot square or smaller. There were three thousand submissions. On January 15, he found out that he'd be one of 457 artists in the show. They had accepted one piece of his, a self-portrait. He wrote to Jean Pierre, "Now I have something to put on a resume."

But what this acceptance triggered internally, which he decided he could tell no one, was a sense of himself in time: "a sense of the aging self, a sense of how much I want to do and experience, no country in the world could hold that much."

He was still sad about his argument with Dolores. He decided that he'd vented his anger and frustration at her for not being what she could be when, really, he was mad at himself for not living up to his own potential. "I guess what scares me more than anything else in my life or in my box of fears is that I won't be able to exercise my senses, my leanings in the time period of my living." He was soon in touch with his mother again.

On a small paper bag he made notes for an installation or performance (never realized). He would appear shirtless, carrying a piece of timber from the piers like Christ going to his crucifixion. He'd attach a clock to the timber. He'd crush animal skulls, shells, and fossils underfoot. And he kept drawing that power plant. Sometimes with one smokestack, sometimes with two.

He'd started a new project—portraits of men. This went on for months, with Brian his most frequent subject: Brian blindfolded. Brian in a bow tie. Brian at the barbershop. Brian at home. Brian on the sand, against a wall, in a car, lying on grass, shooting up. Brian as St. Sebastian at the pier, standing in what used to be an office or a cubicle. And of course, Brian as Rimbaud. He began shooting more Rimbauds at the end of February. Brian remembered always complaining, "I don't wanna," because he worked nights and David was constantly after him to "'get up, get up.'"

Fire ravaged the pier warehouse at the end of January 1980. When David went to inspect the damage a few days later, he found that some of his graffiti had gone up in flames. In the main section of the covered pier, he found an old ratty couch on an upraised ledge and a barrel cover set up on a box "like some wino's living room." Upstairs the entire roof had burned. Steel girders twisted like snakes poked into the sky. Some areas were impassable now, "rooms and rooms of crushed plasterboard, cinders, ash heaps, a couple walls with strange graffitied frescoes done in crayons of altars and angelic faces and swooning winds and muscular bodies."

He noted in his journal on February 8 that a sheet of corrugated iron had been nailed over the walkway that led into the covered pier. He did at least half his cruising closer to home now, along the waterfront in Brooklyn. But mere iron would not keep determined men off the pier for long. On March 6, David was back at the warehouse watching drag queens pick their way through the charred wreckage while a group of men scoured the place for copper to sell. The guy he made it with that night was built like a weight lifter and had a couple of large feathers hanging from one shoulder of his jacket by a piece of string. David wrote, "[This] decoration . . . perplexed yet gladdened me for it threw meaning into his image, as if it were a tribal gift." Later he drew a picture of it in his journal.

David had begun to feel distance growing between him and Brian, though on certain days it would seem "okay" again. He was also editing more of his life from the letters to Jean Pierre, which he still sent once or twice a week. Naturally he'd never mentioned his sexual encounters, though I don't think either of them expected fidelity. But when he met a French man at the piers who took him to Los Angeles for a couple of days, he told JP only that he *might* go—that he'd been told he could find work there. JP apparently responded with some concern, because David's next letter assured him: "I thought I would possibly go to Los Angeles only if I cannot come to Paris by summer. . . . Remember I love you." (Actually, Los Angeles had been "a kind of refuge," he told the journal, "from thoughts about Paris and the constant limbo I feel I'm in.") He didn't tell JP about the drugs either. David tried heroin for the first time in late March. He was with Brian and friends of Brian's including Sister Roxanne, "nurse of the Netherworlds," who selected the best needle from a fistful of hypos and shot them all up. Just days earlier, he'd injected cocaine with Brian and his friends from the Empire Diner, then gone to the Mudd Club—which David thought "bourgeois" but, he wrote in his journal, "with friends it's endurable." He told JP only about dancing there and about escaping a mugger in the subway by leaping into an F train just before the door closed, then finding himself surrounded by homeless men, asleep across every seat.

David also met the poet Tim Dlugos that March and showed him the Rimbaud series. Dlugos wrote to his friend, the writer Dennis Cooper, who was then in Los Angeles editing a journal called *Little Caesar*. As Cooper remembered it, "Tim said, 'I bought this hustler last night and he showed me some of his stuff and it's really good.'"

A hustler?

"Maybe it was 'trick.' I don't know," Cooper said. "But Tim sort of made it seem like he had bought him at the piers."

If David had gone back to selling himself, he never said so. A "trick" could refer to someone he'd picked up. But David might not have been averse to a little cash "gift." He certainly had not paid for the trip to Los

Angeles with the French guy. The upshot was that, in April, David sent a package of sixteen Rimbaud photos and a couple of his monologues to Dennis Cooper, who agreed to publish all of them. There would, of course, be no payment.

At the beginning of May, David went out with John Hall to shoot pictures of trash in the squalid alleyway called Extra Place that ran behind CBGB's. He'd been there a few days earlier, and he couldn't help but notice that the rotting fish he'd photographed then had been stripped to the bone. As he approached a discarded sack of clothing, he realized that it was actually a man, and a gigantic bum called out to tell him he'd be in trouble if he photographed his sleeping friend. The bum pronounced himself sick of "you people coming down here and making money off us." David told him he was just photographing the trash and had never sold a photo. So the bum told him that if he really wanted a story, he should write about "conditions," the fact that sixteen hundred men a night couldn't find a bed in a shelter. And young kids were coming to the Bowery dives and taking the spaces—when those kids could work. His sleeping friend was eighty-six years old and made about ten dollars a day washing car windows on Houston Street. As did he. David asked if he could come back and record their stories. Sure, said the bum. His name was Maurice.

David hadn't abandoned his monologue project. In fact, he'd added a piece about a sexual encounter he had in February with "a young tough" who probably hadn't slept inside for a week (by David's estimate). They met on a bench along the river, where the guy was having trouble rolling a joint because his fingers were so frozen. David helped him, and then they walked down a ramp to have sex in an abandoned playground.*

Even if they didn't become monologues, David was still making notes on intriguing marginal characters. Like the drag queen at the Silver Dollar with a cardboard suitcase under her feet and a cigarette held between shaking fingers, "writing letters with a chewed pencil and stuffing them nervously into envelopes destined for Texas." Or the ravaged old "Genet"

---

* "The Waterfront 2 A.M. New York City" appeared in the posthumous *Waterfront Journals*.

character who invited him to see his room in the Christopher Street Hotel, a room about twelve feet square and plastered with news photos of President Jimmy Carter, the First Lady, Carter's mother, and the American flag. A large flag covered most of the guy's mattress. He pulled out a greeting card featuring a seminude woman, "like a Vargas *Playboy* painting." On this he'd written a letter to the president's mother, explaining to David: "How do I know she didn't look like this when she was younger?"

But if David ever found Maurice again, there's no record of it. He did end up with a photo showing the lower part of a man's body in a pile of trash.

The day he took that picture, he and John Hall went to Squat Theater on Twenty-third Street to see James White and the Blacks. The doors had opened at nine, but these were the days that clubs had to add the word "sharp" if there was any chance of the show beginning close to the advertised time. James White (a.k.a. James Chance) showed up at twelve thirty. David wrote a long description of his performance and the feelings of aggression it aroused in him. White snaked out into the audience touching people. He was famous for attacking spectators. When he grabbed a woman's sweater and pulled her about a yard, David wanted to punch him. "I was gonna grab him by the hair if he fucked with me," he then decided. "That's the intense stuff he inspired—didn't feel good contemplating it—just thought he was both brilliant and a creep." Hall felt certain that the people there must have known White's reputation for these assaults. Dirk Rowntree analyzed it as "a method of making you impatient for freedom—feeling the limitations or boundaries of your freedom by exiting from his self-made boundaries into yours."

Soon after Dennis Cooper accepted his work for *Little Caesar*, David wrote to Sarah Longacre, editor in charge of the centerfold at the *SoHo News*, wondering if she'd be interested in considering his Rimbaud photos. She would. He met with her on May 7, after he'd spent the afternoon making new prints in a darkroom on Prince Street. She immediately asked if she could use the image of Rimbaud shooting up to illustrate a story they were doing on heroin. (It ran in the very next issue, one column wide.) She loved the whole series, but told David she wasn't sure enough New Yorkers would know who Rimbaud was. She needed time to consult with the editor in chief.

That same week, between his meeting with Longacre and the appearance of junkie Rimbaud in print, David finally got a job. He ran into Jim Fouratt at Julius's bar. They knew each other from hanging out late nights at Tiffany's coffee shop. Fouratt had just opened a new club, Danceteria (with business partner Rudolf Pieper), and David asked if he might work for him. Fouratt told him that the only position still available was busboy. Fine, said David. He was so elated to get this job he nearly fell over a chair.

That night at Julius's, he also met Arthur Bressan Jr., a filmmaker. David was thinking about making a Super 8 film. Arthur was all for it, said that's how he'd started. They rambled around the Village, ending up at the Hudson River, where they had sex out on one of the piers. David would realize a couple of days later that he hadn't even seen Arthur's face clearly, but at the end of the evening Arthur had held David's hand. David reacted to this gesture with "almost bewilderment insofar as people rarely do that in this city, much less when they hardly know you, and I really dug it." He met Arthur again a couple of days later, feeling self-conscious because of the "honesty" they'd shared in talking and touching. They went to the pier, and Arthur told him he wanted to make a film about child abuse—actually a film about a man making a film about child abuse, in which a fourteen-year-old boy leaves his cruel parents and finds love with the filmmaker.*

Arthur thought that when kids had sex with older guys, they grew up suddenly—even adopted the mannerisms of an older person, while the older guy became more childlike. David thought this perceptive, based on his own experiences. He flashed back to teenage times when he'd been on the street: "The older men I'd lain down with and the recollection of my movements, my mannerisms with them, those scenes in dim-lit rooms in Jersey swamp motels manipulating a cigarette in my fingers and reflecting on my life and past while talking in a purposefully more sophisticated manner, out loud to the man unseen in the bathroom combing his hair before a fluorescent-lit

---

* When Arthur made this film (*Abuse*) a year or two later, David appeared in it for about ten seconds, giving a man-on-the-street interview on the topic.

mirror." David was quite taken with Arthur and gave him the two Rimbaud prints he requested. However, Arthur thought that David wasn't really a still photographer; he should be "doing cinema." Nowhere does David say that Arthur made mostly porn films. Maybe that wouldn't have mattered to him.

Arthur was at least ten years older than David and took a paternal approach. David had never been truly appreciated, Arthur told him, and had a sadness about him, a loneliness. David didn't agree with this. The line that came into his head immediately was "I never feel loneliness," but he didn't say it out loud.

The affair with Arthur Bressan lasted most of May. That month, David sent fifteen cards or letters to Jean Pierre. He waited for a decision from *SoHo News*, and he began working at Danceteria on Friday and Saturday nights.

He was soon dismayed by his new job and disgusted with the clubgoers. His duties included keeping bartenders supplied with iced Heineken or Bud, carrying broken sacks of ice between floors, emptying garbage cans, pulling bottles or whole rolls of paper towels from toilets, mopping up vomit, and diving "through human walls of sweating pounding thrusting dancing bodies to sweep up broken bottles." Arthur told him that the club goers thought destructiveness was anarchy, and if someone told them to do whatever they wanted with a window, they'd just break it. In a letter to JP, David complained, "Fou! The punk new wave people are becoming very boring to me. . . . [They] destroy anything they desire, break chairs, doors, light fixtures. I have to clean up after them. . . . These people have no imagination concerning what to do with freedom." It was in this letter that David told Jean Pierre he'd met a filmmaker who was showing him how to use a movie camera.

The film David planned—silent, black-and-white, Super 8—would be all about eroticism in everyday life, i.e., cruising. But also about repression, represented by cops bursting into a room. A naked man would be bound to suggest "that waterfront/bar sexuality can be seen as either a result of, or an attempt to break the weight of social/political restraints." He wrote two scripts for this film, which he never made.

Just before meeting Arthur, he'd written to JP: "I do not think I will be in love again in my life, except with you. These are honest words." And they were. His anxiety about the long separation from JP seemed to intensify during the affair with Arthur, especially after he decided that Arthur wanted him only for sex. "I'm still very much in love with Jean Pierre," he wrote in his journal near the end of May. "I still desire the chance to leave here and live with him in Paris. Jean Pierre was the first man to be completely relaxed and loving with me. Unafraid of my personality or my creative movements. There was room with him to love and live and grow and change. Time has put a distance between us. And my meeting Arthur filled up that kind of empty space." He hadn't even gone to the piers in two and a half weeks. But he felt that he didn't have Arthur's real attention. Something was missing.

Ever since David left Paris, he and JP had tried to figure out some way to get back together. Like dual citizenship—which would have allowed David to work in France but would also require his mandatory service in its military. Then there was the idea of entering a French university, but David didn't have the money. That May, they had one last pipe dream between them: David would get a position with UNESCO. Jean Pierre knew a woman who worked there and she promised to help, but David had none of the skills or education the agency required.

It would have been easy to lose touch completely. David still had no telephone. Letters usually took about a week to arrive and sometimes as long as three. But now that David finally had some income, he hoped to visit France in August. He and JP had, of course, not seen each other since the previous August.

One day in Sheridan Square, David ran into his old friend Jim McLauchlin, a.k.a. Jimmy James Strange. McLauchlin had spent the past two years in India, as a Bagwan. He'd changed his first name to "Anado" and was driving a cab. "I was dressed in all orange clothing and had a religious medal around my neck—you know, total cult city," McLauchlin remembered. And he decided that of all the people he'd known in New York, David was the one to whom he could give a book by his teacher. "David was a spiritual man, despite all the anger," McLauchlin observed. That was the last time they saw each other.

David spoke on the phone around this same time with his old roommate Dennis DeForge, and was upset to learn that DeForge had been attacked and nearly killed on the Brooklyn Bridge. David thought of his own close call at the hands of the madman posing as a cop, and he remembered Lee Adler's brutal murder. "Death coming so close to myself, to people I have shared part of life with. . . . Being in my midtwenties I sense the incompleteness that an unexpected death would be. I fear death and disablement, I feel the fear and horror of death coming close to friends."

He was, however, moving away from his Court Street and West End friends and into a new orbit. Years later, when his old buddy John Ensslin showed up at St. Mark's to hear him read, David acted, said Ensslin, "like a ghost from the past had just walked in." Ensslin had moved to Colorado and into a journalism career, and he could see that David did not want to reconnect.

Around June 1, 1980, the *SoHo News* finally let David know that it wanted to run four of his photos in its centerfold: Rimbaud at Coney Island in front of the parachute drop. Rimbaud holding a small pistol in front of a "Jesus Is Coming" mural. Rimbaud at the pier with the torso-hypo graffiti. Rimbaud with a wounded hand.

Sara Longacre asked him to write something poetic to accompany the pictures. He gave her about two hundred words, with lines like "And some of us take off our dreams with our shoes and live in grand cities in day and night while still others move like sailors in a squall, passing among small islands and murmuring their imperfect truths to the shorelines."

The $150 payment was the first he ever received for his art.

The day the paper came out, June 18, David walked for ten blocks with a copy before he had the nerve to open it. He loved how it looked. That issue of the *SoHo News* also carried an interview with Jayne Anne Phillips, which he pasted into his journal because she'd articulated *exactly* what he was feeling. She said of her book *Black Tickets*:

If it is about anything, it's about displacement, deracination and movement—and the kind of distortions that happen when this movement is going on. Alienation is probably an end result of that kind of transience—I don't think that it's a bad thing to experience but it's become a national mood. Now it's possible for people to be absolutely in one place for years and feel as though they don't belong there. . . . A lot of the voices [in the book] have to do with that kind of alienation that happens when you're involved in a culture but you're isolated within it. . . . If you can deal with aloneness in a way that finally lets you be unafraid, you're prepared . . . for the big transformation and you know certain things about it before it even happens—not only death but passion as well.

He was printing Rimbaud photos into July. In the end, he had fourteen contact sheets, roughly five hundred images. He mailed twenty or thirty prints to JP, asking him to take them to a couple of magazines in Paris.

He had become head busboy at Danceteria and now worked three nights a week.

In July, the "Times Square Show" opened in a run-down former bus depot and massage parlor on Forty-first Street and Seventh Avenue with a hundred-odd artists including Jean-Michel Basquiat, Keith Haring, Jenny Holzer, and Kenny Scharf. A motorized James Brown cutout (by David Wells) danced just inside the door, setting the tone. This too was a Colab event, but a legal one.

Mired in inertia at the end of the seventies, the art world was aching for an act of artistic rebellion to kick it in the teeth. The astonishing success of the "Times Square Show" proved how bored everyone had become with sleek white walls, the formalist paintings hanging on them, and the hushed propriety in art's presence. Jeffrey Deitch's review in *Art in America* praised the show's presentation and accessibility, how direct it all was: "entertainment, sexual expression or communication of political messages." How wrong it would have looked in an elegant or even a clean setting. "Art must come to be marketed with the kind of imagination displayed by this exhibition's organizers," Deitch declared. These lessons from the "anti-space" would soon be confidently applied in the East Village.

But if David was even aware of this show, he did not mention it. He was still preoccupied with the riverfront, and the nonstop show around Sheridan Square: The woman at Tiffany's coffee shop painting the frames of her sunglasses with purple nail polish. The drag queen from the previous year's "hell hath no fury fight" (on Christopher Street with another queen) buying pills. Homeless men searching the garbage outside a bar for beer cans that weren't quite empty. Someone in an apartment building at two A.M. throwing firecrackers at the winos on the stoop, though the winos were so drunk they barely flinched. The man with steel blue eyes on Christopher Street standing in front of the church with the wrought iron fence, then walking with David down to the warehouse that had caught fire. "He pulled me down to take him in my mouth."

"Passing by the river awhile later . . . I threw a penny over the water and watched it sink—threw a penny in the river for history, for time and future archeologists and studying civilizations." To David, this collapsing wreck would always be a monument. In just a few years, he would paint a picture called *Soon All This Will Be Picturesque Ruins*, featuring multiple images of the Acropolis as a backdrop to a crumbling building and a couple of the alien heads he created at the beginning of his career. Often he spoke of "the compression of time." To him, Rimbaud was easily transposed to his New York. And we were all in the Acropolis, thinking it permanent.

At the pier, he'd seen some chunk of his own graffiti leaning against a wall. One day in July, he filled two pages of his journal with descriptions of the "vagrant frescoes" still visible, the men moving over charred floors, the sexual motions in rooms that he passed—and he climbed a ladder to an unburned section of the roof where men lay sunbathing nude. He stood facing west and there he had a moment of feeling himself connected in defiance and exhilaration to all of America and all of its history from this epicenter of queer freedom. "I pulled myself up through the roof overhead and stood above the city and saw . . . the red hint of the skies where the west lies; saw myself in other times, moving my legs along the long flat roads of asphalt and weariness moving in and out of cars . . . dust storms rolling across the plains and the red neoned motels of other years and rides and the distant darkness of unnameable cities."

# 8 NIGHTCLUBBING

**For its brief** moment in time, the first Danceteria was New York's hottest club. (Two more incarnations of Danceteria would follow.) The *East Village Eye* even anointed it part of the neighborhood: "exhibits the Lower East Side aesthetic (stiletto heels, purple hair, and pointy sunglasses), although it's located on 37th between 7th and 8th."

Employees worked four nights a week from eight P.M. to eight A.M. David hated this job, but he liked his co-workers. Fellow busboys Chuck Nanney and Jesse Hultberg became good friends, and by midsummer, David had pulled Brian into that fold. One of the other busboys was Keith Haring, then a month or two away from beginning his chalk drawings in the subway. Another was Peter McGough, who would soon become known (with partner David McDermott) for both his art and his dedication to living a late-nineteenth to early-twentieth-century lifestyle.* Poet Max Blagg tended bar. Zoe Leonard, a photographer whose work was destined for the cover of *Artforum*, worked coat check. The doorman was Haoui Montaug, who later MC'ed the No Entiendes cabaret, introducing the world to everyone from Madonna to Karen Finley. Artists Pat Ivers and Emily Armstrong designed and programmed the first "video lounge" in all of clubland and documented the bands. Steve Brown, later a friend of David's and soon to edit the film *Wild Style*, sold tickets at the door.

Maybe working with this community of strivers gave David a push. Maybe a regular schedule helped. But that summer, David pulled out his monologue project again and asked Max Blagg to look at it. Blagg was

---

* McGough and McDermott lived in the early 1980s in a building on Avenue C with no electricity or telephone and dressed as Victorian or Edwardian gentlemen. See http://www.revelinnewyork.com/peter.

impressed and sent the manuscript to a friend in England who ran a small press, Aloes Books.

David had also been gravitating into musical projects since he'd started the job—and he entered a cassette he described as "experimental" in some unidentified competition. While a friend played guitar, David applied himself to some "invented drums," adding sirens and arguments he recorded on the street. He didn't win, but soon after that he began talking to friends about starting a band.

Constant exposure to the bands featured at Danceteria had only reinforced his idea that he and his friends could do just as well, or better. So what if he couldn't play an instrument or read music? By 1980, it seemed like half the people in downtown Manhattan were in a band. No musical skills? No problem! Old rules and categories had cracked open behind the head-banging force of punk. All over the East Village and beyond, the impact of punk's DIY aesthetic was evident. It questioned the basics: What was music? What was fashion? What was art? Anything went and anyone could do it.

The busboys made five dollars and change per hour; tips from the bartenders added sixty to a hundred each night. Once he had an income, David began contributing to the rent at Vinegar Hill, and he finally saved enough money for a ticket to France, though not enough to come back. Jean Pierre would have to pay for that.

Both had declared themselves nervous to see each other again. That August, hearing JP's voice for the first time in nearly a year over a pay phone at the Paris airport, David felt confused, almost angry. "Angry at the loss of his image: the one I'd grown slowly over the year, the image of the tough angel." The tough angel or thug saint was a romantic and sexual ideal for David. But could anyone truly be that?

Waking up at JP's new apartment in Montmartre after fourteen hours of sleep, David felt he'd come to stay with someone who was both completely familiar and a total stranger. At first, they had some big arguments over nothing, started by David and, as he put it, "carried by my sense of being dazed and confused as to what I was feeling." It took him nearly a week to snap out of it, or "loosen up."

They spent several days in Normandy visiting Pat. David photographed JP there for his "portraits of men" series. He had also photographed him in Paris in front of the Eiffel Tower, wearing the Rimbaud mask. On August 11, David wrote to Brian to tell him he'd taken a walk through Les Halles thinking, "Where am I going? What's to be done? What was this last year . . . these reservations in the face of mere living?" He did not mail the letter.

David and JP then spent a blissful week in Montgalliard, a small village in southwest France, with some friends of Jean Pierre's, Marie Jeanne and her husband, Septun. It would have been hard to find a more ideal vacation spot for David. Their first afternoon there, Marie Jeanne pulled out her box of treasures found in the surrounding hills: hundreds of small multifaceted quartz crystals, giant snails turned to rock, fossilized mussels and clams, a stone almond, four tusks and a tooth from a wild boar. David was soon out photographing the bleached jawbones of a rabbit and some prickly flowers, expecting to find vipers. They never materialized but he hoped to catch other snakes after Marie Jeanne informed him that there were some in the hills as thick as a bicep, seven feet long, and a hundred years old. David didn't find those either. Marie Jeanne speculated that the wild boars had eaten most of them. She cooked a local specialty for him and JP: snails grilled over a fire made from vine cuttings, seasoned with crushed chili pepper and sprinkled with hot pork fat, served with homemade wine. David managed to choke down some of this gourmet treat, though he described it as "dripping with slime."

At the top of the trail past the village's stone houses sat a slab of concrete "embedded for unknown reasons on the side of the hill." David and JP went up there one night to make love, afterward smoking and "watching the drifting beacons of car lights follow invisible roads." The town was so poor they'd had to close the school and the church. The iron key was still in the church door, and Marie Jeanne told David he could take the head of a baby Jesus he found there. The head enthralled him, as its "vacant blue eyes never stared directly at you no matter how you turned the head."

Leaving France after a month with Jean Pierre was less emotionally devastating this time. Still, David felt anger over the constant separation. "This cutting off of emotions because of laws, governments, and borders."

JP drove him to the airport, and David found an empty employees' bathroom where they had sex one last time. This left him with ten minutes till his plane took off, so they rushed. At passport control, he looked back to see JP, "something indefinable draining from his face."

For his first twenty-four hours back in Vinegar Hill, he felt terrible. He wanted to cry. "If anything in this world can mean something it's my being with him." He'd loved the week in Montgalliard among people with no pretensions. He felt he was surrounded in New York by the "pseudo-individuality" of new wave and "bourgeoisie set values." Of course, Europe was repressed, Paris a police state. "Yet away from the blatant exhibitionist energies of the NYC music scenes, gay scenes, I feel uncontrollably sane. I've got to return to him and allow myself to change to a more subtle existence for nothing else but my love for him and my own peace of mind."


His life did change suddenly in the autumn of 1980, but not in the direction of subtlety. First, Brian had returned from his own vacation in Provincetown and announced that he wanted out of Vinegar Hill and that he wanted to live alone.

Then, on David's first day back at work, he learned from Max Blagg that Aloes Books would publish the monologues, which he'd decided to call *Sounds in the Distance*. Blagg's friend Jim Pennington liked the project because it showed that "deep angst is not just for the literate and educated," and he liked the structure—"short pieces, almost routines, the moment dominant, no time or place for narrative, and only a faint smell of jism." He had already published work by Kathy Acker, William Burroughs, and Paul Bowles, but Aloes was, for Pennington, "a spare-time occupation." He worked for a commercial press as printer-in-charge and was able to print the Aloes books there after hours or in downtime. He provided the free labor and got the paper "on a quid pro quo arrangement involving unpaid overtime." Occasionally he requisitioned the paper, though he "couldn't go mad." Aloes would print five hundred copies of *Sounds in the Distance* and would make no money. David too would make no money, nor had he asked for any.

Within days of hearing from Pennington, David also began meeting in earnest with Blagg, Brian, and Jesse Hultberg to put a band together. They were preparing for a night a few weeks away when Danceteria employees would get a chance to perform at the club. Half the band—Brian and Jesse—could play an instrument, and that was more musicianship than some groups had. Still, Blagg remembered the band beginning as more of a performance group. He was already doing his own poetry with musical backup (as he did years later when he played a poet on television, in a Gap ad). But Blagg was not part of this particular band for long. The main thing he contributed was the name. He came to one of their meetings with a whole list of possibilities. Though David liked Sissies from Hell, they settled on 3 Teens Kill 4—No Motive, taken from a *New York Post* headline.

They never did play Danceteria. On Saturday, October 4, 1980, police raided the club and shut it down for selling liquor after hours without a license. Blagg, Brian, Jesse, Zoe Leonard, and Keith Haring were among the twenty-seven employees arrested. David had come downstairs to warn Blagg, who simply didn't move fast enough. Nor did Chuck Nanney, who'd been promoted to bartender. But Nanney managed to see his arrest as an absurdity. For one thing, he was so emaciated from drug use at the time that his handcuffs kept falling off. And he thought the cops were . . . nice. "They let us all go into the bathroom one at a time to do anything we might need to do." Like get rid of the drugs they were holding. Meanwhile, David had mingled with the customers, who'd been told to get out or face arrest. For him, one of the few employees not going to jail, the evening was horrific. He wrote in his journal that he'd noticed people with bloody faces. Later he told Brian that he was trying to figure out how to make a Molotov cocktail and blow up the paddywagon without hurting anyone. Then he saw a friend in handcuffs—Iolo Carew, another busboy—nodding toward the door, mouthing the words, "Leave. Leave." So he did.

The next day, October 5, David moved from Vinegar Hill to the East Village, the neighborhood he would call home for the rest of his life. He'd taken a room at 159 Second Avenue with his old friends from Bookmasters, Susan Gauthier and her boyfriend, Steve Gliboff.* For him, though, the move was of little note because he was so depressed and disturbed over what had

---

* The building's front door is on Tenth Street, facing St. Mark's Church.

happened at Danceteria. He wrote to JP on October 8, "This week has been the worst time in my life." He felt so worried and alone. He wished he could talk to JP and asked if he'd heard anything yet about the UNESCO job he was still hoping to get. That month he would send Jean Pierre twenty-three letters and postcards. On October 10, he wrote to say, "Everything here has fallen apart." His life. His friends' lives. No one knew whether the club would continue now that it couldn't sell alcohol. Meanwhile, his new roommates were fighting. That Friday, though, Danceteria reopened and he returned, promoted from busboy to security.

On October 15, he sent four new monologues to Jim Pennington at Aloes and told him he wasn't satisfied with the title. How about *Monologues from the Road* or *Drifter's Notes* or *Everything Is Outside* or . . . Pennington decided to stick with *Sounds in the Distance*. Then, David told Pennington he wanted to dedicate the book to Jean Pierre and—shockingly—his parents. Or, as he put it, "[for] Dolores McGuinness and for my father, *dark shadow on the viridian seas.*" Pennington knew nothing of David's childhood—he just thought the book didn't need a dedication. "A bit presumptuous of me," he said, "but David didn't object." Pennington had to cut the number of pages, anyway. "Otherwise we would have had to send the binding out." As it was, Pennington could not get it printed until 1982.

Meanwhile, David decided to enter a photography contest sponsored by Foto Gallery, after learning that Larry Clark, best known for his photos of outlaw teens, would be one of the judges. David was done with Rimbaud now. He would enter some of his portraits of men, like the picture he'd taken in August of JP holding a large white flower. He thought it his best photo. By the end of October he wasn't just printing pictures; he was back to rehearsing with the band and writing lyrics. Every night that he was not working, he went to the piers. Susan Gauthier remembered that he would leave the apartment at midnight or one A.M., and when he came back in the morning, he would tell her about things he'd seen and characters he'd met.

Then, on October 31, someone called him from the club to tell him not to come to work. Danceteria was closing.* Though suddenly unemployed again, David was now more preoccupied with the photo contest. Soon he

---

* It did not reopen in its next location until 1982.

*When David entered this photo of Jean Pierre Delage in a contest late in 1980, he regarded it as the best picture he'd ever taken. (David Wojnarowicz Papers, Fales Library, NYU)*

would report to Jean Pierre that his mother had entered the same contest and had already been rejected—which made him nervous.

That weekend, fresh out of a job, he went to see the work of his fellow unemployed busboy Keith Haring, who had a studio at nearby P.S. 122, at First Avenue and Ninth Street. Chuck Nanney remembered, "David was really kind of obsessed with what Keith was doing, but I don't think Keith was ever very friendly with David." Haring was still two years away from international fame.

When I first visited old Public School 122 with artist friends in the late 1970s, it was not yet a performance and studio space. We scavenged through abandoned classrooms full of old flash cards, battered books, and other discarded school supplies. Community groups in the not-yet-gentrified East Village had invited artists to take the old classrooms as studios in order to keep the building occupied, and in 1979, performances began in what had once been the school gymnasium.

That same year, Ann Magnuson opened Club 57 in a church basement on St. Mark's Place, a block and a half away. Under her direction, this refuge for the unsuburban created a style other neighborhood clubs would soon emulate. Many of the performances at Club 57 parodied pop culture. Its *Sound of Music* starred John Sex, for example. Other nights, clubgoers screened bad and beloved old television shows or kitsch artifacts like *The Terror of Tiny Town* (an all-midget musical western). Even the theme parties became performances; the "Twisting in High Society" evening, for example, meant that everyone came in formal attire and played Twister. Certain events may have been more fun to write into the calendar than to witness— like Lance Loud hosting a punk rock quiz show, "Name That Noise." But the joy of it was that you never knew what to expect. By 1980, young artists like Haring, Kenny Scharf, and Tseng Kwong Chi were regulars.

The Pyramid Club opened that December, and soon became home to the edgiest drag queens in New York, like the Lady Bunny, RuPaul, International Chrysis, Hapi Phace, Tabboo!, and Ethyl Eichelberger. But the great distinction of the Pyramid was that it did not become a gay club, despite the go-go boys and drag queens dancing on the bar, the many performances by the above-named queens, and the fact that gay men were in charge. This was an artists club—for those who were "queer" in every sense of that word.

It presaged an East Village scene in which the gay-straight split would become just another broken boundary. The summer 1980 issue of The *East Village Eye* included "Gay Shame by David McDermott, Noted Member of the Queer Elite" attacking the "clone" aesthetic: "First of all the whole Gay lifestyle is an anachronism left over from 1972," McDermott declared. "No one cares anymore if you are Gay or not, we care about who you are. You Gay Culture Fags have made a culture that can only be your culture, because we do not want your sex-quiche, sex-moustache, sex-quaaludes, whips, penis-sex-literary pretentious love . . ." And so on. Meanwhile, Keith Haring was out stenciling "Clones Go Home" on sidewalks leading from the West Side, signing it "FAFH," for the imaginary group Fags Against Facial Hair.

Nightclubs of this era became both clubhouse and romper room to young artists of all kinds, with their outré acts, films that would never play a multiplex, and bands whose names were the best thing about them. In this era of cross-pollination, painters played in bands, musicians acted in films, actors tried visual art, and they were all hanging out together.

The new Super 8 films by Scott B and Beth B, James Nares, Vivienne Dick, and others often played nowhere but in the clubs, and they embody an important point about the scene. While some films were quite accomplished, Super 8 has its limits, and many of them looked like films made by artists, starring artists, just to entertain their friends: other artists. Nares's *Rome 78*, for example, features McDermott (a painter) as the demented pip-squeak Emperor, while Lydia Lunch plays Empress in her baby-faced dominatrix mode. Through most of it, traffic is clearly audible in the background as various Romans decline and fall. The risk taking, the micro-budgets, the outlawry, and the willingness to look amateurish in all these enterprises made for an ambience of tremendous energy and creativity. This feeling pervaded the little boho coterie centered in the clubs and visible on the street.

David did not hang out at Club 57, but he'd chanced into a world that was ready to welcome him—or at least let him be who he was.

In November 1980, the Peppermint Lounge opened with Jim Fouratt booking the bands. David applied for a job and again became a busboy, working five days a week, seven P.M. to five A.M. Jesse joined him at the Pep, while Brian found work at an after-hours spot called Berlin and then moved on to the Mudd Club.

Meanwhile, the old Danceteria staff decided to throw themselves a benefit on December 2 at a Tribeca club called Tier 3. This would be the first gig for 3 Teens Kill 4. As Brian remembered it, they prepared three songs and had about ten people in the band—other co-workers. David made posters for the benefit featuring one of his "portraits of men": Iolo Carew, lying on his back exhaling a big cloud of smoke. David said later that it reminded him vaguely of the spirit leaving the body. Iolo would become the first person he knew to be diagnosed with AIDS.

The night that David, Jesse, and Brian walked through Lower Manhattan wheat-pasting these posters on walls and streetlights, they talked about continuing with 3 Teens. "The band was always based around Jesse and Brian and David and their friendship and their background and their sexuality," observed Julie Hair, who soon joined them as 3 Teens' drummer—though she had never played the drums or any other instrument. Hair had moved to the New York City area in 1980 with boyfriend Tom Cochran, who was managing the band Tirez Tirez. One night she went to Peppermint Lounge and bumped into someone she'd met years earlier through a friend—Jesse Hultberg. Jesse introduced her to David. The first thing she said to him, after hearing his amazingly deep speaking voice: "You should be in a band." Once Hair agreed to join 3 Teens, she went to Midtown and bought herself a Korg rhythm machine, thinking she'd be an interim player. Instead she not only stayed with the band but also joined two others—Noch Nichts and Bite like a Kitty.

To anyone who asked David what instrument he played in 3 Teens, he always replied, "Tape recorder." He also sang, played percussion, and manipulated little toys for sound effects. But his tapes of traffic and street talk and random bits from the radio—that was his unique contribution. Of course, he'd also been writing lyrics for years, and now that he'd given up poetry, he cannibalized old poems for lines like "We are all essential laborers / you will die soon enough. / I will not live long / all things will change and move on." This became part of a signature 3 Teens song titled "Hunger." Lyrics he'd written in Paris now had a place too. "Luis Bunuel / . . . can ya enter this cell" became part of "Wind-Up Clock." However, all songs were credited to the whole band, not to any individual.

"We tried to keep it all even," Hair explained. That was the philosophy of the band. They were anti-star. They wanted no lyricist, no lead singer, and no lead guitarist. They would switch instruments during their shows. Brian was a strong keyboard player who also played a good rhythm guitar. Jesse was a gifted multi-instrumentalist who sang beautifully. Hair taught herself to play the rhythm machine and then the bass, but David never became proficient on any instrument. Hair remembered that David felt insecure about his musical abilities. One day he said, "I'm being reduced to shaking a can of beans." This became "The Bean Song," featuring the lyric "I'll bet you wish you could shake a can of beans as well as me."

By the end of 1981, however, they'd decided they needed an accomplished guitar player and added Doug Bressler. The guitar they'd been us-

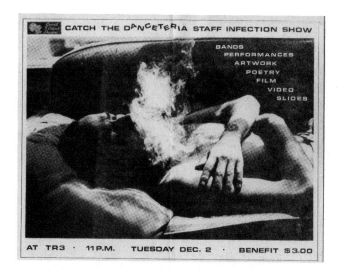

*David created this poster, with a photo of his friend Iolo Carew exhaling smoke, for the benefit where he performed with an early incarnation of 3 Teens Kill 4—No Motive. (David Wojnarowicz Papers, Fales Library, NYU)*

ing, Bressler said, "was a piece of junk, and it wouldn't stay in tune." They not only didn't have quality instruments; they didn't seem interested in acquiring any. The electric guitars would be crackly. "You'd show up at a gig and the amp wouldn't work. Stuff like that," Bressler said. "It was really low-tech. And they were proud of it. That was part of their thing." Hair began to play a thirty-dollar violin that had one string, placing it horizontally on a walker and sawing away. "Early on we used to joke about how we could take all our equipment to a show in a garbage bag," Hair said, "because it would just be a lot of toys and crap." As they continued to switch instruments during their gigs, tension developed over Bressler's resistance to handing over his "gorgeous Les Paul to people who devalued it completely." He remembered being encouraged not to hide behind his guitar, and being told, "You've got to pick up something that's outside your comfort zone."

Despite all this, 3 Teens were way more than three-chord wonders. They had a distinctive sound, very rhythmic and chant-y and percussive and spare, but filled with musical and verbal ideas. Bressler wondered later if he'd ruined the band with his musical stylings. "There was this whole movement in music, like the Young Marble Giants," he said, "where you really were supposed to hear the white of the canvas. And that was very much true in early 3 Teens."

They played their first solo gig at La Rocka Club in the West Village the end of February 1981.

On January 4, 1981, David wrote to JP that he'd "spent the night talking with a new friend about life/photos etc—rare that I have a chance to just talk and listen to interesting things." On the 7th, he again mentions "new friends" and how certain people inspired him to keep working. On the 9th, he finally named a particular new friend: Peter Hujar—and that he enjoyed talking with him about "photography, life, etc." It's quite possible that they actually met in late December. Naturally David never discussed his sexual escapades in letters to Jean Pierre. If he ever referred to those men, they were "friends" and not named. Hujar was in a singular new category David couldn't have named at that point. Hujar would prove to be the most important person in his life.

Early in January, David learned that one of his photos had been chosen for the Foto Gallery exhibition, though what he mostly felt was disappointment that the judges had not picked his portrait of JP. Instead, they'd chosen a picture he'd taken outside the Beaubourg of a kid with James Dean tattooed across his back. This same photo was set to appear on the cover of *Sounds in the Distance*, and that week, he also learned that William Burroughs himself had agreed to blurb his little book. David didn't seem happy or even impressed by any of this.

His life now was "desperate, surreal, awful, and slightly wondrous," he wrote in the journal he'd barely touched since the Danceteria bust. He finally went back to it on January 21, 1981, trying to make sense of things. After the bust, it seemed, "everything became groundless, apt to fall apart at any moment, nothing offering security or permanence." He noted: "It wasn't just the arrests or the eventual loss of work, but rather a period of time in which I grew tired of all the scenes I'd been involved with."

He wrote about meeting Hujar in the Bar at Second Avenue and Fourth Street. "He stared at me and I looked back several times. I guess I wanted him in a strong way." When they got to Hujar's loft at Second Avenue and Twelfth Street, he handed David a book, saying, "This is the kind of work I do." David was stunned to see a volume he'd been drawn to years before—*Portraits in Life and Death*. Hujar's photographs of artists, drag queens, and others who intrigued him were utterly straightforward and empathetic. Along with his friends, Hujar included photographs of mummies in the catacombs at Palermo.

They may not have exchanged last names at the Bar, but David now knew very well who this was. "Hujar" appears, mysteriously, on a list David made in August 1979 while working on the Rimbaud photos, along with items like "brian's collage/pistol" and "parakeets in woolworth's"—and across from each of these, a film speed.

Whatever that was about, David felt that he had an image of Hujar the artist that blocked him from seeing Hujar the person. But over a series of days David let that dissipate. And then what he saw in Hujar was a kind of mirror image; they were both desperate and confused, but David felt he still had hope about the future, and Hujar did not. Maybe because David's art was still developing, while Hujar's art was fully formed and his career had never flowered.

David showed Hujar some of his work, but doesn't say what. Rimbaud? The portrait of JP? The monologues? Whatever it was, Hujar seemed disinterested or maybe just unaffected. At least, that was David's impression, though it would prove to be untrue. In any situation that was even slightly ambiguous, he would seize upon the worst interpretation. One night, he stopped by Hujar's loft to film him for his first Super 8 movie, "Heroin"—silent, three minutes long, and one of the only films David ever completed. If Hujar made the final cut, he played one of the people passed out or dead on various floors and sidewalks. David said only that he left the loft that night feeling a lot of anger about the state of his own work, feeling that he was basically a failure, that he wasn't "capable of affecting change in anyone other than friends." But then, he asked himself, what was it that he wanted to change? Maybe his images were too aggressive. "I seem to really desire some way to seduce people, make them feel at ease and yet make them renounce all the terrible things of the earth and say: Yes, this is what is true."

On the day he did this journal writing—January 21, 1981—Hujar called to tell him he had syphilis. So David went and got his shot and wrote, "[I] am in a state of pain and reexamination of all I once held as my life, not because of the shot but because of the weariness of all these daily routines. . . . But I continue the only ways I know how, always with looking over my shoulder for that chance to change direction and run, escape, depart."

It was a depressive's reaction, but something had lit a fire in him. Susan Gauthier observed that David's life definitely changed when he met Hujar. "Someone saw that [David] was a true artist." She couldn't quite articulate how it changed except to say that David was "full-on" after that, in regard to his work—and he stopped going constantly to the pier.

Truly, everything was beginning for him, but David couldn't see it. Early in February, he learned that Keith Haring had selected him for two group exhibits he was curating, one at Club 57 ("The Erotic Show") and one at the Mudd Club ("The Lower Manhattan Drawing Show"). He was also in rehearsals for 3 Teens' La Rocka gig. And at the end of the month, Dennis Cooper's journal, *Little Caesar*, finally appeared in bookstores with sixteen Rimbaud photos and two monologues. This on top of winning the photo contest and finding a publisher for *Sounds in the Distance*.

David fixated on the glass half-empty, on the fact that he still spent most of his waking hours as a busboy and was in love with a man he rarely saw. (Jean Pierre came to visit for eight days at the beginning of March, and David still entertained fantasies about moving to Paris to work for UNESCO.) He was also unhappy with his home life. "Susan and Steve are sweet but I don't feel very comfortable with them," he wrote to JP. He did not share this with his roommates, of course. Years later, Gauthier still puzzled over the fact that David would never eat dinner with them. Gliboff was such a great cook, she said, yet David ate nothing but peanut butter and jelly sandwiches, or sometimes an egg.

In March, he met a fella at his newest cruising ground, Stuyvesant Park, on Second Avenue five blocks north of where he was living. For the two weeks or so that this affair lasted, David suffered and obsessed over a familiar issue: "Fear to show myself completely to somebody who I desire.

That it will drive them away or that it will give them cause to become disinterested."

He realized now that when he was afraid to share his feelings, he put them into his work. He'd shown this man, Bill, some of his photographs, and Bill thought them disturbing or weird. "I feel kind of tense about that, and he's already asked me if I hustled after looking at some of my monologues, and it was very difficult to say 'yeah.'"

In the midst of this affair, David ran into Hujar one night at the Bar, which functioned as a social club for gay men in the East Village. David told him he was making a portfolio, but first he was going to throw away any drawing he'd made that was aggressive or upsetting. Hujar counseled him not to throw out any drawings. "I shouldn't start compromising and trying to adapt to other people's taste, that no matter what my taste is and what my ideas are, or what my work looks like, if it's good, there'll be somebody who'll pick up on it," David said Hujar told him in a taped journal entry. "And last night, I was standing around here at five, six in the morning, looking through the portfolio, looking at my photographs, just leafing through boxes, and I was really startled. It was like the first time that I sat down and looked at these drawings in ages and ages, since I did them and I realized they are good, and there's absolutely no reason for me to deny them or correct them or throw them away or bury them. They're my life."

He hit another low point that spring of '81. Peppermint Lounge laid him off for twenty days, then rehired him for just two days a week. Business was slow. Some artist, never named, engaged him to paint his house in the Hamptons, but David had little to show for it after paying for train fare and meals.

In April, Gauthier and Gliboff told him they had solved their financial problems and wanted more privacy. Could he please move out? He didn't have the money to do this. In May, Jean Pierre sent him some francs. David was now using his money to eat in restaurants because he didn't feel comfortable using the kitchen at home. Nor did he feel comfortable typing there. (Again, this was David's interpretation, and Susan Gauthier was surprised to learn of it—from me.) Nor could he afford to develop photos or print.

One morning, though, happy over a good dream, David called Jesse Hultberg's place and Zoe Leonard answered the phone. She was there taking nude pictures of Jesse, and told David to come on over: "I'll take photographs of you too."

In one of the last long journal entries David would write for years to come, he gives a rare description of friends hanging out. But he probably wrote it because he began a short affair with Zoe that day and was trying to figure out what it meant.

When David arrived, she was trying to clip a lamp onto a floor-to-ceiling pipe, staggering and weaving because she'd taken four Quaaludes. Jesse posed on a bed illuminated by the blue light of a television. Then he began to read aloud from a trashy novel ("*Hot Hips* or *Love is My Business* or some such," David wrote). Jesse tape-recorded this while David and Zoe provided orgasmic sound effects. David took one Quaalude. Zoe went into the other room to lie down and asked David to lie down next to her. She told him she was depressed. She showed him the bruise on her arm where she'd been shooting up. She said she wanted to leave New York.

Zoe was a bit unsettled by this journal passage when she read it years later. "I was bottoming out here," she told me. "I was definitely tricking at the time, and I was getting really strung out. I'd been shooting a lot of coke and then—I was the one with the bag of Quaaludes. But my feelings for David were incredibly warm and sincere and real. I felt a kinship with him."

Zoe too had had a rough childhood, leaving what she called "a really neglectful and difficult household" at age fifteen and enrolling herself in an alternative high school (City-as-School). Though she never graduated, she soon had a number of classmates crashing with her at the East Village apartment she'd rented. (The one who stayed longest was Jean-Michel Basquiat.) She was younger than David—nineteen at the time their fling began.

Zoe told David that day that he always acted like he didn't really like "some of us." He replied, "No, it's not that," and explained: "I have this whole area of myself I can't share or talk about. . . . Because of that and because I don't want to lose that part of myself, I just get distant. I feel so different from most people I know."

When Zoe initiated sex, he hesitated, telling her, "I'm enjoying this,

I'm feeling this, but I'm trying to understand it." Zoe said she didn't think it right to call what they had a "romance" or an "affair." It was "an extension of this sense of connection, a sense of being kindred spirits, as artists." She estimated that they slept together maybe three more times, but said that "it clearly wasn't going to go anywhere sexually." Mostly they talked about art and their messed-up childhoods. They would sit on the West Side piers. They'd take pictures. "It was very kind of tender," said Zoe. "I don't know another word for it."

At that time, Zoe considered herself bisexual. Looking back on it, she said she felt drawn to David because "he had this depth to him. And even when he was lighthearted, he was sort of solemn." She added: "Also, I think my desire for him was about finding my queerness, finding my own gayness. The way I came out into being an artist and becoming who I am was really through the Mudd Club and punk rock. I really didn't grow up with any kind of understanding of a lesbian culture, and I just loved the whole way that gay men were with each other."

Shortly after this, Zoe left the country for a year and a half. The drug use and sex work had taken a toll. She said, "I just had this feeling: If I don't get out of here, I'm not going to make it."


In the eighties, every wall, Dumpster, and streetlight in the East Village was aflutter with wheat-pasted flyers advertising gigs at assorted hellholes and hot spots. David had taken it upon himself to design the signage for 3 Teens and sometimes for other bands. He'd make a collage or use one of his photos, then spend the wee hours slapping the flyers up all over the neighborhood. After a while, he realized that rival bands were ripping his posters down. This, he told me, was why he started doing stencils. You could spray your message anywhere. Abandoned cars. Doorways. The sidewalk.

Then he started using stencils on paper. Often he went to Julie Hair's place to work—though she had the classic tiny tub-in-the-kitchen tenement. Since Hair and her roommate had already stenciled their own floor, "it was a place he could come and be messy," she said. Hair remembered him stenciling on maps, or doing what she called "glorified posters for our gigs."

David liked street art. He told me about seeing Jean-Michel Basquiat's

"SAMO" graffiti and Keith Haring's subway drawings: "It was the first thing I connected with in terms of the art world because I had disdain for what I sensed of that world. I just didn't believe they were dealing with anything real."

"Julie Hair had a box of international symbols in stencil form. I thought, Oh, we should do stencils that they forgot, such as burning houses. You know, images of resistance or violence. They never make international symbols like that, so let's develop the burning house, a falling man, the target-face person, and little soldiers."

Political art at the time often focused on American support for repressive military regimes in Latin America. David began applying his political yet enigmatic non-advertisements to downtown walls in 1981. He liked going to SoHo and spraying war imagery on gallery doors—an art guerrilla leaving a trail of El Salvador for those wafting toward the Schnabels. Though he would use some of these military images in early paintings, the stencil that registered most was more personal: the burning house.

Artist Jane Bauman was one of several friends who used to go out stenciling with David. "You don't stencil alone," she said. "You need somebody there as a lookout." Usually it was spur of the moment, a plan made when they ran into each other on the street. "The East Village was like a small town," Bauman recalled. "Walk outside and there were all your friends." They'd head out after midnight, venturing as far afield with their spray cans as Tribeca. "He would alter other people's stencils too. A lot of us were doing that. Adding your own little flavor to it."

Years later, he admitted that stenciling hadn't exactly been effective as a political gesture. "It definitely got construed as a whole other thing—as my attempt to get into the art world," he said. "But at the time I thought it was a great rude thing and I never counted on showing in the art world. I didn't think my work was developed enough. I felt, with my lack of education, that wasn't something that was possible."

Even so, Julie Hair remembered that after some art critic disparaged either David's stencils or the idea of stencils in general, David decided to make a less subtle assault on this world he thought he would never enter. "I think that's why he wanted to target Castelli," she said.

One afternoon that spring, the two of them dumped a pile of bloody

*3 Teens Kill 4—No Motive: Clockwise from David, they are Doug Bressler, Jesse Hultberg, Brian Butterick, and Julie Hair. (Photograph by Mark C)*

cow bones on the stairway outside the Leo Castelli Gallery at 420 West Broadway, the "power building" that housed many of the top dealers. On the walls of the first-floor landing, they quickly stenciled an empty plate, a knife, and a fork. (David told me they'd added war stencils too; Hair did not remember doing those.) They littered the bones down the staircase—which wasn't used all that much. Most people took the elevators, so few people would have laid eyes on this installation. And they never heard about any reaction at the gallery.

This mostly unseen piece became legend, and stories circulated about blood dripping down the steps. That did not happen. After David collected the bones from the meatpacking district, he brought them to the framing shop where Hair worked, and they encased them all in plastic. There was still meat and fat on some of the bones but no dripping blood. They were basically shrink-wrapped. They transported them to SoHo heaped in a red wagon they found on the street.

David saw this as the first in a series of "action installations," which would "trespass the boundaries of art world activities." He wanted to organize another in which friends would show up at Macy's in military fatigues, with one person blindfolded, and they'd stage a mock execution by firing squad. Just to literally bring home what was happening in certain parts of Latin America. Friends talked him out of it.

By June, he was uncomfortable enough at 159 Second Avenue to try spending the night with friends like Jesse Hultberg or with men he picked up for sex. To Jean Pierre, he wrote, "I rarely come home. Only if I have no other place to sleep."

He also mentioned to JP that he was reading a book by Renaud Camus, *Tricks*, the French writer's account of twenty-five one-night stands. And David joked, "I looked for you in it." In one of his increasingly rare—and now undated—journal entries, he described taking the book to Hujar, who'd once photographed Camus and was curious about *Tricks*. "As I neared the building I could see strobic flashes of light issue from the windows. . . . Upstairs Ethyl [Eichelberger] was sitting on a chair below some extremely bright floodlamps, huge painted face topped with an enormous wig shaped like a bundle of laundry. I said hello and gave Peter the book and left. At the door I turned to him and said, It's gonna be a great decade. Ethyl shouted: I HEARD THAT!"

David would spend years reworking the story of his connection with Hujar, not because anything changed but because of his core issue—how much could he reveal, even to himself? By the time I interviewed him in January 1990, more than two years after Hujar's death, he thought it the central connection in his life. He told me that the sexual affair had been brief, but that they then began "a very complicated friendship/relationship that took time to find a track to run along." He told me that with Hujar, who was twenty years older, he eventually began to feel easier with himself. "He was like the parent I never had, like the brother I never had. He helped me drop a lot of the shit I carried from the streets—the pain, the fear, the guilt.

Stuff I could barely speak to people about. I remember revealing to him that I'd been a hustler our second night together. We were having dinner, and I fully expected him to reject me. And I remember he just said, 'So?' And we got into this long conversation where I just revealed all my fears." Certainly, Hujar was not the first to learn of David's hustling days, just the confessor who ended up mattering.

"There was a density to the emotional contact between us that was great," David recalled, "and that was what was most valuable. After a couple years knowing each other, it really solidified."

Eventually he would say of his art career: "Everything I made, I made for Peter."

# 9 THE POVERTY OF PETER HUJAR

**They developed a** way to signal each other—I'm here—at crowded gatherings: two fingers up like rabbit ears behind the head.

Hujar would eventually come up with a list of the ways in which he and David were karmically connected, but it wasn't something he wrote down. All his friends could remember him saying was that both he and David had redheaded mothers. That was the least of it, of course.

Peter Hujar was born in Trenton, New Jersey, in 1934 to parents who soon abandoned him. His father, Joseph, reportedly a bootlegger, actually absconded before he was born. His mother left for Manhattan, where she worked as a waitress in a diner after turning the infant Hujar over to her parents, Ukrainian immigrants who lived on a New Jersey farm. Hujar did not learn to speak English till he entered kindergarten. And while he remembered his grandparents as loving, especially his grandmother, he went to live with an uncle after the grandparents died, in an environment that was "worse than Dickensian," according to his friend Fran Lebowitz. "His uncle had a lot of children," Lebowitz said. "They would all sit down to dinner and all the other children would get chicken. Peter would get a piece of bread. On Sundays, the uncle's children would get ice cream, but not Peter."

While he lived in New Jersey, his mother would show up every week or so with whatever money she was contributing for his care, loudly complaining about it. Unlike David, Hujar did not often speak of his childhood. The detail above about his mother comes from Stephen Koch, who first met Hujar in 1965 and eventually became executor of his estate. When Hujar made his will and insisted on leaving one third of the net proceeds of all photos to his mother, Koch was taken aback. He asked why. She had never made one gesture of support to Hujar. She never once visited while he was sick. She would not attend the funeral. Hujar answered, with a fury, "I'll pay her back every penny."

Hujar had moved to his mother's place at 340 East Thirty-second Street in Manhattan by the time he was twelve or so. His mother had remarried, and his new stepfather had a drinking problem. Or she did. Or they both did. Hujar left home while he was still in high school on the night his mother threw a bottle of beer at his head.

"He walked out the door, and he never went back. He lived on somebody's couch," said Steve Turtell, who met Hujar in 1971. "Somebody put him up for the last few months of his high school career. He attended his own graduation and sat in the audience, and when they called his name and no one stood up to get the diploma, Hujar sat in the back slowly clapping, and he was the only person applauding. He loved telling that story to me." Hujar told Lebowitz, however, that he moved out when he was fourteen and had his own apartment in the West Village. He pointed out the building to her numerous times.

Hujar had attended the School of Industrial Art (later called the High School of Art and Design), knowing he wanted to be a photographer. There he had the good fortune to encounter a teacher—the poet Daisy Aldan—who recognized his artistic potential. According to Koch, she is the one who urged Hujar to start doing apprenticeships in commercial photography studios. He became very technically skilled in the darkroom, a master printer.

Steve Turtell heard one story from Hujar about an attempt he made to connect with his mother after his career took off in the sixties. He wanted her to know that he was making it. He wasn't a nobody. So he told her that he was now friends with Andy Warhol. And she said to him, "Oh, isn't he that fag?" It's unclear how much contact Hujar had with her after that. Still, she had the power that mothers have. David once told me, outraged, that she'd often told Hujar he was ugly. And Hujar believed it.

"He never thought that people found him attractive," said another old friend, critic Vince Aletti. In reality, Hujar was so handsome, charismatic, seductive, and engaging that often, when Aletti introduced people to him for the first time—it didn't matter whether they were men or women—they'd be on the phone to Aletti the next day, burbling, "That guy is so fabulous. I love him!" Hujar was unable to take that in. He never believed that people actually valued his work, either, even when they told him they did.

In 1956, Hujar took photographs at a Connecticut school for developmentally disabled children. These were the first photos to become part of his oeuvre. This was also the year he met artists Paul Thek and Joseph Raffael. When Raffael won a Fulbright in 1958, he took Hujar with him to Italy. In Florence, Hujar found a Catholic institution where he took more pictures of neurologically impaired children. He was not yet doing portraits. His pictures show the children at play, and if they are visibly "different"—some have Down syndrome, for example—they are not caught up in their difference. They are not grotesque. They are who they are, and Hujar identified with them. "His experience of himself as a hurt child from a damaged family was lifelong and very powerful," Koch said. "The beauty of things broken and damaged was what he was interested in. The reverse of Robert Mapplethorpe, who was interested in things that were perfect."

In 1963, Hujar was back in Italy with a Fulbright of his own, traveling with his lover Paul Thek, photographing the catacombs at Palermo—where the corpses are dressed up and posing. Eleven pictures of these mummies, along with twenty-nine portraits of living people, ended up in the one book Hujar published in his lifetime, the one David saw: *Portraits in Life and Death*. "We no longer study the art of dying, a regular discipline and hygiene in older cultures," Susan Sontag wrote in her introduction to this book, "but all eyes at rest contain that knowledge. The body knows. And the camera knows, inexorably. . . . Peter Hujar knows that portraits in life are always, also, portraits in death."

By the mid-sixties, he was connected and respected in the New York art world. Warhol filmed him for one of his "screen tests," in which individuals sat in front of a stationery 16mm camera for the duration of a hundred-foot roll of film. Warhol's other subjects included Edie Sedgwick, Marcel Duchamp, and Bob Dylan, but he shot hundreds of these "tests," and they weren't all of famous people. He did, however, select Hujar for a compilation taken from the screen tests called *The Thirteen Most Beautiful Boys*.

When Stephen Koch met him in 1965, in Susan Sontag's living room,

Hujar had just spent the day photographing Jayne Mansfield. Koch was fascinated by Hujar's observations about this star—her relationship to the camera, her relationship to her own body, her relationship to the entourage she'd brought along. At this point, Hujar was working for Harold Krieger, a commercial photographer best known for big advertising campaigns and magazine covers. It was the one time in his life Hujar had a middle-class income.

Soon after this came the shoots for *Harper's Bazaar* and *GQ*, the master class with Richard Avedon, and what seemed the beginning of a successful career. But, as more than one friend told me, Hujar was his own worst enemy. One of his last fashion assignments—maybe *the* last—was a swimsuit spread. He was sent to Florida, and instead of hiring models, he went to the beach and found some teenagers to just hold the suits up. They didn't even put them on. The magazine's publisher was appalled.

Hujar didn't reject fashion, and he wasn't opposed to doing commercial work. He simply had his own ideas about what to do and how to do it. Nor did he wish to be poor. In fact, he resented being poor. He just wasn't willing—and maybe he wasn't able—to do the things that would allow him *not* to be poor.

"I watched Peter wring out a pair of blue jeans he had just washed in his own sink and hang them over the curtain rod to dry," Steve Turtell recalled. "He washed his laundry in the kitchen sink because he couldn't afford the Laundromat, or wasn't going to spend his money on that. He was willing to live on just about nothing—in order to do nothing but his work."

Koch called him "the poorest grown-up I have been personally close to in my life."

Early in the seventies, Hujar moved to a loft at 189 Second Avenue, formerly occupied by his friend Jackie Curtis, the legendary drag queen and Warhol "superstar." Here, where he would live for the rest of his life—where David would then live for the rest of his—Hujar began photographing friends like Charles Ludlam, Ray Johnson, and Ann Wilson for *Portraits in Life and Death*. "It was like a monk's cell," said Turtell. "He had what he needed and nothing more." Bed. Table. Desk. A few chairs.

Even so, Turtell said it took him years to figure out how Hujar was financing this minimal lifestyle. "He took cash advances from the credit cards he had managed to get when he was a fashion photographer," Turtell said. "He had high credit limits on these cards, and he would eke out a small amount, pay back the minimum, and take the cash advance only when he needed it and depend upon the kindness of his friends and the occasional grant and an occasional sale and an occasional job that he would be willing to do."

Hujar was always analyzing his own relationship to money. "He believed that there was a flaw in him that made him wish to be poor," said Koch. "He had this conviction that people get exactly what they want. So when he said, 'I have to figure out how to make money,' that wasn't about 'what phone calls I have to make.' It was about 'How can I settle it with myself? I have to figure out how to forgive myself.' But he never did."

Hujar was also convinced that certain names lent themselves to fame. Alliterative names, for example, like Marilyn Monroe or Jasper Johns. Friends would scoff, "And Andy Warhol?" No matter. For him, the point was that "Peter Hujar" was a terrible name. So he rearranged the letters to create the anagram "Jute Harper." This was the name, he decided, that would make him rich and successful, and at some point in the eighties, he created a small body of work under that name, with David's help. It was soft-core porn done for greeting cards that could be sold in Christopher Street shops—for example, David and an unknown man dressed in sailor suits with their hands at each other's flies. Hujar never made money from this venture either.

He lived so creatively on nothing. He was proud of how creatively. Who needs two sets of sheets? Take them off the bed, wash them, and put them back on. Who needs cleaning fluid for windows? Take a newspaper page and wet it. "He knew every trick that poor people know," Lebowitz said. "Like, when you send a bill in, don't put a stamp on it. They'll either pay the postage due or send it back and then you have more time." He ate lots of brown rice and vegetables. He ate lots of tuna casserole. Many friends remembered him coming regularly to their place for meals. Aletti, who moved in across the street in 1976, was then writing for *Rolling Stone* and went to rock 'n' roll press parties several times a week. Often he took Hujar along, and they'd fill up on hors d'oeuvres.

Hujar knew everyone and attended many parties, but he'd complain, "I don't have a Sam Wagstaff"—referring to Robert Mapplethorpe's very rich and well-connected boyfriend. And if Hujar didn't have that, Koch observed, "he'd have to court people, or at least not be difficult with them. Not throw them down the stairs. Not go into rages."

Many of those close to Hujar had witnessed these rages. Koch was at the loft one night when an uninvited guest stopped by and would not leave when Hujar asked him to—so Hujar actually did throw him down the stairs. Aletti remembered a conversation with Hujar at the loft during which they disagreed—Alettti couldn't remember on what but thought it unimportant—when suddenly Hujar picked up the chair he'd been sitting on. Aletti said, "He broke it into splinters in front of me. Just smashed it on the floor and kept smashing it and smashing it until there was just nothing more to break, and I was sitting there just frozen." Turtell saw Hujar smash a bar stool against a wall one night at SNAFU, after Hujar had bumped his head on a pipe in the club's basement. "Twice, to my knowledge, Peter broke bar stools," Lebowitz said. She recalled an incident when two gallery owners from Paris took him out to discuss showing his work, and it ended with Hujar swinging a bar stool at them. "Trying to break it on people who are trying to further your career—that's Peter," she said.

Of course, he wasn't physically violent as a rule—just impolitic. One night at a party, he was introduced to Cecil Beaton, highly regarded for his photos of everyone from Marilyn Monroe to the queen of England. Beaton said, "I understand that you are a very fine photographer." Hujar replied, "I hear the same about you," and walked away. He took his camera along to another party, where he photographed a few people. The artist Peter Max was there and kept asking to be photographed. Max was of no interest to Hujar, who ignored him until Max finally said, I'll give you one of my pictures. This probably occurred in the early seventies when Max's psychedelic graphics were ubiquitous, even appearing on the New York City phone book. Hujar told Max he did not need one of his pictures since he had a phone book.

Hujar's ideas about art, in particular, were not flexible. He would announce, for example, that Rudolf Nureyev was not a dancer in his soul, but Eleanor Powell—*she* was a dancer in her soul. This he considered inarguable.

"He was always on the lookout for someone that he thought of as a genuine artist," Turtell said. Only a small group qualified, in Hujar's opinion. For example, he greatly admired Ethyl Eichelberger—who had once been James Roy Eichelberger, who had once been the lead character actor at Trinity Repertory Company, who had once been on track for a successful conventional acting career, but gave it all up to join the Ridiculous Theatrical Company and later to play "the great women of history" in assorted downtown dives. Ethyl had decided: This is my path, and there's no questioning it. That's what got Hujar's attention.

During the time he was preparing *Portraits in Life and Death*, he usually went to Turtell's place for Sunday brunch. "He would make lists of who was going into the book on my breakfast table," said Turtell, who was very close to Hujar in the seventies. They were never lovers, but "the kind of friends who could listen to each other breathe on the phone." For this project, Hujar wanted people with "a certain kind of isolation built into their personalities," Turtell said, people whose art came out of that profound isolation. As Hujar's did. "Peter had a kind of fundamental isolation that he could never escape. And he knew it. It was the source of his suffering. It was also the source of his art and his insight." *Portraits in Life and Death* is now a collector's item, but it found its way to the remainder bins during Hujar's lifetime.

He had disdain for the whole process of selling himself. Fran Lebowitz pointed out that he also had a profound distrust of authority and that "he couldn't make a distinction between someone who owned some little photography gallery and the Pope." In the seventies, Hujar had two solo shows at Marcuse Pfeifer's gallery, at the time one of the few galleries devoted to photography. She also put him in a group show. This was the most attention he ever received from a gallery during his lifetime, and he chose to leave it. "It was not easy to sell his work," Pfeifer said, though he had a few savvy collectors including Avedon. He seemed bent on self-sabotage. Pfeifer once accompanied him to the Port Washington Library, where he was supposed to talk about his work (probably the only time in his career he was invited to do so), and he hadn't prepared anything. He got up and had no idea what to say. He left Pfeifer to show at the Robert Samuels Gallery but had some sort of blowup there. Aletti heard a story about Hujar breaking a frame and walking out in a huff. He did not have another show in New York until David persuaded his own dealer, Gracie Mansion, to take him on in 1986 for what proved to be the last exhibit he would have before he died.

But then, Hujar always sensed that he'd be better known after he was dead. He was also enough of a snob to claim that he didn't want his name bandied about by people who didn't really know what he'd achieved. He liked to tell stories about "the real one." As in, "Forget Marlene Dietrich. Greta Keller taught Dietrich everything she knew. You have to listen to Greta Keller." He saw himself as a "real one," and he was willing to sacrifice everything to be that.

"In the long run, Peter got exactly what he wanted," Turtell said. "He once said to me, 'I want to be discussed in hushed tones. When people talk about me, I want them to be whispering, *"Peter Hujar."*'"

Hujar once invited the London-based drag troupe Bloolips to pose. This was in 1980, while they were in New York performing *Lust in Space*. They went dolled up but only in street makeup. (They often wore whiteface and glitter onstage.) The Bloolips spent hours at the loft but Hujar decided it just wasn't working. "We couldn't 'reveal,'" said ex-Bloolip Bette Bourne. "As an actor, you have to reveal. And Hujar's big thing was that you had to re-veal. I know that now, but I didn't know it at the time. In other words, blistering, blazing honesty directed towards the lens. No pissing about. No posing. No putting anything on. No camping around. Just flat, real who-you-are. And then he could go inside. That's what the actor tries to do as well. You must strip down all the nonsense until you get to the bone. That's what Peter wanted and that was his great, great talent and skill."

Hujar loved drag and photographed many a queen, usually with great success. He was able to show that drag isn't just a man in a dress, that drag isn't about artifice—it's about identity, and the clothing is part of it. That's clear in one of Hujar's masterpieces, *Candy Darling on Her Deathbed*. Pho-tographed just a few days before she died in 1974, Candy is lying there in full regalia with the long-stemmed rose Hujar had brought her, and she's so glamorous, so "flat, real who-you-are," that it isn't apparent at first glance that she's in a hospital bed.

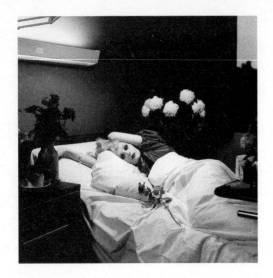

*A Hujar masterpiece:* Candy Darling on her Death Bed, *1973. Vintage gelatin-silver print, 14 × 14 inches. (© 1987 Peter Hujar Archive, LLC. Courtesy Matthew Marks Gallery, New York)*

Hujar had developed his ideas about portraiture by looking at classical paintings, in which the sitter simply looks at the painter. Many of his photos were composed that way, though sometimes the person was doing some physical activity or pose. Gary Schneider, who posed for Hujar naked with his legs over his shoulders, analyzed the technique as Hujar "waiting for the person to come to him and him just being very present." Hujar was looking for genuine connection. "Everybody thought they were his best friend," Schneider said, "so all of a sudden you were inside his camera with him. For me that was a major moment. Very sexual, very sensual, and very intimate. And I think that's why he got those portraits that feel like he's in some kind of really private space."

Schneider was a photographer himself, and—through Hujar—got a job at a major photo lab serving the fashion industry. Schneider regarded Hujar as his teacher, because this man who could become so tongue-tied when discussing his own work could actually articulate things that were much more esoteric. "He taught me how to locate the meaning of the image and how to manipulate the print, in the darkroom, to tell that story," said Schneider. "He could explain how the bright and dark areas of the print guide the eye."

Schneider turned out to be very gifted. From '79 on, he processed all of Hujar's film, though Hujar never paid him. (He gave him photos in exchange.) When Hujar was shooting on the street, Schneider would go with him and be the eyes in the back of his head. Then when Hujar went to the darkroom, he'd make a print and correct, correct, correct, until he'd overcorrect and emerge with seven prints, and Schneider would help him choose the right one. "That's how I learned to see," Schneider said.

In 1981, Hujar convinced Schneider and his partner, John Erdman, to open their own lab—with Schneider in the darkroom and Erdman doing everything else. Schneider and Erdman were among the few friends of Hujar's who also became friends of David's, and eventually Schneider began printing David's work. But threads of the lab story are relevant to the larger story of Hujar's influence. Or, as Erdman said, "Hujar would decide what you should do—and it's amazing how far you would go to live out what he thought you should do."

Schneider and Erdman had just set up shop in their St. Mark's Place apartment, a ten-by-ten room, when they were approached to print Lisette Model's work. She was a master of street photography with work in major collections all over the world. Hujar was the one who got excited, while Schneider worried that he wasn't equipped to do it. "Peter always had a grand plan," Schneider said. "He wanted me to learn how to print her prints because she was this grand master. He pushed me to do it." As it turned out, Model loved Schneider's work, and he printed her photos for the rest of her life.

The lab grew fast, and they soon moved to a larger space on Cooper Square, which Hujar helped them set up. But Erdman had begun to sour on the friendship—and he'd known Hujar since 1969. "He made us open this lab. He was like a Svengali with Gary, and I just knew it wasn't right for us. We weren't businessmen. We came out of the art world," said Erdman, who had been a performer with Richard Foreman, Yvonne Rainer, and Robert Wilson. "We started to lose money right away." This despite the fact that they were soon printing for Avedon, Irving Penn, Francesco Scavullo, the André Kertész estate, a few of the Magnum photographers, and Steven Meisel (specifically, Madonna's *Sex* book). Theirs became *the* lab for black and white, with an international reputation. Schneider too was a master printer, the only other person Hujar would have trusted with his own work.

But Erdman said, "The more successful we became, the more money we lost. It got more and more out of control."

No doubt this is because Schneider approached the work as an artist, not as a technician. "I really believed that no one needed to know how long it took me to make a print," he said, "as long as the print I presented to them was infallible. I never brought an artist in and said, 'Is this good enough?' I never had a print rejected." But they were working seven days a week for long hours—and Schneider went through lots of expensive photo paper to get to those infallible prints.

At one point, they offered to make Hujar a full partner and brought him in to help, since he was desperate for money and they were desperate to make the lab work. Hujar printed for two days. Then Schneider, at work in the next darkroom, heard a loud scream and a crash. Hujar had thrown himself at the door and broken it, then run from the lab. Two days later, he came in to apologize, saying he'd snapped when forced to expend such care making prints for a photographer (well known but no one named above) whose work he thought inferior to his own. Now he understood—the lab enterprise was impossible.

"Too late!" said Erdman.

"But," said Schneider, "I actually love printing. It's the perfect counterpoint to doing my own work. So in the end, I'm grateful to him. Because the lab was really his construct."


One day, Schneider and Erdman ran into Jim Fouratt on the street.

Erdman had first met Fouratt right after Stonewall, during a march down Christopher Street. Back before he was a nightclub impresario, Fouratt had been a founder of the Gay Liberation Front. Erdman hadn't seen him in about ten years, not since Fouratt had broken up with his then-boyfriend Peter Hujar.

He invited Schneider and Erdman to come with him that night to see someone read, a guy he was working with at Danceteria. A busboy with the unpronounceable name of Wojnarowicz.

"Three people were reading," Erdman recalled. "The other two were well known. David was the B-side. And it was like the first time I saw Patti

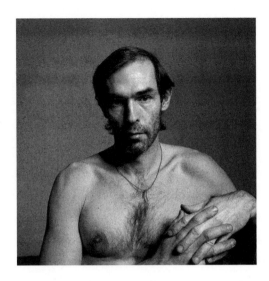

*Hujar took this* Self Portrait (with a string around his neck) *in 1980, not long before he met David. After Hujar's death, David placed this photograph next to his front door so it would be the last thing he saw when leaving home. Pigmented ink print, 20 × 16 inches. (© 1987 Peter Hujar Archive, LLC. Courtesy Matthew Marks Gallery, New York)*

Smith. The performance was genius. The words were genius. I really thought I knew good performance, and this was A-plus."

David and Hujar had not yet met each other. This reading probably occurred in 1980, but decades later Erdman still remembered that David read a story from his hustling days about going home with a parolee, only to have the police show up so David had to jump out a window. It became one of his monologues: "Boy in Horn & Hardart's on Forty-second Street, New York City."

"I was an instant fan," Erdman said. "Totally hooked. I thought, this guy is unbelievable."

Hujar felt an immediate kinship with anyone who'd come out of an abusive childhood. So he and David had that connection, but not only that. "David's story and his range of emotions and intelligence were fascinating to Peter," said Vince Aletti. "He was not somebody that Peter could just move past. I sensed from Peter that he had found somebody, that if the lover part didn't work out, that was OK, because there was something much more important there. And it was rare to get that sense from Peter."

David had not made a good first impression on Aletti, however. "There was always a certain feeling of jealousy of the new boyfriend. Like, why couldn't it be me? Which I think a lot of Peter's friends secretly felt," Aletti said. "But I remember thinking that David was not very good-looking, that he was kind of gawky and not particularly interesting—or verbal. I'm sure I wasn't in the best frame of mind to meet him at that point. But—it's funny. As soon as I saw Peter's photos of him, I realized what Peter saw in him. Then I could see how sexy he was. It was like seeing him through Peter's eyes in those pictures, and suddenly I thought, oh my god, this guy is amazing. And I basically just got over myself because Peter was so taken with him, and clearly there was something very solid there."

Stephen Koch said that Hujar had a strong talent detector. "He knew that David was the real thing—and in Peter's opinion, a big talent that needed development and guidance." That, along with the fact that David was a hurt child. "Those two things were just an irresistible combination," Koch said. "There was going to be art coming out of this. Peter's gathering sense of being somewhat dead-ended would be relieved by David carrying on." Koch thought that Hujar was in love with David and would have liked the sexual relationship to continue, but "he adjusted, moving into the paternal role, and when he found the paternal role, it actually was very fulfilling for them both." Indeed, David seemed to reinspire Hujar, who became very productive in the eighties before he fell ill.

One night Hujar took Schneider with him to see 3 Teens Kill 4. "I have no recollection of the music at all, but there David was and Peter was fixated," Schneider remembered.

"Almost from the beginning," said Erdman, "you could see David's lovingness to Peter, and you could see that he was infatuated with Peter as a person, but you could feel the un-sexual nature of it on his side. As for Peter, it never wavered. He was constantly interested. And it never got ugly. That was clearly not what was meant to be. He just adored David. Just adored him."

One night, Schneider and Erdman went to Hujar's place for dinner.

And he showed them some doodle David had done. Schneider remembered it as a drawing on the door. Erdman remembered a piece of paper. Neither of them could remember what David had actually drawn.

"Peter thought it was just utter genius," Schneider said.

Erdman said that whatever it was, he didn't remember liking it. "But Peter said to us, 'David left it, and I have told him he has to become a visual artist.'"

# 10 A UNION OF DIFFERENT DRUMMERS

**In June 1981,** David went to an event called Noisefest to hear Y Pants or maybe Sonic Youth, and there he met Kiki Smith. They instantly became best friends, often meeting for breakfast, and talking on the phone two or three times a day. David did not live long enough to see the international acclaim ultimately accorded to Kiki Smith. When they met, she'd had work in groundbreaking exhibitions like the "Times Square Show" and "New York/New Wave," but she didn't yet have a gallery. She was working as an electrician's assistant.

David told Kiki that he was painting in an abandoned pier off Spring Street and offered to take her to see it. They didn't go that night, but soon after. She remembered seeing a large painting of a boomerang and a large bird. This was a full two years before the Ward Line Pier Project "opened," only to be instantly shut down by the police. Brian Butterick remembered, however, that back when he and David were still working at Danceteria, David told him he'd just discovered a new pier. Susan Gauthier recalled that David invited her to see it while he was living with her, but she declined.

Chuck Nanney visited the pier early on. He hadn't seen David since the Danceteria bust, but one day they ran into each other at the sex pier. David brought Nanney down to the Ward Line Pier. There wasn't much work there at the time. He remembered seeing some Krazy Kats that David had done. And he saw Kiki's piece. She'd chosen a small room with holes in the ceiling where the plaster had all fallen down, "so it was like walking on icebergs," as she put it. Light coming through the holes made "perfect circles on the floor" that she outlined with paint. Once a day, the light and the paint would align. So—a conceptual piece.

David had picked the Ward Line Pier (a.k.a. Pier 34) because it wasn't a cruising ground. At least, not during the day. And he could be alone. One day he'd watched a huge dog run the football-field length of the main room, toward New Jersey, and he'd followed the animal but never found it, so he began to think the place magical. He'd also investigated Pier 28, just a bit farther south,* and discovered thousands of cardboard cartons filled with files from—he thought—the city prison system. "Psychological profiles of prisoners, documentation from murder scenes, surveillance photographs, court transcripts," he told me. "It was all from the fifties, and that material was so heavy visually that my reaction was not to touch it." But he went through some of the material with Kiki. She remembered this trove as "a one-and-half-story mountain of people's information." It included psychological tests administered by the Psychiatric Clinic of the Court of General Sessions, in which offenders had been compelled to draw both a man and a woman. David and Kiki took many of these drawings.

They planned to silk-screen them onto fine paper and poster them in the streets. They even got a grant to pay for the materials. "I think we sort of lost interest in it halfway through," she said. They never did paste them up in the streets, but did make some prints. And Kiki taught David how to silk-screen.

Years later, many who were part of the scene would recall the day they read a one-column article in the *New York Times* headlined "Rare Cancer Seen in 41 Homosexuals." It appeared on July 3, 1981. Photographer Nan Goldin's recollection has always seemed especially poignant. Still a couple of years away from meeting David, Nan was on Fire Island with a gaggle of friends, including Cookie Mueller, a "queen" of downtown—writer, wild woman, and actress in early John Waters films. Cookie read the article out loud, and, said Nan, "We all kind of laughed."

"Gay" cancer? The second paragraph carried the reassuring news that "there is as yet no evidence of contagion."

This news story was pegged to a report from the Centers for Disease Control released on July 4: "Kaposi's Sarcoma and *Pneumocystis* Pneumonia Among Homosexual Men—New York City and California." News reports

---

* Pier 34 was at Canal Street. Pier 28 would have been the one near Spring Street.

were focusing on KS, the rare cancer that manifested in purple lesions. Most of these patients had severe defects in their immune systems. But how could that cause cancer? Doctors didn't know, but a CDC spokesman said there was no apparent danger to nonhomosexuals. One theory already floating was that the illness had been caused by poppers—amyl nitrite, a drug used to enhance sexual pleasure.

At the time the "gay cancer" article appeared, David was again between homes. He'd moved out of 159 Second Avenue at the end of June '81 with no place to go, though Susan Gauthier insists she wouldn't have let him leave had she known that.

He was in the midst of recording songs with the band. He was bursting with ideas. But now he spent a lot of time just walking around, dropping dimes in phone booths trying to find a place to stay for a night. As he wrote to Jean Pierre, "I wish I could find the way to stop feeling that time is running away."

JP sent more francs. And David considered selling his camera. All this as Foto Gallery let him know, mid-June, that not only would his photograph be exhibited but that he was also one of its ten prize winners. By mid-July, however, he still hadn't gone to the gallery to see what he'd won. He was afraid the dealer would make him pay for framing the picture.

He had the camera with him the July day that he broke into the abandoned sixteen-story Christodora building, a former settlement house on Avenue B. His old buddy, John Hall, had already been in there a couple of times. He showed David how you could get out onto the roof at the Charas/El Bohio building on Ninth Street and then crawl through a window into the Christodora. They explored. Walls were crumbling and sand had accumulated on some of the steps. Downstairs they found a big swimming pool full of black water, with stuff floating in it. In the vandalized library, books and papers covered the floor. In the theater space, they took their clothes off and posed in a decrepit corner—David seated, John standing. David would later embed three copies of this photo in a painting called *Fuck You Faggot Fucker* (along with one of Brian posing as St. Sebastian). David also photographed Hall wielding a club in a broken-down bathroom (clothed) and standing on what seems to be a balcony (naked).

They were in the library, clothed and looking out a window onto Avenue B, when a truck pulled up and someone proceeded to unweld the front door. A man Hall described as a "power yuppie" came upstairs and found them. "We said something like, 'Ah, we're just looking. We'll be out of here soon,'" he remembered. The yuppie remained calm. He didn't ask how they'd gotten in, or how they'd get out. When he left, he welded the front door shut again.

That July the East Village gallery scene very quietly began.

Patti Astor, still months away from filming *Wild Style*, had a day job working for her friend Bill Stelling at his roommate-referral service. One day Stelling asked Astor if she knew of any artists who might want to show at the tiny storefront (eight feet by twenty-five feet) he was using as a textile studio. She did. Astor had already met some of the graffiti artists she'd be working with on *Wild Style*. That summer she threw an "Art Opening Barbeque" at her apartment on East Third Street across from the men's shelter, and Futura 2000 spray-painted a mural on her wall. "The entire art world showed up!" she would later declare. If not exactly "entire," the party did include future big names like Jeffrey Deitch, Keith Haring, Fab 5 Freddy, and Kenny Scharf—who customized her kitchen appliances during the party by gluing little figures to them.

For the first show in Stelling's space at 229 East Eleventh Street, however, Astor recommended her ex-husband Steven Kramer. She did not plan to involve herself; she knew nothing about selling art. So Stelling ran the gallery for the first month with another friend. They put up twenty Kramer drawings at fifty dollars each, and sold them all. Astor decided to participate in the second show, in September, which went to Scharf, then a recent School of Visual Arts graduate.

Astor may have known little about the business of art, but like some of the others running the first East Village galleries, she was an artist at heart—and she knew how to get a party started, how to create a sense of permission and play. She decided that each artist should get a chance to choose a new name for the tiny space and to completely change the decor. So it was Scharf who dubbed the space Fun Gallery that September. There he introduced his mutant Hanna-Barbera characters to a world that wasn't quite ready for them. He sold just one, for fifty dollars.

When Fab 5 Freddy Brathwaite got the next show, he thought about renaming the place Serious Gallery. That's when Astor realized she'd have to change her stationery every month. So the name remained Fun, but Astor stuck with her idea of letting each artist do whatever he or she wanted with the space—a policy that continued when they moved a year later into more square footage at 254 East Tenth Street. Jean-Michel Basquiat, for example, chopped the space up with half-constructed walls. Scharf did a black light installation for his second (rapturously received) show. Haring and his partner LA2 painted their trademark squiggles over everything in the gallery, including Astor's outfit, and even the snow outside.

After bouncing around for six weeks, going home with tricks or crashing with friends, David moved in with Tom Cochran, "the manager of our band," as he described him in a letter to Jean Pierre. Cochran had broken up with Julie Hair and moved to an apartment upstairs in her building at 36 East Fourth, near the Bowery. It had the same floor plan as Hair's tiny railroad flat, a classic tub-in-the-kitchen arrangement. In rooms on either side of the kitchen, Cochran and David each had a loft bed. The whole thing was about 325 roach-infested square feet. They shared a toilet in the hall with the occupants of another apartment. David would live in this bolthole for nearly four years.

He let JP know that he did not have enough money to come to France. He also told him, by way of reassurance, that he had a private part of himself that few would understand—but that was the part he could share with JP. Jean Pierre sent a rather anguished letter in September, one of the few from him that David kept, confessing his disappointment and his nervousness about the state of their relationship. David still felt that he loved JP. "To be honest with you," he wrote, "I sometimes meet people that I like very much, but I never meet any person with your qualities." He hoped to come to Paris that winter. But the eight days they'd spent together in New York that March would be the extent of their contact for 1981. JP had met Hujar during that March visit. 'I felt something between them," he recalled. He'd worried then that his relationship with David was in danger because of Hujar—though he did not express this to David.

In the last substantial piece of journal writing he would do for years, David wrote on September 1 about meeting a fella at Stuyvesant Park. There he'd run into Hujar, who was also cruising. "I sat next to him and we talked for a few minutes. One night when he was feeling down, we'd gone into the west park and built a little fire like scouts on one of the walkways feeding it twigs and leaves for about half an hour, laughing while other guys in the park stared at us like we were nuts. After awhile we parted. . . . I hadn't planned on meeting anyone but then I saw this young guy."

Whatever distance had grown between David and Jean Pierre at this point was only about . . . distance. And the fact that David's life was changing so quickly he could not articulate it even to himself. In the middle of September 1981, David decided to quit the band. He needed time for his writing, his painting, his photography. Besides, "Brian, Jesse and Julie . . . have a way of seeing the world that is very different from me. Too much cynicism," he wrote to JP. (Doug Bressler had not yet joined.) David informed the band of his decision and reported "some anger." But then he changed his mind. He did not leave the band. Yet.

That October, he got a chance to create a gallery-friendly version of the Castelli "cow bone" action for a group show called "Hunger" at Gallery 345, a space on Lafayette Street near SoHo that specialized in political art. He asked Hair to collaborate.

On the street, they found a wooden chair and a wooden crate the size of a smallish refrigerator. They painted the crate black and set it on end so it would open fridge-style. In homage to Robert Indiana's *EAT/DIE* diptych, they painted "EAT" on one side of its door and "DIE" on the other—adding stencils of planes, burning houses, and a large falling man. Inside they placed a large transparent bag of cow bones and a stereo.

They intended this to be an interactive installation, with a visitor wearing headphones while seated on the wooden chair they'd painted and stenciled. Hair couldn't remember what the visitor was supposed to hear on the headphones. Most likely it was one of David's tape collages, with bits recorded on the street or from the radio, but 3 Teens did have a song called "Hunger." *We are all essential laborers . . .*

David did not meet as many kindred souls at Peppermint Lounge, "the Pep," as he had at Danceteria. But a bartender he bussed for, Sophie Breer, became a friend. He worked two nights a week for minimum wage, so he was dependent on the bartenders for tips. She gave him hundreds a night. When punk icon Johnny Rotten hassled Breer one night, standing on her shoe and not letting her move, David came up and threw a drink in his face. Other nights he'd do things to amuse her. He would make mice out of napkins and lemons. Once he brought in a cock-a-bunny and let the costumed roach out of its jar at three in the morning. "This little 'rabbit' running down the bar," he recalled. "The ears make them top-heavy, so they learn to obey the edges of the table." His cock-a-bunnies were creepy-cute, a riveting combination. Breer decided she wanted to film David making them.

One weekend in November 1981, she rented a Betamax, which she didn't exactly know how to use. "I did cocaine and drank and shot skits all weekend long. I have forty-eight hours of mostly crap, but it was fun. Remember, I was twenty-one years old." She'd asked David to come over Sunday morning with "supplies." She had decided on a *Romper Room* approach. David—with his rounded scissors, Q-tips, rubber cement, and a jar with six or eight cockroaches—obliged her with a kindergarten-style presentation, cutting tiny ears from a piece of paper, pulling the cotton end off a Q-tip for a tail, and applying these accoutrements to a reluctant roach he named "Benny." The roach spent some time running around on David's arm before acquiring his ears and tail. David remained deadpan throughout. "Oops, I glued his back legs together."

"Are you trying to take the 's' out of 'pest'?" Breer asked him. She filmed it with "the camera flying all over . . . trails of light. . . . I didn't know how to zoom." But she ended up with a thirteen-minute video piece, *Waje's Cockabunnies*. At the end, David got out the piece of pie he'd brought along, to show that you could easily pick a roach off your slice if you'd given it rabbit ears. He then induced Benny to check into a roach motel.

Back at the Pep, Breer secured a bartending job for her then-boyfriend, Tommy Turner—later one of the directors in the Cinema of Transgression. He and David bonded. Turner was a physically beautiful guy with an affinity for the dark side, obsessed with black magic, medical deformities, murder, and taxidermy. He wasn't a freak, Breer said, just someone who was truly curious. He'd trained as a geneticist. David called him "one of the sweetest heterosexual guys I've ever come in contact with." David had taken Tommy Turner and Sophie Breer ("in my eighties spandex") to the meat-packing district after work one night to scout for cow bones. She didn't recall them finding any. But usually David and Turner went off on adventures by themselves.

They'd leave the club at four or five in the morning and head into Alphabet City to climb the fire escapes of burnt-out tenements. That was the only way into abandoned buildings whose doors had been sealed with cinder blocks or bolted shut with steel. He and Turner explored the hastily abandoned half-melted slum apartments where there'd been arson fires. Sometimes they'd find people sleeping in there. "We'd try to find a stick before we went inside," Turner remembered. Just in case. They witnessed the drug trafficking—one cinder block being pulled back from a door, a hand reaching out for money, then the hand coming back with a small glassine envelope. Turner had not yet become a junkie. Some nights he went along as lookout while David stenciled. One weekend, he and David decided to go to "the country," by which they meant Roosevelt Island and the weeds and trees surrounding the abandoned insane asylum. They entered the broken buildings there to photograph what David called "weird discards of civilization."

David also met two friends of Turner's when they came to hang out at the Pep. One was Richard Kern, who hadn't yet begun to make the violent exploitative films that would bring him a kind of underground fame. David thought Kern a "sexy apparition . . . a dark-haired guy with a corruptible face." Was he straight? David asked Turner, who snickered, "Why don't you find out?" The other friend was Montana Hewson. (Or "Montanna," as David consistently misspelled his name.) The night Montana first came to the club, wrote David, he was wearing a white T-shirt "awash with perspiration and floor grime." He was skinny, with a turkey neck, a hawk head, a jutting chin, and "a las vegas card shark's smile." Montana was an artist David thought multitalented. He was a gay man who fell for straight men like Kern. He was self-conscious about being unattractive. And he was committed to self-destruction. Montana would prove to be the ultimate outcast in David's whole history of interest in outcasts. But that story comes later.

In January 1982, "gay cancer" was renamed GRID, for "gay-related immune deficiency." On the 12th of that month, writer Larry Kramer met with five other men at his apartment to form Gay Men's Health Crisis.

David knew one person who would be diagnosed that year with GRID—Iolo Carew from Danceteria. Years later, David couldn't remember ever hearing much about GRID, this "vague thing that was affecting twenty-some people." And he really liked Iolo, who he felt was being shunned. So he went home with Iolo one night and had sex with him. Telling me all this in 1990, David added that what they did "could only be described as safe sex." But that was all intuitive, he said. "There were no guidelines. So I did that that one night, and then I went back to having unsafe sex."

No one was using the term "safe sex" in 1982. And "no guidelines" hardly describes it—but by 1990 who could remember how ignorant we'd all been just a few years earlier. During the seven months that this disease was called GRID, scientists at the CDC were telling reporters that there was no evidence that this was an infectious disease, and that its sexual transmission was mere hypothesis.

David and his roommate Tom Cochran lived in the rear of their Fourth Street building, and David had the room with the window, ten or fifteen feet from the back of the firehouse on Great Jones Street. Cochran would sometimes come home to find all the lights out and David standing at the window with friends. Maybe Hujar. Maybe Brian or Jesse. They'd be watching the firemen take showers. Cochran seemed to find that amusing. He was straight, of course, but sexuality didn't become an issue. They'd made a "no sex in the apartment" rule. The only tension that came up was over fumes from the spray paint David was using to make his stencil pieces. It would drive Cochran out for a walk with his dog.

In January 1982, David answered an open call at Public Illumination Gallery for artwork that measured ten by ten inches. He submitted a stencil piece with a burning house at the center for "100 Works, 100 Artists, 100 Sq. In," which the gallery accepted and then sold for one hundred dollars.

David knew he had to find studio space. He often went to the White Wave coffee shop on Second Avenue for breakfast, and there he became friends with the woman who would wait on him, Jan Mohlman. When she found a storefront studio on Houston near Eldridge, she asked David to share it. "I had a kind of fluke brief art career," said Mohlman. Meaning, she did an album cover for the Bush Tetras and it ended up in *Artforum*, which led to her inclusion in a few shows. She painted, then started working with mosaics, and she did backdrops for Bush Tetras gigs. But she did not take her art making very seriously. Even so, she liked hanging out at the studio and offered to pay two-thirds of the three-hundred-dollar rent.

Mohlman, who went on to teach psychology at the university level, observed that David had intense one-on-one relationships, and many people felt close to him, including her. "We were in some ways like a couple. We could spend such amazing time together. I really felt like he was one of the people in my life who loved me unconditionally." Some years later, David reminisced in a journal entry about his friendship with her: "I was working as a busboy in clubs and felt like the alien among a species of people I couldn't understand—it was also a time of intense relationship with Peter. Jan gave me my first bike in years, an old sturdy delivery bike from the 40s or 50s—15 dollars from some thief she ran into and we took late night rides to Staten Island among the darkened hills and homes and Wall Street plazas Dubuffets mushrooms circling til dizzy around the fountains at World Trade Center til the crabby guards came screaming at us to stop we rode around anyways."

Sometimes Hujar would drop by the studio. He and David were so intensely bonded, Mohlman said, "they rarely had to use spoken language. They just seemed to communicate so much with silence and proximity. Peter would come down and look at the artwork in the storefront and he would just stand there in silence and study it."

She remembered David working with stencils. "I started to see the soldier motif. The camouflage motif. The science-project paintings with the antigravity theme." (All three appear, for example, in *Science Lesson*, with its large and small floating bodies.) And he'd begun to paint on found objects like maps and trash can lids. Mohlman also remembered him talking about work he was doing in some abandoned pier, but she never went to see it.

Marisela La Grave was a student at the International Center for Photography in 1982. Assigned to document a site of her choosing for her class on color, she was halfway through the semester and still hadn't found a place. She kept going back to the Hudson and walking the waterfront. One day, probably in March, near Canal Street, she noticed something through a broken window on Pier 34. "There was a figure painted on the wall. A big-scale figure that touched wall and ceiling, and then there was more than one, and then as I started getting close and breaking into the fence and breaking into the pier, I realized that I had found paradise."

No one else was there. La Grave had no idea who'd put the art on the walls, but she'd found her site. She came back with photo equipment and began documenting the work. She was in one of the smaller rooms when she heard voices and picked up her tripod to use as a weapon. In walked David Wojnarowicz and the painter Luis Frangella, going, "Hey. What's up?" La Grave may have been the first of the many photographers who would eventually document Pier 34 (the Ward Line Pier). David and Luis squired her around through the other crumbling rooms to show her everything they were working on.

They also took her farther south to Pier 28. "That was a very difficult pier to trespass because the floor was collapsing," La Grave said. Pier 28 was also the location of the documents David and Kiki had plundered. La Grave called it "very officelike. Mostly just paper and boxes." David would continue to work there alone after the art world discovered Pier 34.

Jane Bauman, one of the artists who'd gone stenciling with David, remembered visiting the pier during this phase with David and Luis. "The

*David leaping in front of an early piece at Pier 28, south of the Ward Line Pier and never as public. (Photograph by Marion Scemama)*

three of us would go down to the pier and sometimes we'd work on each other's pieces, but in a playful way. That was the most playful I ever, *ever* saw David. He was so comfortable in that milieu, so relaxed. Serious but childlike. Not 'childish' but 'childlike.' It was his Disneyland. Going into all the different rooms—it's like, This is Frontierland. There's Tomorrowland. Something really innocent came out when he was working there with Luis. That was some of the prettiest, most alive work that he ever did. It was when he seemed the happiest."

One piece David did was a wall-size color version of the *Rimbaud Masturbating* studies he'd drawn while living in Paris. Next to that was a large face, another early David work. He was learning how to be a painter here. He and Luis did not really collaborate; their styles were too different. But Luis taught him something about how to paint. Luis was an expressionist with a line that was both fluid and confident, and he often worked big, painting with a brush or a roller on the end of a stick. "Luis really understood the scale aspect of working in a public space," said La Grave, who grew close to him. They were both from South America and would go out for drinks and Spanish conversation. She remembered David's admiration for Luis—"for the control that he had of the line and how he managed the proportions and perspective." When David eventually covered a whole wall at the pier with a gagging cow head, "that came out of their relationship," she said. "He was saying, 'OK, watch me do a bigger scale.'"

For a while, the gagging cow was a Wojnarowicz trademark. He explained it as a cow "exploding with fear." It was a cow going to slaughter. Back in the East Village very late one night, Tommy Turner watched as David spray-painted one big enough to cover the entire intersection of Second Avenue and Twelfth Street. So Hujar could see it from his window. Another night, possibly in a different year, Chuck Nanney watched as David spray-painted not a gagging cow, but "a friendly cow," as Nanney put it, in that same intersection. This cow had a thought bubble, and in that bubble, a hamburger. David cracked up as he drew it, as he thought about Hujar looking out his window in the morning and spotting the joke. He painted at least one more "friendly cow" there, this one thinking of a television. That one he wrote about in a short piece "for Sophie," where he first talked about cruising Stuyvesant Park and then about coming down Second Avenue to see "the telly cow head seven feet tall and some boy outside La Bamba"—the bar on the corner—"screaming at me to grow up and get some crayons . . . and don't fuck up the street . . . I walked at him like I was gonna spray-paint a cow on his forehead and he split."

Gracie Mansion's "Loo Division" opened on March 30, 1982. This became the scene's best-known origin story—an exhibit put up around a toilet, a party that turned into a gallery.

Gracie was then Joanne Mayhew-Young, an artist with a job in a commercial SoHo gallery selling prints and posters, but she'd already done other projects that functioned as wry commentary on the way art is presented and sold. One Saturday afternoon, for example, she and her friend Buster Cleveland rented a limo for a few hours, parked it at the corner of West Broadway and Spring, and sold Buster's collages out of the back seat. At the SoHo gallery where she worked, she and her co-worker Sur Rodney Sur took over the

*One of the "friendly cows" David drew for Peter Hujar on the intersection of Second Avenue and Twelfth Street, photographed from Hujar's loft. (Courtesy of P·P·O·W Gallery, New York)*

space behind the windows—space where they stood to change the displays—and hung a friend's art there, clipped to coat hangers. Spectators had to open a door and walk in sideways. It was not visible from the street.

Gracie was then living at 432 East Ninth in a fifth-floor walk-up with a tub in the kitchen, though she had the luxury of a loo actually inside her apartment. There she decided to exhibit "photographic work prints" by her friend Timothy Greathouse. She invented her moniker,* made up letterhead for a nonexistent Gracie Mansion Gallery, and wrote a tongue-in-cheek press release stating that in an age when a single painting could cover "the entire interior of a normal apartment"—and who could afford it anyway—"Gracie's 'less is more' gallery offers private seating . . . allowing the viewer to relate 'head' on with the work." It was a real show but it was also the parody of a show.

But in March 1982, there wasn't an East Village scene to provide context. Fun Gallery hadn't attracted much attention in its first seven months. Gallery 51X opened the same month as the "Loo Division," in Rich Colicchio's

---

* Gracie Mansion is the name of the New York City mayor's residence.

apartment on St. Mark's Place, but flew under the radar. Colicchio worried about zoning, the legalities—and what would happen if he got too much attention.

Gracie avoided such issues by opening the Loo Division for just the one day—and after that, by appointment only. She did not intend, at that point, to ever run a gallery. The "Loo Division," though, posed all the questions that would later be brought up by the East Village scene: Did art have to be so pretentious? So intimidating? So expensive? So huge?

Gracie liked to say that she was created by the media. Her press release caught the eye of Howard Smith at the *Village Voice*, who covered the "Loo" opening and asked her, what's your next show? That's when she decided she'd do another.


Filmmaker Ivan Galietti was another who found himself entranced by the poetic ruin of the sex pier. He'd been born on the island of Capri, near Pompeii, and in the pier's labyrinths and caves, its decay, and its sexually explicit "frescoes," Galietti saw the phallic cults of pagan times. In 1982, the city scheduled the crumbling structure for demolition. (The warehouse finally came down in September 1983.) Keen to preserve it, at least on celluloid, he began filming *Pompeii New York* in early April. The Pyramid Club held a "Save the Pier" benefit to help Galietti raise money.

He didn't want to "shoot voyeuristically from a corner" for a surreptitious documentary. Instead he recruited players from the Bar on Fourth Street and asked them to re-create what they'd done at the pier. David was one who immediately agreed to participate, though he appears only briefly: He'd brought an unidentified friend along; he walked over to this friend and started rubbing his chest. Galietti ended up with about half an hour of edited footage from Pier 46. He had even found a "cruising" passage in Dante's *Inferno* to add to the voice-over.* He kept filming the waterfront over the

---

* "When we were so far from the jungle / That it was completely out of sight, / We encountered those souls / Walking along the pier. / Each of them looked at us / As in the evening men are wont / to stare at one another / under a new moon light, / and sharpened their brow / like the old taylor, / squinting at the needle's eye." From canto XV, stanza 5, in the translation on Galietti's website, http://www.romanhattan.com/film.html.

years, but decades later, *Pompeii New York* was still unfinished, more talked about than seen and thus another legend.

David's moment in the film struck me as purposeful, brisk. But then, he was busy. Galietti filmed him on April 4—the same date that's marked on the master tapes for the first and only 3 Teens Kill 4 album. So he was also working in the recording studio that day. And Jean Pierre was about to arrive for his first visit in more than a year.

JP stayed for two weeks. A few days after he left, David recorded himself, talking into his Walkman. He'd just done some heroin. Because Brian and Jesse were doing it. Because he'd been able to get some at work. Because he'd been told it was weak stuff, and he wanted to experiment. He seemed to be after "disordering the senses" in the spirit of Rimbaud, though he concluded by the end that it hadn't worked. "I don't think this tape really achieved anything in terms of speech or ideas or logic or thought." However, after a slurred and rather incoherent beginning, interrupted by bouts of nausea, he reflected on his life the way he once did in his journal writing. It was a catalog of woe. He felt he'd lost the ability to be happy, to be romantic, to be energized, to dream. He wondered if it had all started when he'd fallen in love with Jean Pierre, then couldn't live with him. And then realized that he was afraid of that—afraid "that loving someone and living with him will ruin me."

He wanted to start writing again, but felt he needed to be "fully alone" to do that, not living with a roommate in a tiny space. He was in turmoil. As he explained on the tape, sometimes he wanted to be by himself and sometimes he loved people so much. Sometimes he wanted to walk out the door, just disappear and start a new life somewhere else. Sometimes he thought he was struggling in a way that would keep him struggling for the rest of his life. Sometimes he talked to the winos in the neighborhood and he could tell that they'd once had abilities to create things that might even exceed his, yet there they were—homeless. Sometimes he thought of his own death but always projected it as way in the future. And then there were times when he thought it could be soon. But he didn't think about death much. "It won't let itself be thought of."

"I didn't really enjoy doing this," he concluded, "taking the junk." He preferred speed. But he continued to experiment with heroin, a drug he romanticized. In Paris in 1978, he'd asked his sister to photograph him "shooting up" in front of the Eiffel Tower. He had tied off an arm with his neck scarf and posed with a BIC pen as the supposed needle.

That spring, the artist Ed Baynard set about curating a show for the SoHo gallery, Alexander Milliken. He wanted painters who were both figurative and expressionistic, like David Salle and Francesco Clemente, mixed with artists then considered graffitists, like Basquiat and Haring. And he kept wondering who'd done the burning house stencil he'd seen all over SoHo and the East Village.

One day he was walking down St. Mark's Place when he saw Peter Hujar seated at an outdoor table at Dojo, a cheap vegetarian restaurant. Baynard and Hujar had known each other for at least twenty years. Baynard explained what he was doing. The group show. The burning house. The artist he couldn't identify.

"I know who it is," Hujar said. He gave Baynard the unfamiliar name.

Baynard asked, "Does he paint?"

"No, not yet," Hujar told him. "But he's thinking about painting."

Baynard then called David, who invited him to the storefront studio on Houston. He said yes to participating—something like, this would give him the impetus to do a painting. He bought a Masonite board and created a diptych around an image of Hujar.

David had photographed Hujar on a couple of occasions—specifically, Hujar lying on his back. These pictures were eerily similar to the very last photos David would ever take of him, moments after Hujar's death. But in 1981, he photographed Hujar lying on the floor of his loft and then, another day, Hujar lying on a boardwalk in a dark shirt, eyes closed. It was this image that David began to incorporate into his first paintings. He made it into a stencil. For this first diptych, *Untitled (Green Head)*, he made two red squares, one made from red brick. In each, Hujar is lying on his back in a blue shirt. In one, he has a green head. In the other, he has a yellow head that's exploded into fragments. Around him David stenciled his military images—running soldiers, planes, a burning house.

*David used this photo of Peter Hujar to create a stencil he then used for* Hujar
Dreaming, *for installations, and for more than a dozen other early paintings.*
*(David Wojnarowicz Papers, Fales Library, NYU)*

"I bought the painting," Baynard said. "But it never occurred to me till
much later how full and resolved this was for a first painting. Totally resolved."

Baynard called his show "Fast." It was one of those group exhibitions
that galleries like to mount in the summer before everyone heads to a
Hampton, but it was more distinguished than most. The eighteen artists included Anselm Kiefer and David Hockney, along with those named above.
Each showed just one piece. Milliken printed a small catalog with an essay
by Susan Putterman, who offered the first critical assessment of David's art:
"Using images of urban terrorism and violence, he constructs a universe
devoid of moral reason. Although flatly and uniformly painted, the fore-
shortened figure [Hujar] creates a sense of anxiety. . . . Wojnarowicz spot-
lights society's inability to adhere to its own structures and confronts the
viewer with a vision of anarchy and insanity."

David created at least fourteen other pieces using this same image of

Hujar, most notably *Peter Hujar Dreaming/Yukio Mishima: St. Sebastian,* one of his signature early works.

Alexander Milliken was intrigued enough to offer David his first solo show. He began working on it that summer.

The same day the "Fast" show opened at Milliken, David had another opening to attend on nearby Lafayette Street.

Public Illumination Gallery had set up its own summer extravaganza, called "411," with four one-week, one-person shows. David was one of the four. "They were all elaborate installations, deliberately over the top," said gallery director Jeffery Isaacs, who was then using the name Zagreus Bowery. ("Bowery" also edited the pocket-size *Public Illumination* magazine.) "The idea was that since people mainly go to openings, we'd do an opening every Friday for a month," he said.

David's show was all stencil work, applied directly to the walls of the tiny storefront. "I lived with my wife in the windowless room behind the gallery," Isaacs said, "and I distinctly remember being not too wild about the spray-paint fumes. He only had a couple of days to do the installation, because of the '411' schedule. I remember him working alone and me having to explain to him that no, he couldn't work overnight, as we had to go to bed. The installation included a cassette player with an audio track playing. I don't remember what."

David's imagery was all aggression and vulnerability. He used running soldiers in three sizes, a small burning house, many small bombers, a figure who holds one bent arm over his head, a large falling man, a rampaging wolf, the prone Hujar. Isaacs said that since it was the last of the four installations, he couldn't resist leaving a small section up in a corner until he vacated the space in autumn 1983.

This was a period when David was taking photos of blindfolded men, and he used one of those images on the flyer he made for this show. Were they facing a firing squad? He never spoke or wrote about what these images meant to him.

*  *  *

(*Courtesy of Jeffrey Isaacs*)

That July, the Centers for Disease Control decided that, with GRID diagnoses coming in at the rate of 2.5 a day, it better start calling the disease an epidemic. Its scientists also had evidence now that GRID could be transmitted by blood. However, the Food and Drug Administration did not want the CDC meddling with the blood industry, which was the FDA's turf. As Randy Shilts explained, "Many at the FDA did not believe that this so-called epidemic of immune suppression even existed." Indeed, the FDA would not license a test allowing blood banks to screen their products until 1985.

In the summer of '82, the CDC was at least able to jettison the GRID acronym—which many there refused to use—when someone came up with acquired immune deficiency syndrome, or AIDS.

David bought his art supplies at the venerable New York Central and got to know one of the clerks there, Dean Savard. "I realized this guy knew just about everything there was to know about paper," David told me. Like how different papers would react to spray paint. And then, David added a bit hesitantly—because Savard was still alive when we spoke—"he was giving art supplies away to anybody he thought was OK. He'd pack up a hundred sheets of paper, tons of paint brushes, and write up a bill for two dollars."

One day when David came to the store, Savard told him he was opening a gallery. So David went over to 526 East Eleventh and had a look. "I just
loved that it was in this little storefront. I liked the energy of him and the
guy he was working with." That was Alan Barrows. Savard was then a
painter, using the storefront as a studio and living in the tiny back room,
where he'd installed a loft bed over the meager kitchen utilities.

Barrows and Savard had met in Philadelphia while Savard was attending the Pennsylvania Academy of Fine Arts and working in an ice cream
store. Barrows was a customer at that store until he decided that working
there, with Savard, would be more fun than waiting tables somewhere else.
They were never lovers. But two months after Savard moved to New York
late in 1980, Barrows and his partner followed.

One night Barrows and Savard went to an opening at Fun, where they
talked to the gallery's co-director, Bill Stelling. This was the first Fun, a
small basement room on Eleventh Street. Barrows thought it "kooky" that
someone had decided "let's just hang things on the wall and have a show."
But Stelling suggested that Barrows and Savard do it too. Why not start a
gallery? Savard had certainly met lots of artists at New York Central. So
they decided, why not. They opened their gallery in May 1982, publicizing
the early shows with flyers made from press type and wheat-pasted onto
buildings or distributed at the Pyramid Club.

Savard came up with the name. He told Barrows that on the way to
work one day, he passed a woman standing on a milk crate, absolutely crazy
and yelling out to no one in particular: "The Russians are coming! They're
going to invade! It's going to be fucking civilian warfare in the streets of
New York!" So, Savard told Barrows, they could call it "fucking civilian warfare." Barrows laughed at this recollection. They ended up calling it Civilian
Warfare Studio, at least while Savard was still living there. "It was a very
amateur beginning," Barrows said. But that too appealed to David, who said
the gallery at first was sort of a goof, but "it felt very comfortable." At that
point, David recalled, Savard didn't have any big illusions about where this
would go. It would be many months before Civilian sold so much as a
poster. Barrows and Savard both kept their day jobs and opened the place
nights and weekends. Once the scene got rolling, however, the gallery

quickly acquired a reputation for showing, as one critic put it, "the rawest, harshest work of quality in the East Village."

On September 15, 1982, Civilian Warfare Studio opened "Hit and Run Art," its "third group show," featuring Bronson Eden, Dean Savard, and David Wojnarowicz. This may have been the last time Savard showed his own work. He quickly figured out that he was better at dealing. Eden designed a computer game called "Suzi Head Goes to War," which ran on a monitor in the window. The game got such a reaction, Eden said, "That convinced Dean to make me a regular." David told me that he showed *Science Lesson*, specifically because it was so large—almost fourteen feet long and eight feet tall. He'd had to "work on it in sections and flop it" at the Houston Street studio. Once they installed the piece in Savard's storefront, David said, "Your face was almost in the painting, so it was kind of hilarious. It was like a joke for us."

Eden worked with Savard at New York Central. He'd dropped out of sight while going through a divorce and thought his art career was over. Then he met Savard. "Within two years I was showing in Europe. Dean changed my life. But—he was also a heroin addict, a real pirate. It was a lifestyle. He used to wear these big, bulky overcoats so he could carry stuff out [of the store]. That's how he paid for his heroin addiction, and he also used it to grease his way through the art world in the early days. Gave away a lot of free art supplies to people.

"For me," Eden said, "the East Village—a lot of it was about Dean Savard. I remember an opening in maybe '84 when the scene was really hot, and he just looked like an angel. Like something from another planet. He was wearing mascara, a jacket with no shirt, and he had this white hair that stuck out in all directions. He was just so charismatic and so smart. He was like a nova. He was incandescent. But he was much more influential in the early years. Later on he made some pretty bad mistakes. He screwed up. And then he died."

The September 1982 issue of *Arts* magazine carried the first art world acknowledgment that something was stirring in the East Village: an article by Nicolas Moufarrege titled "Another Wave, Still More Savagely than the First."

His thesis: What rock musicians had been to the sixties, artists would be to the eighties. In the East Village, Moufarrege saw signs of art with "mass appeal," more entertaining, more understandable, more relevant. We were done now with seventies "severity," all that minimalism and conceptualism. "Everything is moving so much faster: waves, volcanic eruptions, high voltage currents. Boomtown, a pulsing heart within the metropolis, the East Village, Manhattan, where different drummers unite in a Zeitgeist despite their varying and very personal rhythms. The need to communicate is overwhelming; in more important ways than literally, the boundaries of art have gone beyond the stretcher and the canvas." By now there were six spaces to cite: Nature Morte, East Seventh Street Gallery, and Life (which would soon become Life Café), along with Fun, 51X, and Gracie's "Loo." (Civilian Warfare was still off the grid, a "studio" and not yet a gallery.)

Moufarrege came from Beirut by way of Paris, stopping at Harvard for a master's degree in chemistry before moving to the East Village. He was the scene's excited first champion—and an idiosyncratic artist in his own right. He painted on needlepoint canvas and did large embroideries that recycled and recombined imagery, from Picasso to Spider-Man, in thread. His "Another Wave" article contains what could be his manifesto. Or it could be David's. Or it could belong to many of the other artists from this scene, at least in the early days:

> I want to draw. I want to paint. I have something to say, to everyone and as many as I possibly can. I am doing it on the streets, I am doing it in my room, I am doing it underground. I am doing it on the trains, on the billboards, in the mail. The palaces are full. But new ones are being built: in the nightclubs and in the bathrooms. I will work with and on whatever I can lay my hands on. I will carve on a tree or on a rock. I will use paint, chalk, or any stick that leaves a mark. I will draw pictures and color them. I will write words, in my language and in yours. I will build toys. I will make sounds and instruments that make sounds. I will rap and I will sing and I will dance to it all. I want you to know my name. I want you to know my sign.

# 11 RAMPAGES OF RAW ENERGY

**By 1982, P.S. 1** was recognized internationally as the most prestigious venue to emerge from the "alternative space" movement. The former elementary school in Long Island City, Queens, had enough room to house both adventurous exhibitions and artists' studios. The "New York/New Wave" show there in 1981 had rocked the art world by showcasing a bit of the raw creativity then emerging from various "downtown" clubs and streets; jaws had dropped before the paintings of Jean-Michel Basquiat.

When a curator from P.S. 1 visited David's studio in 1982, he was selecting work for an upcoming show on animal imagery. Given how little David had shown at that point, and how little of that was about animals, it's amazing that he even got a studio visit. But David felt he belonged in "The Beast Show." When he wasn't chosen, he was pissed.

On October 17, David went to the opening at P.S. 1 with Hujar. He'd spent the morning at Tommy Turner's apartment, making about thirty cock-a-bunnies, which he carried to Queens in a plastic can with holes in the lid, stashed in his shoulder bag. He walked into the exhibit pulling out a few "bunnies" at a time, dropping them amid the Warhols and Clementes. One artist had made "a sculptural city," as David described it. "I remember dropping a handful on that, so cock-a-bunnies were running through this city," he said. "I dropped them on sculptures and pedestals. I dropped some in the administration office on the secretaries' tables. Eventually someone would notice. They'd see this microscopic rabbit running, and it created all this commotion." Guards began chasing them down while David went to see Moufarrege, who had a P.S. 1 studio. Moufarrege and Hujar were old friends. And Chuck Nanney was Moufarrege's boyfriend. Nanney remembered David walking into the studio and depositing his last two cock-a-bunnies on a table, saying, "Check this out." From then on, he included this contribution to "The Beast Show" (an "action installation") on his résumé. David had an adversarial relationship with the art world, even as it opened its doors to him.

That month David curated a show himself, at an East Village cafe called Lucky Strike. Artist Jean Foos—whose cool abstractions never fit the scene's prevailing style—said that David told her, "Bring a big painting!" Foos ended up in a couple of what she called David's "free for all" shows, including the biggest and best of them: the Ward Line Pier Project. There was a part of David that longed to be a protector and provider, and he constantly promoted the work of his artist friends. He never wanted to make a studio visit. He just told them, "Bring something!"

He brought his collaborations with Kiki Smith into his first solo show at Civilian Warfare and got her into the group show "Climbing: the East Village" at Hal Bromm. Among his papers, I found a photocopy of a piece they'd done together—David's footprint, David's image of a tornado and Kiki's childhood story about buying her classmates' souls. Kiki couldn't remember if they created the piece for a specific show. "But he did a lot of things like that where he somehow included me in his access to the universe," she said. "I was one of the people he tried to take along with him."

Gracie Mansion had had two more Loo Division shows—E. F. Higgins III on May 4 and Stephen Lack on June 16. When the *New York Post* picked up on her press release for the latter and ran a blurb on Page Six, a mob showed up for the opening. People were lined up down the stairs of her apartment building and out onto the street. "There were even people on the roof. My landlord flipped out." That was it for the Loo Division.

Gracie decided to make some real money—as a cocktail waitress in a bar on St. Mark's. She called in sick to the SoHo gallery for a few days, long enough to realize that she was "absolutely unqualified to be a barmaid." But when she quit, the bar owner offered to give her the space upstairs for a gallery, rent-free for a month if she fixed it up. "I was young and stupid and thought that was a really great deal," she said. The space upstairs was a beauty parlor turned storage space. She'd have to move all the hoardings and take down the mirrors that still lined the walls. Gracie

*The opening of Gracie Mansion's "The Famous Show" in November, 1982, with* Hujar Dreaming *suspended from the ceiling. (Photograph by Gary Azon)*

organized help from the artists she intended to show. They worked for a month. She called this space the Lieu Division and the first exhibition "Beyond American Standard." (American Standard makes toilets.) The opening pulled in such a crowd that she had to turn people away at the door, many of whom ended up in the bar downstairs. The owner decided to give her another month.

That was unexpected, and she had to pull a show together in a week. She decided—OK, portraits of famous people. "Word just went out—bring in stuff," said Gracie. "People just arrived. I'd set the work up against the wall. 'OK, that's good. You can be in the show.' That's how it happened." She ended up showing more than a hundred pieces, jamming the walls floor to ceiling. David arrived late on the day of the installation, with much of the show already hung. *Hujar Dreaming* ended up suspended from the ceiling by wires in the four corners. At the opening, artgoers again waited in line on the narrow stairway, and this time they crowded out into St. Mark's Place, blocking traffic.

The success of "The Famous Show" inspired the bar owner to start charging Gracie a thousand dollars rent, quite high for 1982. She stayed one more month.

She contacted astrologer Esther Stanway, known as "The Star Lady," to ask, "Should I open an art gallery?" (Each question cost two dollars.) The Star Lady sent back a page-long handwritten letter: "By all means follow the high road to bringing expression in beauty to a weary, disillusioned world. . . . This studio must be unique and with a high degree of SERVICE offered. It must follow without fail a SINGLE PURPOSE and bring a form of ART into every home now drab and without color. . . . Do place beauty upon a commonplace article and send this message into the world and your efforts will be rewarded fourfold."

Gracie found an empty storefront renting for five hundred dollars at 337 East Tenth, facing Tompkins Square Park, and moved there in March 1983, with Sur Rodney Sur as her co-director.

I met David in 1982, late one night at the *Artforum* office. He was not supposed to be there. Keith Davis, the magazine's designer, let him in and brought him to the back room where the two of us were working, alone and on deadline. David had come by to borrow money from Keith.

I knew nothing then of David's painting, his writing, his band—only that he was the guy doing those stencils I'd seen around the neighborhood. David set something down, some paper he and Keith discussed. He had one of the deepest voices I'd ever heard, but I don't remember any specific topic apart from money. I do remember his body language, his focus. He was a force, and made a strong impression quickly. He wasn't there long. David and I became acquaintances.

My colleague Keith proselytized constantly at the *Artforum* office for the East Village scene—especially for Civilian Warfare. (As I recall, the editors ignored him.) Keith had become friendly with Dean Savard. He knew many artists besides David and eagerly collected their work. One night at a Fun Gallery opening, he even persuaded all the graffiti artists present to "tag" his leather jacket.

Then, in November 1982, *Artforum* published Rene Ricard's "The Pledge of Allegiance," an article about Fun Gallery and its artists. Ricard made a case for Lee Quinones and Futura 2000. He found a way to appreciate the unbearable lightness of Kenny Scharf. But the pictures on the wall were just part of the story. Ricard's piece was really about stardom, illusion, and the shifting tectonic plates that determine what is valued in the art world. In hindsight, it reads like a warning: "The feeling of new art is fugitive, like the Fun: here for the moment, gone forever. It's only truly valuable before it's surrounded by the mystique of money, while it's still owned by culture, before it becomes booty."

Jean Pierre Delage shared hundreds of David's letters and postcards with me when I saw him in Paris, but he withheld some from 1982. That's when he had an affair with Jesse Hultberg from 3 Teens, and David was furious. "I made a big mistake," JP said.

Jesse had been visiting Paris with his parents, and according to him, it wasn't even an affair. "I never tried to have a relationship with Jean Pierre. I stayed in his apartment for a couple of days because my parents were staying somewhere in the Fifteenth [Arrondisement] and I liked his place better." When Jesse returned to New York, he and David had a big argument—Jesse pointing out that David hadn't exactly been faithful. "David overreacted big-time in typical David fashion," Jesse said. "He was a hypersensitive person, and you could cross his limit by just looking at him the wrong way." He and Jesse remained friends, however.

David and JP did not break up either. Not ever—said JP. For years, they continued to visit each other. But the contact changed. David continued to write to him about once a month. JP told me that he did not know where he'd put those subsequent letters.

In the last piece of their correspondence I have from 1982, dated November 5, David told JP that he was busier than he'd ever been in his life—and that he'd quit the band. It was around the time that the 3 Teens record finally came out—a record financed by Bobby Bradley, manager of the Pyramid Club, as a kind of money-laundering scheme. All two thousand copies were sold.

It was an autumn of such ferment and portent. The movie *Wild Style* screened for the first time. Keith Haring's show at Tony Shafrazi Gallery made him an international star. A young photographer from Boston named Nan Goldin hauled her slide show, *The Ballad of Sexual Dependency*, to Club 57 and the Pyramid. Limousines clogged East Tenth Street outside Jean-Michel Basquiat's opening at Fun. As for David—along with the three-man exhibit at Civilian, the cock-a-bunnies at P.S. 1, and his painting hung from the ceiling at "The Famous Show"—he was getting ready for his first one-man exhibition at Alexander Milliken, opening December 4, 1982.

It would prove not to be a good fit for either artist or dealer. The gallery card shows one of the Hujar stencil pieces. "I was really happy with some of the images I made," David told me. "Things dealing with homosexuality, and guys arming themselves as defense against government's intrusion in their sexual lives, things dealing with myth—self-created myth." Alexander Milliken liked David's work enough to buy two pieces for himself (*Falling Man* and *Culture in Variation I*), but David complained about the gallery director's ambivalence—that some days Milliken said he was glad he'd done the show and other days he said showing David's work was a mistake.

"I wasn't sure I liked the work," Milliken said, "and I wasn't sure I *didn't* like it." Milliken was in a transitional phase himself, uncertain about which direction he wanted to take the gallery. He asked David and artist Richard Hambleton (who'd also been part of "Fast") to curate a show for January '83 called "Three Part Variety." David brought in Kiki Smith, Chuck Nanney, Jean Foos, and his only remaining friend from *RedM* days, Dirk Rowntree (who was Foos's boyfriend). He and Hambleton also invited Tseng Kwong Chi and Nicolas Moufarrege, among others.

Milliken wanted to see what would come in. "To see if anything grabbed me," he said. "It didn't. It didn't. And I remember I was almost embarrassed at some point to have some of that stuff up. I was heading in another direction." He realized that he didn't like raw work. It wasn't just

David, or the "Three Part Variety" artists. He wouldn't have wanted to show Julian Schnabel either. Or Francesco Clemente. Ultimately he found his new direction with furniture artist Wendall Castle and metal sculptor Albert Paley, "artists who were masters of their medium," as Milliken described them.

He and David parted by mutual agreement.

David was still constantly broke. The Midtown incarnation of Peppermint Lounge closed late in '82. Jean Foos got David a job at *Art News*, where she was working as a freelance production artist. She couldn't remember his exact task there, but it involved making phone calls. He lasted a day or two, then quit.

He was a workaholic who couldn't hold a job. Or, he just knew how he should *not* be spending his time. Though as Foos said, "I don't know how he managed." His share of the rent on East Fourth Street was only about $125. But still.

David told me, "The thing I carried till I was twenty-seven, twenty-eight, was always the sense that I was one step away from the street. It had to do with a lot of depression from being a busboy or a janitor. Really feeling like I had all this stuff that I was carrying that I wanted to express or to communicate somehow, and I wasn't finding the forms for it. Or the form I did find wasn't enough to lift me out of that kind of [menial labor]. I didn't know how to go about it. Peter was really helpful in encouraging me to show work even though it was really raw and rudimentary. I *would* always be one step away from the street. I couldn't last in certain jobs. It just was horrifying to me or made me feel dead."

He went back to journal writing early in 1983—for two days. He recorded nothing but a few anxious dreams: A little kid with explosives tries to toss them under the robes of some adult, but only blows off his own hands. Jesse and Brian tell him they're moving away, leaving him. He's homeless. He's traveling long distances but he's lost. "It was miles and miles back that I took a wrong turn."

\* \* \*

David had met artist Mike Bidlo at "The Famous Show." Bidlo was then just establishing himself as an appropriation artist, re-painting existing modern masterpieces and re-presenting incidents from artists' lives. For example, in *Jack the Dripper at Peg's Place* (1982), he carefully re-created the art-historical moment—in a room at P.S. 1—when Jackson Pollock urinated into Peggy Guggenheim's fireplace. For "The Famous Show," he covered a readymade suit with Pollock drips and hung it on the wall. He'd also added Pollock drips to a vintage black satin gown of Gracie's for her to wear to the opening.

Bidlo's work was conceptualism with an edge, but based on art history, and he cared about the craft of it. When I first met him at his studio in the early eighties, he showed me "the paper Pollock drew on." He'd found the artist's original supplier on Long Island. To do the drip paintings, he'd studied how to thin the paint with just the right amount of turpentine and stain the canvas to simulate thirty years of aging. So—worlds apart from David? Actually, they shared a certain attitude. Bidlo told me that his project was "a pie in the face of the art world—all that sacredness and hermeticism. Like *Les demoiselles d'Avignon* [a Picasso in 1907, a Bidlo in 1983]. You can't even smoke in front of that painting. All the classics of modern art—they're removed from the people." In 1983, he also repainted Pollock's *Blue Poles* outside the Met—on pieces of masonite, which he then distributed to spectators. He went on to paint a *Blue Poles* in Germany "so they could have one too. Evey country should have a *Blue Poles*."

One night Bidlo and David got to talking about "the horrible constrictions of being a young artist trying to show in New York," as Bidlo put it. And David told him about Pier 34. So Bidlo and David came to collaborate on opening the pier to other artists. David must have known that the art-for-art's-sake purity of the project could be lost, but maybe he didn't. He had such an idealistic view of other artists. At least he did then.

Early in 1983, Pier 34 came alive with working artists. (The site's most persistent documentarian, Andreas Sterzing, began photographing there in March.) David's best-known work from the pier was cartoon imagery painted directly on the wall. He did the large gagging cow, a pterodactyl whose wings reach across two walls, and a masterfully deconstructed cartoon strip featuring superheroes and Krazy Kat, generic courage and catastrophe, and a final word-balloon: "Every day my mind grows keener, my good arm stronger, my silly government more futile." He painted the edges of broken windows. He planted grass in rooms with dirt floors. (He would say later that these were the gestures he loved most.) The room with a big Luis Frangella head on the wall overlooking an emerald green lawn was particularly striking.

He told Marisela La Grave: "This is the real MOMA."

On an intact window, David painted an art dealer cockroach declaring, "My name is Tony Shafrazi. . . . My name is Mary Boone. . . . I am your hope." And above that the message: "Artists: stay in control of your work . . . heart + minds."

In May, Richard Goldstein ran a small item on the pier in his *Village Voice* column—just a deep caption under Hujar's photo of the gagging cow. He did not reveal the location. But that was spreading by word of mouth, and the scene began to spiral out of control.

Bidlo and David decided that "the intentionality of the show should be established." So they prepared a statement, written mostly by David. A first draft in his handwriting appears on a paper he found in the abandoned structure—a customs declaration from the New York Cuba Mail Steamship Company:

> Some of us bring in materials to work with. Some work exclusively with found materials. People are affected by light, by wind from the river, by the subtle deterioration of the surroundings, by the movement of strangers through broken doorways, by the shift of sky and water from blues to greys in the evenings, by elements of risk and danger, by suddenly discovered work where hours before there was none.

It's a celebration of freedom reminiscent of his paens to the sex pier. Here there was no electricity and no running water, but also no rent, no curator, no dealers, and no sales. All work was anonymous.

In the final version of this statement, released to the few reporters who were then interested, he and Bidlo added:

> In the Fall of 1982 we felt we needed to do something. We had several possibilities. One of them was to start off a show that would allow

anyone the chance to explore any image in any material on any surface they chose. This is something no gallery would tolerate, nor be large enough to accommodate. It would be a show that by its very nature would not be considered a show. What we are weary of is the tendency in artists in building a show to be more interested in division and selection rather than anything resembling a sense of community. . . . People who lived in this city for years said it was the first time they experienced fulfillment in terms of contact with the art scene and strangers. People shared supplies, energy, thoughts. Given the surfaces to work with—crumbling walls of plaster, earth floors, metal walkways and hundreds of windowpanes—the work came out in rampages of raw energy.

The police became aware of the art activity when a dead body was found one day—not an artist, but someone who'd been dumped at the pier, shot and stabbed. The authorities then tried to seal the entrances. Nevertheless, said the statement from Bidlo and David: "Work continues . . . new people arrive every day . . . word spreading about a show that can't be considered a show." They acknowledged that there had been difficulties, frictions. "Everyone had to in some way learn to give up the desire for possession. Possession of territory, of walls, of materials, of approach to creative impulse." But not everyone could do that.

By summer, Andreas Sterzing observed, the energy had changed. The pier was two stories high with thirty or forty rooms fronting a warehouse as big as a football field—but it just wasn't big enough. By the time I made it down there myself, with Keith Davis, he was telling me stories about artists having fistfights over which space they were going to get. Some had painted over other people's work. Collectors were coming in with saws and cutting chunks out of various walls. There'd been parties. And fashion shoots. I remember hearing that someone had spilled champagne down a shaft into the Holland Tunnel. Still, Keith told me, I should pick a wall and paint my masterpiece. I declined, but artists continued to work there for as long as it stood. David had fled the hubbub, however, absconding to Pier 28 farther south. Bidlo didn't work at either pier. He had a studio at P.S. 1 and made some Pollock canvases that he brought over and stuck on a wall.

David and Bidlo had once joked about having an opening at Pier 34. They never did because they knew it was too dangerous. Unknown to them, however, a group calling itself the Anonymous Artists Alliance distributed leaflets inviting everyone to a wine and cheese party at the pier on June 4, 1983. Port Authority police raided the gathering, arrested four people, and confiscated the one freestanding work of art they found: a statue of a figure slumped over with its head on its knees. (Neither David nor Bidlo was present.) Richard Goldstein reported in his *Voice* column that four revelers had broken through a locked door and entered the venting tower over the Holland Tunnel, which set off alarms. Police again tried sealing the Ward Line Pier, which worked about as well as sealing the sex pier. The artists were soon back. But a petition had been filed in federal district court to demolish the place. Goldstein reported that the structure was sitting atop "piles so eroded that the state's chief engineer warned of its possible collapse."

Years later, in 1999, when *Artforum* devoted a special issue to East Village art—its rise and fall—the editors chose a photograph of David at the pier for the cover. At first, I thought it odd that they'd selected a space outside the neighborhood, but I supposed it illustrated that the East Village scene was a state of mind. And many of those involved in the Ward Line Pier Project ended up showing in those galleries. The pier was definitely the neighborhood's satellite, embodying the scene's best aspirations, then sharing its meteoric fate in an even more condensed period of time. Piers 34 and 28 were both torn down in 1984.

That spring—while the pier had its brief golden age, while Gracie Mansion opened her storefront space on Tompkins Square Park—nearly everyone was still oblivious about the mysterious new illness called AIDS. The notable exception was writer Larry Kramer. In March 1983, he published his landmark piece, "1,112 and Counting," in the *New York Native*, the city's gay newspaper. "If this article doesn't scare the shit out of you, we're in real trouble," Kramer began. "If this article doesn't rouse you to anger, fury, rage, and action, gay men may have no future on this earth." He wrote that between January 13 and February 9 of that year, there'd been 164 new diagnoses—and 73 more deaths. Nearly half of all AIDS cases in the country were in New

York City. Doctors didn't know what caused it or how to treat it. And no one was doing anything.

Letters came in to the *Native* denouncing Kramer as "alarmist."

In April, AIDS was mentioned in the *East Village Eye* for the first time. Cookie Mueller had been writing her health advice column, "Ask Dr. Mueller," for about six months by then, addressing concerns like "I have herpes," "I have amoebas," "I have so much pain in my sinuses," and "What should I do if someone OD's in my presence?" That April, she wrote that she didn't want to comment on AIDS because it was too serious. "But there is one thing I have a burning desire to say and then I won't even mention it again. If you have AIDS, seek help from doctors other than ones connected with the A.M.A." She had three friends with AIDS, she wrote, who'd been "virtually cured" by chiropractor-nutritionists, and she'd give out those names to anyone who contacted her. At this point in the epidemic, it wasn't even bad advice. Medical doctors didn't have a clue.

That same month, Mayor Ed Koch finally agreed to meet with representatives from the New York AIDS Network. Gay Men's Health Crisis, part of that network, could send two people, and GMHC's president decided that Larry Kramer would *not* be one of them. An outraged Kramer resigned from GMHC on April 14. On April 20, Koch met for the first and last time with the AIDS Network and said he would declare "a state of concern" during the week of the GMHC fundraiser. But the city would provide no actual services.

The day after this meeting, artists and clubgoers packed a benefit at Danceteria for "the ailing Klaus Nomi"—as the *Eye* delicately described him. Nomi had become a star in the downtown clubs even as "downtown" invented itself in the late seventies. He sang a startling countertenor while presenting himself as a creature from another planet: finlike hair, high forehead, dark lipstick, triangular tuxedo jackets, robotic movements. His illness seemed otherworldly in its horror. His friend Joey Arias recalled going to visit him in the hospital: "They made me wear a plastic bag. . . . I wasn't allowed to touch him. . . . He developed Kaposi's and started taking interferon. That messed him up real bad. He had dots all over his body and his eyes became purple slits. . . . He had cancer in his stomach. Herpes popped out all over his body. He turned into a monster. It hurt me so much to see him."

In late June 1983, New York City's health commissioner, Dr. David Sencer, reported a "leveling off of cases" and suggested that gay men might be "getting immune" to the disease, that perhaps AIDS was "not as infectious as we may have thought." Meanwhile, the chairman of the city's Human Rights Commission, Isaiah Robinson, told the *Daily News*, "There is no epidemic."

Klaus Nomi died on August 6—of "a disease whose myth exploded through thoughtless babble and media saturation," said the obituary in the *East Village Eye*, an obituary that did not mention the word "AIDS."

# 12 "WILL THEY ALLOW ME ON THE MOON?"

**He liked painting** directly on the world. It was a gesture of defiance—this work done on some decrepit pier or busy intersection or gallery door, this work destined to be destroyed. For his first one-man show at Civilian Warfare, David painted or printed everything on found materials: driftwood, garbage can lids, supermarket posters. And this too was a way of responding to official reality—to what he would later call "the pre-invented world."

He'd been stenciling on garbage can lids since sometime in 1982. Various friends remembered walking the neighborhood with him when he confiscated a lid, or scouted for good ones to take. He wanted them aged or dented so they looked like they had a history. According to Chuck Nanney, it was Hujar who got him to always replace what he was taking, who told him the super would have to do it otherwise out of his own pocket. So David went to the hardware store and bought a new lid to replace each one he took.

In spring of 1983, David spent a day at Jones Beach with Keith Davis and Elayne Kling, a friend of Keith's who was then working at Fun Gallery. Keith brought a big bag of tempera paint with him. "We spent the day picking up pieces of driftwood and painting them these crazy colors," Kling said. Then they built a monolith from these vivid logs, a huge haphazard structure that attracted spectators from way down the beach. At the end of the day, they packed as much painted driftwood as they could fit into Kling's car. At the last minute, she grabbed one that David had turned into an alligator but left behind. "I'm keeping this," she told him. She's certain that this was the day David first began making his driftwood totems, though, as Kling put it, "he expanded on them back at the studio." Indeed, the finished pieces were complex—often stylized snakes or fish painted with the iconography he'd been developing: globes, targets, cowboys, falling men, and so on.

David had left the storefront on Houston Street early in '83 for a studio at the Clocktower, a gallery and studio space affiliated with P.S. 1 but located in Lower Manhattan. He was also working at Keith's loft on Suffolk Street. Keith had silk-screening equipment and technical expertise, and he loved being part of the process. "Keith always had art supplies around," said Steve Doughton, who was close to both Keith and David in the mid-eighties. "He was always encouraging people to come over. 'Paint something, and I'll put it on my wall.' He had a little workshop. I remember them printing the food posters there." In his wanderings, David had found the place where supermarkets had their big window ads made. He told Steve Doughton that he'd watched the guys work and admired their skill, their speed, "just whipping off these stencils freehand with X-Acto knives, cutting into some kind of transfer medium." When Elayne Kling came in one day to help Keith and David print both the Romulus and Remus piece (*True Myth*, on ads for Domino sugar and Kraft grape jelly) and *Jean Genet Masturbating Metteray Prison* (on an ad for ground chuck), she saw that they had boxes of those food posters.

More than half the images in that first solo Civilian show were printed or painted on these posters. *Savarin Coffee*, for example, re-creates frames from the pier cartoon that ended with the word bubble "Every day my mind grows keener . . ." *Tuna* features a cowboy outlaw, and *Slam Click*, a man in a prison cell printed over deli ads. David explained years later that he'd used the food posters because they marked a specific time (with their prices) and represented consumption—moral, mental, psychic, and physical consumption. The supermarket ads represent the wallpaper of our lives, while the unspeakable surfaces in David's images of violence, repression, and desire.

David complained that, during his first show, someone at the Milliken Gallery had said to him: "Why can't you be like Keith Haring—full of fun?" David's work was full of sex and violence—politics expressed at the level of the body. He painted distress. Soldiers and bombers. Falling buildings and junkies. His images had the tension of some niceness opened up to its ruined heart. In the montage style he began to develop, David would expose the Real Deal under the artifacts—wars and rumors of wars, industrial wastelands, mythological beasts, and the evolutionary spectrum from dinosaur to humanity's rough beast.

The Civilian Warfare show opened on June 4, 1983—the day of the police raid on Pier 34.

Between the end of 1982 and the end of '83, David had three one-man shows at three galleries—Milliken, Civilian, and Hal Bromm—while also participating in fourteen group exhibitions, not including the Ward Line Pier Project. In the context of the eighties art boom, this was not so unusual. Artists like Basquiat, Haring, and Schnabel were selling work as fast as they could crank it out. Still, after years of struggle, David was suddenly attracting attention. He would be written about now. He would become a public figure.

This brought him up against one of the central dilemmas in his life: How much could he say? What could he reveal?

Hujar always said that an artist should have an artificial biography. As Vince Aletti explained, Hujar thought such factoids did not matter. Because who really cared? "So he had fun often just making up some kind of slightly believable but odd early history for himself. Each bio was slightly different." On the CV he prepared for his last show, for example, Hujar said that he'd been born in Cairo.

This was also an era when many in the art world—Lydia Lunch, Gracie Mansion, Sur Rodney Sur—played with their identities or flat out reinvented themselves. But there's a light, jokey touch to Hujar's fakery, and a kind of cheekiness to the name changes, while David was engaged in creating camouflage. He'd entered a world where he felt like an alien, acutely aware of being uneducated and working class. He told me he'd felt intimidated at Milliken. He wasn't his own idea of what an artist should be. He thought his work at this point was raw and rudimentary. Hujar pushed him to show it anyway.

David began to create an image for public consumption that wasn't quite who he really was. He simplified his story. He took real events and moved them back in time to make them more terrible. He began crafting this persona right from the first show at Milliken. He would be the street kid, the abused child. A draft of the press release from the Milliken gallery states that David's visual language is informed by world events, but that this is filtered through "his own survival experience, which includes his leaving home and going out on [sic] the world alone at the age of nine." The biographical statement on page two says he came to New York at nine and left home a year later. He revised the age he left for the streets in later versions. But, while David actually moved to Manhattan when he was eleven, he *always* said he was nine—including in sworn testimony given in U.S. District Court in 1990 when he sued the American Family Association.

David told me that he'd discussed hustling early on because it would have helped him when he was younger to know that someone else in his world shared his frame of reference. But then he said, "There was an element of mythmaking, which I can't say I'm not responsible for. Also I think [the hustling story] was used by some people to hit me over the head and by others to find me very attractive on some level." There's nothing in Milliken's press release about hustling. Or Civilian's. David was unusual in speaking about it at all. Early in the eighties, artists who had worked in any part of the sex industry were just beginning to admit it or use it as subject matter, and women (like Diane Torr with "Go-Go Girls Seize Control," 1981) led the way.

Keith Davis interviewed David, probably in spring '83, because as the tape begins, they're discussing work that ended up in the June show at Civilian. ("Ol' Romulus and Remie," David says. "Looks good.") Keith wanted to help David in any way he could, and he'd wangled some kind of interview assignment. It never appeared in print, but Keith tells him, "They want me to ask you questions about symbols in your work. The kind of information I want to get at is what aspects of your life experience indicate how authentic your images are."

This was the first interview David ever did. Several minutes in, he tells a couple of—well, they have to be jokes, but Keith doesn't take them that way. First, David says he used to hitch into New York City to ride "the elevated" in second grade. An incredulous Keith replies, "Second grade?" Then David tells him he started hustling in third grade. "This bunch of farmers that had a club down at the end of this wheat field near my block used to pay me to jump out of birthday cakes, get it on with half the farmers. Who were widowers, because their wives had died chopping down twenty-seven truckloads of hay every day." That one is rather perversely funny, but Keith doesn't laugh. He just says, "Third grade?" Yes, and Bob Dylan began travel-ing with a carnival at the age of thirteen (as he used to tell interviewers). David never told these whoppers again.

Keith recorded a couple of hours of conversation, David talking about Times Square, about being a kid on the lam, telling many of the same sto-ries he would tell other interviewers over the years, including me. He has the same affect with Keith that he has in the Biographical Dateline printed in the *Tongues of Flame* catalog. Hard-bitten. Blasé. As if he'd been through hell and he didn't care. He tells Keith he left home at age nine or ten. But when Keith asks why, he ducks the question. He starts talking about how his brother ended up in a boys' home. As for his mother, he says, "There were times that I'd just walk out of the house for the night, and my mother would be screaming her head off for something, and I'd just say whatever I said and just take off and end up somewhere down around Times Square getting picked up by some guy." (That could have happened—when he was fifteen or sixteen, not nine or ten.) He does not say much else about life at the Hells Kitchen apartment except that home was unstable. That's what he would reveal to a good friend. It's more than most interviewers got.

In August, he met with Robert Pincus-Witten for an *Arts* magazine article. The writer found David to be "diffident and taciturn" and wondered "how much of his uneasy manner consciously plays to a myth in formation." That same day, Pincus-Witten also visited artist Stephen Frailey, whom he described, by way of contrast, as a "privileged boy at his ease." Still, he was unsure what to make of David and his evasions. "To build a sociology around him is awkward—to infer it, easy—as the few facts offered up are of such high profile," Pincus-Witten wrote. "I don't for a moment doubt them, though scads are glossed. He's been on his own since childhood, rejected by a New Jersey family at nine. From what little he says (that's a problem: he hints, not to be flirtatious, but to maintain distance), he had no use for them and they apparently had even less for him. Survival was dependent on itinerancy and vagabondage. . . . A reasonable model is Genet."

I think there's a simple explanation for David's "mythology." He did not want to talk about living family members. It was too complicated and too painful. Instead, he followed the outline he'd established in the unfinished "street novel" he'd written in Paris. Discuss the brutal father, now conveniently dead, and go directly to Times Square. In the novel, he's a runaway with no siblings and a mother who's disappeared, while the dad he flees is clearly modeled on his own.

Coincidently, by the time David did these first solo shows and first interviews, he was completely out of touch with everyone in his family, including his sister. Unknown to him, Pat had remarried that year and moved. He would visit Paris in early '84 and not be able to find her. David had not seen his brother, Steven, since their father's funeral in '76. He'd called his half-brother, Pete, one night from the Peppermint Lounge, just to tell him how much he hated the job. That was the first time Pete had heard from David in years, and they would have no further contact until late in 1991.

Susan Gauthier, who still saw David occasionally, was one of the first people David had ever opened up to about his past, and probably one of the few to get the real story. Hustling? Yes, but not till his teen years. "He put out there what he wanted people to believe, and he wanted to be something of an enigma," Gauthier said. "He had fun with it. He really didn't want people to know who he was. So he was very aware of what he was doing. He wanted to be a puzzle that nobody could figure out."

By the end of his life, David had a reputation as someone who would speak out and hold nothing back. When it came to politics—absolutely. I think people also had the impression that he was telling "everything" because he spoke so freely about sex. But sex was easy for him to talk about, and it wasn't everything. He *never* told everything.

Artist James Romberger popped into the Civilian Warfare storefront to show his drawings to Dean Savard, probably in the fall of '83. Savard wasn't there. But down on the floor was someone who looked like a lumberjack: David in a flannel shirt, hacking at a log with a hatchet. David put down the totem-in-progress and said, "*I'll* look at your work." He liked Romberger's stuff. He thought Civilian should show it. He'd mention it to Savard. James Romberger and David were destined to work together later in various ways. But the point here is that David took an almost proprietary interest in Civilian Warfare. Its funky confines felt like home, and he wanted the place to succeed.

*Alan Barrows (left) and Dean Savard outside Civilian Warfare Gallery on East Eleventh Street. Barrows has a "friendly cow" patch on his sweater and one of David's burning house stencils is visible on the window. The sculpture is by Greer Lankton. The gallery's sign includes three stencils of Hujar. (Photograph by Marion Scemama)*

He and Keith Davis made a distinctive sign for the exterior of the storefront—no name, but three squares, each with a stencil of Hujar. David had also brought Marisa Cardinale to the gallery in early '83 and told Savard to hire her.

Marisa had been working at the Second Stage Theater as "assistant to the assistant to the assistant stage manager," as she put it. She knew David from the Kiev, a cheap Ukrainian restaurant on Second Avenue where she always seemed to run into some combination of him, Hujar, and Ethyl Eichelberger. Apparently David just had a feeling about her: This person is competent; this person is responsible. Marisa had an art history degree but no gallery experience, and she admitted to being a terrible typist. At Civilian, that would not matter. They had no typewriter. Savard wrote everything out by hand on the Civilian Warfare stationery they made at the Xerox shop.

The gallery also had no record-keeping system, and when Marisa started, Savard was still living there. Marisa said that David brought her in because "they had started to make some money, and it was all just sort of disappearing." David was already worried about getting paid.

It was an era when things could be tried, and there was space for the tryout. So photographer Allen Frame and multimedia artist Kirsten Bates decided to form a theater company called Turmoil and began looking for material. Bill Rice suggested that they look at David's *Sounds in the Distance*.

Rice had been acquainted with David for years, and he thought the monologues "stunning." Rice was a painter and an actor, a sort of underground renaissance man. A few years older than Hujar, he'd somehow found his niche in the so-called Blank Generation. He began acting in no-wave films when he was almost fifty, working with Scott and Beth B, Amos Poe, and Jim Jarmusch. He would soon find his way, with David, into Richard Kern's Cinema of Transgression. Onstage he appeared in plays by downtown luminaries like John Jesurun, Jim Neu, and Gary Indiana. Meanwhile, he was in the midst of compiling some two thousand pages of notes on Picasso's *Desmoiselles d'Avignon*, determined to prove that it was originally based on men. For his day job, he worked as a researcher on a scholarly study of Gertrude Stein. By 1983, he was one of about three tenants left in a building at 13 East Third Street, across from the men's shelter, and he'd opened his backyard to underground theater by writers like Indiana. That summer, Rice decided to open his "garden" again, and Turmoil hoped to work there.

When Bates approached David for permission to use *Sounds in the Distance*, he seemed, she said "taken aback." By the time he met Frame, he'd apparently gotten used to the idea. Frame said, "David was very excited about having us adapt it but wanted to be hands-off. He hadn't had any experience in theater." Bates and Frame worked together to adapt and direct eight of the monologues. They called it *Turmoil in the Garden*. David could barely stand to watch. He got Kern to come with him and they crawled into an abandoned building near Rice's backyard and watched from a fire escape. Apparently that got him past his embarrassment, since he came twice more and sat in the audience. Frame said he seemed "captivated."

Rice's backyard was mostly broken asphalt sheltered by a few ailanthus trees, and accessible through his apartment. Frame and Bates experimented with the staging. One performer delivered a monologue from a fire escape. Their cast included Nan Goldin, her then-boyfriend Brian Burchill, and Rice himself. They lit the small space using extension cords strung over backyards from the La Mama theater on Fourth Street. The garden had room for about fifteen lawn chairs, folding chairs, and broken-down seating scrounged from the street.

Inside his emptying building, Rice had commandeered one of the vacant apartments to use as an exhibition space. It was more salon than gallery, since it wasn't open to the public. David became one of many artists who showed work at those soirées.

Carlo McCormick met David at the Pyramid Club, during Pet Night. David had entered a cock-a-bunny in the contest for the most horrible pet. Carlo recalled someone else entering a ferret. And maybe someone had a rat. Any dog in the contest would have been ugly, or, as Carlo put it, "a breed associated with bottom-feeders." He remembered Pet Night as an event the Pyramid sponsored "to celebrate the squalor and poverty of our lives."

Carlo had seen the "Hit and Run" show at Civilian with David, Savard, and Bronson Eden. And he'd attended the opening of "The Beast Show," where he'd seen guards chasing cock-a-bunnies. (He was sure David had brought in hundreds.) So he approached him at the Pyramid. "I was like, 'My god, you're David,' but David didn't like people doing that to him. He jumped out of his skin."

Carlo—who quickly became a major critic, curator, and promoter of the East Village scene—wrote his first piece for the *East Village Eye* on the closing of the Ward Line pier, and one of his first reviews on David's show at Civilian ("homoerotic and dramatic urban and military images done with skill and energy"). The *Eye* had not reviewed neighborhood galleries before this.

Midway through '83, however, the scene had begun to solidify and would not be ignored again, with the *Eye* functioning as house organ. When Club 57 closed that spring, the performance scene also moved into a new phase, as 57's trash-and-vaudeville ambience spread to other venues. Its stars had no trouble finding gigs elsewhere, but in the East Village they tended to play at the Pyramid Club. In July, for example, the *Eye* reported on John Sex singing "Only the Lonely" there with his pet boa constrictor Delilah draped around his torso. Ann Magnuson could pack the place practically on word of mouth alone.

That same month, Carlo curated an event for Limbo Lounge, a tiny club on the north side of Tompkins Square Park: fourteen consecutive one-night, one-person shows. David was one of the artists (as were Mike Bidlo, Keiko Bonk, and Rhonda Zwillinger, for example), and here one could definitely smoke (or drink or vomit) in front of a painting.

The East Village was the art world's surly teenager, ready to tromp all over the unspoken etiquette established in "grown-up" galleries. No one would walk into Leo Castelli's space and ask, "How much is that Rauschenberg?" It wasn't done. Money and status were the elephants in such rooms where top dealers sold top artists to top collectors. In the East Village, prices were discussed right up front. Often you could get something for fifty or a hundred dollars. A completely sold-out Rodney Alan Greenblat show at Gracie Mansion had work starting at five dollars. I once saw a dealer get work out of some dinky back room, spread it over the floor, and ask, "Is this

*Sur Rodney Sur and Gracie Mansion outside the gallery on East Tenth Street.*
*She is wearing the evening gown to which Mike Bildo added Jackson Pollock*
*drips. (Photograph © Andreas Sterzing)*

the right size? Want something in blue?" Then, the East Village galleries
were not just open on Sunday—but that was their big day. At openings, most
of the artgoers were actually out in the street, since so few could fit inside.
And at Civilian, Savard always served vodka, never white wine. What was
not yet called "branding" revolved around such superficialities. At the same
time, the whole East Village setup was a critique of elitism. When I wrote,
in 1984, about what was happening in my neighborhood, I declared that
new ideas were being explored here about what a collector, a dealer, an artist, and a gallery could be. Looking at it after more than twenty-five years,
I'm not sure anything really changed. The art world has a magical ability to
absorb every critique, and make money on it.

Ultimately 176 galleries would open in the neighborhood (not all at
once, obviously). Landlords were eagerly endorsing this unlikely trend by
offering former bodegas and social clubs—and sometimes apartments for

the dealers—at remarkably low rents. I'll never forget the young dealer who took me to her filthy, unheated apartment a few doors away from her gallery, served me instant Bustelo in a dirty cup, and then announced, "This is how we live on the Lower East Side." She'd lived there for six months, after growing up on the Upper East Side. Poverty was apparently a cool new lifestyle, but it wouldn't be for long. As this dealer proudly declared, "We're raising the property values."

Gracie Mansion had started her career as a dealer by looking at the mechanisms involved in presenting and selling art, and she set up another sly commentary in September '83 with her "Sofa/Painting" show. Because when you're not elitist, you end up dealing with art buyers at the other end of the spectrum, those who say, "I need something that looks good over the sofa."

David was one of the six artists she invited to create both a sofa and a painting to hang above it. She gave each artist twenty-five or fifty dollars to help in the purchase of a couch. David found one on the street—a legless banquette that might have come from a diner. He set it on two milk cartons. On the seat he placed a piece of Plexiglas, covered on one side with his complaint about the art world. Yes, he already had one: Too many people wanted to show him. Or, were "trying to seduce him," as Gracie put it. That meant Civilian and Gracie and Hal Bromm. On the other side of the Plexiglas he obscured those words by painting red, green, and white branchlike forms along with a screaming head and a small image of his own head. On the back of the sofa, he painted a cityscape in black and yellow, with a globe in the sky. The painting on the wall above the sofa showed a figure climbing a tree with one stump of a branch. "It's him, trying to get away from all of us," Gracie explained.

David sold work in 1983 through all three of the galleries named and blamed above, earning a total of almost seventeen thousand dollars. He had a gross income of about twenty-six thousand dollars in '84, but he was never rich. As usual, he embodied contradiction: he was irritated by the art world; he was also relieved that he finally had a way to make a living and worried that the whole thing could evaporate at any moment.

David's strange relationship with money began to manifest as soon as he made some. He would give it away without a second thought to a needy friend. Then sometimes, he'd be nearly broke again. He had no concept of financial planning. He never had a savings account. He never had an IRA. He did not have a credit card until almost 1990. Near the end of his life, he confessed to a friend that he had never known how to balance a checkbook. If possible, he would have avoided using money altogether. He preferred trading. He certainly would not consider making art just for money. But then, he wanted the purity of that intention to be matched by a purity of acquisition in collectors. They should care what the work meant! It made him angry, even disgusted, that people would buy work as an investment once it was validated by certain critics. Though he was never remotely as bad as Hujar on this score, his attitude led him into a certain amount of self-sabotage.

He could not walk easily into his success. He had begun to get very prickly.


In autumn 1983, a second wave of galleries opened, including P·P·O·W and Pat Hearn. The scene wasn't percolating up from the streets anymore. The new galleries were run by people who'd always wanted to be dealers, and many came armed with backers or business plans. Hearn even remodeled her space. I remember passing it one midnight with friends right before it opened and stopping, astonished at the gleaming new facade that looked so out of place on Avenue B.

Halloween saw the opening of 8BC, soon to be a centerpiece of the East Village club scene, but then just an unheated basement space in a hundred-year-old Loisaida* farmhouse. The owners had removed most of the first floor, leaving the back end of it to serve as a stage. Spectators stood in the basement, heads craned back for a view, taking care to avoid the trickle of an ancient creek bisecting the dirt floor. Named for its location on Eighth Street between Avenues B and C, the club was in one of the few occupied buildings on the block.

In October the *East Village Eye* did a cover story on the nascent scene,

---

* This Spanglish pronunciation for "Lower East Side" was often applied to Alphabet City.

featuring twenty short pieces on artists who were now "hot commodities." One was David. Writer Sylvia Falcon mentioned both *Sounds in the Distance* and an art "attuned to the bitter details of life." She'd first encountered his work in the *SoHo News*—that centerfold "in which he compared himself to Arthur Rimbaud." Now he was embarrassed by that claim, he told Falcon. "He does not share Rimbaud's boyish enthusiasm for evil."

For his November show at Hal Bromm—a Tribeca space that would soon open an East Village branch—David made more totems and hauled a pile of sand into the gallery so he could place the things on a facsimile of a beach. Among his new paintings was *Smuggler*, a sailor painted over a photo of a riverboat. This was the image chosen for the poster, and there David added a block of text. He had abandoned his writing at this point, but I recognize some of the lines from his journals. The images don't exactly cohere, but they're vivid, like "the drag queen in the dive waterfront coffee shop turning towards a stranger and giving a coy seductive smile which reveals a mouth of rotted teeth."

When Hallwalls Contemporary Arts Center in Buffalo invited Gary Indiana to introduce two new writers in its reading series, he selected David and Joe Vojtko. At the beginning of November, the three of them flew to Buffalo. In an article commemorating his friendship with David, Vojtko recalled that the three of them met at the Kiev for breakfast before heading to the airport and there they began discussing "the purple death, the plague," the disease they still knew so little about. David informed them that the first sign of AIDS was "white stuff on your tongue."

The three got to know each other that weekend in Buffalo. Vojtko wrote, "David and Gary were exchanging ideas and biographical information a mile a moment. I knew Gary well enough to know Gary was totally smitten." It would get complicated later, but back in New York, David and Gary remained the closest of friends, in Vojtko's estimation, for "many weeks, if not months."

Chuck Nanney had known both David and Keith Haring since the three of them were busboys together at Danceteria. Nanney recalled that David loved Haring's subway drawings—to the point of obsession. But Haring had brushed aside any overtures of friendship from David. "In fact," Nanney said, "I think he was kind of rude, because at some point David became really angry about Keith Haring."

During the interview taped by Keith Davis, David complained that Haring had "stolen" his image of a naked man with a dog's head. It was in the piece David contributed to "The Erotic Show" at Club 57 in 1981 which Haring curated. "I didn't feel comfortable using the man-with-dog's-head image anymore after his became well known," David said.

But as Nanney explained it, David's antagonism had nothing to do with art. "I think David wanted a kind of acceptance from Keith that he never got, and that turned into bitterness." Feeling excluded could make David apoplectic. Nanney recalled a day that he'd gone out to look for old comic books with French artist Hervé Di Rosa—a straight guy both he and David had a crush on. When Nanney showed David the comics he'd found, David went off on a tirade: How could Nanney not invite him? How could he show him this stuff after excluding him? When Nanney tried to tell him that the jaunt had been spontaneous, not intended to exclude anyone, David went on ranting: "This happens to me all the time!"

"I think it was part of his frustration, his wanting to feel connected to the scene that was still evolving around Keith Haring and feeling ostracized and not welcomed into that," Nanney said. "It was kind of around that time that he became really anti-Keith and started going around town drawing radiant babies." That was Haring's trademark image.

Nanney, who worked at the Mudd Club with Haring after the Danceteria bust, said Haring was angry when someone else began drawing the babies. "Everybody was talking about it, and Keith was like, 'I didn't tag here—who's doing this?'"

David thought that was hilarious. "He had a strong mischievous side that sometimes was impish and delightful," said Nanney, "and sometimes just—inexplicable."

Nanney and his boyfriend, Nicolas Moufarrege, spent time hanging out with David and Hujar—at the Bar or going for walks in the neighborhood. "David had this favorite game he always wanted to play, because he always knew Peter's result," Nanney said. He would ask, If you could have one piece of art from any artist from any time, what would it be? Nanney and Moufarrege would choose something different every time. But Hujar always said the same thing: either one of Keith Haring's subway drawings or an Andy Warhol film, preferably *Chelsea Girls*.

"David would always wait for Peter's answer, and he'd be like, 'Can you believe that?' He'd go into this whole routine: 'He doesn't even want a piece of mine. He wants a Keith Haring drawing.' He would do this every time so he could go into this mini-rant."

Hujar would just laugh.

In December 1983, Kiki Smith had her first show, in the exhibition space at the Kitchen, an arts organization known for supporting experimental work in many disciplines. She had decided on a multimedia installation about domestic violence, "Life Wants to Live." David helped. "We got pig's blood from the butcher on Seventh Street and covered ourselves with blood and then we made prints of our bodies," she said. While covered with blood, they passed a camera back and forth, taking close-ups of their bodies, then did the same with a Super 8 camera. Kiki also wanted to do CAT scans of their bodies, but when they went to a man with medical-imaging equipment, he said, why don't you do X-rays? So they did X-rays of themselves pretending to beat each other up. She added a stethoscopic recording of a heartbeat.

The X-ray technician didn't have them wear lead shields at any point, then said something about how they should have covered their genitals "if you're reproducing." Kiki told him they weren't reproducing. "I remember David was very angry at me for a very long time," she said. When they discussed it later, he said something like, how come you don't want to have children with me? This had nothing to do with sex; they weren't lovers. This had nothing to do with children; he didn't want children (though he said that if he did, he'd want to have them with Kiki). This had everything to do with his readiness to feel dismissed and rejected.

The Europeans weren't afraid, Alan Barrows remembered. They'd walk into the neighborhood, while the New York collectors kept their limos parked right outside the galleries. Europeans were among the first buyers at places like Civilian, scooping up work before the art establishment even took the scene seriously. German television had already sent a camera crew in 1983.

Near the end of that year, David left for Europe with Dean Savard and Alan Barrows. A dealer in Amsterdam wanted to meet with them. Then they took the train to Cologne, where the Anna Friebe Gallery was putting together a February '84 group show of East Village artists. Friebe's son drove them to Bonn, where they'd been invited to meet with a curator at the Rheinisches Landesmuseum. David and Barrows went on to Berlin for New Year's. Savard, smitten with Friebe's son, returned with him to Cologne.

A German journalist had given David a phone number for filmmaker Rosa von Praunheim in Berlin. Barrows had never heard of him, while David still had enough of a crush on Rosa to feel tongue-tied. (During their chance encounter at the GAA firehouse in 1972, they had not spoken.) Rosa didn't know who they were but helped them anyway. He arranged for a friend to give them her apartment while she moved in with Rosa for two weeks. Years later, Barrows recalled it as a wonderful trip. "David had to go everywhere," Barrows said. "In Amsterdam he took me to a male brothel. For rent boys. He wanted to see what it was like. He wanted to see the kids that were there." They didn't hire any of them. David just wanted to see it. Then, in Berlin, David wanted to see a female brothel. "That was creepy," said Barrows. "It was in a bad area, and these women were just ugly. But he wanted to see it." They went to the parts of East Berlin that were still bombed-out. They walked around both Amsterdam and Berlin looking at graffiti. David photographed everywhere they went—the landscape but also Barrows. He painted on Barrows's shirt, painted on Barrows's sneakers. He painted on the souvenir maps.

One day in an Amsterdam bar, David sat doodling on cocktail napkins with a Magic Marker as he griped to Barrows on a familiar topic: all the attention that Keith Haring was getting. And his stuff was so easy! To demonstrate, David drew the radiant baby on one of the cocktail napkins. Apparently he did a convincing job. The bartender looked over and gasped, "It's you!" He began running over with free drinks for David and Barrows. Then he took the cocktail napkin and put it up behind the bar. David didn't say anything.

\* \* \*

David arrived in Paris on January 9, 1984. He stayed with Jean Pierre till February 22, but JP was at work during the day. And David didn't know where his remarried sister was till she wrote in March to give him her new address and last name.

Then Gary Indiana showed up. He told David he'd written an article he didn't even want to write just to get money to come see him. "It wasn't true," Gary said later. "I just told him that. I had a big crush on him, and I thought, 'Oh, we'll have an affair in Paris.' But then the very first day, he made it clear that that wasn't what he was interested in. I didn't want to spend all my time with him because I still had this crush, but he wanted to spend all his time with me because he didn't know anybody else. It was really stupid."

They began working on a script for a Super 8 film to be called *Taste of the Black Earth*. Like all of David's subsequent scripts, it's a list of images: a Tuileries statue appearing on a Metro track, a Pont Neuf guide boat at night, a face covered in bandages that slowly unravel. Though the project was never finished, they shot some footage, which David eventually gave to Gary, who threw it away. He couldn't recall their overarching idea but remembered that David found an odd abandoned winery in a remote neighborhood and wanted to paint on the walls there, then film some scenario. Judging from David's contact sheets, they also visited demolition sites, rail yards, meat markets, and stores selling odd curios.

In David's version of what happened in Paris, which he published in the *East Village Eye* nearly two years later, he doesn't mention the film but says that after several days, Gary became hysterical and threatened to kill himself if David didn't return his feelings.

Gary tells it differently, but on January 25, he did send David a letter of apology. "I've treated you very shabbily," he wrote. "Almost everything I said to you yesterday was horrible and manipulative and cruel. If you can forgive me it would make a great deal of difference to me."

Asked what he was apologizing for, Gary said, "Probably something utterly trivial." He did not want to see a copy of the letter to refresh a painful recollection.

"Our relationship in Paris was really depressing," he said. "[David] would call in the morning and ask me to meet him for breakfast. We always went to the Café de Flore, and then as the day went on, he would become more and more silent and would yawn. And it was almost like I could feel that he hated being around me, and I couldn't really understand why we were spending all day and into the evening together. The best I could figure out is that I spoke French better than he did, and he just needed somebody to negotiate little practical realities for him." Eventually, Gary left for the Berlin Film Festival.

David went back to his journal writing during this trip, though he stopped again as soon as he returned to New York. He made sketches and recorded dreams, writing nothing about Gary except for one possible enigmatic appearance in a dream. Somebody calls, sounding upset, and tells David, "You have just one minute." David thinks it's Gary and demands, "Gary? Answer me!" But there's no answer.

The images that stand out in the rest of the dreams have to do with hiding and with shame: In one, he's just walked on the moon, giddy with joy, and is told he can go back. But he worries, "Will they allow me on the moon if they realize who I am completely?"

# 13 PRESSURE POINT

**Those of us** who lived among the alphabet avenues in the 1980s grew accustomed to hearing a certain refrain: "Works! Works! Works!" The drug paraphernalia could be rented for just a couple of dollars, and needles littered the sidewalks and gutters. Neighbors complained about all the dealers at the corner. You had to elbow your way through the crowd in broad daylight and would be offered five kinds of heroin on the way to the grocery store. "That corner"—Second Street and Avenue B—"no longer belongs to the city of New York," someone from a group of Loisaida block associations told the *New York Times* in the summer of 1983.

Heroin was a social drug in the eighties, and Alphabet City was its round-the-clock supermarket—or, as the police called it, "the retail drug capital of America." Finally it was easy to find a taxi, people joked, what with so many cabbing in from elsewhere to buy drugs. David had described one kind of transaction—the cement block pulled from a sealed-up door and a hand reaching out. It could be that open, with a line of buyers down the street. But often the dealers hammered some cavelike entrance into a sealed building and allowed customers inside to line up on a rickety stairway lit with votive candles. Upstairs something would usually be rigged at a door or landing to keep buyer and seller from actually seeing each other. Or, if the stairway was gone, someone lowered a bucket for the money, counted it, then lowered the bucket back down with product. Millions of dollars were changing hands.

To an outsider like me—a non-drug user—this was a world of gothic scenery. I'd see ruined buildings down the street a-flicker with candles every night. These were the forbidding cryptlike shooting galleries. Often I saw users on the street, dipping and swaying like cobras. One day I walked out to see someone who'd ODed sprawled on the sidewalk, surrounded by a crowd debating whether he was dead or alive. He'd turned blue. Just then, an ambulance rolled up and the EMTs calmly revived the guy. As if they did it every day, and they probably did.

The most unexpected feature was the din, at least in summer. One night I visited a friend who lived across from one shooting gallery and next to another on East Third. We could barely hear each other over the screams from the street: "Works!" when the coast was clear, or "Bajando!" ("It's coming down") when cops were near. Cars with out-of-state plates were lined up as if headed through a drive-in bank.

Community groups had been clamoring for more cops for years, and occasionally they'd get them—standing on corners along Avenue A, when everyone knew the action was on Avenue B and beyond. Certainly the police made arrests. Sometimes there'd be a whole line of perps standing against some abandoned building with their hands up. But they'd all be back the next day. So, when the NYPD began Operation Pressure Point in January 1984, I did not expect much to change. But this would prove to be more than just another sweep. Operation Pressure Point lasted for a couple of years. By January 1986, the NYPD had made 17,000 arrests in the neighborhood, more than 5,200 of them for felonies, while seizing 160,000 packages of heroin. The courts couldn't even keep pace. New U.S. attorney for the Southern District, Rudolph Giuliani, stepped in to prosecute low-level street dealers one day a week in federal court, where they got longer sentences than they would have in the state courts.

Why did law enforcement suddenly get so serious? As the operation began to squeeze dealers out, longtime neighborhood resident Allen Ginsberg told the *East Village Eye*: "It's seemed to me to be the policy for the last 20 years to destroy the community of the Lower East Side. Apparently the supply of junk has been manipulated by the powers that be to drive the poor out of the neighborhood: use the junk population to burn down the area. The deed is done." That sounds like a conspiracy theory, but it jibed with what I witnessed.

When I lived between Avenues C and D in the seventies, I was aware of some drug dealing, but it was nothing like the open-air drug bazaar of the early eighties. Everyone I knew who'd been flushed out of Loisaida because of drugs—because they couldn't take one more break-in or mugging—fell into the "working poor" category: struggling artists or Puerto Rican families. In the early 1980s, the East Village lay at the cutting edge of the gentrification process.

After David returned from Europe at the end of February 1984, he visited the art piers with a French photographer, Marion Scemama. This was the beginning of a passionate friendship that lasted for seven years—but a relationship of such ups and downs that for several of those years they were not on speaking terms. They went to the piers so Marion could photograph David for a French-language magazine, *ICI New York*. David took her both to Pier 34, which she'd visited the previous summer with so many others, and to Pier 28, which few people had seen. (The derelict structures were still six or seven months away from demolition.) Marion had been active in left-wing politics in Paris, and they got to talking about the Red Army Faction, the West German terrorists sometimes referred to as the Baader-Meinhof Gang. During this conversation, Marion felt something click between her and David.

A couple of weeks later, Dean Savard called her to ask if she could photograph David for his next Civilian show. They were doing a poster, and David had suggested hiring her. Feeling too shy to go alone, Marion asked her friend Brigitte Engler to accompany her to the tiny Fourth Street apartment where David now lived alone. (Tom Cochran had moved out, probably at the end of '83.) The central room, the kitchen, was filled with new sculpture. Plaster heads. Not yet painted. David was using the oven to dry some of them. Marion photographed him seated among the heads, wearing shades and puffing on a cigarette, the essence of boho cool. Then they smoked pot and talked until two in the morning. From that point on, David called Marion nearly every day. They'd meet for breakfast and talk for hours over coffee after coffee.

Beginning with Kiki Smith—or maybe with Peeka Trenkle and Susan Gauthier—David had relationships with certain women that were very intense but never sexual. Marion filled that slot now that he and Kiki had retreated from each other a bit. He was still seething over her comment that she wasn't going to have children with him, while she'd begun to feel that it

*Marion Scemama in 1984.*
*(Photograph © Andreas*
*Sterzing)*

wasn't good for her emotionally to be, as she put it, "so deeply invested" in a relationship with a gay man. Nor did she identify with the aesthetics of the East Village or want to be part of that scene.

At the time of my interviews with David in 1990, he and Marion were in one of their "up" phases. He explained that they had a "friendship that was beyond friendship," that when they met "we were both dealing with a lot of dark stuff, working out things from our pasts." He thought she had an interesting mind.

Marion introduced David to Catherine Texier and Joel Rose, who'd just started their insanely labor-intensive Lower East Side fiction magazine, *Between C & D*. The publication was actually a fanfold computer printout sealed in a ziplock bag with handmade East Village art on each cover. (Price: four dollars.) For their second issue, released in summer 1984, they accepted a piece David wrote about his hustling days, "Self-Portrait in 23 Rounds."

\* \* \*

Even though the neighborhood galleries embraced everything from graffiti (at Fun, for example) to conceptualism (at Nature Morte, for example), I knew what people meant by an East Village "look"—a kind of cartoony figuration, painted quickly, probably meant to register quickly, often helped to that end by simple shocking imagery. By that standard, the quintessential East Village artist was Rick Prol, whose paintings all featured skinny men in business suits with knives stuck through their necks, or some variation on that theme. Prol also curated one of the quintessential East Village group shows, "Underdog" at East Seventh Street Gallery, which included David's work. The same issue of the *Eye* that covered the NYPD's Operation Pressure Point also carried interviews with Prol and another artist Mark Kostabi. They made it clear that a deep cynicism had already infected the scene.

Prol said he'd gone through art school hearing that painting was dead, but "then painting found itself again by letting itself be stupid." As for curating, artists were willing to do anything, Prol declared. "You give them a group show called 'Shit in a Road' and they'd paint pictures for it."

But Prol's was the voice of innocence compared with Mark Kostabi, who liked to say that his middle name was "Et." ("Mark-et." Nudge, nudge.) He told the *Eye*: "Paintings are doorways into collectors' homes." He was still a few years away from opening his own version of Warhol's Factory, Kostabi World, where assistants would manufacture his work for him—a practical approach for someone who regarded his paintings as mere "product." Kostabi would later claim to be a satirist. And maybe he was. In August 1985, while a gaggle of East Village artists painted a mural at the Palladium nightclub, Kostabi threw fifty bucks in singles out over the dance floor and watched people dive for dollars. The problem was that Kostabi's persona rather overwhelmed his actual artwork. A documentary on him that appeared in 2010 was titled *Con Artist*.

By March '84, some thirty galleries had opened. At Fun, Patti Astor and Bill Stelling had taken to wearing sweatshirts that read "The Original and Still the Best." Nicolas Moufarrege, that early enthusiast, published a piece called "The Year After" in *Flash Art* that summer. The key word was now *deal*, he reported, when last year it had been *show*. "The underground Bohemia of last year is now an all-out new establishment with all the intrigues that this engenders," he wrote. While he thought there were good artists at work, "there are too many fastly painted pieces; neo-expressionism and 'bad painting' have made it easy for many to pick up the figurative brush." He hoped this did not signal "the beginning of an era of 'souvenir' art and tourist boutiques."

Nowhere was the blatant commercialism of the scene embraced more openly than in a now-classic piece by Carlo McCormick and Walter Robinson that appeared in *Art in America* that summer. "Slouching Towards Avenue D" cheerfully described the East Village as a "marketing concept" suited to "the Reagan zeitgeist." The neighborhood itself, with its poverty, drugs, burnt-out buildings and crime, they called "an adventurous avant-garde setting of considerable cachet." I found this statement shocking, but they were also naming something real. Tour buses would soon arrive to show the curious-but-timid what the artists had wrought amid the rubble. *Art in America* allotted twenty-eight pages to a celebration of the scene's history and artists. Then, two pages went to Craig Owens for his retort: "The Problem with Puerilism." In Owens's view, the East Village was "an economic, rather than esthetic, development." But had anyone pretended otherwise? He decried the appropriation of "subcultural productions" (graffiti, cartooning). Was this an East Village problem? He criticized the scene as a "simulacrum" of bohemia. But it felt real to me.

What can be seen in hindsight was that reality and hype were tumbling over each other so quickly that both reactions were possible. The whole concept of marginality was in flux here. The media spotlight pushed cultural change at such a velocity that bohemians barely had a chance to stew in their legendary juices before someone was there trying to decide if they were the Next Big Thing.

On April 23, 1984, Health and Human Services Secretary Margaret Heckler appeared in Washington with Dr. Robert Gallo to announce that he had found the virus that causes AIDS. This should have been good news. Instead it marked one more spot where progress had snagged. French scientists at the Pasteur Institute had actually isolated the virus almost a full year earlier. In other words, a couple of months before the death of Klaus

Nomi. Not that it would have helped Nomi. There were no treatments. But the news that this was an infectious disease might have been useful to know, even if no one could say for sure how it was transmitted.

Gallo had shown in 1980 that a retrovirus he called HTLV caused a rare form of leukemia. His hypothesis was that a related retrovirus caused AIDS. The Pasteur Institute scientists sent Gallo samples of their retrovirus, which they called LAV, in July '83 and again in September, to establish that it was *not* a leukemia virus. Gallo announced at the end of that year that he'd discovered the cause of AIDS: HTLV-III. The assistant secretary for health asked him not to make the finding public just yet. It was an election year and credit for the discovery was to go to the Reagan administration, to the president who would not even utter the word "AIDS."

By March 1984, however, the Centers for Disease Control had proven that HTLV-III and LAV were one and the same. The CDC director let the news slip in a March 28 interview with the *New York Native*: The AIDS virus had been discovered—by the French. The *New York Times* picked up on that and ran a story on April 22. Which forced Heckler and Gallo to make their announcement the next day.

Ultimately, the French scientists got the Nobel Prize in Medicine, while it was Gallo who demonstrated that the virus first isolated at the Pasteur Institute is the virus that causes AIDS. So everyone contributed, but the controversy over credit had a negative impact on research. As Randy Shilts pointed out in *And the Band Played On*, scientists working internationally on AIDS were forced to take sides, and certain good virologists opted out to avoid the politicking. Meanwhile, it was time to develop an antibody test, and while Gallo sent samples of the virus to pharmaceutical companies, he did not send any to the CDC until the end of 1984 because the agency had leaked news of the discovery and he saw it as allied with the French.

In April 1984, however, very few people understood the significance of these events or the magnitude of the crisis about to engulf them. The issue of the *Native* that broke the story on the virus did not even give it a cover line. It was just one more theory at that point. More coverage went to the possible closure of the bathhouses.

\* \* \*

On April 15, 1984, Mike Bidlo re-created Warhol's Factory in the attic at P.S. 1.

Bidlo appeared as Warhol and spent the evening making silk-screen prints of "Marilyn" to give out gratis. Silver foil covered the walls. Naturally, the not-quite-Velvet Underground performed. Keiko Bonk—a painter, musician, and friend of David's—put the band together and played Nico. Julie Hair was John Cale while David played Lou Reed and sang a creditable rendition of "Heroin." He also dropped acid for the first time in his life. Dean Savard wafted through the crowd dressed as Edie Sedgwick. Rhonda Zwillinger appeared as Valerie Solanas. Many who'd been there commented later on the crush and the rhythmic bouncing on the floor—remembered indelibly because they thought it was going to collapse.

That month David was engaged in finishing work for his show at Civilian. He had made twenty-three plaster heads with, as he put it, "a couple of extras that were separated from the series," which he called *Metamorphosis*. They looked like the alien heads he'd started to include in a few paintings. No two were alike. A few were covered with maps or parts of maps, others were painted, the colors of the eyes changing "according to what colors mean spiritually," he said. Then halfway through the progression, the heads showed signs of distress: bandages, blood, black eyes, incineration, and finally one "fell off the shelf." A twenty-fourth head sat on the floor in a doctor's bag, an old one. He said the piece was about the evolution of consciousness. With perhaps the attendant consequences. He'd been thinking, twenty-three genes in a chromosome; a twenty-fourth causes mongoloidism. (That was also the reasoning behind the story that was about to appear in *Between C & D*, "Self-Portrait in 23 Rounds.") Some of the individual heads were photographed, but the piece as a whole was never documented. David threw one of the "extra" heads into the Hudson as a sort of offering.

He'd begun to refine his private symbol system. He continued to work with maps, which remained forever mysterious to him as an acceptable version of reality. Ripping them could be a metaphor for so many things, like groundlessness and chaos. He'd stopped working with garbage can lids and driftwood. The new sculptures used animal skulls, skeletons, mannequins.

To look at David's early work is to watch him figuring out how to be an artist. A painting he did in 1983 called *The Boys Go Off to War* is a kind of diptych, and the imagery is simple. On the left half are two men, naked to the waist, perhaps in a bar (since one holds a drink), perhaps lovers but at least friends (since one has his arm around the other). On the right are two gutted pigs. With the paintings he did for the 1984 Civilian show he was really beginning to develop his collage approach. For example, *Fuck You Faggot Fucker* features, again, a male couple. The background is all maps but the only one clearly visible is behind the couple at the center. Created with a stencil, they stand waist-deep in water, kissing. Directly below them is a scrap of paper found by David, on which some anonymous homophobe has written, "Fuck You Faggot Fucker," around an obscene doodle. He's embedded that in the painting. At the four corners are photographs: one of Brian Butterick as St. Sebastian, photographed at the pier; three of David with John Hall, naked at the Christodora.

David's show with the plaster heads, other sculptures, and new paintings opened on May 5, 1984. Though none of the principals, including David, knew it at the time—this would be his last solo show at Civilian. I remember the opening because everyone stood out on Eleventh Street watching David inside, finishing the work. He'd hung the show earlier, placing the heads on a wall where he'd painted a big bull's-eye. Then he left, and the twenty-three heads started to slide off their shelves. The wall was just Sheetrock with no studs. Savard and Marisa took them all down in a frenzy and rehung them on the opposite wall, where Savard repainted the bull's-eye. Then they had to rehang everything else. David, who'd probably been sitting in some restaurant, came back furious. He didn't like Savard's bull's-eye. I remember him standing inside with a paintbrush—opening delayed. What he said to me about it later, though, was that he liked the way that broke the art-world rules. You couldn't go to an opening in SoHo or on Fifty-seventh Street and find the artist still standing there with a bucket of paint.

Earlier that day, David had argued with Alan Barrows about *Fuck You Faggot Fucker*. Barrows remembered, "I said, 'David we can't have that name.' It really bothered me. And he said, 'Well, that's the name of the painting.' I said, 'Can't you change it?' I was thinking of these prissy people

*David installing the plaster heads at Civilian Warfare on May 5, 1984.*
*(Photograph by Philip Pocock)*

coming in." The critics. The collectors. The art crowd. They'd be offended. David adamantly refused.

He then responded to Barrows with a work of art, though Barrows didn't know it until he saw the piece at a New Museum retrospective six and a half years after David's death. There was the familiar image of the two men kissing, this time stenciled over two contact sheets. The one on the right shows Jesse Hultberg at the pier; he's naked in most of the pictures and either wearing a dog mask David made or posing as St. Sebastian. No doubt David intended to contrast Jesse, who was literally willing to expose himself, with the reserved Barrows. The contact sheet on the left shows Barrows in photos David took during their European trip. In one, right near the center, Barrows is sticking his finger down his throat over a plate of bad food at the Berlin airport. So, Barrows realized, "because I had trouble with it, he's forever connected me with that image, and now this"—it's simply called *Untitled*—"is in the permanent collection at the Whitney."


The Civilian show sold pretty well. David was becoming, in the words of Dennis Cooper, "a lion of the scene." And around this time begin the stories of his frightening and often irrational rage.

It was sometime in '84 that David got mad at Chuck Nanney and stopped speaking to him—snubbed him on the street, wouldn't return phone calls. Nanney couldn't figure out why. Finally their mutual friend Steve Brown let Nanney know: "David came over to your apartment while he was tripping, and you looked at him funny." Nanney was astonished. And hurt. The rift was patched up eventually. They had so many mutual friends that it was hard to avoid each other. But they never actually discussed what had happened, and, said Nanney, "Something odd started to happen to our relationship after that."

Then came an explosion at his ex-lover, old roommate, and onetime bandmate, Brian Butterick. One night Doug "Wah" Landau (who later opened King Tut's Wah Wah Hut) pulled up at the Pyramid Club and asked, "Want to go to Provincetown for a couple of days?" Brian did. David piled in too, and Jesse Hultberg. They left after four A.M. when the club closed.

In the course of the four-to five-hour drive, Brian said something sarcastic and, he thought, innocuous. He did not remember the content, except that it had nothing to do with David. But David, seated in front, turned to him so enraged that his face had turned purple. He said something about how Brian was acting like a jaded old queen "and he peppered it with some really hurtful personal stuff," Brian said. David wouldn't drop it, either, until someone else in the car yelled, "Enough!"

"Everyone else was signaling to me when David's back was turned," Brian said. "Like, 'What the hell is going on?' It was so vitriolic and directed towards me, and I didn't understand why he was mad. It wasn't even about him."

By now, Brian was one of David's oldest friends, and he'd never seen him behave like this before. "He was usually held back," said Brian. "With bad emotions. Good ones too. He had never lashed out at me."

The two of them never discussed this incident. "I didn't go there, because it was so nutty," Brian explained. "I talked about it to the other people in the car."

It was a preview of things to come.


Like most villages, this one reveled in gossip. At some point, a delicious story circulated that Gary Indiana had written a feature on David for *Art in America*, but then got so furious with him that he went to the magazine's office and ripped the type off the boards. Carlo McCormick called it "common knowledge at the time." Gary denied it, and Betsy Baker, then editor of the magazine, said that nothing like that ever occurred.

But what had happened between Gary and David in Paris didn't end there. Gary was still in love, and now when they met on the art-world circuit, David acted as if they hardly knew each other. As Joe Vojtko put it, "The more Gary kept trying, the crueler David became." Vojtko said that for many months, even years after, when he ran into one of them on the street, David or Gary would complain for what seemed like hours about the other. Vojtko thought they were both irrational on the topic.

David told people that Gary was stalking him. Marisa Cardinale remembered David coming into the gallery to discuss this, but she couldn't recall specific incidents. "I remember more the emotional tenor," she said. "I remember fraught conversations. Like, 'What am I going to do? How am I going to get him to stop?'"

Judy Glantzman, part of the Civilian stable and later a good friend of David's, confirmed that "David was unnerved."

But Gary adamantly denied that he did any stalking, and when David later wrote about Gary in the *Eye*, he did not mention stalking. Instead he complained, for example, about Gary leaving fifteen screaming phone messages in one night. Gary said he has never called anyone that many times in a day, but in a short letter to David he wrote, "I'm sorry I terrorized your answering machine Saturday night. The more direct thing would have just been to scream in your face." David also charged that Gary was writing him letters of "up to twenty pages outlining how I was still a prostitute."

"We said a lot of things to each other," Gary said. Which isn't exactly a denial, but there is a surviving letter (of five and a third single-spaced pages) in which Gary says, "If you can't cop to the fact that everyone is corrupted by the need to make money, maybe it's because you've never transposed your experience of being a hustler to the market for works of art. . . . Don't you imagine that part of your public image, like Kathy Acker's, has ANY-THING to do with your willingness to expose yourself sexually, and the sexual attraction to you of the viewer/reader/spectator, whatever?"

David was writing letters too. Once the two of them made up—years after this—they agreed to destroy each other's letters, which Gary did. David either did not or he overlooked a couple—quite possible since he always lived in chaos.

But until the end of his life, David believed that Gary had spread stories about him that hurt his career. He thought, for example, that Gary told people he was a junkie. Gary denies this—and it's not clear that such news would have discouraged anyone's interest. Look at Jean-Michel Basquiat, a notorious heroin addict who practically had collectors lined up at his studio door. David also claimed, for example, that Gary put other critics up to writing bad reviews of his work. Gary denies it, and it's hard to imagine any critic taking such direction.

I have spoken to everyone in the art world who's in a position to know, asking them to speak off the record if they must, but to answer the question: Did Gary hurt David's career? What everyone has told me is that David hurt his own career. Whenever his work was most in demand, he would stop painting.

In 1984, Lydia Lunch moved back to New York after spending several years in Los Angeles and London. By the age of twenty-four, Lydia had worked with more than a dozen bands, starting with Teenage Jesus and the Jerks, starred in at least a dozen underground films, and become a pioneer in what would later be called "spoken word." As a self-described catastrophist and contrarian, Lydia liked to rant. Underneath the fierce persona, however, Lydia—like David—was as much a seeker as an agitator.

That spring, she invited David to participate in several spoken-word events she set up at the Pyramid Club: "Readings from the Diaries of the

Sexually Insane and Other Atrocities," "The Grand Finale of the Memorial Day Parade of Idiots," and "The Weekend of Emotional Abuse." Other participants included Vojtko, Richard Kern, Thurston Moore, and Victor Poison-Tete. David probably read from his monologues. He'd written some new ones based on stories he'd heard from Bill Rice and Alan Barrows.

Reminded years later of her menacing titles, Lydia laughed. She'd forgotten them but had a clear memory of what mattered back then to her and the artists she was close to: "We were just so disgusted with the hypocrisy of everything, whether we were talking about sex or money or the police state or personal relationships. Everyone felt that they had to do these performances, had to paint these pictures, had to make these films. They were driven to get it out of their system. To expel into the world what was trying to kill us or silence us or just beat us down.

"We lived with a toxicity in our blood or in our brain or in our psyche that drove us in an explosive way to try to create," she said. "We were going as fast as we could because we didn't think we were going to be around much longer. It's not only about AIDS. It's that you didn't think you could last because you were going to burn out one way or another. It seemed that it was already written for you. That you better do as much as you could right now. Maybe because some people had already gone through so much and they couldn't take much more."

Lydia didn't know a lot about David's life but was drawn to the immediacy of his work. "He made it sound like 'I experienced it, I wrote it, I took it to the stage.' That was very attractive to me," she said. "He was just a spontaneous performer or artist. Not trained, like myself. Not trained. So in a sense we came from a similar background or maybe a mind-set. There were a few people that were really hard-core people just because they were hard-core from circumstances beyond their control. David was one of those. You knew that the experiences were written deeper than the paper he was reading from."

Vojtko recalled performing with his boyfriend, David Said, at one of Lydia's "Weekends of Emotional Abuse." They'd prepared a piece about AIDS, "Secret Love (From a Room at the End of Everything)," using money to record tapes of ambient sound that should have been applied to their overdue electric bill. Fellow readers like Kern and Henry Rollins had attracted what Vojtko saw as an aggressively heterosexual crowd that night. Over the weeks of performing with Lydia, Vojtko remembered, he and Said and David had grown bolder in their "willingness to push the limits and to flaunt the grimy details of [their] sexuality in ways that made the humorless straight crowd uncomfortable." On the night Vojtko and his boyfriend did the AIDS piece, they brought it to a cacophonous crescendo, banging on metal and breaking furniture. "Half of the crowd was weeping and applauding, and the other half was shouting obscenities and throwing things at us. It was just the kind of reaction that Lydia liked best."

Later in the dressing room, Lydia divided the door money among the performers. David tried to give Vojtko and Said his share, saying that he was selling paintings now and didn't need the money. Vojtko and Said told him they appreciated the gesture but couldn't take it. At home later, Said went into his backpack for cigarettes and was astonished to find a wad of twenty dollar bills—more than David's share of the door.


In June, when Luis Frangella traveled to Buenos Aires to visit family, David went with him.

"The colors here are colors that brought me close to fainting," he wrote in a letter to Hujar. He loved the drives with Luis into the countryside and the jungle. They stayed for a couple of days near Iguazú Falls and went hiking. David ventured out into a raging stream above the falls, his feet on bamboo while he held a vine overhead—as Luis screamed, "Come back! You'll be swept over the falls if you slip!" David laughed at him. Until the bamboo broke. He managed to pull himself back to dry land, heart in throat, and found Luis "in the forest too sick to watch me anymore."

He hadn't gone to Argentina to work, but David rarely stopped working. No doubt it was Luis who arranged for him to show at the Centro de Arte y Comunicación. David created *A Painting to Replace the British Monument in Buenos Aires* on a street poster—burning race horses running below a large smoking alien with one eye a British flag, the other an American flag. One of the other pieces he made, *Altar for the People of Villa Miseria*, refers to a shantytown he'd visited with Luis, where he'd seen "huge families picking around mountains of smoking garbage." The major elements in this sculpture: a human figurine seated in a wood cabinet painted pink. A red hand reaching for that human. A loaf of bread on the shelf below, cut in half and sewn together with red thread. All of this on a plinth. A Mayan statue sits at the base of the plinth. Above it all hangs a torn red banner. In a real departure, perhaps an experiment, David also painted about twenty watercolors in a sketchbook, mostly landscapes, which he never chose to exhibit.

He hoped he could come back to Argentina, he wrote Hujar. He would learn the language and travel the continent. But something changed in his relationship with Luis during this trip, according to Marisela La Grave, the young photographer who'd met them at the pier. David and Luis had had an affair, and Marisela thought that Luis broke it off during this trip or maybe just after. He discussed it with her. David and Luis remained friends, however.

David got back to New York on July 8. A couple of weeks later, Jean Pierre came to visit. According to Marion Scemama, David had decided that his relationship with Jean Pierre was over, but he didn't know how to tell him. So David proposed that they take a trip—the three of them. He rented a car and drove them first to Virginia Beach, then to the Outer Banks—two spots he'd come to love during an earlier vacation with Kiki Smith, probably in '83. As Marion remembered it, David was nervous and paranoid for much of the trip. One day in a restaurant, when Marion and JP began conversing in French, laughing at something, David stood up and went to sit at another table. One night David left them alone at the hotel for most of the night. Then there was the fight in the car when David said something so insulting to Marion (she couldn't remember what) that she demanded to be let out so she could take the train home. He let her out, then came back and got her. "David could be really mean with people when he didn't know how to handle the situation," she said. Jean Pierre didn't seem to remember any of this, but he is also the sort of person who doesn't want to speak ill. He maintained that he and David never broke up.

In 1984 Richard Kern began making Super 8 films like *The Right Side of My Brain*, a collaboration with Lydia Lunch. She plays a woman drawn to in-

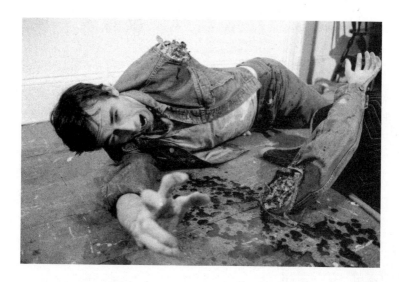

*David in Richard Kern's* Stray Dogs. *(Photograph by R. Kern)*

creasingly abusive men—though they're never abusive enough for her. In the film, she loves how she feels with a man when she's "squirming under his fist." It would have looked like a work of pure misogyny if Lydia herself hadn't written the script.

The Cinema of Transgression reveled in depravity, deliberate ugliness, and amorality. A line from *Right Side of My Brain* summarizes the whole ethos: "We'll take the bad with the bad and make it worse." Some of the films that came out of this movement were just silly, but Kern had enough talent to create others that were truly horrifying. Most of his films revolve around sexual power plays, with an emphasis on bloodletting and self-injury.

Kern asked David to appear in "Stray Dogs," one of the four sections of a film called *Manhattan Love Suicides*. David plays a man identified as "a fan" who's obsessed with an artist (Bill Rice) and follows him home. For some reason, the artist allows this demented fan into his apartment. David wildly overacts—mugging, leering, and twitching. The artist paints while the fan jerks off. Then the fan approaches, and the artist pushes him away. The fan begins literally to explode, first bursting a blood vessel in his neck, then losing an arm. That gets the artist interested. He wants to draw the fan, now lying in a puddle of gore. The cheap special effects are one of the film's major charms. David loved playing out this cartoon version of repressed emotion. It was done over a weekend, and David kicked in $250, which probably covered most of the budget.

When David analyzed his attraction to the Cinema of Transgression later on, though, he didn't even discuss the movies. He said that he'd found a group of people who saw "unarguable truth" in violence.

The art world had turned upside down. Suddenly, a Fifty-seventh Street gallery could close while full-page ads in *Artforum* might be purchased by the occupant of an unheated shoebox between Avenues A and B. It took me quite a while to realize that this was largely an illusion. No one had actually uncovered a pot of gold in the East Village. Hardly any of these tiny galleries made big money. Hardly any of them would survive the scene.

Civilian Warfare, for example, was a hot gallery with a horrible cash-flow problem. The gallery had no backers, and no one working there had any business training. Major collectors would walk out with a number of pieces and promise to pay, for example, a thousand dollars a month. The gallery had to pay rent, utilities, and three salaries, along with the artists whose work had been sold. "We didn't understand the ramifications," Marisa said. "You can't call your artist and say, 'We sold ten pieces,' and then not be able to pay them. We wouldn't have been able to pay them in years, at the rate money was coming in. . . . And I was making, like, two hundred dollars a week."

Back in more innocent times, someone had once come in and paid cash for a piece—a large sum. Savard was there, and Marisa, and David. Maybe Barrows too. "We laid the bills out end to end because we had never seen that much money before," Marisa said. "I don't remember how many thousands of dollars, but it took up a lot of the floor."

In March 1984, however, David deposited a check from Civilian for forty-five dollars, and it bounced. In May, he sold quite a bit of work from the plaster-heads show, but the gallery could not afford to give him his cut. Not all of it, at least. Marisa remembered David and Savard arguing over it.

One day David came into the gallery and saw a receipt push-pinned to a shelf in the back—a receipt for a limousine ride. Savard and Gracie Mansion had taken a limo together to an event uptown, and they were dividing the cost, so Gracie had brought the receipt over. Apparently Savard had some sort of explanation but David couldn't hear it. "He was livid. Just screaming," Marisa said. "We were spending this money, and he hadn't gotten paid. He could not be talked down. He stormed out."

Savard's drug problem hadn't yet begun to wreak havoc with their everyday operations. It was his spirit that was driving Civilian Warfare. People who knew the gallery's directors would describe Alan Barrows with words like "steady" and "mature" while Dean Savard was "charismatic" and "outlandish." Judy Glantzman analyzed it this way: "Dean's strength was also his weakness. That very far-reaching ambition and imagination made Civilian what it was. He was a visionary." But then he'd go too far. He reveled in hyperbole. The gallery's summer show that year was called "25,000 Sculptors from Across the U.S.A." Glantzman estimated that there were maybe a hundred pieces crammed into the storefront. And that was amusing. But she also remembered being with Savard at the home of some important collectors one night and feeling embarrassed by his absurd fabrications. That particular night it was "we've sold five hundred thousand dollars' worth of work."

"He was a pathological liar," said Barrows, who believed Savard's stories for years and then suddenly saw that they didn't add up. Marisa agreed: "He told gigantic lies. He said he'd been raised in Vietnam and was airlifted off the roof of the embassy at the end of the war. He used to bleach his hair and people thought he was Scandinavian—they couldn't wrap their mind around the fact that a man would bleach his hair. So he told those people he was born in Sweden." He'd told Alan that his father was in Kuala Lumpur.

In August the *East Village Eye* reported that Civilian Warfare was going to buy a building—another fantastic lie from Savard. What did happen that summer was that Savard and Barrows decided to leave their storefront for something bigger. They weren't playing anymore. (They definitely had a typewriter now, though according to Barrows, "Someone probably gave it to us.") And they had to keep up appearances in the ever more glamorous and growing scene. Savard seemed to feel especially competitive with Gracie Mansion, and she was moving to a larger space on Avenue A while turning her old storefront on East Tenth into the Gracie Mansion Museum Store.

Savard and Barrows found a place on Avenue B and Tenth Street where they would pay $900 rent instead of $550. They hired someone to renovate the space, then couldn't pay him.

David went to Marisa and asked her if she would start a gallery. Luis came to her with the same idea. But she didn't want to own a gallery. She stayed with Civilian and was there the day David came to the new space on Avenue B and demanded his slides and his clippings. "He said he was going to have a show at Gracie Mansion," she remembered. "It was terrible. Dean cried."

David walked the one block to Gracie's with his loose slides, press releases, and clips in a shopping bag.

# 14 A BURNING CHILD

**With his installation** at Gracie Mansion Gallery in November 1984, David began addressing the events of his childhood for the first time.

He covered a child mannequin with maps. He added flames to the child's arms, legs, and back. The burning child runs across the bottom of the sea. David brought sand into the gallery to create his ocean floor, and added aquatic plants made from newspapers. At the back of the sandy area he placed a map-wrapped cow skull clamping a small globe in its jaws. Suspended above this from the ceiling was a shark covered in maps. Looming over it from the back wall—the specter the burning child ran from—was a large four-paneled painting of an ocean liner titled *Dad's Ship*. On another wall, he depicted impending doom on a larger scale with his painting *Soon All This Will Be Picturesque Ruins*. He lit the scene with tiny white Christmas lights and added a soundtrack he'd done with Doug Bressler from 3 Teens.

The day of the opening, scheduled for six P.M., David didn't show up to install the work until five thirty—with Marion Scemama and Greer Lankton in tow. The opening was delayed for at least an hour and a half while they worked.

David had decided to include some of Greer's work—six human figures, maybe a foot tall, with arms raised in supplication or distress, made from wire frames wrapped in black tape. Greer was a transsexual who made dolls that addressed issues of gender and identity—their mutability. They could be "sissies" or hermaphrodites or Siamese twins, usually anatomically correct. She had had the first show at the new Civilian on Avenue B, but apparently it hadn't sold too well. David put her in his installation because she needed money. The cow skull and Greer dolls were sold as a package. According to Sur Rodney Sur, the collector who bought them threw Greer's dolls away and kept the Wojnarowicz. But Greer got paid.

David had also been invited to show with Greer at the Timothy Great-house Gallery in January '85. David told Greathouse that he would do it only if he could collaborate with Marion. She was an unknown but Great-house wanted David enough to agree. "It was unbelievable," Marion said. "I never showed in my life. David was the first person who said to me, 'but you're an artist.' This guy made an eruption in my life and changed every-thing about how I considered myself."

One night David and Marion went to a desolate site under the Brook-lyn Bridge to stage a photo. David wanted it to look as if he'd been beaten. Queer-bashed. He lay back against an abandoned bathtub, a dazed look in his eye and fake blood coming from his mouth. Marion lit the scene with headlights from the truck they'd borrowed to drive there.

They would use this in one of their collaborations for Greathouse, and in a poster they were making for *Between C & D* magazine. David wanted to pair the photo with a text about a recent court decision ruling that homo-sexuals had no constitutional right to privacy, probably a reference to *Bow-ers v. Hardwick*, then winding its way toward the Supreme Court.* David also spoke of how a person could get away with murder by saying the victim was a queer who tried to touch him. So in his text, he becomes the aggres-sor. "Realizing that I have nothing to lose in my actions, I let my hands be-come weapons, my teeth become weapons. . . . In my dreams . . . I enter your houses through the smallest cracks in the bricks that keep you occu-pied with a feeling of comfort and safety. . . . I will wake you up and I will welcome you to your bad dream."

Marion went home and processed the film immediately. Then she spent the night printing. "I start getting scared about having taken this photo" she said, "because I thought maybe one day he's going to die this way. Because when you're European, you have this image of Americans who just can come from nowhere, come with a gun and kill somebody if they don't like what he represents. I thought maybe I took a fiction photo but one day it could be reality. So I called David. It was early in the morning, and I

---

* Michael Hardwick had been arrested for having consensual sex with another man in his own bed-room. In 1986, the U.S. Supreme Court upheld the anti-sodomy law under which he had been ar-rested, ruling that the right to privacy did not extend to sexual conduct if it involved homosexuals.

said, 'I'm kind of scared of this photo.' He said, 'But do you like it?' I said, 'Just come and see it.' It was six or seven in the morning, and I showed him the photo, and he said, 'Wow that's great.'

"But I said, 'Are you sure you want to use this?'

"He said, 'Yes, of course. Why?'

"And I said, 'I feel a kind of responsibility about this image. Imagine that one day this happens to you.'

"And he got really, *really* angry. *Really* angry. I mean, later I understood that David could become angry at a point where you were not expecting it. But this was the first time he yelled at me: 'How can you say that? If you say that, it means you *want* that for me!'"

So David began 1985—his year of fury.

He'd always had a temper, but now he was leaping into rages that were both irrational and damaging to some of his closest friendships. He and Marion went on to make four or five pieces for Greathouse. They produced the poster for *Between C & D* (which was folded into quarters and slipped into each ziploc bag). They remained on speaking terms. But David withdrew. Marion didn't understand it. She just knew that suddenly "something was gone, something was broken."

Years later, David tried to analyze his ups and downs with Marion, and he made the following notes about this first break with her: "Couldn't leave me alone—together all the time. I asked for a week alone. I thought I was going to kill myself or that she was pushing me to kill her. Asked for week. She said yes. She called screaming about poster collaboration in show. I rejected her."

David did put the poster in a group show without telling her. Then she happened to see him on the street and asked why. He replied, "I don't need to tell you everything." That made her so angry that she went to Keith Davis's loft, where they'd stored the posters, and crossed her name off each one with a black marker. "It was a way of saying, 'OK, I don't want this to be considered a collaboration.' Which was infantile," Marion says. "Later Keith told me that when David saw that, he laughed." However, David told people later that *he* had crossed off Marion's name. Whatever the case, this was the beginning of discord.

\* \* \*

Allen Frame had continued to experiment with *Sounds in the Distance* after the run in Bill Rice's garden. He took it to Berlin during the film festival there and staged it in someone's loft. Then at the end of November 1984, he directed *Sounds* at BACA Downtown in Brooklyn. The new cast included Steve Buscemi, Mark Boone Junior, John Heys, and Richard Elovich. They didn't get reviewed, but Frame was gratified by the packed houses and positive feedback from theater people.

This time, David did not hesitate to attend, and as Frame put it, "he was not that gracious." Frame had been much more ambitious this time. He had fifteen actors instead of eight. He had sets. One actor stepped out of a locker room at the back for his monologue. Another stepped out of an office party. One woman performed a monologue zipped up to her neck in a steam sauna. Onstage until intermission was a sculpture by Robin Hurst—a house sitting on a train trestle.

Frame asked David what he thought, and David responded, "Do you have four hours?"

David's complaints amounted to the fact that he didn't want these monologues reinterpreted. He could accept the locker room and office party ideas, but he certainly hadn't gotten a story from anyone in a steam sauna; he wouldn't have been interested in such a person. And how could the truck driver monologue be assigned to a woman—who then played it as a lesbian trucker? Changing the gender changed the content. On the positive side, one actor sounded so much like the guy he'd originally talked to that David was floored.

Frame felt disappointed that David saw things so literally but dutifully took his "notes" back to a couple of the actors—who were not happy to hear them.

David spent most of January 1985 in Paris, and while there he purchased some real human skeletons along with a baby elephant skeleton. He shipped them in one big crate to Keith Davis's loft. Keith seemed to have infinite patience for any adventure or demand, if art was involved. When he left David a phone message saying, "Termites are coming out of the elephant; we have to bomb it some more," he did not sound perturbed. David told people that the baby elephant had died in a game preserve, crushed in a closing gate or maybe electrocuted on a fence.

In February David bought a car—a green '67 Chevy Malibu station wagon. He'd been renting cars periodically ever since he first had some money. Often he just drove to New Jersey with Hujar or Steve Doughton or Marion Scemama or some other friend to visit junkyards and swamps. He loved looking for snakes, frogs, and bugs. David and Hujar were especially fond of the industrial wasteland near the Meadowlands and another such site along the Hudson at Caven Point. They would both take pictures.

Almost immediately, David began adding tchotchkes and totems to the dashboard of the Chevy. Doughton recalled that among the very first was a figure of the leprous St. Lazarus, attended by helpful dogs. Then came the items that seemed to have floated off one of his paintings—a small skull to which he'd added bulging eyes and fangs, globes, dinosaurs, a bust of Jesus wearing a crown of thorns, assorted monsters, and a hollow green, red, and yellow frog. He once told Tommy Turner that the spirit of the car lived in the frog and had to be fed. Look inside, he told Turner, who found himself staring at a mound of dead grasshoppers, moths, bees, and other bugs collected from the grill and the windshield. A Day of the Dead skeleton decorated with baubles hung from the mirror. Over the glove compartment he eventually pasted a bumper sticker reading "I Brake for Hallucinations."

One night near the end of February, a big crowd gathered at 8BC for an art auction to benefit Life Café, a sort of community canteen that was having trouble paying its rent. The *New York Times* sent a reporter to cover this exotic event. The club, "a dark ruin," was packed. The unnamed auctioneer had accessorized his full-length evening gown with a beard and red horn-rimmed glasses. Bidders held up not paddles but numbered paper plates.

The dramatic highlight came during the bidding over a sculpture by "David Wojnarowicz—the hottest among hot East Village artists." It was a cat's skull, two inches high and covered with maps. Bids jumped in $25 and then $100 increments. When they hit $800, the auctioneer cried, "Push it to a thousand! Think what you'd be doing for the community!" It topped out at $1,100 to wild applause.

The custom at benefits was for artist and beneficiary to split the proceedings, though an artist could always decline to take his half. David *did* take his $550, but not for himself. Early in March, he stopped in at the old Civilian Warfare storefront, which had become Ground Zero. Now living in the tiny back room were James Romberger, the artist who had once mistaken David for a lumberjack, and Marguerite Van Cook, then pregnant with their child.

James and Marguerite had become dealers almost by accident. Late in the summer of '84, they'd curated an exhibit at Sensory Evolution Gallery called "The Acid Show"—so-called because they handed out LSD at the opening. The show was such a hit that it moved to a nightclub called Kamikaze for a short run. One of the artists they'd included was Dean Savard, thrilled to be able to show one of his own paintings for a change. Walking home from Kamikaze one night, they ran into Savard on the street. Civilian was about to move to Avenue B, and Savard said, why don't you take the Eleventh Street space and bring the Acid Show there? He handed them the keys.

James and Marguerite ran Ground Zero in the spirit of the original galleries. "We're not serious art dealers," Marguerite told no less than the *New York Times*. "We do and show what we like." David had heard from Marion Scemama that Ground Zero needed money at least as much as Life Café did. He had never even met Marguerite until the day he came by and handed her a check for $550. She did not allow herself to look at the check while he was there—thinking, wow, maybe it'll be for fifty dollars.


The day after David wrote that check, he went to the opening of the 1985 Whitney Biennial. He had two paintings in the exhibition. He had wanted this since his first year at Civilian, and they couldn't make it happen in '83, when he was such a beginner. Now, just two years later, he was one of two "East Village" painters in the show. (The other was Rodney Alan Greenblat.) He'd arrived.

And he was terribly unhappy.

I remember running into him on the street—either after the plasterheads show at Civilian or later that year when the Whitney announced who'd made it into the Biennial. When I congratulated him, he had such a look of distress on his face. He told me he just hated the art world. And then, I believe the exact sentence went: "If I were straight, I'd move to a small town right now and get a job in a gas station."

Dennis Cooper also ran into him on the street, probably after the Biennial opened. Cooper, of course, had published some of David's *Rimbaud in New York* photos and some of David's monologues in his literary journal, *Little Caesar*. Cooper had moved to New York in 1983. He and David weren't close, but Cooper always went to see his shows and he didn't like the new work—the burning children, the kissing men, the shark. It was all so obvious, he thought. He liked the early work and thought David had "lost the quality of complete and pure alienation that had given his talent its bite and specificity." So Cooper analyzed it in *Artforum's* special issue on East Village art, published in October 1999. When he saw David on the street that day in 1985, he expressed these misgivings, "half expecting one of his famous bursts of temper," Cooper wrote.

Instead, Wojnarowicz sat down with me on a stoop and launched into a tormented, self-righteous, hour-long harangue that has, ever since, struck me as definitive of East Village Art's brief moment, for better or worse. He said that his success was destroying him because he couldn't reject it in good conscience. He'd dreamed of this kind of recognition and had even fantasized about exactly the kind of black-sheep art world that the East Village scene encompassed in theory, a situation where art could be anything at all, and where walking into a gallery would always involve a disconcerting, confrontational experience with an uncompromised, individual vision. But this belief had been contingent on the idea that New York was secretly full of artists who had as clamorous a sensibility as his own. Instead, he found himself surrounded by peers whose talent was merely raw, and raw only by virtue of economic hardship, but whose sensibilities were as coddling and self-indulgent as those of the Salles, Fischls, and Longos who populated the official art world. As a consequence, similar delusions of greatness had settled over the scene. In response, he'd rebelled against his peers by giving his work a social conscience and physical grandiosity, both to counteract the ongoing romanticization of the homespun and to embody what he imagined an "East Village art" should be. But his rebellion had backfired. The political sheen had given critics and curators a way to pigeonhole his work and had led them to misdiagnose his personal rage as the spearhead of a movement with which he felt no camaraderie whatsoever. He said he was going to quit making art, and stormed off.

Of course, David did not quit making art. He just quit painting for the rest of 1985. The only picture in his oeuvre with an '85 date is *Attack of the Alien Minds*, shown in the Biennial; that's dated 1984–85 and features the same alien head he used in his May '84 show at Civilian. A couple of exceptions were paintings he included in the installations that occupied him that year—which really began with the burning child fleeing *Dad's Ship*, at Gracie Mansion. These are the scenarios he created after that: Parents eating their children. Parents being murdered by their children. (That was both an installation and a film.) Then, a burning child fleeing the apocalypse. He also began work on a film about a murdering "satanic" teen. A fourth installation, in a show that raised money for a child victims' fund, featured a kid being hunted down like an animal.

What he realized later was that his newly secure foothold in the art world had relieved all that pressure just to survive—the pressure that had kept him from facing his past. "It was a rough time for me," said David when I interviewed him. "I had more money than I'd ever had in my life. Which gave me access to time, gave me access to movement . . . and it shook up a lot in my life. I hit a really dark period. I think I became somewhat self-destructive, just—you know, I was hitting against that whole childhood." He had tapped into a huge reservoir of neediness and rage.

In 1985, he didn't just make one installation after another about imperiled children or dead families; he began to lash out at people who were "like family."

Jim Stark, soon to start producing Jim Jarmusch's films, decided to become the next to take on *Sounds in the Distance* after he saw the show in Brooklyn. He knew nothing of David's reaction to that version. He just thought the material could use a bigger production and maybe get to a bigger audience. He enlisted a young director, Molly Fowler, who'd never heard of David but was fascinated by the monologues Stark showed her. Then they went to Gracie Mansion to look at David's artwork.

"I fell in love with what I saw," Fowler said. "I knew there was real power in where he'd been and what he'd seen." Her thought was to incorporate David's life into the script, "to keep each monologue on its own and use him to draw us from character to character." She asked if she could spend some time with him.

"We met in various all-night restaurants on Second Avenue," she said. "I don't think we ever met before eleven o'clock at night, and we would sometimes talk for three or four hours about his life, about where the various characters came from, what he remembered about them, and how they'd affected him."

A new version of *Sounds in the Distance* would open in November, but Fowler soon realized that, for David, these meetings at the beginning of '85 were less about a theater piece and more about his need to tell someone his story.

Peter Hujar began a new project, setting out to photograph what he called "tribes," meaning a kind of surrogate family. "Peter was amassing around him people that shared his ideas about life. That was your immediate tribe," John Erdman said. "He loved to talk about his tribe." Hujar had invited Erdman, then working more than full-time at the photo lab with Gary Schneider, to put such a group together. Erdman never did and always regretted it. Hujar soon got bored with the whole idea and stopped the project.

But he was thinking "tribe" when he photographed David in a group shot with Chuck Nanney, Steve Brown, and Steve Doughton. Hujar selected these people. Nanney remembered him saying, "You guys are inseparable and you have this really intense relationship that I admire, and I just want to capture this moment."

David agreed to it, but had he assembled his own group, he might have included Keith Davis, for example. Some of his message tapes from this era survive, and the two Steves, in particular, seem to have called almost every

*Peter Hujar had begun to photograph certain of his friends and their "tribes" when he took* David Wojnarowicz and Friends *in 1985. From left: Steve Brown, Chuck Nanney, David, and Steve Doughton. Vintage gelatin-silver print, 20 × 16 inches. (© 1987 Peter Hujar Archive, LLC. Courtesy Matthew Marks Gallery, New York)*

day, sometimes more than once. Apart from art world activities and voyages to the Jersey woods, one thing the four of them did together was go bowling. David bowled with "a natural grace," said Doughton. "When he released the ball, it would touch the floor almost silently. He had a fair amount of power in his delivery too."

They went to Hujar's loft to pose on March 19. "He gave us no directions," Doughton said, "and I remember feeling awkward. I think we all felt awkward." A couple of days later Hujar called them over to see the print. "This is a shitty portrait," he announced. "I'm trying to capture what you guys have, and it's not there." He began pulling out other pictures to illustrate what he meant. He had one of himself and three other photographers, jumping.

"Do you want us to jump?" asked Nanney.

"I want you to act like you know each other," said Hujar. But he did not reshoot the picture.

Nanney ended up thinking it was funny, saying, "Instead of getting what he wanted, which was us exuding togetherness, he got the walls between us."

Shortly before the Biennial opened, the first AIDS antibody test became available. Gay groups immediately announced their opposition to testing—until there could be guarantees of confidentiality. Not that the test would be easy to get in New York in any case. Other cities set up drop-in centers where the procedure could be done quickly and often anonymously. Other cities allowed physicians to use private labs. But under health commissioner David Sencer, New York had what many regarded as the most restrictive testing policy in the country—along with the most AIDS cases. The antibody test could be conducted "only by a city laboratory on referral from personal physicians" and it took months to get the results, reported the *New York Times* when the policy finally changed at the end of 1985. Sencer was the health commissioner who'd told reporters in February that there was no AIDS crisis, that no education about the disease was needed, that "the people of New York City who need to know already know all they need to know about AIDS."

In her April 1985, *East Village Eye* column, "Dr." Cookie Mueller answered a letter from a gay man who'd just broken up with his boyfriend and felt like a dinosaur at the bars. She told him it was OK to be more selective. "And don't worry about AIDS, for God's sake. . . . If you don't have it now, you won't get it. By now we've all been in some form of contact with it. . . . Not everybody gets it, only those predisposed to it. If everyone got it that was introduced to it, half the population of New York would be on death's door by now."

After a couple of negative letters came in, Cookie responded that she simply wanted to speak against paranoia and fear. "I'm sorry if I offended anyone." At this point, no one knew how likely it was for someone infected with the virus to actually get AIDS, or how quickly that might happen. With health officials like Sencer in denial, ignorance was not Cookie's fault, but it was her problem. She died of AIDS in 1989.

Newly ensconced at 155 Avenue B, Civilian Warfare managed to get a ten-thousand-dollar credit line from Citibank. "This poor bank officer probably lost his job over it," Marisa Cardinale said. "He really believed in the East Village." She was able to write checks at last—pay for the renovation, pay some artists, and pay rent until the end of '84.

Operation Pressure Point had not yet pushed out the drug traffic, and Avenue B still qualified as the Wild East. So the typewriter they'd finally acquired was soon stolen. "Somebody unplugged it and walked out with it," Alan Barrows remembered. "Somebody stole my jacket that had my keys in it. I had to change all the locks. Greer Lankton lost a sculpture that was in the gallery, a little baby. This couple came in with a baby carriage, and when they left, the mother was holding the baby in her arms and pushing the carriage out." They realized later that the couple had put Greer's sculpture in the baby carriage. Greer was devastated. She began wheat-pasting the neighborhood with flyers that said: "Sissy Baby Stolen. Reward."

The January '85 rent check bounced, and from then on, Civilian paid cash in bite-size payments. By spring it was $450 or $250 or $200 at a time.

In February '85, Civilian sent David a check for $337.50—and it bounced. He may have eventually been paid. No one remembers. But in April, he dreamt that he'd fought with Barrows and Savard over the money they owed him. It was part of his only journal entry for 1985. He woke up angry, not remembering details except that at the end of the dream, he showed Barrows the IOU they'd given him. "It's like some strange poetry," David wrote. "Won't stand up in court."

The contrast at the gallery between Barrows and Savard grew sharper now as Savard's drug addiction escalated, while Barrows, after experimenting, had stopped cold. At first, Marisa Cardinale recalled, Savard had just a "friendly" problem where, for example, he might pay her forty bucks he owed her, then ask for twenty back because he'd just "seen someone." He'd disappear and come back, announcing that he now had two dime bags to share with her but he'd been shorted and he'd been charged "all that for just this." So she knew he'd already used some of what he'd bought. And then he'd say, "Don't tell Alan. It makes Alan crazy."

For a while, Judy Glantzman lived upstairs from Savard and his boyfriend, Steve Adams. She remembered Savard knocking on her door sometimes "late at night and saying, 'You know, I just need twenty dollars for'—and it would be something like 'for eggs.'"

"Your work would get sold and you'd never hear about it," said Bronson Eden, "because Dean would use the money to buy junk."

"He was taking money from the gallery," Barrows said. "He was taking checks out of the back of the book so we wouldn't know there was money missing, and then the accounts wouldn't jibe." Usually that was small money, ten or twenty dollars. But then he started stealing things. For example, Barrows learned that Savard had stolen someone's purse and was passing bad checks written on the purse owner's checking account.

Barrows and his partner (also named Steve) had hired a friend of Savard's to clean their apartment, not realizing that this woman, Martha, was actually Savard's drug buddy. Barrows and Steve went out of town and returned to find that Martha and Savard had moved in. Savard was standing there in a necklace that Steve had inherited from his grandmother. He'd been stealing their clothes and their jewelry. Soon after they got Savard and Martha out, Barrows and Steve went to their local video store to rent a movie, only to be told that they had not returned that pile of porn movies they'd rented. Savard, of course, had used their account to get those films, then sold them. Barrows said of Savard: "It was like watching somebody become a vampire."

Savard announced that he and Martha were going to Provincetown to clean up. Bronson Eden remembered the day Savard made his grand reentry at the gallery, declaring that he was now off drugs and everything would be different. This probably occurred around the beginning of April, when Eden and Steve Doughton had a two-man show at Civilian. At the opening, Martha came in and gave Eden a congratulatory hug. "As she was hugging me, this guy came in and put his hand on her shoulder," Eden said. "It was a cop. She'd just bought heroin someplace, and he busted her right there in the gallery. The cat was out of the bag. Dean was still on drugs."

When Barrows's mother came to visit him at the beginning of May, he broke down crying one night and told her what was happening with Savard. She suggested getting his family involved. A couple of days later, they staged an intervention at Barrows's apartment. Any focus on drug addiction got derailed, however, when Savard's parents learned the (to them) startling news that Savard was gay. Barrows's mother was the one who told them. She also declared that there was nothing wrong with it and that they should accept it. Barrows couldn't remember how the topic even came up. He did remember Savard's father announcing, "We are going to take the gay out of you," and then driving Savard home to Connecticut.

The next issue of the *East Village Eye* reported, "Dean Savard is taking an extended vacation from his gallery to travel, relax, and work on his own art."

That spring Judy Glantzman left Civilian for Gracie Mansion. She knew nothing of the intervention, but saw that "Dean was so far gone, it wasn't going to get better." She and David had been Civilian's two biggest earners.

In April, photographer Timothy Greenfield-Sanders began inviting artists, dealers, and critics from the East Village scene to pose in a series of six group portraits he called *The New Irascibles*. He'd been out looking at art with his friend Robert Pincus-Witten and told him, now that the scene was so big, wouldn't it be interesting to document the first generation of artists, the second generation, the first dealers, and so on. Pincus-Witten joked that such a project would become "the central document in the history of world culture." They laughed, but Greenfield-Sanders followed through, and Pincus-Witten helped him make the lists.

For each grouping of twelve to fifteen people, Greenfield-Sanders used the same visual composition seen in Nina Leen's historic 1950 portrait of the abstract expressionists, *The Irascibles*. Greenfield-Sanders's pictures would run in *Arts* magazine with an article by Pincus-Witten describing how much in the scene had changed since 1983. David ended up in the cover shot—the first artists from the first galleries—with Judy Glantzman, Greer Lankton, Mike Bidlo (center, where Jackson Pollock sat in the origi-

*Timothy Greenfield-Sanders,* The New Irascibles—Artists 1, *1985. Gelatin-silver print, 14 × 14 inches. Back row from left, after David: Futura 2000, Mark Kostabi, Craig Coleman, Greer Lankton. Second row from left: Judy Glantzman with knee up, Stephen Lack, Mike Bidlo, Luis Frangella, Arch Connelly, Rhonda Zwillinger. Seated at front, from left: Rodney Alan Greenblat, Joseph Nechtval, Richard Hambelton. (© Timothy Greenfield-Sanders 1985)*

nal, assuming Pollock's pose), Futura 2000, Mark Kostabi, Rodney Alan Greenblat, Luis Frangella, and others. Rick Prol overslept and missed the shoot, thus joining the "second generation," and he told Greenfield-Sanders he would never forgive himself.

Everyone understood that history was being recorded here. Glantzman remembered the buzz around the scene about "who was going to make it

*Timothy Greenfield-Sanders,* The New Irascibles—Dealers 1, 1985. *Gelatin-silver print, 14 × 14 inches. Back row from left: Alan Barrows, cut-out of Dean Savard, Rich Colicchio, Gracie Mansion. Second row from left: Elizabeth McDonald, Bill Stelling, Sur Rodney Sur, Mario Fernandez, Peter Nagy. Front row from left: Doug Milford with knee up, Patti Astor, Nina Siegenfeld, Alan Belcher. (© Timothy Greenfield-Sanders 1985)*

into the pictures, and what cut would you make it into." The rivalry, the jealousy—it was unpleasant, she thought, even nasty, and it was new. She and David were acquaintances at this point, not yet friends, but her feelings echo what David had confessed to Dennis Cooper around the time of the Biennial. "I remember 1985 as the end of the East Village," Glantzman said. "The whole thing had broken down."

"What was ending was the intimacy," Greenfield-Sanders said, "the sense that everyone knew everyone else." New galleries were still popping up in old storefronts, but they were not there to present a wry commentary on the art world. They *were* the art world, and they had swallowed the art playground.

Greenfield-Sanders asked Glantzman to bring in the wood cutout she'd made of Dean Savard. (She had just done a show at Steve Adams Gallery called "Glantzman Cuts Up Her Friends," sixty-six cutouts of artists, critics, and collectors at three-quarters lifesize.) That got Savard into the photo of "first dealers." Just so, one of Nicolas Moufarrege's embroidery pieces represented him in the critics' portrait. For a couple of months, he had been in the hospital and was said to be suffering from "a terrible pneumonia." It was *Pneumocystis*.

Moufarrege's death from AIDS on June 4 sent a shock wave through the community. I spoke to people who hadn't known him personally who could still recall just where they were when they heard the news.

For some reason, he'd been hospitalized in the northern end of the Bronx, far from his friends. Nevertheless, David did go to visit. This would have been his first look at what it could mean to be sick with AIDS. Chuck Nanney also visited, though he and Moufarrege had broken up more than a year earlier. The breakup was so bad they wouldn't speak when they ran into each other on the street or at openings. So Nanney made the trip with some apprehension, but Moufarrege clearly had no memory of whatever had gone wrong between them. He had Kaposi's lesions on his face and some form of dementia. He actually seemed happy, Nanney remembered. "He was able to respond, but then part of his conversation would be all non-sensical, and then he would apologize for it and—it was so hard."

Hospital staff would come in "practically wearing hazmat suits," said Nanney. "The nurses didn't want to be around him. They didn't want to touch him."

Myths about how the disease was transmitted would persist for years. Along with fear. Along with stigma. Moufarrege's obituary in the *New York Times* said he died of pneumonia.

Hujar was closer to Moufarrege than David was, so he must have gone to visit him as well, but that's conjecture. Nor can we know what inspired Hujar and then David to see a nutritionist that spring. But in those days, diet was one of the few ways anyone could think of to combat the disease if they had it—or to keep from getting it if they didn't. That spring they both began what Hujar, in a phone message to David, called a "lymph fast."

This may have had nothing to do with AIDS, however. (David told a few people that spring that he'd been tested for what was still called HTLV-III and was negative, though as previously noted, it was not yet easy to get such a test.) He was unhappy enough to be looking for a major life change. In a couple of handwritten pages found among his papers, he wrote, "I feel lonely and . . . fear that I am totally unlike other people, that I haven't the ability to trust them completely . . . that I am emotionally drifting further away from myself and my abilities to show emotion. I think that I am unloved . . . and the longer I am not in a relationship the further I am cut off from emotions and I want to be with people but I cut myself off from people . . . and never let anyone near except for Peter and I think if he were not there I would go crazy."

But the day he wrote that, he'd awakened with such wonder from a dream in which he could fly. Now he felt that he was beginning "to get out from under the havoc and meanness I see in people in the art scene. Something from my conversation with Peter yesterday when he showed me my qualities—that unlocked the beginning of change. The cigarettes etc are what I need to stop in order to keep the change stronger."

By the beginning of May, David was at work on an installation in the Anchorage beneath the Brooklyn Bridge. He was one of fourteen artists selected to show that summer (from two hundred applicants) by Creative Time, an organization that brings art into public spaces. Until the city shut it down for national security reasons in 2002, the Anchorage was one of the most spectacular spaces an artist could hope to work in. The fifty-foot-tall vaulted ceilings, stone floors, windowless brick, and overhead traffic hum made for an ambience that could be all gothic gloom or cool cave, dungeon or cathedral, depending on the art.

David's piece was installed in one of the "most confined and sinister spaces," according to the brochure handed out for that year's Art in the Anchorage. Here he created a cannibal tableau, a family dinner in hell. Two skeletons sit at either end of a long table. One of them, painted red, applies bare wires from a radio to a yellow skeleton stretched before it. The other skeleton looks blue but is at least partly covered with maps. This one has a blue baby doll raised to its mouth. Blood drips down the torn tablecloth. There's a centerpiece of burnt wood; around it, debris, half-drunk glasses of wine and a bottle of Night Train (with Ronald Reagan's face on the label). Dry leaves and other detritus litter the floor. Behind the blue skeleton there's a roadside scrum of weeds, old tires, and another skeleton at least partly covered in maps. This one is seated in one of the tires, a globe between its knees and a gun in its mouth.

David hired his friends Steve Doughton and Philip Zimmerman to help him create what he simply called *Installation #5*. (They gathered garbage and painted the skeletons.) He never talked to them about what the piece meant, but it's rather crudely apparent. The predatory parents. The alcohol, burning, and blood. The waste surrounding it all. Suspended over the center of the dinner table is the skeleton of a child, ascending into heaven in a white dress and a garland of flowers. "She appears unusually pure and unmutilated compared to the other child skeletons," wrote Mina Roustayi, the one critic or journalist who spoke to David about what the thing meant. Roustayi told David that she thought *Installation #5* related to "the global nature of problems like greed, nuclear war, child abuse, and the instinct for self-extinction." That was valid, he told her, but in fact he'd based the piece "on his childhood and life experience."

That month, *Life* magazine published a feature on East Village art with a photo of David spread over two pages. He'd staged this picture months earlier, setting up at dusk in one of Alphabet City's many vacant lots, this one with low hills of dirt and the usual garbage. Marion Scemama knew someone with a truck, and they'd carted the elephant skeleton, a human skeleton, a burning child, and a few cow skulls covered with maps to this location, then lit a fire in a wire trash receptacle. Marion thought the magazine chose "the most stupid photo. He's sitting there painting a skull."

In New Jersey that month, Steven Wojnarowicz's wife, Karen, happened to see the magazine and showed it to Steven, who learned then that his brother had become an artist of some renown. Steven managed to track David down by phone. When David learned that his brother was working for the American Automobile Association, he told Steven that he sometimes used maps in his work. Could Steven get him some maps? Yes. He could. It was the first time they'd spoken since their father's funeral, eight and a half years earlier.

They arranged to meet at a restaurant on Forty-second Street. "I remember sitting down to talk to him, and David said, 'You don't know I was a child prostitute.' He was hitting me with everything, trying to see if he could just turn me away," Steven remembered. "And I said, 'Well, that's OK. I still love you. You're my brother.'"


Sometime around May 22, David left town in the Malibu. He gave up the apartment on Fourth Street and told Tom Cochran, who still held the lease, that he didn't know if he was coming back to New York. Most startling, he left without telling Hujar.

"He disappeared," John Erdman said. "I saw Peter a lot, and he was always wondering where David was, wondering what it meant, wondering if he was going to come back. He wasn't angry. He was never angry at David, ever, about anything. I remember Peter talking about it and I remember thinking, poor David. He really had to do something to get out from under Peter's thumb. Peter was controlling him or trying to like crazy. He saw him as an offspring and he wanted him to do what he wanted him to do. You saw David getting quieter and quieter. You saw him pulling in and withdrawing. At the same time, you could see that he adored Peter but didn't know what to do. I don't think they had any specific fight. David just had to get out of there. He had to get out from under Peter."

David intended to spend the summer on the road with Steve Doughton and Philip Zimmerman, the friends who'd helped him at the Anchorage. "We had this romantic idea of moving to New Mexico," Doughton said. Not to live together but maybe to live near each other.

Doughton and Zimmerman were also artists interested, like David, in tough elemental and mythic imagery. Doughton sculpted figures from wood, human blood, excrement, and semen. He thought that both he and David had been much influenced by Zimmerman, whose work Doughton described as "devotional, sometimes made out of his own blood and found objects." Zimmerman worked with alchemical, magical, and religious symbolism and had created, for example, many paintings of figures on fire. Invited at one point to show his work to a curator at a New York museum, Zimmerman unfurled a painting of a life-size devil standing in flames with the inverted heads of Lincoln, Washington, and Kennedy at the devil's feet like glowing coals, and a burning church atop the devil's levitating head. "I got thrown out of the curator's office," said Zimmerman. David liked that. He thought it was funny. In 1984–85, Zimmerman was making tiny paintings out of bug parts, fingernails, cat whiskers, gold, paint, dried bats, bones, human blood, spiderwebs, dried bread, and dust. He and David would discuss, for example, the symbolism found in existing belief systems like voodoo or Santeria and how an artist could, in Zimmerman's words, "articulate an internal paradigm but use symbols from older traditions." All three of them collected objects like animal skulls, but also traded them and gifted them.

Their plan was to head for the Southwest, where David wanted to visit the Hopi village of Oraibi, Arizona. Then they'd drive up the west coast and loop into the northern plains, stopping at Yellowstone. First, though, they would travel to Louisiana to visit Steve Brown, who had planned to join them on this summerlong trip until he got a job on a film called *Belizaire the Cajun*.

The trip was an utter debacle. Doughton said later that he and Zimmerman should have seen it from day one, when David came to pick them up and said, "What the fuck!" as they brought out boxes of books they were going to read and sculptures Doughton was taking to a show in Portland. "He made us haul half the stuff back," Doughton recalled. "Then we get to his house and he's bringing just as much as we had, including a typewriter. This car is just loaded to the gills. We're all making sculptures, and we're going to be doing art on the road, so we need our materials. It was just absurd."

Nothing practical had been thought out. Doughton and Zimmerman each had about $120 to their name. Even more ominous was the news that

David was still following his new diet and had decided that the trip would give him a good chance to detox. "We start this road trip," Doughton said, "and David is all of a sudden a vegan, not smoking, not drinking coffee, not drinking beer, not eating sugar, and he's just being a real asshole." David's true drugs of choice were caffeine and nicotine, his favorite dinner was steak, and he sometimes seemed to be living on candy bars. Now he was headed across the country drinking spirulina and a barley grass supplement called green magma.

Something again seemed to be cracking inside him. He'd behaved terribly in April when Steve Brown left for Louisiana and his film job. David and Doughton had helped Brown with last-minute errands before he caught his train at Penn Station. Brown was in a foul anxious mood, and David spent the day needling him. Doughton thought it was because the two had had a brief affair: "David really loved Steve Brown. And the feelings were not returned." So, as they ran their errands, David elbowed Brown and raised his eyebrows every time they passed a guy, like, "there's a hottie for ya." Brown told him to knock it off, so David did it more, with any male they passed—child, old man, or bum. "There's one for ya." Brown begged him to stop. David simply switched to something more irritating. He pulled out a black permanent marker and started writing "For a good time call Steve" or "I love cock! Ask for Steve" with Brown's real phone number—tagging every surface they passed, from signs to parking meters, while Brown threw fits. Finally Brown became hysterical and started crying, and Doughton asked David to stop.

David stopped. They got to the train platform and helped Brown load his luggage on board. He had reserved a little compartment for himself with a foldout bed and a small desk. He talked about how he was looking forward to watching the landscape roll by while he worked on a script. He apologized for overreacting, after David apologized for writing the graffiti. David and Doughton then went outside to wave goodbye. The train began to inch away. Brown had his face up to the window blowing kisses. Suddenly, David whipped out the marker and wrote "QUEER" on Brown's window in huge letters. Said Doughton: "I'll never forget the image of Steve jumping up and down in his little room, veins bulging in his purple face, and the sound of his muffled screams as the train disappeared down the tracks." David was doubled over, laughing.

That was the prelude to a full summer of blowups between David and his friends. Doughton, though, said, "We were not battling 24-7. Many of our experiences were great and among the best of my life." They camped in the Blue Ridge Mountains, visited the shore near Virginia Beach, and one day, driving west of Richmond, spotted a bottle tree. They backed up to take a look at the dead tree festooned with bottles on its branches, driving up to a house on a bit of a rise. This turned out to be a highlight of that summer. An old man came outside. They told him they were artists and had noticed his tree. He then invited them into his house and showed them his own amazing work. Zimmerman said the man had taken "dolls with pink plastic flesh and long blonde nylon hair and given them new faces made out of sawdust and Elmer's glue. So the figures had dark crude and crusty faces with a shock of flaxen blonde hair coming out of the top. Others were robust women carved in wood from pieced boards with these same crusty sawdust and glue faces. They had teapot lids for hats. He also made animals out of logs and stuck real antlers on them." David bought one of his deer. Doughton and Zimmerman each bought one of the woman sculptures. The man had signed each of the figures: AbeL Criss. They found out later that he was a rather well-known folk artist, Abraham Lincoln Criss. He was selling his pieces for about twenty dollars each.

They meandered on toward their rendezvous with Steve Brown in Louisiana, dipping into Alabama and north into Tennessee, visiting Graceland and Loretta Lynn's country store and a rattlesnake exhibit set up in cages along the side of the road. But what stood out in both Doughton's and Zimmerman's memories was their growing friction with David. He criticized their driving when he himself was none too good behind the wheel, in Doughton's opinion. David never looked more than twenty or thirty feet ahead, so he was always slamming on the brakes or swerving at the last minute. He stopped constantly to take pictures of roadkill, no matter the situation. "He'd cross three lanes of freeway to photograph a dead animal," Doughton said. Also, David always drove with the windows open, even when it rained, because, Doughton observed, "he hated having glass between him and the world. He hated being in a bubble." But these were endurable irritations. The real tension began when they stopped for the night. David grew increasingly angry because Doughton and Zimmerman would refuse to undress in front of him.

*Philip Zimmerman (left) and Steve Doughton in the only photo David took of them together during the rancorous cross-country trip in summer 1985. (David Wojnarowicz Papers, Fales Library, NYU)*

This was not about sex. "He thought we were having a secret life apart from him," Zimmerman explained. Doughton is straight and Zimmerman is gay. They were roommates and best friends, but never undressed in front of each other either. Still, Zimmerman thought, they were about as intimate as a straight man and a gay man could ever be. "We were almost symbiotic," he said. "It is hard to explain, but we had an understanding about each other and a connection that David was jealous of."

They got to Lafayette, Louisiana, at the beginning of June. Steve Brown was happy to see them, though he acted a little miffed at first over David's prank. Lafayette is on the western rim of the Atchafalaya Swamp, where they spent a few days trying to find alligators—and restaurants that served gator steaks. (They found none.) David still wasn't officially eating meat, but he hadn't lasted long as a vegan. One of their first nights on the road, they'd stopped at an all-you-can-eat seafood buffet and David packed away three plates of crab. In Lafayette, they went to what was probably a wrap party for the movie and feasted on crawdads.

One day they went into the Atchafalaya with a guide. Zimmerman said, "David was in heaven, looking for alligators and water moccasins. He just had amazing empathy for animals and their innocence. His best stories were about innocent creatures who were tormented by their owners, then rescued by [someone who] would give the evil humans their comeuppance" David identified with such animals. He took photos in the swamp, but they found no alligators and finally had to go to a gator farm to see some.

One night they went to a Black Flag concert and were astonished to see a drag queen walk into the roiling crowd of slam dancers. When some muscular jock pushed the queen to the floor, Brown yelled, "Let's get him!" Doughton recalled that Brown punched the jock while feeling him up until a bouncer pried them apart and that "David was laughing hysterically and snapping photos." For years after, David would not show them the pictures. When he finally did, they saw that these were not vacation snapshots, not a record of friends' antics. David had framed most of the photos to show just legs and torsos, to make people unidentifiable. "He reduced this wild experience to anonymous sweaty male bodies in some bizarre state of rage and ecstasy," Doughton said. Even then, David was making his art. A few years later, one of these photos ended up in a piece called *Spirituality (for Paul Thek)*.

Before they left Lafayette, David and Steve Brown had another fight. Doughton thought it had to do with "David feeling that his love for Steve was one-sided. According to Steve, David said, 'The only way you'd love me is if I were a cold son-of-a-bitch.'"

They were in Texas when David gave them the heave-ho. Neither Doughton nor Zimmerman could remember what finally pushed David over the edge or even what city they were in when he drove them to the bus station and announced, fuck you, you're getting out here.

They'd had a terrible blowup at the hotel in Lafayette. "I don't remember the cause of it, but David was angry with all three of us and stormed out of the room," said Doughton. "The three of us sat there trying to figure out what was eating him. I suggested that it wasn't us, that it was unresolved anger about something from his past. Suddenly the door burst open. David had been listening. He rushed in shouting at me, 'You wanna know what it is? It's *you*. You're selfish. It's you and your selfishness!'"

Zimmerman and Brown left the room so Doughton could hash it out with David. But Doughton couldn't remember David giving him any examples of his selfishness. Nothing was resolved. "At one point, I decided that I wanted to nail him so I told him that he reminded me of my father," Doughton said. "It was a low blow, and I knew it. Later, in the fall when we patched it up, he told me that those words hurt and asked me if I meant them. It's not that my father was a bad guy. David had met him and liked him. He said he just hated to have his faults compared to those of any father."

Soon after they crossed the state line into Texas, David was driving up a long incline when he suddenly swerved onto the shoulder. "Steve [Doughton] and I started to giggle," Zimmerman said, "because David had just lambasted us for our poor driving skills. He got so enraged—I was sitting in the back—and when he turned around to snarl at me, I almost didn't recognize him. His face had turned purple, and his eyes were bugging out. It was actually scary."

When they parted at the bus station in San Antonio or Dallas or wherever it was, Doughton and Zimmerman were relieved. "David was tough to be around," Doughton recalled. "The rage he was going through at that point was just incredible."

Doughton bought a ticket for Portland and had a dollar left. "I spent it on a bag of sunflower seeds."

David drove on alone toward Albuquerque. Once there, he sent the first of two postcards to Hujar, and their wording suggests that he had already been in touch by phone, that Hujar knew who he was traveling with. "Me and the guys split up in different directions," wrote David. "I guess it was for the best. . . . I'm too wound up crazy to travel with them."

David called Keith Davis to tell him that he'd jettisoned Doughton and Zimmerman—"such jerks." Would Keith like to fly out to meet him? They could travel the Southwest together and head up the coast. Keith thought that sounded great. By mid-June he had joined David in the desert. From the time they'd first met, Keith had been very attached to David. They'd also had an affair at some point, though that may have been very brief. Keith was having a tough year. He'd ended a long-term relationship, and his

*Keith Davis with souvenirs, most of them probably David's, during the
cross-country trip in summer 1985. (David Wojnarowicz Papers,
Fales Library, NYU)*

business was in trouble. He'd started Swimming Pool Productions with the
goal of bringing fine artists into his graphic design practice. For example,
he hired Hujar to photograph ads for a high-end clothing store called Di-
anne B. (Hujar had used David as his model wherever it was appropriate:
David shirtless and wrapped in a luscious blanket. David in the sort of
white shirt he would never wear in real life. And so on.) Keith put David's
gagging cow at the pier on the back of an Evan Lurie album. And he was
designing Nan Goldin's celebrated first book, *The Ballad of Sexual Dependency.* Keith had started the year hoping he'd make enough money to pay
off his mortgage. By October, he would declare the enterprise a failure.

David's contact sheets from this leg of the journey show him and Keith
in Monument Valley and in Death Valley. "We made it alive through Death
Valley," David wrote in his next postcard to Hujar. "Peter I feel crazy but I
think of you and hope I can work this all out—my problems and such. Love
you. Ciao, David." He continued to photograph roadkill along with his Western obsessions, like kachina dolls and newspaper stories about snake injuries.
In his pictures, he and Keith reach the coast and the forests, and whatever
has gone awry between them by the time they got to Oregon does not show.

Keith was good friends with both Zimmerman and Doughton. They were all Oregonians. Keith told Doughton later that David had been "flying into fits of rage." But the tension all came to a head when Keith and David stopped to spend the night with Zimmerman at his parents' house in a town southeast of Portland. (Zimmerman said he and David were "OK" at that point, or enough OK that he could have them spend the night, but he sensed tension between David and Keith.) "My parents had only one extra room," Zimmerman said, "and Keith and David weren't going to sleep in the same room, probably because they'd been fighting. My parents have this awful sofa bed in a room full of spiders. Keith got the good room, and David had to sleep on the spider bed. He was furious about that."

As soon as Keith and David arrived in Portland the next day, Keith got out of the Malibu and didn't look back. He called Doughton.

"I get this phone call from Keith," said Doughton. "He's like, 'I've been driving with David, and he's such a fucking asshole.'"

"I said, 'Tell me about it. I hate him.'"

"And Keith said, 'I do too. I hate him.'"


David drove back to Albuquerque alone and spent at least a week there. The Malibu needed repairs. He called Richard Kern and Tommy Turner to tell them that he'd separated from some other friends who were jerks. Would they like to join him on a trip through the South? They thought that sounded like fun.

David met Kern and Turner and Turner's wife, Amy, at the Memphis airport. All three of them were using heroin, and Kern admitted to being dope sick for the duration—probably about ten days. He remembered going to Graceland, David's second visit of that summer to Elvis's grave, and then going to Charleston, South Carolina, at a time of flooding. Receipts indicate that they overnighted at a truck stop in Georgia and visited the Outer Banks.

At some point between Portland and Memphis, David had given up his self-imposed diet restrictions and gone back to coffee, cigarettes, red meat, and sugar. That may have helped to smooth some jagged edges. But, years later, what Kern remembered most about this trip was David's anger.

David paid for all the hotel rooms, so they always got one room with two double beds. Tommy and Amy Turner took one. David thought he and Kern should share the other. Kern told him, "I'm not sleeping with you, dude. I'll be laying there feeling weird all night, so I'll sleep on the floor." Kern suggested they take turns. The next night, David could take the floor. "After a couple days of this," Kern said, "we're sitting in the car, and David's like"—Kern made a huffing sound—"just like in the movie." Meaning *Stray Dogs*, where the David character rages silently until he literally explodes.

Their last stop was Washington, D.C. David went off to the Smithsonian with Turner, and they arranged to meet Kern later. Without telling them what he planned, Kern went directly to Union Station and caught a train to New York. David and Turner waited an hour. According to Turner, David was relieved when Kern didn't show up. Later, David remembered his travels with Kern and the Turners as the good part of his summer.

He got back to New York on August 2 and went to see Keith Davis, an encounter Keith then wrote up in his journal: "I knew [David] would have to call me to get his check book. But I had no idea he would still be full of the shit I experienced out west. More of the line about me sharing responsibility for what happened. . . . He said that he will be spending less time with art world people like Philip [Zimmerman], Steve [Doughton] and me. And that there were no problems with Richard Kern, Tommy or Amy so there must be something wrong with us—Steve, Philip, Keith. Real shit. I couldn't even respond. Fuck him." Later that day, he added, "I don't feel any sadness for David. I wish he were dead."

The strictures against "art world people" did not apply to Hujar. On August 7, David sent him a postcard: "Dear Peter, It's time to get together."

# 15 HELLO DARKNESS, MY OLD FRIEND

**David didn't just** damage relationships that mattered to him that year. He set out to do things in 1985 that—if they didn't damage his career—they also didn't help. Of course, he never saw it that way. In a 1989 interview with Barry Blinderman, published in the catalog for his retrospective, David complained, "After the initial wave of acceptance, culminating in the Whitney Biennial, came the tail end of the cycle when suddenly, for a period of time, nobody was interested in what I was doing."

No one in the art world paid much attention to his dead-family scenarios. David could not make himself take advantage of his slot in the Biennial. The politic course would have been to make some new paintings, have a solo show. He could have capitalized, but for him, that was not a reason to make art.

Meanwhile, the East Village scene had almost imperceptibly begun its decline. Fun Gallery closed while David was away. Anthony Haden-Guest described Fun's June '85 show, "Sink or Swim," as "a jaunty *cri de coeur* to collectors, asking them to help . . . cope with rising rents. Nobody bought a thing." Patti Astor and Bill Stelling boarded up the gallery with a sign that read "NO MO FUN." When *New York Magazine* reported two years later that Fun had closed because they couldn't pay a shipping bill from the Zurich Art Fair, Astor wrote a corrective letter to the editor, declaring they'd found backers to pay the bill, but that the scene had lost its charm. "When the money moved in and track lights became more important than meaning, I no longer felt inclined to cast pearls before swine," she declared. Astor was in Hollywood by then, at work on a film called *Assault of the Killer Bimbos*.

As if to prove that the scene had not exactly become SoHo, however, another blonde bombshell stepped into the breach. The Lady Bunny kicked off the world's first outdoor drag festival, Wigstock, with her rendition of "I

Feel the Earth Move Under My Feet" that Labor Day at the Tompkins Square bandshell. Wigstock began simply as an extension of the nearby Pyramid Club and brought club regulars (Tabboo!, Hapi Phace, Lypsinka, John Sex, Ethel Eichelberger, John Kelly, et al.) into the open air. Inebriated club denizens (including Bunny and Brian Butterick) had dreamt it all up the year before while horsing around at the bandshell in the middle of the night, though no one could remember enough to claim the idea as his or her own. "It's all such a blur" admits the official Wigstock website.

Such frivolity no longer seemed to have a place at the galleries.

Civilian Warfare limped along with Dean Savard back and unrecovered from his heroin addiction. Memories differ on just when the second intervention occurred, this time at the gallery. Friends got him there one day on some pretext and dramatically rolled the gate down. There stood not just Alan Barrows and Marisa Cardinale and Steve Adams and maybe some Civilian artists but also Dean's parents, brother, and sister-in-law. "Dean was furious at me, furious at everyone," Marisa recalled. "And he had a right to be." His mother had brought Dean's prom picture this time to prove that he wasn't gay. "It was horrible," said Marisa. "Because this turned into a misguided journey into coming out for the parents, Martha [his drug buddy] ended up in Connecticut with Dean, which his parents wanted to happen because they believed that Martha was his girlfriend. Of course, Dean as a junkie, and Martha as well, used this as a diversion." They kept up the pretense that they were a couple, their drug use was never addressed, and soon they were back on Avenue B.

By August, Civilian stopped paying rent altogether. Marisa remembered that their landlord, Timothy Greenfield-Sanders, would come around looking for Savard—whose new idea for saving the gallery was to move to Eighth Street, across from the nightclub 8BC. "Like, we'll get away from Tim by moving around the corner?" she said. "Everything was junkie decision-making. You think to the next fix."

When Savard's brother Perry and sister-in-law decided to move into the city, he found them an apartment next to the gallery and moved in with them. And began stealing from them. Marisa returned from her vacation that summer to learn that she was out of a job. The gallery couldn't afford to pay her. In October, Barrows and Savard signed an agreement to leave 155

Avenue B before November 1 and to pay the back rent of $2,700 within six months. They moved Civilian Warfare to a storefront at 614 East Ninth Street, but it was no longer a gallery that mattered.

In the October issue of the *Eye*, Carlo McCormick published "East Village R.I.P."—startling news when the same issue carried listings for forty-seven neighborhood galleries. "East Village art is dead," Carlo declared. "We, who were the first to take credit for the birth of East Village art, now want to be the first to take credit for killing it. But this is what the East Village has always been about, taking credit for other people's work and ideas. After two years of intense coverage of the scene, the *Eye* has officially run out of gimmicks to repackage the same old drivel."

That fall, both the Steves—Doughton and Brown—made up with David when they returned to New York. When Doughton later threw away the two plaster heads David had given him from his last Civilian show—one down the air shaft outside his apartment at Eleventh Street and Avenue C, one out the window of his vehicle while he sped through the desert—he was merely purging, he explained. He felt weighed down by his possessions. He did not carry any anger at David.

Philip Zimmerman, however, kept his distance from David for more than a year, explaining that "David had gotten so strange." David and Keith Davis eventually repaired their relationship, though it's unclear when, and the joie de vivre between them never returned. David stayed true to his word; for the rest of the year, he would hang out mostly with Richard Kern and Tommy Turner.

Once more, David had nowhere to live, and he crashed with Kern for the month of August. "I recently got thrown out of my apartment of four years by a plague of gentrifying artistes," David wrote in the first of four pieces he did for the *East Village Eye*. This wasn't strictly true, of course. His old roommate Tom Cochran had offered him the lease on the Fourth Street place, and David had turned it down. He didn't want to commit. But now, he needed to complain. He needed to show his wounds.

He needed to get into that dark place reachable via drugs. David had never done a lot of heroin. He still preferred speed. He enjoyed psychedel-

*Richard Kern on the set of his 1986 film,* Fingered. *(Photograph by Tony Coke)*

ics. But now his major companions were both junkies. One day, he went to buy heroin with Kern on Eighth Street between Avenues C and D, then "a good place to cop," as Kern remembered it. Back at his apartment, they shot themselves up and got no high, just a bubble of flesh rising on David's arm. There was no telling what they'd actually injected. "I remember us both sitting there going, 'This sucks,'" Kern said. "I used to sell ecstasy some on the side, so I had a bunch of ecstasy. I said, let's try shooting this up and see what happens." They banged up the ecstasy. "It was like *Star Trek*—when you go to warp speed," said Kern. Ideas for a film project began ping-ponging between them.

"I really want to figure out how the kids of today got so screwed up," Kern told David. Specifically, he was fascinated by Lung Leg, soon to become the snarling cover girl on Sonic Youth's *Evol* album. (Kern had just shot the video for Sonic Youth's "Death Valley '69.") Kern hoped to interview Lung about her childhood. They'd do a film about a messed-up family. David responded, "Yeah, yeah, yeah. I've got skeletons. We can use skeletons. Everyone'll be dead."

Then the drug wore off, but Kern told David, let's do this. The film would become *You Killed Me First*, in which Lung Leg plays a girl who slaughters her parents. "When I first met Lung, she had a big X carved in her hair," Kern said. "I wanted to make something just with her because she seemed so weird." Lung was just ten years younger, but as Kern saw it, that decade had erased the hippie and the glam rocker from consciousness. Lung resonated to the darkness and din of industrial bands like Einstürzende Neubauten. "Punk had gotten all mutated," as Kern put it.

In the article where David griped about losing his apartment, he mentioned his first meeting with Lung at a local gallery. "She was carrying around a live toad with plans to sacrifice it in a movie she was gonna make but it had a heart attack from what I heard and now resides in cryonic suspension in someone's freezer," he wrote, adding that Lung did "cool drawings" of demons and that she'd performed at an East Village club, playing bass with a bone in a pickup band doing "We Are the World."

Lung Leg (actually Elizabeth Carr—no relation) thought that Kern interviewed probably five or six people "about their parents" and then combined those accounts for *You Killed Me First*. But, she told me, "about fifty percent of it was directly from David Wojnarowicz's childhood."

On September 26, David read at 8BC "in tandem with some typically grisly Richard Kern films," according to the *East Village Eye*. The evening was called "There Will Be No Fire Escape in Hell."

Then, on October 12, 8BC closed—a huge loss to East Village nightlife and another sign of the scene's incipient demise. Owners Cornelius Conboy and Dennis Gattra had certainly upgraded from the log cabin ambience of two years earlier—when they'd had a dirt floor and no heat, and didn't meet a single licensing requirement. They'd staged some fifteen hundred performances, they'd become a rec room for neighborhood artists, and now they were told they needed, among other headaches, a zoning variance.

Given the honor of being last performer, Ethyl Eichelberger rushed over from the Pyramid Club, where he had a job dancing on the bar. I happened to be waiting outside when Ethyl came striding down Eighth Street at three forty-five in the morning in a long green robe, a big wig, yellow hose, a yellow rose tucked between his falsies, and elbow-length red gloves, carrying an accordion case. Ethyl began the swan songs around four: "Will you remember my name tomorrow? Will you remember my trials, my tears, and my sorrow?"

\* \* \*

AIDS, it was said, now had a human face. Rock Hudson announced from Paris late in July that he was undergoing treatment for the illness. He died in October.

The media was also following the struggles of Ryan White, a thirteen-year-old hemophiliac with AIDS who wanted the right to attend school. On his first day of class, he was allowed only to listen in via telephone.

In September, the Centers for Disease Control started recommending condom use, at least for heterosexuals, adding the caveat that "their efficacy in reducing transmission has not yet been proven."

At the end of the year, however, the CDC stopped all funding for AIDS education. As Randy Shilts reported, conservatives in the White House decided that "the government should not be in the business of telling homosexuals how to have sodomy."

In September 1985, David moved into an apartment at 225 East Second Street between Avenues B and C. Tommy Turner helped him carry the baby elephant skeleton over from Keith's loft on Suffolk Street. They covered it with a sheet because David didn't want his new neighbors to get odd ideas about him. "So he's trying to be real nonchalant," Turner said, "and all these people in the street are going, '*mooooo, mooooo.*'"

Despite the ongoing machinations of Operation Pressure Point, this was still basically the epicenter of the world heroin trade. "It was like Needle Park," said artist Jane Bauman. "The front door was always broken, and the mailboxes had no locks on them. There was always trash in—I hesitate to call it a lobby. There were lots of junkies hanging out. Lots of panhandlers. It was really crummy, but it seemed like that's how we were all living." David never even got mail at this address apart from his phone and electric bills. Bank statements, for example, still went to Keith's place. (When he left town to drive across the country, David had had all his mail forwarded to Keith's.) On the bright side, David now had about twice as much space as he'd had on Fourth Street. Bauman remembered paint peeling off the walls, and David's clutter: "Papier-mâché, stencils, spray cans rolling around on the floor, and a feeling of intense artistic activity amidst all this derelict, run-down, shabby falling-apartness."

That fall David found another way to talk, if obliquely, about his childhood when he began writing a script with Tommy Turner based on the infamous "satanic teen," Ricky Kasso—a drug-abusing heavy metal fan and stone-cold murderer. In June 1984, Kasso killed an acquaintance, repeatedly stabbing him and gouging his eyes out. Kasso did this in front of witnesses, apparently while tripping, then bragged about it, and for the next two weeks, he took other teens into the woods near his Long Island home to view the decomposing corpse. Finally one girl called the police. Kasso hung himself in jail. He was seventeen.

The tragedy was a tabloid sensation, inspiring several movies (notably *River's Edge*) and heated commentary. Why hadn't any of the kids "told" sooner? Did heavy metal music have satanic content? Could it lead to suicide?

"Me and Montana were cracking up about the articles," Turner said. (Montana Hewson was the "turkey-necked" guy David met, with Kern, at the Peppermint Lounge.) Turner said he would sometimes come home from work to find that Montana had pinned a "satanic teen" piece from the *Post* or *Daily News* to his door. Then Turner began discussing the case with David. In April 1985, Kasso's alleged accomplice went on trial. He was acquitted, but for several weeks the story was back in the news every day.

Here was another suburban kid who'd run away from a violent father and indifferent mother, who slept in parks and friends' houses, but who didn't have David's inner resources. Kasso had been arrested for grave robbing, he ingested hallucinogens every day, he always carried knives, and he claimed he could communicate with the devil. His parents tried to have him committed. David and Turner saw Kasso as the ultimate aimless, alienated kid, and both could identify with that to a certain extent.

But there was more to it for David. He'd begun collecting articles about murderous children, especially those who'd killed their families. (Kasso had reportedly threatened his own sisters.) Now that David had allowed his rage over his childhood to surface, he wondered, Why hadn't he, or somebody, picked up one of his father's guns and shot him? Why hadn't he fought back?

Turner said that once they'd decided to make the film, David wanted to include material based on "friends who had strange problems growing up." Which sounds like the Kern film. But here the "strange problems" would be given to Kasso's friends. The finished script followed the actual case in many respects. David and Turner even drove out to Kasso's hometown to interview teenagers at a local park mentioned as a hangout in some of the news accounts. Their screenplay, however, added the devil as a substitute father figure and carried on into the afterlife. Kasso had promised to follow his victim to hell.

They wrote the treatment at David's Second Street apartment in three nighttime sessions, blasting Black Sabbath for inspiration. Turner remembers Steve Brown joining them for at least two nights, before declaring the project "fucked up" and "the devil's work." Steve was so upset he went to Hujar to discuss it, and Hujar advised him to just tell David how he felt, not to worry about seeming "uptight" or "Catholic." Steve never did acknowledge working on the screenplay. He later told an interviewer that he and David fought over the film after he heard about Caven Point. That was one of David's favorite abandoned industrial sites, in New Jersey along the Hudson. David and Turner went there location scouting, since it had so much they could potentially use: a swamp, junked cars, a deserted Coast Guard post, and a cemetery. But walking in, they saw a life-size doll in a white dress hanging from an old bridge, a noose around her neck. Steve was spooked when he heard about this. He told David it was a sign that the film would bring evil into the world. He told Doughton, "Fuck this. Tommy's just into death, death, death. He's into shooting up drugs, and David is too, and I'm out of here."

David had begun spending time with Karen Finley. Maybe three times a week, he'd show up at her apartment on East Third Street at seven A.M. with coffee. Sometimes they would go out for breakfast. Sometimes they would drive out of town to a swamp or a forest. But mostly, they talked. David knew Finley's performance work from the East Village clubs. In those raw early monologues, she spoke without euphemism about rape, incest, abandonment, brutality, emotional damage, and other subjects for which there are no polite words. She exposed the victimizer's monstrous impulses; she validated horrors the victim could barely speak about. As Finley once said,

"There are a lot of people walking around in pain from something that happened to them when they were seven, and now they're forty-two years old and they carry it with them every day. Somehow I bring that pain up to a conscious level. I think that's one of my jobs."

Finley observed that David liked the emotions her work brought out in him. And at this point in his life, when he felt so skinless, he opened up to her about his most painful secrets. He told her that he hadn't just been beaten by his father; he'd been molested. Finley did not ask him for details, and he didn't go into them. Then he told Finley what had happened with his mother after his siblings left home. Though it may well have been inadvertent on her part, David perceived her to be sexually provocative. She occasionally walked around in see-through negligees, and once she came to the door naked. He did not say that his mother molested him or even touched him, but as he saw it, she hadn't maintained the boundaries women usually keep with a teenage son. This had created confusion and anxiety. It's what may have led him to begin spending nights on rooftops and in parks, and then, in stranger's hotel rooms.

He talked to Finley about his street life, his sadness, his history of relationships, his queerness but also his feelings for women, which were sometimes sexual. David had begun to question his whole identity. He told Finley he wondered if the different abuses he'd suffered with each parent had turned him into a queer. In the eighties, homosexuality was still regarded as a psychological deviation. As *People* magazine observed after a certain sex symbol had been diagnosed with AIDS: "In some parts of Rock Hudson's America it is still a fairly radical proposition that someone can be both good and gay." Finley recalled, "David was questioning whether he could be in a relationship with a woman. Was it possible that part of him didn't develop?"

Mostly, Finley just listened. "I think he was talking things out with himself," she said. "What is a relationship? What is sexuality?" Though she wondered at first why David needed to tell her these things, she concluded, "It's comforting to talk to someone who isn't shocked, who doesn't feel pity." He also tried to start arguments with her, but she didn't engage.

"I did not have a childhood like David's by any means," she said, "but I had the trauma of suicide and mental illness in my family, and I had the idea of taking that energy and making it transgressive, into an artwork. We both felt that coming to the East Village and creating work came out of a different need than it did for other artists, like if we weren't creating the work, we would be going crazy."

David did not want to be seen as a victim, said Finley. "We would have conversations about that. How do you reveal this information? What do you do with it? How do we take the experiences we've had and transform them into good? Or how can you transform pain into compassion? How do we transform it into creativity?"

"He was searching for what was him," she said, "to separate that from what was put upon him."

David had told these same secrets to his old friend Susan Gauthier back in the seventies, and he'd told his sister, who found it all very hard to believe. If he did not divulge these stories about his mother to anyone else in his life, he still had a need to vent about her in a more general way.

Nan Goldin ran into David one day in 1985 at the gas station on Fourth and Bowery. After he filled his tank, he offered her a ride. Nan had met David years earlier through Kiki Smith, and she'd appeared in the first incarnation of *Sounds in the Distance* at Bill Rice's garden, but that day in the car was the first time they'd had a conversation.

"He just let forth and started to talk about himself and his life and his mother," Nan said. "He said he hated her. He passionately hated her and blamed her for so many things, like not coming to look for him when he was stolen by his father.

"That meeting in the car was very, very intense for me. But then we would meet for breakfast and he would talk to me about his life, and I'd go over to his house sometimes. His anger wasn't just at his mother and his past, although that was vehement, and he talked about it often. There's almost no one he didn't get furious at. And that rage was all-consuming."

Nan also knew Hujar, whom she regarded as a great influence and teacher. She observed that the only relationship David had that didn't turn into rage was his relationship with Hujar.

\* \* \*

Around the time Carlo McCormick wrote "East Village R.I.P."—August or September 1985—he received an invitation to curate yet another East Village show, this one at Neapolitan Gallery in Richmond, Virginia. His immediate reaction was "forget it, this is gross now," but he told them he'd do it if it could be an installation. He'd bring the artists. So Carlo recruited the painters Luis Frangella, David West, Christof Kohlhofer, Marilyn Minter, James Romberger, Marguerite Van Cook, David Wojnarowicz, and his own partner, the experimental filmmaker Tessa Hughes-Freeland. She documented the weekend. "And we just destroyed the space," said Carlo.

The idea was that the artists would spend the weekend working in teams, painting directly on the wall. Marguerite described the gallery as pristine, with stained glass in the balcony and polished wood floors. But the setup was strange. "They didn't feed us, just put cases of beer and liquor in the middle of the room," Marguerite said. For lodging, the artists had a big empty mansion with no beds. In fact, no furniture of any kind. James and Marguerite had come with their four-month-old son. They put a rug down in the middle of the gallery and people took turns playing with him.

David West thought maybe some people slept the first night, adding "I don't think they even had blankets for us. I mean, they were afraid of us. They thought we were just freaks." He remembered the case of beer being handed over when they left. "Because they just couldn't wait for us to be out of there."

Carlo provided the key ingredient, handing out hits of acid. Marilyn Minter, just out of rehab with eighteen days clean and sober for the first time in ten years, was the only one who abstained. She spent the weekend eating candy. Minter and Christof Kohlhofer worked together with an overhead projector, and so wanted the lights dimmed, which annoyed some of the others. But that was a minor irritant compared with the awful accommodations. No one remembers sleeping the second night.

Marguerite recalled Luis painting with his usual facility, such elegance, making beautiful marks, teamed up with David, "a pragmatic painter . . . and so damn in-your-face," using what Marguerite called "revolting colors." (For one thing, he used the cheapest of cheap paints.) The existing documentation shows some rather monstrous imagery. David wrote a description in what seems a stray page of journal writing: "I painted this six foot decapitated head spewing guts and hellish material from its screaming mouth oh shit acid kickin' in what's this brush in my hand some extension of my brain and all these demon things springing out like cartoon animation." James and Marguerite did a comic strip at the bottom of one wall, the actual size of a comic book page, a worried conversation in paint about what might happen to their son if the government reinstituted the draft. As James saw it, everyone else was "going crazy, just making a mess." David West began inserting a character he called Needlenose around the space. He described this half human, half mosquito as "our little buzzing spirit of futility and malice." David Wojnarowicz joined him in adding those to the mix. Soon everyone's images were overlapping and West started writing, "Fuck your mother, fuck your father" over everything. As Marguerite saw it, West's slogans and Luis's "ornamental threads of continuity" held the disparate imagery together.

Back home, these artists (with Keiko Bonk replacing Minter) dubbed themselves the Wrecking Crew and did two more shows where they'd drop acid and paint around the clock at James and Marguerite's Ground Zero Gallery. They didn't seem to care what anyone thought of these shows or if anyone even saw them. James described them as "purely an outpouring of the id." But in Richmond, where it began, they probably did the most actual "wrecking," spilling paint on the beautiful floor and drawing on the walls with pencils, felt tips, and spray paint, "invasive materials you're going to have a hard time getting rid of," as Marguerite put it. James suggested that it might have been revenge for the way they'd been treated. Carlo admitted, "We were a little immature about it."

When *Flash Art* commissioned Carlo to write yet another East Village roundup, he got David to collaborate on it. They decided to feature, said Carlo, "anyone who was not making an object to sell in a gallery." David started the piece with the image of a flashbulb bleaching the life out of a scene. "We were basically saying that the art world, so driven by money and fame, cast this blinding soul-sucking light on artists," Carlo said, "so we were moving to the shadows where certain artists made work that was so extreme they inherently resisted such market forces."

Therefore, they discussed the odd drawings of Lung Leg.

And Tommy Turner's rat bags. He worked in a medical lab where he had access to abundant dead rats, though he had to skin them and tan them at home. Each bag used two. The front rat kept its paws; the back rat kept its tail and had its head folded over to close the bag. Turner lined each with red silk or satin and attached a leather strap. He had also made an entire jacket of rat pelts, tails intact, by sewing their tanned hides to a jean jacket.

David and Carlo also lauded the unknown Montana Hewson. He had covered the windows of his apartment with hundreds of photocopies of planes crashing. He had written a film script related to voodoo myths and deities, "making use of the psychological properties of light." He had covered his lamps with construction paper chains of "spiritual figures from voodoo history . . . jagged frenetic energy explosions, bodies in lotus positions with enormous hard-ons."

They wrote about Tessa Hughes-Freeland, then just beginning her association with the Cinema of Transgression with short films like *Baby Doll*. (Two go-go dancers get ready for work and discuss their job, intercut with footage of their dancing feet.) Tessa happened to be married to Carlo, but David really liked her work and even bought her her first good Super 8 camera when they passed someone selling it on Avenue A.

Naturally, the article included Kern. "His films stripped all the tedious build-up from Hollywood movies whose essential draw for the ticket-buying public was five minutes of graphic violence," David wrote later. "His films *were* the five minutes of blood-letting and mayhem. He also explored the power plays embedded in the sexual act."

Carlo speculated that they may have also discussed Kembra Pfahler and others then working the margins. But none of this was what the *Flash Art* editors had in mind, and they rejected it.

On November 6, the most ambitious production yet of *Sounds in the Distance* opened at Limbo, which had moved from its tiny club space on Tompkins Square to become Limbo Theater on East Ninth. This time ten actors presented twenty-two monologues, held together by a twenty-third character called the Listener—the David proxy. Molly Fowler had added slides of

David's work and music by 3 Teens Kill 4. She even thought of their guerrilla rehearsals as an homage to David. They'd "borrow" a space, using, for example, empty classrooms at John Jay College of Criminal Justice by just walking in and pretending they belonged there.

Tessa Hughes-Freeland remembered David being upset by the production. Tessa saw it too and thought the main problem was that the David character never conveyed any sense of why those stories had been collected in the first place. As Tessa put it, that character "didn't really have a hunger."

David did not speak to Fowler but wrote her one or two letters. A reply from her was among his papers and only hints at what he'd criticized. The piece hadn't come alive visually, she wrote in her reply to him, and if she had it to do over, she'd chop it up less and change the narrator. She also pointed out that he did not participate in the process in any way after their late-night talks.

Fowler thinks that he then wrote her a second letter, because the main thing she remembers hearing from him is that he found the show too painful to watch because it was too real. He couldn't take seeing those people again.


In November '85, the *Eye* published David's second column, most of it devoted to Tommy Turner—specifically, his little-seen Super 8 film about mind control, *Simonland*, and his job at the lab, "cloning genes and subjecting hundreds of them a week to embarrassing amounts of dread diseases," as David described it. And most of all, *Redrum* (*murder* spelled backward), Turner's zine devoted to various ghastly ways to die. The one issue I happen to own (price: one dollar) has Ricky Kasso on the cover and includes David's appropriated eleven-page *Archie* comic, in which Veronica suggests, "Why don't we take acid and go kill rich pigs." In David's rewritten word balloons and altered pictures, Archie and friends become another band of murdering teenagers.

Turner's project and worldview fascinated David at this point in his life. He wrote, "It's that thin line that interests [Turner]; what is it that separates mass murderers from people who internalize aggressive forms of anger. . . . There is so little that separates us."

*Tommy Turner (Photograph by Jennifer Tull Westberg)*

He recalled the teenagers who'd picked him up in a stolen truck and threatened to kill him when he was hitchhiking back from San Francisco in 1976. David first wrote about that incident right after it happened. Then he said he just wanted to get out of it "alive enough" to tell the story, and that living through it had been a rush. He said nothing about anger. Rewriting, rethinking, refeeling the story in the autumn of '85, he declared that, if he'd had a chance, he would have blown the kids' brains out.

In Turner and Kern, he'd found a couple of artists interested in exploring the ugliest, darkest aspects of human behavior. Their films created bleak worlds devoid of caring, love, or goodness.

David was beginning to consciously connect his family's pathology to a larger worldview. He added an anecdote in the *Eye* about watching a cop kick a dope-sick junkie while arresting him: "And I'm feeling rage 'cause in the midst of my bad mood this cop is inadvertently reaching in with his tentacles and probing in ice-pick fashion some vulnerable area from years ago maybe when my dad took me down in the basement for another routine of dog chain and baseball bat beatings or when he killed my pet rabbit and made me eat it . . . blam . . . blam . . . blam."

David didn't just identify with that junkie. If there was ever a time in his life when he was going to do more than "dabble" with heroin, this was it.

One day, after shooting up, David's arm turned green, and he showed

*Untitled*, 1981. Black-and-white photograph and spray paint on wood, 11 x 19 inches. (Private collection) The dog mask and stencils here are characteristic of David's early work: the burning house, the military planes, the figure with one arm up as if warding off a blow.

*Untitled (Green Head)*, 1982. Acrylic on masonite, 48 x 96 inches. (Private collection) This painting, created mostly from stencils, is the first David ever exhibited. He went on to use the Hujar stencil in many other pieces from this period.

The gagging cow drawn on the wall of the Ward Line Pier, 1982–83. (Photograph © Andreas Sterzing)

*Science Lesson*, 1981–82. Spray paint and stencil on room mural, 96 x 168 inches. (Private collection)

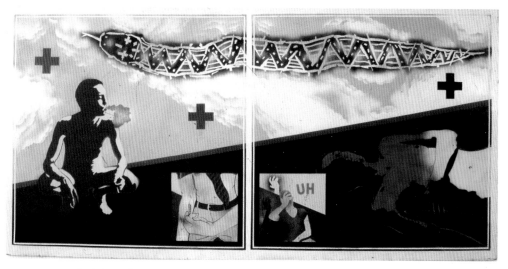

*Junk Diptych*, 1982. Spray paint on masonite, 48 x 96 inches. (Private collection)

*Peter Hujar Dreaming/Yukio Mishima: St. Sebastian*, 1982.
Acrylic and spray paint on masonite, 48 x 48 inches. (Private collection)

The deconstructed cartoon drawn on the wall of the Ward Line Pier, 1983. On the piece of wood attached to the wall, just right of the cartoon, David wrote: "I prepared myself for this world the way one prepares a couch or bed for an expected lover." (Photo © Andreas Sterzing)

*Tuna*, 1983. Acrylic and collage on
supermarket poster, 40 x 30 inches.
(Private collection)

*Untitled (Pampers)*, 1984. Acrylic on
poster, 44 x 32 inches.
(Private collection)

*Screaming Bird Lid*, 1983. Acrylic on garbage can lid,
19 inches in diameter. (Private collection)

*Fuck You Faggot Fucker*, 1984. Black-and-white photographs, acrylic, and collage on masonite, 48 x 48 inches. (Private collection)

*Fish Totem*, 1983. Acrylic on found wood. (Private collection)

David's work in 1985 was all about dead families and imperiled children. Top, a detail from *Installation #5* at Art in the Anchorage. A blue skeleton (not visible) at the other end of the table is eating a baby. (Courtesy of the Estate of David Wojnarowicz and P·P·O·W Gallery, New York) Below, the dead family from the film *You Killed Me First*, a collaboration with Richard Kern installed at Ground Zero Gallery. (Photograph by Marion Scemama)

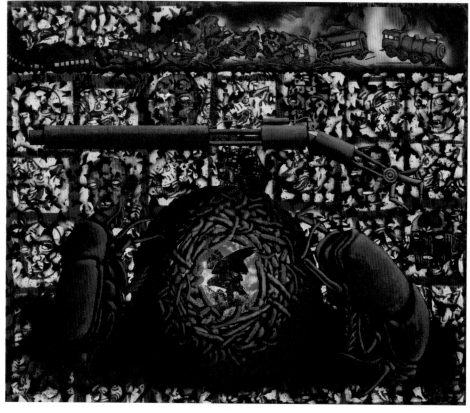

See opposite page

*Something from Sleep II*, 1988–89. Acrylic and collage on canvas, 36 x 36 inches. (Private collection)

Opposite, top: *Some Things from Sleep: For Jane and Charley*, 1986. Acrylic on masonite, 48 x 72 inches. (Private collection)

Opposite, bottom: *Dung Beetles II: Camouflage Leads to Destruction*, 1986. Acrylic, spray paint, and collage on masonite, 67 x 80 inches. (Private collection)

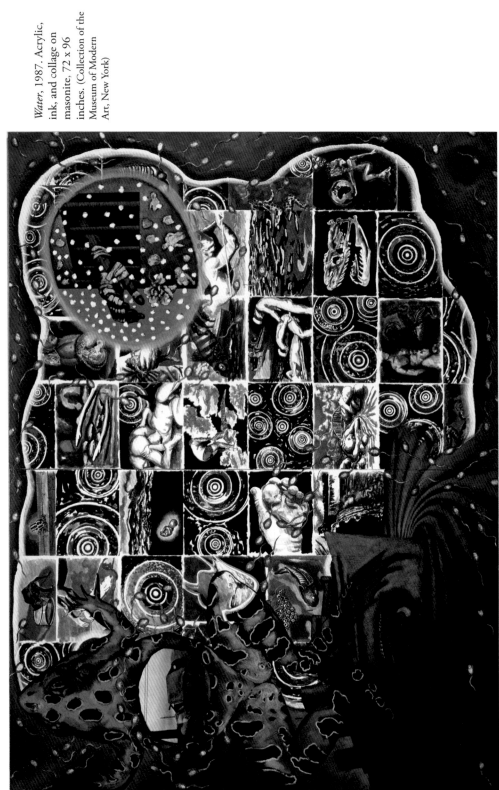

*Water*, 1987. Acrylic, ink, and collage on masonite, 72 x 96 inches. (Collection of the Museum of Modern Art, New York)

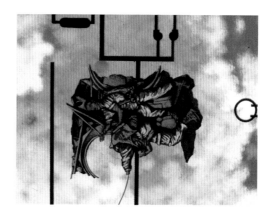

Above: Detail from *Wind (for Peter Hujar)*, 1987. While David did many photographic self-portraits, this is the only one he ever did in paint.

Left: *Wind (for Peter Hujar)*, 1987. Acrylic and collage on wood, 72 x 96 inches. (Collection of the Museum of Modern Art, New York)

"If I had a dollar to spend for healthcare I'd rather spend it on a baby or innocent person with some defect or illness not of their own responsibility; not some person with Aids..." says the healthcare official on national television and this is in the middle of an hour long video of people dying on camera because they can't afford the limited drugs available that might extend their lives and I can't even remember what this official looked like because I reached in through the t.v. screen and ripped his face in half and I was diagnosed with Arc recently and this was after the last few years of losing count of the friends and neighbors who have been dying slow vicious and unnecessary deaths because fags and dykes and junkies are expendable in this country "If you want to stop Aids shoot the queers..." says the governor of texas on the radio and his press secretary later claims that the governor was only joking and didn't know the microphone was turned on and besides they didn't think it would hurt his chances for re-election anyways and I wake up every morning in this killing machine called america and I'm carrying this rage like a blood filled egg and there's a thin line between the inside and the outside a thin line between thought and action and that line is simply made up of blood and muscle and bone and I'm waking up more and more from daydreams of tipping amazonian blowdarts in 'infected blood' and spitting them at the exposed necklines of certain politicians or government healthcare officials or those thinly disguised walking swastika's that wear religious garments over their murderous intentions or those rabid strangers parading against Aids clinics in the nightly news suburbs there's a thin line a very thin line between the inside and the outside and I've been looking all my life at the signs surrounding us in the media or on peoples lips; the religious types outside st. patricks cathedral shouting to men and women in the gay parade: "You won't be here next year - you'll get Aids and die ha ha..." and the areas of the u.s.a. where it is possible to murder a man and when brought to trial one only has to say that the victim was a queer and that he tried to touch you and the courts will set you free and the difficulties that a bunch of republican senators have in albany with supporting an anti-violence bill that includes 'sexual orientation' as a category of crime victims there's a thin line a very thin line and as each T-cell disappears from my body it's replaced by ten pounds of pressure ten pounds of rage and I focus that rage into non-violent resistance but that focus is starting to slip my hands are beginning to move independent of self-restraint and the egg is starting to crack america seems to understand and accept murder as a self defense against those who would murder other people and its been murder on a daily basis for eight count them eight long years and we're expected to pay taxes to support this public and social murder and we're expected to quietly and politely make house in this windstorm of murder but I say there's certain politicians that had better increase their security forces and there's religious leaders and healthcare officials that had better get bigger dogs and higher fences and more complex security alarms for their homes and queer-bashers better start doing their work from inside howitzer tanks because the thin line between the inside and the outside is beginning to erode and at the moment that this thirty seven foot tall one thousand one hundred and seventy-two pound man inside this six foot frame and all I can feel is the pressure all I can feel is the pressure and the need for release

*Untitled (Hujar Dead)*, 1988–89. Acrylic and collage on masonite, 39 x 32 inches. (Private collection)

Two images from *The Sex Series (for Marion Scemama)*. Both are *Untitled*, 1989.
Gelatin-silver print, 16 x 20 inches. (Courtesy of P·P·O·W Gallery, New York)

*Where I'll Go After I'm Gone*, 1988–89. Black-and-white photographs, acrylic, spray paint, and collage on masonite, 45 x 64 inches. (Private collection) David's face appears at lower left.

*Fear of Evolution*, 1988–89.
Black-and-white photographs,
acrylic, string, and collage on
masonite, 42½ x 36½ inches.
(Private collection)

*I Feel a Vague Nausea*, 1990. Black-and-white photographs, acrylic, string, and text on board, 60 x 48 inches.
(Private collection)

*When I Put My Hands on Your Body*, 1990. Gelatin-silver print and silk-screened text on museum board, 26 x 38 inches. (Courtesy of the Estate of David Wojnarowicz and P·P·O·W Gallery, New York)

Nan Goldin, *David Wojnarowicz at Home*, NYC, 1990. (Courtesy of Nan Goldin)

it to Hujar. They were sitting in a restaurant, and Hujar told him, "I don't ever want to see you again."

David gasped. "What?"

"Don't ever come to my house again," Hujar said. "I won't be friends with you if you're going to do that."

David burst into tears. "I just feel so terrible about living," he sobbed. "I feel too self-conscious about living, and it's driving me crazy."

Hujar reached over and rubbed David's arm.

David never used heroin again.

That fall, James Romberger and Marguerite Van Cook moved their Ground Zero Gallery to 339 East Tenth Street, on the north side of Tompkins Square Park. David was one of the artists they talked to about doing a show. "I had a motto," Marguerite said. "'Go harder.' Whoever we invited, I wanted them to present the most profound, challenging work that they could. Something outrageous. Something they'd never get a chance to do anywhere else because no one in their right mind would let them do it. I think that's one of the reasons that David showed with us." David decided he would do an installation at Ground Zero that incorporated Kern's *You Killed Me First.*

Kern shot the eleven-minute film over two days in mid-October. Then employed as an assistant to artist Charles Hinman, Kern had the cast come to Hinman's loft while the artist was out of town. They needed a space that looked "grown-up," Kern said, unlike the shabby dumps where all of them lived. There was never a script as such—everyone improvised—but Kern put together a list of scenes based on the interviews he'd done.

David got the chance to play a version of his own father, and he recruited Karen Finley to play the mother. Lung Leg, in a filthy T-shirt and uncombed hair, had the lead role as the daughter who slaughters her family during Thanksgiving dinner. She tells them she hates them while Dad carves the turkey. Then several flashbacks show why. Her parents despise her creepy boyfriend, Cheese (Montana Hewson). They want her to be like her good-girl sister (Jessica Craig-Martin). Her dad comes home with a gun and shoots it off in the living room. Then he kills her pet rabbit and chops it up with a cleaver. The final outrage is that her mom finds her artwork (which looks very "East Village") and rips it up. The daughter gets the dad's gun and shoots each of them, shouting, "You killed me first!"

Maybe David found it therapeutic to restage both a childhood trauma and a murderous fantasy. He had chopped the rabbit with such fury during filming that he left notches in the butcher block. Kern spent a full day sanding the table down and then staining it to erase the evidence.

David tried to look at what this brought up in him when he did his next piece for the *Eye*. Walking home from the shoot, he wrote, "I was still shaking somewhere deep inside." He saw his father as a master of both physical and psychic violence. He thought he'd put that behind him, but he found that psychic violence could extend its effects through time, particularly "when some other character enters your life and through unconsciousness or design manages to push some of the emotional buttons that have survived the erasure of memory. In trying to put myself into my dad's head, in trying to manufacture his violence and self-hate, I found myself laying open a strange energy, something that rose out of thick scars into the glare of lamps and refused to be identified."

David then went on to discuss the psychic violence inflicted on him by someone he identified only as "a well-known writer." Most people around the scene knew he meant Gary Indiana—as did Gary himself. The placement here is telling. It explains why David reacted to Gary in a way that was rather out of proportion with reality. David claimed, for example, that Gary had made "veiled threats" to physically attack him. He wrote about feeling helpless and fearful. Certainly Gary had tremendous energy. He was a force. He was also a slight man about a foot shorter than David and in no way a physical threat.

David wrote, "I realized around this time that the fear I felt from his attacks were connecting invisibly to fears I developed as a kid at the hands of my dad. The messages weren't all that different: nothing I did was any good."

"David really distorted things in that article," Gary said. "At the time, it was more embarrassing than it was hurtful because I just thought, well, people are disposed to believe this kind of thing. They're not liable to read this article with any understanding that there might be another side to it. I just thought it was lashing out, a really immature way of lashing out."

Looking back, he felt that their relationship had amounted to "sort of a mutual and shared craziness."

"It seemed to me that David was always casting himself as the victim," said Gary. "He always seemed wounded. But I understand it better now, because when you've been hurt by other people, you become almost skinless."


In November, Gracie Mansion got David a commission from Robert and Adriana Mnuchin, major collectors and patrons of the arts. David was to create an installation in their basement.

He hired Steve Brown, Steve Doughton, and Amy Turner to help him collect debris. They spent several days combing through collapsed buildings and rubble-strewn vacant lots in Alphabet City, Harlem, maybe even the South Bronx. They then hauled a car door, a battered old Vespa, the shell of a television, punctured tires, broken windows, old bricks, and scraps of barbed wire into the Mnuchins' Upper East Side town house. David's friends talked about how he enjoyed this—bringing rubble from various blighted neighborhoods into the rich guy's house.

David probably had more than his share of class rage. But the Mnuchin installation was not a piece of tantrum art. He created an apocalyptic scene that was completely in keeping with the other installations he did that year. He also wrote a four-and-a-half-page, single-spaced exegesis to parse what every bit of this piece meant.

"I have grown up in a series of violent circumstances," he explained by way of introduction. "I choose not to turn completely away from this kind of energy even though my life has changed to a degree where I could easily cushion myself from these impulses in the outside world. I would rather look and study and explore these impulses so as to arrive at some kind of personal understanding with them."

David painted a gleaming cityscape across the river from a shoreline strewn with wreckage, skulls dangling from a tree, a skeleton seated in front of a campfire, a flying snake with a human head, a large predatory spider, and the burning child on the run. He said he'd sketched Manhattan from the Brooklyn shore, but it actually looks like he's standing in New Jersey, given the skyscrapers at the tip of the island. A giant figure in a map-covered asbestos suit stands in the city with a hose that gushes fire. He has pulled up a building and set it on fire, but there's no other human activity over there. The rest of the action is on what I'll call the Jersey shore with all the wreckage. Here the "picturesque ruins" are three-dimensional. David painted some debris in the foreground of his cityscape, then extended it with what his friends collected on the street, adding papier-mâché rocks painted to match the stylized rocks in his cityscape.

He added a soundtrack, a tape collage made with Doug Bressler from 3 Teens—apparently mixing sounds like marching feet, children's shouting, and mortar attacks. The installation was very detailed. For example, he'd hidden a tiny farm complete with trees, cows, pigs, horses, and chickens inside a ruptured tire, explaining, "This is a personal image of an outdated idyllic place. . . . One can remove [oneself] from a hostile environment and focus totally on the peacefulness of the new environment but as time goes by this illusion of peace cannot continue totally unhampered by what we escape from."

Indeed, the piece could be read as a metaphor for his state of mind. The emotional focus is the burning boy, again covered with maps and tongues of flame on his arms and legs. He runs toward the skull tree, an image that comes from the Mayan legend *Popol Vuh*. David misremembered the story, however. In the Mayan version, a young woman goes to look at a tree in the underworld where the severed head of a god is hanging. The head spits on her hand, impregnating her with twins who evenutally become the sun and the moon. David's retelling was the myth he needed at that moment. A kid goes into the underworld to find life and comes to a crossroads where there's a tree hung with skulls. When the kid spits on the tree, the skulls either become humans or start talking. (He couldn't decide which.) But "the tree helps the kid towards rebirth."

David spent five days at the beginning of December creating an installation for "The Missing Children's Show" in Louisville, Kentucky—an exhibition created to raise money for the Kentucky Child Victims' Trust Fund.

There isn't much documentation, but one report in a Louisville newspaper called David's piece "a macabre representation of child snatching."

*Marguerite Van Cook and James Romberger, 1985. (Photograph by Karen Ogle)*

He'd brought the yellow skeleton with him from the Anchorage show and suspended it facedown from the ceiling over a black chair with flames painted on it. "The chair is hell," David told a reporter. "It's a metaphor for the aftermath of that kind of act." He had a crawling battery-powered doll, with a globe for a head, on the chair's seat, restrained by a string. In front of it were targets like those used on a firing range, with a deer pictured at center. "The image of the deer being hunted is transferred to the kid," David said. On the back wall he painted a field of cow carcasses, beheaded and slit open. On a wall to the side, he added his trademark large gagging cow.

Five other East Village artists had been invited to Kentucky to work in an old factory undergoing conversion to apartments, the closest thing the curator could find to an abandoned New York building. The art would be destroyed when that renovation occurred.

Judy Glantzman created one of the other site-specific pieces and shared a hotel room with David. This is where they actually became friends. Someone loaned David a 1950 Chevy, and at night he and Glantzman would cruise Louisville, talking. Back in New York, they started meeting for breakfasts that took hours.

The day David returned from Louisville, however, he began working on the installation for *You Killed Me First*. He and Kern drove around to building sites and stole cement blocks and mortar. Ground Zero was a long skinny space. Toward the back, Kern built a cement block wall with a broken window in it. Spectators looked through that window to see the Thanksgiving dinner table, three seated skeletons wearing the characters' outfits from the movie, pigs' blood (from a local butcher) splattered everywhere, and the film playing on a monitor. David and Kern then dragged garbage, dead leaves, and dog turds from Tompkins Square into the front part of the gallery, to make it look like an alley complete with graffiti and a No Parking sign on the wall. David added purple light and wired it for sound. "Foghorns," said Marguerite. "Rats and stuff," said Kern.

People had to pass through that to peek in the window at the dead family. Some walked in and got completely disoriented. Some didn't get past the door. "It smelled bad and was just kind of genuinely revolting," Marguerite said. "We were sitting in the middle of this war zone for a month."

David spent Christmas '85 with Richard Kern and Tommy Turner. They drove to Virginia Beach in the Malibu, stopping to buy fireworks at a roadside stand.

"Weirdest Christmas of all time," Kern said. "Tommy had a whole sheet of acid and we ate the whole sheet."

David brought his typewriter along and about half an incoherent page survives: "what you were talking about before a half cat half dog that ate a poodle and was sweeping out the cloisters man . . . none of the last fifteen or twenty minutes happened." Out on the beach, he started breaking the wood sticks off the bottle rockets. Without that to guide them, the rockets flew crazily, one looping back to explode right over their heads. Armed with his Super 8 camera, Turner drew a big pentagram in the sand with a stick and write "Satan Teens" so he could film it.

Back in New York, David wanted to pick up on Turner's "written in the sand" idea for the opening of their film. He drove around collecting discarded Christmas trees in the Malibu. At Caven Point, he'd found a car that had apparently been pushed from a bridge, its front end stuck in the mud. He and Turner filled that vehicle with the Christmas trees and wrote "Satan Teens" with spray paint on the ice near it. "The idea was to burn the car and then the heat would melt the ice and dissolve the words," said Turner. "Then we'd run the film backwards so it would look like the words were emerging from the liquid." By the time they got this set up, it was dark. When they came back to film it the next day, Turner said, "There were fires all over the place. And firemen." Their Christmas trees were still there in the half-sunk car, but they could hardly set that ablaze under the circumstances. So they just walked around, grabbing other images such as a dead dog teaming with maggots. The mysterious fires, the repellant carcass, their thwarted idea—it made for a suitably bleak ending to a painful year.

# 16 "SOMETHING TURNING EMOTIONAL AND WILD"

**On New Year's** Day 1986, Tom Rauffenbart drank champagne all day while he cooked suckling pig, collard greens, and black-eyed peas for dozens of friends. It was probably eleven thirty or twelve that night when he left his apartment, wired and drunk, to walk to the Bijou, a porn theater on Third Avenue near Thirteenth Street. And there he saw that guy again, the guy he'd described to a friend as so ugly he was beautiful.

He was Tom's type, tall and lean with a long face and buckteeth. Tom had encountered him at the Bijou sometime in November '85, and they'd had sex in a bathroom. "Sometimes you can do that and it's awful," Tom said, "but with him it was so sexy." Though they hadn't talked much, Tom had mentioned that he'd lived in the East Village since the sixties, and then he heard that startlingly deep voice for the first time: "You must have seen a lot of changes." They did not exchange names.

When Tom saw him again on New Year's, he thought maybe the guy wouldn't be interested again. But he was, and they went into the same little bathroom and began to have sex when Tom asked, as he rarely ever did, "Want to go to my house?" Out on the street, they said their names.

"Tom."

"David."

As they walked to Tom's place on East Ninth, they told each other what they did. David said he was a painter.

Tom replied, "Oh. A house painter?"

David seemed bemused. Tom didn't know a thing about art, and he'd ignored the galleries popping up around him in the East Village. Ironically enough, he worked for the city's child welfare department, where he'd spent ten years "in the field," going to allegedly abusive homes and deciding on the spot whether to take the children out with him. By the time he met David, he was in management.

"We spent the night together, which was really erotic and wonderful," Tom said. "I invited him to stay over, and he said, thanks, because he was living in a place where there were a lot of junkies around and it wasn't that comfortable walking home. This was unusual. I rarely invited someone to stay. I usually wanted them out.

"I remember waking up the next morning. I had to go to work, and I just kept looking at him in bed. I was filled with all this emotion. I made a cup of coffee and stood in the doorway watching him sleep, just thinking how wonderful this guy looked and just being really moved. I hadn't been moved by anybody in quite a long time, but this guy really touched something in me, and I don't know what it was. I could just feel this electricity going on. And I just wanted to touch everything that touched him. I'd never done anything like this before but—I smelled his shoes."

Later that day, January 2, Peter Hujar's show opened at the Gracie Mansion Gallery. David had insisted on this, and Gracie agreed despite Hujar's reputation in the art world as "difficult."

A couple of years before this, Timothy Greathouse had offered to show Hujar's work with Nan Goldin's, when she was not yet famous. Greathouse then canceled Goldin to give Hujar a solo show, and Hujar canceled out of loyalty to Goldin.

So he had not had a solo show in New York since 1981.

"The rumor was that Peter hated all his dealers," Gracie said, "that he was worse than David, that he was impossible to work with." But this time, everything clicked. According to Gracie, "Peter was a sweetheart."

Hujar's old friends, Gary Schneider and John Erdman, remembered how happy he was. "He was totally in awe of Gracie," Schneider said. "He thought she was this brilliant light in the East Village." Erdman added, "He thought Gracie was enormously glamorous, and he was shocked that she would do a show of his."

Gracie turned the practical matters over to Sur Rodney Sur, who had a particular knowledge of and interest in photography. Sur asked Hujar what he wanted.

To show a hundred photographs.

Sur told him to bring them in and lay them out, and they'd do it. "We pretty much said, 'Do what you want, and we'll make it happen.'"

Sur explained, "I installed our shows, but I said, 'I'm not going to hang a hundred photographs behind glass, all perfectly neat.' So we hired a very expensive art installer who installed for Pat Hearn, and they did the whole thing beautifully. It was laid out exactly the way Peter wanted, and he was thrilled. Totally thrilled. Because he got the show to look the way he wanted. And I think we sold two prints out of that show. They were six hundred dollars apiece, and no one would buy them."*

In the opinion of Gary Schneider, this was Hujar's best show, and though no one knew it at the time, it was also his last show. Gracie had basically given him a retrospective, and she paired him, in her back room, with Al Hansen, an important Fluxus artist from Hujar's generation and someone Gracie had known for years.

In another decade, another season, the show would have been regarded as an event, but in 1986, the art world ignored it.

The one exception was *Village Voice* critic Gary Indiana, who wrote a piece called "The No Name Review," in which he discussed several exhibitions without naming a single artist. As Indiana explained, "Open a fucking art magazine and there's one proper name after another after another. The proper names just start to stand in for whatever it is you're looking at. Everybody becomes a brand in the art world. It was something that was particularly bothering me at the time."

Given that whatever hurt Hujar would hurt David, the two of them probably saw Gary's review as revenge for David's *East Village Eye* piece, which was still on newsstands as this show opened. Maybe Hujar was even thankful not to be named, since his portraits were described as "those serene, elegant, haunting views of dead people and living people who look dead." Even his pictures of animals were maligned. Gary quoted someone he calls "N" who evokes Alfred Eisenstaedt's portrait of Nazi propaganda

---

* Two other prints were traded, one going to Keith Davis, for example, in exchange for some design work.

minister Joseph Goebbels and claims that most of the people photographed by Hujar looked like Goebbels. "So did the duck. So did the dog."

Tom called David on January 3 and they decided on a first date. They would drive to Robert Moses State Park on the western end of Fire Island. Tom got his first look at the beat-up Malibu, with its saints and monsters on the dashboard and, at this point, two cat skeletons in the back.

They walked the beach in the bitter cold, and David picked up a bird wing. It was a friend's favorite image, he said, without mentioning the friend's name: Peter Hujar. Then he picked up some metal bits. "For my rust collection," he explained, while Tom thought but didn't say, "What?" They drove on to a marina, where they sat outside drinking coffee, and Tom confessed to the most violent—and most uncharacteristic—moment of his life. After eleven awful months with his first boyfriend, Tom snapped into such a fury one day that he blacked out, and when he came to, he was pounding his boyfriend's head on the floor. David would later tell Tom that he had wondered then if he was getting involved with a psycho. They were still strangers, but felt enough of a connection to begin forging past the unexpected and mysterious in each other.

For the next two or three weeks, David came to Tom's place almost every night. "I was totally crazy about him," Tom remembered. "I was just so emotionally moved by this guy. And erotically. It was wonderful, terrific sex. It was great being around him too. And I'd be crazy at work all the time. I couldn't stop talking about him."

David began to sort out his own feelings as he wrote his fourth and final piece for the *East Village Eye*:

Walking back and forth from room to room, trailing bluish shadows, I feel weak; something turning emotional and wild and forming a crazy knot in the deep part of the stomach. And on the next trip from the front of the apartment to the back I end up in the kitchen turning once again and suddenly sinking down to the floor in a crouching position against the wall and side of the stove in a blaze of wintery sunlight; it's blinding me as my fingers trace small circles through the hair on the sides of my temples, and I've had little sleep, having woken up a number of times slightly shocked at the sense of another guy's warm skin and my hands having been moving independent of me in sleep; tracing the lines of his arms and belly and hips and side. . . . So here I am heading out into cold winds of the canyon streets walking down and across Avenue C towards my home with the smell and taste of him wrapped around my neck and jaw like some scarf.

David did not tell Tom he was writing this. Nor did he show it to him. Tom found it by chance when he picked up a copy of the *Eye*. He could not remember what they then said to each other. Probably little. While David found it easy to rage at someone, positive feelings were not only hard for him to articulate but also frightening.

He went to talk to Karen Finley about Tom. "He was scared about his feelings and what to do about them," she said. "I think he was afraid of love because what he had experienced as love from his parents was abuse. With a human who's been damaged by inappropriate sexuality and the power of abuse—we know that the human psyche becomes schizoid and splits, and he would do that. But I told him he was nuts if he walked away from Tom." She encouraged him to tell Tom his fears.

During the last week of January, David called Tom at work, said he had to see him and wouldn't say why. "I immediately thought, well, he wants to break up," Tom said. They arranged to meet at Veselka, a Ukrainian place on Second Avenue. "David came in and he was just a nervous wreck," said Tom. "I'd never seen him like that. And I don't remember exactly how he put it, but the message was that he was really scared. He had all these feelings he didn't know what to do with, all this churning, and he felt lost. I remember being so relieved. Like, is that all? And I said, 'We can take it slow, because I'm confused too. There's so much emotion going on here, I don't know what I'm doing either.' And I remember he went, 'Oh. OK.' Of course, we immediately went to my house and fucked."

David's account of this appeared in a letter he wrote to Luis Frangella in Argentina. After years of not allowing himself to get into a relationship, he wrote, he'd let himself go and now he'd just talked to the guy in a restaurant "and he said something about not seeing each other so much." That was David's version of "We can take it slow."

By the end of January, David had moved into a fifth-floor walk-up in Richard Kern's building at 529 East Thirteenth. He had declined Tom's offer to help, saying he had friends who could do the hauling. This was the beginning of a pattern. David would keep Tom separate from nearly everyone he knew.

As Tom once described the contrast between himself and David's boho friends: "I was settled, I cooked, I had furniture." He wasn't just being facetious. Tom had never gone to the Second Street apartment. But on a first visit to Thirteenth Street, he saw that David had a couple of hardback chairs, a futon on the floor, paint, clutter, and a baby elephant skeleton. "Nothing comfortable anywhere," Tom remembered. And he told David, "You have to buy a bed."

Like Jean Pierre, Tom was middle class and utterly dependable. He was nine years older than David. He loved cooking and the comforts of home. "David met me at an opportune time for him," Tom said. "He thought his career might be dead, and he was fed up with the world he had been in, and in a sense, he hid away with me."

They decided to go to Montreal together the last weekend of January. Tom had always wanted to go there in the winter. So on the appointed Friday morning, he went to Grand Central and bought their tickets and waited. David never showed up. He'd gone to Penn Station. They didn't reconnect until lunch at an East Village sushi bar, and David offered to pay for airline tickets to Montreal. Then they looked at each other and said, "We're crazy. Let's go to the Caribbean."

Neither of them had ever been there. They went to Tom's house, called an airline, and asked the ticket agent, "What's a good place in the Caribbean?" So began their improvised odyssey to the Virgin Islands. From a guidebook bought at the airport, they settled on St. John's as a final destination. The trip became a honeymoon, and nothing could destroy the glow or the afterglow. Not the wait in San Juan's airport from three A.M. to six for

*Tom Rauffenbart photographed by David on the beach at St. John's. (David Wojnarowicz Papers, Fales Library, NYU)*

the flight to St. Thomas. Not Tom learning to drive stick shift on St. John's as they climbed hairpin turns up a mountain in a rented Jeep. Not learning that the room they'd reserved was unavailable. They loved the inn they found by chance. They abjured the chichi restaurants for great local cooking. They had sex on various beaches and in the ocean. At night they could lie on the sand and see a million stars. It was so romantic.

They amazed each other with how public they were, having sex not just on the beach behind some rocks but also in the minivan driving them back to the airport, where they jerked each other off in the back seat. "We were just so aroused. We were outrageous," Tom said. They didn't change out of their bathing suits till they got back to San Juan, where they were still walking around with big erections. Someone came up to them and said, "You guys were the scandal of the St. Thomas airport." They waited for their flight back to New York in a coffee shop, where Tom said to David, "I'm falling in love with you," and David said nothing. His eyes filled with tears and turned red. He looked away.

"It was fine with me, that response," said Tom. "I just remember his whole face went into shock." They boarded their plane. Both liked aisle seats, so David sat in front of Tom. During the flight, David reached his hand back. Tom grabbed it. They held hands.

David wanted to paint again. He did not mention that he'd devoted a year to "imperiled child" or "dead family" scenarios when he explained his hiatus from painting to the *New Art Examiner*. "The attention and money for me was getting in the way of any kind of clarity, and I needed to pull away," he said. "All of this media stuff, you get lost in it. You can take it too seriously and become self-conscious. It seemed like a joke at a certain point. People just come into the gallery and take what you put out and they don't even look at it. You just become a workhorse filling a list. You self-imitate to meet demand." His main journal for 1986 is all sketches, lists, and ideas for paintings. He seemed infused with a new confidence and focus.

Early that year, he began preparing for an April show at Gracie Mansion he would call "An Exploration of the History of Collisions in Reverse." David was beginning his mature work here. There would be no more stenciling on a poster, though the title of a painting he'd done in 1984, *Soon All This Will Be Picturesque Ruins*, still functioned as a theme. That painting was simple, even crude, however, while the new work was dense and multilayered, loaded with messages and storylines about a civilization hurtling toward apocalypse.

*Crash: The Birth of Language/The Invention of Lies* is emblematic, its central image a steam locomotive that is about to collide with a very small planet Earth. Parts of the train are cut away, and the biggest scene visible inside it, the focus of the whole painting, is a dead human tied facedown in the desert and now serving as carrion for two vultures. References to his own past work are embedded throughout—a floating alien head, a burning building, a ground of supermarket posters visible in bits behind the train. In front of the locomotive, above planet Earth, is a skeleton with a lizard head and possibly a human body. Letters of the alphabet explode above that head but form no words. There's more, but that describes the major "action."

David would have been able to say what every single image meant to him. Nothing in his paintings was ever arbitrary, nothing was by chance.

The train, in his cosmology, symbolized the acceleration of time. He chose that—over, say, airplanes—because trains were the instrument of westward expansion; they had wiped out a culture. (A pueblo and a kachina are visible inside one of the locomotive's wheels.) In another of these "history paintings," *Some Things from Sleep: For Jane and Charley*, the side of a locomotive is cut away to reveal a baby, floating in water and still tethered to its umbilical cord. Jane Dickson and Charley Ahearn were about to have a baby, and Dickson described David as "enthusiastic" about that. But in David's view, each new human joins the collision course humanity is on.

The "history paintings" seem to follow naturally out of the Mnuchin installation, down to the gray pile of debris, mostly old machinery, that dominates *Excavating the Temples of the New Gods*. One image in this painting is a head of Christ with crown of thorns, made to look like one of David's "alien heads," green and floating over a background of paper currency. Corrupted spirituality is a new theme. While he was still using supermarket posters, maps, and other paper ephemera to symbolize what people accept without question, his new imagery included Western landscapes, Native American objects, gears and other industrial detritus, hybrid creatures (some combination of animal, human, and machine), and repellant animals with serious jobs (vultures, dung beetles). He was still fascinated by relics and rubble.

He explained a couple of years later that he saw machines as fossils of the industrial age. "For me, the image of the gear or the defunct machine is the image of what history means, reached through the compression of time," he said. "Scientists have discovered that if the head of a moth is cut off, it can still continue to lay eggs. Somehow I don't think civilization is all that different. . . . Society is almost dead and yet it continues reproducing its madness as if there were a real future at the end of its collective gestures."

Though he hadn't articulated it in 1986, he had found the subject matter that would preoccupy him for the rest of his life. Broadly speaking, this was what he called "the wall of illusion surrounding society and its structures"—false history, false spirituality, government control. His shorthand for it was "the pre-invented world." He explained that phrase in *Close to the Knives*:

The world of the stoplight, the no-smoking signs, the rental world, the split-rail fencing shielding hundreds of miles of barren wilderness from the human step. A place where by virtue of having been born centuries late one is denied access to earth or space, choice or movement. The bought-up world; the owned world. The world of coded sounds: the world of language, the world of lies. The packaged world; the world of speed in metallic motion. The Other World where I've always felt like an alien.

When David talked with Tom, he often mentioned a particular good friend, Peter. "One day," Tom said, "it hit me. Could this be Peter Hujar?"

David told him it was funny, because just recently Hujar had said to him, "Are you talking about Tom Rauffenbart?"

Tom and Hujar had had an affair early in 1974 that lasted a couple of months. When they met, Tom knew that Hujar was a photographer. "But I didn't know anything about his world," said Tom. He did know that "the man had no money, ever." He too had seen Hujar wash his jeans out in the sink and dry them on top of a radiator.

One night they went out and Hujar asked Tom if he'd be willing to close his eyes and let Hujar guide him around. "It was great fun for about two hours," Tom said. "We'd stop places and he'd say, 'Feel this and try to tell me where you are.'"

Then Tom discovered that Hujar knew certain people who were more or less famous and that he was taking pictures at Warhol's Factory. "So I was getting the sense that this guy was sort of a mini-celebrity," said Tom, "and that was intimidating to me. We had some really nice dates, but I just got more and more frightened, more and more self-conscious. It became hard to talk. I remember one time saying to him, 'I'm just so impressed by who you are and I don't feel like I'm anything,' and Peter said, 'Well, I've actually been fascinated by you.'"

For the only time in his life, Tom started keeping a journal—which he later found too painful to read. Hujar called him one night and invited him over for dinner. "I asked what he was making, and he said, 'Tuna noodle casserole.'" (At a certain point in Hujar's life, that was the dish he made every night.) Tom, who was trying to learn to assert himself, said, "I hate tuna noodle casserole. No, I'm not coming." The affair ended soon after. Not because of this spurned invitation, but because, Tom said, "I would panic inside and lose myself."

For years afterward, this was the relationship Tom most regretted losing. And now, Hujar was David's best friend. Tom thought, "Oh, great. Peter will tell him what an asshole I am."

In fact, Hujar thought that Tom would be good for David, that David needed stability and Tom would give it to him. Now he'd have regular meals and maybe take better care of himself.

But Tom could sense all the fears and insecurities he'd had in his relationship with Hujar starting to build again in this new relationship with David. "I was getting moody and depressed," Tom remembered. "I was still drinking, and I was afraid to tell David what I felt. I thought he would hate me. It was just horrible." Tom went into therapy that spring. "I knew that if I didn't do something about this, I was going to lose this guy."


David's show of "history paintings" opened at Gracie Mansion Gallery on April 27. "People were literally fighting in the gallery over these paintings," Sur Rodney Sur recalled. "It was horrific. I'd never seen anything like it." Major collectors had come in before the doors officially opened and before David arrived. So, he didn't hear people arguing: "*I* want that one." The difficulty, Sur said, was "when you have two people fighting over the same painting, how do you decide who gets what?"

While David missed this feeding frenzy, everything was sold by the time he showed up. He was stunned. This was exactly what he'd complained about—people buying but (he assumed) not apprehending. Gracie remembered that someone had come in a limo. "And to think that somebody would buy something who had come in a limousine—he both loved and hated it," she said. Gracie had done her job. David was "hot," and all the pieces went to major collections. His response to this good fortune was to announce that he would again stop painting. He told Gracie, "It's over. I'm just going to work on my writing."

Then he told Tommy Turner that he wanted to make a giant spider for the window of the gallery, and this creature would be preying on a man while a fan blew money out its rear end. Gracie was the spider. "Sucking me dry," he complained to Turner.

The day after the opening, David left town with Tom. They went back to St. John's.

David had found the relationship that would sustain him for the rest of his life, and he'd found a new direction for his work. Even so, he hadn't quite finished with the ugly preoccupations of the previous year. He and Tommy Turner worked on their Super 8 "satanic teen" film off and on through the first half of 1986.

Jim "Foetus" Thirwell offered them a song he'd written about Ricky Kasso. He called it "Where Evil Dwells" and said they could have the music if they made that the title of the film. Turner and David agreed that it was better than the title *Satan Teens*. They worked out a new title shot. David stapled a piece of transparent plastic between two broom handles, and a couple of assistants held it up in front of a suburban house while David wrote the words "WHERE EVIL DWELLS." He and Turner felt that Ricky Kasso and friends had used drugs and their own twisted take on black magic to rearrange what David called "the imposed hell of the suburbs."

They shot footage of satanic teens around a campfire and of the Kasso figure chasing the kid he would kill. They filmed the Kasso figure gouging the eyes from what is clearly a rubber mask. So it was ham-handed. It was also a horror film of unrelenting gloom, with images of grave robbing, burning cars, and dead or dying animals.

The most original scenes are set in heaven and hell. (Kasso warned his victim that he would follow him into the afterlife.) The script describes heaven as a "bourgeois restaurant," where Jesus, played by Rockets Redglare, sits gorging at a banquet table. A maître'd bars the satanic teen from entering.

Then there's hell, which turns out to be as barbarous and ghastly as advertised. A number of people have been tied upside down to a locomotive engine, where they're hit by a man in a hockey mask. Fires burn in barrels. A motorcycle with one Hell's Angel and two female minions circles slowly. There are people in masks, people with whips, someone in a goat's head, much smoke and chaos. The Devil (played by Joe Coleman) makes the film's most indelible impression, whether standing on a railroad bridge and exploding the firecrackers attached to his chest or plucking a live white rat from a tray and biting its head off.

They shot the underworld scene on June 28, 1986, after wheat-pasting flyers around the East Village advertising for "inhabitants of hell: junkies, weightlifters, starving bums, suicides . . . human oddities, sleepwalkers . . . screamers, scrooges playing with money . . . anything you want to be or are and wish to have immortalized forever." Such volunteers were to meet at a particular spot along Tompkins Square Park for shuttle service to hell. David had found an abandoned warehouse along the river in a not-yet-gentrified Williamsburg. Turner instructed the assembled hellhounds not to tell the locals what the film was about. "Tell them we're filming *Miami Vice*," he said. One of the actors couldn't contain herself, however, and told some neighborhood kids that they were making a movie about Satan. The kids ran for their older brothers and fathers, who marched down to the warehouse just as filming ended. "It almost turned into a fight," Turner said. "They threatened to push David's car into the river." Somehow David managed to diffuse this situation, but Turner could not remember how.

John Erdman, who played the father of the satanic teen, remembered them shooting the home scenes at an apartment on Front Street in Lower Manhattan. And then something happened between David and Turner. "Something awful, I felt," said Erdman. "David never said what. But he pulled out. He was enraged."

Turner did not recall this, but speculated, "Possibly the drug thing was bothering him." Turner's heroin addiction had intensified. When David wrote years later about making *Where Evil Dwells*, he did not say that he'd been angered by anything but that Turner "was being pulled around by his addiction and sometimes failed to show up for filming."

Turner estimates they had eight hours of footage in the end, but the film was never finished. He and David created a thirty-four-minute "trailer" without sync sound to show at the 1986 Downtown Film Festival. With no sound, though, it's not coherent. A slightly damaged Howdy Doody appears, apparently to narrate, becoming one more inexplicable image. A couple of years after this, a fire at Turner's apartment destroyed the sound tape, whatever footage he'd stored there, his rat-fur jacket, and nearly everything else he owned. Turner escaped the blaze carrying little but his infant son, Talon.

David and Turner spoke a few times about going back to work on *Where Evil Dwells*, but with this film, David seems to have maxed out on dealing with both family trauma and someone else's death wish. There were limits to what one could learn from the tragic but witless life of Ricky Kasso.

He was no longer infatuated with the worldview of Kern and Turner. He began to withdraw from Kern in particular, even though they were neighbors. Kern thought David was angry because he wasn't using him in any more of his films. "And the fact that the drug thing just got worse and worse," Kern admitted. David, meanwhile, had cut way down or even eliminated his own use of speed and psychedelics. The night David and Tom Rauffenbart left the Bijou together, David was on ecstasy, as he told Tom later. But Tom never knew David to take drugs. "Two sips of champagne and he would feel off," Tom said. "Even aspirin bothered him."

David wrote of this period in *Close to the Knives*:

Death was everywhere, especially in my apartment, a gentrified space right above [Kern's] place. In my depression, I kept thinking it was [Kern]'s fragmented state of mind that was pumping death vibes up through the floor. Later I found out a woman with three kids had occupied my apartment before I got there. She apparently died a slow, vicious death from AIDS. I felt like the connection between me and this circle of friends was getting buried in veils of disintegration; drug addiction creates this vortex of psychological and physical fragmentation that is impossible to spotlight or put a finger on. [Kern] was wrestling with it and at the same time seemed unconscious of it. I thought he was becoming a creep. . . . [Turner] was getting more erratic and transparent in his addiction. . . . I felt myself at a point where I needed to either define certain boundaries for myself or get away from my life as it was.

Anna Friebe was one of the German dealers who'd been an early supporter of the East Village, and that summer she offered David a solo show. He left for Europe on July 23 and stayed until September 7. He visited Paris, but for most of that time he was in Cologne creating more "history paintings" for the Friebe Gallery.

*Late Afternoon in the Forest*, for example, continues the general theme of apocalypse and ruin. One of his hybrid creatures—part bird, part airplane—has crashed in the forest. Behind it sits a large alien head with its lips sewn shut. Visible in the torn fuselage of the bird-plane is a bit of gothic architecture, all arched doorways, and from it crawl a couple of red fire ants with human faces. Maybe only the hybrids survive in this future. Everything 100 percent human here seems to be an artifact, and it's all quite small—the Greek statue of a man fighting a centaur, the Indian chief that looks like something bought from a souvenir stand, the Parthenon visible in an upper corner.

David was living and working in the gallery, since it was closed for the summer. Before Anna Friebe left town, she asked one of her other artists, Rilo Chmielorz, to look in on him occasionally. "We connected in a strong way," Rilo said. It felt like "an eternal association." David made a piece to give her, painting his symbols for Earth (the globe), wind (a cloud with a face, blowing), fire (a devil), and water (a snowman) on a German supermarket poster. They had intense conversations. They went to the zoo. She remembered that he was suffering from insomnia.

In *History Keeps Me Awake at Night (for Rilo Chmielorz)*, he stenciled a sleeping man onto maps at the bottom of the piece. (He would use this sleeping figure in several subsequent paintings that suggest dream imagery.) The history he dreams of here is all violence—a criminal with a gun (the image commonly used in target practice), a headless warrior atop a headless horse, a one-eyed monster, and so on. The same monster appeared in a piece done earlier that year for the Gracie Mansion show—*Queer Basher/Icarus Falling*. *History Keeps Me Awake* is a painting about fear, from the violence he dreaded as a gay man to catastrophes that threaten us all, in his view. The titles of other pieces also convey the dystopic vision of America he'd taken as his subject in 1986: *The Newspaper as National Voodoo: A Brief History of the U.S.A.*; *The Death of American Spirituality* (begun in '86 but completed in '87).

Art historian Mysoon Rizk pointed out that as David developed his iconography, he began using animals to depict, among other things, "certain

Sisyphean characteristics of the human condition. . . . Crawling bugs, in particular, appear regularly in his work, often as tenacious protagonists or super-sized heroes invoking an eternal sense of time." Just so, David created two *Dung Beetle* paintings in 1986. Both feature two large scarabs rolling dung around a picture of an American eagle, and in both paintings, disaster strikes an outmoded form of human transportation—the crashed Hindenburg in one, a steam locomotive exploding off the tracks in the other. Rizk observed that in David's work, "even human apocalypse is unable to prevent nature's incessant struggle and cyclical compulsions."

Back in New York, Tom remembered David working on Super 8 film projects during this period. Tom sometimes assisted or posed.

David was creating an image bank. He recorded Tom lifting a baby doll from a bucket and dropping flowers into water. He filmed a doll in stark black and white with a strobe going. He had Tom pose with bandaged hands, sometimes holding coins. He filmed and photographed Tom with his lips sewn shut. "It won't hurt much," David would joke. He attached the red string with glue and used red food coloring to simulate blood.

Tom began introducing David to the wonders of Zagat, to the city's best steak houses, for example, since David loved steak. Another favorite spot was Union Square Cafe, the kind of great but pricey restaurant where David had never eaten before. Tom also loved cooking for David, and he introduced him to such middle-class concepts as "thread count."

David still spent many of his nights at Tom's. Tom gave him a drawer but they never officially moved in together. "It would have been hard without a thirty-room apartment," Tom said. "Neither one of us was easy to live with." They had their first fight while changing the bed. Tom liked the sheets tucked in. David asked why, and Tom said, "There is no why."

"I hate those kinds of answers," David steamed.

Every morning, David would announce that he'd had some dream while Tom would groan to himself, "Oh great," but tolerate the telling. "David never slept well in all the years I knew him," Tom said. "He'd talk in his sleep and thrash around. He was always worried that he was going to smack me. One night he did. I wasn't upset because I knew he didn't mean

*David editing Super 8 film at Tom's house. (Photograph by Tom Rauffenbart)*

it, but he did haul off and whack me. Some nights I'd wake up, and he'd be giving some long dissertation. I'd try to talk back to see if he'd answer, but he never did."

David told Tom that he wished he never had to sleep. He would prefer to be awake all the time. "He was almost afraid to lay down and sleep," said Tom. "It's probably when all the demons in his mind got let loose."

In April 1986, the *Eye* ran a cover story titled "The East Village Yuppie." As the subhead put it, "Into our post-apocalyptic playground come the renovators, the upscalers, bringing tidings of America's New Order. . . . Survival has replaced self-expression and upward mobility is no longer optional."

Meanwhile, Ground Zero Gallery maintained its highly original and completely impractical operations. At the beginning of the year, scenemaker and would-be gossip columnist Baird Jones asked if he could exhibit his photos of Mark Kostabi posing with celebrities. James Romberger and Marguerite Van Cook agreed on the condition that he keep the pigs' blood from *You Killed Me First* on the walls. That spring they showed Dragan Ilic, carrying out his farcical directive that they rotate all the paintings by ninety degrees every twenty minutes "to simulate a zero-gravity environment." Then Mike Osterhout did an installation called *Hell*, painting the walls red, covering the floor with gravel, building a fire in the middle of the gallery, and adding a screen door. "We had all these punk kids coming in, sitting around it like it was a campfire," Marguerite said. But the fire department came daily. From the park across the street, Ground Zero appeared to be on fire, and someone called it in every day. The firefighters had to respond, even though they knew what it was, so James and Marguerite decided to shut the piece down after a couple of weeks. Then when Marguerite did a show of her own work, she and James covered the front of the gallery with silver Mylar so it reflected the park. For an inside wall, Marguerite created a life-size photo of the Pyramid Club by placing the negative in a slide projector and getting a whole team of friends to roll developer onto a huge paper, then carry it—in pitch-dark—to a bathtub they'd filled with fixer. She put that photo up and hung her artwork on it.

The Wrecking Crew did a show at Ground Zero that summer, with the artists working from the afternoon until sometime the next day and possibly tripping, though Marguerite wasn't sure everyone dropped acid. "David did a nice big cop eating skulls," James remembered. "A big cop head. It was really hard to paint on the bricks, so everybody was making these ugly marks. David's thing looked the best because he had the smooth wall."

"We all did whatever we wanted," Marguerite said. "With some flying Needlenoses. I mean, there were general themes of rebellion. Then the psychedelic effect of the artwork got viewers so crazy. We did some performances in there. I think we had Nick Zedd do a poetry thing, and the readings were energized by the environment. There was so much movement within the artwork it unsettled people. It exposed a wildness in the viewers that we were unprepared for." By that fall, the gallery had moved to its last location, on East Ninth Street, and the Wrecking Crew did its final show, working outside in the backyard. David was probably out of town, since he did not participate.

In September, the *East Village Eye*, house organ to the scene, became simply the *Eye* in an attempt to broaden its appeal. It published its last issue in December, then put out a sort of greatest-hits collection of landmark pieces in January, and folded. The scene was clearly melting away, though in 1986 it was hard to see that because no one wanted to. Perhaps Wrecking Crew participant David West offered the best metaphor when he suggested that it was like the sound of a gong reverberating long after it's been rung.

Early in October 1986, David went to West Palm Beach, one of three artists selected to paint a mural on a courtyard wall at the Norton Gallery of Art. His *Some Day All This Will Be Picturesque Ruins; Four Elements* would be obliterated when the show closed. But of course, he had always enjoyed painting something that he knew would be destroyed.

In the mural, symbols for all four elements hover over a Southwestern landscape, and there's a kind of narrative at work about the destruction of Native American culture. A tornado (wind) destroys a kachina doll. The devil (fire) represents the invading white people. And so on. Earth is a globe with an emerging brain, while a snowman represents water. He'd been working this out in his mind for a few months. In another *Earth, Wind, Fire, Water* painting done earlier that year, he created a similar scenario, using a cloud with a face to represent wind.

He would really figure out how to combine "ruin" with the elements in the much more sophisticated *Earth, Wind, Fire,* and *Water* paintings he completed in 1987. But the mural in Florida had to be counted a success given that the Norton Gallery extended the "Walls" show for eight months. Its press release quoted David explaining his work: "It's just recordings, so that if life were to be wiped out, these records would still exist."

Both James Romberger and David had been invited into a summer group show in SoHo curated by Michael Carter, editor of the East Village zine *Redtape*. When the gallery director came to Ground Zero to pick up James's piece, he saw one of Marguerite's, liked it, and left with some of her work as well.

"An hour or so before the show opened, they took my painting down and put up a painting by the [gallery] owner's wife," said Marguerite. "Carter had an issue with this, and things took a turn for the worse. By the time we got there, they had thrown Carter up against a wall, and he was bruised and shaken up." Carter did not recall being manhandled or hurt. But he was thrown out of his own show, along with Marguerite. He had a co-curator, however, who finally prevailed upon the owner to let them back in. Marguerite asked for her work to be returned, either that night or the next day. She was told that the back room was locked.

When Marguerite told David what had happened, he returned to the gallery with her—furious and carrying a sledgehammer. "David took his painting off the wall and told them to give me my work back," she said. "He swung and made a hole in the wall, and then they opened up the back room quick enough. We carried my work out. David's too."

David then discovered that his painting *Dung Beetles* had been damaged. In late October, he went back to the gallery with Tom, who knew nothing about the sledgehammer incident. "David had this huge argument with the gallery owner," said Tom. "'Are you going to repair my piece?' And the guy was saying no." Tom realized later that David had planned this out carefully, because they'd come in on a day when the gallery was getting ready to install a new show. There stood all those pristine, freshly painted, empty white walls. David suddenly pulled out a tire iron, which he must have concealed inside his jean jacket, and announced: "That's what you do to my painting, this is what I do to your wall."

"He smashed about five big holes in the walls," said Tom, who had not known that David was carrying the tire iron. Tom stood there dumbfounded as David stormed out, and the gallery owner screamed at him.

Outside Tom and David met up with Rilo Chmielorz, who was visiting from Cologne and staying at David's apartment. "We had dinner together and we were speaking the whole time about what happened at the gallery," Rilo said. "It was Tom who calmed down David a bit. Tom had both feet on the ground."

When David decided to go to Mexico for the Day of the Dead, he asked Tommy Turner to come with him. He would pay for their tickets. He hoped that Turner could break his heroin addiction and thought a trip away from his drug connections and routines would help. Also, Turner had traveled in Mexico before, while David had just dipped a toe in, swinging through Tijuana and Chihuahua on the bus trip he took in 1975 while vacationing from Bookmasters.

Each of them packed a Super 8 camera, a 35mm camera, and a journal. Early on October 28, they flew to San Antonio, then caught a bus to Laredo, where they spent the night. "Over dinner, David and I discussed the different things we may feel over the next three weeks," Turner wrote that first night in his journal, "especially concerning respective problems we will leave behind in U.S.A. necessarily." David seemed prepared to cope with Turner's withdrawal, and Turner seemed prepared to endure it. He'd slept through most of the trip from New York, so he sat up writing in his journal that night while David went to sleep. Suddenly David sat up, still asleep, and said, "No . . . life as a bird. Like over a wall. A small wall of feeling. A logging ball. The fast left right. A quiet now. A quiet month." Then he dropped back onto the pillow. Turner could not get all the lines down because David had spoken so quickly, but he noted, "Wow. I can't believe it. David dreams in poetry."

The next day, they crossed the border into Nuevo Laredo, Mexico. In David's journal entry, which is brief, he mostly recorded observations of people they encountered, and as usual, he was interested in damaged people, like a guy he calls "the elephant man." He wrote, "Half his face was a hideous color and texture like a truck tire left in a campfire for half an hour." David followed him, noting the reactions he elicited. He and Turner took the train from Nuevo Laredo to Mexico City. Once on board, they were shaken down by cops who checked them "for pistols." David handed over 160 pesos, the equivalent of twenty cents.

David had started referring to Turner as "a beacon" because everywhere they went, someone would come up to him and offer him drugs. Turner would say no and David would tease, "Everybody knows." Turner got through his first two days of withdrawal, consulting his tarot deck, trying to find a spiritual path out of addiction. "I'm going to scorch out my past on top of the Pyramid of the Sun, impregnate my future on top of the Pyramid of the Moon," he wrote, in anticipation of their planned trip to Teotihuacán, the ancient sacred site and Aztec ruin.

Once they got to Mexico City, Turner came down with dysentery and began hallucinating. He saw a statue of a three-headed nun flying right at him, saying, "Why do you think I'm dinner?" A tortoise made of cactus tried to stab him. Some Mexican cards he'd bought now seemed to have faces on them, all staring malevolently. "I was saying all this stuff out loud," Turner remembered, "and David was cracking up, writing it down." Some of these images ended up in a painting David made when he returned to New York, *Tommy's Illness*.

Turner recovered after a day, and they took a bus north to Guanajuato, where both shot some film at the town's Mummy Museum. Later David printed a still from this footage, a dead child with an open mouth that he called *Mexican Mummy (Munch Scream)*.

On November 2, they went to watch Day of the Dead rituals at a cemetery in the Coyoacán section of Mexico City. Turner reported in his journal that he no longer had any withdrawal pain. He felt great. "Flowers everywhere," he wrote, "incense clouding crucifixes, baby angels painted with blue house paint. . . . Me and David felt very self-conscious filming this stuff." This had been Frida Kalho's neighborhood, and they found her museum, but it was closed for the holiday.

They had more chances that day to think about mortality. As they walked away from Coyoacán, they passed shattered buildings and wreckage still there from the September 1985 earthquake, which had killed some ten thousand people. They climbed aboard a bus "to film unobtrusively," Turner wrote. "Yea right. My regular camera sounds like a bank vault being slammed when the shutter closes." On their way to the cemetery that morning, they'd passed a seedy-looking circus, and that's where they wanted to go next. "David was hoping very much to see a bear ride a tricycle," reported Turner. "No such luck. The same three guys did everything. Acrobats (missed almost every attempt), clowns, musicians, lion tamers, and motorcycle daredevils." David filmed all of this.

They found a cabdriver who agreed to take them to see Mexican masked wrestling and act as a sort of interpreter for three thousand pesos

*Film still ["legless beggar"] from* A Fire in My Belly, *1988–89. Black-and-white photograph, 26 × 31½ inches. (Collection of San Francisco Museum of Modern Art)*

(roughly four dollars) per hour. Turner described an anarchic scene at the arena, fighting that kept spilling out into the audience, a wrestler called La Erupción with "a volcano erupting on his chest and flames shooting [up between] his eyes. Me and David were filming like locos." Then they both nearly lost their cameras. First a security guard accosted Turner and pulled him into the lobby, demanding to see a permit. The cabdriver intervened, and it all got straightened out for a bribe of a thousand pesos. As Turner sat back down, a couple of other guards grabbed both his camera and David's. They were told that they would have to give up their film. Again the cabbie intervened and worked it out but they had to stop filming.

David was not insensitive about using a camera here. While he wrote nothing in his journal about the Day of the Dead, the circus, the wrestling match, or the mummies, he did reflect on his own voyeurism, and the fact that it was a luxury he could now afford. "If I were penniless, I'd be just another person hustling for food there," he wrote. "So in filming in Mexico I pushed the voyeurism to the limit, always shooting through a zoom lens whenever possible, from car or bus windows; points of elevation, third story windows, shop balconies, cliffs, etc." He was most interested in the street characters and wrote that the best thing he saw in Mexico City was a man walking into a fancy restaurant, carrying his right shoe up to a table of wealthy diners and lifting his leg so they could see that he had no foot, "just a blood red bone covered in tissue thin skin—looked like a cow bone, the kind you see on 14th street in barrels."

On November 3, he and Turner took a bus to Teotihuacán. David was excited because he'd heard that there were fire ants there. He had brought props with him: watchfaces, coins, a toy gun, a toy soldier, a small Day of the Dead skull, a candle, a sign, a crucifix. Once they reached Teotihuacán, they separated. Turner went to the southern end of the site to meditate and do a tarot card reading atop the Pyramid of Quetzalcoatl. David found nests of big red fire ants somewhere between the pyramids to the sun and moon. He placed the objects he'd brought with him there, took pictures, and filmed the images that would so upset the Catholic League eighteen years after his death. He filmed the pyramids and the Avenue of the Dead. At the end of the day, he and Turner climbed to the top of the Pyramid of the Moon during a thunderstorm and tried without success to film the lightning.

David didn't talk about what the ants meant to him, just as he hadn't talked about any of the other things he'd filmed and photographed. "He was just grabbing images," Turner said, "and he'd use it later." When he printed the fire ant pictures in 1988, he explained, "Ants are the only insects to keep pets, use tools, make war, and capture slaves." In these photos, they represent human activity within pre-invented structures: time (the watchfaces), money (coins), control (the toy soldier), violence (the toy gun), language (the sign), and spirituality (the crucifix). His photos of ants crawling over an artificial eye (knowledge) and over a photo of a naked man (desire) were taken on another occasion (and the eye photo was printed at a smaller size). Writing about *Untitled (Ant and Eye)*, he explained that humans often treat nature as an abstract concept, hardly noticing the ground they walk on. "Using animals as a form to convey information about scale or intention is to take that power away from the human and return it to the life forms that have been abstracted into the 'other.'"

The next day, November 4, David flew into a rage at Turner over the loss of a receipt. It was another inexplicable blowup. Turner wanted to call his wife, Amy, because she was in the hospital. The hotel required a fifty-dollar deposit, which Turner paid. Then David told him he would hang on to Turner's receipt, and Turner gave it to him. Turner never completed the phone call, because Amy didn't pick up. So that evening, David said, go get your money back. Turner said, give me the receipt. The fight started there. Apparently David had lost the deposit slip but attacked Turner for entrusting it to him. "What a stupid thing to do!" And so on.

On November 5, they went to the airport together to fly to the Yucatán. They already had their plane tickets, but at the airport David announced that he'd had it with Turner and could no longer travel with him. He would go elsewhere. He handed Turner, then nearly broke, a few hundred dollars. Turner thought that "very kind." He flew to the Yucatán, alone and astonished. He spent about a week there. "I knew David's history of traveling with people," said Turner. "That it could go awry. But we had always gotten along." Turner had to take a bus back to New York from the Yucatán. He borrowed money from other tourists for the ticket.

Without Turner, David probably stayed in or near Mexico City. He sent Tom a postcard from there: "Hey Cookie, I wish in moments I could live down here with an endless supply of film—being on my own is a bit lonely but filled with strange adventure. Wish you were here and we was driving. Sometimes the slowness of busses is too much."

David arrived home on November 18 and began to work on paintings inspired by the Mexican trip. He had promised James and Marguerite a show at Ground Zero, scheduled to open January 10.

In *Close to the Knives*, he wrote, "When I returned to New York City I saw [Turner] about two weeks later. He was in town a couple days and his eyes were heavily lidded from dope. I started avoiding him after that."

Turner, however, is sure he stayed clean for several months.

Sometime in 1986—no one remembers when—Dean Savard reappeared in the East Village, living in an old Dodge van parked on Tompkins Square. According to Dean's brother, Perry Savard, their parents bought him the van. "My parents basically said, this is the last thing we're doing for you."

Alan Barrows remembered that the point was to get him a van so he could leave New York and get cleaned up. And he did leave town for a while, but "he couldn't stay away," said Barrows. Drugs were still so easy to get in the neighborhood. Savard had with him all the paintings that artists had given him during his years at Civilian Warfare, and he began selling them out of the van to get drug money. "Eventually the van wouldn't run anymore, and he sold the van," Barrows said. "After that, I guess he probably lived in abandoned buildings. By that time, I couldn't have anything to do with him. When you watch somebody go down the hole, they can pull you in with them."

Barrows decided in December that he had to close Civilian. By then, Savard had disappeared completely. The two had been partners, but Barrows was left holding all the debt. "I had to declare personal bankruptcy," he said. The gallery owed more than a hundred thousand dollars, most of it for advertising, but also for back rent and payments to artists.

Barrows left New York in 1987 when his partner got a job offer in Washington, D.C. "I felt like Ratso Rizzo, that character from *Midnight Cowboy*, spitting up blood on the bus," he recalled. "It took me a long time to recover mentally from everything that had happened in New York."


The day after New Year's 1987, Tom Rauffenbart came home to find David sitting at his dining room table.

·"He was very withdrawn," Tom said. "I knew something was wrong, but he wouldn't tell me. I tried to draw it out of him, and then he just broke down in tears. He was a wreck. I finally grabbed him. I was hugging him, and he said, 'You can't tell anybody. You can't tell anybody. Peter has AIDS.'"

# 17 SOME SORT OF GRACE

**The chest X-ray** revealed a lesion. So, on New Year's Eve, Hujar had a bronchoscopy with biopsy to determine why he couldn't get a full breath, why he always felt so exhausted.

Of course, he had no health insurance. Someone he knew arranged for him to see an eminent lung specialist, who did not charge him, and David paid for the lab work. When the doctor called Hujar right after New Year's to say "Come to the office," Hujar refused. He demanded that the results be read to him over the phone. And so he learned that he had PCP, or *Pneumocystis*, therefore AIDS. He called Stephen Koch, who remembered, "He was overwhelmed and in despair and howling, in terrible shape."

And he called David. "I remember picking up a television, and I was going to throw it through a window," David told me. "Then I stopped myself." He walked the two blocks to Hujar's loft, in shock, not knowing what to say. It was odd—and he would come to feel this about his own diagnosis too—how the buildings didn't collapse and the traffic kept moving and you still had to make yourself breakfast.

"You can't shut out the sights and sounds of death," David wrote of this moment later in *Close to the Knives*, "the people waking up with the diseases of small birds or mammals; the people whose faces are entirely black with cancer eating health salads in the lonely seats of restaurants. Those images hurl themselves from the corners of a fast-paced city and you can't even imagine death properly enough to tell this guy you understand what he's railing against. I mean, hell, on the first day that he found out he had this certain virus he bent down to pick up a letter addressed to him that had fallen from the mailbox and he turned and said, 'Even something so simple as getting a letter in the mail has an entirely different meaning.'"

Fran Lebowitz and Lynn Davis took Hujar to Columbia Presbyterian on January 13. According to Lebowitz, a "saintly doctor" got him admitted to a private room in the posh Harkness Pavilion. He was being treated like a rich person, which cheered him up. He asked Lebowitz to buy him some pajamas, since he did not own any. "Pale green with dark gray piping," he specified. She spent a full day hunting for such an item. On January 15, Vince Aletti found him resplendent in blue pajamas with white piping, purchased at Paul Stuart. "She could have gone to Mays," Hujar told Aletti, naming the proto-Kmart on Union Square.

On the uptown subway Aletti had run into David, who was carrying art supplies to further alter a small painting on the wall of Hujar's hospital room. To this picture of some Rockefeller Center buildings with the Atlas sculpture out front, David had already added "a mangy bug-eyed dog and a folksy character with a pig on the sidewalk," Aletti wrote in his journal. That day David added a monkey face in the treetops—because this amused Hujar. Hospital staff did not seem to notice. On the way back downtown, Aletti asked David if he was more afraid of getting AIDS now that an ex-lover had it. "He said he was more worried about the contacts before Peter," Aletti wrote.

With the PCP responding to treatment, Hujar was discharged after ten days. According to Koch, David had been a constant visitor, "practically sleeping on the floor."

He took the letter confirming Hujar's diagnosis and stenciled on it a smaller version of the two men kissing from *Fuck You Faggot Fucker*.

David's "Mexican Diaries" opened at Ground Zero a few days before Hujar went into the hospital. Tom Rauffenbart remembered that David had worked quickly, wanting to help James Romberger and Marguerite Van Cook make some money. But they didn't know who David's collectors were, so they didn't invite them, and they bought no ads. Nothing sold.

David had created five new paintings with images from Mexico. Two of them pick up on a theme in the "history paintings"—the destruction of indigenous culture. *Portrait of Bishop Landa* was typically allegorical. Landa was the fanatical Spaniard who imposed Catholicism on the Mayan people, tortured those who did not accept Christ, and burned as many

Mayan codices and images as he could find. David painted a street performer breathing fire at the center of this piece, a Mayan priest cutting the heart from a human sacrifice on the left, and, on the right, a papier-mâché head of Christ resting on a cluster of live firecrackers. He connected both religions with violence. David later told Romberger that he had destroyed this painting, an act of poetic inevitability given the subject matter. The burning papier-mâché Christ head appears in the film he would soon begin editing, *A Fire in My Belly*.

*Mexican Crucifix* also contrasts two spiritual systems. Christ on the cross appears on the right (paired with an eyeball that is also a globe, a planet Earth with veins) while the Aztec goddess Coatlicue is on the left (paired with a brain). Coatlicue was the earth goddess who gave birth to the moon, the stars, and many a god (like Quetzalcoatl). She was also a destroyer, in her skirt of writhing snakes and necklace of human hearts and hands. Between Coatlicue and Christ, David painted, among other things, the steam locomotive that meant, in his iconography, the arrival of the future, of civilization, of death.

The other few paintings were more personal than anything he'd done since starting the history work. *Tommy's Illness* is a surreal scrapbook of their shared travel—Turner, in the center, is surrounded by the imagery he hallucinated while ill with dysentery along with small Mexican versions of various Hollywood monsters. Spanish headlines and newspaper cartoons are barely visible behind it all. For the Ground Zero show, David suspended a marionette in front of this painting, a cartoonish souvenir bandito holding pistols. A similar puppet appears several times, dancing and finally burning up in *A Fire in My Belly*.

*Street Kid* was based on an encounter David had in Mexico City. A boy threatened him with a knife, then ran off. David noticed that the boy's other hand was bloody, bandaged, and holding a few coins. David could identify. This painting is the first in which he directly connects the sensations of doom and crisis he himself felt as a street kid with his sense of a corrupted wider world headed for ruin. He collaged Mexican "Wanted" posters, lists of lottery winners, *lotería* cards (La Corona, La Bota, La Sirena), wrestling posters, and headlines like "Sacriligio!" around a large, bandaged bloody hand on the right and the figure of a knife-wielding boy on the left. Images of a bandaged hand dropping coins or catching coins appear throughout *A Fire in My Belly.*

David's small painting of a monkey walking along dressed in a red suit comes directly from the circus he filmed in Mexico City. This monkey also appears in *A Fire in My Belly*—somersaulting, riding a goat, always on a leash. David said that he painted the monkey because it looked so lonely. Hujar loved this painting, and David gave it to him. He kept it next to his bed.

New York City hospitals and Gay Men's Health Crisis had begun advocating with Mayor Ed Koch in 1985 to do something about the growing population of People with AIDS who could no longer work and needed public assistance. PWAs were being turned away at welfare centers, where some workers would not even touch the forms they filled out. The few who managed to get into the system often died before they received any benefits.

Anita Vitale became the first director of the city's new AIDS Case Management Unit in January 1986, the month David and Tom became a couple. Fear of the illness was so intense at that point that when its offices opened at the welfare center on Fourteenth Street, the AIDS CMU had to maintain not just a separate entrance and separate bathrooms but also separate air-conditioning. Walls were extended to the ceiling to ensure that no one would breathe the same air.

Anita was Tom Rauffenbart's best friend. They had worked together in the city's child welfare department for many years. Tom called her early in '87 to say that David had a dear friend sick with AIDS. Could she help him? When Anita went to meet Hujar at his loft on February 14, she'd already put the paperwork through to get him Medicaid, food stamps, and a rental allowance. She came by to see what else he needed, and they ended up talking for hours. Hujar showed her his photos. She remembered his burning eyes and how weak he was already. And how stubborn. He'd been seeing Dr. Emanuel Revici, who treated AIDS patients with fatty acids, sometimes combined with elements like potassium or selenium. Revici (who died in 1998 at the age of 101) had developed this approach while treating cancer patients. He's still celebrated in the world of alternative medicine, the subject of a hagiography called *The Doctor Who Cures Cancer.* But Revici also gets a chapter in a book called *Doctors from Hell* and the Quackwatch website debunks his approach in no uncertain terms, noting that "state licensing authorities placed Revici on probation in 1988 and revoked his license in 1993 after concluding that he had violated the terms of his probation."

Anita had decided to become Hujar's caseworker. Even while managing the whole program, she had clients. There was such a backlog of people who needed help. Occasionally she accompanied him to Revici's office. Azidothymidine (AZT) the first drug developed to treat AIDS, had just become available, but many regarded it as toxic, and it had terrible side effects. Hujar refused to take it. "He didn't want any orthodox treatment," Anita said. Certainly there was one thing he could get from Revici that he could not get from a conventional doctor, and that was hope.

David set up a meeting of Hujar's friends who wanted facts about AIDS, still such a new horror. This meeting, at Aletti's apartment, included Fran Lebowitz, Gary Schneider, John Erdman, Stephen Koch, and probably others. Anita came to speak and brought a colleague, Peter Ungvarski, then in charge of the AIDS Home Care Program at Visiting Nurse Services. They talked about what to expect—for example, the kinds of opportunistic infections they might see in someone with a severely impaired immune system. The PCP Hujar suffered from, Anita told them, was "the least of the worst" because at least there was a treatment for it. She had provided Hujar with a home attendant, but that hadn't lasted too long. Like many others, he didn't enjoy having a "stranger" in his apartment.

Erdman said that after this meeting "David took the lead and set up a loose immediate schedule of caregiving, but that was temporary. Peter always had someone coming in to cook, though mostly not us from that meeting. Peter was very popular and the line was long to feed him. David seemed to orchestrate everything, except food."

Several times a week, though, David took Hujar to breakfast at a nearby Second Avenue coffee shop. Occasionally Anita joined them. "I think David saw him every day," Anita said. "Sometimes twice."


Writer and firebrand Larry Kramer came to speak at New York's Lesbian and Gay Community Center on March 10 and drew a large crowd.

First he asked two thirds of that audience to stand and told them they would be dead within five years. He reminded them of the article he'd published exactly four years earlier, "1,112 and Counting." Now the number was 32,000. And counting.

In an echo of that essay, he declared, "If my speech tonight doesn't scare the shit out of you, we're in real trouble. If what you're hearing doesn't rouse you to anger, fury, rage, and action, gay men will have no future here on Earth. How long does it take before you get angry and fight back?" He talked about a government that was murderously indifferent and a Food and Drug Administration that moved at a glacial pace to approve anything.

"I think we must want to die," Kramer harangued the crowd. "I have never been able to understand why for six long years we have sat back and let ourselves literally be knocked off man by man—without fighting back. I have heard of denial, but this is more than denial; this *is* a death wish."

According to eyewitness Maer Roshan, Kramer ended the speech by asking, "What are we going to do?" "Suddenly," Roshan said, "a slight woman in the back stood up and shrieked, 'Act up! Fight back! Fight AIDS!'"

Two days later, some three hundred people met back at the center to form the AIDS Coalition to Unleash Power, ACT UP.

On March 24, hundreds of new activists charged onto Wall Street at seven A.M. after hanging an effigy of the FDA commissioner in front of Trinity Church. They tied up traffic and handed out copies of Larry Kramer's speech along with a fact sheet labeled "Why We Are Angry," focused on the official indifference toward finding a treatment for this illness or educating people about it. Seventeen people were arrested in front of the FDA's Wall Street office.

David dreamt that he was helping to sell Hujar's photos. This was his sole journal entry for '87 before November.

For some reason, he tries to get a literary bookstore like the Gotham to sell the pictures. A man there tells him they don't have room; it's a small shop. "I seize a person nearby. 'Can I talk to you privately? . . . Peter has AIDS and needs the money, and he has a few beautiful portfolios completed.'" The man he's grabbed says, "Maybe." The photos are in color and have religious content—Buddhists in India, and a church where Hujar had had a "strong experience." Then David sees that the pictures are already in the back of the store, stacked in a pile.

Hujar recorded the dates and subjects of his photographs in a cheap eight-by-five-inch spiral notebook. He made one entry after his diagnosis: John Heys on March 2, 1987. Heys was an old friend and a performer probably best known for his portrayal of Diana Vreeland. Hujar had photographed him many times. According to Stephen Koch, "John Heys desperately needed a photograph done while Peter was sick, and Peter agreed to do it, and that is the last picture he ever took."

Gary Schneider processed the film, one roll, and either Schneider-Erdman or another commercial lab printed the photo.

Tom knew that Hujar was David's best friend, but said that at the time of the diagnosis, he did not understand "the depth of that relationship."

Tom had never even seen them together, although he'd been involved with David for a year at that point. After Hujar got sick, though, the three of them met a few times for dinner. Tom cooked over at Hujar's loft. "It became clear that these guys were cemented somewhere," said Tom. "They were like extensions of each other. They were so similar. Each had a kind of presence, a depth. It radiated from them."

Typically, David never wrote or spoke much about him while Hujar was alive.

But David had a dream he labeled "recurring," and Hujar was there in two of the three accounts of it he wrote down. It seems to speak to their connection. This was a dream about ancient lakes with caves beneath their surface. In the dream, David was always traveling toward them, and they were always in a different location.

In the first written account, David began in a churchyard where a fat priest guarded a pile of gold bars. He could feel that he was in an Aztec or a Mayan city, walking with Hujar. "I suddenly realized where I was. I had a faint recollection of the lakes." Rounding a curve, he encountered a woman selling ancient Mayan carvings and fossils and tree branches covered with turquoise paint. "Beyond her were the lakes, but she now owned the land

and didn't want anyone walking around." David was upset. "All I wanted was to find the lakes and show Peter."

The second account was a dream within a dream. That is, David woke (in the dream, not in reality) and Hujar was there, turning to him in the shadows and saying, "Where did you see them? Think about it, and I'll get us there." David knew that Hujar was referring to the deeper dream he'd just woken from, a dream about the lakes.

"I look at Peter strangely with a slight smile," David wrote, "as if I know he'll bring us there because he can see into my images, something like psychic dialogue. He walks down this path with me. . . . There's one doorway with two Indian chiefs standing on each side of it. . . . I walk through with him and both of us burst out laughing. I feel so happy that we can transfer thoughts without talking." They were in a semi-forest. "A feeling of centuries behind the scene. Something from the Aztecs. Something from Indians. A place of refuge."

The image of the distant lake, the one he could never reach, figures, of course, in one of the last pieces David ever made, described many chapters ago, but it bears repeating. Over a photo of skeletons exposed in an Indian burial ground, he silk-screened words inspired by his yearning for connection and his fear of impending and constant loss: "When I put my hands on your body on your flesh I feel the history of that body. Not just the beginning of its forming in that distant lake but all the way beyond its ending . . ."

When Hujar left Columbia Presbyterian, he thought there must have been a mistake in his diagnosis.

"Peter thought AIDS didn't exist," John Erdman said. "And if it *did* exist, it wasn't what they said it was. He thought it was some anti-gay media invention, even while people were getting sick around him. So when he got diagnosed, he thought, 'Well, this probably isn't a fatal disease,' because he didn't believe the publicity."

Vince Aletti remembered that period after the first hospitalization as one of the best he ever had with Hujar. "For the first time in years, we hugged, held hands, cried together, sat and talked about how much we cared about each other," Aletti wrote in Hujar's obituary. "We said things we'd always taken for granted or were just too cool to put into words. Peter was radiant with emotion, our visits so passionate they were almost sexy. In the first months, meeting was an event, and Peter had events every day. All the friends he'd kept at arm's length came around, grateful for a chance to be unashamedly loving, to cook a meal, to shop and clean and listen. And we said to each other, that now, finally, Peter knows how much people care about him. Peter accepts."

On April 6, Aletti met Hujar for dinner at a health food restaurant. Hujar declared that he was now meditating three hours a day, and he got Aletti to sample some wheatgrass. Hujar was in a pleasant mood. As they were leaving the restaurant, he announced, "You know, I have a feeling that in a year, a year and a half, I won't have AIDS. It won't be in my body." He said that he personally knew someone who was beating this illness. Aletti recounted the story in his journal. There'd been an experiment in San Francisco with a hundred AIDS patients. Half were told they had a fatal disease; the other half were told they had an unknown disease. Then all were given an antiviral diet. Of the fifty told that they had an unknown disease, fifteen were still alive. Of the fifty told that they would die, all but one *had* died. That one was the man Hujar knew, still alive because he refused to accept that the illness was fatal. He had kept himself alive with his mind. "Peter says that if you really want something, it will come to you," Aletti wrote.

By late spring or early summer, however, Hujar's attempts at optimism had passed. "When he remained still sick, still plagued by money problems, not knowing where this was going, and not knowing how to get better," Aletti told me, "then started this whole odyssey of trying to find a cure for himself. All these nutty crackpot cures." Someone even had him drinking his own urine, mixed with supplements. David reported this to Anita.

"He ended up getting very angry in general at what was going on with him," said Aletti, "and then just more generally angry at everyone."

In April, David and Tom made their third trip to St. John's. This time they decided that, instead of just passing through the San Juan airport, they would stop and spend a few days in Puerto Rico.

David wanted to film a cockfight. They found a place in San Juan that

Tom described as "upscale" and "classy," the top of the line for this activity. But they had a few days before fights were scheduled, so they drove off to explore the island. They found a special beach. They visited Loíza, a town originally settled by Africans, where they tracked down a local artist whose posters they'd seen in a store. They both bought work from him.

On their way back to San Juan from the west coast of Puerto Rico, they ran into a heavy storm and flooded roads. At one point, they got stuck in a puddle and had to hire some kids to push them out. Tom found an alternate route through the mountains, so they avoided further floods, but they got back to San Juan too late for the cockfight. "David was miserable," Tom said. "I mean, fucking miserable as only David could be. Inconsolable." Then as they drove through town, Tom happened to spot a large drawing of a cockfight on a building. "As luck would have it, they were just starting their day's fights," he said. "Thank god."

This was a neighborhood place, shabbier and thus more interesting to film. The proprietor not only gave David permission to shoot the fight but also let him go back to where the handlers were prepping the birds, attaching razor-sharp spurs to their legs. David included this footage in A Fire in My Belly. The cockfight must have seemed essential to him because it gave him an animal-versus-animal fight. He already had animal versus human (a bullfight filmed off a television) and human versus human (Mexican wrestling).

"We almost broke up twice during that trip," Tom said.

As they moved from the romance phase into building a relationship, they fought and argued a lot. And what were the fights about? "I don't think they were about anything," said Tom. "What would happen is, somebody would say something to set the other one off. Then the other one would go into a mood. Then the one who'd set it off would try to cajole the other one out of the mood, and it wouldn't work. It would get ugly, and the intensity of these fights was just very, very strong."

If the fights were about something specific, they could handle it. They could work it out. But most of them were about "crazy stuff," Tom said, "and a great many were my fault. That's one of the reasons I went into therapy. I could kill a relationship within six months with my moods. Awful. I certainly got a lot better as time went on, and I was going through therapy, and I stopped drinking the way I'd been drinking. I really worked at it."

In May, Tom went to New Orleans with his stepsister. He and David had not settled whatever they were arguing about at that point. "So when I came back, he was waiting for me, and he was already in a mood," Tom said. Soon after, Steve Brown showed up and helped David move all his belongings out of Tom's apartment. With no explanation. "That was a dramatic move-out," said Tom. "It was rather unpleasant. I thought we were breaking up.

"This was the first relationship I think either of us had where we were working through things that had probably been haunting us all of our lives. We were both quick to lose our tempers, and once you're there, you're just not listening. And we went through lots and lots of those moments. I think neither one of us actually knew how to have a relationship.

"I don't know how the hell we kept pulling it back together. There was a lot of agita. But we stuck it out. Sometimes I'm amazed that we did."

Tom was clear about his feelings for David. "He was the love of my life. I've never met anybody who I was so emotionally changed and moved by." But David would never say how he felt about Tom. "We struggled in those first couple years," said Tom, "over 'who am I to you?'" One night during this time of Hujar's illness, Tom and David had dinner at a restaurant across the street from Hujar's loft, and it came up again. "What is this relationship about? Where do I belong in all this?"

David told Tom that he had three priorities: "My work, Peter, and you. In that order."

"I remember thinking, 'I have to decide whether I can live with this,'" Tom said. He never felt resentful of Hujar or the time David spent with him. He also knew that David's work came first, that he couldn't survive unless he made things. "I decided I could live with it."


David was at work on what he sometimes called his "Mexican film." He had images to shoot in New York, like coins dropping from a bandaged hand and sides of beef moving through the meat market. Then he began editing.

James Romberger was probably one of the first to see *A Fire in My Belly* early in 1988. "[David] had me sit in front of his big TV, next to his baby elephant skeleton, and insisted that I watch his Mexican film. What followed was an assault on my senses, a view of a world completely out of control. The strobed, often violent scenes of wrestlers, cock and bull fights, lurid icons, impoverished dwellings, clanking engines, an enslaved monkey, cripples begging for coins, for bread, a burning, spinning globe—it was a picture of indifference to the value of life, Mexico as a grinding machine of poverty and cruel spectacle. I didn't enjoy the experience."

David explained what this work meant to him in a 1988 letter to Barry Blinderman, the curator who was putting together David's retrospective:

> The film deals with ancient myth and its modern counterpart. It explores structures of power and control—using at times the fire ants north of Mexico City as a metaphor for social structure. . . . I explore spectacle in the form of the wrestling matches that occur in small arenas in the poor neighborhoods where myth is an accepted part of the sport; the guys with fantastic masks are considered the "good guys" whereas those without masks are personifications of evil. These images are interspersed with cockfights and TV bullfights. There are sections pertaining to power and control; images of street beggars and little children blowing ten foot long flames among cars at an intersection. Images of armored trucks picking up bank receipts. Images of loaves of bread being sewn up as well as a human mouth—control and silencing through economics. There are invasive aspects of Christianity played against images of Day of the Dead and the earthquake buildings and mummies of northern Mexico. There are symbols of rage and the need for release.

David spent one day working with Doug Bressler, from 3 Teens, on a soundtrack for the film. They combined atmospherics, Bressler's guitar, and sounds David recorded in Mexico (street noise, Spanish talk from the radio, a televised soccer game, a mariachi band, and so on). About halfway through the score, he begins to whisper something inaudible over a small drum and a gradual crescendo of guitar until words do begin to come through: "Go inside your own head, and you can do all these things—easy as drawing blood out through a needle." The score has everything from machinelike riffs to burbling water to what seems like a funeral march, some of it haunting, much of it arresting, but there's no overarching theme. Bressler couldn't recall whether he'd even seen the footage before they started working, and David didn't talk about what the film meant to him. A cassette labeled "Mexico soundtrack" was found in David's archive at NYU's Fales Library. He had never synced it up with the footage. "It may not have met his quality standards or been what he intended," said Bressler. "That's how he was. Often you weren't completely in on the whole picture."

David created at least two scripts for *A Fire in My Belly*. Really they were just lists of images. He had begun to make these "lists of associations" for almost every project, whether a film or a piece of visual art. Most of the time, one image was not enough for him, though there are notable exceptions. But usually his work was collaged and layered, and if he used photos, it would be multiple photos arranged to resonate off one another. He wanted to surround a subject. He wanted to peel back layers.

But he never found a way to do that with film, an inherently linear medium. His films are the weakest part of his oeuvre.

Even when it's nonnarrative, even when it's a collection of images, the filmmaker has to create a flow and establish some thread that pulls you through. David certainly knew how to make a potent image—a spinning eyeball, a kid breathing fire, coins dropping into a bowl of blood, ants on a crucifix. But if the meaning of each image isn't instantly clear, and those images simply follow one another at brutal speed with much repetition, the work just doesn't cohere.

With *A Fire in My Belly*, he intended to address this problem. As he explained to Blinderman, "What I explored in the film is the workings within surface image; so I split open continuous images and placed studio shots or other related images within the splice—the film uses spliced-in images almost as subliminal messages but each image is used at least long enough to register on the brain; sometimes longer." He intended to create the cinematic equivalent of layering or collage, but it doesn't work. David may have realized this. That would explain, at least, why he never regarded any of these "image" films as finished.

In the catalog for his 1990 retrospective, David lists *A Fire in My Belly* this way: "went through two versions then disassembled for other projects." What remains in his archive is a thirteen-minute silent "film in progress" with title and end credits. It's divided into eight parts, each introduced by the image of a steam locomotive. In his final script, some of these sections have labels: aggression, hunger, religion, celebratory death, prostitution. He's also trying to work the four elements into this plan. The death section is labeled "wind," for example. Not that he actually followed his script, but it shows how ambitious this project was. He was trying to pack the universe into it. Most of what Romberger describes above is still there, and then some. Like screaming tabloid headlines, Aztec pyramids, a dancing bandito marionette, and two seconds of fire ants (on dirt). David also left an "excerpt" from *A Fire in My Belly*, seven minutes of footage found on another reel. This imagery is even more intense. Here's all the ant action (apart from the above-mentioned two seconds), as they scurry over coins, bread, a Day of the Dead skull, and a crucifix. That's intercut with images of mummified corpses, lips being sewn, legless men walking on their stumps, a hustler stripping, a cheetah pacing, a giant roach dying, the bandito marionette burning, and so on.

In Mexico, he found a bit less of the "pre-invented world," an unvarnished Catholicism, an acknowledgment of mortality (in Day of the Dead), and actual picturesque ruins. He loved the images he collected there but he needed time to understand their resonance.

With *A Fire in My Belly*, David had begun to work out core ideas that came to fruition later. Many of the Mexican images ended up in work he created for his 1989 show, "In the Shadow of Forward Motion." The *Fire in My Belly* script represents, for example, his preliminary thinking for the "Ant Series." Religion and aggression and prostitution in the script become spirituality, violence, and desire in the ant photos. Also, in the hunger section of the script, he wrote the words "silence through economics." That's the title of a multiple photographic piece he completed for the '89 show. Images from *A Fire in My Belly* also ended up in *Spirituality (for Paul Thek)* and *The Weight of the Earth (Parts 1 and 2)* and in slides for his performance *ITSOFOMO*. The red-coated monkey appears again (painted) in *Seeds of Industry*, along with some of the photos. He also printed some of the film

*Tom Rauffenbart, Anita Vitale, and Peter Hujar at Coney Island on the day they also went to Queens, with David, to find Hujar a "cure" for AIDS. (Courtesy of Anita Vitale)*

stills. Then, he gave the seven-minute excerpt to Rosa von Praunheim, who incorporated a great deal of this disturbing footage into his 1990 film about AIDS, *Silence = Death*.

Early in May, Hujar told Aletti that he was feeling a loneliness and a need for people. Friends were coming to see him every day. But then they would leave, and he would feel so alone. Aletti told Hujar it sounded like the same depression he'd fallen into periodically over the past ten years. Hujar seemed to agree. It worried him. He was trying to survive by thinking positively, and this depression could affect his ability to get better.

David and Tom were now sharing an old Toyota once owned by Tom's mother, though David still had the hardy Malibu. On a weekend in late spring, they drove with Hujar and Anita to Coney Island, where they walked the boardwalk, visited Sideshows by the Seashore, and had lunch in nearby Sheepshead Bay.

Then Hujar told them he'd read a story in one of the tabloids about a healer in Queens. She could perform miracles, he said. He had to find her.

She was in Flushing Meadows Park every weekend. That's all he could remember, but he insisted, "We have to go. She can cure me."

So they drove to Queens as a storm developed. They couldn't find out anything more about who or where this healer might be in a park whose acreage is significantly larger than Central Park's. They drifted aimlessly through thunder and lightning. "We all got disgusted," said Anita.

"We finally just gave up," said Tom, "and Peter got pissed off. Then David got mad. We'd had a nice time in Coney Island, but this thing, this quest, just set everybody off."

In June 1987, *New York Magazine* reproduced the group portrait of the East Village scene's first dealers taken by Timothy Greenfield-Sanders for his "New Irascibles" series in 1985. Of the thirteen people in that picture, ten were out of business.

Among the galleries that hadn't closed, half a dozen were about to catapult out of their cramped East Village spaces to the next frontier, Broadway below Houston. And more would follow. Jay Gorney, part of the third or maybe fourth wave of dealers and one of the few still in business in the twenty-first century, told *New York* writer Amy Virshup, "The galleries that showed 'East Village art' closed because they weren't showing terrific art. They had a media run and now that media run has ended. If you're doing well here now, it's time to move on."

Ground Zero had closed by then, and didn't move on. Its last location was a basement space, and damp, so James Romberger and Marguerite Van Cook had decided to put gray carpet down. "We all got into the same trouble when we formalized our spaces," Marguerite said. They could no longer allow artists to fling paint around or build campfires on the floor. "I think none of us had much energy, given what was going on," she said. "It didn't seem important to paint Needlenoses all over the walls when people were dying down the road."

Romberger began to work with David on a project they'd been discussing for years. David wanted to tell the story of his life. He wanted it to be a comic book, so that young gay people would realize that there was someone else who'd survived the things they were going through. David gave Romberger the monologues about his own childhood that he'd written for *Sounds in the Distance.* Romberger had it worked out in pencil form by the beginning of 1988, when he and Marguerite went off to spend the next half year or so in Belgium.

On June 5, I ran into Keith Davis for the first time in many months. I can be precise about the date because this encounter so disturbed me that I wrote it down in my journal. We stopped to talk on the traffic island at Bowery and Houston. Keith looked uncharacteristically scruffy, in old clothes with a scarf tied over his head pirate-style. On the end of his nose was puffy bluish-purple lesion. I was horribly shocked. My first impulse—not acted on—was to ask what had happened to his nose. As if he'd tell me that he'd fallen off his bike, and it was all going to get better. But I knew the lesion was Kaposi's sarcoma. I knew instantly that Keith was going to die.

He asked if I was on my way to the Richard Kern films playing on Fourth Street, an odd question since I was headed in the opposite direction. So I told him I was on my way to a Lydia Lunch performance in SoHo, and we stood there chatting about Lunch and Kern—inanely, I thought, given the gravity of what was really going on. He was so weirdly upbeat.

"So how are you?" I finally blurted.

"Oh, I have AIDS." He pointed to his nose: "This is Kaposi's."

I grabbed his hand and arm. "Oh, Keith."

He shrugged off my reaction, completely cheerful. His doctor had him on a new experimental drug, and he'd gained thirteen pounds. "I'm gonna beat it," he said.

I learned later that he was seeing Dr. Emanuel Revici.

I learned later that he'd known he was sick since the previous fall, and just hadn't told anyone.

"When Keith finally told me about his diagnosis," David said when I interviewed him in 1990, "I remember I was going every day to help Peter, and it was so overwhelming, emotionally and physically, that—I didn't know what to do. I knew I couldn't do with Keith what I was doing with Peter, in terms of being that emotional contact. I felt terrible about it, but I knew I would crack."

Philip Zimmerman became Keith's principal caregiver. Zimmerman's relationship with David had been strained ever since the disastrous cross-country trip in '85, and they hadn't seen much of each other. He was working as an assistant in Keith's graphic design business. "As he got sicker, I was there more to help him deal with his illness," said Zimmerman. "Then David started to come back around." He and Zimmerman reconnected.

Keith agreed to pose for Rosalind Solomon's project "Portraits in the Time of AIDS." "She took this beautiful portrait," Zimmerman said. "I mean beautiful and horrible. She brought a big one over to the house, and when I came into work that day, the portrait was sitting up on the cabinet, and Keith was just completely devastated because he really hadn't been able to see clearly or objectively how disfigured he was by the KS. I just really felt from that point on there was a rapid decline. Psychically it did something to him, this portrait. It really disturbed me. He set that up and then he set up a mirror beside it."

Sometimes children approached him on the street and asked if he was a clown. He would say, "Yes. I am."

The last time I spoke to Keith, he was about to fly to Oregon for his parent's fiftieth wedding anniversary. He said his doctor had told him not to go, but he was determined. Keith was very close to his family. He called his parents every few days. "A fiftieth anniversary only comes once," he told me, still sounding positive about his own prognosis: "That thing they say, 'Always fatal.' That's just the media. 'Two years to live.' That's the media. Some people have lived for five years."

Hujar went back into the hospital on July 9 with a recurrence of *Pneumocystis*, or PCP. According to Stephen Koch, who took him to Cabrini Medical Center, Hujar turned to him as they were leaving the loft and said, "I've decided that you should have the pictures. Send little Madeline to college." Hujar knew that Koch and his wife wanted a child. (And once she arrived, they duly gave their daughter the middle name Madeline.) Koch had talked to Hujar about making a will and found him a lawyer. The will was drafted while Hujar was at Cabrini and signed when he got back home.

Lynn Davis called Aletti to tell him that Hujar had been admitted and that she'd never seen him weaker. "She says he asked that no one come and see him, that no one call," Aletti wrote in his journal. "He said he didn't want to answer any questions." Hujar *did* want to see David—and Anita, who went to visit him at Cabrini that night. What he apparently wanted from her was help getting out. But she couldn't get him out. He needed the pentamidine treatments that were usually administered by IV. "Awful stuff," said Anita. David came and again altered the hospital decor, adding creatures to the pictures on the wall. Based on a receipt for the phone in the room (paid for by David), Hujar came home again on July 17.

"Sometimes they sent them home on oral medications," Anita said. "But for me, that hospitalization marked a downturn. That marked, for me, his decline, starting that summer. He began to talk about himself in the third person. He would say things like, 'Pete's scared.' 'Pete's dying.'"


Just days after Hujar left Cabrini, Keith Davis was admitted. Maybe he'd contracted pneumonia in Oregon or on the long flight back, but he was in the hospital within a week of returning to New York, and he deteriorated quickly. He was having trouble breathing. He had a high fever and dizziness, and he was too weak to walk. David came to visit every day, as did Zimmerman. Family members flew to his bedside. A lawyer came in to help him draw up a will. Zimmerman told me, "I still have a piece of paper with his weak and shaky handwriting that says things like 'give to family,' 'give to Philip.' He was on a ventilator and could not speak."

The will is dated July 22. The next day, he had two cardiac arrests. He'd left no directive, no "do not resuscitate." Doctors put him on life support at the direction of his anguished family.

"There were so many days of waiting for him to die the third and final time," David wrote in *Close to the Knives*, "and we'd been talking to him daily because they say hearing is the last sense to go. Sometimes alone with him, the nurse outside the room, I'd take his hands and bend over whispering in his ears: hey, I don't know what you're seeing but if there's light move toward it; if there's warmth move towards it."

Zimmerman remembered the days dragging by—it seemed like weeks—as it became, he said, "increasingly difficult to maintain the hope for a turnaround." Doctors told the family that in all likelihood KS had spread throughout his body, including his brain. There were a series of conversations, said Zimmerman, "a series of letting-gos that finally allowed the family to agree to the withdrawal of life support."

On July 27, a doctor came in and removed Keith from various tubes and pumps. Zimmerman was there, and one of Keith's sisters, and David. Then, Keith went so quickly. As David described it, "The guy on the bed takes two breaths and arches his back almost imperceptibly, his lips slightly parted. I have hold of one leg and his sister one hand Philip another hand or part of his arm and we're sobbing and I'm totally amazed at how quietly he dies how beautiful everything is with us holding him down on the bed on the floor fourteen stories above the earth."

I've always been struck by that image. "Holding him down." As if he might have floated away. Keith was thirty-two years old.

The next day, friends came to an open house at Keith's loft on Suffolk Street. It was a jolt: here the funky, aggressive East Village art that Keith so loved and championed, there the sweet, bewildered retirement-age farmers who were his parents. This juxtaposition seemed to illustrate the new world of disharmony we were about to inhabit as we lost so many people who were not supposed to be dead.


The day before that open house, Vince Aletti stopped by Hujar's loft and found him propped up in bed holding two big crystals Fran Lebowitz had given him. He held one over his heart, one over his belly. "He was wondering if maybe he was dying," Aletti wrote in his journal. "I tell Peter I can't see that. . . . I can't feel it really happening."

At Keith's open house, David had told me he was doing something with Hujar related to yoga. He had seemed so positive about Hujar's prognosis.

"But you had to be," Gary Schneider told me. "You had to support his alternative processes. He wouldn't allow anyone else around him."

Hujar so needed money that his friends were trying to recruit people to buy prints from him but, said Schneider, "if they came to the door and they said one word wrong, Peter would tell them, 'Fuck you, get out.'"

John Erdman recalled that Hujar's anger got worse and worse as the year went on. "He threw out one of the people cooking for him—banned him from coming back because he used one square too much of paper towel."

One day Schneider made pasta primavera and was pulling leaves from a bunch of basil while Hujar complained that he wasn't doing it fast enough, that he shouldn't pull the leaves off one at a time. "He was screaming at me," Schneider said. "At a certain point, I gave up cooking for him because it was just too painful."

Hujar talked to his friends about killing himself. He would throw himself off a building, but he couldn't decide which one.

"He became a different person," Erdman said. "Everything just fell apart for him. And it was scary."

"There were physical outbursts," said Schneider.

Schneider and Erdman were out with him at a neighborhood restaurant, when Hujar picked up a glass of water and threw it at a waitress, for no reason. She understood what was going on, said Erdman. "It was so on the surface. You could see that he was sick, and you could feel him just radiating rage."

On August 15, Hujar asked Aletti to go shopping for him. After Aletti went to five different stores to find the best peaches and the right beets, he listened to Hujar complain about other people's shopping. For example, he had sent Stephen Koch out for white corn, and since Koch couldn't find any, he brought back yellow. Then Hujar informed Aletti that he'd made a will, and he'd named Koch as executor. Early on, he had asked Fran Lebowitz to be executor. She told him, "Peter you're not dying." After that, he went back and forth between Koch and Aletti. At one point, he had told Aletti that he would choose him. "He admits he changed his mind about me because I wasn't seeing him very much," Aletti wrote in his journal. Then Hujar told Aletti he would probably change his mind again and launched into "a list of [Koch's] petty transgressions like the white corn incident." Aletti told him the decision should not be based on whether he had visited enough or whether Koch had purchased the right corn. Hujar should imagine Aletti as his executor for a few days and see how it felt.

The next night, Aletti came to make or get dinner for Hujar and inadvertently crossed a line when he commented on how quickly a couple of Tylenol had reduced Hujar's fever.

"It doesn't change the PCP," Hujar said.

"Right, you're just treating symptoms," Aletti said.

"Let's not argue," Hujar said.

"Are we arguing?" Aletti wondered.

Hujar began mimicking Aletti's remarks about aspirin and told him to just leave.

Aletti said he'd make him dinner and moved to hug him. Hujar was, Aletti said, "batting [him] away, then jumping out of bed teeth bared, enraged, yelling, 'I don't care if I felt good in May! I'm dying!' and looking for things to throw." Aletti waited for Hujar to settle down, then washed the dishes and asked again what he wanted to eat. Hujar said he'd just eat bananas.

"I told him he didn't need to be a martyr. I wanted to make sure he had a meal," Aletti wrote. "He got up slowly and worked himself into a rage again, flailing at his rolodex on top of the TV, white saliva coming out of his mouth, waving his arms and telling me he's dying and he just wants me to leave and never come back."

Aletti could not calm him down. Hujar walked Aletti to the door and shut it behind him. Very upset, Aletti called David and a few other friends to discuss what had happened.


David's show "The Four Elements" opened at Gracie Mansion Gallery on September 17. James Romberger remembered seeing Hujar there, "in a terrible state, just completely fucking vaporizing." But Hujar wouldn't have missed this for anything.

Critic Lucy Lippard called *Wind (for Peter Hujar)* "one of Wojnarowicz's most transcendent paintings, emotion distilled."

David explained this painting to me once in his typically oblique way. It was all about portals (an open window) and extinction (a dinosaur) and destruction (a tornado). The open window with curtain blowing, top center, came from a horrifying dream—"a dream of death that shook me"—about a friend in Canada. I now know that he was speaking of the dream he had in Paris about Michael Morais, in which a spirit entered a room where Michael and Brian Butterick were both sleeping, and the "thing" passed over

Brian and went straight into Michael. Later David found out that Michael's wife had given birth to a stillborn child on that day. (Michael would die of AIDS in 1991.)

"The horrifying thing was something I couldn't even paint," David told me. "It was a sense of something moving past me very quickly, and whatever it was filled me with a great deal of fear, but it started out with this window with all this light behind it, the wind blowing the curtains into the room. This was in the later part of Peter's illness." A red line coming through that window attaches to a newborn baby, based on a photo of his brother Steven's new baby. *Wind*, in part, is about rebirth. The other end of that red line is attached to a paratrooper jumping from a plane (above the baby). Right behind the paratrooper is David himself, in probably the only self-portrait he ever painted. (His other self-portraits were photographs.) The lines of circuitry in the painting came from what he described as a "nuclear reactor handbook" he found in Argentina. That was wind at its worst—explosions, the wind that follows. That and the tornado painted at bottom right—wind that destroys. He also painted a wing based on Hujar's favorite image, the Dürer wing. When David first met him, Hujar had a postcard of the Dürer, along with a mummified seagull wing, hanging over a mirror. Hujar had always wanted that image tattooed on his arm—in sepia, so it would disappear when he got a tan. David would have the wing carved onto Hujar's tombstone.

With these masterful paintings, David had found a way to explain the world using the iconography he'd developed. For example, *Water* contains more than two dozen individual paintings, or maybe film stills, that combine biology, his own history, and a great melancholy. Fish, frogs, skulls, explicit sexual images, a small monkey trying to drink from a petri dish, concentric circles around pebbles hitting a pond, a baby sinking below the waves where "Dad's ship" patrols—all are organized in a grid inside one drop of water. "Dad's ship" shows up in the background in two of the other small works and also outside the water drop, where a large ship moves through the ocean, its hold peeled back to reveal a fossil. At the top right, a bandaged hand drops a flower from a prison window surrounded by snowflakes. Also appearing in the ocean and around the grid—a great deal of sperm.

The Museum of Modern Art now owns all four of the "Elements" paintings, but in 1987, Gracie Mansion said, "Nobody was interested. I called all these people who had wanted his work, this huge waiting list—and they had moved on to something else. I sold one piece." That was *Wind (for Peter Hujar)*. The rest of the exhibit, also unsold, included *Mexican Crucifix*, *Tommy's Illness*, and a new painting titled *The Anatomy and Architecture of June 19, 1953 (for Julius and Ethyl Rosenberg)*. It couldn't have helped that *Arts* magazine published a piece that very month that lumped David in with artists from the dissolving East Village scene "who seem to have been making better work three years ago." The article pissed David off. He had very little income in 1987.

But he kept to his habit of leaving town the day after a show opened, flying to New Orleans with Tom for a long weekend.

One day Hujar went by himself to eat at Bruno's, a coffee shop at Second Avenue and Twelfth. David heard from Hujar how Bruno himself had approached his table and said, "Are you ready to pay?" and then made Hujar put his five-dollar bill into a paper bag. Bruno came back with the change in another paper bag and tossed it on the table, declaring, "You know why."

"At first I wanted to go into Bruno's at rush hour and pour ten gallons of cow's blood onto the grill and simply say, 'You know why,'" David wrote. "But that was something I might have done ten years ago. Instead I went in during a crowded lunch hour and screamed at Bruno demanding an explanation and every time a waitress or Bruno asked me to lower my voice I got louder and angrier until Bruno was cowering in back of the kitchen and every knife and fork in the place stopped moving. But even that wasn't enough to erase this rage."

Hujar stopped seeing Dr. Revici in August. He had decided to try AZT. The drug had to be taken every four hours, so Anita had to call him every day at four A.M. Apparently, he had his alarm set for midnight but could not manage resetting it.

One day at breakfast, Hujar told David that he'd seen a news report about a doctor on Long Island who was injecting AIDS patients with typhoid vaccine. The idea was that this would spark the immune system into work-ing again. Hujar insisted that he would visit this doctor alone. He would take the train from Penn Station. At this point in his illness, Hujar could barely cross a room without falling. Still, it took three days of arguing before he consented to let David and Anita drive him there on a Saturday.

David wrote about this trip in *Close to the Knives*. He wrote to bear witness about the epidemic, but also to deal with what these moments brought up inside him. He got sick writing about Hujar's illness. He came down with shingles. It had been so wrenching to admit to his anger—at Hujar who was imparting one last lesson to David. How *not* to die. Since David saw him more than anyone else did, he took the brunt of the rage. Still, his account of Hujar's struggle is both harrowing and compassionate, one of the classic pieces of testimony to emerge from the AIDS crisis.

On the day of their trip to Long Island, David and Anita spent an hour and a half getting Hujar dressed and into the car. Before they'd even left Manhattan, Hujar began to complain angrily that there was a faster way to get there. Then he insisted he had to piss at a gas station where there was no bathroom, staggering off to urinate in a flower bed in what David saw as unfriendly territory. He refused to wear a seat belt. "Don't touch me, it hurts."

When they arrived at the doctor's house, David dropped Hujar and Anita off in front and went to find parking. "In the distance," David wrote, "I could see Peter staggering on the front lawn flailing about in rage. He staggered towards Anita then turned and teetered to the roadside. . . . By the time I reached Anita he was in the distance, a tiny speck of agitation with windmill arms. I asked her what had happened. 'I don't know, one minute he was complaining how long the ride took and when I said that maybe you did the best you could he went into a rage—he threatened to throw himself in front of the traffic. The saddest thing is that he's too weak to throw a proper fit. He wanted to hit me but he didn't have the strength.'"

They caught up with him, calmed him down, and got him into the doctor's office. The waiting room was filled with men Hujar recognized from other waiting rooms, since the AIDS grapevine led PWAs from one supposed cure to the next. This actually cheered him up. David and Anita looked at each other in disbelief.

"Finally the brains behind the business called us into his personal office," David wrote. "It looked like it had been decorated by Elvis: high lawn-green shag carpets, K-mart paintings and Woolworth lamps. Lots of official medical degrees with someone else's name on them. . . . The doctor asked Hujar how he knew he had AIDS. 'After all, you may not have it.'"

Hujar stumbled through a disjointed medical history, angrily refusing help from Anita. Then, while Hujar was in another room getting his typhoid shot, David asked the doctor to explain the theory behind this treatment. The doctor then admitted that he was really a research scientist and talked about the thymus gland, "wherever it is," and drew a diagram of circles divided by a line: "Say ya got a hundred army men over here; that's the T-cells. . . ."

On the way back to Manhattan, they stopped at a diner. David told Hujar about this unsettling encounter with the scientist. "He looked sad and tired," David wrote. "He barely touched his food, staring out the window and saying, 'America is such a beautiful country—don't you think so?' I was completely exhausted, emotionally and physically from the day, and looking out the window at the enormous collage of high-tension wires, blinking stop lights, shredded used-car lot banners, industrial tanks and masses of humanity zipping about in automobiles just depressed me. The food we had in front of us looked like it had been fried in an electric chair. And watching my best friend dying while eating a dead hamburger left me speechless. I couldn't answer."

Back at the loft, David and Anita asked Hujar if they could do anything, if he needed anything. When he responded with an angry "No," they left. David learned later that Hujar had called Aletti almost immediately and said, "I don't understand it. They just put me in bed and rushed out."


Hujar had continued to discuss his will with Aletti, needling him over whether he'd have the time to be an executor, interrogating him about what he would call any future books about the work, and sometimes exploding in rage. After one phone call that ended with Hujar slamming down the phone, Aletti wrote him a note saying he just wanted to be his good friend now, not his executor. "I don't want to be constantly on trial with him," Aletti wrote in his journal. "I felt he was using the will as a wedge between us."

On October 11, Hujar's fifty-third birthday, Aletti came early to prepare for the party, "smothering my dread in determined cheer," as he later wrote in Hujar's obituary. "And while I set out paper plates and plastic cups, he started to talk about dying. He wondered how long his friends would grieve, how long we'd remember him. He wasn't needling or fishing for sympathy, only clearing the air. We were gathering to celebrate his last birthday, and he wasn't going to pretend otherwise. For a few hours, though, he might allow us to cajole him into a mock-festive mood, and as guests arrived, he deflected their edgy merrymaking with gentle good humor. When his bed was surrounded by apprehensive friends, still tensed for the misstep that would send Peter into a tirade of denunciation, he looked up, smiled, and said, 'Pretend you're at a party.' And for awhile, we were."

On the next day, Columbus Day, Anita came to visit. "We started to talk about his dying," she said. "I asked, 'What would you like, and do you want me to write it down?' That's when he told me he wanted to be buried in the Catholic Church. He wanted to have just a shroud. He wanted to be buried in a plain box. He wanted a Mass. I wrote it down."

Anita had brought a priest, part of a hospice team, to see Hujar early in the year. Hujar asked the priest more questions than the priest asked him. What was that life like? Did he have sex? Anita witnessed this encounter, the priest getting more and more embarrassed. He never came back.

"He embraced Catholicism at the end," Schneider said. "But before, he was an atheist." Hujar had long been interested in Siddha yoga, however, and went to retreats or at least classes at the SYDA Foundation on the rare occasions when he had money. He kept pictures around his bed of SYDA founder Swami Muktananda, along with photos of Kalu Rinpoche and the Tibetan Buddhist Karmapa, and two pictures of Pio of Pietrelcina, an Italian priest with the stigmata who was said to work miracles.

"He was grasping," said Schneider. "He didn't know what to do. He was lost."

* * *

On October 22, David took Hujar to a neighborhood clinic to see a urologist. He'd been having pain while urinating and for the past day could not urinate at all, despite feeling an almost constant need to do so. They waited for several hours. When they finally met with the urologist, he exhibited what David saw as impatience, constantly cutting Hujar off as he tried to explain his problem. Finally he told Hujar he was going to insert a tube into his penis. Hujar asked if it would hurt. The doctor said there would be no pain, just discomfort.

In a letter of complaint David sent to the clinic, he wrote, "Peter's reaction was of shock and much pain. I tried to calm him down while the doctor continued. At some point, Peter could not continue the exam—he sat up very upset and told the doctor to get away from him. The doctor reacted as if his life were being threatened." Hujar barely had enough strength to crawl onto the examining table. But the doctor ordered him to leave and summoned a security guard.

David told the doctor he should have a little compassion; the guy just couldn't take the pain. The doctor and the guard then ordered David to leave the examining room. (Hujar already had.) David declared that he would not go until he had both their names. The guard demanded to know David's name and blocked him from leaving the room, ripping up the paper with his name and the doctor's. "He then said he was calling the police and would have me arrested for harassing the doctor. He went on and began manufacturing false charges that he would give to the police when they arrived." David began yelling out the door for help. Finally the guard stepped aside. David went to the waiting room, where Hujar sat. The guard came out and called the police.

David left with Hujar before the police arrived, and went home to write his letter.


One day Hujar sent Schneider into the darkroom to get something. Schneider walked in and stopped in his tracks.

"He had left the trays in the sink uncovered and all the chemicals had dried up and crystallized at the bottom," Schneider said. "He had literally closed the door and not gone back in. I just stood there. It was a powerful, powerful image."

Schneider had always known Hujar to be absolutely fastidious about the darkroom, but apparently he just suspended all work the day he got his diagnosis. "I just stood there. I was riveted," said Schneider. "And all of sudden I hear, from his bed, 'What's taking so long?'"

Early in November, when Aletti came to visit him, Hujar said he thought he'd seen him less than any of his other friends. (Aletti disagreed but didn't say so.) So, Hujar asked, "Are you afraid of my dying?" Aletti sat on Hujar's bed, tears running down his face, telling him there would be a terrible feeling of loss. Then Hujar almost started to cry. Almost. He said that every time a friend visited, he wondered if he would ever see that person again.

Hujar brought them back down to earth by again invoking the will, the changes he might make. He thought maybe he should cut his mother out—she who had never once visited during his illness. He should put Aletti in as executor. He should say the negatives couldn't be used for a hundred years.

Hujar had wavered on his decisions ever since making them, but he never did change the will. Koch said, "Peter assigned roles to people in his life, and I was the bourgeois brother. He left the estate to someone who he thought would make it successful." Aletti had already been named alternate executor, and Hujar had told Koch that he must consult with Aletti if he was ever unsure about the quality of a print, because Aletti had such a good eye. He had decided that his mother and David and Koch would split the net proceeds, after debts were paid and Koch got the first fifteen thousand dollars for his work as executor. But according to Koch, David refused to accept any income from the estate. "He never said why. Just 'I don't want the money.'"

What dismayed many of Hujar's friends—what Erdman called "the horror of his life at the end"—included a kind of internalized homophobia. Hujar told Erdman one day that if only he'd had money growing up, he might have been straight, because you needed money to take a girl out. Hujar had actually had one or two relationships with women. He just wasn't straight. But clearly, when he wasn't in a rage about having AIDS, he was pondering, "Why me?" or "Why us?"

"He thought there was a curse on all gay people," Erdman said.

Schneider added, "He thought we were all going to die."

This explains the rather cruel backhanded compliment he gave Koch the day he told him to "send little Madeline to college." He also said, "You're no good, but you're the best I have."

Hujar asked Fran Lebowitz to make his funeral arrangements. David called her and said, "Don't go by yourself. I'll come with you."

Lebowitz had met David before Hujar became ill, but had not paid much attention to him at first. "That's the first time I really thought that he was an unusual person, morally," she said of his offer to help with the funeral. "David was an exceptional moral presence."

Hujar wanted to be buried from Frank Campbell's, an Upper East Side funeral home that had arranged burials for such luminaries as Judy Garland and Malcolm Forbes. "Peter had incredibly grand ideas," Lebowitz said. "I didn't even inquire there because I knew it was too expensive."

Early in the epidemic, there was only one funeral home in all of New York City that would even take someone who had died of AIDS—Redden's on West Fourteenth Street. Even after other funeral homes changed their policies, many people stayed loyal to Redden's, and that's where Lebowitz went with David.

Hujar wanted a pine box, and the only place they could get one was from an Orthodox Jewish coffin maker. Redden's arranged this. "They couldn't get one without a Star of David," said Lebowitz. "I had a discussion about this with Peter. I became incredibly upset. David was very calm and much more able to deal with it, talk to the guy, and figure out how to get the Star of David off the coffin."

An old friend of Hujar's, Charles Baxter, moved into the loft when it became clear that Hujar could not be left alone for any significant amount of time. On Friday, November 13, Aletti came over to meet Baxter for dinner, only to have Baxter hand him a small note at the door: "Vince, I believe Peter has begun to die." On Saturday, Aletti called and Hujar answered the phone, slurring words, saying he couldn't talk and he was alone. Aletti, who lived across the street, could see from his window that actually David was there, sitting at the blue kitchen table. On Sunday, Aletti went over with fresh raspberries and found that Hujar was up, sitting at his desk with an inventory list of everything in the loft—who would get what. He needed help to get back to the bed. "Do you want the blue table?" he asked Aletti.

Hujar went back into Cabrini on November 16. Koch came to get him and watched as Hujar tottered around the loft, saying, "Goodbye table. Goodbye bed. Goodbye darkroom." But this wasn't supposed to be the end. He was going into the hospital for tests because he was still having trouble urinating and the slightest movement of an arm or leg could trigger nausea. He was supposed to be there two or three days.

The night before Hujar went to the hospital, David had his recurring dream about the lake. He was at the base of a mountain and spotted the dirt road that used to take him there. Years ago, he'd jumped in and swum into an interior cave where he found beautiful stalactites. "But it's like a film in reverse where as I get older, I am getting further away," he wrote. "Each successive dream seems to start at a point just a little further from the dirt road that leads to the lake."

On the 17th, David woke up and wrote in his journal:

Everything about my life horrifies me at this moment, even the room the bed the heat of the pipe running down the wall the vague breeze never quite passing through the cheap curtains, the weight of blankets on me, the persistent need to piss, desire for a cigarette, Peter in the hospital, Tom sleeping in the other room, Peter's friends and my feeling of not being understood by anyone anymore, and I think I should throw myself off a bridge or something, that I can't deal with living the way I used to be able to do—the world is one large fear for me and I feel hot and cold simultaneously and I have no physical comfort in strength of body like when I was 21 and this makes me feel old and wasted like my body is falling apart but so slowly its all I can do to sit and watch it do so.

Five or six days later, he wrote in the journal what would become the beginning of his chapter on Hujar's illness in *Close to the Knives*:

I'm sitting in his hospital room so high up here in the upper reaches of the building that when I walk the halls or sit in the room or wander into the waiting room to have a cigarette—it's the gradual turn of the earth outside the windows, the far plains filled with buildings that have that look of fiction because so high up they flatten out one against the other . . . and leaning against the glass of the window in his room I see dizzily down into the next street and wonder what it is to fall such distances. I'm afraid he is dying.

Schneider and Erdman went to Hujar's doctor to ask how long he had. Earlier that year, they'd booked a Thanksgiving trip to Santa Fe, which would be their first vacation from the lab in five years. Erdman asked the doctor if he thought they could go away for three days. Would Hujar be OK? "And the doctor said, 'He's not going to die this weekend. Don't worry.' And so we went."

On Thanksgiving, on his way to the hospital, David ran into Ethyl Eichelberger. Ethyl had not been to visit during Hujar's illness. Hujar and Ethyl had argued and fallen out. All Erdman could remember was that it was over something "so minor" but had something to do with "selling out." As if either of them could. They had not communicated for at least a year, but when David saw Ethyl on the street, he insisted, "You have to come and see Peter. Now."

Then it was Ethyl who first noticed the change, who said, "David . . . look at Peter."

"And his death is now like it's printed on celluloid on the backs of my eyes," David wrote, "when I looked towards his face and his eyes moved slightly and I put up two fingers like rabbit ears behind the back of my head . . . and I flashed him the sign and then turned away embarrassed and moments later Ethyl said: 'David . . . look at Peter.' And we were all turned to the bed and his body was completely still and then there was a very strong and slow intake of breath and then stillness."

David asked the other friends to leave the room. He asked Anita to guard the door, to keep out the hospital staff. Then with a Super 8 camera, he slowly made a sweep of Hujar's body. Then he photographed the face, the hands, the feet of "this body of my friend on the bed this body of my brother my father my emotional link to the world."

He took exactly twenty-three photographs, and that number was cal-culated. He would mark the envelope for these contact sheets as "23 photos

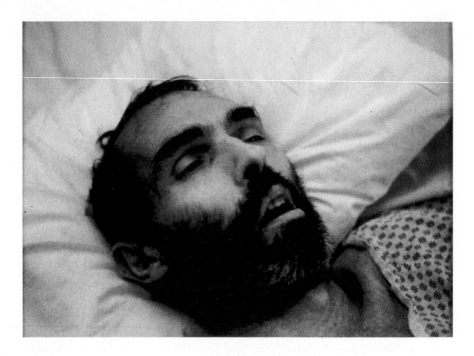

*One of the photos David took immediately after Hujar's death from AIDS. Untitled, 1988. Gelatin-silver print, 24½ × 30½ inches. (Collection of the Whitney Museum of American Art, New York.)*

of Peter, 23 genes in a chromosome, Room 1423." He associated that number with the evolution of consciousness.

Before David left the room, he thought he should say some words to his friend. If there was a limbo or a bardo, he was there now and might be afraid, might be confused, might need reassurance. "But nothing comes from my mouth," David wrote. "This is the most important event of my life and my mouth can't form words and maybe I'm the one who needs words, maybe I'm the one who needs reassurance and all I can do is raise my hands from my sides in helplessness and say, 'All I want is some sort of grace.'" Then David began to cry.

Hujar got his pine box and his shroud. He had also asked not to be embalmed. So the funeral happened just two days later, on Saturday, November 28, at the Church of St. Joseph in Greenwich Village. David wore a suit, which must have been Hujar's. Tom had a fever of 105 and couldn't be there. So David sat next to Timothy Greenfield-Sanders. At some point, whoever was running this service told everyone to join hands. Said Greenfield-Sanders, "I was there holding David's hand, and he was trembling." The burial was at Gate of Heaven Cemetery in Valhalla, New York.

On Sunday—"the third day of his death," David called it—he drove the twenty-five miles back to the cemetery to be alone with Hujar: "Looking at the fresh ground where he lies buried. I see white light, fix my eyes to the plowed earth and see a white powerful light like burning magnesium covering the soil, his body in a semicurled position surrounded by white light floating hovering maybe three feet from the ground. I try talking to him, wondering if he knows I'm there. He sees me, I know he sees me. He's in the wind in the air all around me."

That evening David went to the long-scheduled memorial for Keith Davis at St. Mark's Church. There he ran into Kiki Smith and asked her to come back to Hujar's loft with him. To dance. "I wanted to show Peter some joy, some celebration. . . . We turned on a few lights. . . . Each time I come in a little less of him is there." They put on Albinoni's Adagio in G Minor and tried to waltz, but David couldn't coordinate with Kiki's movements. He felt his body had shut down. Kiki let go of him, turned off the lights, and began whirling through the space. David did the same, "whirling and jumping and driving through the darkness, the window curtains open with the rain roaring through the street . . . and for a moment everything went loose in my head and I was beaming some kind of joy."

Schneider and Erdman were back at the lab on Monday, devastated. "We were just a mess," Erdman said. David walked in. He had them sit down and then recounted the funeral—everything said, the rituals done. "He sort of acted it out," Schneider said. "And it helped."

Then he pulled out a photograph he'd printed for them in Hujar's darkroom. It was a photo David had taken probably years earlier on one of his excursions with Hujar, when they'd drive to Caven Point or some other decrepit site to take pictures.

Hujar had imparted one of his lessons that day on how to live cheaply.

Somewhere in this wreck of a building he'd found a pair of sunglasses. They were old, and they were fogged, but he put them on, telling David, "See. You don't need to buy sunglasses. You can find them."

And at that moment—so Peter Hujar—David had snapped his picture.

Schneider and Erdman stood there weeping.

Soon after, David disappeared. "I wouldn't know where he was," Tom said.

For part of that time, he was at the loft, sleeping in Hujar's bed. Then one day, he came over to Tom's place. "He was just morose and started to cry. He told me he had hooked up with some guy in an S-M relationship, someone he'd picked up in a bar. He was the masochist side of it, and he allowed the guy to abuse him for a while. He told me, 'I was just a pure slave.' He didn't tell me all the details. He just felt so guilty for getting involved."

David had found his bad father to be with, if briefly.

"I remember saying to him, 'I'm glad you told me. I understand how crazy you were, but if it happens again, I don't know what I'll do,'" Tom said. "I guess we both thought we needed to be monogamous at this point. He was really upset about it. But I also could tell he was just lost. It was as if the whole world had come out from under him. And it was clear to me there wasn't anything I could do. I couldn't fill the shoes that were vacated by Peter's death. And part of me resented that, but part of me understood it. It was painful to me that I couldn't help him get over this thing."

Tom gained perspective as time went on. In 1993, he said of David and Peter Hujar: "They were both more than and less than lovers. Peter was the one who saved him, who changed his life in a major positive way. They were kindred souls. Part of David was missing after Peter went."

# 18 ELEGIAC TIMES

**Hujar had wanted** his service to be at the Church of St. Joseph after attending a funeral there in May for his old friend Charles Ludlam, star, director, and playwright for the Ridiculous Theatrical Company. I still recall the horror and dismay that swept through the theater community when Ludlam died of AIDS mere months after his diagnosis. A friend of mine had been to that funeral, and she described how, in all that collective grief, "the church lifted up."

Suddenly we were living in apocalyptic and elegiac times. Every day now began with a look at the obituaries. I could sense the path of the virus around me, the tornado that devastates one house and leaves the next pristine. It was a time to worry about friends—and all the other brilliant, aspiring, wild spirits who'd landed in what we then called "downtown." We were not prepared to see each other die.

Tom Rauffenbart told his doctor that he did not want an AIDS test. That was the general consensus among gay men in 1987. Why be tested when there were no treatments to look forward to—only depression, only stigma. "Everyone was afraid their name would end up on some kind of list," Tom said. But when his doctor suggested a T-cell test instead, Tom agreed. He did not know what a T-cell was. The count that came back was between five hundred and six hundred, indicating that his immune system was somewhat compromised. (A healthy immune system has five hundred to fifteen hundred T-cells per cubic millimeter of blood.) He went to get an AIDS test when he learned that the city's public health clinics would do it anonymously.

And so, two to three weeks after Hujar died, Tom learned that he was HIV positive. When David came over that night, Tom told him, and they both cried.

The struggle for so many now was with how to process all the loss, knowing that there would be more loss.

David had a rubber stamp made that said, "A celebration of Peter Hujar, where he lived, 189 Second Ave, Sunday December 20 1987 1-5," and sent out notices to friends. He had hung Hujar's photographs all over the walls and set up a sort of shrine with candles, Hujar's glasses, and the photos of gurus Hujar had kept by his bed. There were no formal talks recounting poignant or humorous moments with the deceased. Much of the time, David simply stood by the door welcoming people.

He wrote of later "coming back to his place the candle and shrine had burnt down to a beige hard puddle. I told him out loud how sad I am. . . . I can't imagine my life without this man. . . . My conversations with him even when depressed or afraid always had some reassuring calm. Somewhere in the midst of the fear surrounding the problem he could reach right in with little effort and the result was clarity and suddenly allowing yourself strength in a way that seemed right: healthy and real. I felt this sadness all day and night."

David had decided to move into Hujar's loft. He would breathe the same air Hujar had breathed. He would hang on to any vestige. He would leave the phone and utility bills in that name, keep "Hujar" coming to the space. He even saved the junk mail that came for Hujar and at some point tried to stitch it all together to use as background for a piece, the way he used maps. He could hide now, with his name no longer in the phone book. (His mother, for example, never knew where he was living after 1987.) He had his mail from Thirteenth Street forwarded to Tom's house.

Moving to the loft also solved a practical dilemma. He'd been offered a lease extension at his Thirteenth Street apartment, either $982.50 a month for one year or $1,015.86 for two years—rather steep for a dump between Avenues A and B in 1988. His rent there had more than doubled in two years, as his landlord kept getting "rent adjustments" upwards.* That didn't

---

* When David moved to 529 East Thirteenth at the end of January 1986, his rent was $425. In April it was $550. In May it was $850. By 1987, he was paying $901.

bode well. Meanwhile, Hujar's rent was $375. Tom remembered David moving to the loft at the beginning of January 1988.

For years, David had been telling people that his career was in trouble. It was one of the first things he had told Tom about his life as an artist. Schneider and Erdman remembered the only time Hujar ever got mad at David: One night, years earlier, when Hujar had them all over for dinner, David said he was going to have to take a phone call from a journalist who was fact-checking—and this article was crucial because his career was in the toilet. Hujar angrily told him it was wrong to put something like that ahead of dinner with friends. But now, as 1988 began, David's career was genuinely in trouble. He'd had two shows in '87 and sold one piece. The art world had moved on to Neo Geo and Jeff Koons. The East Village was passé, and David was its emblem. He ended 1987 with $166.53 in the bank. Given that David liked to be paid in cash whenever possible, that may not accurately represent his worth. Still, he had a real reason for concern.

On January 20, he applied to the Pollock-Krasner Foundation for a grant, listing his '87 income as $4,125. He also stated that from 1985 to 1987 he had given more than $12,000 to Peter Hujar.

But he did not go back to making work he could sell. Instead, he began a new journal, in which he wrote that he was going to "film the process of grief." He drove out of the city one day to film whatever his intuition led him to, and that was the Great Jersey Swamp, "virgin forest primordial place where dinosaurs once slept—all these heavy storm grey clouds these days—huge dark flapping wet curtains over the stage of this earth." In that passage, he's actually evoked his painting *Wind (for Peter Hujar)* with the images of dinosaur, clouds, and flapping curtains. But then, for him, everything he encountered resonated with emotion, with his feelings for Hujar, which he had probably never expressed while Hujar was alive and struggled to articulate now, through the camera. He ran, "shooting automatic bursts of film," then went whirling through the trees, filming as he spun until he was nauseated. "Felt my body in some strange way its mortality its thumping heart its fear and loss its small madnesses." Later, he said that he

*David took this photo while filming Jesse Hultberg's dream of shirtless men passing the prone body of a man, here played by Hultberg. The scene was part of David's unfinished film for Peter Hujar. (David Wojnarowicz Papers, Fales Library, NYU)*

wished he could have filmed the snowstorm that suddenly engulfed the car on the interstate and the pack of dogs on the road all standing around one dog who'd been hit by a car, who lay there not moving. "In the driving snow, one by one they sniffed at its form unwilling to leave it behind."

Back at the loft, David filmed all the pictures of Hujar he could find, beginning with one little school photo of the unloved kid Hujar had been.

He filmed Jesse Hultberg's dream of shirtless men passing the prone body of a man from hand to hand. Jesse, eyes closed, took the role of the man gently being passed along. He may have filmed this even before Hujar's death. Jesse remembered only that it was an image David wanted. David worked on the Hujar film on and off for about a year, and never finished it. But it goes to the heart of what he was doing with his films. He used the camera to capture something that connected him to the world, that allowed him to react emotionally, and though he had to wait to get the film developed, it seemed instant. It was as immediate as speaking into a tape recorder or pounding out pages at the typewriter, but those two options did not give him a visual image. And he wanted to record each telling detail, like Hujar's bathtub filling with dead leaves that blew in through a vent in the ceiling.

As he tried to understand his loss, he saw that Hujar was one of the first people he ever truly trusted, though he realized, in talking to others, that they'd known a different Hujar. Sometimes he felt he was listening to descriptions of a stranger. The pain he felt confused him, overwhelmed him. David began therapy in January 1988. After his first session, after trying to explain how he felt about Hujar, he drove directly to the Coney Island aquarium to film the beluga whales. He had visited there with Hujar and Charles Baxter, and then he'd been moved by a news photo of a girl granted her dying wish to swim with dolphins. Now he connected Hujar with the "sad innocence" of those whales. "All the mysteries of the earth and stars are contained in their form and their imagined intellect," he wrote in his journal. But their glass case was empty. They'd been shunted off to some shallow pool for a few days, and he left the aquarium immediately. He was obsessed with getting the images he wanted. "When I can't complete an action, I am confused. My emotions won't allow a detour or a wait. It's beliefs like this that kept me alive all these years. And it is in this season that for the first time these beliefs are falling apart. It started with Peter becoming ill."

Around the third week of January, David went back to Mexico with Tom and Anita and a dozen other people to celebrate Anita's fortieth birthday.

Rick Morrison, a friend of Hujar's, knew a woman who rented houses on the beach in Progreso (near Mérida in the Yucatán)—right on the gulf and very cheap. David, Tom, and company rented two of the houses, along with three cars. When they arrived, Morrison was there with his boyfriend, Larry Mitchell, and their friend Bill Rice, the actor and painter who'd once hosted David's monologues in his "garden." They overlapped for a couple of days. Which was good for David because he and Anita were not getting along.

Anita and David hadn't exactly hit it off when Tom first introduced them in 1986. "It wasn't instant dislike," Anita said of meeting David. "It was, 'Who are you and why are you taking Tom away from me?'" But then she and David bonded while caring for Hujar. When they went to Mexico, however, she had just started therapy with someone who urged her to stop taking care of other people, to just take care of herself. "I decided to take that to the next level. I wasn't going to help anyone," Anita said. "And that wasn't me either. That's why the therapy didn't last all that long." David thought she was being cold and mean.

Tom took Anita out to lunch to discuss it, and she changed her approach. From this point until the end of David's life, he and Anita were truly friends. Tom said, "This wound up being—even David admitted—one of the best trips any of us have ever had. We were there for a full three weeks. He and I stayed longer than anybody, but it was really a great trip."

David flew from Progreso to Mexico City for a few days to take pictures. When he came back, he'd brought everyone presents. Anita had never seen him in action before. "David was taking pictures of all the stray dogs and the roadkill and the vultures," she said. "He'd take out his camera and just shoot out the window while driving. It was amazing to me." She asked him about what he was doing. "He said, 'I see the world as just these images—constantly, constantly, and my art is how I organize this.' He was stimulated by everything. He didn't sit quietly much."

David would see vultures aloft and say to Tom, "Let's go see what they found." One day the two of them made a day trip to one of David's favored sites for shooting pictures—a dump. This one was outside Mérida. David climbed up a mountain of decaying garbage to photograph packs of wild dogs and people competing for scraps of food, their mouths and noses covered with bandannas. "There were flies as big as parakeets, and it smelled," Tom said. "I refused to get out of the car." As they drove away, they came upon a vulture in the road, clearly dying. David wanted to stop and pick it up. But there was nothing they could do for it, and Tom said, "David, we are not putting a dying vulture in the back of this car."


Activists in San Francisco had come up with the idea for the AIDS Memorial Quilt in the summer of 1987. Mourners all over the country immediately began sending three-by-six foot panels commemorating lost loved ones to the sponsoring NAMES Project Foundation.

I witnessed the first display of the AIDS Quilt on the National Mall when I went to Washington, D.C., in October 1987 to cover a huge gay rights march. The panels were stitched together into squares of eight and unfolded ritualistically. Step back, grab a corner, turn. It was choreographed. Constructed with varying degrees of craft, some incorporated clothing or other belongings or photographs of the dead. People walked among the squares of fabric, crying. The size of two football fields and destined to get much larger, this was Arlington for PWAs.

David designed a quilt panel for Hujar and worked with Sur Rodney Sur and Melissa Feldman to create one for Keith Davis. On Keith's panel, made from pink tie-dye, David stenciled the two men kissing from *Fuck You Faggot Fucker*. For Hujar's panel, he created a large version of the Dürer wing, with a globe below it, for one half. Then on the half with Hujar's name and dates, he added the image of a figure climbing a tree without branches. This was almost the same image he'd painted for Gracie Mansion's "Sofa/Painting" show in 1983, which she explained as David trying to get away from the various dealers who wanted to show him. But while in the earlier work, he gave himself one short branch. Hujar, even more devoted to self-sabotage, had none.

David also began to design Hujar's tombstone. "He barely even wanted a gravestone," David told me one day at the loft. He pointed at the arched window behind the blue table. "It's that shape, like an Old West tombstone." Just his name, his dates, and the Dürer wing.

David had always thought that he would die before Hujar. He knew he was at risk, and when he got depressed about it, he took comfort in imagining Hujar still there in some room, talking about him, explaining him, not letting him vanish.

And now he faced the possibility of losing Tom. "He was very sweet with me, and helpful," said Tom. But Tom thought that David should get tested too, and one night they had a big fight about it out on Second Avenue near Ninth Street, in front of a funeral parlor. "I thought he was probably HIV-positive," said Tom. "I remember getting pissed off that he'd treat me like I was infected, while he could go on not knowing his own status. I was feeling that what was going on between us was really false. I said, 'You're not taking care of yourself. You could be infected too. What are you doing?' And I was afraid for him. I was afraid for me. It was one of the many hard times in our relationship. We were screaming like banshees. Having AIDS does strange things to your emotions."

David had stopped making art. He felt that he couldn't create anymore. He was horribly depressed.

Meanwhile, Luis Frangella had introduced his dealer in Madrid to David's work, so when Galería Buades invited him to show there in April, he agreed to come a week ahead of time and make several new pieces. Before he left town, though, he wrote down all his fears. The major one, of course: "I'm afraid that I will come down with AIDS." But that spun out into so many others: the fear that this would be his last work before he got ill; that if he sold work in Spain, they wouldn't pay him; that the lump in his arm would turn out to be cancer; that the landlord would try to get the loft back; that he'd have to move in with Tom, where there was no place to work and the cats would get into the paint. Then, he had not filed a tax return, so the IRS might get him. "I have Tom but I'm too fucked up to let myself be loved and maybe so is he. . . . I live like I will die and I wonder how I can shift in therapy when I am so closed up and when I am so self-destructive. . . . I can't let myself hate my mom and dad for what they did. I see it all as my responsibility. Why is this? I'm afraid of my anger that lies buried, afraid if I experience it I will not be able to control it."

He'd gotten a big shock when he started therapy. It turned out that half of what he'd kept hidden were emotions everyone had! A lot of his artwork came out of feeling like an alien. Learning that he wasn't alien at all, he worried that the realization would block him from making his work.

He flew to Madrid on April 8. The paintings he made there were done quickly, and while they were less complex than most—even perfunctory—they were also the beginning of new ideas. *Childhood*, for example, features an empty wire head with orange balls for eyes against a background of clouds. It looks very much like the surrogate mother given to orphan monkeys in test labs. Embedded circles down each side feature some familiar iconography—dinosaur, steam locomotive, erupting volcano, a fetus in a hand. In *Mortality*, an elephant in a pond walks up to a floating elephant fetus. All around this image are both veins (attached to a heart) and vines. Later in the year, he would begin *Something from Sleep II*, an important painting that combines and complicates the imagery from both *Childhood* and *Mortality*.

He began to recover some energy here. He jotted ideas for photo diptychs, paintings, and "sound sculptures" in his journal and made notes to himself like "call Washington zoo for whereabouts of Tasmanian devil in U.S. zoos."

After the opening in Madrid on April 18, he flew to Paris. He may have seen Jean Pierre during his week there, but if so, he did not see much of him. David stayed with his sister, Pat, who was about to have her first child. At six thirty on the morning of April 20, an alarm went off in his sister's bedroom and was not turned off, so he got up and saw that she and her husband, Denis, were gone. He was deeply upset that they hadn't taken him along to the clinic. He cried. He wrote in his journal that he felt unwanted. "I sometimes think maybe it's because I'm queer," he wrote. "Maybe they are afraid of what I carry, if I have AIDS or not. This fear returns often. Maybe they won't allow me to see the baby until some time. . . . I ask myself if it's my imagination . . . because then it could all be something grown out of nothing—the way I sometimes tend to do—when I imagine the worst rejections or actions and project them onto others who I place in power positions. . . . I see myself taking my bags and leaving in anger. I am unhappy with my thoughts. Angry. I want to cry and turn to someone bigger than me—emotionally or physically bigger. Am I a child again in this state?"

While David was beginning to understand that he often saw rejection where none was intended, he still felt completely miserable until Pat's husband called at six P.M. to tell him that the baby had been born. David then went to the clinic. He took a photo of his new niece—which he would soon incorporate into a piece called *Silence Through Economics*. And he tried to imagine "this large creature" emerging from his sister's body. "Pat's belly, the light from the window upstairs, the color of the baby's skin, red, then faint, then red, tiny fingers with tiny nails, little working mouth. Peter. Peter's death. The shape of the earth clouds stars and space. The darkness of the delivery room shadows around the floor and ceiling all the memories in those shadows like films."

He went out and took a long walk.

Maybe that day, maybe the next, David was walking near the Centre Pompidou when Michael Carter, editor of the East Village zine *Redtape*, popped out of a restaurant to say hello. Carter pointed inside to the window table and the person he had been sitting with: Marion Scemama.

"I didn't know if David would come to me, and then he came," Marion said. "So it was weird. All of a sudden, we start like the old days." They hadn't seen each other in two years, but they saw each other every day for the rest of his visit. They went to the catacombs. They walked all over Paris, and one day, passing a store that sold animals, David said, "Let's buy some mice so we can free them."

"We were like kids," said Marion. "We were very happy to meet again, without all the past. Everything restarted as if nothing happened. So he bought four little mice, and we took them to the Jardin des Tuileries." When they saw a cat, they decided they couldn't free the mice there. Marion took them home, where one escaped and she had to recapture it before driving the mice into the country to set them free after David left town.

Marion had learned of Hujar's death from Nan Goldin and thought about calling David then. "But I didn't dare," she said, "because when I left New York, we were not really friends." David told her about his depression and that he wasn't working, and he seemed obsessed with his garbage. He told her he would take his trash ten blocks away, and he tore up everything that had his name on it. This was probably because he was living in the loft illegally, but Marion thought he'd become paranoid.

"I remember I had this feeling that I owed a lot to this guy and maybe he needed me," she said. "I'm not a mystical person, but there was something very strong for me in the fact that we met in Paris by chance. It was unbelievable. That Michael Carter looked out the window at that moment, and that David was passing by—I had the idea that it was not just chance, that it was meant. There was something written somewhere that we had to meet again. And I had the feeling that if something permitted that, it's because I had a role. I had something to do for him."

After David returned to New York on April 26, he and Marion began talking on the phone again—calls that lasted two or three hours. At some point they decided it would be cheaper if she just came to New York.

David decided to get tested for HIV after he came back from Europe. He never said why he changed his mind.

Tom had found a doctor he liked right there in the East Village. Dr. Robert Friedman also happened to be a gay man, and he ended up with a large caseload of AIDS patients. That's where David went for his test. That's where he learned that he was HIV-positive. Not only that—he had fewer than two hundred T-cells, and two hundred was the line of demarcation. In other words, said Dr. Friedman, "David had full-blown AIDS from the time he walked into the office."

However, since he had no opportunistic infections (like Kaposi's or PCP), he was given a diagnosis of ARC, or AIDS-related complex. "It was a euphemism that made people feel better," said Tom. The term was eventually deemed useless.

David's T-cell number would fluctuate. Somehow he got hold of one of his own lab reports in 1990, showing a count of 237. But Tom eventually learned from the doctor that from the time of his diagnosis until his death, David rarely had more than a hundred. David, however, did not want to hear about T-cell numbers. He asked the doctor to just let him know when there were few enough that he could give them all names.

He left the doctor's office on First Avenue that day of his diagnosis and almost immediately ran into Bette Bourne, the lead Bloolip. They'd only met once or twice before, possibly at the Bar or through Hujar, but David immediately went to Bette with his overwhelming news and said, "I'm fucked. What am I going to do?"

"He was sort of smiling," said Bette. "It was very strange. It was one of those smiles of recognition and resignation. He was almost laughing at the horror of it. He was still in shock. We held each other for a bit."

David tried to sort out his feelings by pounding out a couple of pages at the typewriter. The moments after diagnosis "were filled with an intense loneliness and separation," and he realized that "even love itself cannot connect and merge one's body with a society, tribe, lover, security. You're on your own in the most confrontational manner."

He did not make note of the day he was diagnosed. Tom remembered only that it was in spring 1988. But sometime before May 19, David wrote a short disquisition on death in his journal: "So I came down with shingles and it's scary. I don't even want to write about it. I don't want to think of death or virus or illness and that sense of removal, that aloneness in illness with everyone as witness of your silent decline." He had discussed it with Kiki though—you become fly food.

David was thirty-three when he got what was then considered a death sentence. The man who'd run down the street as a boy yelling, "We're all going to die!" had no illusions about "beating" the virus. He expected no miracle. Instead, he began to approach each project as if it were his last.

# 19 ACCELERATION

**David set so** much in motion that summer of 1988, thinking he might soon become too sick to work.

He began to write the piece about Hujar's illness and death. An early draft begins with the words "Rage. Rage. This is something about rage watching the television as some greasy government employee in Texas . . . said if I have a dollar to spend on health care . . . I won't spend it on someone with AIDS. . . . I turn from watching a man I love struggling to save his life." And this leads into his account of the trip to Long Island with Hujar and Anita, four single-spaced pages written in one burst. That would later appear in *Close to the Knives*, while "if I had a dollar" became the first line of text on one of his best-known paintings, *Untitled (Hujar Dead)*.

He'd received a letter from Amy Scholder, an editor at City Lights, asking him to contribute to a special forum on AIDS—its impact on cultural life—in their annual *City Lights Review*. She knew him as a visual artist and expected him to contribute a photo or drawing. Instead he sent a short essay titled "AIDS and Imagination," in which he first described what he meant by the pre-invented world, the regulated world, and how he'd often had the sensation of watching himself from miles above the earth as he moved through this "clockwork of civilization." But with the appearance of AIDS, he now saw everything at once and was acutely aware of himself "alive and witnessing." He incorporated about half of this into the essay on Hujar's death, which he called "Living Close to the Knives."

David and Tom were now attending ACT UP meetings. On June 25, 1988, the NAMES Project brought the AIDS quilt to the Great Lawn in Central Park, with the panels for Hujar and Keith included. On June 26, Gay Pride Day, his old friend Zoe Leonard called David. He told her he'd tested positive, and when she asked what she could do for him, he invited her to come along to the next ACT UP meeting.

He made the film *Beautiful People*, in which Jesse Hultberg gets dolled up in powder and gown, wafts out to a New Jersey lake, and dips his hand into the water, magically turning the film from black-and-white to color. He'd scrawled this note to self: "Seeing drag queens as true revolutionaries who fuck with visual codes of gender." The movie as he left it would have benefited from editing, and it needed a soundtrack. Still, this is a film he came close to completing. It's atypical, though, since it has a narrative.

He began to work in the darkroom with the many photos he'd taken over the years but never printed. Marion Scemama came from Paris for a month that summer with her boyfriend, François Pain. They stayed at her sister's apartment, and though she had assignments for a French photo agency, she was often free to see David. She was taken aback by the condition of the loft. He didn't like to clean, and he hated for anyone else to do it. He seemed to regard it as an intrusion into his privacy. Besides, they might throw something out. Marion cleaned anyway. He drove her to the Great Swamp in New Jersey and took pictures of her in a pond, naked and covered with mud. He took her to a favorite junkyard to photograph old broken cars. "I could feel he was excited, regaining energy," she said. He wanted to get a new exhibition together and asked if she could come back in the fall to help him.

He was also painting that summer. Composer and musician Ben Neill wrote him a letter asking if David would create the cover art for Neill's first LP, *Mainspring*, featuring the experimental instrument he was developing, the mutantrumptet. Neill had seen David's work at Gracie Mansion. "I literally felt like I was looking at a visual representation of what I wanted to do as a musician," Neill said. "He was essentially sampling—borrowing different kinds of visual imagery and putting it together—but it had this sense of mystery and a kind of resonance between the images." Neill sent David the recording, told him he was borrowing from baroque dance forms for this work, and mentioned that he'd become interested in dance diagrams. When Neill arrived at the loft to look at the image, he saw that David had incorporated dance diagrams into the painting, *Something from Sleep II*. A sleeping figure drawn on maps lies at the bottom (first seen in *History Keeps Me*

*Awake at Night*). A system of tubes holds images in place above the sleeper against a background of clouds. In the largest of these, an elephant in a pond is walking up to a floating elephant fetus (first seen in *Mortality*). David painted this elephant image on dance diagrams. Right above the sleeping figure is the surrogate mother's head from *Childhood*. On the right, upside down, is the Cyclops monster first seen in *Queer Basher/Icarus Falling*. At the top is a heart that could have come from a lotería card (reminiscent of the heart in *Tommy's Illness*). David added a new element, a watchface without hands—often a symbol for death. Bits of this painting were covered with torn dollars. Somehow this all worked together as an image of emotion at one remove, emotion under control. It would appear, in May 1989, on the cover of *Artforum*.

He worked on the mock-up of a square thirty-six-page book "in memory of Peter Hujar," *The Angel Inside Me Has Fallen to Its Knees*. This book was never printed, but he completed the design, starting with a cover image of ants crawling over coins and a watchface. On the dedication page, he sketched (in black felt-tip) his painting *Mortality*. He would include all six fire ant photos, thirteen of his paintings, and the text for "Being Queer in America: A Journal of Disintegration." In 1983, he'd made a piece called *The Angel Inside Me Has Fallen to His Knees* as a stenciled self-portrait. That was the year he'd done all the stencil pieces of Hujar.

When David told Gracie Mansion about his diagnosis, she wondered if he wanted that to be known in the art world—a question that made him furious. He was not going to hide it. Gracie then called Barry Blinderman, the former director of Semaphore Gallery who had moved on to become the director of University Galleries at Illinois State. Blinderman remembered Gracie calling to say "Do you know that David has ARC?" and "You should give him a retrospective. Nobody's done one." Blinderman thought it was a good idea. Gracie sent him slides, and Blinderman set about applying for a grant from the National Endowment for the Arts.


The estate of Peter Hujar had been paying rent on the loft since December 1987, while David reimbursed it each month. He had tried to pay the landlord directly, but his check was returned with a note saying that his payment would not be accepted since his name was not on the lease. During the first week of August 1988, David heard from a lawyer representing the landlord who ordered him to leave the loft by the end of the month or face "legal action."

In the case of David's particular building, the landlord wanted to convert it to commercial space and get all the tenants out. Throughout the neighborhood, though, artists had done their job of acting as detergent, and were now to be washed away, along with the rest of the poor. The symbol for it all was the Christodora House on Avenue B, where David had once cavorted naked with John Hall. By 1988, it was filled with high-priced condos. T-shirts reading "Die Yuppie Scum" were ubiquitous in Loisaida. So was the graffiti tag of an upside-down cocktail glass ("the party's over") attributed to the industrial band Missing Foundation, or at least to its leader, Peter Missing. The same East Village streets where artgoers once made their rounds now exhibited raw evidence of the growing crisis in homelessness. Tompkins Square Park had become a tent city, filthy and foul. Homeless people who didn't have so much as a makeshift shelter slept in the bandshell.

On the night of August 7, 1988, the Tompkins Square riot began when police moved into the park to try to enforce a one A.M. curfew imposed by the local community board. Since it seemed quite possible that the tension would come to a head that night, I was there as a reporter. Motley demonstrators trooped defiantly through the park with their "Class War" banners, and then a contingent of mounted police pranced out onto Avenue A. It was twelve thirty Saturday night, a peak traffic hour. I heard an explosion, probably an M-80, and so it began: war in the neighborhood.* I witnessed cavalry charges down East Village streets, a chopper circling overhead, and people out for a Sunday paper running in terror—from the cops—down First Avenue. Rioters smashed the Christodora's front door and liberated a potted tree from the lobby, replanting it across the street in the park. A cop swinging a billy club chased me away from the park, despite my press credentials. The photographer I was working with had her camera smashed. It was an awful night.

The next week, a lawyer for Hujar's estate sent David a letter, reiterat-

---

* For one activist's account of the struggle over East Village gentrification, see Seth Tobocman's *War in the Neighborhood* (Autonomedia, 1999).

ing the landlord's threat to begin proceedings against him "unless we can arrange some kind of agreed upon stay for you. As we discussed before, the estate can not really defend your right to remain in the apartment once proceedings begin."

David never considered leaving, but he would have to fight to stay in the loft.

David had not seen or spoken to his mother since sometime in 1985, his year of creating work about dead families. During his intimate talks that year with Karen Finley, he complained that Dolores was always calling and that he'd cut ties with her. Tom said that after he came into the picture, on the first day of January 1986, he never met Dolores and never knew David to have any contact with her. But in the late eighties, they did write each other once or twice a year. Dolores usually sent a birthday card.

That year she sent her card to David's old address on Thirteenth Street, and it was forwarded to Tom's house. In pink ink, Dolores wished him "universal abundance" and sent her love. She enclosed a letter, saying she thought of him often and hoped he was healing from the loss of his friend. Was he still writing? Was he still painting? "David, I get worried sometimes that we will lose touch with one another and I would of course feel most distressed if that happened." While she respected his decision to keep her out of his life, she wondered if he could give her the address of a friend, someone she could contact if she needed to reach him.

In a postscript, she asked him how Pat and Steven were doing. Both had stopped speaking to their mother in 1981.

David was now occasionally meeting Ben Neill for coffee at Disco Donut on Fourteenth Street. They discussed the book *Pure War*, a conversation between French thinkers Paul Virilio and Sylvère Lotringer. The book is difficult to summarize, but major themes are the impact of speed on a civilization, the way speed dominates everything that moves slower, the potential of a culture to obliterate itself, and how consciousness of that leads to a mindset of perpetual war.

Some of these notions had already manifested in David's work, with its "picturesque ruins," with its locomotives, the instrument of a westward expansion that wiped out Native American culture and that, to him, symbolized the acceleration of time. "He was interested in the whole phenomenon of things speeding up," Neill said, "and I think, for him, that was very much a metaphor for the speed or advancement of his own illness at a certain point." They talked about collaborating and sealed it when Neill was offered a slot to perform at the Kitchen in late '89.

David decided that he would call his next show "In the Shadow of Forward Motion," and the performance with Neill would take the abbreviated (speedier) name of *ITSOFOMO*. He explained the concept in one of his audiotaped journal entries: "Consider that you're in a car speeding along on an expressway. Everything that you see out of the corner of your eye which doesn't register [while you're] in the pursuit of speed . . . is what's in the shadow. It's all the things quietly occurring, within absence of sight."

He was scheduled to have another show with Gracie Mansion that winter. She too was about to move to SoHo, but then her backers pulled out. "Nobody was coming to the East Village anymore," she said. "I had stayed way too long, and I just decided I had to close the gallery." She let her artists know immediately. "David knew he was ill at that time," Gracie said. "He didn't know how much time he had, and he wanted a show right away. He was so pissed off at me." After word got out that she was closing, another backer came forward. But in the month or two between Gracie's telling her artists and finding that backer, David had already gone with P·P·O·W Gallery, which had just moved from the East Village to the eastern edge of SoHo.

ACT UP was planning a big October action at the Maryland headquarters of the Food and Drug Administration to protest the agency's slow pace of drug approval. Hundreds of people now attended the weekly meetings in New York, while branches had formed everywhere from Seattle to Berlin. During its first year and a half, ACT UP had organized nine protests designed to have national impact, along with an unknown number of "zaps." ACT UP was in Washington when Ronald Reagan first uttered the word "AIDS" (after six years of silence), only to call for mandatory testing. Activists tracked Reagan's laughable Presidential Commission on the HIV Epidemic (which included no experts but several people who wanted mandatory testing and/or quarantine). They protested outside the offices of *Cosmopolitan* after the magazine ran an article asserting that straight women were not at risk for the disease. One of the major goals of ACT UP was to find and disseminate the facts about AIDS, from prevention to possible treatments.

As relatively new members, David and Tom were not yet part of an affinity group.* Nor was Zoe Leonard, who'd become a regular at ACT UP, often meeting David there. "David and I started an affinity group call the Candelabras," said Zoe. Tom was in the group and maybe ten other people. No one can remember who came up with that name or why. Each affinity group had to plan its own action and make its own props for the FDA protest.

ACT UP had already been doing "die-ins," and Zoe suggested that their group make tombstones with slogans on them. They could each lie down with one during the demonstration. "Then David said 'foam core and paint,'" Zoe remembered. "I had pictured something much more elaborate, but he said, 'They're signs. Foam core and paint.' We all made them together at my house. The headstones became a real trope in ACT UP. Leading up to that action, David and I were very close, very in sync, and channeling all this emotion into something. I was so happy to have David in my life again in that way."

David and Tom wanted to drive down a day ahead of time, and they volunteered to take Zoe—along with the twenty-five to thirty tombstones. ACT UP was sending buses, but Zoe called David a couple of times to ask whether this or that other person could also get a ride with them, and she could tell that it made him angry. Then on the drive, she kept asking both David and Tom to smoke less, and she thought they were both angry. She was still trying to figure out, years later, how this trip to Washington "ended up," as she put it, "being something that made us not close for a really long time."

---

* Ideally this was a group of five to fifteen people with shared history and goals who could reach consensus quickly, function autonomously if they wished, and watch out for each other during large demonstrations.

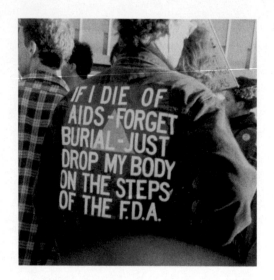

*David at ACT UP's "Seize Control of the FDA" demonstration in Rockville, Maryland, on October 11, 1988. (Photograph by William Dobbs)*

By the autumn of 1988, Tom and David were sharing a Plymouth station wagon that David had bought from his brother, Steven, with whom he had occasional but limited contact. David paid three hundred dollars for the car, and Tom paid for the insurance, and they took turns parking it. "It ate oil," said Tom. It leaked constantly. When David picked Tom up for the drive to Washington, he assumed that David had added oil, but he hadn't. "We busted a rod crossing the Delaware Memorial Bridge," Tom said. "It just blew." So Tom took a cab to the airport, rented a car, and came back to pick up David and Zoe and the pile of foam-core tombstones. They left the station wagon at a gas station in Wilmington, and ultimately abandoned it there. David never owned another car.

Nearly a thousand protesters descended on FDA headquarters in Rockville, Maryland, on October 11. They blocked the entrances to the building. Someone climbed all the way to the roof. One group wore T-shirts that said, "We Die—They Do Nothing." Another group, wearing lab coats spattered with red paint, carried signs that read, "The government has blood on its hands." The Candelabras lay down holding tombstones behind their heads. David's read: "Dead. As a person of color, I was exempt from drug trials." Other tombstones said things like "AZT wasn't enough" and "I got the placebo." David had also painted the back of his jean jacket to read, "If I die of AIDS, forget burial—just drop my body on the steps of the FDA." ACT UP had carefully studied the drug-approval process and produced a detailed list of demands, under headings like "No More Double-blind Placebo Trials" and "Allowance of Concurrent Prophylaxis." It had also prepared an elaborate press kit and received worldwide media coverage. Within months, the FDA had accelerated its procedures.

Tom and David were among the 176 people arrested that day. Police bused them to a gym and handed them paperwork to fill out. They could come back for a hearing, or just mail in a twenty-five dollar fine—which they both did. Afterward, they drove Zoe to the place where she was staying. "David didn't even want me to do that," Tom said. "But I wasn't going to tell her to get out of the car." He never knew why David was so angry at Zoe.

She said, "I just remember at the end of that thing at the FDA feeling like 'What happened? What did I do?' But it was really clear that he had had enough of me. I ended up riding back on the bus."

On October 18, David came home to find an envelope from the landlord's lawyer pushed under his door, telling him that his tenancy had been terminated and that he must leave the loft by the end of November. He made note of the time and date in a journal, but whether he took immediate action is unknown. He had just a few days to finish a major mixed-media piece for a group show.

This piece would change his life. He'd set out to address the epidemic and the emotions it stirred in him. Once he'd filled his "history paintings" with messages about a civilization hurtling toward apocalypse, but now the apocalypse was personal: His community faced ruin. His best friend was dead. His own death seemed imminent. The authorities who could have helped had instead turned their backs.

At the center of this new piece, David silk-screened the deathbed photographs of Hujar. At the edges are supermarket posters so broken up—and intercut with U.S. currency—that they've become abstractions. Sperm shapes made from maps float on top of that. Then layered over everything is one of David's more remarkable texts—a rant, really. It begins:

"If I had a dollar to spend for healthcare I'd rather spend it on a baby or innocent person with some defect or illness not of their own responsibility, not some person with AIDS . . ." says the healthcare official on national television and this is in the middle of an hour long video of people dying on camera because they can't afford the limited drugs available that might extend their lives and I can't even remember what this official looks like because I reached in through the tv screen and ripped his face in half.

It's a text filled not just with rage but with a kind of shocked disbelief at the government's official indifference to the crisis—in fact, the government's official malice. He goes on to parse the homophobia behind that malice, from the governor of Texas joking, "If you want to stop AIDS, shoot the queers," to the devout standing outside St. Patrick's Cathedral during Gay Pride parades chanting, "You won't be here next year. You'll get AIDS and die. Ha ha ha."

But it's also a text about fantasies of fighting back:

And I'm carrying this rage like a blood-filled egg and there's a thin line between the inside and the outside a thin line between thought and action and that line is simply made up of blood and muscle and bone and I'm waking up more and more from daydreams of tipping Amazonian blowdarts in "infected blood" and spitting them at the exposed necklines of certain politicians . . . and at the moment I'm a thirty seven foot tall one thousand one hundred and seventy-two pound man inside this six foot frame and all I can feel is the pressure all I can feel is the pressure and the need for release.

On October 22, the painting went on display in a group show at Milford Gallery called "Still Trauma." There it was seen by Karen Rinaldi, then an editorial assistant at Random House, who happened to be trolling the galleries on lower Broadway. She had never heard of David when she read the text on his painting. "It was one of those moments when you just stop in your tracks," she said. "I was so overwhelmed by the writing." She went to the front of the gallery where there was a copy of the *Journal of Contemporary Art* with another piece by David, "Living Close to the Knives," his account of going to Long Island with Hujar. Rinaldi sat in the gallery and read the whole sixteen pages, telling herself, "I want a book by this person." Eventually she made this happen. The book was *Close to the Knives*.

David's piece was also seen by critic Jerry Saltz, who chose to cover it in his monthly *Arts* magazine column, in which he wrote in depth about a single painting. Wendy Olsoff, who—with Penny Pilkington—had just taken David on at P·P·O·W, cited this article as a turning point in how David was perceived by the art world. He wasn't just the East Village primitive anymore. Saltz called *Untitled (Hujar Dead)* a piece with "the power to change lives."

The persona he projected in this important work—the furious, even monstrous, gay man—would become the image of an increasingly public David. He was so comfortable with rage, so accustomed to it, and he could use it as armor or, at least, a mask.

Behind it, he hid his struggle to face mortality, his fears about what lay ahead. "I feel like it's happening to this person called David, but not to me," he wrote in his journal. "It's happening to this person who looks exactly like me, is as tall as me and I can see through his eyes as if I am in his body, but it's still not me. So I go on and occasionally this person called David cries or makes plans for the possibility of death or departure or goes to the doctor for checkups or dabbles in underground drugs in hopes for more time, but then eventually I get the body back and that David disappears for awhile and I go about my daily business doing what I do, what I need or care to do. I sometimes feel bad for that David and can't believe he is dying."

David devoted himself to the studio now, and that fall he began to generate a great deal of new work for his upcoming P·P·O·W show, "In the Shadow of Forward Motion"—both paintings and complex photo pieces.

David had been intimidated about working in Hujar's darkroom. He felt like a beginner. Some of the Rimbaud photos had been printed by commercial labs, and some had been printed by him. He told Wendy Olsoff that he was proud of those prints but that they'd been hard to do. Then, early in the eighties, he'd worked in Tommy Turner's darkroom. Turner described David as "really adept from the beginning," but David had not printed anything since doing the photos pasted into *Fuck You Faggot Fucker*. David told me that he thought of his first work in Hujar's darkroom as "experimenting."

Gary Schneider and John Erdman encouraged him. "They explained to me that the earliest prints a photographer does are the most interesting," David told me, "because they're full of all the struggle and tension of creating and finding something about how light acts on paper. That when you learn it more thoroughly, you can make amazing things but the energy is totally different."

David did not consider himself a photographer. One essay in *Close to the Knives* begins with his declaration that he once accepted an invitation to speak at the University of the Arts in Philadelphia because they were going to call him a "visiting photographer." And that amused him since, as he put it, "I don't even know how to operate a camera on anything other than automatic."

Still, now that he could "experiment," he had years' worth of negatives and contact sheets to go through. In some of his new photo pieces, he juxtaposed five or seven or even fifteen distinct (not collaged) photographs. They show that David had again become a poet. Maybe he'd never stopped being one, as he worked to get disparate images to resonate. But pieces like *Spirituality (for Paul Thek)* make it clear that, for him, photos functioned as the words he could not construct from an alphabet. As he put it, "I generally will place many photographs together or print them one inside the other in order to construct a free-floating sentence that speaks about the world I witness."

His preliminary sketches and "lists of associations" were always about working out ideas, not "how will I draw this." When he planned the piece dedicated to Paul Thek, who had died of AIDS in August, he knew exactly which images he wanted—for example, Christ with ants, ecstatic slam-dancers in Louisiana, and Iolo (who died of AIDS about six weeks before Hujar did) exhaling smoke.

*Weight of the Earth, Part I* and *Weight of the Earth, Part II* each have fourteen carefully chosen photographs and one small drawing. David thought of these images as frames from "films of living, sounding a particular note like each word that makes up a sentence." These pictures could stand on their own—a hand holding a burning globe, a wrestler flipping through the air, a frog breaking through the surface of a pond and seen from below (legs only), a man standing in a pool of white light, the midsection of a highway patrolman walking past a car window, the sad monkey at

Untitled (Buffaloes), 1988–89. Gelatin-silver print, 27½ × 34½ inches.
(Courtesy of the Estate of David Wojnarowicz and P·P·O·W Gallery, New York)

the circus, a homeless person asleep in a box with only his feet visible—but together they describe something enigmatic, poignant, and difficult about being alive. To him, this was an opera that could have a hundred parts, but at least he'd made two of them. He scribbled a note on a worksheet: "*Weight of the Earth* is about captivity in all that surrounds us." In his "Notes to the Show," he described it as "the weight of gravity, the pulling in to the earth's surface of everything that walks, crawls, or rolls across it" and "the heaviness of the pre-invented existence we are thrust into."

On his first list of some thirty-five or forty possible images for *Weight of the Earth* is one he called "buffalo falling." David had taken the picture in Washington, D.C., at the National Museum of Natural History, where it's part of a diorama illustrating a Native American method for hunting buffalo. Hunters could kill a large number of the animals if they chased them towards a cliff they didn't know about. David recognized this as "a metaphorical image for the title of the show, a sense of impending collision

contained in this acceleration of speed within the structures of civilization." *Untitled (Falling Buffalo)* is now the image most identified with David,
and a detail from it became the cover of *Close to the Knives*. David talked
in his notes to this piece about his anger at the structure of things. But to
me, this image is about the AIDS crisis, about those who ended up going
off a cliff because they did not know that they were headed for one.

David took the negative of the falling buffalo to the Schneider-Erdman
Lab. He told them he'd made five sixteen-by-twenty prints. That was as big
as he could go in Hujar's darkroom, and he thought the prints should be
bigger. Schneider asked him to bring in one of the sixteen-by-twenties so he
could use it as a guide, and David refused. But not because he didn't think
his was good enough. "My versions were an interpretation that he really appreciated," Schneider said. "I think he truly believed that if he didn't try to
control how I produced anything, I would produce something better." Eventually Schneider did see the buffalo print David had made, and he thought
it was "unbelievably beautiful."

The ant photos taken at Teotihuacán also fit his theme—"things quietly occurring" while life rushes past. Again, the ants represented human
society to him. They go about their business, not heeding the symbols for
spirituality (crucifix), control (toy soldier), time/money (watchface/coins),
violence (toy gun), desire (photo of a naked man), and language (a sign).

"In the Shadow of Forward Motion" was the largest solo show David
ever had. Marion Scemama came from Paris twice to help him, first in October and November 1988. She spent hours going through contact sheets,
talking with him about which images were strong and had meaning. She
cut sperm shapes out of maps. She ran errands. She did some printing in
the darkroom. But perhaps most important to David, she understood what he
was doing. "She really did energize him," Tom observed. "There's no question.
At least creatively, the two of them set off sparks with each other."

One day, waiting for Marion to arrive, he began another taped journal.
He talked about his disgust with the art world. "I'm busting my gut to make
these things that are part of my personal truth," he said, and now the art
world would judge them, quite possibly dismiss them. His anxiety over this
made him feel like smashing all his work. He'd wait till Marion got there
and she could witness it. He'd forget about the show. Then he imagined

himself puking over the walls and fixtures and darkroom, putting his head out the window to throw up all over the street. And as he went off on this rant, he actually started to vomit. He couldn't tell if it was "the fear that I've carried through my whole life" that made him sick or if it was the virus. He felt scared.

But when David created a piece for this show about his possibly imminent death, it was surprisingly serene. He used a grid of black-and-white photos showing gears and other industrial oddments—"the residue of the manufactured world I was born into"—as background. *Where I'll Go After I'm Gone* is a collaged and painted piece dominated by a jungle fern on the left. His own face is among the beautifully arranged elements here—with blue moons, a winged foot, a fetus, a Native American doll, a donkey. In his "Notes on the Show," he explained, "I thought if there was indeed a place one goes after death then it could only be a place determined by one's vision of the world; of life; of concerns. Hell is a place on earth. Heaven is a place in your head. The garden is the place I'll go if I die."

He recorded a dream in his journal about meeting a hot guy at ACT UP. "I'm very attracted to him sexually but it's more that I feel like he'd love me and even protect me take care of me," he wrote. Eventually they end up on an escalator extending miles up into the sky and they somehow get separated. "I feel upset and need to find this guy also wondering when I'll tell him about my diagnosis. Suddenly the gladness I feel with contact with him turns to memory of Tom. Sadness and feelings of love for Tom. I think that I don't want to lose him. I can't envision breaking up with him. I wake up sad and exhilarated simultaneously."

On November 25, David brought Marion along to Tom's birthday dinner at Gage and Tollner, a steak house in Brooklyn. This was unusual because most of David's friends never met Tom or even knew he existed. Tom could remember walking around the East Village with David and running into Kiki Smith or Keith Davis—and David would act as if Tom wasn't there. He wouldn't even say "This is Tom," much less "This is my boyfriend." The only friends of David's that Tom really knew were Gary Schneider and John Erdman. Sometimes the four of them would have dinner

*Though Tom and David photographed each other, they were rarely photographed together. This stained photobooth picture of them kissing and the photo on their video rental ID card could well be the only two pictures that clearly show both their faces. (Photobooth: David Wojnarowicz Papers, Fales Library, NYU; Video ID: Courtesy of Tom Rauffenbart)*

together. Tom was acquainted with Judy Glantzman. He'd met Zoe Leonard through ACT UP. That was it. When Tom asked why, David said that he just liked to keep his life private. But it ended up reinforcing how intimidated Tom felt about the art world. "Early on, at least, I was afraid to meet his friends," he said. "I just didn't know who I was in relation to any of them. It was like with Marion. I always felt outside when they were together. David was nervous about that. And then, as I felt bad, he would sense it, and it just was awkward all the time. And I really did sense that—when they were together, no one else existed, and it made me feel pretty superfluous. I remember him yelling at me about it, like it was my fault that I didn't like Marion."

Marion returned to Paris at the end of November, but planned to return in January to help him finish preparations for the show. They continued their marathon phone conversations. One day he mailed her a large print of a ship with a small circular inset showing a blow job, all of it printed to look like a negative. He had folded it into four parts and included a note to say he was experimenting with this. What did she think?

That was the first print David made for *The Sex Series*. He'd gotten the idea to work with negative images after talking with Marguerite Van Cook about manipulations that could be done in the darkroom. She told David about a photo series she'd made by using color slides in the enlarger—a positive would become a negative, though the red light in the darkroom would knock out a certain portion of the light spectrum coming through the slide. So the prints would look like negatives but a little "off." She also explained how to make contact prints and reminded him that if you took the negative holder out of the enlarger, you could burn a circular image into the paper. Or you could make your own negative holder, as she had in order to print from Super 8 film, which is quite small. He seems to have tried all of the above.

The eight photomontages in *The Sex Series (for Marion Scemama)* were immediately hailed as a remarkable achievement. "Motion is of primary importance in these X-ray visions of a world gone awry," critic David Deitcher wrote in *Artforum*, "and a discomfiting sense of time's accelerating passage emerges as its coefficient: a steamship ascends a storm-tossed sea; a military airplane disgorges paratroopers; the Brooklyn and Manhattan bridges converge like luminous arteries seen from the air; a train snakes its way through a desolate region; a massive tornado obliterates a landscape; a clapboard building and watertower are glimpsed as if from the window of a speeding car. Only the shot of tree trunks in a forest, seen from near ground level, hints at stasis and duration. But the fact that these trees are rooted in the flooded terrain of a bayou hints at both death and decay."* Set into each landscape described above are circular images David lifted from Hujar's porn collection. Most have other insets as well—ants on money, a fetus, typed texts, blood cells, part of a newspaper piece about a queer-bashing. Deitcher remarked, for example, on an image of two women embracing— one of the circular images flanking the tornado: "That an image of an embrace should be juxtaposed with one of nature out of control underscores the emotional sense of peril and ambivalence that suffuses the entire series."

Writing in *Art in America*, critic Lucy Lippard noted that David related these insets "to surveillance photos, to suppressed information and to cells seen through a microscope. Most of the circular cameos contain explicit homoerotic or occasionally heterosexual scenes. The reversal to negative

---

* Seven scenarios are described here because the bridges were used in two of them.

suffuses them with a nocturnal glow and generates unexpected sources of light and energy, haloing heads, cocks, bony hands. The larger underlying images are often quite ordinary to begin with . . . but they take on, through the inversion of light and dark, a menacing, oneiric aura."

David wrote in his "Notes to the Show" that he'd been inspired by his rejection from a Paris exhibition about sexuality. He'd collaborated on a piece about attempts to repress sexuality in the age of AIDS, and the curator, an American, told him, "This is not a show about AIDS." David declared that this curator was thought to be a nice guy. "That reminds me of Hitler's passion for painting flowers. I'm in the throes of facing my own mortality and in attempting to communicate what I'm experiencing or learning in order to try and help others I am effectively silenced. I am angry."

When I asked David about *The Sex Series*, he said, "It came out of loss. I mean every time I opened a magazine there was the face of somebody else who died. It was so overwhelming and there was also this huge backlash about sex, even within the activist community. The thought police were jumping out left and right about what's proper. . . . And it essentially came out of wanting some sexy images on the wall—for me. To keep me company. To make me feel better. It was fairly democratic. The lesbians and homosexuals outnumbered the heterosexuals, but I thought that was proper."

And he wanted to see sexy images connected with Hujar, who had thrown away all his porn soon after he was diagnosed. David rescued it from the trash. Much of that collection comes from the fifties, judging by hairstyles. Most shocking in the heterosexual scenes is how homemade they seem, how cheesy and unglamorous—though that isn't detectable once they're negatives. The "man-on-man action" looks a bit more professional and includes pictures from the coy bodybuilder magazines of that era. David told me, "There were some images in there that were really evocative of a time that I always wished I could go to—just for the sexual part of it."

David made just one of each photomontage in *The Sex Series* and then went to the Schneider-Erdman Lab to discuss whether they could be reproduced. "He was really having kind of a breakdown because this was a unique set of prints, and he was worried that they would be sold," Schneider said.

"He was passionately in love with them," Erdman added.

"They're miraculous prints," said Schneider. "That's very complicated masking.* Really difficult. He knew he could never repeat them. And he knew how important they were."

The set David made was twenty by twenty-four inches, probably because he'd found it easier to do all the insets at that size, but Hujar's darkroom wasn't set up to print images that big. Schneider told him to bring in the three hardest (i.e., those with the most subtle tones) and he would make sixteen-by-twenty-inch versions of them. "Avedon and Scavullo and the Kertész Estate would bring me retouched printing—or vintage prints in the case of the Kertész Estate—and I would make a large-format negative plus masks and a new version that was basically a copy print but a really, really high-end version."

"You couldn't tell the difference," said Erdman.

"So I made these three prints for him, and of course it was enormous labor to do, and usually I charged a fortune for that work. Really a fortune," Schneider said. "Because for all of those artists, it was worth it."

"We didn't charge David anything," Erdman said.

"And he was overwhelmed by the quality of them," Schneider said.

The Schneider-Erdman Lab had been processing David's film and making him contact sheets since 1984—and had never charged him. "He made it very clear that he couldn't cope with it ever being a commercial relationship, and it would have to be an exchange relationship of some sort," said Schneider. "He laid that out very clearly. From the beginning. Even with film processing."

"Then after every trip he seemed to come in with hundreds of rolls of film," said Erdman.

"And we were poor," said Schneider. "But Peter kept telling us that David had no money." They'd had the same arrangement with Hujar. Schneider processed his film in exchange for the occasional print.

In 1984, while he was still at Civilian Warfare, David asked them what

---

* The mask protects the photo paper from the enlarger's light. David would have had to create a mask for each circular inset or any other image he embedded, then burn those in while another mask protected the background image.

work of his they'd like in exchange. Schneider wanted *Fuck You Faggot Fucker*, but it was already sold. So he asked for one of the small black and gray watercolors depicting sexual situations in a porn theater, pictures that ended up in David's last book, *Memories That Smell like Gasoline*. Apparently David decided that one watercolor wasn't enough, because he showed up at the lab one day with a huge painting done on a school map. Schneider described it as "vertical poles, men climbing the poles, a big screaming head, a red open mouth, and a meteor in the sky—all the icons." It was the size of an East Village apartment wall, and very fragile. Hujar came by to advise them not to roll it up. They had to put it in a big acrylic box. Eventually they sold it to the Newark Museum.

In preparing for "In the Shadow of Forward Motion," Schneider printed for David for the first time, and David compensated him by giving him art. One falling buffalo. A couple of prints from the "Ant Series." But with *The Sex Series*, David suggested that Schneider-Erdman co-own the edition. Earnings were split evenly between David, the lab, and the gallery.

Dedicating *The Sex Series* to Marion Scemama was "a joke between us," David told me. "She was extremely helpful in getting me out of depression, getting me working. She helped me focus through conversations and excitement about sharing time and making things. So I did it as a thanks— and also to get all her friends to ask, "Why is this homosexual dedicating *The Sex Series* to you? What does this mean?""

David had his retrospective at Illinois State University coming up, but for all he knew, "In the Shadow of Forward Motion" would be his last show of new work, and he wanted a catalog. The gallery budget would allow for only a photocopied effort. Even so, Marion promised to solicit her friend Félix Guattari to write the introduction.

In this country, Guattari—psychotherapist, philosopher, and semiotician—is best known for his two collaborations with philosopher Gilles Deleuze, *Anti-Oedipus* and *A Thousand Plateaus*. In academia and in an art world enthralled in the 1980s by postmodernism, Guattari had enormous cachet. Marion had known him since the early seventies—he was first her therapist, then her friend. In 1988, she and her boyfriend, François Pain, were living at Guattari's place in Paris.

Guattari knew nothing of David's art, but Marion prepared a slide show for him. David called her one night to talk about what his work meant: "Hi, Marion, this is David. OK. If I start out with the idea that we're born into a completely pre-invented existence where everything is regulated . . ." It was a seamless 3,500 words that could have been a lecture, but he was clearly not reading. Marion translated this into French for Guattari, then rendered the resulting essay into English before she returned to New York.

Almost half of Guattari's introduction quotes from what David said on the phone. Still, David was pleased to have some words from this important thinker. He felt that his work had never been taken seriously, that critics and journalists always focused instead on his perilous childhood. That would change with "In the Shadow of Forward Motion." At least, his life story would move to the background more often.

Certainly Guattari described the work with an intellectual framework never before applied to David, with phrases like "the concatenation of semiotic links." But Guattari seemed most moved by the way David was dealing with his diagnosis. "His revolt against death and the deadly passivity with which society deals with this phenomenon give a deeply emotional character to his life work," Guattari wrote, "which literally transcends the style of passivity and abandon of the entropic slope of fate which characterizes this present period."

Again—David never disclosed the terror and dread his diagnosis churned up in him. "I just hope it's not something prolonged and painful, and I hope it's not fearful," he said in a taped journal entry sometime in December 1988. "I just hope it's something I can slip into, like slipping into a tub of water. Warm water. Something restful. But when I think about dying and I suddenly have fear about it, it's fear of going before I'm ready. And then I think, how can I ever be ready?"

He came back to the tape later, talking with a stuffed nose, as if he'd been crying. "I guess what scares me the most," he said, "I feel afraid of what the end of my life will be. It's the idea that I would lose my mind. Maybe the threat all my life of trying to maintain some kind of complete control of myself. Coming from where I come from—all the scenes as a kid hustling and all the scenes from the streets and the times I came close to death and the times that I nearly starved and the times that lack of food or sleep sent my body into a tailspin. . . . And maybe, as somebody suggested, that need for self-control is the mask, this enormous rage that I either carry or may carry from all those experiences. I guess I fear loss of control, that that rage will spill and become indiscriminate in terms of what it attacks. And really and truly I think I'm afraid of losing my mind. . . . I want to be able to provoke some change in whatever limited fashion, whatever small sense of shift that anything I could do or say could create in people, in a person, in numbers, in subtlety and whatever. I just want to be able to make that gesture. And I hope that my mind remains consistently clear despite rage, despite illness, despite weakness or despite comfort or despite pain."

The Hujar Estate's tenancy at the loft had ended on November 30, a date on which it was to turn the unit over "broom clean" and vacant. The landlord went so far as to inform the estate that there was never any intention to renew Hujar's lease either; the loft was being converted into a commercial space. David realized then that he was going to have to hire a lawyer.

On December 20, 1988, he appeared in civil court to fight his eviction from Hujar's place.

The result was a stipulation signed in January that allowed him to remain at 189 Second Avenue, and its wording was rather extraordinary. He would consent to the issuance of a warrant of eviction, but the execution of said warrant would be stayed until January 15, 1990, "by virtue of the fact that respondent Wojnarowicz is currently suffering from and has been officially diagnosed as having Acquired Immune Deficiency (AIDS)." If he still had AIDS on January 15, 1990, and his health had not improved, the stay would be extended for as long as he continued to suffer from AIDS. He would furnish the landlord with written statements about his health from his doctor. "It is further stipulated and agreed by the parties hereto that in the event respondent Wojnarowicz is cured of AIDS or otherwise recovers from this disease, the stay shall be vacated and petitioner may execute the warrant of eviction."

The lawyer who'd worked this out was someone David kept on retainer until early in 1991. The building was about to be converted into a multiplex, and his problems at the loft were just beginning.

Early in January 1989, David and Tom went to New Orleans for the fourth time. Tom had fallen in love with the unique feel of this city and its hybrid culture—even the romantic aura surrounding its deterioration and rot. But above all, he loved the food. He had introduced David to New Orleans during their first year together, and David found that he too loved this city—and the alluring nearby swamps.

They always rented a car. David liked to make day trips into the bayous to look for critters. "No matter where we'd go, he'd pick up a slimy thing," Tom said. On one early visit they found a dilapidated snake farm, and on another visit, an alligator farm where they watched bull alligators feasting on rodent skulls.

They talked about buying a house in New Orleans. David was especially keen on this idea after Lydia Lunch moved there and told him, "People don't even stare at you." It would be a shotgun house, maybe in a neighborhood like Faubourg Marigny. Maybe across the river in Algiers, where they sometimes went to eat. They'd pick a street where it looked like a vampire could live.

It was all talk and such a wonderful fantasy.

On the way to the airport for their flight home, they stopped at a pet store that specialized in tarantulas. David intended to buy some red-legged ones to bring back to New York. Once inside, though, David spotted a couple of box turtles and recognized that one was sick. He also knew that they were an endangered species and illegal to sell. So he bought only the turtles and, though he and Tom were already running late, he insisted that they drive the turtles back into town to the Audubon Zoo, where they could be treated. "We raced back to the zoo," said Tom, "and the staff confirmed that the turtles were in bad shape. They were moved by David's concern and agreed to try to save them."

Back home, David compensated for not buying the tarantulas by rescuing a scorpion from a Lower East Side pet shop. They'd kept it under bright lights, but scorpions like the dark. David made a cave for it from a few lean-to rocks and named it Lucy (short for Lucifer). It left little snow-mobile tracks in the sand of the terrarium, and at night he could hear it scuttling to climb the glass walls. He worried that he hadn't given it a good-enough home, and he wondered how poisonous it really was. When some-one asked him why he wanted such a thing, he told them he wanted to own death, "to have death in my house outside of myself, outside of this virus." Now most of his to-do lists carried the instruction: "Buy crickets." This scorpion food lived in an adjacent terrarium—always singing. It was part of the natural history ambience prevailing at the loft, with its baboon and baby elephant skeletons, small cactus shaped like a brain, globes and plastic liz-ards, framed pictures of frogs and toads. David had a bed and a kitchen table with chairs. That was it, apart from the enormous clutter. Near the front door he'd hung a framed self-portrait of Hujar. Every time he left for the outside world, that was the last thing he saw.

Marion Scemama arrived in New York about ten days before David's show opened. The photos were done by then, but they had to be framed. And he had paintings and collages to finish.

He dedicated to Tom *Something from Sleep III*, an image of a man cov-ered with the solar system, peering into a microscope. This had come to him in Paris, he explained in his "Notes to the Show," after his niece was born. He wrote of looking through his journals at accounts of dreams from past years: "I see the threads of the unconscious revealing to me that this virus was making its way through my body." And he realized that this baby was on its way to replace him. On the day of her birth, he sensed the "historical thread" leading from earliest organisms to dinosaurs and then all of human history. "I saw a vague transparency of my self disappearing beyond the brick and mortar of the buildings surrounding the clinic and the tips of trees beyond the roofs and at some point around then I had this dream"—about the man with the microscope. He had also finished *Something from Sleep IV* (a stegosaurus with letters instead of plates along its spine spelling "W O J N A R O W I C Z"), *Fear of Evolution* (a monkey in bib overalls pull-

ing a globe in a wheelbarrow), and much more for "In the Shadow of Forward Motion."

On February 8, David rolled up at P·P·O·W in a truck with Marion and
all this artwork sometime around three or four in the afternoon. The show
opened at six. So his punctuality had actually improved since the East Village days, but Olsoff and Pilkington were frantic. While they hung the
work, David sat down at the gallery's typewriter and pounded out seventeen
single-spaced pages for the show's catalog, writing what each piece meant
to him. He'd brought Guattari's introduction, along with some of his work-
sheets, with their rough sketches and lists, to show his process. He did not
write from notes. "He didn't labor," Olsoff observed. "It was all in his head."
Nor did he make any changes. The pages went out to be photocopied.

A couple of nights later, David came back to the gallery with Marion
and with photographer Andreas Sterzing, who had a large-format camera.
They spent the whole night there, eating and drinking and documenting the
show. When they left at five in the morning, David told Marion, "I don't
think we should split now. Come back to the loft."

"And so I laughed, and at that point I was really in love with him,"
Marion said. "It was just magic. So we went to his loft, and at the moment
we had to put ourselves in bed, he started getting nervous. I remember that,
because he wouldn't come to bed. So I understood that maybe he was
scared that I would try to have sex with him. So I said, 'Look, David. I feel
you're nervous. So don't worry. I have some Valium. I'm going to take half a
Valium and then you won't be afraid I'll jump on you.' So he laughed and he
said, 'OK, I'll take one too.' Then in the morning, he woke up first. . . . He
prepared breakfast for me. I think he was very relieved to see that we could
sleep in the same bed and just be tender with each other."

Marion was about to go back to Paris and told him, "Do you know one
thing that would make me happy? If you and Tom could see me off at the
airport." So David arranged this, despite knowing that Tom disliked her.

As Marion remembered it, she came to the loft an hour before they
were supposed to leave for the airport. David was giving her a stack of his
photos in payment for all the help she'd given him. "So we looked at them
together. We had fun," Marion said, "and I was in love with this moment of

him, with all these photos he was giving me. And I said—like not kidding but laughing, like playing, I said, 'Oh, let's go just you and me to the airport,' because I wanted to continue this magic thing." That made him so furious that he tore up one of the prints he'd given her and then, after she said no and begged him to stop, he threw the rest of the pictures up in the air. She went out to walk and cry for half an hour. Back at the loft, David picked up all the prints he'd thrown. They patched it up, but David did not forget this.

He wrote about it later, when he was trying to analyze his relationship with Marion. As he remembered it, she had asked him the night before if they could go to the airport without Tom. Or as David put it, "Reject Tom in other words. I said no. She said: 'I gave you so much and ask only one small favor and you reject my request.' I went nuts. Uncontrollable. Ripped up the photos I packed for her. Was relieved that was all. Fear of all my life killing someone if out of control. Ended up going alone I think. . . . Hard to remember now."

Marion thought that Tom had come along in the end. Tom is certain that he did not.

David usually left town immediately after a show opened. He always expected the worst and did not want to hear the reactions. This time he was in New York long enough to understand that the art world had embraced his new work. He felt confused. He was afraid his emotions would become apparent. "My buried rage could surface along with need for the embrace—who knows?"

On February 22, David left for Albuquerque—a rare solo trip. He began a new journal on the flight. "What is it I want or need? . . . I want to create a myth that I can one day become. I want to adjust myself through my work. . . . I am what I do, but not really. I get angry at the pressure of strength. I get resistant to the idea that I should be clear and strong in this part of my life. I want to be raw, I want blood in my work. This is why I don't revise my writings very much. Why I stop short of the ideal construction of painting or photos or whatever."

He spent about ten days in the Southwest, mostly in or near Albuquerque, but he also drove west through the Petrified Forest and the Painted Desert, into the vicinity of the Zuni, Hopi, and Navajo reservations, and ultimately to Meteor Crater. He sent a postcard to Marion from

Holbrook, Arizona. "Sitting in a motel room the swimming pool is filled with red dust . . ."

Had it really been just three and a half years since he'd stayed at this same motel with Keith Davis, and the pool was filled with water?

ACT UP decided to target the Koch administration's miserable record in addressing the AIDS epidemic, and it prepared by conducting a series of four-hour teach-ins for its membership. New York had 22 percent of all reported cases in the country. The crisis was multipronged and included the city's collapsing health care system, the thousands of homeless people with AIDS, and a mayor so fearful and ignorant about the disease that he immediately went and washed his hands after handing a PWA a cookie. To educate its membership, ACT UP created and distributed a hundred-page handbook filled with statistics, analyses of what had to change, and lists of who in city government was not doing what.

On March 28, 1989, an estimated five thousand activists demonstrated at City Hall and blocked the Brooklyn Bridge. The face of Mayor Ed Koch—known for his glib catchphrase "How'm I doin'?"—now appeared on an ACT UP placard that read, "10,000 New York City AIDS Deaths. How'm I doin'?" David was one of more than two hundred people arrested that day. Tom participated early in the action, before work, but was not arrested.

Zoe Leonard came to that demo with the Candelabras. David and Tom were no longer part of that affinity group, but she and David had begun talking on the phone again. Even when they were slightly estranged, she said, she and David could run into each other on the street and decide to have coffee or say, "I'm shooting something. Do you want to help?"

He was the one she wanted to talk to about the questions her activism brought up in her. One day she asked him to come to her apartment to look at some prints. "I was taking all these aerial photographs," Zoe said, "and I confided in him about this conflict I was having as an artist about the intensity of the activist work and the harshness of the reality of the crisis and—I was photographing clouds. There was just beginning to be a little bit of interest in my work. I had been offered a one-person show, and I remember being really confused. Like, what do I do? There's this divide in my life.

And I showed him all these prints. I used to just work en masse, and I had stacks and stacks of prints all over the floor, and he was so kind."

Her voice broke as she recounted what David told her: "Zoe, these are so beautiful, and that's what we're fighting for. We're being angry and complaining because we have to, but where we want to go is back to beauty. If you let go of that, we don't have anywhere to go."

# 20 "LIKE A BLOOD-FILLED EGG"

**Rosa von Praunheim** came to New York in April 1989 to make *Silence = Death*, a documentary about artists dealing with AIDS. He filmed a ritual unfolding of the NAMES Project quilt. He filmed an exhibit by the activist-artist collective Gran Fury. He interviewed artist Peter Kunz, who died two weeks after recording his segment. He caught Emilio Cubiero performing his horrific suicide piece, "Death of an Asshole"—jamming a pistol into said orifice and pulling the trigger. Allen Ginsberg read his "Sphincter" poem, and Keith Haring paused in the midst of painting a large erotic mural to say, "This is about nostalgia. It's not about anything that could happen now." But it was David who became the moral and political center of this film.

He was about to become one of the major voices to emerge from the AIDS crisis. *Silence = Death* returns to him repeatedly for monologues, rants, and interviews, and he used this as a forum to deliver key points he'd been working out in his writing:

"When I was told that I had this virus, it didn't take me too long to realize that I had contracted a diseased society as well . . .

". . . and I'm carrying this rage like a blood-filled egg . . .

". . . if I die of AIDS, I don't want a fucking memorial. . . . Drop my fucking body right on the front steps of the White House . . .

"I don't think having AIDS is something heavy; it is the use of AIDS as a weapon to enforce the conservative agenda that's heavy."

He delivered the monologue with that last line while wearing a white T-shirt emblazoned with the handwritten slogan "Fuck Me Safe." He gave Rosa footage from *A Fire in My Belly* and from the unfinished film about Hujar. He provided a wolf mask and costume in which someone came creeping toward him during the "blood-filled egg" voice-over. (David chased the "wolf" off with a flaming pole.) He talked about Hujar's death and what that loss meant. He talked about his own death, betraying no fear of it. "You become fly food, and somehow that's comforting."

Norman Frisch, then working for the Wooster Group as administrator and dramaturge, met David at a panel discussion organized by Gran Fury. Frisch had been acquainted with Rosa von Praunheim for years and also knew Phil Zwickler, who was acting as line producer on *Silence = Death*. Frisch observed, "David had a lot more control over his sequences than any of the other artists did. Somehow he and Rosa had agreed that David's sequences were really David's film, and that he could do what he wanted."

David asked Marion Scemama to be there too, and to bring her video camera. (At that time, she was coming to New York four or five times a year.) "We had started thinking about a film we could do together," Marion said. "But it would be his film. About death. About AIDS. About the world and sexuality."

One day, while he was still filming *Silence = Death*, he became very angry at Marion. She'd been in New York for a week and they hadn't shot anything for their own film. "He was saying all these bad things about me," she said. "That I was disturbing his life, that I was fucked up—like he used to do sometimes when he was too nervous." She told him she was going to turn on a tape recorder and he should just talk.

What then poured out was all his ambivalence about doing their film. "It makes me very self-conscious to sit in front of a tape recorder and talk about this kind of shit," he began. "The thing about my death, about Peter, about whatever—I mean, I can sit there and do this for Rosa's movie on a certain level because I hadn't really talked about it on tape recorder that much except privately." He meant his taped journals.

"The thing that occurs to me is, so what? We have a documentation of David with rage, we have a documentation of David angry, we have a documentation of David scared, so—all this stuff that I can only imagine is for after my death. And again, it's like, so what? How many thousands of people died of AIDS now? How many documentations do you have to have of this sick, dying faggot sitting in a room, going through whatever shit that he's going through and oh look, he has rage; and oh yes, he has fear; and oh yes, he has a mind; and oh yes, he created these things and some people think they're beautiful, other people think they're full of shit. To be a participant in recording myself for after my death just seems pretty fucked-up."

He addressed Marion at some point: "What is important about this to you? I'm asking you. What do you think comes from looking at images of somebody who's angry because they're dying? What is it about the sound of their voice or the information that they have about panic or fear that's important? Like, what can it do?" She did not reply.

David kept going for another thirty minutes or so. The gist of the subsequent rant was that he didn't want to be pinned down "like a bug on paper" in some film that would claim to be the definitive David. "I get afraid," he said, "that—OK, I'm documenting this stuff, but what about the billions and billions of things that are taking place inside my head and body that I can't document because there's no language for it?"

Marion helped him prepare for each scene he filmed with Rosa. They hadn't decided what form their own video would take. But one thing David talked about, said Marion, was his nostalgia for cruising. One night, he took her to a gay porn theater. She bound up her breasts and wore a hat so she could pass as a man. Once inside the theater, David immediately walked over to some guy and left her hiding behind a pillar. When a man approached her, David came right back. She asked if they could leave. "He wanted me to see how it worked. He wanted to try and make me feel the beauty of two men meeting through anonymous sex. They were closing the theaters, so for him it was an entire culture that was collapsing. That's why he did all those drawings of guys having sex in theaters [later published in *Memories That Smell like Gasoline*]. He wanted to record it before everybody died."

David told her he wanted to do a scene with a guy for *Silence = Death*, "to show how it is between guys—not a sex scene but a sensual scene." When he said he didn't know who he could get to do this, Marion suggested Paul Smith.

Smith was an artist and occasional critic. (He had reviewed David's "Mexican Diaries" show, for example.) They'd been acquainted for years. David had asked Smith to pose the year before for the photos of lips sewn, hands sewing bread, and hands bandaged that he used in *Silence Through Economics*. According to Marion, David had always been attracted to

Smith. This was news to Smith, who said, "He never gave me any clue that he was attracted to me."

He said that David asked him, "Would you be willing to kiss me for this film?" And that David was shy about kissing him. Their encounter in *Silence = Death* is very short in duration and very short on chemistry. David took Marion to see the rushes and they were both disappointed. As Marion put it, "The mystery of sensuality and eroticism was gone." She thought the cinematographer should have done more close-ups.

She and David decided they would do it over—for themselves—with Marion shooting video. She had once had a short affair with Smith, who described himself as "more bisexual than David was." Marion described the subsequent shoot as "hot."

"I was so excited," she said. "Because I had this desire for Paul. I had this desire for David. I love men's bodies. And it was like David giving me something to see about his sexuality.

"There was this intense complicity between David and me," she said, "because I had this camera that wasn't just an object but an extension of David's mind through my eye and my arm. That's when I really understood what my work with David could be. . . . David used to say we were from the same brain. . . . After this, we were not scared anymore of trying to put together this video he wanted to make about him[self]. We started playing with the camera, creating more and more images without knowing yet what we would do with it. . . . The camera literally became a 'desiring machine,' a belt of transmission between our respective fantasies, a way of pushing away the growing feeling of death surrounding us."


That April, letters from outraged members of the American Family Association (AFA) began to inundate Congress.

Andres Serrano's photograph *Piss Christ* had been part of a juried group show, "Awards in the Visual Arts," sponsored by the Southeastern Center for Contemporary Art (SECCA) in Winston-Salem, North Carolina. After traveling unremarked through Los Angeles and Pittsburgh, the exhibition landed at the Virginia Museum of Fine Arts in Richmond and closed at the end of January 1989. Nearly two months later, on Palm Sunday, the *Richmond Times-Dispatch* printed a letter complaining about Serrano's piece.

A local member of the AFA clipped the letter and sent it to the group's leader, the Reverend Donald Wildmon, who then used the AFA newsletter to mobilize a protest. The exhibit had been funded by the Equitable Life Assurance Society, the Rockefeller Foundation, and the National Endowment for the Arts. Equitable reported getting forty thousand letters. Wildmon himself wrote to every member of Congress, enclosing a reproduction of *Piss Christ*.

This Cibachrome print of a wood and plastic crucifix submerged in the artist's urine was one of a series the artist made with bodily fluids. I've always thought the intention was to make something beautiful from what's usually hidden or repellant. Without his titles, the fluids would not even be noticed. *Milk, Blood* (1986), for example, looks like a minimalist painting, a red rectangle next to a white one. Is it possible to challenge the meaning of such loaded symbols? To see them as abstractions? Had the crucifix in *Piss Christ* really been defiled? Or had the urine been sanctified? These are an artist's questions. Wildmon saw only sacrilege.

He would target David within the year.

Before 1989, however, Wildmon had devoted himself to policing pop culture. He began organizing advertiser boycotts in the late 1970s, going after television programs he considered morally reprehensible—*Three's Company* and *Charlie's Angels*, for example. In 1988, he organized the attacks on Martin Scorsese's *The Last Temptation of Christ*, from picket lines in front of theaters to a massive letter-writing campaign. (He claimed he sent some three million letters to his Christian supporters.) Pepsi canceled a commercial featuring Madonna after Wildmon took offense at her "Like a Prayer" video and threatened a boycott. Now, in the art world, he was about to uncover a rich new mother lode of sinners, not to mention fundraising possibilities for the AFA. I don't mean to suggest that Wildmon went at his work cynically, however. He sincerely believed that the country was teeming with anti-Christian bias. He concluded his letter about Serrano with the words: "Maybe, before the physical persecution of Christians begins, we will gain the courage to stand against such bigotry. I hope so."

On May 18, Senator Alfonse D'Amato, a Republican from New York, rose to announce to the Senate that for several weeks he'd been getting letters, phone calls, and postcards about an artwork by Andres Serrano. D'Amato then dramatically ripped up the catalog for the "Awards in the Visual Arts" exhibit and made what would soon become the central conservative argument in the culture war: "If this is what contemporary art has sunk to, this level, this outrage, this indignity—some may want to sanction that, and that is fine. But not with the use of taxpayer's money. This is not a question of free speech. This is a question of abuse of taxpayers' money." He and twenty-two other senators sent a letter to the NEA demanding changes in procedure "to prevent such abuses from recurring." One of the signatories, North Carolina Republican Jesse Helms, also addressed the Senate that day to denounce Serrano. "He is not an artist. He is a jerk. And he is taunting the American people."

David hadn't seen his aunt Helen from Michigan since he was about five years old. That spring Helen Wojnarowicz drove to New Jersey to visit David's brother, Steven, for the first and only time in her life. Pat flew over from Paris. It was shaping up to be a kind of family reunion.

David had planned to be part of it. Then he informed Steven that he was going to confront Aunt Helen and tell her that she had allowed them to be beaten. He was going to tell her he was gay and that he had AIDS.

"And I said to him, you're not going to do that. Then don't come," Steven said. "Do that on your own. If you want to go to Michigan when they get home, do what you want. But this is my home. I protect people in my home. This is my sanctuary, and I don't want to re-dig the dirt here."

Then David asked Steven if he'd told his two daughters that he was gay.

Steven said, "No, they're children. I don't need to do that right now." His daughters were nine and three years old.

So David said, "Oh, you don't like faggots, huh."

"He was in a rage," Steven recalled. "He scared me when he was that way. He said, 'They have to understand the realities of life.' And I said, 'I want my children to believe in Cinderella and Santa Claus as long as they can. The problem with you and me is that we saw the realities of life too goddamn early.' He said, 'I'm coming down!' I said, 'You're not coming down. You come down, I'm calling the police.'"

At some point, Steven called back and left a message: "Dave, I don't want to end this thing this way. I'm telling you, we're misunderstanding each other. And I think we need an opportunity to get together and talk about it. You're flinging shit at me and I'm flinging shit in defense back at you. . . . I don't want to end the thing with a phone call and say, hey this is it. So I'm asking you, please, let's sit down. Let's see if we can arrange to get together. I love you."

Apparently they did speak on the phone, because Steven left a second message to say, "I think you're right. Probably the best thing is for the two of us to walk away. We're just different people, we've got different views on things, and I don't think we understand each other."

But Steven called a third time and said he thought they should get together and talk. That did not happen. Steven ended up feeling rejected—but so did David. He kept the answering machine tape. He actually considered using it in *ITSOFOMO*. But he didn't.

Tom remembered sitting out on a stoop with David, discussing it. "He thought they didn't want him to come because he would embarrass them in front of these relatives," Tom said. "So he felt they were ashamed of him, and that really set him off."

David and Steven never spoke again.

"I always dreamed that in the end the three of us were going to be together," Steven said. "That we were going to walk through this stuff and get out. But it didn't happen that way."


David was still asymptomatic but he saw the doctor regularly for aerosol pentamidine treatments. He could inhale the same drug that Hujar had had to take intravenously when he came down with *Pneumocystis*, or PCP. By '89, doctors were administering pentamidine in mist form to prevent PCP, and it was relatively effective.

Still, David was very aware of the ticking clock. He wanted to do another cross-country trip, thinking this could be the last time he would ever drive from coast to coast. And it would be.

He'd been calling car-relocation services, but they wanted drivers who would keep to a schedule. David wanted to take his time, maybe take an indirect route, and hit some of his favorite spots. He was able to make it happen when Norman Frisch left the Wooster Group for a job with the Los Angeles Festival and needed someone to drive his car from Boston to L.A.

On May 24, 1989, David took the shuttle to Boston to collect the car. An expense list in the back of his journal indicates that he drove to North Carolina before meandering west. He went back to Graceland to buy Elvis slippers, and sent Judy Glantzman a postcard to complain that they no longer sold them. ("I drove all the way there for that.") He visited Cadillac Ranch outside Amarillo and the National Atomic Museum and the Rattlesnake Museum in Albuquerque. He went back to Meteor Crater. He told Glantzman in another postcard that he was skipping Monument Valley so he'd have a reason to come back. He loved the Southwest. As he once said in a postcard to Marion, "This country is so screwed up but the landscape speaks of other things." He was filming images for *ITSOFOMO*. He found fire ants again. One hitched a ride in his camera bag and bit him the next day. But he had the best drive he'd ever had in Arizona. And once he hit California, he headed straight for SeaWorld.

He turned up in Los Angeles a couple of weeks after leaving the East Coast. Frisch had really started to wonder where he was.

On June 8, Representative Dick Armey, a Republican from Texas, sent a letter to the National Endowment for the Arts, signed by more than a hundred members of Congress, criticizing its support for the Robert Mapplethorpe retrospective "The Perfect Moment." What was the agency doing, Armey wondered, to curtail its support of "morally reprehensible trash"? NEA appropriations were coming up for a vote. He gloated that he had only to circulate the Mapplethorpe catalog and he "could blow their budget out of the water!"

On June 12, the Corcoran Gallery of Art in Washington, D.C., canceled the Mapplethorpe retrospective, scheduled to open there July 1. Director Christina Orr-Cahill felt the entire NEA budget was at stake. Besides, she explained, "It would be a three-ring circus in which Mapplethorpe's work would never be looked at in its own right." A small artists' organization, Washington Project for the Arts, stepped in to take the show. The night of June 30, arts supporters demonstrated outside the Corcoran, projecting slides of Mapplethorpe's work on the exterior.

Organized in 1988 at the Philadelphia Institute of Contemporary Art with a thirty thousand dollar grant from the NEA, "The Perfect Moment" had already broken attendance records in Philadelphia and Chicago. Conservative outrage this time gathered around 7 of the 150-plus photographs in the show: 2 of children with their genitals exposed and 5 documenting gay male sadomasochism. "The Perfect Moment" would soon become a symbol of everything the far right found wrong with public arts funding—and with art. Senator Jesse Helms declared that Mapplethorpe's work included "explicit homoerotic pornography and child obscenity," and many of the artist's new critics invariably mentioned that he had died of AIDS.

His S-M photos, part of the *X Y Z Portfolios*, were printed relatively small and not hung on the wall. Museumgoers could easily avoid them if they wanted. Mapplethorpe himself had designed a case for these *Portfolios,* which displayed thirty-nine photographs in three rows. Along the top were the *X* pictures (gay S-M), then in the middle the *Y* (flowers), and at the bottom the *Z* (figure studies of black men). Seen together, the pictures inform each other. All of them seem sexual. But all of them can be read, horizontally or vertically, for their compositional elements. Mapplethorpe wanted to see if he could turn pornographic subject matter into art, and most people probably find the *X* pictures far from titillating. Many of them isolate body parts, where pornography tends to show more of the body, if not a whole scenario. Pornography is an aid to sexual fantasy, while the *X* pictures confront the viewer with dispassionate documentation of sexual extremes. As for the two children he photographed, both were with their mothers, friends of Mapplethorpe's, when he took the pictures. He captured the children's unself-consciousness about their bodies. They are pictures of innocence, the opposite of the photos in the *X Portfolio.*

*New York Newsday* published a column in support of Orr-Cahill on June 21 by archconservative Mona Charen headlined "Sex Photo Ban Involved Taste, Not Censorship." Her first sentence: "Robert Mapplethorpe was a photographer and a homosexual." She concluded, "If you take the king's coin, you live by his rules. But their piteous cries of 'censorship' are not moving. No storm troopers are confiscating their work. They have nothing to lose but their subsidies."

David wrote a letter to the editor the next day. "Charen is mistaken if she believes the cancellation was not a form of censorship because there were 'no storm troopers confiscating the work,'" he said. "In the lands of dictatorships there are never billboards or newspaper ads announcing that oppressive policies are in action. It is always taking place in much more subtle ways such as in the guise of 'taste' or 'morality.' At issue here are depictions of some people's sexuality." Certainly David's work—political, emotional—was quite a contrast to Mapplethorpe's formal, depersonalized studies. But both insisted on homoeroticism as a valid subject for art.


David hoped to publish a book of his essays but had taken no step to begin that process. The day Random House editorial assistant Karen Rinaldi saw *Untitled (Hujar Dead)* and then read David's piece in the *Journal of Contemporary Art*, she flipped through the rest of the journal and realized that she was acquainted with one of its editors, John Zinsser. She called him.

When Zinsser then contacted David to try to set up a meeting, he thought David seemed wary. David said he'd always pictured himself publishing with Grove Press, home to his heroes Genet, Burroughs, and Kerouac. Still, he met with Rinaldi, who told him, "I've never been so blown away in my whole life by a piece of writing. What else do you have?" David gave her the pieces he'd published in various tiny magazines like *Cuz* ("Being Queer in America: A Journal of Disintegration") and *Diana's Almanac* ("Losing the Form in Darkness") and *Between C & D* ("Self-Portrait in 23 Rounds").

"I read it and I fell in love with it, and then I brought it to Random House and tried to get somebody to listen to me," Rinaldi said. She worked in the flagship Little Random division, where her job description included answering the phone, reading submissions, and handling permissions. Since she did not have the authority to purchase a manuscript, she had to find someone within Random House to do that. "I wound up really fighting for this book. I remember one of the older editors saying, 'Karen, are you fucking kidding me? You want to publish what? Forget it.' They all thought I was a little bit crazy for bringing in a box of manuscripts from this downtown artist who was writing this sort of hybrid rant about politics and AIDS and art and memoir." Finally she took it to Erroll McDonald, executive editor at Vintage, a Random House imprint that published paperback originals.

"He said, 'You're right—this is amazing stuff,'" said Rinaldi. "And I said, 'I'll build the book with David. Just help me buy this.' I didn't even know what I was doing. It was my first acquisition. And it was *Close to the Knives*."

David would not sign a contract until he finished the book. But it would happen, and he didn't know enough about publishing to appreciate this coup. He told Zinsser that he was disappointed it wouldn't be a hardcover book. And he wasn't sure he trusted Rinaldi, whom he regarded as an "uptown" person. They didn't really connect until somehow the subject of New York Mets center fielder Lenny Dykstra came up. Dykstra was traded to the Phillies that summer, a crushing blow for many Mets fans. "He was a young, butch gorgeous thug," said Rinaldi. "I was just mad about him."

When she mentioned this to David—who was by no means a sports fan—he pulled out his wallet and showed her that he was carrying a worn photo of Lenny Dykstra. "I love him too," he said.


Suddenly he had a lot to do in whatever time remained to him. He planned to devote the rest of the year to writing, to film and photography, and to *ITSOFOMO*. He also had his retrospective to think about. That would open in January 1990.

David had had some time to reflect on what he now called the "self-portrait film" he planned to do with Marion Scemama. Maybe it didn't have to be a document of himself just angry and scared. "I want to treat myself as a third party," he wrote in his journal, "to look at myself from a distance to see what I am made of like what my gestures and existence is so maybe I can find out who I am, what walls I can explode so as to find or further my own distances or to be able to answer the questions that I am silently screaming. Maybe if I achieve the distance thru film I can see myself clearly enough like from the opposite side of the street from where I'm standing and be able to hear those questions see my limits break my chains self imposed or other-wise."

On July 5, David and Marion headed upstate in a rented car. Sylvère Lotringer, a friend of Marion's, had given them the use of his house in the Adirondacks for the month. David brought all his journals, since he also intended to work on his book—which at this point he was calling *A Self-Portrait in 23 Rounds: A Psychic Walkabout*. For the first three days, they were alone and getting along so well that David told her he now thought he could go to Morocco with her. Marion had been born there, and though she also spent parts of her childhood in Uruguay and France, she had lived mostly in Morocco before going to Paris for university.

Three days into their stay, they drove to the Canadian border to pick up Marion's boyfriend, François Pain, a video artist. Then, two Frenchmen turned up, friends of Marion's and Francois's, along with photographer An-dreas Sterzing and his girlfriend. It seemed to be a vacation. But amid visits to a nearby lake, badminton games, boating, and barbecues, David did not really stop working. He would point a video camera at the barbecue while shrieks of laughter came from the lake and he'd spontaneously compose poetic lines as a voice-over: "Sometimes my mind is an automobile but my heart is a prison. Sometimes the stars in sky make my head hurt." He came up with a more successful prose poem one day when a green bug landed on his finger while they were driving and Marion filmed him in the back seat as he said, "I wonder what this little bug does in the world, what his job is. . . . Does the world know it, if it dies? . . . Does something get mis-placed? Do people speak language differently if this bug dies? Does the world get a little lighter in the rotation?" His 1990 photographic piece *What Is This Little Guy's Job in the World* would feature a tiny frog in David's hand, with text that is nearly the same as that spontaneous voiceover.

On the drive back from the Canadian border, they had seen a turtle in the road, rolling because it had been hit by a car. David, who was driving, stopped to pick it up. A bit of its shell was broken. They put it in the pond behind Sylvère's house, and David went out to check on it every day. He was also filming frogs, fish, and spiders.

When Andreas and company departed after a week or so, he left them his 8mm video camera. It could do freeze-frames, split screens, strobe ef-

*David holding a tiny amphibian during the July he spent in the Adirondacks with Marion Scemama and other friends. (Photograph by Marion Scemama)*

fects, and frames within frames. David had never had anything that fancy to work with, and he spent days experimenting with it. "One day we were driving on the road," Marion said, "and David took the camera and started filming with a strobe effect, going from a hand on the steering wheel to the top of a tree, to the white line on the road . . . a series of fragmented views. The soundtrack was live: laughing, conversation, music. . . . Back home at night, we watched on TV what we shot. David's images were beautiful. François turned off the sound and put a song by the Doors on the tape recorder. 'This is the end . . .' The effect was immediate. It didn't look like a vacation movie anymore but like somebody in a car, getting close to a car accident. Just changing the soundtrack turned the shooting into a video piece about death, tension, and emotion. The tone was set. We knew from that moment that everything we would shoot could be used for other purposes. An amazing ballet began between us with the camera going from hand to hand, shooting each other, trying new forms, new feelings and emotions."

One night they put on Patti Smith's *Horses* and Marion told David about the excitement and sexual tension she remembered from riots she'd participated in back in 1970s Paris, how she'd met a guy in a leather jacket and kaffiyeh scarf who'd saved her from the cops by pushing her into a hallway, where they began kissing and almost had sex, listening to the sounds of screaming, running, and confusion outside while the voice of Patti Smith screamed "Horses" from somewhere on an upper floor. David said, "We should stage that."

"He set up a strobe light, put Patti Smith on again, and asked me to dance topless with the energy of a street fight," Marion said. "The piece would be called *Using My Sexual Energy as a Tool to Fight the State Is as Good a Tool as Any Other*. To tell the truth, when I saw the footage, it looked more like a go-go dance than a street fight. I didn't say anything, but a few days later, it was raining, we were stuck in the house, getting bored. On an impulse, I put Patti Smith on, gave David the camera, and asked him to shoot. I called François and asked him to follow me to the garden. We started dancing in the rain, a strange dance between attraction and rejection, violence and love, fighting and sex. At one point, I threw away my T-shirt and François too. We were topless, jumping on each other, rolling on the wet grass, driven by the Patti Smith beat. David's images were exactly what we could expect: ambiguous enough to question what was going on—sex fever or rape?" David would use these images later in *ITSOFOMO*, contrasting violent images of heterosexuality with tender images of homosexual sex.

One night, Marion filmed David reading to the house cat from *The Pictorial Encyclopedia of the Animal Kingdom*. "And this is Aunt Claws," he said, pointing to a photo of a jungle cat. "That's your mommy," he continued, pointing to a leopard. David described the rest of the cat family, the bad one who'd gone to jail, the uncle in Africa, and so on, then turned to the snake pictures ("Don't ever go near these") and the birds ("These are fun to chase around the yard"). The cat on his lap actually looked quite attentive.

"He really lived his dreams and nightmares," Marion said. "I remember when he woke up, he would be completely in his dreams." He recorded a few on audiotape during this stay upstate, most of them violent. One morning at breakfast, after a night of bad dreams, David delivered a long monologue about his desperation and, yes, his anger over what he was facing. Still asymptomatic, he could only wait to see what vicious path the virus would choose. He could do nothing to stop it. Marion suggested they go to the lake and take the boat out. She would film him swimming. Then he would record his monologue and they'd use it as a voice-over with the watery images. "It's like every emotion we would have, we tried to turn it into a piece, so we could control it in a way," she said.

"I remember at one point, I asked David to swim underwater, and I saw images of his body drifting away, with all the deformations that water produces on a body. Now, when I see these images, I think that they express what has become of David, a shapeless form, a liquid, a blade of air, an element of nature. It's not because David was going to die that we were filming, but because these metaphoric images could serve what he wanted to express of his approach to death. We went back home and looked at the footage. After a long silence, he thanked me for the beauty of the images."

The next day, David built a small white house from cardboard and filmed it in the backyard as he began another of his improvisations: "Inside this house, many things go on. Many people, many lives, many personalities. Some of them dream, some of them don't. Some of them fall, some of them rise." And one of them was a little girl whose dreams nobody understood. His final text for the 1990 photographic piece *Inside This House* would closely approximate this. Then he tried to set the house on fire. He couldn't get it to burn. If he had, it might have resembled his early stencil of the burning house. When he could only get smoke to come out the windows, however, he decided that image was beautiful.

One day while David worked outside in the garden, Marion was in her bedroom editing the audiotape they'd recorded during *Silence = Death*, the one where he said things like "How many documentations do you have to have of this sick, dying faggot sitting in a room, going through whatever shit that he's going through." She said of listening to it at that moment, "The fact that he was angry made me laugh. So I went to the window with the tape recorder and I said, 'David, listen, listen.'" She thought he would laugh too and began playing the tape. "But he didn't laugh at all," she said. "He was really angry. Then he said, 'Why did you do that? I was feeling good.'"

She reflected later that this had been a stupid thing to do. They seemed to patch things up. But David never forgot this moment. A couple of years later, when he made notes about his relationship with Marion, that was on the list of grievances: "archives material I never wanted to see—she could deal with it after my death. She played tape loud in garden after I'd begun to unwind—tape of me angry or talking about death. Rejected her."

On July 31, they drove back to Manhattan, five tense hours in the car with no one saying a word except for driving directions. No one wanted to come back, Marion remembered. She went to the loft with David and they made another attempt to film her dancing to Patti Smith's "Horses." But *Using My Sexual Energy as a Tool to Fight the State* would remain unfinished, along with the two other films he began in the Adirondacks, *Howdy Doody Goes for a Drive* and *Teaching a Frog to Dance*.

Marion returned to Paris two days later and did not hear from David. When she finally called him, he told her he did not want to be in touch with her anymore. The relationship did not actually end there, though it would be another year and a half before David and Marion saw each other again.

David composed a long, rambling letter to Marion, probably late that summer or in the fall, but it's undated and he did not send it. The salient line: "I had to make the break between us because of the point we reach over and over again that ends up feeling very confusing for me." He was trying to figure it out for himself as well as explain it to her.

Artist Manuela Filiaci remembered having David and Marion over for dinner, remembered how they fought. Since Filiaci lived on the ninth floor and the elevator was broken, she could hear them screaming at each other all the way down the stairs. That was earlier in the eighties, not on this visit, but the pattern didn't change. "There was a deep attachment to each other," Filiaci said, "but when some kind of love or attraction is not consummated, there is so much tension." She observed that Marion would get too close; she had no boundaries. And David could be so touchy. "Unless he knew that you really were on his side, he would get so angry," she said. "I think he really cared for Marion, but at the same time he wanted to tear her away. This strange relationship obviously that started with his mother. This love and hate."

Commenting on David's long history of close relationships with women—not just Marion, but also Kiki Smith, Judy Glantzman, Karen Finley, Marguerite Van Cook, and others—Filiaci said, "I think he wanted a woman to love him."

David discussed his relationship with Marion in therapy and finally came up with a letter in January 1990 that he did send:

> Marion, I don't understand everything that is there between us in terms of the place we go where I feel very confused and uncertain about both our needs. I thought at some point it was the intensity of our relationship and that somewhere emotional needs can't connect because of our sexualities. We have talked about this before candidly and I know your feelings on the subject—I can and have accepted your feelings that it doesn't exist with any seriousness in your feelings. I still get things from my [therapist] that there are issues of sexuality that we carry on some level maybe unconscious that end up in confrontations in order to resolve pressures. I don't know what I feel about these interpretations but I also don't know why we hit the same area over again—it is for me a place too confusing and painful to want to chance reliving again and again. . . . I am at a point mentally where I can't take on certain things. I feel a serious and sometimes dark thing that I can't explain to anyone. And I have been dealing with so many things that make that feeling grow larger. And I fear taking on anything more if it contains built-in confusion. So that is why I have stepped back.

His mother had sent him a letter on July 4, 1989, which he probably did not receive until he returned from upstate. It was her first since writing in 1988 to say that she worried they would lose touch.

Evidently he had told her in a letter that he'd started therapy, because she said that she was glad to hear it. And she wanted to tell him something she wasn't sure he wanted to hear: "I am very sorry you have had to experience the terrible things in your childhood. I know how deeply it affected you and I wish with my whole heart and being that it could have been different for you." She regretted not being stronger back then, better able to handle the difficulties she'd faced.

At this point David was at work on the Biographical Dateline for his retrospective's catalog. He regarded it as "a heavy document," knew it probably had mistakes "in terms of timing"—and what if his mother saw it? Apart from writing that she'd encouraged him to paint and draw and that she'd been friends with a woman who had a mentally handicapped son, he had rendered her invisible during the Hell's Kitchen years, "because I can't begin to touch that stuff," he told me. "And if she made it through something and is actually healthier now, I wouldn't want to contribute to unhinging that."

He worried about her. "That's the crux of the problem I have, something that's never been resolved and that I've always carried," he said. "Even through all the weird brutal stuff and the disconnectedness and her lack of care. I've never fully given her the responsibility for what she did because of everything in her background. From what I witnessed, it was an extraordinary amount of pain that she lived with. Also, I can feel the anger after years of blocking it. It's one of the reasons I can't see her. It's too loaded. It's embarrassing to have such a mixture of feelings. I love her somewhere. She did wonderful things despite all the horror in various shades. She really, really encouraged anything creative out of me. Went out on very little money and bought supplies early on. She recently got a license to teach. Did she change? Did she get healthy? I have no idea, yet I don't want to get close enough to find out."

He also knew that he had to tell her soon about his AIDS diagnosis. By the end of 1989, he figured he probably had a year to live, maybe two. He drafted a letter to her that fall:

Mom, I have a lot of mixed feelings towards my relationship with you—I am caught between the understanding of what problems you carried from your experiences with your family and with Ed and also with dealing with three kids, and the experiences of what I carried as a kid. There is no immediate answer for any of those things; I just have so much buried inside me that is scary to touch and at the same time I'm trying to reach it when I am in therapy. I don't feel very healthy mentally although given what my life has been I am doing okay. I've hesitated telling you about this diagnosis because I need the privacy and distance right now. I'm not sure when I will feel ready to get together with you because it feels so loaded with things I haven't been able to resolve. I do think of you and always hope for the best for your life and whatever things you are trying to do.

He did not send this letter.

His community continued to disintegrate. His old friend Luis Frangella—who'd worked alongside him at the Ward Line Pier, who taught him so much about how to paint, who took him to Argentina, who got him a show in Madrid—was ill with AIDS by sometime in '89. The musician and painter Keiko Bonk, who was close to Frangella, remembered seeing David at the hospital. "Luis wanted to die in Argentina," Bonk said, "but the family [let us know] that he couldn't come back because there were no facilities at that time. Nobody was treating AIDS patients. It was really heart-wrenching." By the end of '89, Frangella's former boyfriend Russell Sharon had returned to New York to care for him at home.

David never wanted to be identified as an "AIDS artist" but felt compelled to respond to the devastation around him. After returning from the month upstate, he began to collaborate on a project with Phil Zwickler, the line producer on *Silence = Death*. Zwickler, a writer, an activist, and a film-maker, was probably best known for his documentary *Rights and Reactions*, about the struggle in 1986 to pass a gay rights bill in New York City. David and Zwickler had met during ACT UP's City Hall demonstration. Zwickler also had AIDS.

They decided to make a series of short videotapes titled *Fear of Disclosure: The Psycho-Sexual Implications of HIV Revelation*. They planned to make five of them, exploring the ramifications of admitting to HIV-positive status in five different situations.

In the first, probably made in August '89, a man tells a potential sexual partner. Zwickler relates a story about someone calling him in response to a personal ad. He works the conversation around to asking, "Would you have sex with someone who was HIV positive?" That was done as a voice-over against images of two men dancing shirtless in gold lamé shorts intercut with David's imagery of a spinning globe lit from within and a brain with a clock embedded in it. David and Zwickler described this segment as "Go-Go boys from New York's Pyramid Club bump and grind while sizing up each other's mortality." It's about five minutes long, and they finished it in time for the Gay and Lesbian Experimental Film Festival in mid-September.

The other tapes in the series would cover telling yourself, telling your family, telling your boss, and telling the world. They completed a script for "Telling Yourself," a dialogue between them about the various emotions they felt upon learning they had the virus, their medications, their confusion. They recorded one of the sessions in which they worked on this script, and David sounds very testy. "You had me cross that out on my master copy. Now you say you want it," he complains. "Man, you gotta learn how to fuckin' communicate."

"It didn't take much for them to fight," said Norman Frisch, who occasionally went to dinner or to some event with the two of them. "They were both hotheads, and they pushed each other's buttons. One time out of three, our get-togethers ended in some fight between them, and then a week later, they would have made up."

David and Zwickler planned to each create their own images for "Telling Yourself." As they explained in a memo, "One narrator looks to nature to project and dispel many of the fears he experiences. The other is angry and looks at the streets of NYC as the metaphor for the expression of these feelings." The "angry" one wrote an "image script" for himself that included Times Square, "medicine bottles superimposed on kissing faces," ants crawling on money, Bowery life, gears, and so on. Some of these images he already had from *A Fire in My Belly* and other films. The rest were never shot.

Zwickler may have filmed his part, though "Telling Yourself" was never completed. He was already in poor health. In February 1990, Zwickler developed *Pneumocystis* on his retina. (It usually manifested, of course, in the lungs.) He gradually began to go blind. He then made a six-and-a-half-minute film called *Needle Nightmare*—his monologue about subsequent symptoms, infections, and excruciating treatments paired with the bucolic nature footage that he found so comforting.

They never got started on the other sections of *Fear of Disclosure*. In autumn '89, right after finishing the first videotape, David began writing an essay about the epidemic. Photographer Nan Goldin was curating a show at Artists Space and asked him to contribute a piece to the modest catalog. Artists Space, a major nonprofit arts organization, characterized the exhibition as "a personal reflection on the influence AIDS has had on aesthetics, culture and sexuality among Goldin's peers in the Lower East Side community." Goldin decided to call it "Witnesses: Against Our Vanishing." David's catalog essay "Postcards from America: X-Rays from Hell" would turn him into a public figure.

**The politicians who** opposed arts funding were often the same people who opposed AIDS funding.

Senator Jesse Helms and the California Republican congressman William Dannemeyer were both virulently, self-righteously homophobic. Both fought bitterly against spending a single government dollar on AIDS research, AIDS prevention, or AIDS treatment. Helms masterminded the law that banned people with HIV from entering the country. Dannemeyer backed a California ballot initiative to quarantine people with AIDS—it failed—and he once declared that PWAs emitted spores "known to cause birth defects." In the summer of 1989, Dannemeyer outraged many when he read graphic descriptions of gay sex into the Congressional Record, an effort to alert his colleagues to "what homosexuality really is." He was about to publish A Shadow in the Land, his book attacking the gay rights movement. In 1987, the Senate had adopted a Helms amendment (pushed through the House of Representatives by Dannemeyer) that prohibited the use of federal funds for any AIDS education materials that could "promote or encourage, directly or indirectly, homosexual activities." Donald Francis, a pioneer in AIDS research who was later AIDS adviser to the state of California, called their efforts "truly damaging" in preventing the spread of the virus.

Dannemeyer supported all efforts to defund the NEA, after failing in his bid to rewrite its authorizing legislation so that Congress would have "oversight" of choices made by grantees. He was not leading the House effort to kill the agency, though, leaving that to a fellow Orange County, California, conservative—Representative Dana Rohrabacher. Helms, however, spearheaded the anti-NEA charge in the Senate. That September, he cooked up an amendment aimed at preventing the likes of Andres Serrano and

Robert Mapplethorpe from ever getting another grant. Attached to the 1990 appropriations bill, his amendment outlawed the use of federal money to "promote, disseminate or produce obscene or indecent materials, including but not limited to depictions of sadomasochism, homoeroticism, the exploitation of children, or individuals engaged in sexual acts; or material which denigrates the objects or beliefs of the adherents of a particular religion or nonreligion." Helms got this passed in the Senate by calling for a voice vote when only a few senators were present. But it did not pass in the House.

In late September, the Senate and House conference committee met to work out a compromise. Helms threatened his Senate colleagues with a roll call vote if they dropped his amendment, to get them on the record "as favoring taxpayer funding for pornography." He made good on his threat that very evening, attaching his original amendment to a military spending bill, then directing all pages (who are high school juniors) and all "ladies" to leave the room. He whipped out the Mapplethorpe photos and distributed them around the Senate chamber. Other senators didn't seem cowed. One Republican even pointed out that both Mark Twain and Chaucer would be unacceptable under the Helms amendment.

But content restrictions were on the table to stay. The conference committee simply came up with a modified version of the Helms amendment. Funds could not be used for anything the NEA thought obscene, "including but not limited to depictions of sadomasochism, homoeroticism, the sexual exploitation of children, or individuals engaged in sex acts which do not have serious literary, artistic, political or scientific value." The NEA added this language—known in the arts community as "the loyalty oath"—to its terms and conditions for grant winners. The culture war was just beginning.

"Witnesses: Against Our Vanishing" was a landmark show, among the first to focus solely on artists' personal responses to the AIDS crisis. It had been scheduled to coincide with the first-ever Day Without Art, on December 1, 1989, a day of action and mourning over the epidemic that would be observed in arts institutions all over the country.

In her statement for the catalog, photographer Nan Goldin wrote that when she got out of rehab in 1988, she wanted to reconnect with friends she'd lost touch with during what she called "my last few years of isolation and destruction." Goldin had been so wrapped up in her addictions that she'd paid little attention to the advancing plague. Once she was clean, though, she felt overwhelmed by how many of the people she loved or admired were now sick, grieving, or dead. When Artists Space invited her to curate a show, she saw a chance to give these friends a forum. Certainly by 1989, everyone who'd been part of the downtown scene knew someone who was dead or dying or both. This was a traumatized community.

David had *Untitled (Hujar Dead)* in this show, along with the three photographs of Hujar (face, hand, foot) he had silk-screened into that piece, and four prints from *The Sex Series*. For the catalog, he contributed a photo not in the show, a picture of some graffiti that reads, "Fight AIDS. Kill a quere [sic]."

Kiki Smith's piece featured figures of many naked women and some babies silk-screened onto muslin, in memory of all the sisters "disappeared by AIDS," as she put it. The plight of HIV-positive women had gotten relatively little attention at this point, and her sister Bebe had died of AIDS in 1988.

Styles ranged from that to Vittorio Scarpati's cartoons drawn in the hospital, where he spent months after his lungs collapsed from *Pneumocystis*. If any type of art predominated in "Witnesses," it was portraits, both paintings and photographs. Goldin included some Hujar portraits in the show, for example. Philip-Lorca diCorcia contributed a photo of Scarpati looking spectral in his hospital bed, like he was literally fading, while the bandages covering much of his bare chest and festive balloons hanging from an IV stand look more permanent. Married to Goldin's old friend Cookie Mueller, Scarpati died on September 14, 1989, at the age of thirty-four.

There wasn't much nudity in *Witnesses*, apart from the Kiki Smith piece, Dorit Cypis's photo installation with nude female body parts, and Mark Morrisroe's enlarged Polaroids of naked men. None of this was pornographic, none of it obscene. Indeed the most shocking thing in the show was a description Morrisroe wrote of his treatment in the hospital (reprinted in the catalog), about how he had "smashed the vase of flowers Pat Hearn sent me so I would have something to mutilate myself with by carving in my leg 'evening nurses murdered me.'" Friends with Goldin since art school, Morrisroe had died of AIDS that summer at the age of thirty. In his last portrait, he looks sixty.

Goldin wanted an essay for the catalog from her friend Cookie, the writer, actress, and quintessential free spirit Goldin had been photographing since 1976. But Cookie also had AIDS, and by the summer of 1989, she was walking with a cane and had lost her ability to speak. (Goldin's last photo of Cookie alive was taken at Scarpati's funeral about two months before *Witnesses* opened.) The catalog reprinted a piece Cookie wrote earlier for *City Lights Review*. Half of it was devoted to the last letter she ever received from her best friend, Gordon Stevenson, the no-wave filmmaker (*Ecstatic Stigmatic*) and bass player for Teenage Jesus and the Jerks who died of AIDS in 1982. Stevenson felt that the illness was punishment for being different, for being a "high-risker." For her part, Cookie advised, "Watch closely who is being stolen from us. . . . Each friend I've lost was an extraordinary person, not just to me, but to hundreds of people who knew their work and their fight. These were the kind of people who lifted the quality of all our lives, their war was against ignorance, the bankruptcy of beauty, and the truancy of culture. . . . They tried to make us see."

When Goldin sent David a description of what would be in the show, she added a handwritten note: "I'm so happy you've agreed to write a piece for the catalogue. . . . As for how you want to approach this, it's up to you."

David had begun taking AZT, though it often made him vomit. He still had no opportunistic infections (like *Pneumocystis*). But he knew that it was time to write an essay dealing with his own mortality. As always, he would then step back to look at the context, the landscape devastated by plague—and this time, he would name some villains.

But he began by talking about a friend who'd dropped by unexpectedly, who sat at the kitchen table trying to find language for what he was going through now that his T-cell count had dropped to thirty. David wrote:

My friend across the table says, "There are no more people in their thirties. We're all dying out. One of my four best friends just went into the hospital yesterday and he underwent a blood transfusion and is now suddenly blind in one eye. The doctors don't know what it is . . ." My eyes are still scanning the table; I know a hug or a pat on the shoulder won't answer the question mark in his voice. The AZT is kicking in with one of its little side effects: increased mental activity which in translation means I wake up these mornings with an intense claustrophobic feeling of fucking doom. It also means that one word too many can send me to the window kicking out panes of glass, or at least that's my impulse. . . . The rest of my life is being unwound and seen through a frame of death. And my anger is more about this culture's refusal to deal with mortality. My rage is really about the fact that WHEN I WAS TOLD THAT I'D CONTRACTED THIS VIRUS IT DIDN'T TAKE ME LONG TO REALIZE THAT I'D CONTRACTED A DISEASED SOCIETY AS WELL.

That passage, with its angry desperation, sets the tone. He wrote of how he resisted being comforted, of his need to witness, of his tendency to sometimes forget the disease for whole hours, of the inadequacy of memorials, of trying to "lift off the weight of the pre-invented world," of how important it was to see his reality represented in the culture—on gallery walls, at least.

He also wrote one sentence fantasizing about the deaths of Helms and Dannemeyer: "At least in my ungoverned imagination, I can fuck somebody without a rubber, or I can, in the privacy of my own skull, douse Helms with a bucket of gasoline and set his putrid ass on fire or throw Congressman William Dannemeyer off the empire state building." Elsewhere, referring to the attacks on Mapplethorpe, Serrano, and the NEA, David called Helms "the repulsive senator from zombieland."

He devoted an entire paragraph to local villain Cardinal John O'Connor. The cardinal's name came up frequently among queer activists and at ACT UP meetings. He opposed safe-sex education and preached against condom use. He had representatives on the New York City Board of Education's AIDS advisory committee, where they lobbied to stop all sex education and AIDS education in public schools. He served on Reagan's know-nothing

Presidential Commission on the HIV Epidemic. He prohibited the gay Catholic group Dignity from holding Mass in any church in the diocese; when Dignity members protested by standing in silence during the cardinal's homily at St. Patrick's Cathedral, eleven were arrested, and the cardinal banned them from ever entering the cathedral again. O'Connor fought vigorously against the passage of any legislation guaranteeing civil rights to gay people. He was also strident in his opposition to reproductive freedom for women. While at work on his essay, David read an article in the paper about O'Connor's wish to join Operation Rescue in blocking abortion clinics.

David wrote, "This fat cannibal from the house of walking swastikas up on fifth avenue should lose his church-exempt status and pay taxes retroactively for the last couple of centuries. . . . This creep in black skirts has kept safer-sex information off the local television stations and mass transit spaces for the last eight years of the AIDS epidemic therefore helping thousands and thousands to their unnecessary deaths."

The comments on all three villains would soon be extracted from his 3,700-word piece and excoriated, but he had no reason at the beginning of October to anticipate trouble. Goldin loved the essay. And he had other things to do.

In autumn 1989, David had distractions at home to deal with almost daily. He lived above what had once been one of the great Yiddish theaters, a space the landlord began converting that year into a multiplex. In June, the theater roof collapsed, but most of the irritations suffered by tenants were less spectacular: no lights in the hallway, phone cables cut, interruptions to electrical service, severe leaks, drilling and loud tapping during daylight hours.

The tenants had been keeping a "harassment list" all year, but problems began to intensify in August. For nine days in September, roof demolition created "noise so loud that a normal conversation cannot be heard," the list reported. David got his lawyer involved to try to stop the removal and replacement of the roof. On October 2, the list noted: "Water pouring down D. Wojnarowicz's west wall, down wall in common hall area, and pouring down the stairs." The complaints cited most often were high-decibel noise and leakage.

David wanted to devote the remainder of the year to *ITSOFOMO* and to his upcoming retrospective at Illinois State University. He had a new piece in mind and ideas about the catalog. Barry Blinderman, director of University Galleries, suggested to David that they call the show "Tongues of Flame." He had secured a fifteen-thousand-dollar NEA grant toward the exhibition and catalog.

On October 7, David flew to Bloomington-Normal, the twin cities of central Illinois. He and Blinderman worked on an interview for the catalog, some of it conducted in the car while they drove around town, discussing, for example, the idea Blinderman would eventually use as the interview's title, "The Compression of Time." David said, "You look down there and you see a white car moving by, and now it's gone; the fraction of time that the action inhabited is so brief that all we can do is carry the traces of memory of it. That's what life is. Every minute, we pick up the traces of what just happened; perception and thought and memory are continuous, and yet somehow we make these delineations or these borders between what's acceptable and what's not. Time is not something that's set to a strobic beat. For instance, if you're in a place where violence is occurring—possibly occurring to yourself—time takes on a totally different quality than it would be if you were in an introspective quiet place. Time expands and contracts constantly, and yet we set it to a meter which is completely unreal." Since David was staying with him and his family, Blinderman also saw how sick David was, constantly nauseated from AZT. He was in Illinois for a week.

Back in New York, David asked Jean Foos to design his catalog. She'd just become art director at *Artforum*, but they'd been acquainted since the early East Village days. She'd painted at the pier, she'd introduced him to Keith Davis, and her boyfriend was Dirk Rowntree, one of the few people David was still in touch with from the seventies. David explained that he would be giving her a painting in lieu of payment.

He knew what he wanted for the cover—either a photo by George Platt Lynes or an image that would approximate it. Lynes is best known for his erotic male nudes, photographed when such pictures were completely taboo. (He died in 1955). The picture David loved, though, was not a nude but an image of a man's head in profile. The man appears to be screaming. John Erdman and Gary Schneider owned this photo, and David wanted to buy it from them. "He often asked to see it when he came over," said Erdman, who refused to part with the picture. "I don't know if he was going to use this for the cover of the catalog or if he was just going to study it. But whatever coolness happened between us was because of this. He was angry that I wouldn't give it to him."

David then photographed a number of people standing in strong red and blue light—just their heads with mouths open, as if screaming. The dancers who would be part of *ITSOFOMO* were all photographed that way, as was Steve Brown. David decided to use the picture of Brown, screaming, on the cover of his catalog. Back in 1985 when David was in the Whitney Biennial, Brown teased him about Robert Hughes's panning of the show in *Time*. (Hughes called David's work "repulsive" and declared that edition of the Biennial to be "the worst in living memory.") In an interview with Sylvère Lotringer, Brown recalled telling David that he couldn't wait for the day when *Time* had David's face on the cover with the caption "Misfit or Messiah." David thought Brown was making fun of him, and said he was putting his face on the catalog to get back at him.

David also began work with Foos on a new piece that would appear in the catalog but not hang on the wall in Normal, a school photo of himself as a boy, surrounded by type. "One day this kid will get larger," the text begins. "One day this kid will feel something stir in his heart and throat and mouth. . . . One day politicians will enact legislation against this kid. One day families will give false information to their children and each child will pass that information down generationally to their families and that information will be designed to make existence intolerable for this kid."

This would become one of David's best-known, most widely distributed works, translated into German—he hoped to get it into other languages as well—and also presented with a little girl at the center. Critic Maurice Berger remembered encountering it in a show in 1990. "The juxtaposition of freckle-faced, jug-eared innocence with the poisonous reality of homophobia moved me deeply," Berger wrote. "And while I have been 'out' for almost a

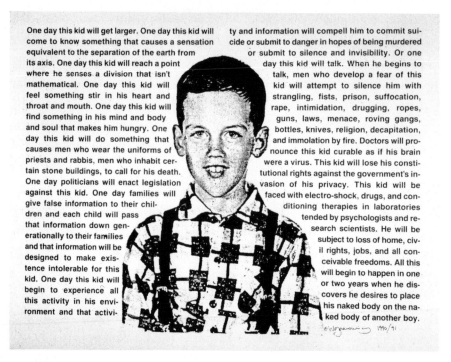

One day this kid will get larger. One day this kid will come to know something that causes a sensation equivalent to the separation of the earth from its axis. One day this kid will reach a point where he senses a division that isn't mathematical. One day this kid will feel something stir in his heart and throat and mouth. One day this kid will find something in his mind and body and soul that makes him hungry. One day this kid will do something that causes men who wear the uniforms of priests and rabbis, men who inhabit certain stone buildings, to call for his death. One day politicians will enact legislation against this kid. One day families will give false information to their children and each child will pass that information down generationally to their families and that information will be designed to make existence intolerable for this kid. One day this kid will begin to experience all this activity in his environment and that activity and information will compel him to commit suicide or submit to danger in hopes of being murdered or submit to silence and invisibility. Or one day this kid will talk. When he begins to talk, men who develop a fear of this kid will attempt to silence him with strangling, fists, prison, suffocation, rape, intimidation, drugging, ropes, guns, laws, menace, roving gangs, bottles, knives, religion, decapitation, and immolation by fire. Doctors will pronounce this kid curable as if his brain were a virus. This kid will lose his constitutional rights against the government's invasion of his privacy. This kid will be faced with electro-shock, drugs, and conditioning therapies in laboratories tended by psychologists and research scientists. He will be subject to loss of home, civil rights, jobs, and all conceivable freedoms. All this will begin to happen in one or two years when he discovers he desires to place his naked body on the naked body of another boy.

*Untitled [One day this kid . . .], 1990. Gelatin-silver print, 30 × 40 inches. (Courtesy of the Estate of David Wojnarowicz and P·P·O·W Gallery, New York)*

decade, the work helped me to accept a part of my queer self that I had never before owned: the gay-bashed, self-hating kid who struggled to survive."

David's essay "Postcards from America: X-Rays from Hell" had been typeset while he was in Illinois. On October 17, Susan Wyatt, executive director at Artists Space, looked at the galleys for the "Witnesses" catalog and read his piece for the first time. She was alarmed. Artists Space had received an NEA grant of ten thousand dollars toward the exhibition and catalog. (The total budget for "Witnesses" stood at thirty thousand dollars.) Wyatt now anticipated difficulties because of the new Helms amendment. She also worried that the essay could be libelous. Artists Space had never even published a catalog piece that used four-letter words. Wyatt felt that she had to protect the organization, but she also wanted to protect the NEA. As she put it later in her written account of this incident: "It's an incredible responsibility when you realize the whole future of the public funding of art has come to rest on your shoulders." That's what she felt was at stake.

She sent the "Postcards" essay to a lawyer on the Artists Space board. Then she called David Bancroft, the NEA program specialist responsible for the grant, and asked if they could change their award letter to state that NEA money would fund the exhibition only—not the catalog. She already had a five-thousand-dollar grant from the Mapplethorpe Foundation and could allocate that money to the catalog. Bancroft didn't think there'd be a problem with that, but said he would call her back.

Meanwhile, the lawyer on her board advised her to get David to take out the names of Helms, Dannemeyer, and O'Connor. He could just say "government officials." But Wyatt realized after a "difficult" first phone call with David that there was no way in hell he would do that.

According to Nan Goldin, Wyatt also called her. "She asked me to censor," said Goldin. "I talked to David. He said he refused to censor. She read me the lines she wanted censored. 'The fat fucking cannibal in black skirts.' The only thing he agreed to do was to take 'fucking' out. And I quickly became aligned with him. First, she talked to me and tried to get me aligned with her. And I didn't initially understand why it was so important to David to keep those lines in. But then of course I supported him a hundred percent."

Wyatt did not recall asking Goldin to contact David, but said, "I tried to keep Nan in the loop. She did get to be very difficult. She got very angry at me." Goldin was still based in Watertown, Massachusetts, near the hospital where she'd recovered, and was commuting to New York. But Connie Butler, who'd just taken a curator job at Artists Space, remembered her as "a really forceful presence. She was very emotional and trying to be protective of the artists and of David."

When David later typed up notes for himself labeled "NEA—Artists Space Flap," he recounted his first couple of conversations with Wyatt this way: "Susan Wyatt calls to ask that I change certain things I refuse she asks disclaimers I refuse she says [Artists Space] will do disclaimers—she tells me her lawyer asks me to sign liability waver in case of lawsuits—I say send it to me."

David went to the Center for Constitutional Rights, where he was advised that the cardinal could sue over the assertion that he'd suppressed safe-sex information. But if the cardinal did that, the CCR would defend David pro bono. He then signed Artists Space's liability waiver, assuming financial responsibility for all "losses, liabilities, damages, and settlements" resulting from his essay.

Wyatt spent the next few days trying to determine whether the NEA would even want credit for funding "Witnesses." Goldin had commissioned new work from some of the artists, but nothing had come in yet, so Wyatt wasn't sure what would be in the show. She speculated that some of it could be sexually explicit. When she couldn't get an answer from NEA staff, she decided to go ahead with crediting the agency—usually standard practice—on the outgoing press releases.

On October 24, NEA program specialist David Bancroft called Wyatt to confirm that she could change the award letter, deleting the catalog from what would be funded. He advised her to simply revise her budget and to formalize the change in writing. (He later called this "Susan's interpretation of our conversation.")

On October 25, Wyatt was in Washington to meet the new NEA chairman, John Frohnmayer, with a delegation from the National Association of Artists' Organizations. Frohnmayer had held the job for three weeks. Now, briefed on Wyatt's queries, he asked to have a word with her in private. Later, when he too wrote an account of all this, he said he did not know at that point that she wanted to excise the catalog funding from the grant, while Wyatt maintains that she told him that day. (Her letter formalizing that change did not arrive at the Endowment until November 7.) Frohnmayer then asked her to remove NEA credit from the catalog and to print a disclaimer. She decided that was only fair. She'd already included a disclaimer on behalf of Artists Space, stating that the organization and its board "may not necessarily agree with all the statements made here."

At this point, no one at the NEA had seen the art to be exhibited. So, on October 30, Frohnmayer sent Drew Oliver, director of the NEA's museum program, to New York to look at slides of the work selected by Goldin and to obtain a copy of the catalog text. Artists Space still didn't have all the work. Before Oliver arrived, Wyatt had gone through the material they did have with the lawyer on her board, who said that the only image that might be problematic was a Hujar photo of a naked baby and advised that they track down the parents. Then Oliver arrived to have a look. Wyatt described him as "pleasant" and "unsurprised by everything." However, that wasn't what Frohnmayer conveyed in his book about running the agency, *Leaving Town Alive*. Oliver "reported back that the images were clearly explicit (that is, they whacked you between the eyes so you wouldn't miss the point), reflected anger toward society about AIDS, and had some nudity," wrote Frohnmayer. "Drew thought that a disclaimer was necessary, because the material was cruder and potentially more problematic than Mapplethorpe's photos."

Frohnmayer called Wyatt just hours after Oliver left Artists Space to request that the Endowment's name be disassociated not just from the catalog but also from the whole of "Witnesses." He wanted both the removal of the credit line from all signage and future press releases and a disclaimer stating, "The opinions, findings and recommendations included herein do not reflect the view of the National Endowment for the Arts." Wyatt thought that was like saying, we don't approve of this show, which we had nothing to do with. It didn't make sense to her, so she refused. But she tried to work out some new disclaimer language that Frohnmayer would accept.

On November 2, she called him with her counterproposal, and Frohnmayer asked her to voluntarily relinquish the grant. She said she would have to consult her board. Frohnmayer then decided that "not acting, particularly when Susan Wyatt had dumped this steaming, writhing mess on my desk, would be a declaration of weakness." So the next day, when Wyatt was again in Washington for a meeting, he had the NEA legal counsel hand her a letter declaring that "certain texts, photographs and other representations in the exhibition may offend the language of the FY 1990 Appropriation Act"—in other words, the Helms amendment. Frohnmayer acknowledged that the grant for "Witnesses" was made in fiscal year 1989 and therefore not subject to the amendment, but, he wrote, "Given our recent review, and the current political climate, I believe that the use of Endowment funds to exhibit or publish this work is in violation of the spirit of the Congressional directive. . . . On this basis, I believe that the Endowment's funds may not be used to exhibit or publish this material. Therefore Artists Space should relinquish the Endowment's grant for the exhibition." In addition, he asked

Artists Space to "employ the following disclaimer in appropriate ways," for example, on all its press material: "The National Endowment for the Arts has not supported this exhibition or its catalog." The Artists Space board met on November 7 to vote unanimously not to relinquish the grant. Not voluntarily, at least. They hadn't yet received a penny of it.

David, meanwhile, knew nothing of these machinations. He'd signed the waiver accepting financial responsibility for any "damages" caused by his essay, and he thought that was the end of it.

On Monday, November 6, the *Los Angeles Times* broke the story that the NEA wanted its grant money back. The exhibition was "said to include homoerotic sexually explicit pictures and text materials that criticize a variety of public officials." David was not named, nor was he aware of this story appearing in Los Angeles.

So he was blindsided on Tuesday when he got a call from the *New York Daily News*. Was he aware, a reporter asked, that the NEA was about to rescind a grant for the "Witnesses" show because of his essay? The ostensible reason, said the reporter, was that "it's too political." The reporter asked, what's in your essay? David spoke to him at length but would not give him the inflammatory "cannibal" sound bite. Later that night, Susan Wyatt called him. "She tells me not to speak to press—keep focus on show," he wrote in his summary of events. "I relate reporters remarks mention *LA Times* story she says story is untrue none of it has anything to do with my writing—it's the show itself maybe erotic stuff." Wyatt points out that if she said this, it was because she assumed that the NEA had accepted her proposal to separate the catalog from the grant. Therefore the catalog could not be the problem.

That same night, the city elected a new mayor, David Dinkins, first African American to hold that office. The next morning, November 8, David went out to buy a *Daily News*, thinking that certainly that story would overwhelm a little item about an art exhibit. He was shocked to see that the *Daily News* had done a wraparound supplement on the election and beneath that was the regular front page, blaring "CLASH OVER AIDS EXHIBIT." The story quoted Susan Wyatt saying that she'd alerted the NEA, concerned that Jesse Helms "might not particularly like the artwork." Then the piece described David's "photo essay," conflating *The Sex Series* with the "Postcards" essay. "His photos include heterosexual and homosexual acts with accompanying text that describes O'Connor as a 'fat cannibal in a black skirt' and rips the Catholic Church's stance forbidding teaching about safe sex practices," the story said. (The misquote of the "cannibal" line indicates that this reporter did not have the essay but probably had a source inside the NEA.) The only quote from David was "I understand the gallery's fear. But if the grants have already been given out, is the law now also retroactive?"

That day, Frohnmayer issued a statement announcing that he would withhold payment of the grant to Artists Space: "What had been presented to the Endowment by the Artists Space application was an artistic exhibition. We find, however, in reviewing the material now to be exhibited, that a large portion of the content is political rather than artistic in nature." This statement did not mention David or any other artist by name. Nor did it mention the catalog. But when a reporter from the *New York Times* called him, Frohnmayer declared, "There are specific derogatory references in the show to Senator Helms, Congressman Dannemeyer and Cardinal O'Connor which makes it political." When Wyatt spoke to the reporter, she clarified that these references were not in the show, just in the catalog—"strong statements written by the photographer David Wojnarowicz."

When that story ran on November 9, the show hadn't even been installed, and the catalog, if printed, was not yet available. David would not tell the reporters calling him what was in the essay. He had started recording his phone calls with them and others apropos the controversy. Phil Zwickler also came by that day and filmed him as he talked on the phone. His emotions ranged from rage to consternation to sorrow. Occasionally Zwickler panned over to the television, where the Berlin Wall was coming down.

Cardinal O'Connor released a statement that day: "Had I been consulted, I would have urged very strongly that the National Endowment not withdraw its sponsorship on the basis of criticism against me personally. I do not consider myself exempt from or above criticism by anyone."

Wyatt called David with the news. She'd been telling the press that she was sure David would be happy about the cardinal's gesture.

"I find his benevolence questionable," he told her. "If he would completely reverse the church's suppression of safer-sex information and

456 // **FIRE IN THE BELLY**

back off from abortion clinics, I would extend my appreciation to this man. But I think it's a political tactic, and I won't be fooled for a second."

Wyatt told him that Senator Daniel Patrick Moynihan, a Democrat from New York, would get up on the floor of the Senate to support Artists Space but had to see David's text first.

David replied, "You think he's going to get up in support of—"

"Yes I do," Wyatt said.

"Those quotes?"

"I do."

"About Jesse Helms?"

"I absolutely, honestly do."

"It's hard for me to fathom," David told her. "They couldn't get behind a bunch of photographs. Why would they get behind something that is more direct?"

Wyatt called him back later that evening to thank him for challenging her. "It helped me," she said. "It made me think about why a politician has to read a text before he can support freedom of speech."


Cookie Mueller died of AIDS on November 10, 1989, at the age of forty.


On Sunday, November 12, the *New York Post*, a right-leaning tabloid owned by Rupert Murdoch, ran an editorial titled "Offensive Art Exhibit"—about the show no one had yet seen. In high dudgeon, the *Post* declared that funding anything that criticized Cardinal O'Connor was like funding work that glorified Hitler. David clipped this and wrote along the edge: "Just one of many articles and editorials distorting issues." Later he used the editorial in a lithograph, printing a voodoo doll on top of it.

On Monday, Frohnmayer told the press that he regretted using the word "political" when describing the problem with the Artists Space grant. His reason, more precisely, was that between the application for the grant and the installation of the show (not yet seen), there'd been "an erosion of the artistic focus."

The next day, conductor and composer Leonard Bernstein informed the White House that, because the NEA had canceled the grant to the "Witnesses" show, he would decline the National Medal of Arts, which he was scheduled to receive that Friday,

Meanwhile, David was getting increasingly frustrated with Artists Space. "Tired of restraint of Susan while bigots speak unrestrained," he wrote in his notes. He thought they should fight the NEA. Legally, they had a case. Wyatt said Artists Space did consider a lawsuit, though she did not mention this to David. The lawyer advising her warned that it could take years and drain the organization's resources. Also, the NEA was an important funder for them.

David hadn't gone into much detail in his essay about what the "fat cannibal" had actually done. He decided he better get the facts out. David went to see Ann Northrop at the Hetrick-Martin Institute, an agency serving LGBT youth. Northrop worked there as an AIDS educator for teenagers in the metropolitan area. She was also very active in ACT UP, which was then planning its Stop the Church action aimed at Cardinal O'Connor and Catholic conservatism. David wanted to talk to Northrup about the campaign against the church, and they had a long conversation. David also consulted with ACT UP compatriots Jim Eigo and Richard Elovich. He then created "The Seven Deadly Sins Fact Sheet" with specific information on the villains—not just O'Connor, Helms, and Dannemeyer but also Mayor Ed Koch and others. He followed that with "Additional Statistics and Facts," much of it about the Catholic Church. As someone who had been a sexually active teen, David was especially incensed about the archdiocese's lobbying against teaching about safe sex in public high schools. As someone who had been a hustler, David was outraged that at Covenant House, the church's safe haven for teenage runaways, residents could not get safe-sex information or condoms.

On Wednesday, November 15, Frohnmayer came to Artists Space to meet with thirty-five members of the arts community, including Nan Goldin and David. He was one of several to read a statement to Frohnmayer. It said, in part:

What is going on here is *not* just an issue that concerns the "art world"; it is not *just* about a bunch of words or images in the "art world" context—it is about the legalized and systematic murder of homosexuals and their legislated silence; it is about the legislated invisibility and silencing of people with AIDS and a denial of the information necessary for those and other people to make informed decisions concerning safety within their sexual activities. . . . I will not personally allow you to step back from your original reason for rescinding the grant, which was that my essay and the show had a political rather than artistic tone. You are now attempting to jump from one position to another . . . hoping to come up with one that sticks. It is obvious that you are in bed with Helms and Dannemeyer, and that your ignorance or agenda, both of which I find appalling, are clearly revealed by your actions.

Frohnmayer was told by others: "You have politicized the NEA." "You are a coward." "You have sold out the artists of this country; you should resign." Near the end of the meeting, David confronted him again, asking, "What do you think of men who love men and women who love women? What do you think of men who have sex with men and women who have sex with women?"

Frohnmayer told him, "I refuse to answer that; that is private." The new chair of the NEA was a former chair of the Oregon Arts Commission and a Portland lawyer. Though appointed by President George H. W. Bush, he was no right-winger. He was more like the new recruit sent to the front, taking a few bullets and endangering those around him. Under Frohnmayer, the NEA began trying to anticipate and parry critiques from the far right—and learned the hard way that there was no appeasing them.

Few on the "art" side of the culture war saw what was beginning here, while the far right found a uniquely exploitable world: skilled professionals making highly charged imagery they could take out of context. The right-wing frothers soon learned that, yes, nuance could be crushed, intimidation would work, and facts did not matter. Right-wing media would get the lies out unchallenged. (Early fomenters of crisis were the Washington Times and the New York City Tribune, both owned by the Reverend Sun Myung Moon's Unification Church.) Meanwhile, the Frohnmayers and Wyatts of the art world thought they could reason with the right, thought truth would change perceptions. They thought this was an episode, not the beginning of a train wreck. But David, with his rebelliousness and his passion and his hair-trigger temperament and his illness, which had made him even more sensitive to the total blockage in society—he got it immediately.

That day at Artists Space, Frohnmayer got his first look at the show, scheduled to open the next day. "It was a bleak and disturbing exhibition," he wrote. "One could find some penises and some scatological language, but the intent was far from prurient. It wasn't as crude as Drew Oliver had described, but more oppressive and hopeless and depressing."

That night David went to Cookie's funeral at St. Mark's Church, an event that went on for hours because so many people wanted to speak about her.

The next day, November 16, Frohnmayer restored the grant, specifying that the money could *not* be used for the catalog. Some fifteen hundred people mobbed Artists Space that evening for the opening of "Witnesses: Against Our Vanishing," while Art Positive, a collective organized to fight homophobia and censorship in the arts, demonstrated against the Helms amendment out on the street.

David did not attend.

Allan Frame, who had photographs in the show, said, "The whole fanfare was about him so I thought, 'Wow—he's not even there.' I went home that night and called him. I'm glad I did. He was just alone at home. Nobody had called." Frame had had little contact with David since directing *Sounds in the Distance.*

But David had considered attending. Phil Zwickler came back to document the day, and David told him he'd been up all night finishing a personal statement about the controversy and "The Seven Deadly Sins Fact Sheet" to slip into the catalogs. He could drop that off before the opening, but realized there might be cameras around that night. He didn't want his face out there. As he told Zwickler, "If a nutcase like Dannemeyer can occupy a position in governing this country, imagine what's walking around the streets."

Besides, he had another statement to finish, this one to the Artists Space board, detailing his distress over its agreement to separate the catalog from the show for funding purposes, thus severing his words from contact with taxpayer dollars. He didn't know that Wyatt had suggested this herself back in October. He thought that Artists Space had given Frohnmayer a way out by agreeing to it. If the board had said no, David wrote in his statement, "[Frohnmayer] would have had no choice but to agree to fund the entire show with catalogue included thus sending a message across the board that we still retain our civil rights and our constitutional rights even in the face of possible loss of funding." He delivered it to Artists Space the next day.

On November 22, conservative columnist Ray Kerrison compared David and his supposed religious bigotry to Louis Farrakhan (leader of the Nation of Islam and a notorious anti-Semite) in the *New York Post*. The same day, in his syndicated column in the *Post*, Patrick Buchanan attacked David, the NEA, Frohnmayer, and "Witnesses: Against Our Vanishing," which he described as "a New York exhibit of decadent art, i.e. photos of dying and sometimes naked homosexuals." Buchanan also invoked Farrakhan, who'd been condemned by liberals for calling Judaism "a gutter religion." Now none of those liberals would stand up to David and "the militant homosexuals' rhetoric of hatred against Roman Catholicism."

David worried about the impact this firestorm would have on his retrospective in Normal. That day, he composed a three-page single-spaced letter to the dean of Illinois State University's College of Fine Arts, explaining why it was important to him that "Postcards from America: X-Rays from Hell" be included in the "Tongues of Flame" catalog.

"Have you ever woken up one morning and read in the daily paper that you have lost your constitutional rights against the government's invasion of your privacy?" he wrote. "I did—within the last four years the Supreme Court made such a decision in regards to homosexuals." He laid out facts and statistics about AIDS, about the Catholic Church's stance, which he regarded as "murderous," and about the actions of Helms and Dannemeyer, which had also cost people their lives. He did not consider his outrage over these issues to be radical. He knew that the dean and Illinois State University might now be under pressure because of the NEA funding for "Tongues of Flame." "I sympathize with what that pressure feels like, in which our individual characters are called into question in a political climate that seems to care little about the basic issues of truth contained in what I might have to say. . . . I would appreciate your help in supporting my right of free speech under the First Amendment."

On November 23, David went to New Orleans with Tom. He returned on November 29, in time to participate in a reading at Artists Space with Eileen Myles, Richard Hell, and several others. David wore a Reagan mask and placed his text inside a copy of *Horton Hears a Who*.

On the first Day Without Art, December 1, he read unmasked at the Museum of Modern Art. Also on the program was Leonard Bernstein, playing three pieces he'd composed in memory of friends who'd died of AIDS. Lavender Light Gospel Choir performed. Actress Jane Lawrence Smith (Kiki's mother) read a piece selected by Philip Yenawine, who was the museum's director of education and also part of Visual AIDS, the organization behind this observance. But Yenawine thought David's reading was the most powerful moment. Yenawine had asked him to read from his targeted essay, a section related to its real subject: mortality.

"I worry that friends will slowly become professional pallbearers," David read,

> waiting for each death, of their lovers, friends and neighbors, and polishing their funeral speeches; perfecting their rituals of death rather than a relatively simple ritual of life such as screaming in the streets. . . . I imagine what it would be like if friends had a demonstration each time a lover or friend or a stranger died of AIDS. I imagine what it would be like if, each time a lover, friend or stranger died of this disease, their friends, lovers or neighbors would take the dead body and drive with it in a car a hundred miles an hour to Washington D.C. and blast through the gates of the white house and come to a screeching halt before the entrance and dump their lifeless form on the front steps. It would be comforting to see those friends, neighbors, lovers and strangers mark time and place and history in such a public way.

# 22 WITH A TARGET ON HIS BACK

**David became the** third artist targeted in the culture war, just as he was entering his last months of relative vitality. His letter to the dean at Illinois State indicates that he anticipated more trouble, and more would come. What mattered to him in the meantime was getting certain messages out.

He and composer-musician Ben Neill had about a week of rehearsal at the Kitchen before *ITSOFOMO (In the Shadow of Forward Motion)* opened there on December 7, 1989, roughly a year after they'd begun their discussions at Disco Donut.

David had come up with an overarching theme for the show: the formation and collapse of the "one-tribe nation." This was one of his tropes and had to do with homogeneity and conformity. As he put it in *Close to the Knives,* "To speak of ourselves—while living in a country that considers us or our thoughts taboo—is to shake the boundaries of the illusion of the ONE TRIBE NATION. To keep silent is to deny the fact that there are millions of separate tribes in this illusion called AMERICA. To keep silent . . . is to lose our identities." What he wanted to do in performance would be the equivalent of breaking a collage apart, moving the elements around, and commenting on them. He planned on a recurring motif of life and death images. To that end, he created a big papier-mâché egg and six to eight sperm, all of these covered with maps. The performance began with him cranking a big gear that pulled the sperm toward the egg. Periodically during the piece, he cranked it closer. Near the end he included a filmed sequence of a snake killing and ingesting a mouse.

"We came up with this formal conceit of the gesture of acceleration on all these different levels," said Neill, who used that conceit as a structural element in his music and in pacing the visual material David brought into the piece: images on four video monitors at the front of the stage and slides on a screen at the back. Most of the visuals had been pulled from photo pieces like *The Weight of the Earth*, films like *A Fire in My Belly*, and paintings like *Fear of Evolution*. David wanted movement in the piece, slithering, hopping animal movements that he knew he couldn't do. So Neill brought in a choreographer he knew, and her small dance company. About halfway through the piece, David made himself a wolf mask from that day's *New York Times*, along with a newsprint tutu he tucked into his belt, and did a little dance. He moved a strobe over a prone dancer's body, and confronted a "politician" standing on a ladder. But mostly he read some of his texts. *ITSOFOMO* ended with the music and movement and imagery building to a frenzy while he shouted out the words from *Untitled (Hujar Dead)*: ". . . and I'm carrying this rage like a blood-filled egg . . ."

Neill played live computer electronics and his mutantrumpet (three bells, seven valves, a trombone slide, and interactive computer electronics). He'd gone to record a hollering contest in his native North Carolina, "these tribal yodeling hillbillies," and sampled that throughout. He had a percussionist, Don Yallech, on vibraphone and timpani, the latter triggering other electronic sounds. "For its time, it was technologically advanced," Neill said.

They were able to tour the piece over the next couple of years, taking it to San Francisco, Seattle, and Minneapolis. When *Tongues of Flame* came to Exit Art in New York, they performed there too. But they never used the dancers again. Neill said David wasn't happy with how that had worked. "I think it made the piece get a little out of control," Neill observed. "Neither one of us had experience working with that kind of performing force. We never used any of the theatrical elements again, and it became more like a rock band—a trio onstage with the videos. David did more freestyling in terms of improvising the texts, and he took on way more of a central role."

At the Kitchen, they had the standard four nights to perform. On the last day, December 10, David spent the morning at ACT UP's big "Stop the Church" demonstration in front of St. Patrick's Cathedral. Bill Gerstel, the musician who'd replaced David in 3 Teens Kill 4, happened to be one of thousands of demonstrators on Fifth Avenue. He remembered a tall skinny man in a ski mask wiggling his way to the front and throwing himself at a police barricade to knock it over. The crowd then surged past the barrier and the masked man ran around the corner. Gerstel decided to follow him to see who he was. He found David, mask off, sitting on the ground against a building, out of breath. With a performance to do that night, he couldn't risk arrest.

In the *ITSOFOMO* program, David inserted a page devoted to facts and statistics about AIDS, especially the role played by the Catholic Church in choking off the flow of safe-sex information. In David's opinion, the facts were enraging, and they would be to anyone. He hated it when people attributed his anger to what he called "my diagnosis."

David worked on one writing project that he never finished but that may have helped him to deal with the rage he felt about the right-wingers piling on to attack him. They were far from done with him, but given the cast of characters he used in the project, called "The Private Lives of Saints," he would have written it at about this point in his troubles. "Private Lives" was intemperate, to say the least. Part of it was a film script in which the president, Jesse Helms, Cardinal O'Connor, and others of their political persuasion engaged in orgies, murder, drug taking, and general depravity—the Cinema of Transgression meets Capitol Hill.

But that was play. He had serious messages to get out. So he agreed to appear on a local public affairs show, *The Eleventh Hour*—on the condition that no one see his face. He wore his Reagan mask throughout the interview, taped at Artists Space, and hit listeners with lots of statistics, later edited to a few voice-over sentences.

Asked to explain the mask (in a section that did not air), David said he thought it would be ironic for viewers to get their facts from the president, who had not said the word "AIDS" through six and a half years of an epidemic that killed twenty-one thousand Americans, and who'd thus inspired the phrase "Silence=Death."* Also, David was now even more fearful about being queer-bashed. After Patrick Buchanan's *New York Post* column calling the show "decadent," with special opprobrium for David, and Ray Kerrison's *Post* column comparing David to Louis Farrakhan, Artists Space received a bomb threat and had to evacuate the gallery.

---

* The phrase "Silence=Death" preceded the formation of ACT UP, which then made furious use of it. See http://www.actupny.org/reports/silencedeath.html.

David had clearly prepared a set of talking points for this taping—the virus did not have a sexual orientation, the virus was running rampant in minority communities, the cardinal preferred coffins to condoms, and so on. He spoke for at least half an hour, but wearing the Reagan mask, hidden except for his buck teeth and the gap between them, he looked a bit goofy. In the end, *The Eleventh Hour* gave him three and half minutes.

For most of that time he faced *Untitled (Hujar Dead)* on the Artists Space wall and read the text about the blood-filled egg, without the mask, while the camera focused on his back and on the clenching, unclenching fists at his sides.

Early in 1990, he traveled to Philadelphia to lecture at the University of the Arts as a "visiting photographer," and there in the audience sat Dean Savard, covered with Kaposi sarcoma lesions.

They probably hadn't seen each other since Savard left Civilian Warfare. He was living in Philly, driving a cab. When Savard later passed through New York on his way to see his parents in Connecticut, he and David got together for dinner.

David felt nauseated for the first part of this meal. "I do have tremendous emotional reactions to the physical problems people have with this disease," he told me. "It's more a psychological thing because of my own fears about what I face."

Savard told David that when his parents came to take him to rehab all those years ago, he'd offered to gas up the car and then he just kept driving west while they stood waiting in front of the gallery. He'd gone all the way to Hawaii and spent a year there. Now he had so much KS that he could be a firehouse dog, he said. One of his legs was especially bad, and might have to be amputated. He'd gone to his local swimming pool with a friend, and as he dove in, a woman there with her kids started screaming at them, "Outta the pool!" Then he saw all these other parents yanking their kids out while his friend rolled on the ground laughing, saying, "Gotta bring you more often," because she'd never seen so few people in the water. Savard was off dope, but just in case things got really bad, he had a "secret stash . . . guaranteed to kill me nicely."

David typed this up and labeled it "Dean's monologue." There's no telling how much of it is true.

"Witnesses: Against Our Vanishing" closed on January 6, 1990. David's retrospective, "Tongues of Flame, would open at Illinois State University on January 23. With this suddenly controversial artist headed to Normal, the *Village Voice* planned a cover story and assigned a couple of features. I was to write about David's life while art critic Elizabeth Hess went to Illinois to write about the show. I did my three interviews with him early in January 1990.

We sat at what had once been Hujar's blue kitchen table—though little blue was visible under the stacks of paper, books, plastic toys, and general clutter. Off mic, he told me he'd gone back into therapy. And he was a little apprehensive about this journey to the heartland. As I turned on the tape recorder, he hid the phone under some clothing and blankets on the bed so the ringing would be less audible. It rang constantly. The answering machine clicked. The crickets chirped.

David flew to Normal a few days before the show opened. He'd followed up his letter to the dean of the College of Fine Arts with a phone call to curator Barry Blinderman. David thought Blinderman also deserved to know that a certain essay now in the "Tongues of Flame" catalog had become radioactive.

Blinderman responded, "No problem." The administration of Illinois State University would stand behind him. He told a reporter, "I'm simply carrying out the grant we received to the letter. We're an educational institution. It's not our job to squelch controversy."

The grant application Blinderman submitted late in 1988 stated: "David Wojnarowicz's impassioned, intensely colored images cry out against oppressive socio-political contingents, and address societal and sexual taboos. . . . Wojnarowicz's presence at our museum will provide our audience with an experience that may challenge or disturb them. We feel that one of our responsibilities is to reinforce the appreciation of art that transcends decorative function." He included slides of David's work and a copy of "Living Close to the Knives," the essay about Hujar's death. Blinderman figured the project budget at $57,200 and applied to the Endowment's museum program for $23,300.

The NEA's peer panel approved a grant of $15,000 in February '89, a couple of months before Reverend Donald Wildmon orchestrated the letter campaign against *Piss Christ*. This panel, which also approved the grant for "Witnesses: Against Our Vanishing," would have consisted of art world professionals from all parts of the country—curators, academics, and critics, for example—people familiar with the work of the artists and the reputations of the institutions applying. The panel would have convened in Washington, D.C., for several days to make choices based on artistic merit. Set up as a Great Society program in 1965, the NEA was designed to disseminate money for the arts across America. For example, its funding allowed dance companies to tour and world-class nonprofit theaters to thrive far from Broadway. It helped to support orchestras and museums and poetry festivals in communities that didn't have the economic base to fund them. And it allowed a small museum at a Midwestern university to give a New York–based artist a retrospective.

"Tongues of Flame" would test a familiar right-wing assertion. Jesse Helms and his cronies liked to characterize what they contemptuously called "the arty crowd" as either purveyors of perversion or some jewel-encrusted elite, a symbiotic gang of highbrows and lowlifes. According to Helms and crew, this crowd's pornographic, sacrilegious art experiences were resentfully funded by the tax dollars of "average Americans," some of whom might reside in a town called Normal.

On the night of January 23, 1990, more than seven hundred people crammed into the gallery at Illinois State to hear David speak. "It just broke any record that we've ever had, including student annuals," Blinderman said. "It was beyond what fire laws would allow."

Elizabeth Hess described David's talk this way in her piece for the *Voice*:

> In a brilliant litany of questions, answers, statistics, and anecdotes, Wojnarowicz makes connections between his own life story, the defense budget, homelessness, AIDS, sex education, gay and lesbian teenage suicide, abortion, and the real killer—silence. Students sitting next to

me are nudging each other with wide eyes. They can't believe their ears. "If I tell you I'm a homosexual and a queer does it make you nervous? Does it prevent you from hearing anything else I say?" screams Wojnarowicz into the mike.

He had surrounded himself with four video monitors playing the footage from *ITSOFOMO*. He ended by reading the text from *Untitled (Hujar Dead)*. Afterward he spent nearly two hours shaking hands, signing posters, and accepting gifts before finally going out for dinner with Tom Rauffenbart and Anita Vitale, who'd come from New York for the opening.

The next morning, he returned to the gallery with Blinderman and Hess, stopping at a McDonald's drive-through for his usual two Egg Mc-Muffins. Hess reported that David gave his order to the disemebodied voice on one side of the building, then drove to the other side to pick up his food. When that window opened and the bag emerged, a voice over the speaker said, "Thank you, thank you. What a great performance!"

He wasn't yet able to take that in. Someone sent a box of flowers to the gallery that day, addressed to David, but after he picked it up, he put it right back down. It was too heavy for flowers! Blinderman took the box out into the hallway and opened it to find, not a bomb, but flowers with a waterpack. Soon enough, David was able to drop his anxiety about what was going to happen to him in the heartland. "A great performance" turned out to be the consensus.

"Tongues of Flame" broke attendance records at University Galleries and got good reviews in the local press. The catalog sold out. David decided to stay an extra week, because the "average American" was so supportive—sending him letters, approaching him in restaurants to thank him. "It was my moment as a rock star," he told me later. He also said he thought people were hungry for information, and if someone stood in front of them and told them directly, "This is my experience," the average American would listen. The Associated Press ran a story on the show headlined "'Degenerate' Art Exhibit Creates No Complaints."

"He endeared himself to the community," Blinderman said. "He made such an impact. After you hear a voice like that, it changes you." Bloomington-

Normal's first ACT UP chapter formed while David was there, and held its first meeting at the gallery, surrounded by his work.

Blinderman recalled him being friendly, meeting with anyone who wanted to meet with him. "People just went crazy over him," said Blinderman. "So charismatic, sensitive, humble, and vulnerable. So open. And he enjoyed the attention because it was sincere."

David had arrived in Normal with a shopping bag full of sheet music, fake dollars, and supermarket posters to use in the lithographs he would create at Normal Editions Workshop, the University's print atelier. He'd been planning another version of "The Four Elements." On this visit, he began work on *Earth and Wind* (a brain emerges from a globe on a background of sheet music; a songbird and tornadoes on a background of dollars), but then turned to a more urgent piece. This new lithograph had the *New York Post's* "Offensive Art Exhibit" editorial on one half, dollars on the other. He drew a voodoo doll on litho stone to be printed over the editorial, skeletons and a globe to be printed over the dollars, and a circle filled with blood cells uniting the two halves.

After its run in Normal, "Tongues of Flame" was scheduled to travel to the Santa Monica Museum of Art, Exit Art in New York, and Temple Gallery at the Tyler School of Art in Philadelphia. Blinderman was able to send the NEA a rapturous final report:

> Perhaps the most satisfying aspect of the Wojnarowicz exhibition was watching the profound effect that the artist's work and the attendant controversy had on our audience. Community members who had never stepped into the gallery before flocked in to see the work in person, after having read and heard so much about it. We received support and praise from town officials and university upper administrators, including the mayor of Normal and the President of Illinois State University. . . . The public's enthusiastic acceptance of a so-called "difficult" show gave us great hope that the terms "average American taxpayer" and "playing in Peoria" could at last be redefined. In addition, hundreds of students of all disciplines at I.S.U. wrote papers on the social, moral and legal aspects of the exhibition. Some law students even did dissertations on

the topic. As was the hope of our Dean of the College of Fine Arts, *Tongues of Flame* proved to be a unique educational experience for our immediate audience and people all over the country.

Meanwhile, back in Washington, John Frohnmayer had decided to tell people what he might have said during the Artists Space meltdown: "Tongues of Flame" had been funded before he got there, and he did not have to comment on it. Frohnmayer was only off the hook until the self-appointed watchdogs found their next "degenerate" artist. And David wasn't off the hook at all.

Patrick McDonnell was an Illinois State graduate student in the Art Department who worked at University Galleries and acted as preparator for David's retrospective, unpacking the work and helping to hang and light it. He and David had met during David's first visit to Normal, the previous October. Patrick knew nothing about David's work, and they didn't speak until David started laughing at a piece Patrick had made from an empty Etch A Sketch; on it he'd spray-fixed a drawing of an armless man with a huge erection. Patrick had just come out. The piece was about his frustration over being gay and never acting on it. For the remaining days of that October visit, said Patrick, "if there was a moment that we had to share, we were having it."

When David arrived before the opening in January, he said to Patrick, "Take me through the show and tell me what you like and what you don't like."

"I still didn't know anything about his work. So I took him over to this one piece and said, 'This looks unfinished.'" It was one of the driftwood totems.* "David said, 'Really!' And I said, 'Yes. This piece looks like you just stopped.' David went into the office and he grabbed some brushes and paint and brought them out to me, and he said, 'Here. You finish it.'" Patrick declined.

One night David went to see *Driving Miss Daisy* with Patrick and his

---

* Probably *Totem 3* (1983) on page 123 of the "Tongues of Flame" catalog.

roommate, Anna Marie Watkins. When they got back to Barry Blinderman's house, where David was staying, he said to them, "I don't want to become friends with you guys, because I'm going to die. It's not right to impose that on someone."

Patrick told him he'd had friends who died and he'd almost died himself, and it didn't matter. "I wanted to be near him and I told him so," said Patrick. "I felt like I could relate to him on so many different levels." For one thing, Patrick had spent time as a kid living on the streets of Houston—along with his mother and siblings. His father had abandoned the family. His mother was schizophrenic. They lived intermittently with Patrick's grandmother, but she was incapacitated and poor. So the kids all cleaned houses and mowed lawns to get money for food, and when that didn't bring enough, they'd borrow from the neighbors, who knew they weren't going to get it back. Their grandmother would throw them all out when the mother became particularly difficult. Sometimes the mother would find a guy to move in with, and he'd provide for a while, then get tired of it, and they'd try going back to their grandmother. Patrick and his siblings also lived briefly with an uncle and did a couple of stints in foster care. He attended seventeen different schools, thinking everyone lived that way. Finally, at the age of seventeen, with two years of high school to go, Patrick moved in with his brother's ex-girlfriend, who gave him the first stress-free environment of his life. Eventually, he was able to get a full scholarship to Texas A&M at Corpus Christi.

David was a revelation. Patrick had bought into all the stereotypes about gay men, and David didn't fit any of them: "He was just himself, and that's what I wanted to be." Patrick was nine years younger than David. They spent a lot of time together just talking, going out for breakfast, driving around town. David would tell him, "You're driving Miss Daisy." This was the last major friendship David developed in his life. He treated Patrick as though he were a younger brother, encouraging and advising him. He tried to be the mentor Hujar had once been to him. "He wanted me to make a way for myself that I didn't have as a child growing up," Patrick said. When he told David, for example, that he wanted to drop out of graduate school, David urged him not to, saying, "You'll regret that." In the end, Patrick was glad he took that advice.

"He wanted me to explore my sexuality beyond what I had," said Patrick. "I really wasn't dating anybody, but there were some guys I wanted to date, and he would say, 'Well, ask 'em, Patrick.'" He even suggested an ice-breaker: "Tell them you know the famous artist from New York, and you can introduce them."

Patrick told David about "the Square," a gay cruising area that extended from the courthouse in Bloomington to an adult bookstore in Normal. He commented that the men who went there were desperate. David said, "You know, Patrick, you're a prude. Those men are not desperate. They happen to know what they want, and they're going to go get it. You tell me all the time what you want, and you're not going to go get it, so fuck you."

"So," Patrick said, "I took that challenge." He started cruising the Square with David. "We never picked anybody up. We would just look." Sometimes they would drive around town and see an attractive guy and start howling or woofing.

David told Patrick stories about the days when he went to the piers for sex. When he wanted to find a run-down site like that in Bloomington or Normal so he could stage a photo, Patrick took him to an old warehouse in an abandoned railyard. There David photographed Patrick in a headdress made from maps, kind of a Krazy Kat with a long nose that said "culture." He'd made masks like this for himself in years past. This time he added a clown collar fashioned from large fake dollars, painted Patrick's arms blue with darker blue spots, and had him wear a polka dot shirt. "Pose like Coco Chanel," David told him. He called the resulting Cibachrome print *A Formal Portrait of Culture*.

One day Patrick and David went to a coffeehouse in Normal, and David began to talk about the problems he was having with the building conversion engulfing his loft. They'd opened a hole in his roof and water was leaking through it. "I said to him, 'David, what is stability anyway?' Because I was kind of reflecting on *my* horrific childhood, having everything constantly taken away from us. And this moment of the roof leaking at his house—it would pass. I was saying, 'We all have to understand that life throws you curveballs.' And he just came unglued in that restaurant. In front of everyone."

David exploded into one of his purple-faced rages, yelling that he wasn't talking about 'stability,' that Patrick wasn't listening to him, that he had a fucking hole in his fucking ceiling. Everyone in the restaurant turned and looked. Patrick said, "OK. Calm down. Sorry I spoke."

And David was able to recover. He told Patrick, "I'm sorry. I don't know what comes over me. I do that all the time. I've been working on it with my therapist."

Keith Haring died of AIDS on February 16, 1990, at the age of thirty-one.

California representative Dana Rohrabacher had developed a new strategy in his campaign to kill the National Endowment for the Arts.

Early in February he sent a "Dear Colleague" letter to every member of Congress, condemning the agency for funding Annie Sprinkle's *Post Porn Modernist*, a performance in which the former porn star talked—graphically—about her experiences as a sex worker. Above Rohrabacher's headline, "The National Endowment for the Arts Is at It Again!" he ran a quote from Sprinkle's show: "Usually I get paid a lot of money for this but tonight it's government funded." That was a joke. Sprinkle had never applied for a grant, much less received one. But the show was a perfect vehicle for generating outrage among enemies of the agency.

On February 13, the American Family Association took out a full-page ad in the *Washington Times* headlined "Is This How You Want Your Tax Dollars Spent?" and using Sprinkle's comment that her show was "government funded," then listing about a dozen supposed NEA outrages, a list riddled with misrepresentations and errors. For example, "Witnesses: Against Our Vanishing" was described as "an art exhibit in which angry homosexuals denounced Catholic clergyman John Cardinal O'Connor." The NEA quickly released a fact sheet to correct all the mistakes. When the AFA bought its next full-page ad, in *USA Today*, it had to cite its sources, most of them right-wing publications not known for their fact-checking departments.

Susan Wyatt had an appointment with Congressman Rohrabacher on February 20. She was there to advocate for the arts. And he would ask,

"What's your religion?" But when she first got to his office, everyone was looking at Rohrabacher's latest "Dear Colleague" letter.

"They were all so thrilled, and they showed it to me," she said.

His new letter, again sent to every member of Congress, condemned the NEA for supporting David Wojnarowicz's "Tongues of Flame," described by Rohrabacher as "an orgy of degenerate depravity." His missive carried an image of Jesus shooting up that had been clipped from the corner of *Untitled (Genet)*, the collage David created in 1979 while he was still living in Vinegar Hill. That piece wasn't even in the exhibition. As with *One Day This Kid* and photos from the *Rimbaud in New York* series, the image appeared only in the catalog. Rohrabacher asked his colleagues to consider whether their constituents would want their tax dollars subsidizing a show of such work. He wrote, "The art is sickeningly violent, sexually explicit, homoerotic, anti-religious and nihilistic."

The conservative weekly *Human Events* ran a short piece on this "NEA-funded blasphemy" a few days after Rohrabacher circulated it. *Human Events* then used it in a subscription offer to members of the American Family Association. The image from *Untitled (Genet)* also became a featured outrage on Pat Robertson's 700 *Club.*

Since David left for Berlin and then Paris on February 21, he knew nothing about this until he returned March 3 and spoke to Blinderman.

A young man had come to University Galleries after hearing about David's work on *The* 700 *Club.* "I feel the show is bad," he told Blinderman. "I want to take it down."

Blinderman talked him out of it. "I ended up going into this big art historical argument." He invoked, for example, Matthias Grünewald's Isenheim altarpiece, painted in the sixteenth century for a monastery where monks cared for people with skin diseases—so the suffering Christ in that painting shows symptoms of skin disease. "It's because he's the man of sorrows," Blinderman argued. "He takes on the suffering of the world. So if Christ were to appear physically today, one of the sicknesses he would have to take on would be drug addiction."

"Here I am—a secular Jew," Blinderman said. "But as an art historian, I had to learn a lot about Christian art, and I love it." He reminded the man that Jesus had said "you who are free of sin cast the first stone" and "turn the other cheek" and "judge not and be not judged." He spoke of compassion and humility and sacrifice. The man looked baffled, but he left.

"Tongues of Flame" was on view in Normal until March 4. On March 5, 1990, President George H. W. Bush sent the image of Christ with hypodermic to John Frohnmayer with an "eyes only" note stapled to it. The president stated, "I know you are as offended as I am by the attached depiction of Jesus Christ. I think you have been doing a superb job, so I send along this note not in any critical vein whatsoever, but simply to inquire if there isn't something we can do about excessive cases like this."

Frohnmayer told the president, "Yes, I was offended by both the work and the man, since I had encountered him directly at Artists Space where he was very angry and abusive toward me personally. Our original legislation, however, warns the Endowment to avoid imposing . . . a single aesthetic standard or to direct artistic content." Frohnmayer thought this a wise policy, and he would fight to defend it from Helms.

When Frohnmayer related the incident in his book, though, he admitted that he had not been offended by this work. He understood it. "In fact, an image of Christ with a needle in his arm, particularly when he is not holding the needle, is consistent with an interpretation of Christ taking on the sins of the world—hardly a blasphemous concept."

That March, Jesse Helms directed the General Accounting Office to investigate a list he provided of the NEA's "questionable activities," among them "Tongues of Flame."

While he was in Normal, or shortly after, David made notes in his journal for what he thought would be new photo pieces: "FLEURS DU MAL . . . Photo blow-ups of color flowers (Hawaii book, Louisiana book). Sew in images and information on homophobia, AIDS issues, sexual issues, invasions, distortions, health papers." Ultimately these ideas developed into the flower paintings in his last show.

During the trip to Berlin, where he was in a group show, he stayed for three days with Andreas Sternweiler, co-founder of the world's first (and only) gay museum. Sternweiler later sent him photos of the Nazis destroying the Institute of Sexual Science, an organization that had advocated for women's liberation and gay rights. Nazis burned the institute's books as part of a government censorship program, so David contemplated a piece linking this event with the Helms agenda.

In one of the airports where he waited on this trip, David wrote, "I won't grow old and maybe I want to. Maybe nothing can save me. Maybe all my dreams as a kid and as a young guy have fallen down to their knees. Inside my head I wished for years that I could separate into ten different people to give each person I loved a part of myself forever and also have some left over to drift across landscapes and maybe even go into death or areas that were deadly and have enough of me to survive the death of one or two of me—this was what I thought appropriate for all my desires and I never figured out how to rearrange it all and now I'm in danger of losing the only one of me that is around. I'm in danger of losing my life and what gesture can convey or stop this possibility? What gesture of hands or mind can stop my death?"

Dean Savard died of AIDS on March 30, 1990, at the age of thirty-one.

David got a letter from Montana Hewson, the friend of Tommy Turner's and Richard Kern's who'd had a small role in *You Killed Me First.*

Montana wrote after the Artists Space imbroglio hit the papers in his home state of Texas, but he didn't know David's address. He sent the letter to Artists Space, and David finally got it either just before or just after he went to Normal. He decided then that, for the last chapter of his book, he'd do a profile of Montana, "a guy I psychically felt connected to because of the way he didn't fit. I wanted to touch that thing that I knew he carried."

He sent Montana his address and phone number and told him he'd like to come visit, to ride around some back roads with him and talk. Montana could call him collect. After David heard nothing back, he sent a postcard in March. Then at the beginning of April, he received a mysterious letter addressed to "David W—" with no return address. The full text read, "David W—In response to your card, I regret to tell you that Monte committed suicide about January 18, 1990. His dad."

David thought about the last line of Montana's letter: "No fair dying before I do." It dawned on him that Montana had been dead by the time he wrote him back. He decided to do a chapter on him anyway, to write about self-destruction, about the circle of people around Montana he'd once been part of.

He hadn't been in touch with his Cinema of Transgression friends, Turner and Kern, since Hujar got sick. As David put it, "Emotionally it was too ugly to be taking care of a guy who was battling to live and then hang out with people that were jamming shit in their arms or throwing themselves into the varied arms of death." Kern had moved to San Francisco and cleaned up but had recently returned to the East Village. Turner would eventually get completely off drugs, but at this point he was on methadone. David set up interviews with each of them and with Sophie Breer, she of *Waje's Cockabunnies*, since they had all known Montana better than he had.

He wanted to ask each of them: What attracted us to the dark things? Things most people recoil from? What was this death wish? What were the drugs about, really?

Montana had been this paradoxical character who, as David put it, "built an elaborate shrine over a mouse hole." He would not kill a cockroach. Yet he claimed to have murdered a drug dealer who ripped him off. (This can in no way be substantiated.) He was creatively and disturbingly self-destructive. And he had stolen money from Tommy and Amy Turner to buy drugs. That was the transgression that haunted him till the end of his life. When Turner came to see David for his two interviews, he brought Montana's letters—one after another begging forgiveness. Turner talked to Montana on the phone and forgave him, but it didn't seem to assuage the guilt.

Montana had lived in such extreme circumstances—sleeping at least part of one winter in Central Park, for example. He'd also lived in a building on the Lower East Side where, thanks to a fire next door, he had no heat and no unbroken windows. So he put blankets over the windows and kept a toaster oven propped up on a bureau. Then there was the ten-by-ten foot room in the residential hotel, where he had a bed and a hot plate and saved all his garbage. Newspapers stacked up the wall. Rows of bottles filled with piss. Montana was hopelessly in love with the heterosexual Kern. So, before his first suicide attempt—shooting ten bags of heroin—he wrote Kern a letter to say, "You can have my synthesizer. I'll leave the door unlocked. Take pictures of me dead." His second attempt, much grislier, involved massive blood loss but a neighbor found him in time.

David had always romanticized those he regarded as "thug saints." But there was more to it here. David was impressed, perhaps overly so, with Montana's writing and drawing. He saw him as an artist, as someone who rebelled against the structure of things. When David called a friend of Montana's in Texas, Mary Hayslip, to get what information he could about the suicide and what led to it, he explained that writing about Montana would give him a chance to confront his own alienation. "I feel like I've gone through my whole life pretty uncomfortable with what it is to live in the world," he told her, "so in this writing, I just want to talk about those mixed feelings of either being human or not being human." David too had thought about suicide, but in Montana, his worst impulses were magnified to the nth degree. This was someone who rebelled so hard against the structure of things that he'd rebelled against being alive.

The letter from Montana's father really shocked him. "I felt like my soul was slammed against a stone wall," he wrote in his essay, the longest by far in *Close to the Knives*. "I started crying, something I haven't done in months. There was something about the last half year, about all the deaths in the air. I'd been wondering if death has become so constant that I will never feel anything again. I fear losing the ability to feel the weight and depth of each life that folds up, sinks, and disappears from our sight. I thought of whether anyone will be able to feel anything about my death if it takes place. Is it all becoming the sensation one feels when they pass a dead bird in the street and all you can do is acknowledge it and move on."


Robert Mapplethorpe's beleaguered retrospective "The Perfect Moment" opened in Cincinnati on April 7. I was there to cover it and will never forget the moment when the police came bursting into the Contemporary Art Center, pushing away the artgoers and knocking down velvet ropes as if chasing some deadly criminal.

The police cleared the museum, which was on the second floor of a downtown mall and had been full to capacity. Between those thrown out and those who'd been waiting to enter, many hundreds of people soon stood on the mall's ground floor. Museum director Dennis Barrie came out to address them, covering his face with his hands and telling them, "It's a very dark day."

The sheriff announced later at a press conference that the museum was now obligated to remove the offending pictures. The next morning, a Sunday, lawyers for the Contemporary Art Center went to a federal judge for a temporary restraining order. The judge ordered the police not to remove pictures, close the exhibit, or intimidate the people who wanted to see it.

Barrie and the museum had been charged with "pandering obscenity" and with "illegal use of a child in nudity-oriented material." According to *Miller v. California*, a decision about obscenity should be based on "community standards." At trial that fall, the prosecutor would suggest to the jury that maybe the record-breaking eighty-one thousand spectators had come from out of town.

But on April 7, the hundreds of people who stood outside the Contemporary Art Center began chanting to a surprised-looking police force: "We're the community standard! We're the community standard! We're the community standard!"

Reverend Donald Wildmon, the Mississippi-based director of the American Family Association, had ordered himself a copy of the exhibition catalog for "Tongues of Flame." Here was something he could use to further the Lord's work of killing the National Endowment for the Arts. Though he reported later that the catalog made him kind of sick to his stomach, he persisted in ferreting out fourteen images—Christ shooting up plus thirteen pictures of alleged sexual activity. One of them was *Rimbaud Masturbating*, but all the others were fragments of much larger pieces. Six were negative insets from *The Sex Series*, one was a severely cropped still of the disco dancers from *Fear of Disclosure*, one was a purification ritual involving urine and a cow, and the rest were chopped from the complex and much larger paintings *Water* (from *The Four Elements* series) and *Bad Moon Rising*.

Wildmon pasted these bits onto two legal-size pages and added text with the headline "Your Tax Dollars Helped to Pay for These Works of Art." The fact is that tax dollars paid for none of the work. David never in his life applied for an NEA grant. He earned a total of five hundred dollars from "Tongues of Flame"—his speaking fee. Even that didn't necessarily come from the NEA, since its grant covered less than a third of the show's cost.

On April 12, 1990, Wildmon mailed envelopes labeled "Caution—contains extremely offensive material" to every member of Congress with the two-page pamphlet of images and a long letter informing them that the enclosed information would soon be mailed to "3200 Christian leaders (heads of denominations, bishops, superintendents, etc.), 1000 Christian radio stations, 100 Christian television stations, and 178,000 pastors." These "key leaders" would be asked to distribute the material further.

Wildmon suggested that the NEA had broken the law by funding "Tongues of Flame" in violation of the Helms amendment. He declared that the NEA acted as a government censor since only work chosen by elitist panels was funded, and he repeatedly quoted Frohnmayer out of context. But his main point was this: "The NEA has been isolated from mainstream American values for so long that it has become captive to a morally decadent minority which ridicules and mocks decent, moral taxpayers while demanding taxpayer subsidies. Congress must either clean the NEA up or abolish the agency altogether."

Frohnmayer wrote Wildmon a letter on April 20 that began, "Members of Congress have shared with me your letter dated April 12, 1990. I am sure you will want to contact each of them again and correct the many false impressions you left. I know your zeal for this subject is great, but I hope you also remember the Commandment against bearing false witness for which all of us who are Christians and Jews must some day answer." And he added that images like this were not going to be funded on his watch.

David didn't know about the mailing until Blinderman called on April 19 to describe what it looked like and read him the text. David was angry and upset. The next day, he got a call from the *Washington Post* and told the reporter he thought the people attacking him were "repressed five-year-olds." The mailing did not represent his work. "They're making pieces of their own," he said.

When the *Post* reporter called Wildmon, the reverend admitted that the images were cropped, but he asked, "Does that make them less obscene?"

He never responded to Frohnmayer's plea to correct "false impressions." Instead, on May 1, Wildmon sent another letter to every member of Congress, which began, "The National Endowment for the Arts helped fund the child pornography contained in the enclosed sealed envelope." There he placed copies of Mapplethorpe's two pictures of children and copies of photos taken by Ricardo T. Barros of his nude wife and children. The latter had run in *Nueva Luz*, an NEA-funded photography magazine. Wildmon promised that this information would soon be mailed to his list of "key leaders" and they would be asked to disseminate it further.

On April 21, David left for a long-planned trip to Mérida in the Yucatán with Tom. There he found the material for the end of his book, his postscript to "The Suicide of a Guy Who Once Built an Elaborate Shrine over a Mouse Hole."

Tom had seen a poster for a bullfight. David wasn't sure he felt like going, then decided he would. His first impulse, he wrote in his journal, was to offer money to spare the animal, but he didn't have that kind of money. His twenty-three-page "postscript" interspersed his account of this bullfight with various sharp memories: The violence he'd experienced at the hands of his father. Keith Davis on his deathbed getting a last-minute phone call from his estranged boyfriend. The earliest photo he had of his mother—the one she'd inscribed at the bottom with the word "Self." The ritualized slaughter he and Tom witnessed in the bullring that day came to a terrible end as the bull, twisting and turning before the assaults of the banderillero, broke its own front left leg. "The matador shakes his head in sympathy and disgust," he wrote. "He arches his feet and points his sword at the bull in an affected graceful, arched motion. He takes aim with his X-ray eyes on that invisible point between the rolling curves of the bull's shoulders, the true point where the entrance of the steel blade will still the heart. Smell the flowers while you can."

"The pain I feel is to see my own death in the bull's death," he wrote. He was also still thinking about Montana's suicide and why it had hit him so hard—"despite my having successfully managed to freeze out the weight of various other deaths in the last five years," as he put it. "I felt I stood the chance of going crazy and becoming a windmill of slaughter if I allowed myself the luxury of experiencing each of those deaths with the full weight accorded them. [Montana's] manner of death opened a door to all that I've been speaking of."

He noticed children in Mérida selling wild roses. His photographic piece *Hell Is a Place on Earth* would tell the rest of the story, how at dusk the children would sit in a local park eating the petals of the flowers they hadn't managed to sell. That was the text incorporated into a close-up of a bumblebee.

He and Tom stopped at the Mayan ruins of Chichén Itzá, where David filmed a long column of leaf-cutter ants, each carrying a green slice of leaf back to the nest. They spent the night there and Tom went off to see the light show put on at the ruin, but David did not feel well and stayed behind at the hotel. "He knew something was wrong [physically]," said Tom. "All the little things that usually cheered him up weren't working. David used to love to go shopping for little trinkets and things, but—he said he just didn't care anymore. Nothing like that mattered. So he was really depressed. I think he was more afraid than he ever admitted."

They went on to Playa del Carmen, where they were going to meet Anita Vitale. One night, David dreamt that he was back in Times Square. He wondered what his purpose was there. He couldn't remember where he lived. In the dream, he found two baby birds in a cardboard box and tried to figure out how to take care of them. Where could he get an eyedropper? Then, walking west across Forty-second Street, he began to scream. "It is a sad great deep scream and it goes on forever. It lifts and swells up into the air and the sky, it barrels out into the west and my head is vibrating and the pressure of it makes me blind to everything but the blood running in rivers under my skin, and my fingers are tensed and delicate as a ten-year-old's and all my life is within them and it is here in the midst of that scream in the midst of this sensation of life in an uninfected body in all this blurry swirl of dusky street light that I wake up."

They brought piñatas to the airport to greet Anita, but all three of them hated Playa del Carmen. They drove off to the rough ruins at Cobá, surrounded at one point by thousands of small yellow butterflies. David insisted that Tom drive at a snail's pace but casualties were inevitable, and he would groan each time one hit the windshield. They went to the beach at Xel-há and did some snorkeling. This had never made sense before, since David could barely see a thing without his glasses. But Tom had bought David a gift—goggles that had his prescription. At another beach, David lay in a hammock, and Tom realized it was the only time he'd ever seen David relax on a vacation. "He was swinging very slowly, with his finger in the sand, and I whispered to Anita, 'Look, look, look. He's just laying there.' And we were shocked. Neither of us had seen that before. Usually he was on the go. Always running."

David told them he was too depressed to enjoy himself. He wanted to leave. In Cancún, Tom went with him to see if they could arrange a ticket back to New York, but they couldn't get it done. While they were with the travel agent, she told them there was a suite available at the Sheraton in Cancún. It could easily accommodate three people, and the price wasn't bad. They had not expected to like Cancún but actually quite enjoyed it for a few days. David even went parasailing off the beach. But when they went out to shop, he still wasn't interested. He left before Tom and Anita did, but that was part of the original plan. He had to get back. Still, said Tom, "He was definitely off. The spark was leaving."

That was David's last trip to Mexico.


He got back to New York on May 1. On May 2, he went to the *Village Voice* office, where a reporter showed him a fax of a photocopy of the original AFA mailing, which easily gave him enough of an idea of what had been done to his work. He was outraged. As he would say many times over the next two months, his work had been turned into "banal pornography," stripped of its artistic and political content. And these bowdlerized images had reached way more people than his real art ever had. He began to have trouble sleeping.

He called John Carlin, the former art critic for *Paper* magazine who'd become an entertainment lawyer. "I gave him some basic copyright info, but told him it wasn't my area of expertise," Carlin said. Carlin had just founded the Red Hot Organization, which that fall would release its first CD, *Red Hot and Blue*, to raise money for AIDS charities. He suggested another lawyer and stayed in touch with David as the case developed, trying, he said, "to help him understand the counterintuitive aspects of the law as best I could." David actually applied for copyrights on all the pieces Wildmon had used on May 11, something that would never have seemed necessary to him before this.

When he discussed the issue with Wendy Olsoff, one of his dealers at P·P·O·W, she contacted her brother Jonathan Olsoff, an attorney with Skadden, Arps, Slate, Meagher & Flom, a major corporate law firm with an extensive pro bono practice. Olsoff quickly decided to take David's case, and brought in Kathryn Barrett, a colleague at Skadden Arps who specialized—as he did—in intellectual property. They were joined by David Cole, then an attorney with the Center for Constitutional Rights who specialized in First Amendment issues.

The culture war was about to intensify on several fronts. On May 13, the National Council on the Arts convened. This group of presidential appointees with more or less distinguished careers in the arts met quarterly to advise the chair on agency policy and, usually, to rubber-stamp grants recommended by peer panels. This time, Frohnmayer told them, there were some problematic grants in the solo-performance category. "Holly Hughes is a lesbian and her work is very heavily of that genre," he told them. Tim Miller's work was "aggressively homosexual." John Fleck was said to have urinated into a toilet onstage during a performance. And Karen Finley had just been labeled "a nude chocolate-smeared young woman" by conservative columnists Rowland Evans and Robert Novak. The council tabled a decision on the four artists, but took action to terminate two grants to the Institute for Contemporary Art in Philadelphia, the organizer of Mapplethorpe's show "The Perfect Moment." Killing a grant was an unusual move by the council, quite possibly unprecedented, and it was widely understood in the art world to be punishment.

David couldn't afford to get completely distracted by the culture war. He had to finish his book. He also had an installation to make for "The Decade

Show," opening May 12, 1990. This survey of the 1980s was an unusual collaboration among three institutions: the Museum of Contemporary Hispanic Art, the New Museum of Contemporary Art, and the Studio Museum in Harlem. The focus was "identity."

The New Museum gave David a small room with the fourth wall open. David had hired Judy Glantzman to help him. They drove to the Palisades together in her car to collect twigs, leaves, and branches. He knew what elements he wanted to include, and he'd sketched a very complex, very labor-intensive plan in his journal. Then he cut that back after feeling his way in the space allotted him. "The wild thing about David—watching him work," Glantzman said, "was that he would smoke four thousand cigarettes, the deadline was getting closer, I'm a nervous wreck, and he's sitting still smoking, but he's working. His wrist wasn't working but his brain. And then the piece came out fully formed."

He called the piece *America: Heads of Family/Heads of State*. At the center he suspended a large papier-mâché head, blindfolded with the word "QUEER" written in red paint across the forehead. Below it were two video monitors on a stand, running some of the *ITSOFOMO* footage. He placed images around that stand—a photo of anti-gay picketers with signs like "AIDS is a Punishment from the Eternal Father" next to a photo of Nazis destroying the Institute of Sexual Science. For the sides of that video stand, he'd enlarged some of the hate mail that started coming into University Galleries in Normal after his work was discussed on *The 700 Club*, in the weekly *Human Events*, and in the AFA mailing. Laid out in front of that on a kind of nest made from branches and flowers was the child skeleton wearing a white dress. He placed a large print of *One Day This Kid . . .* on the back wall, with photos of politicians like Reagan and Helms and pictures of his own parents on the side walls. Between the video setup and *This Kid*, he'd created a kind of village on a leaf-and-twig-strewn floor, with a couple of small houses covered with dollar bills, his globe where the only country is America (repeated in all hemispheres), a doll reclining in a Plexiglas cube, a child's chair with branches growing from it—and nestled at the center, *Horton Hears a Who*.

\* \* \*

On May 18, 1990, David's team of lawyers filed for a preliminary injunction in U.S. district court to stop Donald Wildmon and the American Family Association from further publishing or distributing the two pages of severely cropped images.

Then on May 21, David's lawyers filed a complaint charging Wildmon and the AFA with "unauthorized copying, deliberate distortion and mutilation of, and misrepresentation of seven works of art" and "false and malicious defamation of the character, reputation and professional standing of Mr. Wojnarowicz." They were asking for a million dollars in damages on each of five legal claims.

That same day, David wrote to Philip Zimmerman, the friend who was with him when he witnessed the death of Keith Davis. Zimmerman had just tested positive for HIV, and he told David in a letter that he would consider suicide before going out the way Keith had David wrote back.

> Despite some of my fears I feel I am approaching the spectacle of my own death with interest in everything around me. I see my own contradictions and feel less afraid of them, I see my weaknesses and my strengths and they are becoming important to me. It's hard to define what I am trying to give you here; I guess its reassurance in whatever you do. I think it's beautiful what you carry and what you make and all the impulses that you outline because they reek of life. I would like to be parting air with my body's movement for years and years even in exhaustion, but in the event of my possible death . . . I feel kind of satisfied in mapping down my interior world with each thing I make. I'm realizing that there is something elementally important in bringing what is deep inside to light. It can ease things for others. It can ease the pressure of being alien in the visible structure that we had no hands in creating. . . . Philip, I have no threshold for physical pain and have always wondered in the last couple years what to do if I reach a point of pain I can't endure. I think living has been painful to an extent in this society that was and is blind to who and what I am, but its been a bearable pain because it simultaneously revealed me to myself over

these years. I hold on to my body's life and feel reluctant to think much about giving it up.

On Memorial Day weekend 1990, David went back to Normal to finish work on the lithographs. Though he would be back in New York by June 2 or 3, he worried about leaving for even a short time because of the ongoing work at his building. The landlord now wanted to put in a new boiler, to replace the radiators with baseboard heaters, and to install new double-glazed windows. He wrote to the lawyer he had on retainer to say he felt vulnerable. Some tenants had been going through eviction proceedings. His gas had been shut off without notice. It had taken three weeks to get a lightbulb changed in the hallway. He'd had to endure a lot of carbon monoxide and thick black soot from heavy equipment idling for hours along the sides of the building. Noise and vibrations had been intense at certain periods.

Not mentioned to the lawyer—and more irritating than threatening—the hookers who worked his corner at night were so noisy that he kept a carton of eggs on top of the refrigerator to throw at them. Sometimes he painted the eggs black.

David arrived in Illinois with a gift for Patrick, Gran Fury's "Read My Lips" T-shirt with an image of two men kissing. "I put it on immediately," said Patrick, "and we were going to a gun shop to buy police targets." That would be the background image for *Fire*. "David said to me, 'Wait. You're going in there with that shirt on?' He didn't want me to get hurt. I said, 'Why not? They're just going to look at me like I'm some freak—if they even notice.' Actually, they didn't bat an eye. I bought the targets. David didn't come in with me. He sat in the truck."

Patrick worked with him on the lithographs. David had never done one before, and he had some trouble with the touche technique that can give a lithograph the look of a watercolor. He told Patrick he couldn't control it, and he didn't like it.

Someone had let them into the workshop at ten P.M. and they were alone. Patrick asked, "Did they show you the crayons?"

David brightened. "Crayons? They've got crayons?"

David told Patrick to draw the snowman for *Water*. "He let me into his work," said Patrick. "That was a *huge* gesture for me. He told me he wanted me to believe in myself. 'Believe in your vision,' he would say. I didn't know I *had* a vision."

Donald Wildmon sent an urgent five-page letter to the 425,000 members of the American Family Association, telling them that "David Wojnarowicz, the homosexual creator of the NEA-funded 'Tongues of Flame' catalog—which featured 'Christ the Drug Addict' amidst hardcore homosexual photographs"—was now suing him for a million dollars. "This is the most important letter I have ever written you," Wildmon told his members. "I am asking you to make as generous a gift to AFA as possible."

He pointed out how the "left" had repeatedly used the courts "to take away the rights of Christians while promoting the 'rights' of pornographers, atheists, child molesters, abortionists and homosexuals." He was not asking for help to pay off the million dollars. He would win this lawsuit. No, he wanted contributions to set up a "crack team" of Christian lawyers.

"The AFA Legal Team will not only react to actions made against Christians," he promised, "but initiate actions that will put the pornographers and child abusers and homosexuals and humanists on the defensive."

In a "VERY IMPORTANT!!!" flyer enclosed with the letter, Wildmon stated that he'd made an error. The "radical homosexual artist/activist" was actually asking for five million dollars.

That spring, before David heard about the AFA mailing, he'd learned that he and Phil Zwickler had won a New York Foundation for the Arts grant of five thousand dollars for *Fear of Disclosure*. It isn't clear how much they actually received, since neither was able to complete the public service event required of NYFA recipients.

Zwickler was then working as editor of the People with AIDS Coalition Newsline. "When the Wildmon thing came up, he thought that David had an opportunity to become a very public figure," said their mutual friend Norman Frisch. "He thought David should be doing a lot of press, making appearances, and David was just too weighted down and overwhelmed and angry to be in public very much. He was not making himself available to people."

Frisch's work with the Los Angeles Festival brought him to New York frequently, but he'd been unaware of the Wildmon case. "David explained to me how he had been personally singled out as the devil by this guy," Frisch said. "He really felt victimized by it. Through his writing, he worked it out. He fought back. But at this point, he hadn't done that writing yet. And he was afraid of what was coming down on him. He was very paranoid about people trying to get at him, so he was not responding to the press or to activists who wanted to push him upfront. He just wasn't ready to go public. He thought, you know, people were going to try to kill him."

Frisch witnessed big shouting matches between David and Zwickler about the right way to conduct the politics of the response. "Phil was a very volatile person and not a good patient when he was ill," said Frisch. "On top of everything else, he was losing his eyesight, which made him very, very fearful that he was going to lose his independence. And he realized that this was really the end of his career, so he became even more volatile. When he and David would disagree, they would kind of explode at each other. They'd get into a big argument about who was sicker. David would say, 'You don't realize how fucking sick I am and how bad I feel, and I just don't have the energy for this.' Phil would say, 'I'm sicker than you, and I have the energy for it.' Then they would start with what drugs they were on and what infections they had. They would try to outdo one another with their symptoms. It would have been comical if it wasn't so sad."

In June, David signed his contract for *Close to the Knives*. The five-thousand-dollar advance was small but he didn't care. He didn't think he had a lot of time left. He just wanted the book to get out there.

Arguments for both sides in *Wojnarowicz v. American Family Association* were laid out that June in the pretrial briefs. Lawyers for Wildmon and the AFA responded to the complaint with several motions to dismiss. For example, Wildmon's lawyers asserted that no artwork had been mutilated, only reproductions. That the reverend's descriptions of the pictures as "part of" the "Tongues of Flame" catalog indicated that they were details of larger pieces. That, in any case, the whole piece did not have to be shown: "One may criticize Hitler for the gas chambers without being required to compliment him on the trains running on time, even if it is argued that the failure to so compliment him gives a distorted view of his regime. So one may criticize an artistic creation for the moral repugnance of a part of it without being required to evaluate the rest as to its artistic merit." They argued that David's reputation had been enhanced, not damaged, by their attack on him. That if he was going to take NEA money, he couldn't cry foul when some of his work was shown to Congress. That Wildmon's criticism of his work was political and therefore "protected" speech, which the artist hoped to censor. Most startling was their point that even if Wildmon really intended to label David a pornographer, that was not defamatory since "pornography can in many instances exist as a protected art form."

Then, barring dismissal, they wanted a change of venue so the case would be tried in Wildmon's home state of Mississippi. To support the latter motion, Wildmon's lawyers stated at a status conference on May 30 that the reverend had mailed only one copy of his broadside into the Southern District of New York—and that to Cardinal John O'Connor. The discovery process (ordered by the court over AFA objections) revealed that he had actually sent 210 copies into New York state, including 63 to newspapers and 25 to radio stations.

Motions for dismissal and change of venue would be addressed at the beginning of the trial, set for June 25. In mid-June, David and Reverend Wildmon were each deposed by a lawyer from the opposing side, part of pretrial fact finding.

Wildmon had assembled a small team of religious right lawyers to defend him. Joseph Secola, the lawyer for Operation Rescue, deposed David. Often a future witness will try to say as little as possible, but the transcript of David's deposition is notable for answers about his work and process that go on for pages. Secola finally complained, "I'm getting narrative responses to almost every question I ask." He wanted to establish some things that could be used at trial. Had the AFA actually called David a pornographer? David wouldn't say the word "no" but—no, they'd only made him look like one. Secola pulled out a copy of the letter David had written to the dean at

Illinois State explaining why it was important to him that the "Postcards" essay be included in the "Tongues of Flame" catalog. David had addressed it "to the Dean and whomever else it may concern." Who was "whomever else"? Had it been widely distributed? (No.) Wildmon's lawyers were also using the *Village Voice* article I had written about David as a defense exhibit because I said he'd used Hujar's porn collection to make the small circular insets in *The Sex Series*. Secola wanted to know if this was accurate. David replied that he would call them "sexual images," not porn. It didn't seem like much was discovered by either side. Wildmon, deposed by Kathryn Barrett, readily admitted that he'd gone through the catalog, plucking out images he thought would be most offensive to "the average taxpayer." He also testified that he had mailed just over six thousand copies of the pamphlet; the pictures were simply too offensive to send to 178,000 pastors.

David's lawyers had charged the AFA with libel, with two counts of copyright infringement, and with violating a New York state law against altering, defacing, mutilating, or modifying a work of art and then presenting it as the authentic work of the artist. The lawsuit also charged that the AFA's misleading description of David's work violated a federal law against trademark violation and false advertising.

On June 25, the trial began with Judge William C. Conner dismissing the latter charge. He ruled that it applied to false statements about a competitor's product and the AFA was not selling a product. He did not throw out anything else. He would not allow the trial to move to Mississippi. And he would dispense with opening statements since he'd read all the preliminary papers. This was a nonjury trial, and a no-nonsense judge who clearly wanted the proceedings to move right along. Judge Conner showed little patience for political posturing from either side.

Some of David's friends were seated in the gallery. Tom had taken the day off from work. I was there to cover the trial for *Artforum* and noted that Wildmon stayed out in the hall as David began testifying about how his work had been misrepresented. He had brought in an actual-size replica of *Water* to show how large and complex it was, how little had been excerpted. There were no surprises in his testimony.

The proceedings got spikier during the cross-examination by Wildmon's lawyer, Benjamin Bull, once part of Charles Keating's Citizen's for

Decency Through Law, and later senior counsel at Pat Robertson's American Center for Law and Justice and chief counsel for James Dobson's Alliance Defense Fund. Bull queried David, for example, about the letter he'd written to the dean at Illinois State. When David's lawyers objected, Bull explained to the judge that he wanted to show that David "was fully aware" that his work was going to be criticized. "I submit there is an inference that it could have been copied and shown to Congressmen as part of that criticism," Bull said. But the judge excluded it.

Bull then went through the catalog, directing David to read lines from his own essays and those written by critics, attesting to the centrality of sexual imagery in his work. Then there was the interview with Blinderman, where David said, "If my work is going to reflect my life, then I'm going to put sexuality into my work." And what about *The Sex Series*? Wasn't sexuality an integral part of it?

Bull also wanted to make the case that the AFA had had little impact on David's career. So he asked if it wasn't true that museums steered away from sexually explicit work, especially work about homosexuality. Wasn't it true that major museums would not show his work, with or without an AFA mailing? When David said he didn't know that to be true, Bull directed him to his own "Postcards" essay, in which David had written that what Helms and D'Amato had done was just an extension of standards formed in the arts community itself, where visible sexual images were usually for the straight, the white, and the male, and where Mapplethorpe had been one of the few to break through. Bull inquired about David's 1989 income of thirty-four thousand dollars—hadn't he earned most of that after "Witnesses: Against Our Vanishing" opened. (No!) But didn't he have shows coming up? "Tongues of Flame" was touring. And wasn't it true that no one had canceled the exhibit? And hadn't the price of Mapplethorpe's and Serrano's artwork gone up?

David's lawyers were allowed to call only one expert witness, and they chose Philip Yenawine, MOMA's director of education, who brought some perspective to the questions above. "Sexual explicitness as this [AFA mailing] represents Mr. Wojnarowicz to make is anathema to museums, and they won't present it," he testified, for example. "More people have heard his name than have seen his work. If they think this is what he does, they will in fact refuse to show it." He established that David had created a great many pieces with no sexual representations. As for Mapplethorpe and Serrano, Yenawine said that they were both more established in the art world and that the pieces of theirs attacked by the right had been presented in their entirety, not in fragments.

Yenawine's testimony would have impact but, he told me later, he "felt muzzled from the standpoint of saying, 'David is not going to recover from this. He is not well, and whatever damage has been done to his career, he's not going to have time to repair it.'" This had been a moment of self-censorship. Said Yenawine, "I didn't want to say in front of David that he was dying."

Wildmon's lawyers tried to keep the reverend off the stand. They'd announced that he would be their only witness, so David's lawyers said they would wait to question him during cross-examination and rested their case. Technically, they could call no more witnesses. Then Wildmon's lawyers announced that they would call no witnesses at all. David's lawyer David Cole put the matter to the judge, who decided that he had induced plaintiff's counsel not to call the reverend, so he would allow it. Bull registered his objection, but the gray-haired reverend had to take the stand.

This man so adept at intimidating corporate leaders and members of Congress was, in person, more mousy than magnetic. To make the libel charge stick, David's lawyers had to prove that Wildmon had acted with "actual malice." With his questions, Cole tried to establish "malice" by showing that the reverend excerpted the parts of larger pieces he thought people would find most offensive and by failing to correct the misrepresentations Frohnmayer had pointed out in his letter about "bearing false witness." The judge didn't seem to be buying this.

During cross-examination, Bull then tried to make the point that Wildmon was no art critic, just a concerned citizen. "Would you know the difference between a collage and a portrait?" Bull asked. The reverend said no. Would he object—as a taxpayer—to any sexually explicit images, even if done by, say, Rembrandt? The reverend said, "Yes I would."

At the trial's end, the judge declared that he had given them an accelerated trial and would now give them an accelerated ruling on the May 18 motion for a preliminary injunction. That was granted. The AFA was enjoined from any further publication or distribution of the pamphlet, since, said the judge, there was "a reasonable likelihood" that it "could be construed by reasonable persons as misrepresenting the work of the artist with likely damage to the artist's reputation and to the value of his works." He would rule later on the complaint alleging libel, copyright infringement, and violation of the New York Artists' Authorship Rights Act.

Bull leaped to his feet to say that this injunction violated the First Amendment and would have a "chilling effect" on the American Family Association. Judge Conner, who characterized himself as "not entirely unacquainted with the First Amendment," assured Bull that the AFA could publish anything it wanted about David Wojnarowicz's work, as long as it was true.

After court adjourned, David told a reporter, "I consider this a vindication of sorts."

But it had been startling to see Wildmon's team appropriate every argument artists had used against their would-be censors: the First Amendment, the specter of fascism, even the "chilling effect." What this short trial showed so clearly was that the culture war was really a battle between two irreconcilable ways of looking at the world.

During the week of this trial, NEA general counsel Julie Davis was on the phone, polling every member of the National Council on the Arts about the four performance artists they'd discussed at their meeting in May. A majority voted to kill the grants recommended by a solo-performance peer panel, but the final decision would be up to Frohnmayer. Later he would be self-critical about how he'd handled this: "Instead of saving the Endowment by demanding that Congress and the administration support the arts, warts and all, or giving up and admitting that our society is not strong enough to withstand controversy, I was trying to find middle ground that would appease everyone."

So on June 29, 1990, Frohnmayer announced that he was defunding Karen Finley, John Fleck, Holly Hughes, and Tim Miller. These artists, soon known as the NEA Four, would file a lawsuit against the Endowment and Frohnmayer that September, charging that their grants were denied for political reasons.

Finley was long gone from the East Village by this time, but she and David had reconnected when he filed his lawsuit. They'd been talking politics. "He was a very big supporter to me when I started having my legal problems," Finley said. "I would talk over the decisions I was making. And from my perspective, I didn't feel that I had many artists I could talk to about it. We had been friends before, but at this time we became colleagues. He would know what I was talking about, because he was living it. He gave me strength."

# 23 "DESPERATE TO BRING A LIGHT"

**Between the end** of the trial and the end of 1990, David created his last pieces of visual art. He still had none of the opportunistic infections that so often afflict people with compromised immune systems, but he knew he was getting weaker.

"I have reached a point where my life feels like it fits in a tiny funnel, and I can see something of its shape and form and end and that is the worst feeling in the world," David wrote that July to Judy Glantzman, who was upstate for the summer. "I always needed room to drift or dream and my sense of mortality and Luis' illness and phone calls bringing more slices of reality/mortality into my home just sent me over the edge."

Luis Frangella, being cared for at his New York apartment by his ex-boyfriend Russell Sharon, could barely speak. "He could just push out a few words with a whole lot of effort," Sharon said. "There were very few people he would allow to be near him." David was not one of them.

Glantzman had written from upstate because David was acting so strangely when she left town, and she wondered if things were OK between them. David explained in his letter that he had a character trait that sometimes made him keep people at bay. "It's the big wall of fear that I can't seem to circumvent and I realized that somewhere I couldn't connect with you and I felt angry at what I carried and the fact you were leaving and life was going on around me."

He had committed to two exhibitions at P·P·O·W, the first an installation to be done with friends and the second a solo show of new work.

But first—he worked that summer with printmaker Richard Deagle on a diptych called *Untitled for ACT UP*, something the organization could use to raise money. In 1989, Deagle had created one of ACT UP's better-known placards—the picture of Mayor Ed Koch next to the words "10,000 New York City AIDS Deaths. How'm I Doin'?"

David selected the images for this piece and Deagle did the labor, printing them with activist Joe Wollin. David wanted to use the text from *Untitled (Hujar Dead)* on top of a picture from a Red Cross lifesaving manual, one man on the ocean floor and another floating just above him. This could be viewed as intended, one man saving another—or as something erotic. *Untitled for ACT UP* would not be the standard diptych with side-by-side images but would have one image above the other. For the bottom piece, David wanted a map of the United States with a target on it. He thought they needed something there to balance the text on top, so David suggested stock quotes. "I got a *Wall Street Journal*," said Deagle, "where each alphabetical section of stock has the letter repeated three times. I picked the one that says *KKK*, and I said, 'Is this too gimmicky for you?' and David said, 'No I kind of like it.'"

In mid-July, David learned that construction crews planned to work in his loft on a daily basis for two and a half months beginning August 6. They would leave the place "broom clean" each day but he should remove all valuables, as they would not be responsible for the loss, theft, or destruction of his belongings.

On July 20 and 21, he wrote letters to the loft board and to his lawyer, explaining what he'd already witnessed of the crew's habits during earlier periods of work. He had asked that the darkroom equipment be fully protected and they showed up with a filthy piece of plastic full of holes to cover it. He had set part of his day aside for them to come in and measure for new baseboards; a week or two later, they wanted access to do the same measurements again. They'd spent twenty-three days replacing fifteen feet of exposed gas pipe. They'd left his bathroom a mess and thrown a shower curtain and rods into a pile of his paintings. They'd left the loft door unlocked numerous times while the street door was propped open with a cinder block, leaving him vulnerable to anyone who wanted to wander in from the street. Worst of all, he didn't see how he could get his work done for the two upcoming shows.

\* \* \*

His retrospective began its tour, and David wanted to see it in each new location. On July 22, he flew to Los Angeles to prepare for the "Tongues of Flame" opening at the Santa Monica Museum of Art.

He stayed with Norman Frisch on Venice Beach, and Frisch remembered that David arrived "fuming mad"—at Marion Scemama. He and Marion had reconnected, by phone, in late June when she called from Paris on her fortieth birthday. "He was sweet," she said. "Not too surprised." They had begun calling each other again, and she felt they had reconciled. A month later, she felt confident enough to propose that she come and help him in Santa Monica. "He got angry at the way I was asking him," she said. "He felt manipulated. I didn't say 'I'd love to come help you' but 'do *you* want *me* to come.'" David's version is unknown; it's not part of the list of grievances against Marion he eventually wrote out. But it seems to have been one more irrational rupture.

"He was in such a state emotionally when he landed in Venice," Frisch said. "It took him days to calm down." Frisch remembered some intense phone conversations between David and Marion, to the tune of "I never want to fucking see you again." And he remembered David's agitation over the loft. "He was afraid that the landlord might try something if he found out he was away. So he had someone staying there or coming by every day or two." Walking on the beach seemed to help.

It also helped that he loved how the show looked in Santa Monica. "I guess there was more space or nicer space," said Frisch. "He spent a long time installing the show with the staff. He was also painting directly on the walls of the museum, and he was very into it. But I think that was the first time I really saw him not feeling well. That was a struggle for him because he was very excited about the exhibition, and he was going to get press that had not come to Illinois. It was a high-profile venue for him because at the time it was a very hip museum. But his energy was limited." David had occasional bad headaches, he had trouble keeping food down, and he tired easily. He would need to lie down on the cement floor of the museum even as people worked around him.

On the night of the opening, July 27, David gave a reading. There in the audience was Jan Mohlman, the woman who'd shared a studio with him on Houston Street in 1982. She had moved to Los Angeles after the East Village scene ended, and she'd lost touch with David. "As soon as our eyes met, I burst into tears in front of everyone in a crowded gallery," she said. "He was so kind. He spent a good ten minutes just standing with me, making sure that I was OK. I think he was a little freaked out by all this emotion I was displaying. That kind of thing made him uncomfortable, but that might have been the first time I'd seen him in person since he had gotten his diagnosis, and so it was a huge thing for me to see him."

The day after the opening, David left to perform *ITSOFOMO* with Ben Neill, first in Seattle and then in San Francisco, where David stayed for several days. This is probably the point when he actually met Amy Scholder at City Lights, after corresponding with her for a couple of years. She was interested in publishing David's monologues, since *Sounds in the Distance* was long out of print and he had more to add. This project, *The Waterfront Journals*, would appear several years after David's death.

Philip Zimmerman went to see *ITSOFOMO* at the San Francisco Art Institute and found it disconcerting that his old friend had become the Angry Art Star. "It was a rant and people were cheering at the end. This was foreign to the David I knew," said Zimmerman. "It was weird and creepy for me. I didn't enjoy it."

Zimmerman took David to see Anna Halprin's workshop for HIV-positive men. A revered postmodern dancer and choreographer, Halprin believed that movement could be a healing art. Zimmerman's boyfriend, Allan Stinson, had worked with her since the seventies, so Zimmerman joined in, admitting that it wasn't really his style—"a session of rolling around on the floor rearranging your emotions through sketching with oil pastels and yelling at the virus." David watched for about forty-five minutes, then told Philip he'd meet him later. He pronounced it "hokey."

"It was too West Coast weird for him," Zimmerman said. "I understood what David meant, but also in the back of my head I was thinking that maybe something she was working with would click with David—something about neutralizing the rage, that thing that was eating him and making him sicker. He was beginning to get seriously ill, and in my own way I was grasping at straws trying to offer some alternative to what he was getting back in New York. I think that if he had been able to pull out of the stress of New York, there might have been a turnaround. I talked to him about moving to San Francisco for a while. He wouldn't do it. That darkness energized him. While he was here, we would go to Polk Street and hang out in the coffee shops, watching the hustlers and junkies."

David was retracing his steps. He actually stayed at the Y where he'd lived in 1976 while working as an egg sorter. Back then he'd romanticized life in the Tenderloin neighborhood. Now his impulse among the runaways and crack addicts and beaten-down homeless was to withdraw to his "bummy room" and to watch "people being violent with each other from the eighth floor windows," and to find it simply depressing.

David got back from California on August 5. On August 8, Judge William C. Conner dismissed the charges related to copyright and libel in the case of *Wojnarowicz v. American Family Association*. While acknowledging that David's copyright *had* been infringed, the court bought the AFA's "fair use" defense, i.e., that it was free to use the artist's work for the purpose of criticizing and commenting on it. Then, to prove libel against someone who'd been designated (as David had been) "a limited use public figure," plaintiffs had to prove that Wildmon intended actual malice against David, and the court was not convinced.

The court did find, however, that the AFA had violated the state law, the New York Artists' Authorship Rights Act. Wildmon had "largely reduced plaintiff's multi-imaged works of art to solely sexual images devoid of any political and artistic content." The judge cited Philip Yenawine's testimony "that there is a reasonable likelihood that defendant's actions have jeopardized the monetary value of plaintiff's works and impaired plaintiff's professional and personal reputation." He ordered the AFA to send a corrective mailing to everyone who had received the original pamphlet, telling them that the images were fragments of larger artworks. But, because David could not provide evidence of lost income or canceled shows, he would be awarded damages of just one dollar.

He called me and many others that day to say that he'd won this dollar and that, depending on how he felt, he would use it to buy either a condom or an ice cream cone. He got a little chuckle out of that. In fact, he specified that the AFA write him a check, no doubt intending to use it in some future piece. The AFA's check for one dollar remains uncashed among his papers.

That summer David wanted Patrick McDonnell to come to New York from Illinois. He knew Patrick had little money, so he gave him a print, telling him, "Sell this and come visit me." It was one of the supermarket posters with Romulus and Remus. "I didn't know what it was worth and I was embarrassed to ask David," Patrick said. "So I shopped it around and no one would buy it. Then my boss at an art store told me he'd give me six hundred dollars. So I sold it to him. I thought six hundred dollars was pretty good. Then I got to New York, first time I'd ever been there, and David yelled at me immediately. 'That was worth three thousand dollars!* You just gave it away!' He was so mad at me. He said, 'You could have stayed in a nice hotel, and you could have had a much different experience if you'd done it the right way.' And he goes, 'Now you're going to have to stay with Tom.'"

The first morning Patrick woke up in New York, he walked the few blocks from Tom's place to the loft to find that David was distraught. He had just learned about the suicide of Ethyl Eichelberger, the drag performer who'd been close to Hujar.

This was one of those deaths that shook what was left of the East Village community, especially the performance artists. To Patrick, who hardly knew who Ethyl was, David said, "I could have talked him down. He was too powerful a force to give up. He wasn't sick!"

But he was. Few people knew that Ethyl had been HIV-positive for years. Reportedly he could not tolerate the few medications available in 1990. On August 12, he slit his wrists. People then began to recall that at his

---

* The piece would not have been worth three thousand dollars in 1990 but was probably worth more than six hundred.

last show, Ethyl had—for the first time—failed to deliver his signature song at the end of the performance: "We Are Women Who Survive."

By the time of Patrick's visit, David had completed much of *Why the Church Can't/Won't Be Separated from the State*, a large painting that addressed much of what he'd been through over the past year.

According to Patrick, who saw this in progress, David used maps of Iraq as a base. On top of that he painted a river that runs into a tunnel, then circles back around the hill. The water is red before entering the tunnel and it's labeled "artery." The part that's come back around is blue and labeled "vein." So this is a painting about one body, making separation impossible.

He made ten openings in the barren landscape around the river, and in these he inserted photos, stats, and one lithograph, all held in place with red string: three images of men underwater from the Red Cross lifesaving manual, including the one used in *Untitled for ACT UP*; a picture of a Greek statue with right arm bent, a pose he'd once used as a stencil; the photo of graffiti reading "Fight AIDS. Kill a quere [sic]," which he'd contributed to the "Witnesses" catalog; the first page of the Wildmon pamphlet, labeled "Your Tax Dollars Helped to Pay for These Works of Art"; the lithograph made with the *New York Post* editorial; Patrick posing in the "culture" headdress; a small photo of the homophobes who protest at every Gay Pride parade; and the Wildmon fundraising flyer stating that David wanted five million dollars. (This last item he had decorated with a large swastika.) He left one hole empty, with red strings hanging, as if something had been ripped out. Patrick said this was his suggestion when David could not decide on a final photo to include.

Elsewhere David fixed small circles with some of his standard iconography—ants on a crucifix, blood cells, a snake catching a frog, and so on. A small seated skeleton, cut from dollar bills, wears a pope's miter.

The piece completely coheres despite all the disparate elements, though it invites the viewer to spend some time taking it in.

\* \* \*

"Tongues of Flame" was on view in Santa Monica until September 5, and while it was there, religious right activists came up with another line of attack.

Reverend Louis Sheldon had convened a meeting of conservative ministers at a nearby church to "discuss options" a week before the show opened. Sheldon, founder and chairman of the Traditional Values Coalition, wrote to church leaders, "I am told the exhibit includes photos of men having sex with men and animals." Later, he told the *Los Angeles Times* that the meeting had drawn a large crowd and among the actions discussed was a possible class-action lawsuit.

The lawsuit filed in U.S. district court on August 29, 1990, however, made no mention of Sheldon or his group. It was the work of the Rutherford Institute, a legal organization dedicated to promoting the Christian right's agenda through the courts. One of its lawyers, Larry Crain, had represented Wildmon during his deposition.

The lawsuit, *Fordyce v. Frohnmayer*, alleged that the NEA's support for "Tongues of Flame" violated the establishment clause of the First Amendment. Tax dollars had partially paid for a catalog in which a recurring theme, the complaint said, was "sacrilegious, defamatory, and scurrilous depictions of the person of Jesus Christ." Plaintiffs David Fordyce and Yvonne Knickerbocker were devout Christians who regarded the public display of this work as a violation of their right to practice their religion free from government intrusion. Fordyce, a Los Angeles lawyer, told the *New York Post* that he wanted a permanent injunction to bar the NEA from "funding, sponsoring and endorsing works which promote blasphemous and sacrilegious hate material." The plaintiffs also claimed that they had suffered "spiritual injury."

In dismissing the case, the court pointed out that nowhere had they even declared that they had seen the show or studied the catalog. "Plaintiffs have failed to show that they endured any special burdens that justify their standing to sue as citizens." Nor, the court said, did they have standing to challenge decisions made by an agency of the executive branch.

\* \* \*

David probably knew about that lawsuit, but he never commented on it. He spent much of August working on a huge installation at P·P·O·W called *The Lazaretto* with artists Paul Marcus and Susan Pyzow.

Marcus was then represented by P·P·O·W. He and David had met there in the office shortly after David joined the gallery. They vaguely remembered each other from the High School of Music and Art. Marcus recalled David as "the type of kid who'd hang outside smoking cigarette after cigarette." They had not been friends.

He did not know at that point that David had AIDS. Marcus began to talk about his volunteer work with the Montefiore outreach program in the Bronx, where he'd been helping a young Hispanic woman who was dying of AIDS. "The whole experience had knocked me for a loop," Marcus said, "and I remember that I was pretty emotionally trashed at that point. I told him about it, and from there we started to have a real rapport."

They began meeting occasionally at an East Village coffee shop, talking for hours over chicken soup and borscht. "I'm very strong in my political view of things, and as a result have found it difficult to function within the art world," said Marcus. "David was more willing to accept people's differences, and I have problems with that, definitely. I want people to see the light. I *demand* that people see the light and recognize the light and walk towards it."

During one of these meetings, they began drawing caricatures of political figures on the napkins. As they played more and more with this, one of them drew what he called a ship of fools. They knew they wanted to see Jesse Helms on that ship. "It was like throwing a rock into water," Marcus said of their process. "It started rippling out in this free-floating word-association game over the course of three or four of these encounters where one of us would pick it up and just continue to visualize it. We found it totally hilarious. Then it grew into these other compartment. And the sketches grew. The complexity of the idea grew, and we started to take it seriously, seeing it as this sort of morbid, black, poignant way of expressing our sentiments about the whole AIDS situation."

Susan Pyzow, Marcus's wife, came up with the title. A lazaretto is a quarantine station, sometimes a ship. "It's a metaphor for exiling people that society doesn't want around," she said. "Just cast them off, and whatever happens to them, happens."

"There were nights he would come over to our place," said Marcus, "with two pints of strawberry sherbet and smoke a pack and a half of cigarettes and stay from nine o'clock in the evening until four o'clock in the morning, go home, take a shower, come back within a couple of hours and continue the conversation. There was no middle ground with David. There was an intensity about him, which wrapped itself around the shortness of time that he was always conscious of, so when he embraced you, he fully embraced you."

When the gallery went on hiatus in August, Wendy Olsoff and Penny Pilkington turned the keys over to the three artists, who found a few other helpers among Marcus's art students at Parsons. David and Marcus had been collecting stories from people with AIDS about the physical horrors, the victimization, and the discrimination they often faced. (For example, "I spent nine days in a hospital emergency room corridor. They sent me home when I refused a colonoscopy in the hallway.") They began the installation by constructing a labyrinth with black plastic bags. Then they wrote out the stories they'd collected on large sheets of paper and attached those to the billowing walls. This maze led into a grotesque sickroom where, in a corner, a skeleton lay under a blanket on a cot. Decorating the walls around the cot was a screed about access to health care and other issues affecting the politicized body. On a nightstand sat many bottles of pills and a small TV pumping out daytime drivel, crowned on top with an actual dead cockroach. There was garbage on the floor, splotches of vomit, a Raggedy Ann. In the hallway leading from this room, blue hands reached out of the walls. This led to the ship of fools and its papier-mâché passengers—Cardinal O'Connor, Jesse Helms, and George H. W. Bush. They floated across a sea of blood—red satin in which hundreds of small human faces seemed frozen in mid-cry and hundreds of human hands reached out for help. Past this centerpiece came a dancing Howdy Doody, who talked nonstop: "How'm I doin'? Hey, don't look at me. I'm a puppet. I'm a politician. I have a wooden head and sawdust for brains. Hey, ain't my fault people are dying. Is it your fault? How'm I doin'?" Just outside the installation stood three long tables covered with pamphlets, fact sheets, condoms, and needle-bleaching kits from a diverse selection of groups trying to address the crisis. The soundtrack to it all, on a loop, was what David claimed as his favorite song, Louie Armstrong's "What a Wonderful World."

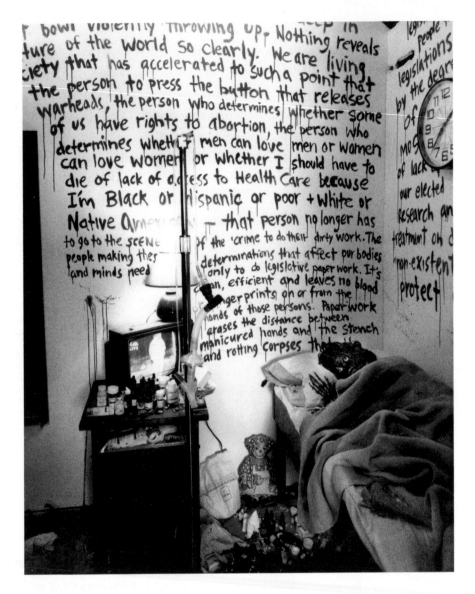

The handwritten text visible on the wall in the installation reads:

r bowl violently throwing up, Nothing reveals
ture of the world so clearly. We are living
ciety that has accelerated to such a point that
the person to press the button that releases
warheads, the person who determines whether some
of us have rights to abortion, the person who
determines whether men can love men or women
can love women or whether I should have to
die of lack of access to Health Care because
I'm Black or Hispanic or poor + white or
Native American — that person no longer has
to go to the scene of the 'crime to do their dirty work. The
people making these determinations that affect our bodies
and minds need only to do legislative paperwork. It's
clean, efficient and leaves no blood
or fingerprints on or from the
hands of those persons. Paperwork
erases the distance between
manicured hands and the stench
and rotting corpses th...

*"The Lazaretto, an installation about the current state of the AIDS crisis,"* 1990.
*(Courtesy of P·P·O·W Gallery, New York)*

The artists had decided that they would present *The Lazaretto* anonymously. "We felt sort of desperate to bring a light to this issue," Pyzow explained. "We were worried that the impact of the show would be diluted or diverted by bringing names into it."

Olsoff called Marcus the driving force behind the construction of this piece. "David got too weak," she said, though he was certainly present and engaged. And he was dealing with the announcement card for the show. Olsoff and Pilkington had driven to Massachusetts to visit artist Carrie Mae Weems. On the way back to New York, they kept stopping at gas stations to call David, because the card had to get to the printer. And they were arguing. David wanted the card to say that the show had been funded by the NEA.

"But that isn't true," Olsoff told him.

David screamed, "This is what I liked about Dean Savard! He would have just done it." Eventually they worked out a compromise. The announcement card said: "Artists involved in this installation have received NEA funds in the past which they have chosen to help support this exhibit."

Above that ran words, probably David's, evoking the ambience of *The Lazaretto*, which would open on September 6, 1990: "You're awakened by a thick societal smoke, you cough, you can't see your hands in front of you, your body is paralyzed, your lungs squeeze tightly, all you can do is whisper, 'help.'"

In the midst of installing *The Lazaretto*, David asked Marcus and Pyzow to take a break with him and go upstate. They were all exhausted and wrung out, after working through a typically brutal and muggy New York August in a space with no air-conditioning. "He insisted that we go to Lake George," Marcus said. "Why? Because of whatever it rekindled in terms of his memories that he wanted to hold on to one more time. Wasn't our idea to go to Lake George. That would not have appealed to me, but it seemed important to him. So we rented a car and just went. And I said, 'David, it's August. Where are we going to stay?' We traveled all the way up there on the spur of the moment, and there was nowhere but this dive that had a spare room. And of course it was only one room, so we were all in there together. That didn't matter to David, as long as he was there. Then he had to take us to all these places that he remembered. He knew the watering hole, he knew where to swim, he knew where to eat.

The "dive" was in Warrensburg, about five miles from where David had spent a month the summer before with Marion Scemama. There's no way to know, of course, if he wanted to remember her or just the general intensity of their month together. Often he simply liked to go back to a place he knew.

\*   \*   \*

Dolores usually wrote to David on or near his September 14 birthday. Her 1990 letter indicates that he had finally told her about his diagnosis. "Your letter was a profound shock to me," she wrote. She had sincerely hoped that he would have no more trauma in his life.

She told him she was concerned about his last two notes. She hadn't understood them. David did not keep copies of those letters, but apparently he'd said something about being depressed, and she'd assumed he was still mourning for Hujar.

She concluded by telling him, "I send you positive energy and love always—you know I am here for you whenever you need me. Love, Mom."

The letter was tucked inside a birthday card that featured a spluttering Daffy Duck: "Admitting your real age? What honesty! What courage! What veracity!"

This was the last time David ever heard from his mother.


Scheduled construction at the loft now threatened to bring unrelenting chaos into his life. There was no way he could do any work there for his November show. He decided to relocate to his new home-away-from-home: Bloomington-Normal. He could again stay with Barry Blinderman and family and find a cheap studio.

He arranged to have a storage unit built in the middle of the loft to hold artwork and other valuables. His upstairs neighbor Dori Poole would supervise the sealing of darkroom equipment and generally keep an eye on everything. The construction company agreed to give him a thousand dollars for airfare and studio rental. He left for Illinois on September 15, the day after his birthday. He stayed for one month.

Patrick took him to the old Montgomery Ward building in downtown Bloomington, where he had a studio and where his roommates had opened a gallery. "It was an old rickety building, with old elevators and grand staircases," Patrick said. His roommates had rented two rooms and a long hallway on the second floor and called it Upfront Gallery. David rented one of those rooms. Patrick described it as enormous with northern light and sixteen-foot hammered-metal ceilings. It also happened to be near the local restaurants David loved, greasy spoons that served steak. David rented a car for about ten days. The studio was in walking distance of both Blinderman's house and Patrick's house, but according to Patrick, David rarely walked anywhere. When he didn't have his rental, Patrick would drive him in his old beater of a pickup truck.

Early on, David went to Walmart to buy a boom box for his studio. While he was there, he spotted a gumball machine full of Super Balls and started loading in quarters and filling his pockets with them. They got into Patrick's pickup and drove out onto a parkway with people traveling fifty-five to sixty-five miles an hour. David wanted to throw Super Balls out the windows. "To shake things up in Bloomington," he told Patrick, instructing him to slow down to thirty-five miles an hour while they launched the balls as far as they could in front of the truck. The balls would bounce, hit the front of the truck, hit the bed, and bounce onto the cars behind them. "He was just laughing. He was having such a good time," Patrick said, "and people were swerving and flipping us off."

David's aggression against the "pre-invented world" had never manifested in such a potentially disastrous way before, but it didn't last long. He had a follow-up idea for a project he and Patrick would do together, traveling the country. "He just thought we were all too complacent," Patrick recalled. "He wanted to go to rural America and camp out in a hotel and get a sense of what everyone did there. Then we were going to make these icons of fear, just these real scary masks, and leave them where people could find them and be stirred by their fear of what this was and where it came from and who left it there." And they'd finance it by applying for a grant. Or so he told Patrick. For David, very aware of the state of his health, this may have been fantasy or even a joke, given his recent adventures in the world of grants.

He created a costume for a new photo series, a kind of skeleton with a monstrous head, a large penis, big spiky-looking hands, and a goggle-eyed crazy face attached to its rib cage. David had Patrick pose in this for what became *Death in the Forest* and *Death in the Cornfield*. "I was afraid we were going to get shot, because we were out on some farmer's land," Patrick said. "I told him, 'David, they're going to bring out the shotgun.' And he goes, 'There's nobody out here.' He was always so willing to take chances. At other people's expense."

A visitor to new territory can have the wrong idea about what's safe and what isn't. One day David sent Patrick into a site that he assumed would be unfriendly, an Army-Navy store. He wanted dog tags printed with the inscription "I really want to farm that blow boy."

"I would do things more daring than he would do," said Patrick. "He's sitting in the truck, saying, 'You're really going to do this?' I said yes. But I don't think I would have done it had he not been sitting in the truck. He put me up to it and I would just do it." Patrick found some sorority girls at work in the Army-Navy store, and they were unfazed by his request.

David was not pleased with the subsequent photo shoot in the forest and cornfield. They began in a wooded area, with David yelling, "All right, you're a monster. Act like a monster." Then, "you're not scary enough!" When Patrick finally settled on rocking, squatting, and reaching like a gorilla, David said, "Yeah, like that. Now yell." The ground was muddy and wet and the feet David made for the costume began to disintegrate. "Screw it," he said. "We don't need 'em." Then all the way back to Bloomington, he fumed, "That was just horrible. That was a waste of time. It's not going to work. It's terrible."

While these photos were never exhibited during David's lifetime, Wendy Olsoff thought they were the beginning of a new direction. "I don't think he felt like it was a finished thing. That's my gut feeling," she said.

He bought a cheap notebook at Walgreen's and began a journal. He dreamt that Hujar was photographing him. David was looking through the contact sheets, "small images of my body near naked, naked, piled around with wet potter's clay. They were beautiful and harrowing. Wet clay with impressions of fingers, hands, pull marks, piling and pounding and at times shot from below my knees, me on my back, some just shots of torso, a large clay hard-on. . . . Peter never photographed me nude. He was always 'protective' in some way of what interpretations or taboos might come towards me, and in the photographing he was observing limits of his own choosing but there was sweetness in his limits of documenting me. In this sleep it felt like he'd freed up that stuff and the resulting images were very sexy and primal and almost what he would have dismissed as 'french' or 'arty' but the sensuality of the wet clay hard-on was pretty wild and even a little disturbing in the questions of who? What hands made this?"

He was creating work in Bloomington-Normal for what would be his last show, and he wanted to change his image. In a letter to Judy Glantzman, he wrote, "I feel like I've been in a place this last year that I don't want to be back in again. I'm sick of the bigot stuff, the press, the reputation as bad boy, etc. I really need to have things come and go on a quieter level." Since people thought of him as the angry artist, he wanted to show that he could make something beautiful.

So he began the flower paintings. But David had never in his career created beauty for the sake of beauty, and he didn't do so now.

According to Marguerite Van Cook, David was very interested in the Decadent movement in literature—Baudelaire's *Fleurs du mal* (*Flowers of Evil*), but also Huysmans's *À rebours* (*Against Nature*). She and David had had a long discussion about *À rebours*. At one point, the principal character, Des Esseintes, collects hothouse flowers "to see the death in them and the decay in them," as Marguerite put it. Des Esseintes is thrilled by plants that seem to have sores and abrasions, that have the look of a half-healed wound, a crusted scar, or gangrened skin. "Des Essientes was mourning his virility," Marguerite said. "He's become weak and wrestles with a variety of spiritual matters. All of which happens as he sequesters himself as his health fails." At one point, Des Esseintes looks at a caladium flower and has, in Huysmans's words, "a sudden vision of the human race tortured by the virus of long past centuries." He means syphilis, but his ability to look at an exotic flower and see "the malevolence of the virus" must have resonated with David. With the flower paintings, he made an unusually sly gesture at addressing the hideous things the AIDS virus could do to a human body. "David was sick of being so dark," said Marguerite, "but at the same time, he was David."

He told Patrick that he'd taken photos at the U.S. Botanic Garden in Washington, D.C. In his Bloomington studio, he projected these slides onto a thin wood board, drew the images, then painted them. He showed Patrick his process, how he used his sketchbooks and journals, telling him, "You need to develop your own methodology, but this is how I do it."

"I'd been trained as a photo realist," Patrick said, "and I talked about how I'd learned to paint—what people told me. We just discussed it." He did not demonstrate anything. David was working on a Hawaiian flower and invited Patrick to critique it. "I said, 'Oh, it's gorgeous. The light is beautiful. I wouldn't change a thing.' I couldn't believe he had done this—the whole plant, the sky—in twenty-four hours, like he hadn't gone to sleep at all. And he said, 'I don't like it. Tell me what I should change.' I couldn't find a thing I would change. And he said, 'You're just flattering me. Let's go to lunch.' So off we went. And I came back the next day and he had changed it. It was even more gorgeous with better light. He had repainted the entire flower."

Of course, the piece wouldn't just be a flower. Each of these forty-eight-by-sixty-inch paintings had small openings where he inserted photos held in place with red string. Each also had two or three blocks of silk-screened text. "The flower paintings were supposed to be very peaceful," Wendy Olsoff said. "Of course, they were layered with his text. He wanted people to linger on the text, so he made it really hard to read. You had to stare at it quite awhile and stay with the painting."

*I Feel a Vague Nausea* features a large blood-red flower with fleshy petals, small black-and-white photo insets of images like the surrogate mother (from *Childhood*) and an X-ray of a heart, with some of his writing from *Close to the Knives*: "I feel a vague nausea stroking and tapping the lining of my stomach. The hand holding the burning cigarette travels sideways like a storm cloud drifting over the open desert. How far can I reach? I'm in a car traveling the folds of the southwest region of the country and the road is steadying out and becoming flat and giving off an energy like a vortex leading into the horizon line. I'm getting closer to the coast and realize how much I hate arriving at a destination. Transition is always a relief. Destination means death to me."

*We Are Born into a Pre-Invented Existence* includes that core text, already featured in *ITSOFOMO* and *Close to the Knives*. The painting of one red flower with a yellow stamen is quite phallic, and among the photo insets around it is the head shot of Steve Brown used on the cover of the "Tongues of Flame" catalog.

For *Americans Can't Deal with Death*, a painting of a pink flower, he wrote a new piece about his visit to the National Atomic Museum, where death is an abstraction, where in the offered documentation you can't see the bodies, "the burnt flesh and sores." He can't deal with the guide who explains the bomb's invention like a proud parent, so he wanders off, watches families snap vacation pictures. If he were in charge, he'd "hook the constant smell of rotting flesh into the air conditioning unit." The other text block is a dream about a kid who has a swollen lump in his armpit. David tells him he needs a doctor. A guy comes in, "acts like he knows me," and David understands that this is Death. He steers him away. "He reappears far away but far away is not far enough."

One night David took a break at a local adult-film joint to watch some porn, wild scenes both gay and straight. As he pulled out of the parking lot, he noticed someone following, flashing his brights at every stoplight.

David ignored him, "not wanting to connect with anyone in this small town figuring that my diagnosis could freak someone out or maybe my semi-notoriety, and any cop or priest or bigot in the state would probably love to arrest me for even breathing on another guy's body." He got to Blinderman's house with the car still right behind him.

David parked and walked over to the driver. The guy said, "What ya up to?"

"Oh I dunno it's hard to explain," David said.

"You married?"

"No, I got other problems. Medical ones."

He noticed that the guy was jerking off as he tried to get David to describe his body. Finally David leaned in the window and slid his hand over the guy's chest, and the guy came.

David walked into the house where everyone was asleep, and found that Blinderman's son Gabriel had fallen out of bed and rolled into the hallway, "looking like he'd fallen off a sled."

This incident recorded in the journal became one of the text blocks on the flower painting *He Kept Following Me*—a piece about what cruising meant to him in 1990 contrasted with the old sense of possibility and freedom, and how he still saw sexuality as a way to embrace the world. The flower he chose is an anthurium, very phallic. He also included text about an encounter at the pier that ends: "In loving him, I saw men encouraging each other to lay down their arms. In loving him, I saw small town laborers creating excavations that other men spend their lives trying to fill. In loving him, I saw moving films of stone buildings; I saw a hand in prison dragging snow in from the sill. In loving him, I saw great houses being erected that would soon slide into the waiting and stirring seas. I saw him freeing me from the silences of the interior life."

Hujar was alive one night in David's dream. His death had been faked, or else he'd revived and gone to live elsewhere. David was at the loft with a Puerto Rican man he'd picked up on the street for sex. They'd arrived to find the scorpion tank full of water. David thought Lucy was dead, but once he spilled the water out, Lucy started climbing the wall. Then David found a second scorpion in a shoe. His mother showed up. "I'm trying to understand what she's there for," he wrote. Then the door opened and Hujar was standing there, looking sheepish.

"Peter comes in and I feel a lot of anger at him for allowing me to believe he had died. Why would he do this? How did he do this? The Puerto Rican guy or my mother had earlier touched the wall of the darkroom and it collapsed like a house of cards. I picked it back up but it was wobbly and rickety. I thought of this now looking at Peter. I'm living in his house and since he has returned, what will he think of . . . all my things, the darkroom's condition, the dirt and dust and pile-up of objects and papers and . . . I can't quite get over my anger at his disappearance, his 'death,' and I'm trying to figure out how to tell him that two scorpions are running around."

Suddenly Hujar walked to the door and said, "I'll see you—good-bye." He was gone. "I realize he may be gone for good. Forever. He may not have planned on staying."

David wanted to do some new photographic pieces for his upcoming show. He bought a large plastic spider with a rather bulbous body and painted parts of it yellow, red, and blue—with a red swastika on the body. He stuck a photo of Jesse Helms's face on the spider's head and photographed it on Blinderman's front porch. David wanted some humor in this exhibit.

He also fashioned a bee from dollar bills and photographed it hovering over a flower made from world maps. This and *Subspecies Helms Senatorius*, Cibachrome prints, would be the only new pieces for his show that did not combine image and text.

The other new work would synthesize all his skills. One day, Blinderman and his wife, Christina Nordholm, took David to the site of a Native American settlement and burial ground near Normal—Dickson Mounds. "This was hallowed ground, and they built a museum over it," Blinderman said. "One could look down into the pit and see these skeletons." Here David took the black-and-white photo that became one of his best-loved pieces after he matched it with the words, printed in red, that had come to him so many years ago: "When I put my hands on your body on your flesh I feel the history of that body. Not just the beginning of its forming in that distant lake but all the way beyond its ending. . . . If I could attach our blood vessels in order to anchor you to the earth to this present time to me I would. If I could open your body and slip up inside your skin and look out your eyes and forever have my lips fuse with yours I would."

In Illinois he dreamt again about the lake. "I returned to that place the reoccurring place where it's been years the sinkholes filled with aquamarine waters, the road of history and infatuations, of myth and killing spiritualities— Christian maybe Mayan and whatever else. I was on the verge, close to it. I talked to people in this sleep and realized I was near my own death, that to finally return to this elusive place meant my death in clarity. Over the years in various sleeps the place got obscured, the forest, the labyrinths of paths, sandy shoals, the fragmented stones, carvings, priests, crosses become entangled in super highway structures and now it was revealing itself with all the detail of reality. And that was at the verge of my final death."

Then the dream changed. He was in a hotel, and he felt that Hujar was nearby or had just left. He thought he caught a "brief fragmented sight of him eating a meal" in a room where three to seven Buddhist monks sat eating.

David worked in Illinois until October 15, and so missed the opening of Luis Frangella's show at Gracie Mansion's new SoHo gallery. By then, Luis was nearly paralyzed, but he still made small drawings on notepads. Gracie offered him a show, which would be his last. He came to the opening in a wheelchair.

In Normal, meanwhile, David had agreed to do a reading at University Galleries on October 9, a benefit for the McLean County AIDS Task Force. He told Judy Glantzman in a letter that he was nervous about it: "Dunno why." In the end, he decided he didn't want his face out there. He wanted Patrick to perform.

David stood behind a wall with a microphone, reading from his galley of *Close to the Knives*. He told Patrick to pretend that he was a cartoon character living in a cartoon jail and that he had to find ways to pass the time. Patrick dressed himself in solid black and painted his hands and his head blue. The top of his head was red with a white stripe separating red from blue. "I was going for a matchstick look," Patrick said.

Some days earlier Patrick had been breaking up glass, in his job as preparator at the gallery, to make it smaller and safer for disposal. David happened by and said, "Stop. We can use that in the show." David arranged to have a fifty-five-gallon drum filled with broken glass and a kettle drum set brought into the gallery. The space was between shows, walls blank, and they put up big sheets of newsprint. David had given Patrick a cue for when he was supposed to start drawing on them. Before that, Patrick banged the drums and smashed the glass. He had a big black marker and a ladder. When he began to draw, he wanted to work quickly. He drew cartoon characters, a big eagle representing American government, and some of David's iconography, like the tornado and the alien head.

"I had never been out in front of a crowd," Patrick said. "What made him think I'd be a good guy to perform? He was pushing me to be this artist that he saw in me." The gallery was packed—standing room only. Patrick was not happy with any of the drawings. Then the last thing he painted was an "exit" and, in the spirit of Wile E. Coyote, he ran into it.

"I did it as many times as I could until I hurt myself. I mean, I literally threw my body into this thing. And that pretty much ramped up the show. After the audience stood up and applauded, I was hooked. I was a performance artist after that. I just loved it. I felt so powerful up there, and it was his words, but it changed my life."

\* \* \*

A pipe broke at the loft four or five days before David was to return from Illinois. Dori Poole, the upstairs neighbor, called Tom, who came over and sloshed through a few inches of water to get to the storage unit that was supposedly guarding David's valuables from the hazards of construction. Dori knew David's temper and she wanted Tom to be the one who took action.

"I decided to pull the stuff out. His stencils were all wet, and all these other things," said Tom, who took them into the darkroom and placed them on the drying racks. "I tried to make sure everything was out of the water. Then the question was, do I tell him while he's away." He decided to wait till David returned, since David was busy and couldn't do anything about it from Illinois.

"He got home and flipped out," Tom said. "I mean, went into a rage: throwing the telephone, screaming, saying it would have been better if I'd let everything just rot—at least then he could sue the shit out of them. And I got so furious I left. Here I'd gone through this struggle with it, and I'd done the best that I could do trying to save the stuff. So I went home and then he called me up and started yelling at me on the phone. I remember yelling back at him that it was not my fault. And slammed the phone down in his ear. Slammed it down. About ten minutes later, he called me back, calm. He didn't apologize, but he was saying, 'You gotta understand.' And I said, 'I do understand. But none of us knew what to do. Your temper—we didn't know whether to tell you out there. The way you've been feeling lately, I didn't know what to do. So if I made the wrong decisions, so be it. But decisions had to be made and I made 'em.'"

David thought about getting an appraisal on what he'd lost. But there's no evidence that he did that or took even the first step toward a lawsuit. Now that his life "fit into a tiny funnel," as he'd put it to Judy Glantzman, that could not be a priority.

He had about two weeks to finish the darkroom work for his show at P·P·O·W. He printed some of the photos he'd taken the previous summer with Marion in the Adirondacks—a caterpillar on a leaf, a honeybee on a stem, his own hand holding a tiny amphibian. He also printed photos of various critters in formaldehyde that he'd taken in Normal at Illinois State's science labs. He matched each of these images with short texts. For example, he placed "what is this little guy's job in the world . . ." on the picture of his hand holding the small frog or toad. In this way, he created a set of eleven unique black-and-white gelatin silver prints.

Gary Schneider printed the skeleton photo David took in Illinois, *When I Put My Hands on Your Body.* It had to be large enough to accommodate silk-screened text. David planned to do two more pictures in this series—large photos with text. He would eventually complete one of the two.

He told his doctor that he had felt so weak and tired while doing the four flower paintings in Normal that he wasn't sure he would have the strength to finish them. He didn't have the energy to make enough new work to fill the gallery. So he decided he would reprint the *Rimbaud in New York* series. When he shot those pictures in 1979 and 1980, he did not have a good camera and certain scenarios were badly lit, so some of the negatives were not good. Printing them was difficult, and he was proud when he pulled it off. The *Rimbaud* series had never been exhibited before. He also turned his controversial 1979 collage *Untitled (Genet)* into a large lithograph.

With this combination of new and old work, his show, "In the Garden," opened on November 2, 1990. Calling it "In the Garden" was a logical choice given the flower paintings, given that all the new photos from caterpillar to *Subspecies Helms Senatorius* came from nature. But it also harks back to something he'd written for his last show about a mixed-media piece, *Where I'll Go After I'm Gone.* "I thought if there was indeed a place one goes after death then it could only be a place determined by one's vision of the world . . . The garden is the place I'll go if I die."

David knew he was getting weaker, but otherwise, the disease didn't yet show. He never had KS lesions on his skin. He was no thinner than he'd ever been. And he kept all thoughts about impending death to himself. He wouldn't talk about it even with Tom, maybe especially with Tom, who said, "He thought I wouldn't be able to put up with it." So David tried to work out his feelings in his journal. The following entry is undated but was written in 1990, probably soon after he came back from Illinois:

> Will my death be terrible and difficult? Will I let go easily as a body
> among the waves or the reeds of a pond? Will I sink below the surface of
> life like a swimmer whose feet become entangled in the undulating

weeds? Will I be embraced by all those who have gone before me? Will I be loved before I go? Will I know it? Will I turn to stone like a grey dot in the field? Will I burrow into the dream of the earth, the humming of the motor works? Will I speak in numbers or symbols? Will I shock myself by dying when I feel it is time, not waiting a moment longer than necessary?

# 24 "LIKE A MARBLE ROLLING DOWN A HILL"

**"In the Garden"** was still up at P·P·O·W when David's retrospective rolled into New York, headed for Exit Art, a large nonprofit space. Co-founders Papo Colo and Jeanette Ingberman had a special appreciation for artists who worked against the grain, against stereotypes, against aesthetic norms. They'd made it their mission to highlight the uncodified and the marginalized.

Ingberman called David "the perfect artist for Exit Art." She had offered him a mid-career retrospective after his troubles began at Artists Space. Told that such a show was already in the works out in Illinois, Ingberman agreed to take "Tongues of Flame" when it toured.

Then she discovered that she was going to have trouble raising the money; David was now a targeted artist. Even colleagues in the nonprofit world were asking her, "How can you do this show? You'll lose your funding!" She collected just a fraction of what she usually did—a donation from the Cowles Charitable Trust. Everyone else said no.

Colo and Ingberman didn't really know David and were surprised to find that this artist with the aggressive sensibility was so reserved, almost shy. He came in one day with several shoe boxes and asked if he could put up some ephemera in a small room. They said they'd be delighted. So David went to work hanging flyers, notes, letters, doodles, personal photos, and posters that traced his history, while Colo installed the rest of the show. They got to talking, and Colo reported that David was installing "an archae-ology of himself."

This show opened on November 17, 1990. A week later, David was back in New Orleans for a vacation with Tom.

\* \* \*

David's physician, Dr. Robert Friedman, was waiting at the barbershop one day when he spotted the December 1990 *Art in America* with the name "David Wojnarowicz" on the cover.

The doctor said to himself, "Gee, I have a patient by that name. That's not a common name." Friedman read the piece, by Lucy Lippard, and realized then that his patient was a rather well-known artist. "I wasn't even charging him. He had no health insurance, and he looked terrible, and I didn't have the heart to ask him for money." He brought the magazine back to his mother, who worked as his receptionist, and told her he didn't know what to do about it.

David really liked Mrs. Friedman. She was always telling him to eat. Sometimes when he came in, she would run across the street to Christine's, a Polish coffee shop, and buy him soup, then make him eat all of it in front of her. "I thought he was just a poor struggling East Village type," said the doctor.

When David came in for his next appointment and began to walk out without paying, as usual, Mrs. Friedman pulled out the magazine and said, "Would you autograph this for us?"

"What?" David said, startled.

Dr. Friedman remembered: "My mother said, 'David, you've been coming to see the doctor for like two years now and you've only paid a couple of times. Don't you think you should do something for the doctor?' I would never have had the chutzpah to say what my mother did. So David went down the block, and he came back and handed me a copy of *The Sex Series*. The whole series in a portfolio." It was David's artists' proof. This was, of course, his preferred method of payment. (Coincidentally, that cover of *Art in America* featured his mixed-media piece *Anatomy and Architecture of Desire*, which he had given to Jean Foos in exchange for her work on the "Tongues of Flame" catalog.)

Dr. Friedman was so busy he did not take the time then to look through the portfolio. "So," he said, "I see my mother and David looking at these big photos, which are highly sexual. And my mother, this Jewish lady from Rockaway, in her seventies, picks up the one of the forest with the circle insert [one man with an erection rimming another], and my mother—I've never forgotten this moment; it made me love my mother even more—my mother looked at the image and slaps her finger across the trees and says, 'This is nature,' and then she points at the insert and goes, 'I guess that's nature too.' And David says, 'You're exactly right.'"

Luis Frangella died of AIDS on December 7, 1990, at the age of forty-six.

On December 18, David requested that a piece of his be removed from a group show, "Art What Thou Eat: Images of Food in American Art," opening that night at the New-York Historical Society. This exhibit of eighty food-related paintings and sculptures included work by such luminaries as Alice Neel, Jasper Johns, and Roy Lichtenstein. What stuck in David's craw was the presence of Mark Kostabi. "I'd never be in the same show with that bigot," he told a reporter.

Once known for glib pronouncements like "paintings are doorways into collector's homes," Kostabi had been branded a vicious homophobe after the June 1989 *Vanity Fair* quoted him saying, "These museum curators, that are for the most part homosexual, have controlled the art world in the eighties. Now they're all dying of AIDS, and although I think it's sad, I know it's for the better. Because homosexual men are not actively participating in the perpetuation of human life."

Kostabi reacted to the public outcry by telling *Newsday*, "I feel terrible for saying something that was an unfair generalization based on a few specific experiences with gay curators and critics that left me very angry. The day of the interview I was in a very bad mood and took it out on a whole group and it was an insensitive and angry remark and I apologize to all who were offended."

Ten days later, he retracted the retraction, telling the *Post's* Page Six that he'd been pressured to apologize by Abbeville Press, which was about to publish *Kostabi: The Early Years*. "They're scared to death. They made me write all these phony apologies," he told Page Six, adding that he still thought the art world was dominated by homosexuals and "that's why there's so much bad art in the world."

When Art Positive, an offshoot of ACT UP, organized in the summer of '89 to fight homophobia and censorship in the arts, Kostabi had been the flashpoint.

"Art What Thou Eat" originated at the Edith C. Blum Art Institute at Bard College, where it opened under the radar in September 1990. (David either didn't know about it, or didn't know Kostabi was included.) Bill Dobbs, an activist with Art Positive, took note of the show's imminent arrival at the New-York Historical Society when an announcement ran with a photo of a Kostabi painting. Dobbs organized an opening-night protest with picketers from Art Positive as well as Queer Nation and ACT UP. David called Dobbs the day of the opening to say he would try to pull his piece, *Tuna*—one of the supermarket posters. He wasn't sure he could, since he no longer owned it. Gracie Mansion did. But she agreed to David's request, and the Historical Society museum director took *Tuna* off the wall during the opening.

That night, Kostabi left a long message on David's answering machine. The core of it was this: "I just wanted to clarify matters and let you know that I'm not the person who I suspect you think that I am, and if you are specifically thinking about that quote in *Vanity Fair*, that was part of a performance art piece and the quote was actually a quote of what other people were saying. I was not quoting my feelings but things that I've heard other people say and it was used out of context, and I explained this about two years ago when it happened. And most of the people, like people at GLAAD and in the gay community—we talked it over and I had pretty much come to an understanding with everyone and I made numerous apologies. Apparently some people are still under the impression that I'm a 'quote' homophobe, or whatever, and I'm sure that will never die down with some people. And I sympathize with their and I presume your anger and I understand that. But I just wanted you to hear from me that that's not the case, that I am exactly the opposite of what you think."

Linda Weintraub, director of the Blum Art Institute and curator of the show, had *Tuna* rehung after the opening. She told a reporter that she had sympathy for David but that "his absence would have compromised the entire show." In fact, the Historical Society had used *Tuna* as the press photo when they sent out the publicity. The final absurdity here was the way the catalog described *Tuna*, as "a comic-like portrait of Superman." The figure painted on the supermarket tuna ad is clearly an outlaw in a green shirt, tying a red bandanna over his face. A small inset in that portrait shows a gun held by someone in a green shirt blowing the head off someone in a blue shirt.

In January, Weintraub sent David a letter: "I am anxious for you to know that the events that took place at the opening of the 'Art What Thou Eat' exhibition have not altered my regard for your work nor my respect for you as a spokesperson for your cause. My insistence that your work remain in the show is based on admiration." She went on to offer him a chance to speak in a public forum at Bard on issues like "the rights of artists to control the sale, exhibition, and reproduction of their works of art after they leave the studio."

"Art What Thou Eat" was up at the New-York Historical Society until March 22. On February 8, the museum director again removed *Tuna*, this time without consulting Weintraub.

On February 1, 1991, "Tongues of Flame" opened in Philadelphia at the Tyler School of Art's Temple Gallery. Wendy Olsoff drove David there to do a reading, similar to what he'd done in Normal, with video running on several monitors.

"I have the worst sense of direction, but I thought, 'I'll just get us to Philly.' I didn't even have a map," Olsoff said. "So David and I are talking on and on about dreams, about life, about death—and smoking so much there must have been smoke coming out the roof. And suddenly I realize we're forty minutes past Philadelphia. I was going, 'Oh my god, we have to find the school,' and I realized, he did not care. I've thought about it since. For him, it was about the journey, the traveling. So I was in a panic and he was not in a panic, and he was not going to help navigate the route at all. I leaned out the window and got directions, and we were significantly late.

"There was a massive crowd waiting for him, because he was a legend at this point. So they had all the monitors set up and the microphones, and David starts getting really angry because the equipment wasn't set up right. Everyone was a little scared of David. But they got it together, and once he started performing, everyone seemed to stop breathing. He had total control. I remember feeling bad, because he gave so much in the performance, and he was really sick."


Early in February, David got a letter inviting him to appear in a Gap ad, for television, to be shot by Matthew Rolston. If he agreed, he would, talk on camera about an issue of importance to him. "The Gap will be encouraging subjects to use this important media access to affect positive social change," said the invitation. Among the others the company had approached were Martin Scorsese, Philip Glass, Spalding Gray, and I. M. Pei. The print campaign included Miles Davis, Spike Lee, and Joni Mitchell. The Gap would pay scale, which many subjects donated to charity. He would wear his own clothes plus one Gap item.

David walked over to the Schneider-Erdman Lab to tell Gary and John.

Erdman remembered asking him, "Are you going to do it?"

And he remembered David's reply: "Are you kidding? That's a sellout. That's so commercial."


David also received a letter that month from Amy Scholder in San Francisco, proposing that he do an artists' book for a new imprint she was editing. Though she was still at City Lights, Scholder had taken on this project with Artspace, whose director, Anne Marie MacDonald, wanted to begin publishing books that paired a visual artist with a writer. They would be the same size and shape as the Golden Books for children. David would be first in the series, providing both words and visuals.

Scholder also invited him to participate in Out/Write, a gay and lesbian writers conference in San Francisco at the end of February 1991. He would be part of a panel titled "AIDS and the Social Function of Art." To that end, he jotted a list of ideas in his journal: "disease on two legs," "self-protective cliques even in the activist community," "the need to have fantasies that don't acknowledge AIDS issues," and more. But he elaborated on only one of the points he wanted to make: "I'm not so much interested in creating literature as I am in trying to convey the pressure of what I've

witnessed or experienced. Writing and rewriting until one achieves a literary form, a strict form, just bleeds the life from an experience. How do we
talk, how do we think, not in novellas or paragraphs but in associations, in
sometimes disjointed currents." On February 24, he flew to San Francisco
for the conference.

He did some journal writing there, none of it about Out/Write. He was
too preoccupied with his depression: Two entries, "Guy on Polk Street" and
"Kid on Market Street," evoke the monologues of old, but David never spoke
to those two for their stories, only noted their apparent suffering and their
potentially imminent deaths.

Soon after his return to New York a week later, David received a four-
page letter from a young writer he'd met at the conference. It began: "Dear
David Wojnarowicz, First off, I want to tell you I think you're one of the
very few people in the world I could fall <u>deeply</u> in love with." The young
man said he now dreamt of David, felt he'd always known him, and spelled
out an elaborate sexual fantasy about him. Though he was currently living
with Dennis Cooper, he thought that relationship was over. He didn't want
to tell Cooper, however. He thought that, first, he and David should "just see
what happens."

David didn't respond for almost two weeks. Then he wrote:

> I haven't answered right away because I've been pretty ill and also
> needed to think about your letter. I was feeling pretty sick at the confer-
> ence and it got worse on the plane home. Your letter really surprised me.
> I mean, you don't really know me at all and it's a pretty intense letter to
> receive from someone I don't know at all either. I don't know what I
> represent to you but I really have none of the feelings you describe as
> having towards me. . . . The stuff you say about your relationship, I
> mean—that's all normal stuff. The intensity at first is always wild because
> you can fill a person up with all associations and projections and myths
> and desires and when they and you reveal the subtle stuff underneath, it
> all becomes kind of mundane or "normal" and the intensity shifts. You
> need to accept that it is always like that and just put your energy into the
> subtle stuff and real communication; your fears, your desires, whatever.
> You should be exploring that with Dennis, otherwise you end up just

repeating it over and over and over. . . . If you knew me at all, you would see that I really don't want a love affair with anyone at this point in my life. I have a relationship that I've been involved with and all the issues you raise about yourself are things I'm dealing with with this guy. I remember when I had crushes on people in the past and the idea of it exhausts me. I'm dealing with all this illness around me and the illness I go through for periods of time so that things like love or stuff like that are issues that I don't have the energy or desire to go through. Like I said, the guy I'm involved with to an extent is where I would put that energy if I wanted an intense relationship. Right now I actually prefer to be on my own for long periods so I can think and deal with issues like my past and my mortality.

Also, he couldn't see going behind Cooper's back. "I just don't move that way." He urged the young writer to work things out with Cooper.

He'd been selected again for the Whitney Biennial, this time with *The Sex Series, He Kept Following Me,* and *When I Put My Hands on Your Body*— the skeleton piece.

He sketched out an idea for a new painting. It would be like *Something from Sleep II,* with the figure drawn on maps dreaming at the bottom, but this time there would be even more things dangling over the bed—all David's signature images, like the burning man, the worker carrying a deer, the burning house, the dung beetles, the locomotive, gears, nude men washing. He labeled it *Dictionary of Good-Byes.*

David would never make another painting, but wanted to finish what he could. In March, he and Ben Neill spent a few days in a Brooklyn studio recording *ITSOFOMO* with a fifteen-hundred-dollar grant from Art Matters. The cover would use a detail from *Fear of Evolution,* the monkey pulling a globe in a wheelbarrow.

His activity gets harder to track here. Most of the journal entries from the beginning of 1991 are undated. One says: "'Like a marble rolling down a hill'—something heard on TV." David had this fatalism about him. His doctor thought that part of him wanted to keep fighting but part of him was

# 7 MILES A SECOND

*Seven Miles a Second, 1993. Ink on paper. Title page (p. 39) of the third section of the graphic novel by David Wojnarowicz, James Romberger, and Marguerite Van Cook. This drawing is an accurate representation of David at home.*

resigned to dying. In another journal passage, David wrote down one of the politically correct tropes of that time: "AIDS is not about death. It is about people living with AIDS." His pronouncement on that: "Bullshit. . . . I demand that we don't slip into denial about Death as an aspect of AIDS."

He visited his friend Phil Zwickler in the hospital. Since Zwickler was asleep much of the time, David drew a picture of him hooked up to an IV with a caption: "He had dementia. One time he woke up laughing. What's funny, I asked. He mumbled: the story in the paper. I picked up a newspaper from the floor. On page 2 the headline said: WOMAN TRIES TO STOP FIGHT BETWEEN TWO 5000 POUND ELEPHANTS. No that's not it, he said, and fell asleep."

David was like a turtle pulled into his shell. He observed but mostly kept people at bay. Even as he wrote and drew to bear witness to the epidemic, he faced, once again, the core issue in his life: How much could he reveal about himself? He found it difficult to communicate what he was feeling even to those closest to him, like Tom. Someone had arranged for David to see a doctor in Boston for some experimental treatment, and Tom kept asking, "Do you want me to go with you?" Tom was more than willing to do that, but David always said no and wouldn't even say when he was going. Then on April 8, he called Tom at work. Tom took his call, as he always did, though he was in the middle of a meeting with several state officials. David said to him, "I'm leaving for Boston in an hour." Tom was shocked—and angry—and he couldn't stop his meeting to have a conversation, so he said, "Good luck."

David then wrote in his journal that he'd called "a friend"—Tom—who'd responded as if David was going "for an overnight vacation." He added, "I'm speechless." David stayed in Boston just the one night. The drug reaction lasted forty-eight hours. It made him nauseated and wobbly. He had a new pain beneath his rib cage, right hand side. But there was more than physical discomfort now. His fear of rejection and his refusal to let anyone comfort him was making him very miserable. "My eyes hurt when I cry so I can't even fucking let it out," he wrote in the journal.

He decided against continuing with the experimental treatment. He began to have unexplained fevers, night sweats, profound weakness. He was getting to that point where he could give all his T-cells names. But then he would rouse himself. He was very determined to finish a couple of projects, like the artists book he titled *Memories That Smell like Gasoline*.

The book would be one last act of transgression. He was thinking about sex, the mystery and power of it, the adventures he'd had. The visual element in *Memories That Smell like Gasoline* would be his black and gray watercolors of sexual encounters set in porn theaters—delicate renditions of hard-core scenes—along with ink drawings that illustrated moments from his own sexual history. He included the drawing made at Zwickler's bedside. The four stories were all about anonymous sex—the sweet pleasures of cruising but also the dangers. There's a constant sense in these texts of at least latent violence, which sometimes turns real and potentially deadly.

The title story is about the night he was in the lobby of a movie theater and suddenly saw a man who'd raped him when he was a teenager. David had been on one of those jaunts out of the city that he used to take from Port Authority, riding a bus into New Jersey to some body of water where he'd walk in fully clothed and float, then hitch a ride back. A man in a pickup truck stopped for him, drove to a remote location, overpowered him, fucked him. David remembered that to endure the rape he had tried, unsuccessfully, to imagine that the guy was sexy or gentle. David thought he might die that night, and when he saw the man at the theater, he shrank in his own mind to boyhood-size and went and hid in a bathroom stall.

He had been a victim of sexual violence and now he was facing death from a sexually transmitted disease—yet for David, holding on to sex was a way of holding on to life, and he was trying to understand the contradictions.

He wrote about sex in the pre-AIDS world—like the time he hooked up with a truck driver while he was on the road. He also included the story, from the 1980 journal, about the night he met a deaf and mute man who followed him into the West Fourth Street subway station and, on the empty mezzanine between the Eighth Avenue and Sixth Avenue lines, began to simultaneously blow him and rob him. David escaped and ran to the lower platform, where he just managed to leap into an F train as the doors closed, and then found himself surrounded by sleeping winos.

He wanted to analyze what he'd seen in this guy and in the other violent, unpredictable men he sometimes found himself attracted to. "It's something about violence as a distancing tool to break down the organized world. It's the weird freedom in his failure to recognize the manufactured code of rules. The violence that floats like static electricity that completely annihilates the possibility of future or security; I'm attracted to living like that," he wrote in this piece, titled "Doing Time in a Disposable Body." David had never been violent with anyone, yet he radiated that impulse in his frightening rages. He knew so much now about how he used his anger in order to survive. Increasingly he had found aesthetic solutions to his early experiences with violence. That was a way to be set free.

The concluding story here, "Spiral," is the last piece David ever wrote. Much of it is about AIDS, hospital visits to the latest dying friend, his reaction to some porn palace where no one's using a condom, and, at the end, a poetic evocation of fading away: "I am growing tired. I am waving to you from here. I am crawling around looking for the aperture of complete and final emptiness. I am vibrating in isolation among you. I am screaming but it comes out like pieces of clear ice. I am signaling that the volume of all this is too high. I am waving. I am waving my hands. I am disappearing. I am disappearing but not fast enough."

He saw his impending death, the secret theme of *Memories*, as the logical outcome of a society that did not value him, did not protect him— and never had.


David called me on April 10 to say that in five days he was going to start driving across the country to do readings from *Close to the Knives*, which would reach bookstores that month. "I carry a whole blanket of fears in my psychology," he told me, "and I think this trip could be a big breakthrough for me." He was going to take a typewriter and a sketchpad and try to relax. Then when he got back at the end of May, he planned to start another experimental drug trial in Boston. In the journal, though, he wrote that he was probably crazy not to cancel this trip. He'd felt nauseated all week.

On April 12, David underwent a bone marrow biopsy to test for lymphoma. They took marrow from his hip, and the next day he was still in pain, "kicked by a tiny mule," he said when he wrote about it in the journal.

He could calm himself by thinking, "I'm here. This is the chair, the bed, the shelf . . ." The cross-country trip was on hold.

"I've been depressed for years and tears since Peter died and Tom's diagnosis and my own diagnosis," he wrote in the journal. "When I was younger I could frame out a sense of possibility or hope, abstract as it was, given my life felt like shit. I've lost that ability. Too much surrounds me in terms of fears . . . the recent loss of mobility where I am too terrified to go long distances for fear of death or illness in unfamiliar environs. Knowing I've been depressed, realizing the extent recently, makes it all more confusing because I don't know, I can't separate what in my fatigue and exhaustion and illness is from depression, what is from disease. One feeds on another until I want to scream."

David's self-imposed isolation was the opposite of what he needed. He thrived on interacting with people. It's why he collaborated so much. But he'd decided that no one could comprehend what he was going through, so he kept to himself, which made him more depressed, which made him feel more isolated.

The big list of complaints he eventually made, the one in which he broke down what had happened with Marion Scemama, would also include the friends who were now telling him things like "You look good, you're a survivor." He added a complaint about his boyfriend: "With Tom, I can't verbalize my illness or dying—he can't handle it. I get so lonely in this illness that I wish I could go to bed and die but I'm afraid to take my own life right now."

The observation about Tom would prove to be quite unfounded, but during this period David wouldn't even tell him if he had a fever. As a rule, he and Tom spoke on the phone every day if they didn't see each other. But one night, David told him, "I feel more alone when you call than when you don't call."

Recalling how irritable and uncommunicative David was about his illness at this point, Tom said, "I think he assumed that people should be able to intuit how to deal with him. As much as I would try to figure out what to do, it was really hard. Clearly something was going on emotionally with him very, very deeply, but you couldn't touch it. I just couldn't get there. So that comment came out of that kind of struggle. But it really hurt. I felt so bad when he said that. I didn't know what to do."

David wrote later in his journal:

I don't know why I feel this, but I do and I have to say it. I can't control myself. Nobody can touch what's going on inside me, so maybe that's the bottom line problem. I have to get used to it, get used to fevers periodically. Sore throat strep throat I'm just beginning to get. Took a little mirror to look at my throat, bent over a lamp and found my mouth full of fungus again. What do I do? [Tom] slammed the phone down and I don't blame him because it was brutally clear what I said but I can't pretend it feels different. When he calls lately it's usually at the end of the day to say goodnight and my head is so filled with fear and darkness it's almost an insult. Everything is scary and I feel shook with the reality of the situation. I AM DYING SLOWLY. CHANCES DON'T LOOK TOO GOOD.

Marion had called David sometime in March. They began speaking again, and the connection intensified in April. David's phone bill showed fifteen calls to Paris between April 6 and the beginning of May. One would call, and after they talked awhile, they'd hang up and the other would call back, so they could share the cost. One night they talked for four hours.

David told her about wanting to do a book tour, but by the end of April, he'd narrowed that down to one stop: San Francisco. He also wanted to re-visit his favorite spots in the Southwest. He asked Marion to come with him. "This will be my last trip," he told her more than once. "My last trip."

"I was kind of scared to do it," she said. "I knew how hard it would be. He was sick and I didn't know if I would handle it, but at the same time, I didn't think I could say no."

During one of their phone calls, he told her, "I have a list of things to discuss with you before we decide to do this."

Marion thought, how American! "But in fact it was great," she said, "because we had to define what kind of relationship we had, what kind of relationship we didn't want to have anymore, and what kind of relationship we dreamed of having during this trip. Then I said, 'I should have my list, because you're hard to deal with too.' But I didn't prepare a list. I may have asked about two or three things, but the main thing I said was, 'I want you to swear, really swear, that whatever happens during this trip, you will never reject me the way you did before. I went through a strong depression. It has been too hard for me.' . . . And he laughed and said, 'No, no, no, I promise.'"

They planned to fly to Albuquerque and rent a car. Marion came to New York several days beforehand and helped David get ready—doing errands, the legwork. Every day when six o'clock came around, though, he would ask her to leave the loft because Tom was coming over. Marion didn't think this was odd. David was about to leave town for three weeks, so of course he'd want to spend time with Tom. Then one day, Tom was on his way over and she was still there. "I didn't understand why David was so nervous," she said, "but I left." She went to see someone in the neighborhood and came back along Second Avenue just as Tom and David were leaving the building. "I was going to walk over to them and say hello to Tom," she said. "David saw me, and I could see him freaking out." He signaled at her to walk away. Then he and Tom crossed the street. "That was an image I kept in my mind."

Tom knew that David was traveling with Marion but he thought they were meeting in New Mexico. He did not know that Marion was in New York. Nor did David tell Tom that this was going to be his "last trip."

Phil Zwickler died of AIDS on May 7, 1991, at the age of thirty-six.

On May 8, David and Marion arrived in Albuquerque. They rented a car and drove to Monument Valley, which was probably their first stop. But then they headed for Las Vegas. According to Marion, there was a show there that David wanted to see. It had been running for ten years, or maybe twenty or thirty. People had played the same roles for decades. That was all she could remember of David's description. As they drove, David joked that maybe they should get married. In Las Vegas, it only took five minutes. What would François think, he asked. Marion wondered what Tom would think.

She said that she'd actually broached the idea of marriage earlier, maybe in '89. She couldn't remember the date, but they'd written some letters about it. After his diagnosis, he worried about how he would afford health care, since he had no insurance. She told him that if they married, he would be able to get free health care in France. They fantasized further. They'd live in a loft together. They'd generate income by making T-shirts. Tom would move in too, and Marion would get him a job as a cook—she knew people. "We lived in this dream for two weeks, three weeks," she said, "but if he had asked me, I would have done it. I think it made him feel better to know that there was this possibility."

So they were approaching Las Vegas, she said, "with odd but sweet feelings for each other," and they stopped for gas on the edge of town. They were within sight of the glitz and the kitsch when they saw a girl walk out of a convenience store with a big frozen drink that was pink and green or blue—something so aggressively artificial it seemed the symbol of the city. David asked her if she really wanted to go into Las Vegas.

She said, it's up to you.

He said, let's drive to Death Valley.

She thought maybe if they'd gone into Las Vegas they would have gotten married, and that would have been a mess, "but there was this kind of romanticism sometime between him and me, like we could go together forever."

Certainly when they worked together, they'd been capable of an almost uncanny rapport. But the perceptions they had on this trip often seemed to originate on two different planets.

When David wrote in his journal about these first days on the road, he said nothing about Las Vegas, marriage, or even Marion:

I'm in a constant flux of anxieties about my body and its exhaustion and strange waves of illness. I feel like my brain and my body are separated and my brain refuses to acknowledge that my body wants to shut down or throw up or burn with fever. Sometimes it hits just a few hours after waking—if I'm lucky it waits until late afternoon or evening. I hate it. And I push myself to keep moving or else consign myself to the bed in surrender which depresses me, makes me angry, makes everything dark until I wish for death to relieve me. I get tense and suddenly everything is too much. I think I'll break down if even one more thing confronts me. Even a simple choice makes me feel like I want to scream and disappear.

I know I need to adjust and accept my body and its levels of energy but it complicates everything. My refusal to accept is the struggle. I feel extremely alone in all this as if confronted with no choice when I should have a choice. I'm too young for this yet I'm feeling old from all the deaths. Phil died a few days ago on the 7th of May. I couldn't feel anything but maybe a little relief for him that it was over. That lasted until evening of the 8th. Then I got scared and sad. Now I can't believe all the death I've seen. It's so outrageous, it's like a long slow fiction that overtakes what you come to know as "life." It's like waking up one morning to see that the sky has disappeared and it never comes back no matter how patiently you wait.

When they drove into Death Valley, they stopped the car to watch a beautiful sunset. They walked a ways and wrote in the sand, "David and Marion Death Valley May 1991." They started speaking about how it would be nice for David to die there. They could place beautiful fabric on the sand and light candles and it would be dusk. Marion would be with him. And Tom. To that, David said, "We'd have to put a curtain up between you."

Marion said, "What are you talking about?"

David told her, "Tom never wanted to share my friends with me, in any way. He doesn't understand my relationship with you."

Of course, David did not really want Tom to know his friends. Marion was not aware of this, since she had met Tom easily enough. So had Patrick. Conveniently, both lived far away. Among David's New York friends, Judy Glantzman knew of Tom's existence but did not socialize with him. The only friends of David's who did so were Gary Schneider and John Erdman. They had even accompanied Tom and David on one of their trips to New Orleans.

More typical was Norman Frisch, who had no idea that David had a boyfriend until sometime in 1991. "He seemed to be keeping Tom in a corner of his life that only he entered," Frisch said. "David was very paranoid about people plotting. I'm talking about his friends. He just didn't want anyone talking about him or planning anything for or about him that wasn't

*David writing in his journal on the last trip. (Photograph by Marion Scemama)*

in his direct control and that he wasn't hearing and seeing. That was part of why he was so insistent on keeping these worlds of people apart from one another."

And that evening in Death Valley, Marion began to sense this. She asked David if he wanted her and Tom to fight. "I wanted to let David understand that maybe he did things wrong," she said. "Maybe he manipulated my relationship with him to get Tom jealous."

Then David told her that Tom did not know they were traveling together, that that was why he'd waved her away on Second Avenue. This was not true. (Before David left town, Tom told him, "Push her off a mesa for me.") But Marion believed David, believed Tom didn't know, and she was upset that Tom didn't know.

She thought that now Tom would hate her—because she was doing the "last trip" and he was not. But the real issue between them was probably not resolvable. "Maybe I was jealous of the intensity of their connection," Tom said. "But mostly, I felt that she wanted to swallow him. Just essentially capture him in some way."

"I almost had tears," Marion said. "I realized I would never be next to

David when he died. I thought of all these things we were supposed to do together." According to Marion, David had asked her to photograph him just after he died, the way he'd photographed Hujar. Now she knew that would be impossible. "So I start getting nasty at David, teasing him, and the charm was finished. That day the charm was finished."

David sent a postcard to Judy Glantzman the day they got to Death Valley, however, telling her, "Marion has been a pleasure to be with. I'm the one I feel must be difficult when I don't feel well." They spent five days in Death Valley, and it isn't really clear when things started to go wrong.

David loved the desert, loved contemplating the emptiness and driving through it at speeds that let him fantasize about becoming airborne. He did not mention Marion in the journal until they were about a week into the trip, so this may have been where the tension began. She had gone for a walk in the desert and came back with a story about a black bird that came walking up, circled her, and then flew away. David remarked that "maybe it thought you were carrion." Marion did not know that word, and when David explained, she was irritated. According to Marion, they did not have a fight but she did not appreciate the joke he was making. As she put it, "Sometimes I don't have humor."

"She gets on my nerves sometimes," he wrote in the journal, "but then again, I don't do well being with anybody these days for too much time. I know she wants it to be different between me and her. I know. But that's the breaks, that's how it is in my body and mind, months and months of isolation don't break so easy. . . . The silence and the tension is rising really it's the music underneath that silence and its stirring the violence I carry . . . fueling whatever potential I have for being a killer . . . and I'm so tempted does she know I'm so tempted to turn the wheel, its just the turn of a wheel, its just a turn of the wrist and we will fly we will burn away we will fall away we will jet away a killer in a jet plane with four wheels and a windshield oh life is so free in America."

They got to San Francisco on May 17. David's old friend Philip Zimmerman, who knew Marion from the East Village days, came to hear him read. He remembered that during this two-day visit "David and Marion were bickering and complaining about each other. One would take me aside and say terrible things and then the other would do the same."

David introduced Zimmerman and Marion to Amy Scholder. He read at the gay bookstore A Different Light, and afterward the four of them walked to City Hall to join the AIDS Candlelight Memorial and Mobilization. Marion walked with Zimmerman and watched as David and Amy engaged in intense conversation all the way there. David wrote in his journal that he had felt an "instant deep connection" with Amy. He thought she was beautiful, sexy, and smart and "if she were a guy I'd maybe marry her." (He said none of this to Amy.) But the next morning, he resented it when Marion called Amy and invited her to join them for breakfast before they left town. "Then she started torturing me with the possibility of taking pictures of Amy and me," he complained. He hated being photographed in public. Marion had also taken pictures the morning before and he'd asked her to stop and she hadn't. This time she said she'd photograph only Amy, but David was tense all through breakfast.

During one of the rare moments when Amy was alone with David, she said, "Oh, Marion's great," and he said, "She's driving me crazy."

As he and Marion drove out of town, headed back to Death Valley, David recounted an incident at a San Francisco porn theater. He'd gone there to jerk off, something he hadn't done in months. A guy sat next to him and put his hands all over him and then tried to suck his dick while David rebuffed him. So David told Marion all the intimate physical details, all the complicated things that had been going through his mind. He felt he had laid himself bare, more than usual. That evening as they drove through Bakersfield looking for a place to eat, she began to tell him about a sexual encounter she'd had in Marrakech when she was traveling with a girlfriend. She'd met two French guys, was attracted to one of them, and ended up having sex with both of them. But she stopped the story at "a point of intimate detail," as David put it. She wouldn't go any further. To David, this was betrayal. "I told her I would never again talk about intimate details of certain experiences if she couldn't tell me about hers. I felt emotional in this. Hurt. I wanted her to <u>hear</u> me. It was a flurry of emotions and it swept into the moving car." They found a steak house with fake Western decor. "She said the fact I pushed her to speak of the details made her suddenly freeze and unable to remember or that she needed time or something."

"I was kidding," Marion remembered. "I was playing like a little girl who didn't know what to say, and then all of a sudden he just blew out, yelling at me, 'How dare you.' Then I started to really freak out. It paralyzed me because then we were back to something heavy. And so I couldn't speak anymore. We went to a kind of pub. It was dark and we had a difficult dinner. We couldn't speak to each other. We tried to make it work, but something was broken."

David told his journal that it wasn't her unwillingness to share intimate details that got to him; it was the "trust broken." He wrote, "My emotional reaction was betrayal and regret, stupid as that may look at a later date. I felt like I was a stranger or she was a stranger in that moment. It could be a child's thoughts, it could be. But it's there and I felt a door closing between us."

They were at a Days Inn in Bakersfield. They were at a stalemate. David asked Marion if she could let it go and she said no. As long as this heaviness was in the air, he said, he didn't want to go on to Death Valley, where the hotel was expensive. Spending extra money to be miserable—no. They could just head back to New Mexico. She said she could take the bus to Albuquerque and wanted him to help her plan this. He decided, "I don't have the energy to plan her trip, to plan the disintegration of this one. . . . I feel like I'm standing in the distance watching this accelerate and grow and implode and yet it seems stupid, what it's all based on."

He called the front desk and said they were staying another day. Then he drove off and left her at the Days Inn. He thought she should decide if she really wanted to split, and he didn't want to sit in the room and listen to her make plans.

He and Marion had not seen each other in nearly two years. "When she was coming with me, all my thoughts were based in old memories of the exciting times, the intense communications that ran deep between us," he wrote in the journal. "Years ago we were almost inseparable. Others were jealous of us because there was a great sense of reality between two people that outlined something of the soul, previous travelers who recognize each other in the cloak of strangers. Two strangers who know each other intimately and instantly upon meeting. Maybe that's why it breaks so powerfully. But this time has been different. I can recognize what I loved in her in the past but something has changed." He decided that he was the one who had changed. And it had to do with "that thing, that form, that location" that had grown inside him through all the loss he'd experienced, beginning with Hujar's death. "I kept waiting for the switch to be thrown, the close-up recognition that she and I had resumed what we dropped two years ago. It never came."

Meanwhile, back at the motel, Marion wrote in her diary, made some Polaroids, and cried. She called her sister and Sylvère Lotringer. She called the bus station. She would return to San Francisco, she thought. So she called Amy Scholder and asked if she could stay with her.

Amy said no, reasoning, "I didn't want to get in the middle of their shit. It was impossible. Then David called me. I told him that Marion had called, and he was furious." This would go onto David's final complaint list—the way Marion would call his friends, even his sister, to get information about him or somehow insinuate herself. He hated it.

Marion also called Philip Zimmerman. "She was pumping me for information about David," he said. "It would have been comical if there wasn't such weird desperation behind it."

Meanwhile, David called Tom to complain.

"I'm sitting in a restaurant and eating alone and writing and the world goes on around me," David wrote. "The Bakersfield world. For a moment I wanted to tell her, Don't go. On one level, I'd rather finish the trip, on another level, I'd rather be alone. I don't have a strong feeling of being able to retrieve enough of a connection to her to make the return trip have lovely meaning. Something has shut down, maybe out of exhaustion, maybe out of despair, maybe I need a catastrophe or explosion. This is not clear at all. I just want it somehow to stop."

Marion said, "He wouldn't help me to leave, but at the same time he wouldn't do anything to make things better. On the second day I thought that we couldn't keep on like this. It was too hard for me, and if I would stop the trip, it would be like a failure. I would feel so bad to leave him and to go back to France. So when he came back in the late afternoon, I had all these Polaroids around me that I did in the hotel room. I was posing, and in one of the Polaroids I was lying on the bed with *Close to the Knives* on my chest, as if I were reading and thinking about the book—a stupid photo in a way. So when David walked in the room, I thought, I'm going to act like everything is all right. So I said to David, 'Look at the photos I took.' And when he saw these photos of me laying on the bed with his book on my chest, he started laughing." Of these fights that started so unexpectedly and irrationally, she said, "After a while we would laugh to make things relieved, because it was too heavy for both of us to handle. And that's what happened. From one minute to another we became friends again."

He wanted to drive through the emptiest parts of the earth. So they returned to Death Valley for a couple of days.

On one of them, they drove out to a canyon and parked. Marion, who shared David's love for toy animals, had a plastic frog, snake, and alligator and said she was going to photograph some animal scenes among the rocks. David told her, "Go by yourself. I'm staying here." She thought he wasn't doing well and wanted to be alone. She left him and walked into the canyon, where she did some self-portraits and staged animal shots. After about a half hour, she went back to the car and found that David had tilted the seat back as far as it would go. He lay there completely pale, "like somebody who was really suffering," she said, "like somebody not anymore of this world."

She went up and took his hand, saying, "Come back, David, come back. Don't worry."

"I felt that something was going wrong," she said, "that he was going away, in his mind and in his body. Like he wasn't there. So I started caressing him and talking to him, and then he came back. I don't know where he had been, but he had been somewhere I couldn't reach. And little by little his face started getting color again, and then I asked him, 'What happened, David?' And he said, 'It's nothing—don't worry,' and then three minutes later he was laughing."

They drove the back roads. They drove through Indian reservations, where David always felt like an interloper. But he couldn't stand the tourist areas. By May 24, they were in Flagstaff and the next day Gallup. It was there that David said to Marion, "There's a photo I want you to take."

*Untitled, 1993. Gelatin-silver print, 28½ × 28½ inches. David selected this image from the series of photos taken that day, but it was printed posthumously. (Courtesy of the Estate of David Wojnarowicz and P·P·O·W Gallery, New York)*

He drove them north to Chaco Canyon. He had been there before and knew exactly where he wanted to stage this. "We're going to dig a hole," he told her, "and I'm going to lie down."

They began digging without saying a word, a hole for his upper body and a bit for the legs. They used their hands. The dirt was loose and dry. He lay down and closed his eyes. Marion put dirt around his face till it was halfway up his cheeks and then stood over him, photographing his half-buried face first with his camera and then with hers.

"We walked back to the car, and we sat without saying a word," she said. "He didn't turn the car on. We stayed like this a few minutes, and then we held hands."

Marion decided that this project was a last gesture from him because she would not be able to photograph him at his death. But David never said that. Certainly, he had orchestrated all of his last work very carefully.

They always shared a motel room, with twin beds, and on the last night, David handed a postcard of a hairy scorpion across to her. On the back, he'd written, "Dear Marion, Bruja, Coyote Girl, Despite the rough spots it was a good voyage. . . . I hope I'm healthy enough to see Morocco with you next year. We'll see. Hope you follow your heart and mind and make the films you carry in your body and write the books I know you can write. France would never be the same. Adios. Love, David."

He had drawn some little spectacles on the scorpion. David and Marion both wore glasses. "I asked him if it was me or him, and he didn't answer," said Marion. "He laughed."

David returned to New York in time to attend Phil Zwickler's memorial on what would have been his friend's thirty-seventh birthday—June 1, 1991. That night he dreamt that he called Zwickler's number. And Zwickler answered! David was amazed, and afraid to mention death, as if that would make him disappear again. Suddenly he and Zwickler were seated at a table together. David asked, "How was it?" Meaning death. Zwickler would only look at him but seemed to be suggesting that it wasn't so bad. "The small distance between us was charged with emotion," David wrote. "I was trying to understand everything in the world at once. If he died and was now back physically and able to talk to me, then death was a process that was one of transition or travel. I was just so relieved to see him alive, or at least physical and communicating. I started weeping and then so did he. We cried this short intense clear emotion. It felt like what I think grace is."

# 25 "DISAPPEARING BUT NOT FAST ENOUGH"

**David remained isolated** through the summer of 1991 and into the fall. In late July, he wrote a letter to Judy Glantzman, who was again upstate for the summer. "I was so ill since you left," he told her. "It got pretty extreme where I went so dark that I couldn't call people or <u>speak</u> to anyone other than Tom in order to get help from him." Then he started taking steroids, which magically cured his intestinal problems. He felt better than he had all year. Now he could finish *Memories That Smell like Gasoline*. He attached a letter he'd written her a few weeks earlier at the height of his misery. He hadn't mailed it then because it was so bleak and ugly. He was not willing to go through that again. He'd found a book outlining how to commit suicide. He wanted the option.

At some point, I had heard that David was feeling poorly—and that he wanted no contact with anyone. We were only acquaintances, but I'd felt some connection with him ever since meeting him through Keith Davis, and his work moved me. I decided to call him. I left a message offering to get groceries or do laundry. He would not have to talk to me. I could hand a bag in at the door. He didn't take me up on that.

But he called me on July 29 after he'd started the steroids to tell me that his life had been hellish since the end of the trip west. He'd had constant nausea and constipation and couldn't get out of bed. Now he was supposed to leave the next day for the long-delayed drug trial in Boston, but he'd canceled. It would have meant more biopsies, self-administered injections, and blood drawn every day. Then if he felt bad and didn't show up for a procedure, they'd kick him out. "I totally stopped talking to people," he said. "I wouldn't even tell the doctor what my symptoms were. I'm losing touch with everything. Art—it's all meaningless. It's an issue for me, whether I'll ever work again."

He complained that his doctor was treating him "like an emotional basket case" and would not discuss suicide with him. "He freaked," David griped. "His reaction was 'don't worry, I won't let you suffer.'"

"He was a very difficult patient," Dr. Friedman said. "A million questions. But he was difficult because he was in an impossible situation. The options were so limited. How could he not be angry? How could he not be volatile? How could he not be frustrated?"

David seemed to have as much trouble communicating with his doctor as he did with Tom. He told me that before he started the steroids, he'd been injecting himself with interferon, and "no one knows why." I'm sure the doctor knew why. David just had a hard time hearing what the doctor was telling him. He'd get lost. Or he couldn't take it in. "He'd get overwhelmed and just give up," said Tom, who urged him constantly, "you have to tell the doctor if you don't understand what he's saying." Tom sometimes sat down with David, wrote out his questions for the doctor, then went with him to the appointment.

On August 1, David noted in his journal that the nausea, constipation, and fevers were back. He went through his address book. Most of the people he wanted to speak to were dead.

Sometime in August, a fired destroyed much of Tom's apartment. A neighbor phoned him at work to tell him, and Tom called David to ask him to go look. David rang him back to say, "It's bad."

Tom had left a lamp on. Firemen speculated that one of the cats knocked it over into an old chair, where it smoldered into a small flame. In any case, the place was a mess, mostly from smoke and water damage. Most of the furniture was not salvageable. Part of Tom's large cookbook collection was ruined. A supermarket poster David had given him had water damage. A small painting of a tornado that David had made for him was completely black.

"I didn't know what to do, so I said to David, 'I guess I'll be staying at your house for a bit," Tom recalled. David could not understand why Tom wasn't more upset.

"I was sort of calm. I went and had dinner with him. I was laughing,"

Tom said. "Actually I was shell-shocked. I didn't quite know what to do, but being upset wasn't going to make it any better. I don't freak out. He would explode and scream and throw things. That's not my way—and he was really upset about that. I said, 'Well, David, we're just different.'"

That weekend, about twenty of Tom's colleagues came to the apartment to help carry out the wreckage. David was there too but decided he couldn't handle being around so many people. He went home. Meanwhile, Tom's cat Evelyn disappeared. Someone in the crew hauling things out had left the door open, so Tom worried that she had gotten out of the building. He began hunting for her.

In the midst of the chaos, David called. Marion had put together a sheet of his old photobooth pictures and he'd left them at Tom's house. Where were they? Tom didn't know.

David said, "Those are very important to me. I have to have them." Marion had a copy but he did not want to ask her for it.

"I told him, 'I've got twenty people here helping me, the cat's gone, I can't find her, and as we go through things, I'll see if I have it.' But David wanted me to look right then. I said, 'No, I can't do it.' And he got furious," said Tom. "Then the next thing I know, he's outside walking up and down the street, looking for Evelyn."

Eventually, the photobooth pictures turned up. The cat was found in the empty apartment across the hall, hiding behind the stove.


Nan Goldin had come by to photograph David. He posed next to the baby elephant skeleton in what looks like Hujar's suit jacket, with his hair slicked back. And he's wearing makeup. Nothing heavy—just foundation. When I asked Goldin about the makeup, she explained, "He wanted to wear a mask."

Goldin inadvertently played a role in one last flare-up between David and Marion Scemama. They still spoke on the phone occasionally. One day that fall, Marion called him to say she'd run into Goldin in Paris, and Goldin told her all these things David was saying about her. Things like "she's fucked up, she's crazy."

"I said to him, 'You swore to me that you wouldn't reject me again, and

here you are saying to everybody that I'm fucked up and people believe it,'"
said Marion. "We spoke for an hour or two. We start getting mad at each
other and then we cooled down and he explained certain things to me—
that he went through depression after the trip, that he couldn't deal with
certain things about me, et cetera. When we hung up, we were not saying,
OK it's over. We just cooled down. But that was the last time we ever spoke
to each other."

Goldin wrote David an apologetic letter, saying that Marion had misinterpreted what she'd said.

Occasionally David went to visit Anita Vitale, who was still running the
city's AIDS Case Management Unit. He would sit in her office and they'd
chat, sometimes about Tom as he and David went through their ups and
downs.

One day in the autumn of 1991, David told her that he'd been diagnosed with *Mycobacterium avium-intracellulare* (MAI), a form of tuberculosis usually found in birds. People with healthy immune systems are not
susceptible. For those with fewer than fifty T-cells, however, this was not an
unusual opportunistic infection—and it was David's first such infection.
Years later, Anita could still remember his despondent tone of voice. "Pigeon
shit in my lungs," he called it. Tom did not recall hearing about the MAI
before David entered the hospital. Instead, David told him that he felt like
he was trying to breathe underwater, that something was weighing him
down. But Tom saw that David was terrified.

David knew what it meant when the bird and animal diseases set in:
time to put one's house in order.

Sometime in October, David called his half-brother, Pete Wojnarowicz. They had not spoken in more than ten years. Not since David was a
busboy at the Peppermint Lounge.

Pete was thrilled.

David had simply fallen out of his life, and he never knew why. He
figured that maybe during their last conversation—the night David called
him from the Pep—he'd said something wrong. He'd get the occasional

update from Pat or Steven. He knew about David's appearance in *Life* magazine in 1985. He knew David had AIDS. Pete would say, "Tell him to call me." He'd gotten David's number from Steven and left messages but David had never called back. Until this time. The end time.

Pete worked as a UPS driver. He was married and lived in New Jersey. The Saturday after David called, Pete drove into Manhattan to meet him at the loft. "I got up there and hugged him," Pete remembered, "and I said, 'Why the fuck didn't you call me in all these years?' He just said he was sorry."

They spent the day together talking. About their father, for one thing. David had believed since childhood that Pete and his younger sister, Linda, were the favorites, that their father had only beaten him and Steven and Pat.

Pete told him, "No. Sorry. There were no favorites in that family." He sensed a kind of relief in David, who said, "I'm sorry you had to go through that."

David told him about Hujar—how Hujar had saved his life and made him believe in his work.

Pete admired what passed for decor in David's loft, especially the baboon skeleton. He asked how the hell David ever got that into the country.

David said, "You want it?"

Pete declined. Then when he came back two weeks later, the baboon was gone. David had given it away, and Pete was filled with regret. If he'd known that David wanted to get rid of it, he would have taken it. "Because I didn't really want nothing from him," Pete said. "I was there to get to know my brother, and that was it."


David had been meeting periodically with James Romberger, and sometimes with Marguerite Van Cook as well, to work on the comic book version of David's life story, *Seven Miles a Second*. They'd started in 1987 after Romberger and Van Cook closed Ground Zero Gallery and had completed part one—David's childhood hustling stories—within a year. Romberger spent a long time drawing the second part, working from a sheaf of David's writing about his teenage years on the street, especially the adventures with Willy. That was completed, with Marguerite's coloring, sometime in 1991.

They had settled on the cover. At David's request, Romberger drew him running down Park Avenue, with one foot anchored in the ground, like a tree root, and the world breaking off in front of him. Romberger also drew two circular insets with David-style imagery—a head in flames and a skeleton with brain and eyeballs intact. They had an ambitious plan for lenticular animation on the cover. (This is usually a simple effect, like a winking eye.) The images would shift as the reader moved the book. The kid would be trying to run, for example. "David loved 3-D," Romberger said. But they couldn't get the budget for it in the end, and the insets ended up on the back cover.

The third part was to be about David's current life, but his feelings about what to include seemed to change from month to month. "All I had to go on were the conversations we had when we met," Romberger said. "I tried to enact everything he said. He wanted me to draw him huge on Fifth Avenue smashing the buildings. That's what he said. It seemed logical to make it St. Pat's. But then, I couldn't do the last part. He wanted it to end with a happy day—him just happy to be alive, but there's nothing like that in his writing. His life dictated the ending."

David would complain as he got sicker that if Romberger didn't finish the thing, he was going to come back and haunt him.

He had begun to find places for objects he valued, like the baboon skeleton. At one of their last meetings, David gave Romberger his brown leather jacket. Romberger does not remember David saying anything about why he'd gifted him with this. "It was a significant thing. I mean, it's his jacket. But how much do you want to question somebody," said Romberger. "It was embarrassing. Here's this fucking raggedy-ass leather jacket. It's not like I was going to wear it." He had the impression that David had been wearing it since he was a teenager.

Marguerite said, "He gave James the jacket, for posterity. Because it was symbolic." David had told her that when he wore it, he could listen and watch unobserved. The jacket made him invisible.

\* \* \*

On October 26, David gave his last reading. The evening at the Drawing Center was set up as a tribute to him and as a benefit for ACT UP's needle-exchange program. Those who read selections from *Close to the Knives* included Kathy Acker, Karen Finley, Hapi Phace, and Bill Rice. David himself read a few selections not in the book, like "When I put my hands on your body . . ."

When Acker got up to read, she referred to David as "a saint."

"That made me laugh," Tom said, "but this was a big emotional event for him—and for the audience. He was very 'up' afterwards, very moved by it."

Drawing Center director Ann Philbin, who had organized the event with Patrick Moore from ACT UP, wrote David a letter: "Thank you for providing the soul and spirit of one of the most extraordinary evenings I've spent in a long time. I'm sorry I burst into blubbering tears when I went to thank you at the end but I was one of hundreds walking around the room like a raw nerve. It was truly moving and I feel honored to have been there. How can anyone thank you enough for how you share what you know?"

David had decided on the other two images he wanted to use in the series with the skeleton piece *When I Put My Hands on Your Body*. As in that one, he would match a large black-and-white photo with silk-screened text.

He selected one of the many photos he'd taken over the years of bandaged hands. Gary Schneider made a large print, and over that, a silk screener printed the final section from David's last completed text, "Spiral," concluding with "I am disappearing but not fast enough."

The third image looks like a Japanese temple guardian caught in a conflagration. It's a very disordered scene, with a burnt shoji screen, lanterns on tilted poles, and piles of detritus in front of the guardian. Apparently the temple was not protected. David never completed a text for this.

On November 6, David flew to Minneapolis to perform *ITSOFOMO* at the Walker Art Center with Ben Neill. Jean Foos went along to be the "nurturing helping person," as she put it. David had very low energy, and he had become "suspicious" of Neill. "For no reason," Foos emphasized. (And Neill never knew this.) David was still struggling, in his isolation, with suspicion about many of the people close to him.

Then he was unhappy with his hotel and checked out after one night. He went to stay with Foos, at her sister's house. The major drama that played out during four days there was David's effort to get the sister's Weimaraner to like him. The dog just didn't take to David, which bothered him a great deal. Foos remembered that there was a lot of tension until the dog finally came around.

Patrick McDonnell drove up from Normal with his boyfriend and chauffeured them over the Twin Cities' icy roads. They all went to see Isaac Julien's *Looking for Langston*.

"David slept in a room in the theater building during the afternoon before the show," Foos said. "I had to go get him up. There were many nervous moments wondering if he was up to it. But then he gave an amazing performance!"

Back in New York, David was still stuck in his depression, still morose. "It was sometimes hard to talk to him," Tom said. "No matter what you said, it wasn't good enough. I'm not quite sure what he was looking for. Then I'd get worked up and not know what to do and probably made it worse. It wasn't until he had those two weekends . . ."

The first two weekends in December, David was running a fever of 106 degrees. Both weekends he called Tom in the middle of Friday or Saturday night to say, "Can you come over?" Tom arrived to find him not only running a high fever but also shivering violently. He stayed with David and did not sleep. When it happened the second time, Tom called the doctor, who said to take him to the hospital.

On Sunday, December 8, Tom took David to the emergency room at Cabrini, the hospital where Hujar had died. David, uninsured, was soon enrolled in Medicaid. Two days later, Tom left on a long-planned trip to Mexico with Anita and other friends. David had never wanted to go along. "I was just relieved because he was in a room, he was being cared for, he was comfortable," said Tom. "He was actually happy to be in the hospital that first time."

David spent a week in isolation because the doctor thought he might have tuberculosis. This was a precaution. Tests showed the problem to be pigeon TB, or MAI. Once David received this diagnosis, he was moved to the IV drug users ward—all AIDS patients—because that's where there was a bed, and he called me. "Everything started falling apart lately," he said. "I'm having invasive procedures."

I went to see him. The guy in the next bed kept his television blaring around the clock, which was driving David nuts, but he said of the junkies on the ward, "They accepted me right away." Remarkably, this hospitalization brought him back to his artist self. In a green journal he designated as "rough notes," he started writing observations on the other patients. For example, "'That was my best tattoo . . .' shows me amputated stump 'not much left—it was a dragon.' All I could make out was a wing uttering from the wound."

I went to see David again on Christmas Eve. That's when I finally met Tom, who was seated next to the bed, learning from a nurse about how to administer antibiotics and total parenteral nutrition (TPN) through David's newly implanted Hickman catheter. "It looks like a Christmas tree ornament," David said, staring down at the thing in his chest.

David was cranky. The ward reeked of Elizabeth Taylor's Passion for Men, which had been distributed to everyone as a gift, and it felt impossible to have a regular conversation amid the chaos and noise: TVs blasting, people shouting, carolers bumming everybody out. "It's like trying to get better in a subway car," he complained. "I'm going to write about this."

On his good days, he talked about working again. But he never again had enough energy. In the last entry in the journal of rough notes, added shortly after a line about the Elizabeth Taylor perfume, his handwriting is ragged. He wrote, "My life is no longer filled with poetry and dreams. I can smell rust in the air. Sometimes the fact that we can't deal with death, our mortality—it's the same with cultures—anything that doesn't reflect our faces and soul. We wish to annihilate things when we fail to see ourselves inside it."

Even here, in what I think of as the last journal entry, he felt compelled to connect his situation to the wider world. That had always been his

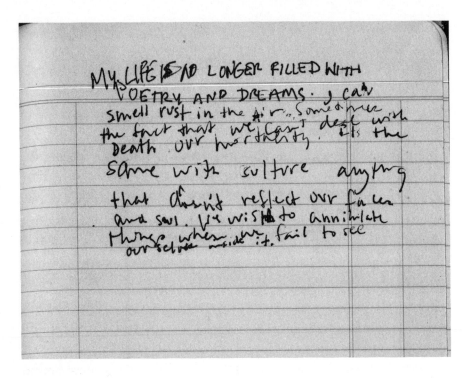

*"My life is no longer filled with poetry and dreams." This last journal entry is undated but follows events he recorded on Christmas Eve, 1991. (David Wojnarowicz Papers, Fales Library, NYU)*

style. His writing, his neo-Beat prosody, was built on the long breath that leaves one body to engulf the endless world and, returning, sees the universe in a single action. Call it a Howl.

When David came home after Christmas, Tom decided that he'd better move into the loft. He would go home to feed his cats and get the mail, but he was now David's principal caregiver. The upstairs neighbor Dori brought a mattress down for him, and they put it on the floor.

David asked a few people to come over for one day to help him go through his things. Among them was Norman Frisch. "He was obsessing about how he no longer knew where things were," said Frisch, "and he was worried about things not getting to the right people after his death. He was in bed most of the time, giving instructions about what he wanted. Or maybe he was sitting at the kitchen table. People would bring stuff over to him and spread it out on the bed and he would decide what to keep or what went where. When it came down to it, there was very little that he was actually willing to part with." He had piles of work prints, however. They were substandard, and he was afraid they could make it onto the market. Those were destroyed.

Given that he now had a catheter in his chest, he had to worry about infection. To that end, he had the friends take out the old terrariums. His scorpion was dead—no need for crickets. The loft was filthy but the friends did more sorting than scrubbing. One pile for journals and notebooks, another for film and video materials, another for anything related to Hujar.

Frisch remembered it being a very long day. "He was in rough shape— not entirely rational, very emotionally raw, easily overwhelmed, taking a lot of pain meds, sometimes drifting in and out."

David still had high fevers and nausea. He would tell me later that his spleen was now so enlarged that it had pushed his intestines to one side. But in this interval, before the second hospitalization, he did not want me to come over.

Karen Finley saw him a couple of times during this period. She said, "He was very suspect. He actually got mad at me for coming over. He told me, 'I don't understand why you're here. What do you want?' He expressed anger. He gave me the ninth degree. He wanted to make sure I wasn't coming over out of pity. Or, people could come over with their own issues about death and be gazing upon him."

This was when she got to know Tom, whom she'd met for the first time the night of the reading at the Drawing Center.

David told Finley that he was very worried about his baby elephant skeleton. She promised him she'd take it. "He knew that I would take care of it, and that I could handle the heaviness of what that was," Finley said. "I always saw it as an image really of him, of his totem. He's the elephant. The elephant never forgets. You know—there's the ancientness of it."

David was doing so poorly that Tom was convinced he was close to death. He could remember sitting in a chair in the loft, crying while David slept.

On January 19, David called me. He was back in the hospital, on a quieter floor. "They lured me in, saying three days," he said, "but I guess it'll be ten."

Tom had told David that, while he was at Cabrini, he was going to clean the loft. "I cannot sleep in this pigsty."

David was resistant. He said, "I have things here."

Tom promised he would throw nothing away. Not even a matchbook. He'd put everything in boxes.

"I finally convinced him to let me clean it up," said Tom, "and I remember looking at the bed and, literally, the foam had taken on the shape of a body. It was a futon or something and it had almost an indentation from where Hujar had been. This was a platform bed, so he was basically lying on wood. I called David's downstairs neighbor and we hauled it downstairs and threw it away." Tom had a real mattress delivered and hired someone to build a headboard so David would be able to sit up in bed. Then he had shelves installed on the windows for flowerpots. Tom washed the floor and cleaned the disgusting stove.

David called me again on January 22. I had not been able to visit him because I had a cold and couldn't risk bringing germs to someone with no immune system. He told me that he had a blood infection now. They'd pulled out the Hickman. "Just pulled it out. It's scary how cavalier they are." He had night sweats so bad that the bed would be soaked. They told him to drink water. "It takes hours to get my hand over to it," he said. Now though, he had come to trust the doctor a lot more. "He's on top of things."

He asked Tom to call his half-siblings, Pete and Linda, to tell them he was in the hospital. From about this point until the end of David's life, Pete and Linda and their spouses came to visit David nearly every weekend.

"I didn't know who Tom was at that time," Pete said. "Then David said, 'He's my boyfriend.' And I said, 'Well, do you trust him?' And he goes, 'I think so.' I said, 'Do you or don't you? You gotta be sure.' Then when I met Tom and I saw Tom—next time I talked to David, I said, 'Why are you worried about him? The guy loves you.'"

\* \* \*

David came home again on January 30, and his top priority was to get over to the Kitchen to see Karen Finley's installation *Memento Mori* before it closed on February 1.

Finley's work is about deep emotion, the feelings that propel someone to use a four-letter word because they can't articulate what they really feel. In this case, she wanted to deal with grief about AIDS, addressed so inadequately at a typical memorial service, and with violence against women.

David went with Tom, Anita, and Philip Yenawine. At the entrance, they were each given a glass of wine at the Spit Bar, then led to a wall covered with flags from every country. An assistant there invited them to spit the wine onto the flag of their choice. The flags had begun to look like they were covered with blood.

David was given a chair and his friends moved it through the installation, allowing him to sit at each station. They came to the Ribbon Gate, where each took a ribbon and tied it to the gate in memory of a loved one who'd died of AIDS. The floor in the Memorial Room was covered with dead leaves. Here was the bedside vigil, illustrated by a volunteer in a bed and another in a chair next to it. Finley had written texts over the walls, "Lost Hope" and "In Memory Of." In the corner was a mound of sand where they could place a lit candle in memory of someone. At the Carnation Wall, they pushed the stem of a flower through a hole in a lace curtain.

The Women's Room addressed abortion rights and violence against women. Finley had written the texts "It's My Body" and "My Own Memories" over these walls. In the corner was a mattress surrounded by dead leaves and flowers. A woman sat there, wrapped in sheets.

Finley told me later that David sat at the Spit Bar for a while and did all the rituals. He told her that being there made him feel human again. "I could tell that he forgot he was sick," she said. "It broke my heart when I saw him reading everything on the walls. He was almost unable to walk."

Afterward David wanted to go to Union Square Cafe for smoked shell steak, his favorite. When they got to the restaurant, they were told that dinner would not be served for another three hours. Knowing that David was too weak to make it to the loft and back, they sat there and waited the three hours.

\* \* \*

I went to visit David at the loft early in February. He sat propped up with some pillows in a blue corduroy shirt. There was an image of an Indian chief on the blanket over his legs.

Tom injected him with some anti-nausea medication and made him chicken soup. Then he left to feed his cats. As soon as Tom left, David told me he was thinking about suicide. It was about quality of life, he said. He'd had two months of treatment with no improvement. Now they were talking about taking out his gall bladder and putting in another Hickman. He hated that "brutal" stuff. He said this as he injected antibiotics into the catheter in his arm, then hooked a small bottle to it. The bottle had what looked like a balloon inside, which would collapse as the medicine flowed out. "That's for the MAI," he said.

Tom had purchased a comfortable armchair, in case David wanted to get out of bed and sit in something besides a kitchen chair. The loft was still incredibly cluttered, with piles of paper everywhere. "I should just throw it all away," he said.

When I saw David in the hospital at the end of January, he'd talked about making art again. He'd felt better. But on this occasion, he told me he could not remember feeling better.

He did have some good news, however. The rock band U2 planned to use his falling buffalo image for a record cover and a video. They were among the musicians on *Red Hot and Blue*, the first CD put out by the Red Hot Organization—founded by David's friend John Carlin to raise money for organizations fighting AIDS. Carlin had sent the band a "Tongues of Flame" catalog, and they loved it.


On February 20, he called to tell me he couldn't get on his feet. His legs were killing him. The doctor was thinking neuropathy, but David hoped it was just because he hadn't exercised in so long. The week before, he'd been tottering at least. Now that he could no longer take for granted his ability to walk, he was afraid to be left alone.

I stopped by the loft to get keys from Tom so I could get in the next day and sit with David. He was lying on his side, and I got a look at his legs for the first time. Toothpicks.

I don't know why he let me into his life at this point. There were many friends he wouldn't see or even speak to on the phone, and in most cases, I also don't know why he cut them off. He and I talked about death on those occasions when it was just the two of us. He was curious about Buddhism. Since I have close friends who are practitioners, I had attended many talks and ceremonies, even a public cremation. I shared what little I knew. He asked if I believed in reincarnation, admitting that the possibility bothered him: "I don't want to come back," he said.

He'd had a visit the day before from Adam Clayton, the U2 bassist. David had taken some Ritalin so he could feel up for that.* The day I was there, he had a doctor's appointment and took more Ritalin—"hoping it would give me strength," he told me. It hadn't worked. He couldn't even stand.

About a week later, Tom called to ask if I could stay with David for the day. Tom had been missing a lot of work. He always took care of what David needed first, so he sometimes went in late or not at all. When I arrived, David was sitting with his feet over the side of the bed, hunkered down, hooked up to the bottle of MAI medicine. I noticed that his elbows, feet, and knees were swollen. Probably from the steroids, he told me. The table next to his bed was entirely covered with pill bottles.

A physical therapist came to help David exercise. They walked once around the perimeter of the loft. The guy had David raise his arms out straight, parallel to the ground, five times. Then above his head five times. After that, David needed to sit down and rest. They repeated this routine three or four times. David paid the guy. He was relieved when he left. Three or four times that day, I massaged David's feet. It helped, he told me. One of his legs was "two-thirds better."

At the beginning of March, Pat came from Paris to visit. And Philip Zimmerman came from San Francisco. David seemed to rally around this time, meaning he actually went outside for a couple of short walks. But he still had depressed, anxious days and terrible nights.

Tom was getting exhausted. "One night I was just desperate to go

---

* People with AIDS sometimes took Ritalin to combat depression and fatigue.

home and be in my own apartment for a night's sleep," he said. Zimmerman said he would stay with David.

David spent the night writhing and groaning, emitting sounds like *I EE I-EE* and saying, "Oh god, please help me." He had a fever, but every time Zimmerman approached him with a thermometer or a cold cloth, David's rage would surface. "Always in the eyes," said Zimmerman.

Around six thirty in the morning Zimmerman called Tom and said, "You've got to come over here. David hates me. He's yelling at me. He doesn't know who I am."

Tom got dressed and walked over to the loft.

Zimmerman was standing against a wall in the kitchen, which was just a few feet from the bed where David sat scowling, "Who is this guy? What's he doing here?"

Tom said, "David, that's Philip. He stayed with you to take care of you."

David said, "Oh!"

Clearly the virus had started its work on David's brain, but at this point, he was still of sound mind most of the time.

On another occasion, though, Judy Glantzman spent the night with the same result: David in bed screaming, "Who are you? What do you want?"

Glantzman could not remember if she even stayed through the night. "It was so scary I couldn't do it ever again."

On March 18, U2 sent a limousine to the loft to bring David to the Meadowlands for their show, along with Tom and Pete and Linda—David's "little brother and sister," as he called them—and their spouses.

The band paired David's falling buffalo photograph with what became one of their signature songs, "One." They released it as a single with David's image on the cover—with all royalties going to AIDS research.

At the Meadowlands, David and his entourage met the band backstage before the show. He was having a hard time walking that night. Bono asked David if he would like to pray with them. David declined. But everyone had been so kind. Pete and Linda were given seats near the side of the stage. The band had arranged for David to have a chair on the platform in the middle of the arena where the tech crew sat, controlling the sound and lighting. Tom stood behind him. As the band began to play "One," the buffalo image came up on the screen behind the drum kit, and Bono called out, "David! This is for you!" Tom choked up.

Eventually, the band would pay for all of David's private nursing costs.

He called me the day after the concert and said, "Parts were great, but it's not my world. It really made me feel my age."

Word was getting around that David was in bad shape.

Doug Bressler, the musician from 3 Teens who had worked with David on the soundtrack for *A Fire in My Belly*, had not seen David in quite awhile but just thought he was busy. "I didn't know how bad his health was because he never talked to me about it," said Bressler, who began to cry as he remembered this. One day Bressler ran into Steve Brown, who told him that David had dreamt about him. Specifically, David had dreamt that Bressler came to visit and flew in through the window. Brown added, "You better go see him. It's bad."

Ben Neill also came to visit. They had talked about doing a video documentary of *ITSOFOMO* with some of David's film footage, parts of the live performance, and maybe some documentation from rehearsals. Neill told him that PBS's *Alive from Off Center* had expressed interest. But David told him, "I can't listen to it anymore." He said what he really wanted was to go for a drive. Neill told him he had a car now. He could take him. David was enthusiastic, telling Neill, "Yeah, I want to take a ride. Let's go somewhere." But he was really too weak.

P·P·O·W sent someone over with the last finished piece—the imploring bandaged hands with the silk-screened text about "disappearing but not fast enough." Penny Pilkington remembered, "He hardly had the energy to sign it."

One day, he asked me if I thought he should contact his mother. Since I knew little about her at that point, I didn't know what to tell him, but thought that if she didn't already know what kind of shape he was in—how good could that relationship be?

Tom said that David told him one day, "I wish I had a mother."

I kept a phone log for my calls at work. Just notes. One from David in April reads, "Threw up. No cat." Tom told me that David decided he wanted a cat, and Tom was trying to give him what he wanted at this point. They took a cab to the ASPCA. "We found one that we both liked, but they told us it was a biter," Tom said. David reconsidered. No cat. Tom was relieved. They cabbed it back to the loft. David struggled up the stairs and collapsed into bed.

Karen Finley came to the loft to pick up the baby elephant skeleton on May 4, the day David went into the hospital for the last time. He had endured two weeks of nonstop nausea. Tom woke up that day sick with a high fever. He felt awful, so Finley agreed to take David in.

When she got to the loft, David was "puking his guts out," she said, and he looked terrible. She called the doctor, who arranged for an ambulette to pick him up. David was so out of it that when he put his jacket on he pulled out his catheter. He walked down the stairs bleeding everywhere, puking into a bag. A neighbor ran for paper towels to stanch the blood. As Finley stood with him on Second Avenue waiting for the ambulette, David could not remember what they were doing out there.

When the ambulette arrived, the driver refused to help David and drove wildly as the blood spurted everywhere. He claimed to not know where Cabrini was. When they got to the crowded emergency room, no one there would help either as David's blood dripped on the floor. Finally, Finley told me, "I threw a hissy fit." Someone then fixed his IV, but no one would clean him up. They handed Finley a towel. David was still puking into a bag. There was nowhere for him to sit. Finley said he looked like he'd passed to the other side.

By the next day, though, he was better. No more vomiting. Four bags of fluid on the IV stand. He had a south view this time. Once he was strong enough to stand up, he could see the roof of his building from the window. David did his last writing during this stay, which lasted for most of May. On a couple of pages torn from a notebook, he wrote "Hospital." I won't quote it all, but this seems most salient:

The world is way out there sort of in the distance vibrating and agitated like a bowl of gruesomeness. They shot me with Demerol and gave me a powerful sleeping pill and then started blood transfusions that took place all night long and I watched the dawn arrive among the southern view of the city. It was quite beautiful as plastic pack after plastic pack of other people's blood emptied into my body. I wish I had language enough to speak what all this is to me. I'm losing my memory at an alarming rate. It's been going on for months slowly at first and now accelerating. Events are lost to me seconds after they take place.

One of the horrors of the disease was its unpredictable course. There could even be moments that seemed like remission along the twisting but always downward spiral—and then there were the ghastly surprises. This time, after a week in the hospital, David's feet swelled up to twice their normal size. He joked that he thought they might explode, that he could feel things breaking in there. He was staring at the awful things when I got to his room. Dr. Friedman walked in, looked like he had not expected to see this, and prescribed a diuretic.

Once medicated, David insisted on a trip to the smoking lounge, hobbling with one white-knuckled hand around his IV stand. He'd been hooked up to IVs or PICC lines for months, though he'd refused to let the doctor insert another Hickman catheter. "Too brutal." But now he had track marks, which he showed me after we sat down in the cheerless nicotine den.

Somehow we got onto the subject of cameras. He told me Hujar had repeatedly tried to show him how to use his Leica, his street-shooting camera, but David could never get the hang of that stuff about F-stops and preferred his automatics. I told him I'd once had a Nikon F, but it was stolen from my apartment, and I'd never found another camera I liked as much. "Really?" he said. "I'll give you that camera of Peter's." I was moved that he would offer such a thing, but did not expect him to remember our conversation. He was clearly losing his memory.

David was waiting for certain infections to clear up. Then, he told me, he would have his spleen and his gall bladder removed. The other person in the lounge, an old guy in a wheelchair, decided to butt in to say he'd just had his gall bladder removed too, and he had this incredible doctor. David, tottering and wincing his way to the bathroom, turned when this man mentioned the doctor's name and said angrily, "That guy nearly killed a friend."

Once David was out of the room, the man in the wheelchair assured me that the doctor was good. His own T-cell count had risen from zero to seven.

When I came back to Cabrini a few days later, David was sleeping heavily. His upper and lower arms, where he used to have IVs, were wrapped in blue bandages. They were infected. I decided not to wait for him to wake up. Tom was there and walked me to the elevator. He told me that David was talking about suicide again. *Because if this is all there is . . . Because if there's no hope . . .* Tom had convinced him to see how he felt after the surgery.

It was Tom's presence that most reassured him now. Tom would enter the room, calling "Hi, handsome" and David would brighten. One day David told me, "I worry he's going to spend the best years of his life taking care of me."

David had surgery on May 22. Tom called me when it was over and said he thought David was going to be upset. "Because the cut was so big," he said, and started to cry.

The next night David called Tom at eleven P.M. quavering, "They're trying to kill me." He was having a bad reaction to the morphine. Tom went to Cabrini and spent the night in the empty bed next to David's.

I went to see him the day after that. He looked so tense, so vulnerable—eyes bugging out, body taut, tube up his nose, not able to say much. "You know what?" he said to me quietly, his voice breaking. "They had me on a five cc drip . . ." He was still getting the morphine out of his system. I took his hand and felt the pulse beating through it, hard and rapid.

A couple of days later, he had someone call me at work to make sure I was coming to the hospital that afternoon. He had something to give me. When I got there, he pulled Hujar's Leica out from under the bedclothes. Overwhelmed, I stumbled through a thank you. "I figured you could do some stories where you did both the words and the pictures," he said.

He had not remembered our earlier conversation about cameras, but he did remember that I was leaving town. I had taken a job in Los Angeles for the summer. Leaving David was my only regret. We did not say goodbye but spoke of how we were both sure we would see each other again. In hindsight, it looks like denial, but I don't think I was the only one who expected him to at least live through the summer. Everything that could be done for an AIDS patient in 1992 was being done, and we all thought the surgery would buy him time.

Dr. Friedman explained that they had operated because "the spleen was enlarged and there could have been a rupture. We thought it was infected, that he had a splenic abscess and that we had to remove it as a focus of infection." What they found, though, is that the MAI had spread through his intestines.

The last time I saw him at Cabrini, David told me that if he got a little better, he would come visit me in L.A. When he shuffled off to the bathroom, the nurse told me they were going to give him another Hickman, but hadn't told him yet. This one would be "permanent."

The day David left the hospital to go home, he had a talk with the doctor. "He was very clear about what he wanted," Dr. Friedman said. "He told me, 'I know that if I go back to the hospital one more time, I will die there. I want to die in my apartment. I want to die in that space.'"

David wanted to make sure that Peter Hujar was part of the photography collection at the Museum of Modern Art, and to that end, he donated four Hujar prints—probably right after he got home from the hospital. In a thank-you letter from the museum dated June 29, 1992, John Parkinson III, chairman of the Committee on Photography, said, "Artists often give their own work to the Museum, but it is much rarer that they give the work of others. Your generous gift has significantly enhanced our collection of Hujar's work and I am pleased to thank you for it on behalf of the Committee and the Board of Trustees."

One night as Tom lay on his mattress on the floor, David looked down at him and said, "You can sleep in the bed. Get in."

"I thought the operation would make things better," said Tom, "but he got sick pretty soon after coming home. Started throwing up black stuff."

David and I still spoke on the phone. On June 22, David called me and said, "Something changed drastically. My brain." Certainly, the dementia had been coming on for a while, but on this day, he felt some physical sensation he couldn't describe beyond "everything's strange, everything's upside down."

He was still following his self-imposed rule of not telling Tom the bad news, not discussing death with him. "He thought talking about death scared me," said Tom, "and there were times when I didn't want to talk about it, because I wanted to keep hope going." So David did not tell Tom that he had felt something change in his brain. But Tom knew something was off. One night he cooked David one of his favorite meals, roast beef and broccoli, and they sat eating at the blue table. "He ate it but I could tell he was somewhere else," Tom said. "He had this goofy look on his face." Not a self-presentation Tom had ever seen before from David. Not the normal David.

One night Tom was sitting on the end of the bed, and David said, "I guess I'm not the star of this movie."

Tom said, "You're not a star in everything but you probably have a good cameo."

Then David asked, "Do I die in this movie?"

Tom paused and then said, "Yes, I think you do."

"How do I die?"

Tom replied, "How would you like to die?"

David looked alarmed, so Tom said, "How about quietly in your sleep."

And David said, "Yeah, that's OK."

In Los Angeles on June 28, I saw part of the Gay Pride parade down Santa Monica Boulevard. It seemed to be at least 80 percent male and white, mostly tanned, buff guys who must have run right over from the gym and then a tiny contingent of pale, scrawny politicos with banners about AIDS. At least that was my impression. I couldn't stand watching too much of this denial of reality. I went home and called David.

"All sorts of weird stuff is taking place," he told me. "I don't know what money I have and what I don't have." He told me he had just been away for a week and a half, driving. He'd done some work in Argentina. Then he went to Normal, where he'd slept in a barn. Contradicting him would have been pointless and cruel. So I asked him why he'd been sleeping in a barn.

"I was trying to do work. But I feel like I try to do too much. I've really been ripped off quite badly." He went back to discussing Argentina, where he'd had a good time. "But I lost something. My direction. My focus. I did an installation at the home of an artist who died on the outskirts of Buenos Aires."

"What was the installation about?"

"About money. About poverty."

As David neared the end of his life, he worried constantly that he was going to end up back on the street, that he would run out of money. Tom told me that at one point David became convinced that nearly everyone he knew was stealing from him. In this phone call, David told me that he couldn't find the check he'd just been given in Buenos Aires, but acknowledged, "I've been ill a bit, having trouble with my head."

He asked me if I ever ran into Luis Frangella. I wasn't quite sure where David thought I was. Luis had been dead for a year a half. I just said no. He told me that Luis was sick. If I went to Argentina, could I take him some money? "Of course," I told him. David seemed relieved.

"I love you and think of you all the time," I said.

"Vice versa," he replied. "Is it horrible to say vice versa? Tom gets upset with me when I say that."

I told him it was fine for me, but maybe in Tom's case he could tell him he loved him.

"I have a hard time with those words," said David. "I've had a hard time readjusting after my trip. I get lost sometimes and don't know where I am. I'm sort of at a crossroads now. I don't know how they're going to treat this. I have so many ulcerations. I want to get things together here at home, pare things down. I'm not sure of anything except I gotta hang on. I could die but I may not feel much different till later, like in October or towards the end of the year."

As we said our goodbyes, David told me that it had been great seeing me in Argentina.


Round-the-clock nursing care began during the last few weeks of David's life.

Early in that phase, Tom woke one night and saw that David was not in the bed. He heard the shower. The night nurse was agitated but not doing anything. (And was soon replaced.) Walking into the bathroom, Tom saw David taking a shower. He was amazed that David had not only walked unaided to the bathroom but managed to step into the big claw-footed tub.

Tom said, "David, what's going on?"

"I'm going to Times Square."

"Ah, well, let me help you get dried off."

As soon as David turned off the shower, he had to sit down on the edge of the tub. Tom wrapped a towel around him. David was almost too weak to stand, but Tom got him back into bed, and by that time he had forgotten about Times Square.

"There was one that got me the worst," said Tom. "He was in bed and I was walking out, and he said, 'Hey, how about if I meet you later at Union Square Cafe and we'll have dinner?' And it hit me. I'm never going to sit in a restaurant with him again."


On June 30, David called me, sounding completely coherent and angry at the doctor. "They're nuts! They want to put me on methadone. It's really toxic," he complained. "I don't like what's going on. If they leave me alone, I'll be fine." He told me that he would probably come see me before the end of the summer.

They had diagnosed another opportunistic infection, something that could be treated in the hospital. Tom's first reaction was, yes, back to the hospital. (David had never told Tom that he didn't want to be hospitalized again and wanted to die at the loft.) But, Tom said, "Looking at him, his mind was gone, and Bob [the doctor] seemed hesitant about it, and I realized that David wouldn't understand, if he was there, why he couldn't smoke. He wouldn't know where he was. He would get scared. Then I finally decided. I told Bob no. But that was a hard decision. That was one of the last things before Bob and I agreed to cut off everything."

Tom called me on July 3 to say that that night they were going to stop the nutrition, the TPN that David was getting through the Hickman. And that David wanted to see me. "It doesn't make sense for him to live like this when all he does is lay in the bed and vomit," Tom said. "The nausea is worse again, and it's clear it won't stop. It's time to let his body take its own direction. What breaks my heart the most"—he began to sob—"is all he's been through. I just don't want him to suffer."

Though David did not know about this decision, he had been clear that he didn't want to hang on artificially. He said to Tom, "They tell me I'll be taking care of a baby elephant pretty soon."

I arrived back in New York on July 9 and went directly to the loft. Overcome with emotion, I was glad to find David asleep. Even his sleep seemed different, heavier. When he woke, he was surprised to see me. I told him I thought it was time for a visit. He didn't question it. He was wearing a bright green T-shirt and orange swimming trunks. He was drugged, in pain, nauseated, and unable to focus. He could no longer sit up without help. He could no longer stand.

He had made for himself a kind of shrine. He'd hung a dozen necklaces on the wall next to his bed, each a different vivid color, thick and sparkly. This man who had dressed most often in jeans and a pocket T-shirt (to hold cigarettes) never wore jewelry, but he'd been collecting it for years. He'd bought charms on his travels, complex special ones, then strung them on a necklace. He gave this to Karen Finley. When he came home from the hospital for the last time, he hung the bright necklaces he'd bought at an Afghani store on Bleecker Street. Then he put on a silver bracelet and a silver necklace with an antique cross and a kachina doll charm. On his last trip out of the loft, he went to a jeweler with his day nurse and bought a solid gold necklace, thick with an Indian weave. He didn't put it on but kept it near.

He still had the same artwork hanging on the wall. It had been there all through his illness—his *Fever*, two photos of the moon above a photo of a skinny anxious-looking dog that he'd taken in Mérida, at a slaughterhouse.

During the two and a half days I spent there, he slept most of the time. Every period of wakefulness ended with him vomiting into one of two plastic dishpans that were always on the bed. He repeatedly inquired about the Demerol pump attached to his Hickman. What was it? Steve Brown stopped

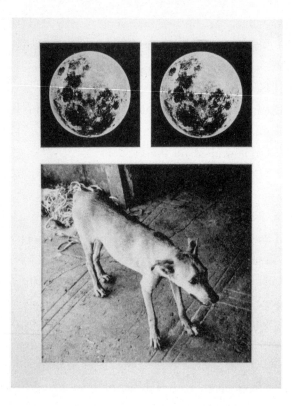

*Fever, 1988–89. Three gelatin-silver prints on museum board, 31 × 25 inches overall. David had this piece hanging above his bed at home through at least the last six months of his illness. (Private collection)*

by and David told him he was thinking about getting tattooed. "Something mythic but kind of contemporary. Machine but flesh."

He slept most of the next day but woke periodically to tell me something. He had just been to Queens, he said, "to see about that commotion. About God. All these people had had visions." Tom explained later that it was a reference to the trip they'd made with Hujar in 1987 to find the healer, to find a cure.

At one point, David said to me, "I'm just trying to figure out where I am."

"Home," I told him.

He looked confused.

"Second Avenue and Twelfth Street," I explained.

"Hujar's place?"

"Yes."

He looked relieved. Later he lurched to a somewhat upright position and asked the nurse, "Is there a bathroom here?"

I met a friend for dinner and returned to find only the night nurse there with the sleeping David. I decided to wait for Tom to return. When he did, he told me he wasn't sure what to do about funeral plans. He and David had never discussed it, and now it was too late. He'd thought about burying him near Hujar, but that was a Catholic cemetery. "I just wish I could hold him and make him better," Tom said and began to cry.

Just then, David woke up, lucid and fully present for the first time that day. He smoked a few cigarettes and drank some water. Tom sat next to him on the bed. We chatted and David kept asking what time it was: ten ten, ten fifteen, ten twenty. Then he got tired and went back to sleep.

The next day, a Saturday, David woke up and asked Tom, "Can you find somebody to get me a diagnosis?" It made Tom cry.

There were many visitors that day, and I stayed away from the bed to give them privacy. Pat had arrived from Paris and was staying in New Jersey with their brother, Steven, whom David had not spoken to since 1989. Every day, Steven drove Pat to the loft but would not come in. Not out of rancor toward David. He was convinced that David did not want to see him, that David had rejected him permanently and would yell at him if he came upstairs. When Steven spoke later at David's memorial, he said that basically he and David had played hide and seek and had played it too well and never found each other.

That day, David got a letter from his English publisher, Serpent's Tail, with a copy of its cover for *Close to the Knives*. Tom began to read the letter out loud to him, choked up after a sentence, and handed it to me to finish. They were using *Hujar Dreaming* on the cover. David stared at it for a long time, loving how it looked with the green type and yellow background.

Did David even know that this was a book he'd written? A painting he'd made? We couldn't quite tell anymore. But because it delighted him, and because he no longer had a short-term memory, Tom was able to bring it back every half hour or so, and say, "David, have you seen the English cover for your book?"

And David would look up in wonderment. "No!" Tom would get it back out. And David would love looking at it again.

He slept most of the time, however, sometimes clenching his fists, making faces. Sometimes he looked very old, but more often childlike and rather dazed. "Oh boy," he'd say about the pain. I noticed how he accepted things, how he no longer asked questions like "Why can't I stand up?" In his moments of lucidity, he described his condition as "not feeling too good." I looked around at the clutter—the yeti on a trike; the crawling baby doll whose head had been replaced with an alligator's; the plastic exploding volcano, kachinas, and dinosaurs; and the framed color photo of a duckling.

Around ten thirty or eleven P.M. David woke and Tom told him about all the people who had been there to see him that day. Apart from his sister Pat, he'd been visited by Brian Butterick, Judy Glantzman, Philip Yenawine, his stepbrother, Pete, and stepsister, Linda, and many others. David did not remember any of it. Tom asked him if he'd seen the English cover for his book. "No!" said David, and Tom pulled it out again. David stared again for quite a few minutes. This would always be new.

Then he got the hiccups. His whole stomach was spasming. None of the tricks that usually stop a hiccup attack had any effect. Finally he started to vomit, and the hiccups stopped. As if his stomach had been trying to throw up but didn't have the strength. David looked down at the scar, healing nicely from the surgery done in May. He said sweetly to Tom, "What were they looking for?"

David had always wanted a ring with a green stone, and he'd found such a stone on one his trips to the Southwest. Tom asked him if he'd like that for a ring and had one made for him with 23 karat gold. "He was really very emotional when I gave it to him," said Tom. "He was out of it, but I put it on his finger and he cried a little bit. Jean Foos was there, and she started to cry on the side. There were so many of those moments while he was sick."

Philip Zimmerman came back from San Francisco, bringing David a turquoise bullet, and remembered him saying, "It would be great if it was made out of meteorite."

Tom and Anita went to Redden's Funeral Home "to pre-plan what had to happen," as Tom put it. He was crying, so Anita gave them David's name and spelled it wrong. Tom corrected it, and they both cried.

As David moved further into dementia, he finally dropped the burdens he had always carried. The rage. The anxiety. The emotional toxicity of his childhood. "At that phase of dementia, he was the happiest I ever saw him," said Judy Glantzman. "He was delighted with life." That might be the saddest thing I ever heard about David.

Back in Los Angeles, I called him on July 14. He actually took the call but sounded very weak. "I'm just feeling so-so," he told me. That was the last time we spoke.

Patrick McDonnell came to visit from Illinois. One day David said that he wanted to sit by the window. Tom was there, with Patrick, Steve Brown, Philip Zimmerman, maybe others. David couldn't walk at all, so they picked him up in a sheet, and David went, "Wheeee!"

"So we started to bounce him and he loved it," said Tom. "He kept going, 'Wheeee! Wheee!'"

One day soon after this, he went into a coma. He was suffering from what his doctor described as "overwhelming sepsis—probably bacterial sepsis with multiple infections, everything from disseminated candida, which is fungus, *Mycobacterium avium*, overwhelming HIV infection, Kaposi's sarcoma, which manifested internally, and probably *Pneumocystis jiroveci* pneumonia."

Judy Glantzman remembered lying on the bed next to him, telling him—since people in a coma can still hear: "David, if you need to go, it's OK" and his face took on the old look of rage, as if to say, I'll go when I'm ready.

David Wojnarowicz died of AIDS on July 22, 1992, at the age of thirty-seven.

This occurred at "Hujar's place" at about nine thirty P.M. Present were Tom, Anita Vitale, Jean Foos, Steve Brown, Philip Zimmerman, and David's siblings Pat, Peter, and Linda.

Once David was declared dead, Pat threw herself on the bed, hugging him and calling his name. She became so upset when the hearse arrived that Tom felt he had to stay with her instead of walking down the steps with David's body.

Judy Glantzman had left to meet with her sister and so missed David's passing, but returned about ten minutes later. When the hearse arrived, Steve Brown and Philip Zimmerman said they would carry David downstairs. Glantzman walked down with them.

As they walked out onto Second Avenue, with David in a body bag, there was one last surreal moment. The singer and composer Diamanda Galás happened to be walking by. She and David had never met, but they'd spoken once on the phone. She shared his commitment to addressing AIDS, in her case through *The Plague Mass*, which showcased her five-octave range and fierce persona.

Galás does not remember being on Second Avenue that night, but she made an indelible impression on Zimmerman and Glantzman. She had walked by, but as they were putting David into the hearse, she spun around and ran back, yelling, "Who is that? Is that David Wojnarowicz?" Zimmerman and Brown didn't answer. What Glantzman remembers is that Diamanda Galás was there at the door, screaming. "As if our feelings were being amplified," said Glantzman. "Hysterical screaming."

# EPILOGUE **THROW MY BODY ON THE STEPS OF THE WHITE HOUSE**

**David's memorial took** place at St. Mark's Church on what would have been his thirty-eighth birthday—September 14, 1992. But at the urging of Judy Glantzman and Steve Brown, Tom opened the loft to David's friends on the Sunday after his death in July. Along with many friends, two members of an ACT UP affinity group called the Marys turned up. Joy Episalla and Carrie Yamaoka had never met David, but they knew Jean Foos. They wanted to talk to Tom about giving David a political funeral.

The Marys had an established reputation for commitment and audacity. These were the activists who rented a room at the Waldorf Astoria so they could throw fake money inscribed with "George Bush—Blood on Your Hands" out the window when the president's car pulled up to the hotel. They'd shut down the *MacNeil/Lehrer NewsHour* to protest the scant attention paid to the war at home, AIDS, while the media covered the war in the Persian Gulf. They'd dumped a coffin full of bloody bones in the Citicorp atrium, with explanatory flyers, on ACT UP's Day of Desperation. They'd organized a march on the Bush home in Kennebunkport, Maine, and helped shut down Grand Central Station during rush hour while other activists hung huge banners ("One AIDS Death Every 8 Minutes"). They met often, they were close-knit, and they regarded each other as family. Then in late '91 and early '92, two of them, John Stumpf and Dennis Kane, died of AIDS and had the usual ungratifying memorials.

Everyone in the Marys read *Close to the Knives*, and when they got to the part in which David suggests, that people drive the body of their loved one a hundred miles an hour to Washington, blast through the White House gates, and "dump their lifeless form on the front steps," the group decided, in Episalla's words, "Goddamn right. That sounds just about right to us." They decided to dedicate themselves to David's idea of making AIDS deaths visible

*David worried that people affected by the AIDS epidemic were becoming professional pallbearers, perfecting rituals of death instead of "a relatively simple ritual of life such as screaming in the streets." (Photograph by Brian Palmer/ bxpnyc.com)*

to the public, and named the new project Stumpf/Kane. During the 1992 Gay Pride parade, they circulated flyers asking for volunteers who would agree to a political funeral, who would "leave your body to politics." There were no takers.

When they came to Tom that day at the loft, he hesitated. He didn't want violence. He didn't want people arrested. Episalla and Yamaoka assured him that they could do this without mayhem. And so, one week after David's death, he had the first political funeral to come out of the AIDS crisis.

The procession began outside the loft, moved down Second Avenue, then east to Avenue A and south to Houston. The Marys had created a banner wide enough to shut down traffic: "DAVID WOJNAROWICZ, 1954— 1992, DIED OF AIDS DUE TO GOVERNMENT NEGLECT." Two women beat snare drums. Others clapped sticks of wood together, but they all walked in silence. Someone had handed out a few sunflowers to carry, while friends held up reproductions of David's work. As they marched through the East Village, people began to step off the sidewalk and join the procession. They had no permit, and the police were involved by the time they got to Avenue A—one squad car with lights flashing, leading them. Marchers walked west on Houston, then north on the Bowery.

Hundreds were marching by the time they got to the parking lot across from Cooper Union (now an undulating glass tower filled with luxury condos), where Yamaoka and activist Tim Bailey waited with a slide projector set up on top of Yamaoka's car, plugged into a nearby electric pole. The slides playing across the wall behind parked cars showed David's name and dates, then a photo of the White House with the passage superimposed about driving your dead friend to Washington, D.C. Dirk Rowntree read the extended version of this from David's most controversial essay, "Postcards from America: X-Rays from Hell," beginning with the words, "To make the private into something public is an action that has terrific repercussions in the pre-invented world. The government has the job of maintaining the day-to-day illusion of the ONE-TRIBE NATION. Each public disclosure of a private reality becomes something of a magnet that can attract others with a similar frame of reference; thus each public disclosure of a fragment of private reality serves as a dismantling tool against the illusion of a ONE-TRIBE NATION." Rowntree ended his reading with that image of the lifeless body on the White House steps. It might be summarized as: My grief as a tool to fight the state is as good a tool as any other.

Episalla and activist Barbara Hughes then took the banner into the street and set it on fire. Friends tossed in the placards they'd been carrying. Friends tossed in the sunflowers. They stood in silence, watching the funeral pyre burn.

The Marys left that evening determined to carry out David's idea. They all committed to having a political funeral when they died. Within the next year, three of them did. On November 2, the night before the presidential election, the Marys carried the body of Mark Lowe Fisher in an open casket from Judson Memorial Church all the way up Sixth Avenue to the Republican Party headquarters on Forty-third Street. On July 1, 1993, the Marys drove to Washington, D.C., with the body of Tim Bailey, planning to march past the White House, but authorities prevented them from even getting the casket out of the van. A couple of weeks later, they carried the body of Jon Greenberg through the East Village, and he lay in state in Tompkins Square Park, casket open. One of the Marys read the speech Greenberg had delivered at the first of these funerals, in which he spoke of the importance of what they were doing with this final act of empowerment and generosity.

In the years after David's death, Tom Rauffenbart sprinkled David's ashes in places that had held meaning for him. He took some to the beach in St. John's where they'd had their first sexy romantic vacation. He left ashes at the loft, sealed inside a wall. He sprinkled some in Paris, in New Orleans, in the Great Swamp of New Jersey, at Teotihuacán, and at what was left of the Christopher Street pier. Then in October 1996, he joined in ACT UP's second "Ashes Action" in Washington, D.C. He got up to the fence and threw David onto the White House lawn.

# ACKNOWLEDGMENTS

*Fire in the Belly: The Life and Times of David Wojnarowicz* is a project of the Creative Capital/Andy Warhol Foundation Arts Writers Grant Program. I am also deeply grateful for the support of the John Simon Guggenheim Memorial Foundation.

I was helped enormously by a Lannan Foundation residency in Marfa, Texas, and by a stay at the artists' community, Yaddo.

Fales Library at New York University became my home away from home during the research phase. I benefited from director Marvin J. Taylor's unstinting support for this project. He and archivists Lisa Darms and Brent Phillips went out of their way to help.

For their help in Paris, I am grateful to Marcelle Clements, Laurence Viallet, and the Centre International d'Accueil et d'échanges des Récollets.

Art historian Jonathan Weinberg shared research he gathered while working on a book about the Hudson River piers and while curating the exhibition "The Piers: Art and Sex along the New York Waterfront."

Bill Dobbs provided documentation on "Art What Thou Eat" that I could not have found otherwise.

I was fortunate to have Donna Mandel and Ann Snitow as first readers of each chapter and can't thank them enough for their close reading, their feedback, and their encouragement.

My editor, Kathy Belden, was a champion of this project early on, and I benefited enormously from her enthusiasm, her patience, and her skill in shaping the narrative.

I also owe special thanks to acquiring editor Karen Rinaldi, who recognized immediately what this project could be.

Photographer Karen Cattan played an invaluable role in organizing and preparing the visual elements in this book.

Special thanks to Vince Aletti, Tommy Turner, and Jean Foos (on behalf of the estate of Keith Davis) for sharing relevant portions of personal journals.

I am also deeply grateful for the sundry crucial ways in which I have been helped and supported during this process by Shelagh Doyle, Tierney Drummond, Karen Durbin, Su Friedrich, Dave King, Amy Scholder, Amy Sillman, Karen Vierneisel, and Marianne Weems.

# NOTES

## Archive

The David Wojnarowicz Papers (MSS 092) at the Fales Library and Special Collections, New York University. Citations for "Fales" refer to the Wojnarowicz Papers unless otherwise noted.

## The Truth: An Introduction

**p. 1 "an obvious attempt to offend Christians during the Christmas season"** http://washingtonscene.thehill.com/in-the-know/36-news/7223-boehner-and-cantor-call-for-closing-of-smithsonian-exhibit.

**p. 1 "I ain't particularly radical"** DW to Glantzman, October 1, 1990, in author's possession.

**p. 2 "a metaphor for social structure"** DW to Blinderman, October 22, 1988, in author's possession.

**p. 3 "selling it back at an inconceivable mark-up"** Edit deAk, "Urban Kisses/Slum Hisses," in *ABC No Rio Dinero*, ed. Moore and Miller, p. 34.

**p. 3 "the last outsider"** Vince Passaro, "The Last Outsider," *New York Times Book Review*, March 12, 2000.

**p. 6 "All this in my work"** Fales Series 3B, Box 5, Folder 215b.

## 1 Where Something Broke

**p. 9 Dolores filed for divorce** *Dolores J. Wojnarowicz v. Edward T. Wojnarowicz*, M99-56, Superior Court of New Jersey, Monmouth County.

**p. 10 the court ruled that it could not decide a religious difference of opinion** *Wojnarowicz v. Wojnarowicz*, 48 N.J.SUPER. 349, 137 A.2D 618 (1958).

**p. 14 "brown stuff" came out of her ears and mouth** DW, *Close to the Knives*, p. 152.

**p. 15 "take it in the yard" and make David "watch him shoot it"** "Biographical Dateline," in *Tongues of Flame*, ed. Blinderman, p. 114.

**p. 15 claiming it was "New York steak"** Ibid.

**p. 15 probably in 1962** Though David situated the shopping center incident in 1961, Ed's record with the United States Lines indicates that 1962 was the only year he was home for Christmas. Service record of Edward T. Wojnarowicz in author's possession.

**p. 17 sitting together behind Lee's gas station** Fales Series 1, Box 2, Folder 27, and *Diaries*, ed. Scholder, p. 199.

**p. 20 broke a whiskey bottle over someone's head** October 15, 1979, in Fales 1, 2, 36.

## 2 Dissolution

**p. 27 "I got yelled at"** Author's interviews with DW in January 1990.

## 3 The Street

**p. 39 "cigars under the flashing entrances"** Fales Series 3A, Box 4, Folder 12, p. 15.

**p. 39 "all directions at once"** Ibid., p. 16.

**p. 39 "knife wielding lunatic"** Ibid., p. 25.

**p. 40 "could hardly recognize myself"** Ibid., p. 26.

**p. 40 "filled with lurid photos"** Ibid., p. 33.

**p. 41 "death trip continually"** Ibid., p. 38.

**p. 41 "We were still new to hustling together"** April 24, 1978, in Fales 1, 1, 6.

**p. 46 a piece for his local paper** http://articles.mcall.com/1992-12-24/news/2880365_1_raymond-blind-man-salvation-army.

**p. 49 described meeting him in the dining hall at the residence** Untitled story in Fales 3, 4, 3.

**p. 49 In one story . . . at the halfway house for a few months; in another, he said he'd been there for a year** "Guy Wakes Up (16 Years Old)" in Fales 3D, 6, 228, and untitled story in Fales 3, 4, 3.

**p. 50 he and Willy stayed with an ex-con** Steve Hager, "From Street to Salon, *New York Beat*, May 9, 1984, in Fales 5C, 8, 23.

**p. 50 finding an abandoned bus on Houston Street** "Guy Wakes Up (16 Years Old)" in Fales 3D, 6, 228.

**p. 51 "or lonely drag queen's palace"** Ibid., pp. 3–4.

**p. 51 two accounts of this sojourn** "Teenage Guy on Canal Street" in Fales 3E, 6, 247, and "Willy" in Fales 3B, 5, 206.

**p. 52 "I almost burst into tears"** "Guy Wakes Up (16 Years Old)" in Fales 3D, 6, 228.

**p. 52 he gave Willy the name "Lipsy"** Fales 3A, 5, 152.

**4 The Secret Life**

**p. 55 "FIRST PHOTOS (AWFUL)"** Fales Series 9A[3], Box 32, Envelope 21, Sheets 33, 34, 35.

**p. 66 "that I at least give my life up to it"** Fales Series 2, Box 2, Folder 1.

**p. 67 prose poem on the Denver bus station** *Coldspring Journal*, no. 10, April 1976.

**p. 67 questionnaire about his poetry life** Fales 3A, 5, 149.

**p. 70 "He'd given up in a way"** DW to Ensslin, September 9, 1976, in author's possession.

**5 At the Shattered Edge of the Map**

**p. 81 an anthology they turned up in a remainder bin** Ronald Gross and George Quasha with Emmett Williams, John Robert Colombo, and Walter Lowenfels, eds., *Open Poetry: Four Anthologies of Expanded Poems* (New York: Simon and Schuster, 1973). David read Filliou's intro while Lackow created his own tiny poem.

**p. 83 One study of the Beat Generation . . . analyzed Huncke's appeal** John Tytell, *Naked Angels: The Lives and Literature of the Beat Generation* (New York: McGraw-Hill Paperbacks, 1977), p. 91.

**p. 84 "She leaked from every pore."** Lydia Lunch, foreword to Thurston Moore and Byron Coley, *No Wave: Post-Punk* (New York: Abrams Image, 2008), p. 4.

**p. 91 "My Father as the Red Lark"** September 28, 1977, in Fales Series 1, Box 1, Folder 4. **answer pages among his papers** Fales 3A, 5, 149.

**p. 96 a response to Pinochet's 1973 coup** http://www.arianeroesch.com/Press/The_Ties_that_Bind.pdf.

**p. 96 "concealing messages behind a false eyeball"** May 8, 1978, in Fales 1, 1, 6.

**p. 99 one trucker who gave him a ride ended up among the monologues** This version of the trucker's story is from David's journal in Fales 1, 1, 19.

**p. 100 "I just had a vision of myself after the tenth grade"** Fales 3E, 6, 257.

**p. 100 two autobiographical pieces Cartwright wrote out in his big grade-school handwriting** The autobiographical pieces Louis Cartwright wrote can be found in Fales 3H, 6, 295.

## 6 The Flaneur

p. 104 "Feeling hyena. Feeling wolf. Feeling dog" August 31, 1978, in Fales Series 1, Box 1, Folder 5.

p. 104 "I ain't eaten in three fuckin' days" September 4, 1978, in ibid.

p. 106 "put my mouth to his and taste wine" September 15, 1978, in Fales 1, 1, 7.

p. 106 "delirious through the side streets of the Louvre" September 16, 1978, in ibid.

p. 106 "a semi-surreal erotic novel" DW to Jezebel Cook, 1978, letter read during interview.

p. 107 "daytime photos of symbols that reflect areas of thinking" October 1, 1978, in Fales 1, 1, 7.

p. 107 afraid of his actual subject matter DW to Cook, letter read during interview.

p. 107 "a wild look of criminality in their eyes" October 12, 1978, in Fales 1, 1, 7.

p. 107 "never thought so deeply as this" October 13, 1978, in ibid.

p. 108 "forever fixed in the non-seeing eye" October 10, 1978, in ibid.

p. 108 "the fusion of society and physical law" October 11, 1978, in ibid.

p. 108 "to learn as much as we can from it" October 17, 1978, in ibid.

p. 109 the distances he'd come in his life October 18, 1978, in ibid.

p. 109 "the experiences are needed . . . necessary" October 22, 1978, in ibid.

p. 110 "brilliant white heart metamorphoses" October 24, 1978, in ibid.

p. 114 "all the frightening bareness I feel" Undated entry, probably November 4, 5, or 6, 1978, in ibid.

p. 116 "a little more than they expected" DW to DeForge, December 7, 1978, in author's possession.

p. 116 "what am I racing towards?" November 22, 1978, in Fales 1, 1, 8.

p. 118 "a sense I may never rid myself of" DW to DeForge, December 7, 1978, in author's possession.

p. 119 "trying to get out of bird appearance" December 10, 1978, in Fales 1, 1, 9, and letter to Brian Butterick on p. 66 in ibid.

p. 119 "I have learned of my own so far" Loose material in Fales 1, 1, 8.

p. 120 "slowed me down and calmed my writings" DW to Ensslin, March 27, 1979, in author's possession.

p. 120 "supportive glimpse into the netherworld" February 12, 1979, in Fales 1, 1, 9.

p. 120 "guaranteed entrance into heaven" Fales 3A, 4, 8.

p. 121 "poodles in the midst of all this" November 2, 1978, in Fales 1, 1, 8.

p. 121 "wished it was fifties all over again" DW to Ensslin, March 27, 1979, in author's possession.

p. 121 wanted to be part of that vibrant, growing scene February 22, 1979, in Fales 1, 1, 9.

p. 124 "contact, sexual or otherwise" April 11, 1979, in Fales 1, 1, 10.

p. 124 "explore things as they move my way" Ibid.

p. 124 "wanted to leave quite badly" Ibid.

p. 125 "spared from the typewriter" Ibid.

p. 125 "part of one's personal myth and therefore true" Christopher Isherwood, *Christopher and His Kind* (Minneapolis: University of Minnesota Press, 2001). The quotes David refers to are on pp. 2 and 4.

p. 128 "seems in hindsight" April 29, 1979, in Fales 1, 1, 10.

## 7 Go Rimbaud

p. 131 "destroys the most subtle responses in human nature" June 14, 1979, in Fales Series 1, Box 1, Folder 11.

p. 133 "places I starved in or haunted on some level" David Hirsch, "New York Adventure," *New York Native*, December 3, 1990, and in Fales 6C, 10, 71.

p. 134 two exposures, one printed Contact sheet in Fales 9A [15], Box 44, Sheet 2.

**p. 135 "to fall through their living room floors into the apartment below"** Undated journal entry, p. 3, in Fales 1, 1, 14.

**p. 136 Dirk photographed them** July 6, 1979, in Fales 1, 1, 11.

**p. 137 "some kinda vision in all this"** Ibid.

**p. 138 "If he's following my scent . . . this'll throw him off"** Undated journal entry, p. 59, in Fales 1, 1, 11.

**p. 139 "made him feel good about his own early life"** DW to Delage, December 19, 1979, in author's possession.

**p. 139 "departing from conventional morality"** Jean Genet, *The Thief's Journal*, trans. Bernard Frechtman (New York: Grove Press, 1964), p. 222.

**p. 140 "ye have done it unto me"** Matthew 25:40.

**p. 140 "It's so simple, the man without the eye against a receding wall"** September 8, 1979, in Fales 1, 2, 36.

**p. 140 "lips traced lines down on the belly"** Ibid.

**p. 140 someone had thrown rocks through the Rimbaud face** September 16, 1979, in ibid.

**p. 140 complaining of odd purplish lesions** Shilts, *And the Band*, p. 37.

**p. 141 he'd written to a friend regarding the hoboes** DW to Seymour, February 16, 1979, in author's possession.

**p. 142 "all these unspoken sentences at the tip of my tongue"** October 7, 1979, in Fales 1, 2, 36.

**p. 143 "the way this living is really constructed"** October 8/9, 1979, in ibid.

**p. 143 "this city rotating with the world on its axis"** October 9, 1979, in ibid.

**p. 143 "pieces of sky along the dark floorboards"** October 22, 1979, in ibid.

**p. 144 "something relegated to the self of the past"** December 11, 1979, in Fales 1, 1, 12.

**p. 145 "plane engines easing into the distance"** December 8, 1979, in ibid.

**p. 145 "I would like to return to Paris"** DW to Delage, December 30, 1979, in author's possession.

**p. 145 "systematically screwed out of decent places to exist in"** Lehmann Weichselbaum, "The Real Estate Show," in *ABC No Rio Dinero*, ed. Moore and Miller, p. 52.

**p. 146 "merger of the South Bronx and the East Village"** Steven Hager, "Patti Astor's 'Wild Style,'" *East Village Eye*, February 1983.

**p. 147 "they intend to stay put and help determine the area's evolution"** Peter Fend, "Letter to *Skyline*," in *ABC No Rio Dinero*, ed. Moore and Miller, p. 59.

**p. 147 "something to put on a resume"** DW to Delage, January 16, 1980, in author's possession.

**p. 148 "my leanings in the time period of my living"** January 15, 1980, in Fales 1, 2, 36.

**p. 148 "swooning winds and muscular bodies"** February 2, 1980, in Fales 1, 1, 13.

**p. 149 "as if it were a tribal gift"** March 6, 1980, in ibid.

**p. 149 "remember I love you"** DW to Delage, April 3, 1980, in author's possession.

**p. 149 "the constant limbo I feel I'm in"** Undated journal entry in Fales 1, 1, 13, and *Diaries*, ed. Scholder, p. 150.

**p. 149 "escaping a mugger in the subway by leaping into an F train"** DW to Delage, March 13, 1980, in author's possession, and March 14, 1980, in Fales 1, 1, 13.

**p. 150 "sex in an abandoned playground"** February 14, 1980, in Fales 1, 1, 13.

**p. 150 "envelopes destined for Texas"** February 2, 1980, in ibid.

**p. 151 "How do I know she didn't look like this when she was younger?"** February 26, 1980, in ibid.

**p. 151 "from his self-made boundaries into yours"** Undated journal entry in Fales 1, 1, 14.

**p. 152 "I really dug it"** May 11, 1980, in Fales 1, 1, 14, and *Diaries*, ed. Scholder, p. 156.

**p. 152 "combing his hair before a fluorescent-lit mirror"** May 1980 in Fales 1, 1, 14, and *Diaries*, ed. Scholder, p. 158.

**p. 153 "to sweep up broken bottles"** May 1980 in Fales 1, 1, 14, and *Diaries*, ed. Scholder, p. 162.

**p. 153 "concerning what to do with freedom"** DW to Delage, May 18, 1980, in author's possession.

**p. 153 two scripts for this film, which he never made** The script in Fales 3F, 6, 271 is typed and looks more finished, but ideas in the second handwritten script, in Fales 3F, 6, 276, seem more developed.

**p. 154 changed his first name to "Anado"** McLauchlin went on to create installations, jewelry, furniture, and assemblages at his home in Mexico. See http://www.madebyanado.com.

**p. 155 "horror of death coming close to friends"** Undated journal entry in Fales 1, 1, 14, and *Diaries*, ed. Scholder, p. 165.

**p. 157 "the kind of imagination displayed by this exhibition's organizers"** Deitch's review of the "Times Square Show" can be found in *ABC No Rio Dinero*, ed. Moore and Miller, p. 12.

**p. 157 chunk of his own graffiti leaning against a wall** June 18, 1980, in Fales 1, 1, 14.

**p. 158 "the distant darkness of unnameable cities"** July 6, 1980, in ibid.

**8 Nightclubbing**

**p. 159 "located on 37th between 7th and 8th"** The description of the first Danceteria is from Malu Halasa, "New and Used Clubs," *East Village Eye*, Summer 1980.

**p. 160 entered a cassette he described as "experimental"** DW to Delage, May 23, 1980, in author's possession.

**p. 160 busboys made five dollars and change per hour** Information about busboy salaries came from Brian Butterick.

**p. 160 "the image of the tough angel"** Fales Series 1, Box, 1, Folder 15, p. 14.

**p. 160 "confused as to what I was feeling"** Ibid., p. 42.

**p. 161 tooth from a wild boar** Ibid., p. 28.

**p. 161 snakes . . . a hundred years old** Ibid., p. 50.

**p. 161 "dripping with slime"** Ibid., p. 15.

**p. 161 "car lights follow invisible roads"** Ibid.

**p. 161 "how you turned the head"** Ibid.

**p. 161 "because of laws, governments, and borders"** Ibid., p. 44.

**p. 162 "something indefinable draining from his face"** Ibid., p. 55.

**p. 162 "my love for him and my own peace of mind"** Ibid., p. 48.

**p. 162 "only a faint smell of jism"** E-mail to author from Jim Pennington, October 12, 2010.

**p. 162 he "couldn't go mad"** Ibid.

**p. 163 when he played a poet on television, in a Gap ad** Max Blagg's Gap ad can be seen at http://www.youtube.com/watch?v=gpXopw4anJE.

**p. 163 Iolo Carew, another busboy** Carew has been identified as both manager and DJ at the club, but Jim Fouratt, who hired him, said he was a busboy.

**p. 164 "for my father, *dark shadow on the viridian seas*"** DW to Pennington, October 15, 1980, in author's possession.

**p. 164 He thought it his best photo** DW to Delage, October 26, 1980, in author's possession.

**p. 165 his mother had entered the same contest** DW to Delage, November 22, 1980, in author's possession.

**p. 165 went to see the work of his fellow unemployed busboy** DW to Delage, November 1, 1980, in author's possession.

**p. 167 spirit leaving the body** Fales 3A, 4, 103 in the explanation for *Spirituality (for Paul Thek)*.

**p. 170 "just talk and listen to interesting things"** DW to Delage, January 5, 1981, in author's possession.

**p. 170 inspired him to keep working** DW to Delage, January 7, 1981, in author's possession.

**p. 170 about "photography, life, etc."** DW to Delage, January 9, 1981, in author's possession.

p. 170 **"tired of all the scenes I'd been involved with"** January 21, 1981, in Fales 1, 1, 15.

p. 171 **across from each of these, a film speed** Fales, 1, 1, 11, p. 72.

p. 171 **he still had hope about the future, and Hujar did not** January 21, 1981, in Fales 1, 1, 15, and *Diaries*, ed. Scholder, p. 172.

p. 171 **"Yes, this is what is true"** January 21, 1981, in Fales 1, 1, 15, and *Diaries*, ed. Scholder, p. 182.

p. 172 **"change direction and run, escape, depart"** January 21, 1981, in Fales 1, 1, 15, and *Diaries*, ed. Scholder, p. 183.

p. 172 **"I don't feel very comfortable with them"** DW to Delage, April 9, 1981, in author's possession.

p. 173 **"will give them cause to become disinterested"** Fales 8B, 16, Audiotape 092.0220.

p. 173 **"They're my life"** Ibid.

p. 173 **Could he please move out?** DW to Delage, April 17, 1981, in author's possession.

p. 174 **"so different from most people I know"** Undated journal entry in Fales 1, 1, 15, p. 98, and *Diaries*, ed. Scholder, p. 192.

p. 175 **"I'm trying to understand it"** Undated journal entry in Fales 1, 1, 15, and *Diaries*, ed. Scholder, p. 193.

p. 176 **"It definitely got construed as a whole other thing"** Author's interviews with DW in January 1990.

p. 178 **"Only if I have no other place to sleep"** DW to Delage, June 5, 1981, in author's possession.

p. 178 **"I looked for you in it"** Ibid.

p. 178 **"I HEARD THAT!"** Undated journal entry in Fales 1, 1, 15, p. 97, and *Diaries*, ed. Scholder, p. 186.

## 9 The Poverty of Peter Hujar

p. 184 **created a small body of work under that name** Cards made by "Jute Harper" are in Fales 6A, 9, 14.

p. 185 **"I hear the same about you"** The incident with Cecil Beaton is recounted in a chapter on Hujar and Paul Thek, "Peter and Paul," in Carl Rollyson and Lisa Paddock, *Susan Sontag: The Making of an Icon* (New York: W. W. Norton, 2000), p. 113.

p. 185 **since he had a phone book** The encounter with Peter Maxwell came from the author's interview with Steve Turtell.

p. 186 **"he couldn't make a distinction between someone who owned some little photography gallery and the Pope"** Melissa Harris, interview with Fran Lebowitz, *Brush Fires*, p. 81.

## 10 A Union of Different Drummers

p. 195 **offenders had been compelled to draw both a man and a woman** http://www.undo.net/it/mostra/44190.

p. 195 **"We all kind of laughed"** http://www.digitaljournalist.org/issue0106/voices_goldin.htm.

p. 195 **"Kaposi's Sarcoma and *Pneumocystis* Pneumonia Among Homosexual Men—New York City and California"** Shilts, *And the Band*, p. 76.

p. 196 **no apparent danger to nonhomosexuals** Lawrence K. Altman, "Rare Cancer Seen in 41 Homosexuals," *New York Times*, July 3, 1981.

p. 196 **"feeling that time is running away"** DW to Delage, July 1, 1981, in author's possession.

p. 197 **gluing little figures to them** "Charlie Ahearn on Fun Gallery," *Artforum*, October 1999.

p. 198 **sold just one, for fifty dollars** Interview with Patti Astor at http://www.at149st.com/astor.html.

p. 198 **sent a rather anguished letter in September** Delage's letter from September 1981 can be found in Fales Series 2, Box 2, Folder 6.

p. 198 **"I never meet any person with your qualities"** DW to Delage, November 1981, in author's possession.

p. 199 **"but then I saw this young guy"** Loose sheets tucked into Fales 1, 2, 36.

p. 199 **"Too much cynicism"** DW to Delage, September 15, 1981, in author's possession.

p. 201 **"one of the sweetest heterosexual guys I've ever come in contact with"** DW, *Close to the Knives*, p. 178.

p. 201 **"weird discards of civilization"** Ibid.

p. 201 **"Why don't you find out?"** Ibid., p. 188.

p. 202 **"a las vegas card shark's smile"** Ibid., p. 183.

p. 202 **"vague thing that was affecting twentysome people"** Author's interviews with DW in January, 1990.

p. 203 **"crabby guards came screaming at us to stop we rode around anyways"** Undated journal entry in Fales, 1, 2, 35.

p. 206 **a cow "exploding with fear"** Gideon Gil, "Artists Work to Help Fight Child Abuse," *Louisville Times*, December 6, 1985, in Fales 6C, 9, 46.

p. 206 **"for Sophie"** Fales 3A, 5, 183.

p. 209 **"taking the junk"** Fales 8B, 16, Audiotape 092.0248.

p. 211 **"confronts the viewer with a vision of anarchy and insanity"** Fales 6D, 10, 78c.

p. 213 **"Many at the FDA did not believe that this so-called epidemic of immune suppression even existed"** Shilts, *And the Band*, p. 170.

p. 213 **FDA would not license a test allowing blood banks to screen their products until 1985** http://www.aids.gov/hiv-aids-basics/hiv-aids-101/overview/aids-timeline.

p. 215 **"harshest work of quality in the East Village"** Timothy Cohrs, "25,000 Sculptors from across the U.S.A. at Civilian Warfare" *East Village Eye*, September 1984.

p. 216 **"I want you to know my sign"** Nicolas Moufarrege, "Another Wave, Still More Savagely Than the First," *Arts*, September 1982.

**11 Rampages of Raw Energy**

p. 218 **"My landlord flipped out"** "Pronto Profile" on Gracie Mansion in Fales Series 6C, Box 9, Folder 49.

p. 218 **"I was young and stupid and thought that was a really great deal"** Ibid.

p. 225 **"suddenly discovered work where hours before there was none"** First draft of the statement on the Ward Line Pier by DW and Mike Bidlo in Fales 11A, Oversize Box 22, Folder 24.

p. 226 **"the work came out in rampages of raw energy"** Final version of the DW and Bidlo statement on the Ward Line Pier is in Fales 6D, 10, 78b.

p. 227 **"warned of its possible collapse"** Richard Goldstein, "Post-Graffiti: The Pier Group Makes Its Mark," *Village Voice*, June 21, 1983.

p. 228 **"It hurt me so much to see him"** Hager, *After Midnight*, p. 119.

p. 229 **"There is no epidemic"** Shilts, *And the Band*, p. 340.

p. 229 **"a disease whose myth exploded through thoughtless babble and media saturation"** Kristian Hoffman, "Klaus Nomi," *East Village Eye*, September 1983.

**12 "Will They Allow Me on the Moon?"**

p. 231 **used the food posters because they marked a specific time** David's explanation of the food posters comes from Fales Series 8B, Box 16, Audiotape 092.0247.

p. 232 **born in Cairo** Fales Series 7A, Box 13, Folder 43.

p. 233 **"going out on [sic] the world alone at the age of nine"** Fales 6D, 10, 78b.

p. 233 **"indicate how authentic your images are"** Fales 8B, 16, Audiotape 092.0227.

p. 234 **Bob Dylan began traveling with a carnival at the age of thirteen (as he used to tell**

**interviewers**) http://www.nydailynews.com/archives/news/2004/06/15/2004-06-15_self-portrait
__bob_dylan_inv.html.

**p. 234 "A reasonable model is Genet"** Robert Pincus-Witten, "Entries: Myth in Formation," *Arts*,
November 1983.

**p. 240 176 galleries would open** This number comes from "The East Village: A Chronology" in
*Artforum*, October 1999.

**p. 242 had never known how to balance a checkbook** From author's interview with Norman
Frisch.

**p. 243 the first sign of AIDS was "white stuff on your tongue"** Joe Vojtko, "Dangerous
Combustibles: A Memoir from a Room at the End of Everything," *Review*, December 1, 1997.

**p. 248 "Will they allow me on the moon if they realize who I am completely?"** January 31,
1984, in Fales 1, 1, 17, and *Diaries*, ed. Scholder, p. 196.

**13 Pressure Point**

**p. 249 "That corner"—Second Street and Avenue B—"no longer belongs to the city of New
York"** Marcia Chambers, "Lower East Side Drug Trade Evades Cleanup," *New York Times*, July
5, 1983.

**p. 249 "retail drug capital of America"** Marcia Chambers, "Going Cold Turkey in Alphabetville,"
*New York Times*, February 19, 1984.

**p. 250 while seizing 160,000 packages of heroin** Jane Gross, "In the Trenches of a War Against
Drugs," *New York Times*, January 8, 1986.

**p. 250 "use the junk population to burn down the area. The deed is done"** Jeff Gottesfeld and
Spencer Rumsey, "Drug Bust! 'Operation Pressure Point' Hits Avenue B," *East Village Eye*,
March 1984.

**p. 253 "they'd paint pictures for it"** Sylvia Falcon, "Let Paintings Be Stupid," *East Village Eye*,
March 1984.

**p. 253 "Paintings are doorways into collectors' homes"** Carlo McCormick, "Sweet 'N' Low,"
*East Village Eye*, March 1984.

**p. 254 "beginning of an era of 'souvenir' art and tourist boutiques"** Nicolas A. Moufarrege,
"The Year After," *Flash Art*, Summer 1984.

**p. 254 "adventurous avant-garde setting of considerable cachet"** Carlo McCormick and Walter
Robinson, "Slouching Towards Avenue D," *Art in America*, Summer 1984. This piece also
appears in *ABC No Rio Dinero*, ed. Moore and Miller, p. 40.

**p. 254 "simulacrum" of bohemia** Craig Owens, "The Problem with Puerilism," *Art in America*,
Summer 1984.

**p. 255 "AIDS virus had been discovered—by the French"** Thomas Steele, "CDC Director Says
Announcement of AIDS Cause Is Forthcoming," *New York Native*, April 9–22, 1984.

**p. 255 "ran a story on April 22"** Lawrence K. Altman, "Federal Official Says He Believes Cause of
AIDS Has Been Found," *New York Times*, April 22, 1984.

**p. 255 "he saw it as allied with the French"** Shilts, *And the Band*, pp. 460–62.

**p. 263 "the kind of reaction that Lydia liked best"** Joe Vojtko, "Dangerous Combustibles: A
Memoir from a Room at the End of Everything," *Review*, December 1, 1997.

**p. 263 "colors that brought me close to fainting"** DW to Hujar in Fales Series 2, Box 4,
Folder 37.

**p. 266 people who saw "unarguable truth" in violence** DW, *Close to the Knives*, pp. 172–73.

**14 A Burning Child**

**p. 271 "I rejected her"** Fales Series 4, Box 7, Folder 13.

**p. 273 sent a reporter to cover this exotic event** Douglas C. McGill, "An Art Auction-Benefit
with East Village Style, *New York Times*, February 26, 1985.

**p. 274 "We do and show what we like"** Grace Glueck, "East Village Gets on the Fast Track," *New York Times*, January 13, 1985.

**p. 275 Cooper analyzed it** Dennis Cooper, "Odd Man Out," *Artforum*, October 1999.

**p. 279 finally changed at the end of 1985** Erik Eckholm, "City, In Shift, To Make Blood Test for AIDS Virus More Widely Available," *New York Times*, December 23, 1985.

**p. 279 "know all they need to know about AIDS"** Shilts, *And the Band.*, p. 533.

**p. 280 no one knew how likely it was for someone infected with the virus to actually get AIDS** http://www.thebody.com/content/art31903.html.

**p. 282 "Dean Savard is taking an extended vacation from his gallery"** Carlo McCormick, "Art Seen," *East Village Eye*, May 1985.

**p. 282 Nina Leen's historic 1950 portrait of the abstract expressionists** A group of New York painters including Willem De Kooning, Jackson Pollock, Robert Motherwell, and Mark Rothko wrote a letter in May 1950 to the Metropolitan Museum of Art protesting the exclusion of abstract artists from a show on contemporary painting. Nina Leen photographed fifteen of the painters in November 1950. The photo appeared in *Life* in January 1951 with the caption "Irascible Group of Advanced Artists Led Fight Against Show."

**p. 286 "The cigarettes etc are what I need to stop in order to keep the change stronger"** Fales 3A, 5, 155.

**p. 286 one of fourteen artists selected to show that summer (from two hundred applicants)** Kim Levin, "Cryptanalysis," *Village Voice*, June 18, 1985.

**p. 287 he'd based the piece "on his childhood and life experience"** Mina Roustayi, "Had You Bought the Brooklyn Bridge . . ." *Brooklyn Affairs*, June 1985, in the Creative Time Archive (MSS 179) at the Fales Library and Special Collections, New York University, Series 1, Box 2, Folder 58.

**p. 289 alchemical, magical, and religious symbolism, and had created, for example, many paintings of figures on fire** See http://www.philipchristianzimmerman.com.

**p. 294 "I'm too wound up crazy to travel with them"** DW to Hujar, circa June 11, 1985, in possession of the Hujar Estate.

**p. 295 he would declare the enterprise a failure** October 7, 1985, journal of Keith Davis, in author's possession.

**p. 295 "Peter I feel crazy but I think of you"** DW to Hujar, June 25, 1985 in possession of the Hujar Estate.

**p. 297 "I don't feel any sadness for David. I wish he were dead"** August 3, 1985, journal of Keith Davis, in author's possession.

**15 Hello Darkness, My Old Friend**

**p. 298 "nobody was interested in what I was doing"** Barry Blinderman, "The Compression of Time: An Interview with David Wojnarowicz," *Tongues of Flame*, ed. Blinderman, p. 53.

**p. 298 "Nobody bought a thing"** Anthony Haden-Guest, *True Colors: The Real Life of the Art World* (New York: Atlantic Monthly Press, 1996), p. 140.

**p. 298 "no longer felt inclined to cast pearls before swine"** Patti Astor, letter to the editor, *New York Magazine*, August 24, 1987.

**p. 299 "It's all such a blur"** http://www.wigstock.nu/history/index.html.

**p. 300 listings for forty-seven neighborhood galleries** Liza Kirwin, "The East Village: A Chronology," *Artforum*, October 1999.

**p. 303 allowed only to listen in via telephone** Lisa Perlman, "AIDS Victim Begins School by Phone," Associated Press, August 26, 1985.

**p. 303 "their efficacy in reducing transmission has not yet been proven"** http://www.cdc.gov/mmwr/preview/mmwrhtml/00000610.htm.

p. 303 **"the government should not be in the business of telling homosexuals how to have sodomy"** Shilts, *And the Band*, p. 586.

p. 305 **he heard about Caven Point** Sylvère Lotringer, "Steve Brown," in *A Definitive History*, ed. Ambrosino, p. 42.

p. 306 **"I think that's one of my jobs"** C. Carr, "Karen Finley," *Mirabella*, November 1990.

p. 306 **"that someone can be both good and gay"** Jeff Yarbrough, "Rock Hudson: On Camera and Off; The Tragic News That He Is the Most Famous Victim of an Infamous Disease, AIDS, Unveils the Hidden Life of a Longtime Hollywood Hero," *People Magazine*, August 12, 1985.

p. 308 **using what Marguerite called "revolting colors"** Mysoon Rizk, "Marguerite Van Cook and James Romberger," in *A Definitive History*, ed. Ambrosino, p. 97.

p. 309 **"springing out like cartoon animation"** Fales Series 3E, Box 6, Folder 257.

p. 310 **"bodies in lotus positions with enormous hard-ons"** DW, *Close to the Knives*, pp. 184–85.

p. 310 **short films like *Baby Doll*** Sargeant, *Deathtripping*, p. 170, and see http://web.mac.com/ tessahughesfreeland.

p. 310 **"power plays embedded in the sexual act"** DW, *Close to the Knives*, p. 189.

p. 313 **"I feel too self-conscious about living, and it's driving me crazy"** Ibid., p. 206.

p. 317 **"The image of the deer being hunted is transferred to the kid"** Gideon Gil, "Artists Work to Help Fight Child Abuse," *Louisville Times*, December 6, 1985, in Fales 6C, 9, 46.

p. 318 **"none of the last fifteen or twenty minutes happened"** Fales 6E, 12, 116.

**16 "Something Turning Emotional and Wild"**

p. 323 **"So did the duck. So did the dog."** Gary Indiana, "The No Name Review," *Village Voice*, January 28, 1986.

p. 324 **"the smell and taste of him wrapped around my neck and jaw like some scarf"** DW, "Losing the Form in Darkness," *East Village Eye*, February 1986.

p. 325 **"he said something about not seeing each other so much"** DW to Frangella, Fales Series 2, Box 2, Folder 9.

p. 327 **"You self-imitate to meet demand"** Judd Tully, "The East Village: Is the Party Over Now?" *New Art Examiner*, March 1986.

p. 328 **"at the end of its collective gestures"** Fales 3A, 4, 69, plus DW discusses the machine symbolism in his work in Fales 8B, 16, Audiotape 092.0247.

p. 328 **"the wall of illusion surrounding society and its structures"** Fales 3G, 6, 280.

p. 329 **"The Other World where I've always felt like an alien"** DW, *Close to the Knives*, pp. 87–88.

p. 331 **"the imposed hell of the suburbs"** Ibid., p. 207.

p. 332 **"sometimes failed to show up for filming"** Fales 3A, 4, 58.

p. 333 **"get away from my life as it was"** DW, *Close to the Knives*, pp. 216–17.

p. 335 **"nature's incessant struggle and cyclical compulsions"** Mysoon Rizk, "Looking at 'Animals in Pants': The Case of David Wojnarowicz," *TOPIA: Canadian Journal of Cultural Studies* ("Nature Matters: Materiality and the More-Than-Human in Cultural Studies of the Environment" issue; Toronto) 21 (Spring 2009): 137–59, and http://pi.library.yorku.ca/ojs/index .php/topia/index.

p. 340 **"respective problems we will leave behind in U.S.A. necessarily"** Tommy Turner, "Travel Log to Mexico," October 28, 1986, in author's possession.

p. 343 **"use tools, make war, and capture slaves"** Fales 3G, 6, 280.

p. 343 **"life forms that have been abstracted into the 'other'"** Ibid.

**17 Some Sort of Grace**

p. 346 **"'getting a letter in the mail has an entirely different meaning'"** DW, *Close to the Knives*, p. 67.

**p. 349 a hagiography** William Kelly Eidem, *The Doctor Who Cures Cancer* (CreateSpace, 2008).

**p. 349 Revici also gets a chapter** Fred Rosen, *Doctors from Hell* (New York: Windsor Publishing, 1993).

**p. 350 "concluding that he had violated the terms of his probation"** http://www.quackwatch .org/04ConsumerEducation/null.html, and see also Stephen Barrett, M.D., "Questionable Cancer Therapies" at http://www.quackwatch.com/01QuackeryRelatedTopics/cancer.html.

**p. 351 Now the number was 32,000. And counting.** If Kramer's number was approximate, it was approximately correct. By the end of 1987, there would be about 35,400 dead. For statistics on AIDS deaths, see http://www.aids.gov/federal-resources/policies/pacha/meetings/march-2008/ hiv-aids-update-in-us.pdf.

**p. 351 "this *is* a death wish"** Kramer, "The Beginning of ACTing Up," *Holocaust*, p. 128.

**p. 351 "'Act up! Fight back! Fight AIDS!'"** Maer Roshan, "ACT UP," *Advocate, 35th anniversary issue*, November 12, 2002.

**p. 351 Three hundred people met back at the center to form the AIDS Coalition to Unleash Power, ACT UP** Kramer, *Holocaust*, p. 137.

**p. 352 back of the store, stacked in a pile** Fales Series 1, Box 1, Folder 18.

**p. 353 "to find the lakes and show Peter"** Fales 3A, 5, 183.

**p. 353 "A place of refuge"** Fales 3A, 5, 174.

**p. 353 "talked about how much we cared about each other"** Vince Aletti, "Portrait in Life and Death," *Village Voice*, December 15, 1987.

**p. 355 cockfight must have seemed essential to him** See the script in Fales 3, 4, 24.

**p. 357 "I didn't enjoy the experience"** Romberger's article can be found at http://www.tcj.com/ hoodedutilitarian/2010/12/wojnarowiczs-apostacy.

**p. 357 "symbols of rage and the need for release"** DW to Blinderman, October 22, 1988, in author's possession.

**p. 358 two scripts for *A Fire in My Belly*** Fales 3F, 6, 277 and 3, 4, 24.

**p. 358 "register on the brain; sometimes longer"** DW to Blinderman, October 22, 1988, in author's possession.

**p. 359 seven minutes of footage found on another reel** The footage shown and then removed from "Hide/Seek: Difference and Desire in American Portraiture" at the National Portrait Gallery came from this "excerpt."

**p. 361 "it's time to move on"** Amy Virshup, "The Fun's Over: The East Village Scene Gets Burned by Success," *New York Magazine*, June 22, 1987.

**p. 364 "if there's warmth move towards it"** DW, *Close to the Knives*, p. 82.

**p. 365 "on the floor fourteen stories above the earth"** Ibid.

**p. 367 "emotion distilled"** Lucy Lippard, "Out of the Safety Zone, *Art in America*, December 1990.

**p. 369 "who seem to have been making better work three years ago"** Dan Cameron, "The Season That Almost Wasn't," *Arts*, September 1987.

**p. 369 "wasn't enough to erase this rage"** DW, *Close to the Knives*, p. 106.

**p. 370 "'didn't have the strength'"** Ibid., p. 92.

**p. 371 "'you may not have it'"** Ibid., p. 96.

**p. 371 "that's the T-cells"** Ibid., p. 97.

**p. 371 "I couldn't answer"** Ibid., p. 98.

**p. 371 "put me in bed and rushed out"** Ibid., p. 99.

**p. 373 "doctor reacted as if his life were being threatened"** DW to Stuyvesant Polyclinic, October 23, 1987, in Fales 2, 2, 13.

**p. 376 "a little further from the dirt road that leads to the lake"** Fales 1, 2, 35.

**p. 379 "the third day of his death"** Fales 1, 2, 27.

**p. 379 "He's in the wind in the air all around me"** Ibid.

**p. 379 "beaming some kind of joy"** Ibid.

## 18 Elegiac Times

p. 382 "sadness all day and night" Fales Series 1, Box 2, Folder 27.

p. 382 $982.50 for one year or $1,015.86 for two years Fales 7B, 14, 53.

p. 382 "rent adjustments" upwards Fales 6E, 11, 112.

p. 383 $166.53 in the bank Fales 7A, 13, 34.

p. 384 "unwilling to leave it behind" Fales 1, 2, 27.

p. 385 "It started with Peter becoming ill" Ibid. and *Diaries*, ed. Scholder, p. 204.

p. 387 the sponsoring NAMES Project Foundation http://www.aidsquilt.org/about/the-aids
-memorial-quilt.

p. 388 "afraid if I experience it I will not be able to control it" Fales 3A, 5, 176.

p. 388 emotions everyone had Author's interviews with DW in January 1990.

p. 389 "Am I a child again in this state?" Fales 1, 1, 20, and *Diaries*, ed. Scholder, p. 210.

p. 390 "the memories in those shadows like films" Ibid.

p. 391 a count of 237 Fales 7A, 13, 21.

p. 392 "in the most confrontational manner" Fales 3A, 5, 160.

p. 392 "witness of your silent decline" Fales 1, 1, 20, and *Diaries*, ed. Scholder, p. 211.

## 19 Acceleration

p. 393 aware of himself "alive and witnessing" Fales Series 3, Box 4, Folder 1.

p. 396 by the end of the month or face "legal action" Fales 7A, 12, 5.

p. 397 "your right to remain in the apartment once proceedings begin" Ibid.

p. 397 Dolores usually sent a birthday card Note that David's mother was now spelling her
name "Delores," though I have stayed with the spelling on her divorce and naturalization
papers: "Dolores."

p. 397 "that we will lose touch with one another" Fales 2, 2, 15.

p. 398 "things quietly occurring, within absence of sight" Fales 8B, 17, Audiotape 092.0278.

p. 401 the FDA had accelerated its procedures Crimp with Rolston, *Demo Graphics*, p. 83, and
http://www.newsweek.com/2008/12/08/gay-rights-2-0.html.

p. 401 leave the loft by the end of November Fales 7A, 12, 5.

p. 401 time and date in a journal Fales 1, 2, 35.

p. 402 "all I can feel is the pressure and the need for release" DW, *Close to the Knives*, p. 60.

p. 403 a piece with "the power to change lives" Jerry Salz, "Not Going Gentle," *Arts*, February
1989.

p. 403 "can't believe he is dying" Fales 1, 1, 20, and *Diaries*, ed. Scholder, p. 212.

p. 404 "how to operate a camera on anything other than automatic" DW, *Close to the Knives*,
pp. 138–39.

p. 404 "that speaks about the world I witness" Ibid., p. 144.

p. 405 an opera that could have a hundred parts, but at least he'd made two of them Fales
8B, 16, Audiotape 092.0247.

p. 405 "the heaviness of the pre-invented existence we are thrust into" Fales 3A, 4, 103.

p. 405 list of some thirty-five or forty possible images for *Weight of the Earth* Fales 3A, 5, 197.

p. 405 if they chased them toward a cliff they didn't know about For a discussion of David's
use of animal imagery see Mysoon Rizk, "Taking the 'S' out of 'PEST.'" *Antennae: The Journal
of Nature in Visual Culture* ("Insecta" issue) 11 (Autumn): 37–50, and http://www.antennae.org
.uk/Back%20Issues.html.

p. 406 "within the structures of civilization" Fales 3G, 6, 280.

p. 407 "the fear that I've carried through my whole life" Fales 8B, 16, Audiotape 092.0218.

p. 407 "The garden is the place I'll go if I die" Fales 3A, 4, 103.

p. 407 "sad and exhilarated simultaneously" November 9, 1988, in Fales 1, 1, 20, and *Diaries*, ed.
Scholder, pp. 216–17.

**p. 409 "hints at both death and decay"** David Deitcher, "Ideas and Emotions," *Artforum*, May 1989.

**p. 410 "a menacing, oneiric aura"** Lucy Lippard, "Out of the Safety Zone," *Art in America*, December 1990.

**p. 410 "I am effectively silenced. I am angry"** Fales 3A, 4, 103.

**p. 410 "just for the sexual part of it"** Author's interviews with DW in January 1990. For source photos see Fales 9D, 66 and 67.

**p. 414 "despite comfort or despite pain"** Fales 8B, 16, Audiotape 092.0218.

**p. 414 "broom clean" and vacant** Fales 2, 2, 15.

**p. 414 into a commercial space** Fales 7A, 12, 5.

**p. 414 "may execute the warrant of eviction"** Fales 2, 3, 27.

**p. 416 "then I had this dream"** Fales 3A, 4, 103.

**p. 418 "Hard to remember now"** Fales 4, 7, 13.

**p. 418 "ideal construction of painting or photos or whatever"** February 22, 1989, in Fales 1, 1, 21, and *Diaries*, ed. Scholder, p. 219.

**p. 419 New York had 22 percent of all reported cases in the country** Crimp with Rolston, *Demo Graphics*, p. 85.

**p. 419 washed his hands after handing a PWA a cookie** Richard Levine, "Koch, in Book with O'Connor, Traces a Conservative Shift," *New York Times*, March 7, 1989.

**p. 419 who in city government was not doing what** The "Target City Hall" booklet can be found in Fales 7D, 15, 132A.

**20 "Like a Blood-Filled Egg"**

**p. 422 "It makes me very self-conscious to sit in front of a tape recorder"** Audiotape of DW in possession of Marion Scemama.

**p. 423 "He wanted to record it before everybody died"** Sylvère Lotringer, "Marion Scemama," in *A Definitive History*, ed. Ambrosino, p. 132.

**p. 424 "the growing feeling of death surrounding us"** Scemama quotes here are from both author's interviews and *A Definitive History*, ed. Ambrosino, p. 132.

**p. 425 to every member of Congress, enclosing a reproduction of *Piss Christ*** Robert Hobbs, "Andres Serrano: The Body Politic," *Andres Serrano: Works, 1983–1993* (Philadelphia: Institute Contemporary Art, University of Pennsylvania) 1994, pp. 17–43.

**p. 425 "the courage to stand against such bigotry. I hope so"** "Reverend Donald Wildmon, letter concerning Serrano's *Piss Christ*, April 5, 1989," *Culture Wars: Documents*, ed. Bolton, p. 27.

**p. 426 "he is taunting the American people"** "Debate in Senate over the NEA . . . May 18, 1989," Ibid., p. 30.

**p. 427 considered using it in *ITSOFOMO*** He wrote "tape of conversation w/Steve Woj" on the script labeled "visual notes" Fales 3G, 6, 284.

**p. 428 "could blow their budget out of the water!"** William Honan, "Congressional Anger Threatens Arts Endowment's Budget," *New York Times*, June 20, 1989.

**p. 428 "Mapplethorpe's work would never be looked at in its own right"** Grace Glueck, "Art on the Firing Line," *New York Times*, July 9, 1989.

**p. 429 "explicit homoerotic pornography and child obscenity"** "Debate in Senate over Helms Amendment . . . July 26, 1989, *Culture Wars: Documents*, ed. Bolton, p. 76.

**p. 430 "depictions of some people's sexuality"** DW to *Newsday* in Fales Series 2, Box 3, Folder 19.

**p. 430 David's piece in the *Journal of Contemporary Art*** Zinsser's co-editor, Philip Pocock, was actually the person who solicited the piece from David.

**p. 432 "break my chains self imposed or otherwise"** Undated journal entry in Fales 1, 1, 21.

**p. 432** "**Sometimes the stars in sky make my head hurt**" Fales 10A, Videotape O92.0009.

**p. 432** "**a little lighter in the rotation?**" Fales 10A, Videotape O92.00015.

**p. 433** "**trying new forms, new feelings and emotions**" Sylvère Lotringer, "Marion Scemama," in *A Definitive History*, ed. Ambrosino, p. 133.

**p. 434** **The cat on his lap actually looked quite attentive** Fales 10A, Videotape O92.00019.

**p. 436** "**tape of me angry or talking about death. Rejected her**" Fales 4, 7, 13.

**p. 436** **did not want to be in touch with her anymore** Sylvère Lotringer, "Marion Scemama," in *A Definitive History*, ed. Ambrosino, p. 139.

**p. 437** "**that it could have been different for you**" Fales 2, 3, 19.

**p. 438** "**I wouldn't want to contribute to unhinging that**" Author's interviews with DW in January 1990.

**p. 438** "**yet I don't want to get close enough to find out**" Ibid.

**p. 438** "**Mom, I have a lot of mixed feelings towards my relationship with you**" DW to Dolores, November 1, 1989, loose pages inside Fales 1, 1, 20.

**p. 440** "**while sizing up each other's mortality**" This short film can be seen at http://www. pzfoundation.org/philzwickler/film/fear.html.

**p. 440** **create their own images for "Telling Yourself"** Fales 3F, 6, 266.

**p. 440** *Needle Nightmare* It's not clear whether Zwickler considered this film finished. It can be viewed at http://www.pzfoundation.org/philzwickler/film/index.html.

### 21 Witnesses

**p. 442** "**known to cause birth defects**" http://articles.latimes.com/1985-12-10/news/mn-15459_1 _enters-senate-race.

**p. 442** "**what homosexuality really is**" Robert W. Stewart, "Dannemeyer Causes Flap in Congress by Describing Gay Sex," *Los Angeles Times*, July 25, 1989.

**p. 442** "**truly damaging**" **in preventing the spread of the virus** Duncan Campbell, "AIDS as an Election Issue," *New Scientist*, January 21, 1988.

**p. 442** "**oversight**" **of choices made by grantees** Robert Atkins, "Stream of Conscience: Andres Serrano's 'Piss Christ,'" *Village Voice*, May 30, 1989.

**p. 443** "**favoring taxpayer funding for pornography**" William H. Honan, "Compromise Is Proposed on Helms Amendment," *New York Times*, September 28, 1989.

**p. 443** **Chaucer would be unacceptable under the Helms amendment** Ibid.

**p. 445** "**They tried to make us see**" Cookie Mueller, "A Last Letter," *Witnesses: Against Our Vanishing* catalog, p. 14.

**p. 446** "**I'D CONTRACTED A DISEASED SOCIETY AS WELL**" DW, *Close to the Knives*, pp. 112, 113–14.

**p. 446** "**Dannemeyer off the empire state building**" Ibid., p. 120.

**p. 446** "**the repulsive senator from zombieland**" Ibid., p. 119.

**p. 446** **cardinal's name came up frequently** See, for example, the summary of grievances in Crimp with Rolston, *Demo Graphics*, pp. 131–38, along with DW, *Close to the Knives*, pp. 125–27.

**p. 447** **banned them from ever entering the cathedral again** See http://www.dignityny.org/ content/social-justice.

**p. 447** "**thousands to their unnecessary deaths**" DW, *Close to the Knives*, p. 114.

**p. 448** "**a meter which is completely unreal**" Blinderman, "The Compression of Time: An Interview with David Wojnarowicz," *Tongues of Flame*, ed. Blinderman, pp. 61–62.

**p. 449** "**the worst in living memory**" Robert Hughes, "Art: Careerism and Hype Amidst the Image Haze," *Time*, June 17, 1985.

**p. 449** **was putting his face on the catalog to get back at him** Sylvère Lotringer, "Steve Brown," in *A Definitive History*, ed. Ambrosino, p. 40.

**p. 450** "the gay-bashed, self-hating kid who struggled to survive" Maurice Berger, "Stonewalled at the Museum," *Village Voice*, August 18, 1992.

**p. 451** "the whole future of the public funding of art has come to rest on your shoulders" Susan Wyatt, "Setting the Record Straight: Diary of a Controversy," in *The Cultural Battlefield: Art Censorship and Public Funding*, eds. Jennifer A. Peter and Louis M. Crosier (Gilsum, NH: Avocus Publishing, 1995) p. 97.

**p. 451** no way in hell he would do that Evelyn B. Leong, "An Interview with Susan Wyatt," *Gulf Coast: A Journal of Literature and Fine Arts*, vol. 6, no. 2, September 1994, p. 50.

**p. 451** "asks me to sign liability waver in case of lawsuits—I say send it to me" Fales Series 7B, Box 14, Folder 57.

**p. 452** for all "losses, liabilities, damages, and settlements" resulting from his essay Ibid.

**p. 452** "Susan's interpretation of our conversation" Robert Atkins, "Black Thursday: Frohnmayer Fiddles, Artists Burn," *Village Voice*, November 28, 1989.

**p. 452** Frohnmayer then asked her to remove NEA credit from the catalog and to print a disclaimer Susan Wyatt, "Setting the Record Straight: Diary of a Controversy," in *The Cultural Battlefield: Art Censorship and Public Funding*, eds. Jennifer A. Peter and Louis M. Crosier (Gilsum, NH: Avocus Publishing, 1995), p. 81.

**p. 453** "pleasant" and "unsurprised by everything" Evelyn B. Leong, "An Interview with Susan Wyatt," *Gulf Coast: A Journal of Literature and Fine Arts*, Summer 1994, p. 53.

**p. 453** "more problematic than Mapplethorpe's photos" Frohnmayer, *Leaving Town*, p. 76.

**p. 453** "a declaration of weakness" Ibid.

**p. 453** "Artists Space should relinquish the Endowment's grant for the exhibition" Frohnmayer to Wyatt, November 3, 1989, in author's possession.

**p. 454** "it's the show itself maybe erotic stuff" Fales 7B, 14, 57.

**p. 455** "is the law now also retroactive?" John Marzulli, "Liberal Arts? A SoHo Gallery Fears Backlash," *Daily News*, November 8, 1989.

**p. 455** "There are specific derogatory references in the show to Senator Helms, Congressman Dannemeyer and Cardinal O'Connor which makes it political" William H. Honan, "Arts Endowment Withdraws Grant for AIDS Show," *New York Times*, November 9, 1989.

**p. 455** "I do not consider myself exempt from or above criticism by anyone" William H. Honan, "The Endowment vs. the Arts: Anger and Concern," *New York Times*, November 10, 1989.

**p. 456** "an erosion of the artistic focus" William C. Honan, "Endowment Head Explains Withdrawal of Art Grant," *New York Times*, November 14, 1989.

**p. 457** "Tired of restraint of Susan while bigots speak unrestrained" Fales 7B, 14, 57.

**p. 458** "you should resign" Frohnmayer, *Leaving Town*, p. 84.

**p. 459** "more oppressive and hopeless and depressing" Ibid., p. 83.

**p. 460** "possible loss of funding" Fales 3A, 5, 163.

**p. 460** compared David . . . to Louis Farrakhan Ray Kerrison, "Art Show Assaults O'Connor and Church, But Our Catholic Governor Is Mute," *New York Post*, November 22, 1989.

**p. 460** "hatred against Roman Catholicism" Patrick Buchanan, "Why Subsidize Defamation?" *New York Post*, November 22, 1989.

**p. 461** "supporting my right of free speech under the First Amendment" DW "to the Dean and whomever else it may concern," November 22, 1989, in author's possession.

**p. 461** "history in such a public way" DW, *Close to the Knives*, p. 122.

## 22 With a Target on His Back

**p. 462** "To keep silent . . . is to lose our identities" DW, *Close to the Knives*, p. 153.

**p. 464** "The Private Lives of Saints" Fales Series 3A, Box 4, Folders 92 and 93.

**p. 464 a section that did not air** Fales 10A, DVD 092.0434.

**p. 464 The phrase "Silence = Death"** Allen White, "Reagan's AIDS Legacy: Silence Equals Death," SFGate.com, June 8, 2004.

**p. 466 "Dean's monologue"** Fales 3D, 6, 223.

**p. 466 "It's not our job to squelch controversy"** Elizabeth Hess, "Frohnmayer's Normal Waterloo?" *Village Voice*, December 12, 1989.

**p. 468 "Does it prevent you from hearing anything else I say?"** Elizabeth Hess, "Queer in Normal," *Village Voice*, February 13, 1990.

**p. 470 "a unique educational experience for our immediate audience and people all over the country"** "Final Descriptive Report: David Wojnarowicz, Tongues of Flame University Galleries of Illinois State University NEA Special Exhibition Grant #89-4442-0376," in author's possession.

**p. 470 he did not have to comment on it** Frohnmayer, *Leaving Town*, p. 114.

**p. 473 "Is This How You Want Your Tax Dollars Spent?"** "American Family Association . . . February 13, 1990," in *Culture Wars: Documents*, ed. Bolton, p. 151.

**p. 475 "hardly a blasphemous concept"** Frohnmayer, *Leaving Town*, p. 121.

**p. 476 "What gesture of hands or mind can stop my death?"** Undated journal entry in Fales 1, 1, 22, and *Diaries*, ed. Scholder, p. 229.

**p. 476 "Monte committed suicide about January 18, 1990. His dad"** Fales 8B, 17, Audiotape 092.0280.

**p. 477 "throwing themselves into the varied arms of death"** DW, *Close to the Knives*, p. 225.

**p. 478 "Take pictures of me dead"** Fales 8B, 17, Audiotape 092.0270.

**p. 478 "being human or not being human"** Fales 8B, 16, Audiotape 092.0240.

**p. 478 "acknowledge it and move on"** DW, *Close to the Knives*, p. 241.

**p. 481 "Does that make them less obscene?"** Kim Masters, "NEA-Funded Art Exhibit Protested: Wildmon Mails Sexual Images to Congress," *Washington Post*, April 21, 1990.

**p. 481 "Smell the flowers while you can"** DW, *Close to the Knives*, pp. 271–72.

**p. 482 "a door to all that I've been speaking of"** Ibid., pp. 270–71.

**p. 482 "this sensation of life in an uninfected body"** Undated journal entry in Fales 1, 1, 22, and *Diaries*, ed. Scholder, p. 224.

**p. 484 "Holly Hughes is a lesbian and her work is very heavily of that genre"** C. Carr, "Artful Dodging: The NEA Funds the Defunded Four," *Village Voice*, June 15, 1993.

**p. 484 "aggressively homosexual"** Frohnmayer, *Leaving Town*, p. 151–52.

**p. 487 "reluctant to think much about giving it up"** DW to Zimmerman, May 21, 1990, in author's possession.

**p. 487 intense at certain periods** Fales 7A, 12, 2 and 2, 3, 27.

**p. 488 "as generous a gift to AFA as possible"** Fales 7B, 14, 64.

**p. 490 Motions for dismissal and change of venue** David Wojnarowicz, Plaintiff v. American Family Association and Donald E. Wildmon, Defendants, United States Court District Court for the Southern District of New York, 90 Civ. 3457 (WCC).

**p. 494 "middle ground that would appease everyone"** Frohnmayer, *Leaving Town*, p. 176.

**23 "Desperate to Bring a Light"**

**p. 496 "and life was going on around me"** DW to Glantzman, July 7, 1990, in author's possession.

**p. 497 selected the images for this piece** *Untitled for ACT UP* can be seen at http://www.actupny .org/merchandise/index.html.

**p. 497 letters to the loft board and to his lawyer** Fales Series 2, Box 3, Folder 27.

**p. 500 damages of just one dollar** The decision can be read at http://www.artuntitled.com/ resource/wojnaro_AFA.html.

**p.** 501 **"He was too powerful a force to give up. He wasn't sick!"** Patrick McDonnell's account can be read at http://the11thmcdonnell.blogspot.com/?zx=3363ab1894f0daae.

**p.** 503 **possible class-action lawsuit** Josh Meyer, "Drawing the Line: 2 Clerics Face Off Over Exhibit in Battle for the 'Soul' of America," *Los Angeles Times*, August 2, 1990.

**p.** 503 **free from government intrusion** http://www.csulb.edu/~jvancamp/doc2.html.

**p.** 503 **"works which promote blasphemous and sacrilegious hate material"** Eli Teiber, "N.Y Artist's Work Is the Focus of Suit Against the NEA," *New York Post*, August 30, 1990.

**p.** 503 **they had suffered "spiritual injury"** http://www.csulb.edu/~jvancamp/doc2.html.

**p.** 503 **"standing to sue as citizens"** Ibid.

**p.** 508 **"Your letter was a profound shock to me"** in Fales 2, 3, 25.

**p.** 508 **arranged to have a storage unit built** DW to Ackerman, August 27, 1990, in Fales 2, 3 27, and DW to Ackerman, September 5, 1990, in Fales 7A, 12, 2.

**p.** 511 **"on a quieter level"** DW to Glantzman, October 1, 1990, in author's possession.

**p.** 511 **"the malevolence of the virus"** This translation of *À rebours* can be found at http://www.ibiblio.org/eldritch/jkh/ro8.html.

**p.** 512 **"Destination means death to me"** DW, *Close to the Knives*, p. 62.

**p.** 514 **"He may not have planned on staying"** Undated journal entry in Fales 1, 2, 28.

**p.** 519 **"not waiting a moment longer than necessary?"** Ibid.

## 24 "Like a Marble Rolling Down a Hill"

**p.** 522 **"not actively participating in the perpetuation of human life"** Anthony Haden-Guest, "The Art of the Hype," *Vanity Fair*, June 1989.

**p.** 522 **"all who were offended"** "Kostabi Apologizes," *Newsday*, May 17, 1989.

**p.** 522 **"so much bad art in the world"** "Not Sorry," *New York Post*, May 26, 1989.

**p.** 523 **"I am exactly the opposite of what you think"** Fales Series 8B, Box 17, Audiotape 092.0263.

**p.** 523 **"compromised the entire show"** Tom Hickerson, "Controversy Rages Over Former Blum Exhibit," *Bard Observer*, February 22, 1991.

**p.** 525 **clothes plus one Gap item** Fales Series 2, Box 3, Folder 29.

**p.** 525 **first in the series, providing both words and visuals** Fales 2, 3, 28.

**p.** 526 **"in sometimes disjointed currents"** Undated journal entry in Fales 1, 2, 30, and *Diaries*, ed. Scholder, p. 235.

**p.** 526 **letter from a young writer** in Fales 2, 3, 28.

**p.** 527 **"deal with issues like my past and my mortality"** Ibid.

**p.** 527 **The cover would use a detail from** *Fear of Evolution* Fales 2, 3, 31.

**p.** 529 **"Death as an aspect of AIDS"** Undated journal entry in Fales 1, 2, 30, and *Diaries*, ed. Scholder, p. 244.

**p.** 529 **a picture of him hooked to an IV with a caption** DW, *Memories*, p. 50.

**p.** 529 **"I can't even fucking let it out"** Undated journal entry in Fales 1, 2, 30.

**p.** 531 **"It's something about violence as a distancing tool"** DW, *Memories*, p. 28.

**p.** 531 **"disappearing but not fast enough"** Ibid., p. 61.

**p.** 531 **probably crazy not to cancel this trip** Undated journal entry in Fales 1, 2, 30, and *Diaries*, ed. Scholder, p. 246.

**p.** 532 **"I'm afraid to take my own life right now"** Fales 4, 7, 13.

**p.** 536 **"how patiently you wait"** May 1991 in Fales 1, 2, 30.

**p.** 538 **"oh life is so free in America"** Ibid.

**p.** 540 **"she needed time or something"** Ibid. and *Diaries*, ed. Scholder, p. 252.

**p.** 540 **"I felt a door closing between us"** Ibid. and *Diaries*, ed. Scholder, p. 253.

**p.** 540 **"seems stupid, what it's all based on"** Ibid. and *Diaries*, ed. Scholder, p. 256.

**p.** 541 **"something has changed"** Ibid. and *Diaries*, ed. Scholder, p. 255.

p. 541 **"It never came"** Ibid. and *Diaries*, ed. Scholder, p. 256.

p. 541 **"want it somehow to stop"** Ibid. and *Diaries*, ed. Scholder, p. 260.

p. 544 **"It felt like what I think grace is"** June 1, 1991, in Fales 1, 2, 30, and *Diaries*, ed. Scholder, pp. 263–64.

### 25 "Disappearing But Not Fast Enough"

p. 545 **"Tom in order to get help from him"** DW to Glantzman, July 27, 1991, in author's possession.

p. 548 **"Marion had misinterpreted what she'd said"** Fales Series 2, Box 3, Folder 29.

p. 551 **"how you share what you know?"** Fales 2, 3, 28.

p. 553 **"wing uttering from the wound"** Undated journal entry in Fales 1, 2, 31.

p. 563 **"Events are lost to me seconds after they take place"** Fales 3A, 4, 29.

### Epilogue Throw My Body on the Steps of the White House

p. 575 **"dump their lifeless form on the front steps"** DW, *Close to the Knives*, p. 122.

p. 577 **"illusion of the ONE-TRIBE NATION"** Ibid., p. 121.

p. 578 **this final act of empowerment and generosity** Information on the political funerals, including film footage, can be found at http://www.actupny.org/diva/polfunsyn.html.

# BIBLIOGRAPHY

Ambrosino, Giancarlo, ed. *David Wojnarowicz: A Definitive History of Five or Six Years on the Lower East Side*. Interviews by Sylvère Lotringer. New York: Semiotext(e); Cambridge, MA: MIT Press, 2006.

Blinderman, Barry, ed. *David Wojnarowicz: Tongues of Flame*. Normal, IL: University Galleries, Illinois State University, 1990.

Bolton, Richard, ed. *Culture Wars: Documents from the Recent Controversies in the Arts*. New York: New Press, 1992.

Cameron, Dan, curator. *East Village USA*. Exhibition monograph. New York: New Museum of Contemporary Art, 2004.

Carr, C. *On Edge: Performance at the End of the Twentieth Century*. Hanover, NH, and London: Wesleyan University Press and University Press of New England, 1993.

Crimp, Douglas, with Adam Rolston. *AIDS Demo Graphics*. Seattle: Bay Books, 1990.

Dubin, Steven C. *Arresting Images: Impolitic Art and Uncivil Actions*. New York and London: Routledge, 1992.

Frohnmayer, John. *Leaving Town Alive: Confessions of an Arts Warrior*. Boston and New York: Houghton Mifflin, 1993.

Hager, Steven. *Art After Midnight: The East Village Scene*. New York: St. Martin's Press, 1986.

Harris, Melissa, ed. *David Wojnarowicz: Brush Fires in the Social Landscape*. New York: Aperture Foundation, 1994.

Hujar, Peter. *Portraits in Life and Death*. New York: Da Capo Press, 1976.

Kramer, Larry. *Reports from the Holocaust: The Story of an AIDS Activist*. Updated and expanded edition. New York: St. Martin's Press, 1994.

Moore, Alan, and Marc Miller, eds. *ABC No Rio Dinero: The Story of a Lower East Side Art Gallery*. New York: ABC No Rio with Collaborative Projects, 1985.

Patterson, Clayton, ed. *Captured: A Film/Video History of the Lower East Side*. New York: Seven Stories Press, 2005.

Sargeant, Jack. *Deathtripping: The Extreme Underground*. Third revised edition. Berkeley, CA: Soft Skull Press, 2008.

Scholder, Amy, ed. *Fever: The Art of David Wojnarowicz*. New York: Rizzoli and New Museum of Contemporary Art, 1999.

———. *In the Shadow of the American Dream: The Diaries of David Wojnarowicz*. New York: Grove Press, 1999.

Scholder, Amy, and Ira Silverberg, eds. *High Risk: An Anthology of Forbidden Writings*. New York: Penguin Books, 1991.

Shilts, Randy. *And the Band Played On: Politics, People, and the AIDS Epidemic*. New York: Penguin Books, 1988.

Stosuy, Brandon, ed. *Up Is Up But So Is Down: New York's Downtown Literary Scene, 1974–1992*. New York and London: New York University Press, 2006.

Taylor, Marvin J., ed. *The Downtown Book: The New York Art Scene, 1974–1984.* Princeton, NJ, and Oxford: Princeton University Press, 2006.

Wojnarowicz, David. *Close to the Knives: A Memoir of Disintegration.* New York: Vintage Books, 1991.

———. *Memories That Smell like Gasoline.* San Francisco: Artspace Books, 1992.

———. *Sounds in the Distance.* London: Aloes Books, 1982

———. *The Waterfront Journals.* Edited by Amy Scholder. New York: Grove Press, 1996.

Wojnarowicz, David, and James Romberger. *Seven Miles a Second.* New York: DC Comics, 1996.

# INDEX

Note: Page numbers in *italic* indicate illustrations. "David" refers to David Wojnarowicz.

*An alien head placard on the funeral pyre at the end of David's political funeral.*
*(Photograph by Brian Palmer/bxpnyc.com)*

# A NOTE ON THE AUTHOR

**Cynthia Carr** was a columnist and arts reporter for the *Village Voice* from 1984 until 2003. Writing under the byline C. Carr, she specialized in experimental and cutting-edge art, especially performance. Some of these pieces are now collected in *On Edge: Performance at the End of the Twentieth Century*. She is also the author of *Our Town: A Heartland Lynching, a Haunted Town, and the Hidden History of White America*. Her work has appeared in the *New York Times, Artforum, Bookforum, Modern Painters*, the *Drama Review*, and other publications. She was awarded a Guggenheim fellowship in 2007. Carr lives in New York.

One day this kid will get larger. One day this kid w
come to know something that causes a sensatic
equivalent to the separation of the earth from
its axis. One day this kid will reach a point
where he senses a division that isn't
mathematical. One day this kid will
feel something stir in his heart and
throat and mouth. One day this kid will
find something in his mind and body
and soul that makes him hungry. One
day this kid will do something that
causes men who wear the uniforms of
priests and rabbis, men who inhabit certain stone buildings, to call for his death.
One day politicians will enact legislation
against this kid. One day families will
give false information to their children and each child will pass
that information down generationally to their families
and that information will be
designed to make exis-
tence intolerable for this
kid. One day this kid will
begin to experience all
this activity in his environment and that activi-